BRITTON

THE FRENCH TEXT CAREFULLY REVISED

WITH AN ENGLISH TRANSLATION

INTRODUCTION AND NOTES

BY

FRANCIS MORGAN NICHOLS M. A.

OF LINCOLN'S INN BARRISTER AT LAW

FORMERLY FELLOW OF WADHAM COLLEGE

VOLUME I.

THE LAWBOOK EXCHANGE, LTD.

Clark, New Jersey

2003

ISBN 1-58477-258-1

Printed in the United States of America
on acid-free paper

The Lawbook Exchange, Ltd.
33 Terminal Avenue
Clark, New Jersey 07066

Please see catalogue at rear of this volume
or our website
www.lawbookexchange.com
for a selection of our other publications and fine
facsimile reprints of classic works of legal history.

Library of Congress Cataloging-in-Publication Data

Britton / the French text carefully revised with an English translation, introduction, and notes by Francis Morgan Nichols.

p. cm.

Originally published: Oxford: Clarendon Press, 1865.

Includes bibliographical references and index.

ISBN 1-58477-258-1 (cloth: acid-free paper)

1. Law—England. I. Nichols, Francis Morgan, 1826-

KD600 .B74 2002
349.42—dc21 2002024326

BRITTON

THE FRENCH TEXT CAREFULLY REVISED

WITH AN ENGLISH TRANSLATION

INTRODUCTION AND NOTES

BY

FRANCIS MORGAN NICHOLS M. A.

OF LINCOLN'S INN BARRISTER AT LAW

FORMERLY FELLOW OF WADHAM COLLEGE

VOLUME I.

Oxford

AT THE CLARENDON PRESS

M DCCC LXV.

PREFACE.

ENGLAND is peculiarly rich in the monuments of its ancient jurisprudence, and in the materials for the history of that great system of law which in the course of so many centuries has grown up among us. But while in other European countries collections of their legal monuments have been carefully prepared and printed at the public expense, the unfinished labours of the Record Commission and the early Year Books recently published under the authority of the Master of the Rolls constitute all our acquisitions in this department which we owe to the aid of Government. On the other hand, that which has been accomplished by individuals in the publication of Judicial Records and Ancient Law Treatises was for the most part done more than two centuries since, when the required materials were scattered and difficult of access, and historical criticism was in its infancy. The valuable series of Treatises on the English Law, written in the twelfth, thirteenth, and fourteenth centuries, has never yet been properly edited. The most important of these works, Glanvill, Bracton, Fleta, Britton, and the Mirror of Justices, and also the two tracts called Great and Little Hengham, have been printed, with little or no care for the most part to secure a good text, and in some instances so negligently as to be frequently unintelligible. And the existing editions are wanting in those aids, such as indexes, convenient divisions of paragraphs, and marginal abstracts, by which the labour of the reader may be materially diminished.

It was one of the unaccomplished objects of the Record Commission to publish 'a correct and uniform impression of our early law writers, such as Glanvill, Bracton, Britton, Fleta, The Mirror, the Old Book of Tenures, and Littleton's Tenures[a].' 'Every lawyer knows,' as was observed in one of the Returns made to the House of Commons Committee on Records, 'how uncouth and incorrect almost all the existing editions of those authors are[b].' And the want which the Record Commission was to have satisfied is one which has been frequently pointed out by those who at various times have laboured in this department of knowledge[c]. The present publication is the result of an effort in some measure to supply the want above indicated; and the Editor has reason to congratulate himself upon having obtained the assistance of the Delegates of the Oxford Press in taking the first step to provide a modern edition of the venerable text-books of our law.

It may be thought by some that when an attempt is made to recall the attention of the student to our old legal authors, he is invited into a field the harvest of

[a] Report of the Select Committee of the House of Commons on Public Records, 1800, pp. 17, 383.

[b] Return of the Society of Lincoln's Inn to the Committee on Public Records, 1800. Report of the Committee, p. 383.

[c] See Reeves' History of English Law, vol. ii. p. 283; Mr. C. P. Cooper's Remarks on the Public Records, vol. i. p. 401; Two Discourses, by Geo. Long, Reader on Jurisprudence to the Middle Temple, 1847, p. 106.

which has been long since gathered in by our antiquaries of the seventeenth century, to whom the whole province of legal antiquities was so familiar. This apprehension, however, will not weigh much with those who reflect that after the labours of Selden, Coke, Spelman, Sir Matthew Hale, and others, an adequate History of English Law is still to be written. Moreover, in the domain of General History, and especially in that important part of History which has only in later times attracted its due share of interest, the history of the social progress of the people, the assistance which might be derived from a more familiar knowledge of our legal Records and Treatises is very far from being exhausted.

It may be asked why Britton has been selected as the first work to be produced in the present form; Glanvill and Bracton being both of earlier date, and certainly not of inferior interest or importance. The most obvious consideration, which led the Editor to the choice which he has made, was the present comparative inaccessibility of the French Treatise. Glanvill has been printed already in a fairly accurate form[d], and an English translation has also appeared[e], while Bracton and Fleta are read, even in the present imperfect impressions, with far more facility than Britton or the Mirror. With respect to Bracton, another reason has had still stronger weight. There can be no question that a far greater benefit would be conferred upon the study of our law by a good edition of Bracton than by the present reprint of Britton. But Bracton is a much longer and a much more important work; its production in a form worthy of its place in literature would necessarily be the labour of many years;

[d] I refer to Mr. Rayner's edition of Glanvill, London, 1780.

[e] A translation of Glanvill by John Beames, London, 1812.

and the Editor felt that an adequate edition of that great monument of English jurisprudence required a more extended knowledge both of our early law and of kindred branches of science than he was conscious of possessing. If at a future time he should be encouraged to undertake the labour of editing Bracton, the experience which he has acquired in preparing the materials of the present publication may be of some service in that more difficult task.

In the preparation of the present work, the Editor has been placed under many obligations. By the indulgence of the late Archbishop of Canterbury, Dr. Sumner, he was enabled to collate in his own chambers one of the best existing manuscripts of Britton. The Warden and Fellows of Merton College have with the greatest liberality permitted him to keep, during the whole period in which he has been engaged upon the book, a most valuable manuscript from their library. To Mr. Henry Bradshaw, Fellow of King's College, Cambridge, he is indebted for many services in facilitating his use of the manuscripts preserved in the Cambridge University Library; and to his friend Mr. Lindley of the Middle Temple, he is especially obliged for advice and assistance in the revision of the work as it has issued from the press.

It is the Editor's wish to proceed after a short interval to the publication of others of the Ancient Law Treatises. How far he may be induced to carry out his intention, will depend in some measure upon the judgment which may be formed by the public of the utility of the work.

CONTENTS.

VOL. I.

BOOK I.

OF THE AUTHORITY OF JUSTICES AND OTHER OFFICERS, AND OF PERSONAL PLEAS, INCLUDING PLEAS OF THE CROWN.

BOOK II.

OF DISSEISINS AND THEIR REMEDIES.

VOL. II.

BOOK III.

OF INTRUSIONS AND THEIR REMEDIES.

BOOK IV.

OF PLEAS RELATING TO ADVOWSONS AND THE PROPERTY OF CHURCHES; AND OF ATTAINTS.

BOOK V.

OF PLEAS OF DOWER, AND ENTRY.

BOOK VI.

OF PROPRIETARY ACTIONS.

INTRODUCTION.

Subject of Introduction.

THE origin of the ancient law treatise here presented to the public is involved in considerable obscurity, and it has been a matter of question among antiquaries from what source it derived the name by which for many centuries it has been known. As far as I am aware, its contents have not been subjected in modern times to any careful or critical examination, nor has its relation to other early works upon English law been precisely ascertained. I propose in the present Introduction, to submit to the reader what traces can be found of the origin of the book; to point out its relation to other treatises preceding or contemporaneous; and to give a short account of the character and arrangement of the work and of the nature of its subject-matter. I shall add a few observations upon the language of Britton. I shall then give an account of the manuscript copies with which I am acquainted; of the earlier editions of the book; and of the manner in which the present text has been formed. A very few additional remarks will be needed upon the subject of the translation and notes with which the present publication is accompanied.

I. *Origin and Authorship of Britton.*

Project of codifying the law attributed to Edward I.

The service which might be done to English jurisprudence by the codification of our laws has at various times engaged the attention of statesmen and lawyers, and there appears to be considerable probability that the treatise of Britton owes its origin to an early project of this kind. It has been asserted that Edward I., whose reign forms so important an epoch in our legal history, conceived the design of reducing the laws of England to certainty by a written exposition, and that for this purpose he composed, with the assistance of some of his judges, a book of laws. This assertion has been made on the authority of a distinguished judge, Sir John Prisot[a], who presided in the Court of Common Pleas in the reign of Henry VI., and whose legal studies must have commenced more than a century after the death of Edward I. It is impossible to determine upon what evidence the Judge's statement rested,—whether it was the tradition of Westminster Hall, or his own conclusion from the contents of the then existing treatises, which had their origin in the time of Edward I. There can be little doubt, however, that the book alluded to as having been composed by Edward was that known as Britton; although Selden has conjectured that it was not the only work of the same nature written by the command of that king[b]. This treatise bears upon the face of it an assumption of royal origin. It claims in its opening words to be the immediate work of the king, and the same pretension is kept continually before the reader, the established doctrines of the Common Law and the practice of the Royal Courts being enunciated throughout as resulting

Britton the result of this project.

Britton written in the name of the king.

[a] *Prisot.* Cest statut [Statute of Westminster I. c. 22.] fuit fait al temps le Roy E. le premier, le quel Roy fuit appurpos daver mis tout en certain et en escripture, et commence de ceo faire livres de et par plus sages homes de Ley deins le Realme, s. Juges, et auxi il fist un livre deux ans proche apres le fesance de cel statut, en quel est reherce tout cel statut. (Year Book, Hil. 35 Hen. VI., p. 42.) The Statute of Westminster I. c. 22 is cited in Britton, l. iii. c. 3. s. 3 (where the marginal reference requires correction). Chief Justice Prisot, 'a famous and expert lawyer,' is said by Coke to have assisted Littleton in the composition of his treatise on Tenures. (Coke, Reports, part x. Preface.)

[b] Selden, Dissertatio ad Fletam, p. 461.

directly from the will of the author. The form thus impressed upon the book is peculiar to it among the English treatises; and it is difficult to suppose that a work would be prepared or published in such a form, at the period to which this book belongs, without express authority.

Similar efforts made in other countries.

Both at home and abroad the age in which Britton was produced was active in the cultivation of the science of jurisprudence; and the most enlightened sovereigns in other countries of Europe had already directed their personal efforts to fix and reduce to a system the confused mass of laws by which their countries were governed. Edward had an illustrious example of royal authorship in the juridical labours of his father-in-law, Alfonso X. king of Castile, whose great work, entitled *Las Siete Partidas*, was about coeval with the treatise of Bracton, having been composed between the years 1256 and 1263. Another of Alfonso's treatises, *Fuero Real*, was completed, as we are informed by a note at the foot of the work, in the year of Edward's early visit to Spain[c]. The code of Magnus VII. of Norway (surnamed *Laga-bæter* or Law-reformer) was promulgated in 1274. This work is, like Britton, written throughout in the king's name, and is said in its prologue to have occupied his attention for a considerable time[d].

Legal writings of Alfonso X. of Castile, and of Magnus VII. of Norway.

Age of Britton.

I have assumed in the above observations, that the king, whose name appears in the introductory sentence of Britton, was Edward I.; and that the work is to be attributed to his reign. Upon this point no question has ever been raised, and the assumption is confirmed both by internal and external evidence.

[c] 'This book was made and ended in Valladolid by the king's command on the thirtieth day of August in the era of 1293, (A. D. 1254); in the year that sir Edward, eldest son and heir of Henry king of England, received knighthood in Burgos from the above-named king Alfonso.' (Note at the foot of Fuero Real; Opúsculos Legales del Rey don Alfonso el Sábio, Madrid, 1836, p. 169.) Another of king Alfonso's works, Espécolo de todos los derechos, probably suggested the name of our 'Mirror of Justices;' but the title of 'Mirror' appears to have been much used in the twelfth and thirteenth centuries. It is remarkable, that, as Britton was the first law-treatise in the vernacular French, the legal works of Alfonso X. appear to be among the earliest monuments of the Castilian language. (Opúsculos Legales del Rey Alfonso, Prólogo, p. 5.)

[d] Magnus Konongs Laga-bæters Gulathings-laug, Havniæ, 1817, Prologus, p. 5.

Internal evidence; language.

The language of Britton is that of the end of the thirteenth century. Upon this some remarks will be found in a subsequent page. The law is, for the most part, the same as that propounded by Bracton in the latter part of the reign of Henry III., with the modifications introduced by the statutes of the first eighteen years of the following reign.

Statutes cited.

Latest statute, 18 Edw. I.

The latest statute referred to is the well-known Statute *Quia emptores terrarum*, passed in the eighteenth year of Edward I.; and this is mentioned as a new law, 'une novele constitucioun[e],' an expression never used in reference to the Statute of Westminster the Second (13 Edw. I.), which is frequently mentioned, or to any other statute. Changes in the law subsequently made are not noticed. For example, in Book I. c. 12. s. 1, the punishment of breaking prison is stated to be death, although this penalty was abolished by a statute of the twenty-third year of Edward I.

External evidence; age of MSS.

If we add to this internal evidence the fact that some of the existing manuscripts appear to be at least as old as the commencement of the fourteenth century, we can have no doubt in fixing upon the twentieth year of Edward I. (A. D. 1291–1292) as an approximate date for the origin of this book. It will be seen in the following paragraph that an earlier date has, upon evidence of a different kind, been attributed to it.

Authorship of Britton.

John le Breton, Bishop of Hereford.

With respect to the authorship of the book, it was formerly the generally received opinion that it was the work of John Britton, or le Breton, bishop of Hereford. 'Britton,' says Lord Coke, 'composed a learned work, and published the same in 5 Edw. I. (as appeareth in 35 Hen. VI.) by the commandment of Edward I., our Justinian; the tenor whereof runneth in the king's name, as if it had been written by him, answerable to Justinian's Institutes, which Justinian assumeth to himself, although it were composed by others. This John Britton was bishop of Hereford, and of great and profound judgment in the common laws[f].'

[e] See vol. ii. p. 39. See also vol. i. pp. 252, 254, where the law is stated as it was altered by the same statute.

[f] Coke, Reports, pt. x. Preface. Subsequently, the same author upon internal evidence corrected his opinion of the age of this book. 'Britton maketh mention of the Statute of Winchester, and of the Statute of

If it were possible to adopt the theory that the book was, as Coke supposed, written by John le Breton, bishop of Hereford, we should be compelled to place its composition at a still earlier date, the bishop having died in 1275 (3 Edw. I.), and to suppose that the numerous passages in which the subsequent statutes are mentioned or alluded to, were a later addition. It will however, I think, be found that the evidence of the authorship of John le Breton is not so strong as to force us to adopt a supposition which an examination of the book renders improbable.

John le Breton died 1275.

John le Breton, bishop of Hereford, has been supposed to be the writer of the present work upon the authority of a passage found in some of the copies of the History of Matthew of Westminster. That passage in the printed copies runs as follows:—'Anno gratiæ 1275. Obiit hoc anno Johannes Bretoun, Episcopus Herefordiensis, qui, admodum peritus in juribus Anglicanis, librum de eis conscripsit qui vocatur le Bretoun[g].' The difficulties involved in the supposition that the book now known as Britton was composed by the Bishop of Hereford who died in 1275, were pointed out by Selden in his notes upon Hengham, first printed in 1616[h]; and the origin and authorship of the book are further discussed by the same writer in the Dissertation appended to Fleta, published in 1647[i]. It is there observed that the sentence relating to Britton is absent in the first edition of Matthew of Westminster, printed in 1567, and in some ancient manuscripts of the author preserved in the Libraries of Lambeth and Westminster. I have myself looked into several ancient copies, and have in every instance found this passage to be wanting[k].

John le Breton, why supposed to be the author.

Westminster II., anno 13 Edw. I. So as he wrote not his book in 5 Edw. I., as Prisot supposed; neither died he in 3 Edw. I., anno Dom. 1272, as Bale, fol. 111, hath mistaken; but he certainly wrote his book after 13 Edw. I.' (Coke, Institutes, pt. ii. p. 569.) Selden also seems to have thought that the Statute of Westminster the Second was the latest statute referred to in Britton; and in order to make the statement of Chief Justice Prisot as to the age of king Edward's book agree with the internal evidence, he suggested that *douze* should be read for *deux* in the passage from the Year Book cited at the foot of p. xvi. (Dissertatio ad Fletam, p. 461.)

g Matth. Westm. Flor. Hist. part. ii. p. 364. (ed. Lond. 1570.)

h Selden's Hengham, p. 129. (ed. 1616), p. 118. (ed. 1660).

i Dissertatio ad Fletam, p. 458.

k The MSS. which I have examined are

Reasons for rejecting the authorship of the Bishop.

Whether the sentence asserting the Bishop's authorship of the book be the words of the Monk of Westminster or of some later transcriber, the principal evidence of its error is to be found in the book itself. References or allusions to the two earlier Statutes of Westminster (3 and 13 Edw. I.) and to the Statute of Gloucester (6 Edw. I.) occur in at least fifty passages of the work, and I have already mentioned that the Statute of Westminster the Third, commonly called the Statute *Quia emptores terrarum* (18 Edw. I.), is also cited. Wingate, who edited the last reprint of Britton in 1640, conjectured that the Bishop might be the author of the Treatise, but that 'the book thus written, being, by command of Edward I., examined and perused by the then Judges of the kingdom, was after the death of the said bishop published in the same king's name, having all the statutes then extant, which did any way concern it, inserted into it.' This conjecture does not in itself appear probable; the passages in which the statutes of Edward I. are mentioned have not the appearance of interpolation; and the influence of Edward's legislation frequently appears when no direct reference is made to the statutes[l].

It may be further observed that it is extremely improbable that any book upon the law should have been written by Edward's command and in his name before the month of May, 1275, at which time the Congé d'élire for the choice of a successor to John le Breton was issued[m]. Edward returned to England from the Holy Land in August, 1274, and was crowned in the same month. Upon his first accession to power he was much occupied in inquiring into and correcting the abuses which had arisen in the previous reign; and a general Parliament was summoned early in the following year for the strengthening and reformation of the law[n]; at which Parliament the Statutes of Westminster the First were

the following: Bodleian, 149, 912; Laud, C. 86; Rawlinson, 177, 186; Hatton, 53; King's Library, 14 C. VI.

[l] See for example vol. i. pp. 147, 252, 254, 255; vol. ii. pp. 11, 153.

[m] See Selden's Notes upon Hengham, p. 130. (ed. 1616), p. 119. (ed. 1660).

[n] Chronicon Thomæ Wikes, p. 102; Parliamentary Writs, vol. i. p. 1.

enacted. It will be seen that the interval between the return of the King and the death of the Bishop was not more than a few months, and these months necessarily occupied with pressing business, including the preparation of some important changes in the law. We can hardly ascribe the assumed scheme for a codification of the law, or the composition of a legal treatise under Edward's direction, to this period of his reign.

Name of Breton borne by other persons in the service of Edward I.

If we are thus compelled to reject the paternity of John le Breton, bishop of Hereford, the questions remain, who was the author of the book, and whence did it derive the name by which it has been so long known. It may be observed, that besides the Bishop, there was at least one other person of the same name employed in the judicial service of king Edward I. John le Breton was appointed in 1300 (28 Edw. I.) one of the Justices for the county of Norfolk to hear and determine complaints of the non-observance of the Great Charter and the Charter of the Forest, and in 1305 and 1307 (33 and 35 Edw. I.) one of the Justices of Trailbaston for the counties of Norfolk and Suffolk, and in consequence of these appointments was summoned to parliament among the Judges and Clerks of the Council in the first and second years of Edward II.[o] It appears probable that this was the same person with Sir John le Breton (or de Breton) to whom, alternately with Sir Ralph de Sandwich, the custody of the city of London was confided by king Edward I. during the interval between 1286 and 1298, when the city was deprived of its liberties and retained *in manu regis*[p], and also with *Johannes le Breton, dominus de Sporle,* one of the barons who signed the letter to Pope Boniface in the twenty-ninth year of Edward I.[q] Bishop Nicholson has suggested, that John

[o] Parl. Writs, vol. i. pp. 399, 400, 407, 408, 497; Rot. Parl. vol. i. p. 218; Foss, Judges of England, vol. iii. p. 61.

[p] Foss, Judges of England, vol. iii. p. 61; Liber Albus, pp. 17, 18, 34, 559; Calend. Rot. Pat. 53, 56, 59.

[q] Parl. Writs, vol. i. p. 104. John le Breton, lord of Sporle in Norfolk, was the son and heir of William le Breton, who held the manor of Sporle in 25 Hen. III. (Plac. cor. Reg. 25 Hen. III. rot. 14 in dorso, cited in Blomefield's History of Norfolk, vol. iii. p. 444), and who died in or before 45 Hen. III. seised of lands at (among other places) Boxsted in Essex, and Blatherwick in Northamptonshire. (Calend. Inquis. post mort. 45 Hen. III. p. 20; Morant's History of Essex, vol. ii. p. 240.)

Sir John le Breton, author of Britton—*qu.*

le Breton who was summoned as a Justice to parliament in the first year of Edward II., was the true writer of the present treatise[r]; but this appears to be a mere conjecture founded only upon the name. If the Judge of Trailbaston, the custodian of the city, and the lord of Sporle were the same person, it can scarcely be taken as certain that he was a professional lawyer, since it appears to have been not unusual to place upon the commission of Trailbaston barons and knights resident in the counties to which it extended, who were not otherwise engaged in the administration of justice[s]; and the same name occurs in the Records in connexion with other duties administrative and military, such as were ordinarily thrown upon the more important proprietors of land. We should rather expect, if there were any materials to aid the search, that the author of Britton would be found among the clerks employed in the legal service of the Crown; and there are one or two passages which confirm the opinion formerly received, that the author was an ecclesiastic, as so many of the judges and officers of the king's courts in his time are known to have been[t].

John le Breton in April, 1261 (45 Hen. III.), did homage to the king, and obtained seisin of the lands held *in capite* by William le Breton. (Excerpta e Rotulis Finium, vol. ii. p. 349.) This William le Breton is identified by Mr. Foss with the Justice of that name, who appears for the last time in the writs of assise, 43 Hen. III. (Foss, Judges of England, vol. ii. p. 262.) John le Breton had a son, John le Breton the younger, who died in his father's lifetime in or before 34 Edw. I., seised of lands at Blatherwick, leaving a third John le Breton, his heir, aged ten years. (Esc. 34 Edw. I. No. 29, cited in Parl. Writs, vol. i. p. 497.) The third John le Breton died in the lifetime of his grandfather, John le Breton, at whose death, in or before 4 Edw. II. (1310), Matilda, daughter of John le Breton the younger and wife of Richard de la Rivere (or Rivers), was his heir. (Esc. 4 Edw. II. No. 32, cited in Parl. Writs, vol. i. p. 497.) Richard de Rivers appears in the *Nomina Villarum* (9 Edw. II.) as lord of Sporle in Norfolk, and one of the lords of Blatherwick in Northamptonshire (Parl. Writs, vol. ii. pp. 304, 391); and he also succeeded to the lands at Boxsted in Essex, subsequently known as Rivers-Hall. (Morant's Hist. Essex, vol. ii. p. 240.) I have been the more particular in this account of the family of Breton, because Mr. Foss has erroneously, as I venture to think, identified John le Breton, the Bishop of Hereford and reputed author of Britton, with John le Breton son and heir of William le Breton. The descent of the estates of William le Breton to the Rivers family in the manner which I have traced, appears to exclude this supposition. If the Bishop was, as is probable, of the same family, I should conjecture that he was a younger brother of William le Breton and uncle of John le Breton, 'lord of Sporle.'

[r] English Historical Library, p. 186.

[s] Foss, Judges of England, vol. iii. p. 29.

[t] See especially liv. ii. c. 5. s. 8, vol. i. p. 240. The commencement of the chapter on Attaints, liv. iv. c. 9, has an ecclesiastical air, but this is also in Fleta. In liv. iv. c. 3. s. 7, the author attributes an authority to the ecclesiastical court, which is not ascribed to it by Bracton or Fleta, and which is contradicted by the practice of a few years later. See vol. ii. p. 180.

II. *Relation of Britton to earlier and contemporary Treatises.*

We owe to the ingenuity of Selden a conjecture respecting the origin of the name of Britton, which, if adopted, dispenses us from seeking for an author bearing the same name as the book. After observing that the surname of Henry de Bracton, the reputed author of the treatise known by his name, was sometimes written Britton, Briton, and Breton, he states his opinion, that the compendium of law called Britton (which he elsewhere describes as the royal abridgment of Bracton increased by the addition of some subsequent statutes[u]), 'took its name from the author out of whose work, in the king's name and by the king's command, it was composed[x].' **Name of Britton derived from Bracton—qu.**

It is impossible to speak with certainty upon such a point as this. It is undoubtedly true that the name of Bracton presents no obstacle to the theory, since it appears that the name of the Justiciary commonly known as Bracton is on the roll of fines indifferently spelt Bratton and Bretton[y]. And it is, I think, open to question whether the letter *c* which occurs in the received form of this name may not have originated in a misreading of the ancient handwriting[z]. On the other hand, the name of the treatise, which in modern times has been generally known as Britton, is variously spelt in the MSS., Bratton, Brettoun, Bretton, Breton. It must also be allowed, that a great part of the materials of Britton was derived directly or indirectly from Bracton. But the smaller treatise **Name of Bracton, more properly Bratton, or Bretton.**

[u] Regium Bractonii compendium non sine insequentibus aliquot Edvardi primi legibus intersertis, Breton et Britton nuncupatum. (Diss. ad Flet. p. 454.)

[x] Et Bracton igitur et Brycton et Britton et Briton, etiam et Breton aliterque, appellatus est. Unde et compendium illud sequentibus aliquot legibus auctum, Britton dictum, nec sine errore manifesto Johanni Bretoun Episcopo Herefordensi annis compluribus ante ejusdem conscriptionem mortuo tribui solitum, nomen velut ab autore, unde nomine jussuque regio descriptum est primario sumpsisse autumo. (Diss. ad Flet. p. 457.)

[y] See Foss, Judges of England, vol. ii. p. 250; Madox, Baronia Anglica, pp. 102, 104.

[z] In MSS. of the thirteenth and fourteenth centuries the double *t* was frequently written like *ct*, the upper part of the first letter being kept below, and the second letter being carried up above the cross line. This is the case throughout the Cambridge manuscript of Britton, Gg v. 12, cited in the various readings as MS. *C*, where in the colophon the title of the book is so written as to read at first sight 'le liure de Brectoun.' Selden mentions another MS. of Britton, in the colophon of which the book is called *le Brecton*. Possibly this may have been merely another example of the double *t*.

Britton not an abridgment of Bracton.

cannot be correctly described as an abridgment of the larger. The form of the whole work, and the arrangement of the heads of subjects, and of the matter under each head, are totally different[a]; and of the great work of Bracton only a small proportion, taken in fragments from various parts of the book, is incorporated in the composition of Britton. Modern examples, however, might be cited to show how a great author may become so identified with the subject which he has successfully appropriated, that his name may be attached to books of a later time founded upon his own work, in spite of a re-arrangement of his materials and of the addition in a large proportion of the labours of others[b].

Authority of Bracton.

The work of Bracton, one of the fullest and ablest treatises upon jurisprudence which this country has ever produced, could not but remain for a long period after its publication the principal authority upon the general subject of English Law. But its great length rendering the labour of perusing it considerable, and the difficulty of finding in a huge closely-written manuscript, without paging or index, the particular matter required for the moment, must in early times have interfered with its practical usefulness to the lawyer; as the same disadvantages, not much lessened by the form in which the work was printed in the sixteenth century, render it unattractive to the modern student. Towards the middle of the reign of Edward I., a strong demand appears to have arisen—whether promoted, as has been conjectured, by the king, or not[c]—for a comprehensive treatise upon the law as then administered in the Royal Courts, which should include in a more compendious form the most useful portions of Bracton. Three treatises are now, or were lately, in existence, which were written about the same time to supply this want. One of these is the well-known Latin work called

A shorter compendium required.

This want how supplied.

[a] Some of the divisions of Bracton are variously placed in the several MSS. This however does not affect the above statement; the principle of arrangement of the two works being different.

[b] I allude especially to the name of Blackstone, as an example *in pari materia*. Other instances might be given, as the small English Dictionaries which pass by the name of Johnson, the "Pocket Johnson," and so forth.

[c] Selden appears to have believed that several summaries of the law, including Britton, Fleta, and Thornton, were compiled by order of Edward I. (Diss. ad Flet. pp. 461, 547.)

Fleta. Another is Britton. The third, a Latin abridgment of Bracton by Gilbert de Thornton, Chief Justice of the King's Bench from 1289 to 1295, which is said to have been composed in the twentieth year of Edward I., is described by Selden in his Dissertation upon Fleta[d]. Of these three works, the treatise called Britton appears to have been the only one which came into general use, the two others having scarcely survived in single manuscripts to modern times[e]. Fleta, Britton, and Thornton.

Fleta has been supposed by some authorities to have been composed as late as the reign of Edward II. or Edward III.[f]; but it has been satisfactorily shown by Selden that that treatise also belongs to the time of Edward I.[g] The internal evidence resembles that already mentioned with regard to Britton; and it is remarkable that in both cases it points to the same date. The author of Fleta refers to the Statute of Acton Burnell (11 Edw. I.) as a recent law[h]. The Statute of Westminster the Second (13 Edw. I.) is also frequently mentioned[i]. Some precedents of proceedings in the Court of the Steward of the King's House in the fourteenth and seventeenth years, and one in the eighteenth year of Edward I. (1289–1290), are cited, the two latest from the Rolls of Peter de Chanvent, then Steward[k]. And finally, in the chapter upon Charters[l] there is an indistinct reference to the Statute of Westminster the Third (*Quia emptores terrarum*) passed in the summer of 1290. It is to be observed, however, that the general tenor of this chapter remains as abridged from Bracton, although considerable modification is required to adapt it to the change of law introduced by the last-named statute; and the writer, who is generally well acquainted with the statutes and cites them in their own words, refers to this most important act of legislation as if he had only Age of Fleta, about 1290.

[d] Selden, Diss. ad Flet. pp. 459, 545. I have not been able to discover in any of the public libraries the work of Gilbert de Thornton, of which Selden knew only one imperfect copy, which was then in his own possession and had formerly been in lord Burghley's library. This copy may possibly still exist in some private collection.

[e] There exists, I believe, only one ancient copy of Fleta, Cotton Jul. B. viii., a MS. of the fourteenth century.

[f] See Coke's Reports, pt. x. Preface.

[g] Diss. ad Flet. p. 546.

[h] Fleta, p. 138.

[i] Ibid. pp. 138, 185.

[k] Ibid. p. 68.

[l] Ibid. p. 198.

heard of its proposal, and did not distinctly understand its purport. He speaks of it moreover as a law not applying to past transactions, but only to the future. Hence, it appears probable that the allusion to this statute was added after this portion of the work was finished; and I am inclined to infer that in the year 1290 the book was in course of preparation.

Author of Fleta, probably an officer in the Court of Edward I.

If we are right in ascribing this date to the composition of Fleta, the fact that the writer shows himself acquainted with the rolls of the Steward of the King's House up to this very year, is significant with reference to its authorship. It must have been composed by one who had access to, or was well acquainted with, the current rolls of the Steward[m]. It is further remarkable that Fleta is more full than any contemporary work upon the subject of the various officers of the royal household, whose powers, duties, privileges, and emoluments are described at considerable length; this portion of the work, and some chapters upon the duties of bailiffs and other manorial officers, being the principal part of the treatise not founded upon Bracton. It is difficult to avoid the conclusion that Fleta was the work of some clerk or lawyer employed in the household of king Edward I.[n] If the statement in the *Proœmium*, that it was composed *in Fleta*, that is, in the Fleet prison, be authentic, the employment of the writer must have recently terminated[o].

Fleta compiled before Britton.

We have already seen that the Statute of Westminster the Third is also the latest statute cited by Britton. So far the internal evidence of Britton and Fleta points to the same

[m] Peter de Chanvent, or Champvent, mentioned by Fleta as *Senescallus hospitii* (or *aulæ*) *Regis* 17 and 18 Edw. I., appears in the same character in the *Placita in Parliamento*, 18 Edw. I. (Rot. Parl. vol. i. p. 17). His name is not found among the summonses of the military tenants until 1296, when he appears as a knight holding land in Sussex (Parl. Writs, vol. i. p. 275), although his name appears as that of a grantee of land from the Crown, 52 Hen. III. (Cal. Rot. Chart. p. 97.) He was summoned to Parliament as a baron in 1300; and died in 1304. See Parl. Writs, vol. i. p. 82; Dugdale, Baronage, vol. ii. p. 27; Cal. Inquis. post mort. p. 180.

[n] Among the officers connected with the Court of the Steward, Fleta mentions one whom he calls 'the King's Clerk holding the roll of pleas of the Household for the King,' and in another place 'the King's Clerk deputed to the pleas of the Household.' (Fleta, pp. 67, 70.) Possibly the author may himself have held this post.

[o] The Fleet is mentioned in the text of Fleta, as the prison to which the Marshall of the Exchequer is bound to deliver prisoners committed for debts due to the King. (Fleta, p. 83.) Selden has suggested that Fleta may have been the work of one of the judges who were fined and imprisoned for corrupt practices in the year 1288. (Diss. ad Flet. p. 548.)

date for their composition. But a comparison of the parallel passages in the two treatises has led me to the conclusion that Fleta was first written, and that this book as well as Bracton was in the hands of the author of Britton, who appears to have more frequently made use of the compendium of Fleta than of the larger work. This conclusion may be tested by any reader who will compare the language of Britton with the parallel places in Bracton and Fleta, which are indicated throughout in the margin of the text[p]. Where there is an error or obscurity in both of the two later writers, which does not appear in their common author, it is difficult to suppose it to be of independent origin; and it is no less difficult to believe that the author of Fleta, who was abridging in Latin a Latin work, and whose abridgment throughout is more full and approaches nearer to the original than the compilation of Britton, should have transplanted an error or obscurity from the French treatise. On the other hand, there are passages which show that, for that part of his work which is ultimately traceable to Bracton, the compiler of Britton was not wholly dependent upon Fleta, but that he also drew his supplies from the original source. It may be added that Britton contains more than one notice of the proceedings in the court of the Steward of the King's House[q], apparently derived from the very full account of that court given by Fleta. I do not think that this subject is mentioned by Bracton.

Fleta used in the composition of Britton.

III. *Character, Method, and Arrangement of Britton.*

The materials so liberally taken by the author of the present treatise from preceding writers are appropriated in a bold and independent fashion suitable to the character assumed by the writer. The various passages are freely translated, amplified, or abridged according to the pleasure of the

Character of the work of Britton.

[p] See especially the seventh and ninth chapters of the third book. See also vol. i. p. 377; vol. ii. pp. 65, 80, 94, 98, 107, 152, 155, 180, 210, 224, 272, 301.

[q] See vol. i. pp. 3, 4, 170, 171, 172.

borrower, and arranged in the new work without reference to their relative position in the old, the object being to recast the materials thus supplied in a more practical form and in a smaller bulk. The important place occupied by Britton in the series of our ancient law-writers depends mainly upon two peculiarities; first, the royal authority under which the book assumes to be promulgated; and, secondly, the fact that it was the first great treatise upon our law written in the vernacular language of the Courts,—the first of the series of books to which the works of Littleton, Fitzherbert, and Plowden belong. The interest of Glanvill is almost purely historical. Bracton stands apart: the theoretical portion is formed in a great degree upon the principles of the Civil Law, though the practice described is English. The author of Britton reproduces much of the practical part of Bracton, but the character of the book is widely different. Its aspect is much more like that of the later text-books; and we feel in reading it that we are nearer to Plowden or to Coke than to Glanvill or the Dialogue of the Exchequer. If much of the work is obsolete, it is in the same way as much of Coke, and even of Blackstone, is obsolete, not because the general maxims have changed, but because the details have been altered by Statute, or one portion of the Common Law has grown at the expense of another[r].

Britton the first French text-book.

Britton still an authority.

Early authority and popularity of Britton.

The language in which Britton was written, and the sanction of the royal name, could not but make the work popular among contemporary students and lawyers; and the number of early and carefully-written manuscripts which still exist bear witness to the estimation in which it was held[s]. I shall shortly have to describe an elaborate commentary written upon it within a few years of its promulgation. Its authority continued for several centuries, and such was the demand for

[r] It will be remembered that Blackstone asserts, that 'the legal Treatises written in the time of Edward I., as Britton, Fleta, Hengham, and the rest, are for the most part law at this day, or at least were so until the alteration of tenures took place.' (Blackstone, Commentaries, vol. iv. p. 426.)

[s] Among the bequests to the Chamber of the Guildhall of London made by the will of Andrew Horn, the author of the Mirror of Justices, dated in 1328, is 'a book called Bretoun,' as well as a copy of the Mirror. Neither of these manuscripts is now in the possession of the Corporation. (Munimenta Guildhallæ Londoniensis, edited by H. T. Riley, esq., vol. ii. Introduction, p. x.)

copies of it, that it was at an early period committed to the press. It would seem, however, that towards the end of the fifteenth and in the beginning of the sixteenth centuries, the great reputation of Littleton's Treatise on Tenures, the large accumulation of decided cases collected in the Year Books, and the Abridgments of those cases subsequently printed by Fitzherbert and Brooke, obscured in some measure the reputation of the more ancient treatises, which were not always found applicable to the law, as it had been gradually altered by usage, legislation, and judicial decisions[t]. Still the older authors were not entirely superseded; and it is well known to every student of our law, that Lord Coke has incorporated considerable passages from Britton and the other treatises of the thirteenth and fourteenth centuries in the several parts of his Institutes.

Decline of authority of the ancient Treatises.

As Britton was the first text-book written in French, so Coke's Institutes was the first important work upon our law composed in the English language. The great authority of his name, the vastness of his learning, and his familiar knowledge of the original materials of our law,—a knowledge so difficult of acquisition, and in which no one in later times could fairly hope to rival him,—have so accustomed his successors to depend upon his works for information as to our older law, that in modern times it has become unusual to recur to the sources from which his learning was derived; and our ancient writers have been suffered to throw only that amount of light upon our jurisprudence which is reflected from them by the pages of Coke. The repulsive form in which alone our earlier authors have been accessible has contributed to confine the researches of the student; and for the practical purposes of legal discussion it has been found a convenient rule to limit the citation of early authorities to those which appear under the sanction of the great Commentator. It is not, however, to be expected that in the vast aggregation of authorities of all ages brought together by Coke, the true features of the juris-

Position of Lord Coke in relation to the earlier authorities.

[t] See Fitzherbert, Abridgment, tit. *Garde*, pl. 71; Plowden, Commentaries, pt. i. ff. 58, 357, 358; Selden, Dissertatio ad Fletam, p. 455. Compare Brooke, Abridgment, tit. *Dum fuit infra ætatem*, pl. 5; Standford, Plees del Corona, Preface, and f. 20 *b*.

prudence of a more remote time can be discerned; and the student, who desires to know the real nature of the laws expounded by Glanvill, Bracton, and Britton, must have recourse to the original sources, and will frequently find it necessary to correct an erroneous impression derived from the confused information of later writers.

Object and method of Britton.

The object of the compiler of Britton, as somewhat ambitiously stated in the opening paragraph, was nothing less than to reduce into writing the entire Common Law of England.

Defect of his arrangement.

His method of arrangement is not adapted to a philosophical treatment, and, in the true spirit of an English lawyer, he approaches his subject from a practical point of view, fixing his regard upon the remedies to be administered by the legal practitioner rather than on the rights attributed to his client. In this respect he offers a contrast to Bracton, whose arrangement, borrowed from the Justinian Institutes, is entirely different. It will be remembered that in the Institutes, the law is arranged under the four heads of the Law of Persons, Things, Obligations, and Actions. In Britton the whole of the law is treated with reference to the legal proceedings by which it might be enforced, the principal division of the subject being into Personal Pleas or Actions, including Criminal proceedings, and Real Pleas. In this arrangement the Rights of Persons find no separate or special place, but are incidentally treated under other heads, such as Naifty or Villenage, Wardship, and Marriage; the first of these subjects being introduced as a supplementary chapter to the book on Personal Pleas, the others being treated in that part of the work which is introductory to the description of the proceedings in the Assise of Mortdancester. So the subject of the purchase or conveyance of property is introduced as subsidiary to that of seisin, and this as having relation to the Assise of Novel Disseisin; the law of Inheritance is discussed as a matter preliminary to the Plea of Right, in which alone a disputed succession could be tried; and the subject of Obligations is treated in the chapter upon the actions of Debt and Trespass.

IV. *Summary of the Contents of Britton.*

Subjects treated by Britton.

Such being the principle of arrangement, I shall proceed to state shortly the chief matters which are discussed, and the order in which they occur. The work commences with the King, both as the author of the book, and as the source of all legal jurisdiction, and then proceeds in the first chapter to describe the Royal Courts and Officers of Justice. The second chapter is devoted to the duties of the Coroner, whose functions, as representing the rights of the Crown, were of considerable importance, and by the Statute of Westminster the First were required to be discharged by one of the most lawful and discreet knights of the county. The Coroner is accordingly described in Britton, as 'a principal guardian of the king's peace, bearing record of the pleas of the Crown, of his own views or inquests, and of abjurations and outlawries.' The primary object of his office appears to have been to keep watch over the profits of the Crown. He was bound to inquire concerning treasure-trove, wreck, whales, and sturgeons, and to secure them for the king's use. The inquest in cases of sudden death had a similar purpose, to see that the Crown was not deprived of its emoluments arising from the forfeiture of the chattels of felons and outlaws. The Coroner alone bore record of outlawries in the County Court; his presence was required whenever judgment of death was passed in a court of private jurisdiction[u]; appeals of felony were commenced before him[x]; and his inquest extended to cases of rape, which was from ancient time a matter of royal jurisdiction, and consequently of profit to the Crown[y]; and to cases of wounding, which might possibly lead to death, and upon which, if the wound was serious, an appeal of felony might be founded[z].

The Sovereign. *Prologue.* The Royal Courts. *li.* i. *chap.* 1. Coroners. *li.* i. *chap.* 2.

The third chapter describes the manner of proceeding in the opening of the *Iter* or Eyre of the Justices Itinerant. These magistrates are represented as holding their sessions

The Eyre. *li.* i. *chap.* 3.

[u] Britton, vol. i. pp. 17, 18, 37, 56.
[x] Ibid. pp. 12, 110, 112.
[y] Leges Hen. I. c. x. § 1, c. 13. § 6; Glanvill, l. i. c. 2; l. xiv. c. 6.
[z] Britton, vol. i. p. 98, 123.

Duties of the Justices Itinerant.

in every county once in seven years[a], when they not only heard and determined the civil and criminal business ordinarily taken by Justices of assise and gaol delivery, and the common pleas of the county where they sat, which were adjourned before them by the Justices of the Bench, but were also charged with duties of the highest political consequence. The limitation and suppression of local and feudal jurisdictions was a material object of the policy of the Plantagenet kings, and the Justices Itinerant were entrusted with an important part in carrying out this policy. Their first business was to inquire concerning franchises claimed by bishops, abbots, earls, barons, and others in the county, and any liberties which were not distinctly claimed in writing on the first day were taken into the king's hand[b]. They took notice of the extortions and malversations of Sheriffs, Coroners, and other officers of the Crown, and of those who held similar offices in fee; of claims to local usages contrary to the common law[c], and of the usurpations, excesses, and errors of local and private jurisdictions, and exercised the power of amercing the offenders[d]. The Eyre was attended by all the prelates, noblemen, and free-tenants of the county, and the peasants were represented by the provost and four men of each township; but it would seem that where there was a liberty within the county having the privilege of an Eyre held exclusively for its district, the inhabitants of the liberty were sent home after the first day, the bailiff only remaining in attendance on the Justices[e]. The fourth and twelve

[a] Britton, vol. i. p. 3. The septennial period mentioned by Britton appears to have been only approximately observed in practice. See Foss, Judges of England, vol. ii. p. 192. There was no *Iter* in London between the 4th year of Edward I. and the 14th of Edward II., a period of thirty-five years, (Liber Custumarum, p. 290); but there were probably special reasons for the long cessation in this case: and I am informed by Mr. Horwood, that in a MS. of the University of Cambridge, Dd. 7, 14, there are reports of an *Iter* of 22 Edw. I., which are headed, 'Placita apud London̄ in Itinere de Middelsexe.' The account in the *Liber Custumarum* shows how unpopular and oppressive these Commissions could be.

[b] Britton, vol. i. pp. 19, 20; Year Book 30 Edw. I. Appendix to Preface, p. lviii.

[c] Britton, vol. i. pp. 84, 85.

[d] Ibid. pp. 75, 79, 90, 91; Cornish Iter in Year Book, 30 Edw. I. pp. 241, 258, 501, 545.

[e] Britton, vol. i. p. 22; compare p. 75; Bracton, f. 117 b, 118; Fleta, p. 23 (§ 8); Chronicon Petroburgense, p. 119. The sittings of the Justices Itinerant were of considerable duration. The Eyre of Northampton, 13 Edw. I., lasted ten weeks, and that of London, 14 Edw. II., twenty-four weeks and three days. (Chronicon Petroburgense, p. 118; Liber Custumarum, p. 285.)

following chapters are occupied with the Criminal Law, as administered at the king's suit before the Justices appointed by the Crown. The seventeenth chapter is upon the privilege of Sanctuary, and the practice of Abjuration before the Coroner, upon which the criminal who had taken refuge in a church, having confessed his felony, had liberty to depart the realm. The five succeeding chapters conclude the business of the Eyre and the various matters, civil and criminal, concerning which the Justices were charged to make inquisition. These are divided under the five following heads: first, Troveures, or objects found, under which head the rights of the Crown, the lord of the manor, and the finder, in treasure and other objects found are partially discussed; secondly, the king's proprietary rights, seigniories, wardships, marriages, escheats, and the like, the object of the inquiry of the Justices under both these heads being to assert and enforce the royal prerogative; thirdly, Franchises, under which head the manner of proceeding against usurpers of feudal jurisdictions and other liberties is described; the fourth head, 'Of diverse wrongs,' includes fortification of houses without licence from the Crown, neglect of repair of roads and bridges, and many other minor inquiries of the Eyre, the greater part of which were also made at the Sheriff's Tourns, and in Courts Leet. The concluding head of inquiry has reference to the delinquencies of the King's Officers in defrauding the Crown or oppressing the subject. The four following chapters describe the proceedings in Appeals of Treason, Homicide, Robbery, and Mayhem, and the mode of punishing these offences at the suit of individuals[f].

Criminal law. *li.* i. *chap.* 4–16.

Abjuration. *li.* i. *chap.* 17.

Treasure-trove, &c. *li.* i. *chap.* 18.

Proprietary rights of the Crown. *li.* i. *chap.* 19.

Special franchises of subjects. *li.* i. *chap.* 20.

Minor enquiries made at the Eyre. *li.* i. *chap.* 21.

Offences of king's officers. *li.* i. *chap.* 22.

Proceeding by appeal. *li.* i. *chap.* 23–26.

Three chapters only are devoted to civil actions of the personal class. The twenty-seventh chapter, which is entitled 'Of Attachments,' treats of the proceedings and process in actions of trespass and account in the King's Courts. The twenty-eighth describes the proceedings and mode of pleading in the

Civil actions. *li.* i. *chap.* 27–29.

[f] The age at which an appellor was exempted from offering to prove his accusation by his body, that is, by battle, is placed in the text at seventy years. See vol. i. p. 100. We should probably substitute *lx.* for *lxx.*, though the latter is found in the best MSS. The other authors fix the period at sixty. (Glanvill, l. xiv. c. 1; Fleta, p. 50, § 25.)

Replevin. *li.* i. *chap.* 28. action of Replevin, in which the Sheriff had jurisdiction. The twenty-ninth chapter is devoted to the action of Debt, whether brought in the King's Court, or, for a sum under forty shillings, in the County Court or Hundred, and treats incidentally of the law of Obligations. The same chapter also contains a notice of the Court of the Steward of the King's House, whose jurisdiction was confined to felonies and trespasses which had been committed, and for which the prisoners were attached within the verge (that is within twelve miles of the royal residence, wherever it might be), and to debts contracted by writing in which the debtor expressly bound himself to the jurisdiction. This chapter concludes by a short reference to other causes of personal actions.

Debt. *li.* i. *chap.* 29.

Law of Obligations.

Court of the Steward of the King's House.

Sheriff's Tourn. *li.* i. *chap.* 30.

The thirtieth chapter describes the jurisdiction of the Sheriff exercised in the Tourn, at which all the freeholders of the hundred in which it was held were bound to be present, except earls, barons, clerks and women, who were exempted by the Statute of Marlborough from this attendance[h]. The same chapter also describes the proceedings in Views of Frank-pledge, and the manner of enforcing the law requiring the subjects to be enrolled in tithings, and to take the oath of fealty to the king. The next chapter, which is entitled 'Of Measures,' contains the provisions known as the Assises of Bread and of Beer, and describes an inquest made by the king's 'Officer of Measures within the royal verge.' This officer appears to have been styled Clerk, or Keeper, of the Market; and his duties were generally united with those of the Coroner of the Verge[i].

Assise of bread and beer. *li.* i. *chap.* 31.

Clerk of the Market.

Villenage. *li.* i. *chap.* 32.

The chapter which follows, upon Naifty or Villenage,

[h] Stat. Marl. (52 Hen. III.) c. 10; Britton, vol. i. pp. 184, 178, where the words, 'somouns comunement deyvent venir,' should probably be translated, 'being summoned by general summons ought to appear.' See vol. ii. p. 339. In the same page at the end of s. 1, the word 'nos' should, I think, be omitted in the clause 'en nos hundredz.' This reading is authorized by MSS. *S* and *C*. The meaning would then be, that in hundreds (held in fee) and other minor liberties the courts were called Views of Frank-pledge. The courts held twice a year by the Abbot of Peterborough in the eight hundreds belonging to that monastery were called 'Sheriff's Tourns.' (Chronicon Petroburgense, pp. 109, 114.)

[i] Fleta, p. 71; Britton, vol. i. p. 4; Coke, Inst. pt. iv. p. 273. In the 28th year of Edward I. the 'profits of the market,' received by Richard de Bremesgrave, clerk, *custos mercati regis*, and derived principally from fines for trespasses in weights and measures, amounted to 153*l.* 11*s.* 8*d.* See Liber Garderobæ, 28 Edw. I. pp. 4, 8, 62.

forms in some manuscripts the first chapter of the second Book. In others it constitutes a separate Book, not included under either division of Personal or Real Actions. In others, again, it forms the last chapter of the first Book. I have thought it more convenient to adopt the last arrangement. The plea of Naifty, in which the question of status was decided, was, in relation to the alleged villain, an action of a personal nature, while it partook of the character of a real action in reference to the lord, who claimed the defendant as a chattel annexed to his freehold. It will be seen that the chapter on villenage exhibits a condition of law extremely favourable to the gradual enfranchisement of the peasantry.

Real Actions. *li.* ii–vi.

The subject of personal actions, and the other matters which according to the author's method of arrangement are treated as subsidiary thereto, being concluded in the first Book, the remaining five Books are occupied with Real Actions and the several matters brought under that head. Real Actions were either possessory or proprietary. The former were employed when the possession of the defendant was wrongful, as arising from a recent act of invasion, which could be testified by an inquest of the neighbouring freeholders. A proprietary action was resorted to, where the defendant had acquired by process of time, by judgment, or in some other way a title to the possession which could only be divested by the most solemn proof of the absolute right of property. The subject of possessory actions naturally precedes that of proprietary actions, which were the ultimate remedies given by the law.

Real Actions, possessory and proprietary.

Assise of Novel Disseisin. *li.* ii.

The proceeding called an Assise of Novel Disseisin was, as its name implies, a judicial inquiry instituted at the suit of a person who alleged himself to have been at a recent period wrongfully dispossessed of the subject of litigation. This action forms the principal subject of the second Book; but as the act of disseisin, or dispossession, implies a previous possession, the subject of seisin, or possession, and of the acquisition, or purchase, of land by feoffment, or gift, accompanied with delivery of possession, is discussed as introductory to the Assise. This introductory matter is prefaced by a

Purchase and Possession of land. *li.* ii. *chap.* 1–10.

Acquisition of property. *li.* ii. *c.* 2.

chapter upon the acquisition of property in general, and the *lt.*ii.*chap*.3. various modes by which a legal ownership is obtained. The third chapter is upon the subject of gifts or feoffments, and *lt.*ii.*chap*.4. the conditions necessary to their validity. The fourth is upon joint or common purchase; the distinction between jointenancy and tenancy in common appears to be of later growth. *lt.*ii.*chap*.5. Among the remaining introductory chapters one is devoted *lt.*ii.*chap*.6. to conditional gifts or purchases, another to the title of a *lt* ii.*chap*.7. donor by reversion and escheat, another to acquisitions by *lt.*ii.*chap*.8. villains and the rights of their lords arising therefrom, and another to the form of a charter or deed of feoffment. The

Livery of seisin. *lt.* ii. *chap.* 9.

ninth chapter describes the acts necessary to a transfer of possession. This was a matter of essential importance in the ancient conveyance of land, since, if there was any ground for holding that livery of seisin had never been completed in the donor's life, his heir might set aside the title of the purchaser, and the smallest circumstance was relied upon to show that the transfer was, either in intention or in fact, imperfect. Hence, a careful practitioner distrusted a purchase unless the tenement was first entirely vacated by the removal of the donor's family and goods; and it was not considered safe to permit the donor to reside in any capacity upon the land which he had conveyed[k]. Livery of seisin was generally made by the donor or his agent putting into the donee's hands in the presence of witnesses the handle or ring of the door of the principal house, so that he might open it and shut himself in; where there was no house, the ceremony was completed by the symbolical delivery of a rod or glove or

Advowson in gross.

other like object[l]. On account of the impossibility of delivering seisin, it appears to have been doubted in the time of Britton whether an advowson could be conveyed without a manor or other corporeal tenement to which it was ap-

Rent charge. *lt.* ii. *chap.* 10.

pendant[m]. The tenth chapter deals with the conveyance of a seigniory or reversion, and the grant of a rent-charge.

[k] Britton, vol. i. pp. 259, 262, 265.

[l] Ibid. pp. 261, 262; Archæologia, vol. xvii. p. 311.

[m] Britton, vol. i. p. 267. The word 'glebe' was then used to designate the land to which the advowson was appendant, vol. ii. pp. 173, 184, note.

Disseisin. *li.* ii. *chap.* 11, 12.

The subject of Purchase and Seisin being thus disposed of, we are next led to that of Disseisin or Dispossession. The various instances of disseisin and other analogous acts which gave occasion to the assise of novel disseisin, and the cases of dispossession in which that assise was not admitted, are discussed in the eleventh and twelfth chapters. The thirteenth describes the primary remedy for disseisin which was sanctioned by our early law, namely, the ejectment of the wrongdoer by the act of the person dispossessed. This was lawful only if accomplished within a limited time, four days being allowed to collect arms and friends, and the fifth to recover the possession; but if the disseisee was absent from the country, the period was extended[n]. The fourteenth chapter, entitled 'Of Views in Disseisin,' opens the proceedings of the assise, in which the jurors, who were freeholders of the neighbourhood, were directed in their summons to be at a certain time and place before the King's Justices to make recognizance upon their oaths, whether the plaintiff was disseised of his freehold according to his plaint, and in the meantime to view the tenement. This process of View, which was conducted under the direction of the plaintiff, who was bound to point out the boundaries of the land he claimed, was of obvious importance when the jurors were expected to found their verdict, not upon documentary or other evidence, but upon their own observation of the manner in which the land had been enjoyed[o].

Remedy by reentry. *li.* ii. *chap.* 13.

View. *li.* ii. *chap.* 14.

The next chapter is principally occupied with the appearance of the parties in court, and treats of the authority of attorneys, and of bailiffs by whom the defendants might be represented in this action. The declaration of the plaintiff and the pleadings of the defendant, or tenant, as he is called, are described in the four following chapters. The twentieth is occupied with those cases in which the action was concluded by a verdict upon some collateral point raised by the

Process in the Assise. *li.* ii. *chap.* 15.

Pleadings. *li.* ii. *chap.* 16—19.

Assise turned into Jury. *li.* ii. *chap.* 20.

[n] Britton, vol. i. pp. 294, 295.

[o] The Coustumier of Normandy, which describes a system of law very closely resembling that found in Britton, gives an interesting account of the process of View, with more details than are given in our English books. The view of Baronies, *fiefs de haubert*, and *sergenteries* was not to be made without knights, provided they were to be found in the neighbourhood. Coustumier de Normandie, c. 95.

pleadings, and the recognizance of the assise was consequently not taken upon the principal question of disseisin. In these cases the assise was said to be 'turned into a jury,' and the most important consequence of this change of proceeding appears to have been, that in general the verdict of a jury was not subject to the process of attaint, by which a verdict taken upon the assise might be set aside[p]; the inquest of a jury being in theory a species of arbitration, to which the parties voluntarily bound themselves, though in fact their submission was enforced by the alternative of defeat in the litigation[q]. The twenty-first and twenty-second chapters describe the Trial of the assise, and the nature of the Judgment pronounced in it.

Trial and Judgment. *li.* ii. *chap.* 21, 22.

Servitudes or easements. *li.* ii. *chap.* 23.

Common of pasture. *li.* ii. *chap.* 24–28.

The assise of novel disseisin applied not only to land, but to some incorporeal hereditaments, being easements or servitudes appurtenant to land, in which the plaintiff had a freehold. The nature of Servitudes in general is therefore discussed in this place under the name of 'Appurtenances;' and the most important of all easements, namely Common of Pasture, and the various remedies given by the law for disturbance of common either by the owner of the soil, by a stranger, or by one of the commoners, are treated at some length. Rights of way and water, and the remedies for their infringement, are discussed under the head of 'Nusances;' and the disturbance of the franchise of market comes under the same title. A short chapter at the end of the Book is devoted to the imperfect remedies then given by the law to vindicate the right of a farmer or lessee to possession of the land during

Nusances. *li.* ii. *chap.* 30–32.

Rights of lessees. *li.* ii. *chap.* 33.

[p] Britton, vol. ii. p. 222. In the passage in vol. i. p. 335, which appears to be contradictory, the word *james* ought probably to be substituted for *jalemeyns* in the second line of the page. This correction is authorized by MS. *I.* The reading in the text is found in MS. *LMSG.*

It is singular that Britton appears to take no notice of the 38th chapter of the Statute of Westminster the First, which enacted that the king should, *de son office*, grant attaints upon inquests in actions concerning freehold, when it should appear necessary. Fleta interprets this law as providing for attaints upon juries where freehold was concerned, as well as upon assises, but only *ex gratia principis*. (Fleta, pp. 335. 336.) Lord Coke on the other hand appears to suppose that before this law, whereas attaints were generally allowed in personal pleas, they were granted in pleas real only upon special suit to the king, and considers that the object of the act was to make that of course, which was before a matter of discretion. Coke, Institutes, pt. ii. p. 237.

[q] Britton, vol. i. p. 334; vol. ii. p. 157.

his term. It may be observed, that, while admitting the incompleteness of his remedy, the author sets the right of the lessee to his term as high as that of the freeholder to his freehold[r].

Abatement and intrusion, the subject of the third Book.

Disseisin and disturbance are injuries done to a person previously in possession of a tenement. Where one having a right to possession upon the death of his ancestor or predecessor is prevented from taking possession by the usurpation of another, the wrong is called an Abatement or Intrusion. The remedies provided by the law for this species of invasion of a possessory right form the subject of the third Book. The principal of these remedies was the Assise of Mortdancester, by which an heir was enabled to claim the possession of an hereditament of which his father, mother, uncle, aunt, brother, or sister, died seised. If the ancestor stood in a more remote degree of kindred to the claimant, as being his grandfather, greatgrandfather, or cousin, the possessory action was called a plea of Ael, Besael, or Cosinage. And where it was necessary to go back to the seisin of the ancestor in the fourth degree the possessory right was exhausted, and the only remedy was by a proprietary action.

Tenures; profits of seigniory. *li.* iii. *chap.* 2–5.

But inasmuch as the claims of heirs were qualified by, and were frequently in conflict with, the feudal rights of the lord of the fee of which the lands were held, and the rights of the lord depended upon the nature of the tenure, the subject of Tenures, and of Wardship, Marriage, Homage and Relief, the principal fruits of seigniory, are discussed in the introductory chapters of this Book. And since inheritances were frequently divisible either by common law between sisters, or by special custom between brothers, the means provided by the law for securing each parcener in the enjoyment of his or her proper share, either jointly with the others, or by a partition, are also discussed in the same part of the work. The proceedings in the Assise of Mortdancester are then described. The action named after the writ of *Quod permittat*, by which an heir being in possession of his land was assisted to recover an

Rights of coheirs *inter se*; partition. *li.* iii. *chap.* 7–9.

Proceedings in Mortdancester. *li.* iii. *chap.* 10–24.

Quod permittat. *li.* iii. *chap.* 25.

[r] See vol. i. p. 416, vol. ii. p. 113, and compare vol. ii. p. 124, note.

easement appertaining to it, of which his ancestor died seised, is the subject of a short chapter, which is followed by another upon the varieties of action called Pleas of Cosinage, Ael, and Besael.

Action of Cosinage. *li.* iii. *chap.* 26.

The fourth Book comprehends the assises and actions relating to property of an ecclesiastical character, and the process of attaint applicable to set aside the verdict given in an assise. The first six chapters are occupied with the Assise of Darreign Presentment, or Drein Present, as it is called in Britton, whereby the question of the possession of an advowson was determined by the issue, 'who last presented in time of peace.' The assise of 'last presentation' being essentially founded upon possession of the right by the plaintiff or his ancestors, was of no avail when the plaintiff's title commenced by gift or otherwise since the last clerk was presented. The ordinary remedy in such cases was by *Quare impedit,* when the plaintiff claimed the property of the advowson, or by *Quare non permittit,* when he claimed only the usufruct. These actions are shortly discussed in the sixth chapter. The seventh and eighth are devoted to the Assise of *Utrum,* by which the question was tried, whether land was the property of a church or constituted a lay fee. This assise is described as the clergyman's writ of right, and was applicable to the land attached to a parish church which was held by the parson *nomine ecclesiæ,* and not to the properties of cathedral and conventual churches, the dignified holders of which had the same remedies by the ordinary writ of right as if they were lay fees, and could found their claim in the same way upon the seisin of their predecessors as the lay demandant could upon that of his ancestors.

Assise of Darreign Presentment. *li.* iv. *chap.* 1–6.

Quare impedit; Quare non permittit. *li.* iv. *chap.* 6.

Assise of *Utrum.* *li.* iv. *chap.* 7, 8.

Attaint. *li.* iv. *chap.* 9–12.

The verdict of an assise finally determined the right of possession, and, in the case of an assise of *Utrum,* the right of property also, unless the jurors of the assise were convicted of perjury by the process called an Attaint, in which the verdict of the original twelve was submitted to the judgment of twenty-four jurors, who were required to be taken from the higher class of freeholders. This proceeding forms the subject of the four remaining chapters of the fourth Book, and is introduced in the ninth chapter by some general observations upon the nature of an oath.

Oaths. *li.* iv. *chap.* 9.

In ordinary possessory actions the demand proceeded upon an allegation of previous possession by the complainant, his ancestors, or predecessors in estate; the claim of a widow to dower out of her deceased husband's lands was founded upon a peculiar title, and was enforced by special remedies. The law of dower is discussed at some length in the first three chapters of the fifth Book. This law was in the thirteenth century less favourable to the wife than it became in later times. It was the common practice to appoint upon the occasion of the marriage the particular lands which the wife was to enjoy as her dower, and such an appointment was valid against the heir, provided it did not exceed a third of the land belonging to the husband at the time of the marriage. If the dower was so 'established' at the church door, the wife could claim no more, although the husband might after the time of the marriage have acquired a property far larger than he then possessed. A dower might even be appointed in chattels or money, and such a dower, however small, if made with the assent of the wife, barred her from any claim against her husband's land[s]. If, on the other hand, no dower was expressly appointed, the wife was entitled to 'reasonable dower,' that is, to the full third part of the lands held by the husband at the time of the marriage. This was the law as laid down by Glanvill[t]. The seventh chapter of the Great Charter of Henry III. directed, that there should be assigned to the widow for her dower 'the third part of the whole of her husband's land which was his in his life.' This clause is not in the charter of John, and it is remarkable that Bracton still treats the wife's claim as confined to the land belonging to the husband on the day of the espousals[u]. Britton and

Law of Dower. *li.* v. *chap.* 1-3.

[s] It was doubted in the time of Edward II., whether an agreement made at the marriage, that the wife should have no dower at all, would be a valid answer to the demand of the widow. See the note in vol. ii. p. 236.

[t] Glanvill, l. vi. cc. 1, 2.

[u] Bracton, f. 92 (§ 2); Fleta, p. 341 (§ 11). The words of Magna Charta do not point distinctly to an intended change in the law; and if construed according to their terms would extend the widow's claim further than has ever been allowed. Hence, in the

Hengham[x] appear to be the earliest authorities which expressly extend the right to land acquired after the marriage[y].

Various actions for recovery of dower.

The law of dower having been generally laid down, the various forms of action by which the rights of the widow on the one hand and of the heir on the other were determined, are next discussed. Where the person in possession of the land refused altogether to recognize the widow's claim, her remedy was by writ of dower 'whereof she hath nothing.' Where the widow having obtained possession of her dower was afterwards disseised, or where she was in possession of part and excluded from the rest, or in possession of the land and deprived of easements or appurtenances belonging to it, her remedy was by writ of right of dower. The latter action was commenced, like the ordinary writ of right patent, in the court of the lord of whom the land was held, that is, when the husband had himself been seised of the seigniory, in the court of the heir, who was called the warrant of the dower[z]; whence it might be removed into the County Court, and thence before the King's Justices by writ of *Pone*. The plea of Dower *unde nihil habet* was instituted originally in the King's Court, because, when the claim of the widow was contested *in toto*, it was assumed that the validity of the marriage would be in question, and this could only be determined by the certificate of the Ordinary in return to a royal mandate[a]. The proceedings in this action, and the several defences by which it was commonly met, are described in eight chapters. The writ of Right of Dower occupies another chapter, and another is devoted to the plea of Admeasurement of Dower, by which the heir obtained

Writ of dower *unde nihil habet*. *li.* v. *chap.* 4–11.

Writ of right of dower. *li.* v. *chap.* 12.

English version, the words 'in vita sua' are freely paraphrased, 'during coverture.'

[x] Britton, vol. ii. pp. 238, 242; Hengham Parva, c. iii. pp. 85, 87 (ed. 1616).

[y] Between the time of Britton and Littleton a large change was introduced into the law of dower without the assistance of direct legislation. Dower at the church door was no longer confined to the third part of the husband's lands, and might even extend to the whole. (Litt. Ten. s. 39.) And it was held further, that the wife was not bound by this endowment, if after the husband's death she chose to refuse it, and to claim her common right. (Litt. Ten. s. 41.) On the other hand, whereas dower was anciently allowed to the wife of one who became a monk professed, (Britton, vol ii. p. 261,) in later times no dower could be claimed till his natural death. This change was established shortly after the time of Britton; see Year Book, 32 Edw. I. p. 166.

[z] See Glanvill, l. vi. c. 4; Bracton, f. 329; Hengham Magna, c. i. p. 7 (ed. 1616); Britton, vol. ii. pp. 286, 292.

[a] Britton, vol. ii. p. 254.

redress, when the widow by the assignment of the guardian during the infancy of the heir[b], or by her own usurpation, had obtained possession of more than her rightful portion of her husband's land. This latter proceeding was in the County Court, but the pleadings might be removed into the King's Court by the writ of *Pone*.

Admeasurement of dower. *li.* v. *chap.* 13.

Before passing to the subject of proprietary actions, the form of action called a Plea of Entry is described in the three concluding chapters of the fifth Book. This form of action was properly possessory, the cases to which it applied being those in which the tenant, or defendant, had gained an entry into the property by an abuse of the possession derived from the demandant or those whom he represented in estate; but the tenant might convert the proceeding into a proprietary action by pleading that the absolute right to the land in question was vested in such an one, his ancestor, and so tracing its descent to himself; and according to the form of the pleadings, the trial was either by jury, as in other possessory actions, or by battle or great assise, as in the writ of right. The discussion of this form of proceeding concludes the description of possessory actions, and introduces the reader to the subject of the sixth Book.

Plea of Entry. *li.* v. *chap.* 14–16.

This book was intended to embrace the entire proceedings in a Plea of Right. The few existing chapters, which are probably all that were written, exhaust but a small part of the proposed subject. This form of action was founded upon the assumption that either in union with, or separated from, the possession and the right to the possession, there always existed in some person an ultimate or absolute right of property (*merum jus*). The question in whom this mere right was vested could in early times be tried only by wager of battle, until a change of law introduced by Henry II. gave the defendant the option of appealing to a jury of knights, called the Great Assise. The proceedings in a plea of right were dilatory in the extreme, principally owing to the number of essoins, or excuses for non-appearance, which were

Proprietary actions, the subject of the sixth Book.

Delays in a writ of right; essoins.

[b] Britton, vol. ii. p. 238.

successively allowed to the tenant, and which it was customary to use for the sake of prolonging the possession without any reference to their truth in the particular case[c]. In this way the trial was regularly delayed for several years, and if the plaintiff died before the judgment, the proceedings were to be re-commenced anew by his heir. The advantages thus given to the defendant were in some cases regarded as legitimate privileges due to length of possession, recourse being had to a writ of right when, owing to lapse of time, a possessory action would not lie, or where the demandant had lost his possession in such an action.

Question of descent tried in writ of right. *li.* vi. *chap.* 1.

But in disputed successions these delays must have led to peculiar hardship. Such questions were considered too difficult to be determined by a jury in a possessory action; they were therefore triable only by writ of right, and probably supplied the most ordinary examples of this form of action.

Rules of inheritance. *li.* vi. *chap.* 2, 3.

The subject of succession and the Rules of Inheritance are discussed in the second and third chapters of this Book.

Writ of right brought in Court-baron. *li.* vi. *chap.* 4.

The remaining chapters are occupied in describing the preliminary proceedings in the plea of right, which was commenced in the court of the lord of the fee, unless the lord by anticipation remitted his jurisdiction to the king[d], but was generally removed in regular course from the Court-baron to the County, and from the County to the Bench. These proceedings are described in the fourth chapter.

Summons. *li.* vi. *chap.* 5.

The fifth is devoted to the Summons of the tenant, which in a plea of right was required to be performed with special solemnity.

Essoins. *li.* vi. *chap.* 6–9.

The important subject of Essoins is then commenced, and is only partially concluded in the sixth, seventh, eighth and ninth chapters.

Attorneys. *li.* vi. *chap.* 10.

The tenth chapter, which is the last in the book, and concludes abruptly in the middle of a sentence, relates to the appointment of Attorneys to represent the parties in actions, a subject which appears to be introduced as immediately connected with that of essoins, the essoiners or persons charged with the excuses of the parties having the character of attorneys for a limited purpose, and

c Hengham Magna, cc. vi, xi. pp. 28, 62, 63 (ed. 1616).
d Ibid., c. iii. p. 11 (ed. 1616).

attorneys being capable in some cases of causing themselves to be essoined.

There is evidence in the pages of Britton that the work was intended to include a chapter upon the practice of vouching warrants in proprietary actions, other chapters upon exceptions, and a description of the trial by battle in civil proceedings[e]. If completed, it would probably have followed the arrangement of the latter part of Bracton and Fleta so far as those works could have served as guides. But it is remarkable (though I do not find that the observation has previously been made), that both those treatises are also incomplete. In Bracton, the proceedings in a plea of right are pursued only as far as the exceptions or defences pleaded by the tenant. The trial, by battle or great assise, was intended to be afterwards described[f]. The three chapters which are found in the printed book, and, as far as my observation has extended, in the MSS. also, at the end of Bracton, appear to be a fragment not connected with the matter immediately preceding. Fleta, which in this part is an abridgment of Bracton, ends with like abruptness at the same point, and its agreement in this respect with Bracton appears to shew that the same incompleteness which is found in our copies existed in Bracton as it was originally written, or at least as it was known to the author of Fleta.

Britton an unfinished work.

Bracton and Fleta also incomplete.

V. *Language of Britton.*

The French language was at the time when this treatise was composed, and had been for two centuries, the ordinary dialect of the Court and of the governing class of the community. It was consequently the language in which the discussion of legal questions before the royal tribunals was carried on; at the same time the written documents and records were in Latin, and in the Eyre of the Justices the proceedings were partly conducted in English[g], which in the local and popular

French the language of the Court of Edward I.

e Vol. i. pp. 107, 321, 322, 333; vol. ii. pp. 98, 102, 258, 333, 335, 359.
f Bracton, f. 394 *b* (c. 23. § 1).
g See the note in vol. i. p. 23.

courts was no doubt still more generally employed. The received mode of speech, by which the language of Britton and of contemporary and succeeding English authors who wrote in the same tongue is distinguished as Norman French, is perhaps scarcely accurate. The language of William the Bastard and his Norman followers may probably have been a provincial dialect, but the French spoken at the court of Edward I. did not materially differ from that spoken by St. Louis, and the language of Britton resembles very nearly that of Joinville. We may well believe, that the accent of Paris had already become, as it was a century later[h], the standard of the Langue d'Oil. The French which is ridiculed by Chaucer as 'Frenche of Stratford-atte-bowe' was not Norman French: it probably differed from 'Frenche of Paris' much as the French of a modern English schoolboy differs from that of his instructor. To king Edward I., and many of his barons and courtiers, if French was not properly their mother-tongue, it was equally familiar[i]. The jargon, which from the time of Littleton to that of Levinz was the current dialect of our legal writers, and which has also been commonly termed Norman French, was a corruption of the language which in the thirteenth century was common to Northern France and to the higher classes of England. The principal characteristics of this juridical French were not those of a provincial dialect: they were

'Norman French' incorrectly so called.

French of Stratford-atte-Bowe.

Law-French.

h See Chaucer, Prologue to Canterbury Tales, in the description of the Prioress.

i We read in Matthew of Westminster (*sub anno* 1301) that the Archbishop of Canterbury informed the Pope, that his letters had been presented to king Edward I. in full court, 'quas ipse dominus rex reverenter recipiens eas publice legi coram omnibus et in Gallica lingua fecerat patenter exponi.' No better evidence can be given as to the language ordinarily used in king Edward's Court. On the other hand it is worth observing, that in 'Blonde of Oxford,' a French Romance of the thirteenth century, the scene of which is principally in England, the author makes the Earl of Gloucester, an imaginary English character, talk bad French. See Blonde of Oxford, p. 91. The collection of Historical Letters published by Sir Henry Ellis furnishes the means of observing the progress of the English language among the higher classes. Henry IV. writes in French, and Henry V., the conqueror of France, is the first king who writes in English. So in Nichols's Collection of Royal Wills, the first will written in English is that of the same king. The oral pleadings of the Courts of Law were ordered to be in English by Statute 36 Edw. III. c. 15, but Fortescue appears to intimate that this rule was imperfectly observed by the lawyers, (Fortescue de laudibus legum Angliæ, c. 48); and it is well known that French was long retained as the language of legal literature. The last Reports published in French were those of Sir Edward Lutwych, which comprise cases decided in the second year of Anne, 1702. Sir Thomas Raymond's Reports, which include the greater part of the reign of Charles II., and Lord Raymond's, which commence in the 6th William and Mary, are in English.

simply a very limited vocabulary, and a complete degradation of all forms of inflection[k].

Language of Britton not barbarous or irregular.

The text of Britton, as it will be found in the following pages, exhibits a very fair example of the French of the thirteenth century. The language is considerably more copious than the later legal dialect; and shews no trace of the obliteration of inflections by which that is characterized. On the contrary, in the copy from which the text is derived a remarkable accuracy in this respect may be observed. The genders are carefully distinguished when the form of the word, as spoken, is affected; and there is a peculiar example of this, which I do not remember to have seen in any contemporary book, the masculine form *noster* being throughout distinguished from the feminine form *nostre*, which is generally used for both genders. On the other hand, the feminine past participle is not, as in modern French, spelt differently from the masculine, the pronunciation being the same. Thus, *gardé* and *gardez* stand for the modern *gardé gardée*, *gardés* and *gardées*. The old form *li* or *ly* is sometimes used for the masculine article, thus, *li lers*, (in modern French *le larron*). The feminine article *la* frequently becomes *le* before a vowel, the stronger sound being changed for the weaker by a sort of partial elision. The letter *z* is employed with singular accuracy, being scarcely ever found except when a *d* or *t* are lost, as in the plural of the past participle (e. g. *singular*, assigné, *plural*, assignez, sometimes assignetz, *Latin*, assignati), and in the plural of *fee*, *pree*, *plee*, *visné*, and the like (*Latin*, feo*d*um, pra*t*um, placi*t*um, vicine*t*um), and in such words as *peyz* (pon*d*us), *puyz* (pu*t*eus), *purchaz* (perquisi*t*um), *eynz* (in*t*ra, an*t*e). It is not however my intention to enlarge

[k] It was observed by Sir John Davis in a passage in the preface to his Reports, which is cited by Blackstone, (Comm. vol. iii. p. 320), that the Law-French is so easy, that 'the meanest wit that ever came to the study of the Law doth come to understand it almost perfectly within ten days without a reader.' Fortescue has his own method of accounting for the difference observable in his day between the Law-French and the language spoken in France, the latter having in his opinion been corrupted by vulgar use. 'Unde accidit quod lingua jam in Francia vulgaris non concordat Gallico inter legis peritos Angliæ usitato, sed vulgariter quadam rudilate corrupta; quod fieri non accidit in sermone Gallico infra Angliam usitato, cum sit sermo ille ibidem sæpius scriptus quam locutus.' (Fortescue de laudibus legum Angliæ, c. 48.)

upon the peculiarities of the language used in Britton. My object in the few details I have mentioned has been merely to call the reader's attention to the fact, that the language of these early treatises is not so obscure, barbarous, or irregular as has been frequently supposed.

Philological interest of the language of Britton.

I will however venture to observe before leaving the subject, that this ancient dialect is of importance in the history of our own language, and that in this point of view the publication of an Anglo-French treatise of the thirteenth century in a correct form has a certain philological interest. The dialect, whether Norman or Parisian, is that which was actually spoken by our ancestors, and in some instances a knowledge of it may serve to explain the origin of expressions still in use [1].

Glossary.

Regarding the matter in this light, I have taken some pains to prepare a Glossary (which is printed at the end of the second volume), containing the words found in Britton, which are either not used in modern French, or of which the form is considerably changed.

VI. *Manuscripts of Britton.*

List of manuscripts.

The following list of manuscript copies of Britton comprises those preserved in our principal Public Libraries, but is probably far from being a complete catalogue of existing manuscripts of the work. All those mentioned below are on vellum or parchment. Where they are described as folio, 4to, or 8vo, it is to give a general idea of their size, and not with reference to the folding or division of the sheets. In those instances in which the copy has been consulted for the purpose of the

[1] The word *coarse* has baffled the ingenuity of the lexicographers. Johnson has no etymology for it. His late editor, Mr. Todd, refers to a Gothic word, *kaurids*, having the sense of heavy or depressed. Richardson, following Junius, points to the Latin, *cursus*, a thing done cursorily being apt to be coarse. We find in Britton the old French word, *corsu*, with the sense of large or coarse, which is evidently, like the French *corsage*, derived from *corps* or *cors* (Latin, *corpus*). The word *abet* is referred in the dictionaries to the A.-S. *betan*, to improve, make better, but we find in Britton its proximate origin in the old French word *abbeter*, to encourage. We find also in *rehercer* the immediate parent of *rehearse*, which has been derived by the lexicographers from *rehear;* and in the verb, *apposer* to interrogate, the proximate origin of the English *pose*, and *poser*, which have been fancifully connected with the A.-S. *gepose* (said to mean headache), or the Greek παῦσις.

present edition, the letter by which it is cited in the various readings is added to the description.

1. Lambeth Library, MS. 403. A 4to. volume containing Britton alone. It has no title, and the last folio is wanting; see vol. ii. p. 359. Late thirteenth or early fourteenth century. *L.* MS. *L.*

2. Cambridge University Library. MS. Dd. vii. 6. A large folio volume, containing a collection of early Statutes and Treatises, with a marginal commentary upon the treatises. The Britton has the following title, *Incipit summa de legibus Anglie que vocatur Brettone.* The text of Britton is in a hand much resembling the Lambeth MS. The notes were written in after the text, but a large margin appears to have been purposely left to admit them. Early fourteenth century[m]. *N.* MS. *N.*

3. Bodleian Library, Douce MS. 98. A small folio volume, containing Britton with other legal matter. Title, *Incipit Summa que dicitur Brito.* Several folios are missing between the latter part of liv. i. chap. xxiii., and the end of liv. ii. chap. x.; and a folio is missing at the end of the text, which terminates with the words, 'se profre attournee en;' see vol. ii. p. 360. A list of chapters follows which is imperfect at the commencement. Early fourteenth century. *D.* MS. *D.*

4. Lansdowne MS. 575. A small folio volume, containing Britton, an Abridgment of the early Statutes, and a Register of Writs. It has at the commencement a table of chapters divided into four books. No title or colophon. Early fourteenth century. *S.* MS. *S.*

5. Merton College Library, MS. Q. 2. 16. A folio volume, containing a collection of Statutes, Entries, and Treatises. The Britton commences with a table of chapters, having the following heading: *Ceste soume contient deus maneres de pleez principaument. Ceo est a sauer pleez personeus e plez Reaus, de personeus pleez est fet vn liure qe contient* [hiat.] *chapitres dont le primer est ceo—Lyber primus I. De poer des Iustices......* MS. *M.*

[m] This volume contains a calendar, in which the dates of the months of the accessions of the first and second Edwards, 20th November and 7th July, are noted in a different hand. The manuscript was once in the possession of Selden; see vol. i. p. 2, note. As to the notes contained in it, see below, p. lx.

The name of the treatise does not occur. The contents of this volume appear to be all of the time of Edward I. or earlier. Early fourteenth century. *M.*

MS. *G.* 6. Harleian MS. 869. A small folio volume, containing ancient Statutes and Treatises[c]. The Britton has a table of chapters with a heading similar to MS. *M.* The title of the treatise does not appear. There is an inscription of a later date on a fly-leaf: *Iste liber constat Waltero Carleton de Lincoln Gentilman.* Early fourteenth century. *G.*

MS. *C.* 7. Cambridge University Library, MS. Gg. v. 12. A tall 4to. volume containing Britton alone. It has no title or table of contents. Colophon: *Icy finist le liure de Brettoun.* The text of this manuscript contains many errors. Early fourteenth century. *C.*

MS. *H.* 8. Harleian MS. 324. A tall 4to. volume containing Britton alone. This book appears by an inscription to have formerly belonged to the abbey of St. Mary Miraval. It has at the commencement a table of chapters, at the end of which is written, *Expliciunt Capitula del Bretoun.* And at the end of the volume is written, *Explicit liber qui dicitur Bretoun: et continet in se quinque libros.* The text of this MS. much resembles that of *C.* Early fourteenth century. *H.*

9. Corpus Christi College, Cambridge, MS. 258. A small folio volume, containing the Mirror of Justices, and Britton, bound together. The Britton is an earlier manuscript, but has a marginal summary in the same handwriting as the Mirror. Early fourteenth century.

MS. *A.* 10. Harleian MS. 3644. A tall 4to. volume, containing Britton written in double columns. This book appears formerly to have belonged to St. Augustin's Monastery, Canterbury. There is a table of contents, but no general title at the beginning or end, and the name of the work does not occur. The conclusion differs from other manuscripts. See the various readings in vol. ii. p. 361. Fourteenth century. *A.*

[c] This volume has some initial letters, skilfully illuminated. The initial E at the commencement of the text of Britton in the present impression, representing a king expounding the law, was suggested by the letter which occupies the same place in this manuscript.

11. Bodleian Library, Rawlinson MS. C. 898. A tall 4to. volume, containing Britton alone in double columns; formerly in the possession of Francis Tate. It has a table of contents at the beginning, but no contemporary title, nor does the name of Britton occur. This manuscript both in its manner of writing and in the readings and orthography closely resembles the last. Fourteenth century. *R.* MS. *R.*

12. Bodleian MS. 562. A 4to. volume, containing Britton and some small fragments of other legal matter. It has no title or table of contents. At the end is written, *Explicit;* and then in a larger but contemporary or nearly contemporary hand, *In Dei nomine amen ego W. T. imp* (or qu. *nup,* i. e. *nuper*) *generosus Clementis Hospitij*[d]: below, in a different character, *omnium facultatum doctor legitimme.* Fourteenth century. *W.* MS. *W.*

13. Lansdowne MS. 574. A small 4to. volume, containing an imperfect Britton, beginning near the end of book i. chap. 13, and ending in the middle of book vi. chap. 6. Fourteenth century. *T.* MS. *T.*

14. Lansdowne MS. 1176. A 4to. volume, containing Britton, and (in another hand) some early Statutes. It contains a table of chapters, and an original title, *Br*[*e*]*toñ*, of which however the third letter has been erased and written over. At the end, *Expliciunt quinque libri Bretoñ.* Below, in a hand of the 15th or 16th century, is an extract from the Year Book, with the reference, A. 35. H. 6. p. 37 par Prisott. (See before, p. xvi. note.) Fourteenth century. *E.* MS. *E.*

15. Harleian MS. 5134. A small 4to. volume, containing MS. *Z.*

d It does not appear to be known at how early a date Clement's Inn was used as an habitation for students of the law. Dugdale cites an entry of 19 Edw. IV. in which a defendant, alleging that he was misnamed in the plaintiffs' writ, pleaded that he was of Clement's Inn, which Inn at the time of the purchase of the writ, *and long before,* was an Inn of the men of the court of the secular law and of counsellors of the same law. (Dugdale, Origines Juridicales, p. 187, citing Liber Intrationum, f. 108.)

The reader will remember, that Clement's Inn is the place where Justice Shallow pursued his youthful studies and amusements.

> *Shallow.* He must then to the Inns of Court shortly: I was once of Clement's Inn; where, I think, they will talk of mad Shallow yet. (King Henry IV. Second Part, Act iii. Scene 2.)

Mr. Foss calculates that Shallow's youth must have fallen in the reign of Edward III., but can produce no evidence in confirmation of the antiquity of Clement's Inn. (Foss, Judges of England, vol. iii. p. 387.)

Britton, followed by Officium Coronatoris (one folio), and two folios of later additions. The Britton has a table of chapters divided into five books, with the title *Bretoun* at the head, and at the end, *Expliciunt Capitula libri Breton.* Colophon at the end of the book: '*Explicit hic Bretoñ qui diuiditur in quinque libris. Hunc consummatum Bretoñ considera gratum.*' Fourteenth century. *Z.*

MS. *Y.* 16. British Museum, Additional MS. 25,458. A small 4to. volume containing Britton alone. It has no title or table of chapters. On the fly-leaf in a later hand, *Quod yeluerton de Rougham.* Fourteenth century. *Y.*

17. Harleian MS. 529. A small 4to. volume, containing early Statutes, and Britton from the commencement to the beginning of the last chapter of the fifth book. It has no title, but an imperfect table of chapters at the beginning of the volume. Fourteenth century.

18. Cambridge University Library, MS. Hh. iv. 6. A 4to. volume containing Britton with a collection of Statutes of the time of Edward I. The signature, *Ro. Cotton,* 1598, is upon fol. 3. It has a table of contents with a heading similar to that in *M,* and the following colophon: *Ici finist le bretton qe content v. liuers en les queus chescune manere de ple est contenu.* Fourteenth century.

MS. *K.* 19. Harleian MS. 3937. An 8vo. volume, containing ancient Statutes, and a Britton imperfect at the end. It ends in liv. v. chap. 6. Heading in an ancient but later hand, *Incipit Bracton'* (*Bracton'* erased and *Britton* written in a hand of the seventeenth century). No table of contents. Late fourteenth century. *K.*

MS. *F.* 20. Cambridge University Library, MS. Ff. ii. 39. A tall 4to. volume containing Britton alone. It has a table of contents with a heading similar to that in *M,* and a colophon, *Explicit Bretona.* Late fourteenth century. *F.*

MS. *P.* 21. Harleian MS. 870. A tall 4to. volume, containing Britton, with one folio at the end of Maxims from the Civil Law, 'Propocitiones Digestorum,' in Latin. The headings of chapters are in Latin. It has no title at the beginning, nor table of contents. Colophon: *Explicit liber qui dicitur Brattone de Legibus Anglie Omnibus est notum scriptor quod amat bene potum. P.*

The following manuscripts contain parts of Britton.

22. Lincoln's Inn Library. A small folio volume, containing the Cornish Iter of 30 Edw. I., and Entries and Cases of other years of the same king, and also several fragments of Britton[e]. The largest fragment extends from the twelfth to the twenty-sixth chapter of Book II. Early fourteenth century. *I.* MS. *I.*

23. Harleian MS. 489. A small square 4to. volume, containing a collection of early Statutes and Treatises, and Britton from the commencement to the middle of liv. i. chap. 28. Title in rubric: *Bractō̄n* (qu. *Brattō̄n*). Early fourteenth century.

24. Cambridge University Library, MS. Dd. ix. 38. A small folio volume formerly belonging to Reading Abbey, and containing a collection of early Statutes and Treatises. The fragment of Britton begins with liv. i. chap. 6, and ends in the midst of liv. iii. chap. 5. Middle fourteenth century.

25. Balliol College Library, MS. No. 350. A small folio volume containing the Domesday Book for Herefordshire, Glanvill, and an imperfect Britton. The name of Britton does not appear, and the book contains from the commencement to liv. iii. chap. 22. sect. 8. Late fourteenth century. *B.* MS. *B.*

26. Harleian MS. 4656. A small square volume, containing an imperfect Britton, from the commencement to near the beginning of liv. iv. chap. 7. It has a rubric title, *Incipit tractatus qui dicitur Brutonis;* and at the top of every folio is the heading *Brut'*. Fourteenth century.

[e] This MS. is described in Mr. Horwood's Preface to the first volume of the Year Books of Edward I.; in which volume the Cornish *Iter* is printed.

VII. *Printed Editions of Britton.*

Original impression of Britton.

Britton was first printed by Redman, probably about the year 1530; the imprint is without date. The book is a small 8vo. volume about the size of a modern 12mo. Title: *Britton. cum priuilegio regali.* Colophon: *Imprynted at London in Flete strete by me Robert Redman dwellyng in saynt Dunstanes parysshe at the signe of the George.* It is printed in black letter with numerous contractions. Unfortunately an extremely incorrect copy appears to have been used by the printer, and this edition is truly described by Wingate, a later editor, as 'exceeding full of manifest imperfections.' Among other considerable defects is the omission of an entire chapter (liv. iv. chap. 5) in the middle of the work.

Wingate's edition, 1640.

In 1640 a second edition of Britton was printed in a similar size under the superintendence of Edmund Wingate[f], the author of 'The Maximes of Reason, or the Reason of the Common Law of England.' The editor points out in his preface how unintelligible much of the text was as formerly printed, and supplies numerous corrections from some better manuscript than that previously employed; but instead of importing his corrections into the text, he has reprinted the work in the same corrupt form as before, with the exception of 'manifest false pointing and litterall errors,' and has added his amended readings, with the omitted chapter, in an appendix. This edition is in black letter, with the old contractions.

Britton reprinted in France by Houard, 1776.

The above are the only editions which have appeared in England. Britton was reprinted in France in the fourth volume of Houard's Traités sur les Coutumes Anglo-Normandes, published at Paris and Rouen in 1776. This edition is merely a reproduction of the corrupt text furnished by the English copies, and the French editor has not thought

[f] 'Britton. The second edition. Faithfully corrected according to divers ancient Manuscripts of the same Booke. By *Edm. Wingate*, Gent. London, Printed by the Assignees of *John Moore*, Esquire, *Anno* 1640. *Cum privilegio.*'

it worth while either to introduce into his text or to print separately the missing chapter and other corrections supplied in Wingate's appendix. The French edition has however this advantage over the English, that being in a modern type and in words at length, it is more easily perused by a reader of the present day.

VIII. *Formation of the present Text; Translation, and Notes.*

Lambeth MS. (*L*) the basis of the text.

After making myself more or less acquainted with the merits of most of the manuscripts contained in the above list, I had no difficulty in selecting the Lambeth MS. (cited in the notes as *L*) as the basis of a new text of Britton. That copy appears to me to present the text in its oldest form, and is probably contemporary with its first publication. It is also written with remarkable care, and for the most part in words at length, and is free, in an unusual degree, from errors of the pen as well as from corruptions of the text. By the favour of the late Archbishop of Canterbury, Dr. Sumner, I was enabled to have this book for some months in my chambers and to consult it at leisure. The manuscripts next in value to *L* are those cited as *N*, *D*, *S*, *M*, and *G*; all of which appear to have been written when the work was recent. *S* agrees most closely with *L*; *N* and *D* also resemble *L*, but agree still more closely with each other.

Next to *L*, the manuscript most useful to me has been the Merton MS. cited as *M*. This does not agree so closely with *L* as those last mentioned, and in some places the true reading has been preserved in it, where all the other copies are at fault. Having by the liberality of the Warden and Fellows of Merton College been enabled to keep this manuscript by me during the whole time that I have been engaged upon the present work, I have collated it with considerable care, and I believe every important variation in reading which it presents has been given in the notes.

MSS. *C* and *H* resemble each other nearly, and, though ancient, are remarkably full of errors. The printed editions of Britton appear to be derived from one of these manuscripts, or some copy from them. The chapter (liv. iv. chap. 5) which is wanting in the printed text is also omitted in both these manuscripts; I have not observed its omission in any other ancient copy; and in MS. *H*, the chapters are numbered in an early hand, as in the printed copies, from beginning to end without reference to the divisions of Books. The manuscript cited as *A*, with which *R* closely agrees, although carefully written, appears to present the text in a form further removed from the original than any of those already described. This copy has not been collated throughout, but has been consulted in passages where the text appeared doubtful. Some others of the later manuscripts, especially Harl. MSS. 3937 and 5134, differ still more widely from the text as here printed. Having access to so many of the earliest and most accurate copies, I have not thought it worth while to load the page with various readings resulting from the carelessness or caprice of subsequent transcribers.

Manner of forming the text.

The text of the present impression represents that of MS. *L*, corrected throughout, where defective or erroneous, by comparison with other manuscripts. In all cases in which I have deviated from *L*, except very manifest errors of the copyist, the reading of *L*, with the authority for the reading adopted, will be found in the notes.

Conjectural readings.

In a very few instances, where neither my principal copy, nor any other, has furnished a satisfactory reading, I have introduced conjectural emendations. Most of these are both unimportant and obvious; and in all, the reader will find in the notes the sign *conj.*, together with a collation of the readings of various manuscripts. He will thus be enabled to supply such other reading as commends itself to his own judgment. Much of the book being derived from Bracton or from Fleta, a comparison of these authors has frequently served in doubtful cases to fix both the expression and the sense of Britton.

I have thought it convenient to distinguish the *v* from the *u*, and the *j* from the *i*[g], although not so distinguished in the manuscripts. I have also introduced the apostrophe to mark the elision of a vowel, and an accent to distinguish the final accented *e*[h]. In other respects I have followed the orthography of MS. *L* with all its variations, and where words or sentences omitted in *L* are introduced from other manuscripts, the spelling elsewhere most commonly used in *L* is employed[i].

Various readings.

In collating the copies of a work written in a language so fluctuating and uncertain in its forms as the French of the thirteenth century, it is somewhat difficult to select the various readings which appear worthy of notice. If minute differences were to be in all cases recorded, a great part of each manuscript must be printed. I have found it necessary as a general rule to pass without notice variations of spelling and slight changes in the forms of words which frequently occur, as *terminer* and *determiner, accuser* and *encuser, accrest* and *encrest, achesoun* and *enchesoun*, or the like; so also, unless where the sense is affected, I have generally left unnoticed variations in inflection, as in case, number, or tense, or in the arrangement of the words of a sentence; changes in minor forms of speech, as the negative particles *point, pas, mie;* the pronouns *cist, cel, tiel;* and omissions or additions of particles frequently introduced or left out by the copyist *ad*

[g] In ancient MSS. an attempt is sometimes made to distinguish these letters by using the capital *I* when the sound of *j* is required. Thus in MS. *L*, the words *jeo, justice, jurour,* are generally spelt with a capital letter, and sometimes even *jour* and *ja* in the middle of a sentence; and in one instance the word *ajournent*, is written *aIournent*.

[h] In many modern editions of ancient French authors, all the accents, as now used, are introduced; in others no accents are added, but the words are printed as in the original MSS. The middle course which I have adopted is that followed by the editor of the magnificent edition of Joinville's History recently published in the twentieth volume of the French Recueil des Historiens (folio, Paris, 1840), and by the editors of the Monumenta Historica Britannica (fol. London, 1846) in the French portion of their work.

[i] In the case of one word only I have with some hesitation departed from the above rule. The word *ses* (plural of *soen, sa*) is in many MSS. of this time commenced indifferently with *c* or *s*, and in MS. *L* it is always, or almost always, spelt *ces*. This spelling is apt to lead to confusion, and I have therefore thought it better to adopt the orthography which is more usual in other MSS. of the time, and more intelligible to a modern reader.

libitum, as *y*, *en*, *de*, *mesme*. I have also thought it better not to encumber the page with readings, manifestly corrupt, from the manuscripts collated, where there was no doubt about the true text. In this way I have endeavoured to confine the various readings to cases in which either a different sense is offered, or the words or form of expression are materially changed. In those instances however in which I have left the Lambeth MS. to follow some other reading, I have thought it proper to notice comparatively trifling variations; and the same has been occasionally done where a various reading occurred differing slightly from the text, which might possibly appear preferable to it. If any one should think it worth while to criticise this part of my labours, it will, I believe, be found that I have erred on the safer side of introducing too much rather than too little. I should add, that in the various readings I have as a general rule given the words at length, although they may be contracted in the original. The reader will find at the end of the Introduction an explanation of the abbreviations used in this part of the work.

English translation.

In preparing the English translation now printed, I have made such use as I could of the labours of the late Mr. Robert Kelham, formerly a member of Lincoln's Inn, and well known for his works on legal antiquities. Mr. Kelham prepared a translation of the whole of Britton, and having in 1762 printed the greater part of the first book in English with notes, he shortly before his death, which occurred in 1808, gave the remainder of his work in manuscript to the Society of Lincoln's Inn. The printed text, from which Mr. Kelham translated, is so imperfect, that it was impossible that his version should not be full of errors. That now presented to the public has been carefully formed upon the revised text. It has been one of my principal objects to retain as much as possible the form of expression used in the original; especially where the expressions are technical, or such as afterwards became so. This may serve as an excuse for the somewhat antiquated language and construction of sentences adopted.

The whole, both in the French and in the English, is divided into Books, Chapters, and Sections. The last division has been made by the Editor. The two former divisions, though with some variation, are found in most of the manuscripts, and appear, from several passages of the book, to have formed part of the plan of the Author[k]. In the Lambeth MS. the chapters have titles, but no numbers, and the division into books is only indicated by the words of conclusion and commencement introduced between some of them. The division of books found in MSS. *N* and *D*, appeared convenient with reference to the length of the several parts and the arrangement of the subject-matter, and has been accordingly adopted in the present impression. In MSS. *M* and *G* the one chapter on Naifty (Book i. chap. 32) constitutes Book II.; and the fifty-four chapters comprised in Books III., IV., and V., are all included in Book IV., the entire work being divided into five instead of six books. The arrangement in MS. *A* resembles that of *M*, except that there are only four books, the chapter on Naifty being included in Book II.[l]

Division into Books, Chapters, and Sections.

Books.

In the copy from which the old edition was printed the division into books appears to have been omitted, and the chapters in that edition are accordingly numbered continuously from the commencement to the end of the work.

Chapters.

With respect to the division into chapters there is no great variation in the principal manuscripts, except in the opening portion, the first chapter of the present edition, which in the old print is not numbered as a chapter, being in some of the copies, including *N* and *D*, divided into several chapters with distinct titles. I have already mentioned that one entire chapter was omitted in the original impression, the numeration being carried on throughout. This omission, the

[k] See vol. i. pp. 5, 162, 219; vol. ii. pp. 2, 139, 161, 171, 212.

[l] In *M* there is also some indication of this chapter not having originally formed a book of itself, since the fourth Book in that MS., which corresponds in its commencement with the third as here printed, has the following rubrical heading:—*Ci comence le terz lyure de intrusion.*

disregard of the division into Books, and the omission of the first chapter from the numeration, made it appear undesirable to retain the chapters as formerly printed; but for the sake of facilitating reference, Britton having been cited sometimes by chapter and sometimes by page, I have printed the old numbers of the chapters in brackets, and have also given the old paging in the margin.

Notes to the present edition.

With respect to the English notes, I have not proposed to furnish an illustrative commentary on Britton. Such an attempt would have extended the book to much larger limits.

Marginal references to other authorities.

The references to the earlier and contemporary treatises and statutes which are given in the margin of the French text, will enable the student to supply for himself the most valuable commentary. These are confined to the authorities which were, or might have been, known to the writer; and upon some of which the substance of the work is in a great measure founded. In preparing these references I owe much to the industry of Mr. Kelham, who illustrated the portion of Britton which he published in English with very copious marginal notices of authorities of all dates, and in whose manuscript translation similar references are continued in less abundance. The greater number of references are to Bracton and Fleta, which have already been pointed out as the principal sources from which the materials of the book were drawn. Both these authorities are cited by the pages of the printed copies. In my references to the early statutes I have used the edition of the Statutes of the Realm, printed by direction of the Record Commission; and in referring to the written laws of an earlier time, I have used the Collection of Ancient English Laws edited for the Record Commission by Mr. Thorpe.

Editor's Notes.

The notes at the foot of the page, so far as they are supplied by the editor, are principally confined to the elucidation of the text in places where, from its obscurity or ambiguity, or contrariety with other authorities, it appeared to call for explanation.

Notes from MS. *N.*

To the references and notes above mentioned I have added,

in no great quantity, another class of annotations which I trust will be more acceptable to the reader. The Cambridge manuscript already described, and cited in the notes as *N*, contains a commentary upon Britton, which seems to have been written by a contemporary of the author. The age appears not only by the mode of writing, and the character of the law described, but also by more distinct evidence. Thus, in the first folio of Britton, the author in commenting upon liv. i. chap. 1. s. 11, (vol. i. p. 7,) says: 'En la secunde partie defend il, qe nul ny amende faus Iugemens de ses Justices fors qe ly memes ou sun Chief Justice, qui represente sun cors demeyne, sicome Sire Roger le Brabanzun.' If, as appears probable, the author names here the actual Chief Justice of the King's Bench, the note must have been written between the twenty-fourth year of Edward I., 1295, and the ninth of Edward II., 1316[m]. Again, in the twenty-second chapter of the same book, in a note of which the reader will find a translation at vol. i. p. 95, a conspiracy formed in the thirtieth year of Edward I. (1301–2), by Sir Robert de Vere, Sheriff of Northampton, and others, is mentioned in a manner which appears to shew a familiarity with the circumstances[n]. There are several proofs throughout the volume, that the collection was formed by one connected with Northampton, the writs cited being generally addressed to the Sheriff of Northamptonshire, and a fragment of a collection of Customs of the town of Northampton forming part of the book[o]. Occasional references to the opinion of 'some of his companions[p],' when differing opinions are mentioned, would lead us to suppose that the author was either one of the Justices of the Bench, or associated with them as a Judge of Assise. And, if I do not misunderstand the note of which I have given a translation at vol. i. p. 309, and part of which I cite in its original

Age of these Notes.

Volume compiled at Northampton.

Station of the author.

His name, John de Longueville.

[m] Foss, Judges, vol. iii. p. 242.

[n] See also vol. i. p. 27, note *l*.

[o] See also the note in vol. i. p. 174. Some documents illustrative of the administration of the Criminal Law in the time of Edward I. are now being printed from this collection in the fortieth volume of the Archæologia.

[p] Vol. i. p. 236, vol. ii. p. 73. The same expression occurs in a note on liv. i. c. 2. s. 1, not printed in the present volume.

form below[q], the annotator has introduced himself by the name of 'Johan de Longeville of Northampton.'

Facts known concerning John de Longueville.

We are fortunately able in some measure to trace the identity of the person here named, and we find him answer in character and position to that which we should expect of the compiler of the valuable collection in which his name so occurs. John de Longueville, the ancestor of the family subsequently ennobled by the descent of the Barony of Grey of Ruthyn[r], was sent as Burgess for Northampton to the several Parliaments which met in the twenty-sixth, twenty-ninth, and thirtieth years of Edward I., and the first of Edward II. He was also returned to represent Northampton in a special convention of Merchants which met at York on the twenty-fifth of June, 31 Edw. I.; and it was probably the same John de Longueville who was chosen knight of the shire for Northampton in the eighth, and again in the twelfth year of Edward II.[s] In the twelfth and thirteenth years of Edward II. he appears to have been employed as a Justice of Assise, oyer and terminer, or gaol delivery, since his name occurs in two lists of persons who are commanded by writs dated 8 June, 12 Edw. II., and 5 June, 13 Edw. II., to deliver estreats of the rolls of them and their companions assigned to take assises, juries, and certifications, to hear and determine, or do other business, or to deliver the gaols[t]. He was

Judicial employments of John de Longueville.

[q] 'Nota qe tot die la partie premere de cest chapistre qe il y ad plusurs titles de franc tenement, Johan de Longeville de Northampton vus dist curtement qe il ny ad fors qe ii. titles de franc tenement et nient plus.' (Note in MS. *N* on liv. ii. c. 16. s. 1, vol. i. p. 309.) It will be observed that the expression is not 'John de Longueville says' or 'tells us,' but 'John de Longueville tells *you*;' the author's opinion not being otherwise conveyed.

[r] See the Pedigree in Baker's History of Northamptonshire, vol. i. p. 27; Wotton's Baronetage, vol. iv. p. 349.

[s] A Sir John Longueville, knt., probably of Overton, or Orton Longueville, in Huntingdonshire, on the borders of Northamptonshire, was knight of the shire for Huntingdon in the 35th Edw. I., and his name occurs as a banneret of Huntingdonshire in the list of bannerets (with their arms) of the commencement of the reign of Edward II. published by the Record Commission in Parliamentary Writs, vol. i. p. 417. Johannes de Longeville, *miles*, received a pardon as an adherent of the earl of Lancaster, 12 Edw. II., and Johannes de Lungeville, *miles*, was Assessor and Collector of the subsidy for the county of Northampton in the 16th Edw. II. (Parliamentary Writs, vol. ii. div. ii. p. 128, div. i. pp. 211, 278.) Whether either of these knights is identical with the burgess and Justice, I cannot say. The identity of the burgess with the Justice is assumed by the author of the Index to the Parliamentary Writs, and is confirmed by the compilation of legal materials, including a Custumary of Northampton, contained in the Cambridge MS.

[t] Parliamentary Writs, vol. ii. div. ii. Appendix, pp. 137, 147.

employed in the 17th Edw. II. as a Justice to investigate the conduct of the sheriffs and other officers of the Crown; and in the following year he appears as a Commissioner of Array, but unable to act for illness. His death probably occurred in this year, since his name does not afterwards occur in the Records. It can scarcely be doubted, from the offices which he filled, and still more from the appearance which he makes in the present volume, that he was a professional lawyer; and it would seem from his own description that he either resided at the time of the compilation of the book at Northampton, or that his name was known in connection with that place. The manor of Little Billing, in Northamptonshire, where his family was subsequently seated, appears to have been purchased by him in or before the fourth year of Edward II.[u]

His death, about 1324-5.

A commentary upon Britton written by a lawyer who was probably practising at the time of its publication, and who subsequently filled judicial offices, could not but present some features of interest. It consists of an analysis of the contents of each chapter, which for this purpose is divided into sections, with several notes interspersed, explaining, expanding, and in some cases correcting the statements of the author. In perusing these annotations, I have selected such parts of them as appeared important, either as elucidating the text, or as throwing a light upon the history of the law during the time when the book was new; and have added them, as notes, to the present volume. Among them I have inserted some notices of doubtful points and unsolved queries of the ancient annotator, judging that the history and progress of the law is often best illustrated by showing what questions were considered at a particular time to be doubtful, and what arguments were used in favour of one solution or another. I have thought it more convenient to give these notes in an English version, citing the original French only where, owing to the obscurity or peculiarity of the expression, it appeared desirable to do so.

Nature of the Notes in MS. *N*.

[u] Baker, History of Northamptonshire, vol. i. p. 26.

Glossary, and Index.

The Glossary of obsolete French words, which is added at the close of the second volume, has been already mentioned. A copious Index concludes the labours of the Editor, by which it is hoped that whatever information can be gained from the pages of Britton is rendered easily accessible to the student.

ABBREVIATIONS USED IN THE VARIOUS READINGS.

add. MGR. = added in the text of MSS. *M*, *G*, and *R*.

add. in margin N. = added in the margin in *N*.

conj. = the reading in the text is conjectural.

eras. D. = erased in *D*.

hiat. A. = a hiatus or blank space in *A*.

ins. N. = inserted between the words originally written in *N*.

int. G. or *interl. G.* = inserted by interlineation in *G*.

qe [nul] hom *N*, *or* qe [nul *interl.*] hom *N*. The word in brackets is inserted by interlineation in *N*.

oblit. L. = obliterated (struck through with a pen) in *L*.

om. S. = omitted in *S*.

sim. CH. = similarly (i. e. with a slight variation, for the most part in spelling only) in *C* and *H*.

so corr. N. = so corrected (the original reading having been different) in *N*.

so on eras. N. = so corrected on an erasure (a former reading having been scratched out with a knife) in *N*.

so print. = so printed in the former impressions.

so verb. NDSG. = so verbally *NDSG*. (The reading in the text is found in all those MSS. with variation in spelling only.)

N.B. Where the reference to the note is made by a single figure, the various reading affects only the one preceding word, or is an addition to be inserted in that place; where the reference is by two figures, the various reading affects all the words between the same two figures in the text.

Where part of the various reading itself is in italic, it is underlined in the original.

BRITTON.

LIVRE I.

EDWARD, par la grace Deu, Roi de Engleterre[1], Seignur[2] de Hyrelaunde, [3]et Duk de Aquitayne[3], a touz ses [4]feaus et sugez[4] de Engleterre et de Hyrelaunde[5] pes et grace de sauvacioun. [1.]

Stat. West. 1. (3 Ed. I.) Pream., c. 1. Bracton. 1 *b*, 107. Fleta. 16 (§ 4).

Desirauntz[6] pes entre le poeple qe est en nostre proteccioun par la suffraunce de Deu, la quele pes ne poet mie ben[7] estre[8] sauntz ley, si[9] avoms les leys qe hom ad usé en noster reaume avaunt ces hores fet mettre en escrit solum ceo qe cy[10] est ordeyné. Et volums et comaundums qe par tut Engleterre et

1. Coroune et *add. E.* 2. Sire [al. seignur *interl.*] *N.* sire *GSEB.* Syre *H.* e Seygnour *M.* 3—3. *om. MEFWB.* 4—4. feaux e leaux e ses sugges *H. sim. C.* fels e leaus sugez *M.* leaus et suggez *E.* 5. Ireland etc. *AR. sim. Y.* Hyrlaund [saluz. *interl.*] *N.* 6. de fraunche *AR.* 7. *om. ARB.* 8. garde *add. C.* 9. si *om. MEARH.* 10. so *MEWCH.* ci *DAR.* *om. LNGS.*

BOOK I.

OF THE AUTHORITY OF JUSTICES AND OTHER OFFICERS, AND OF PERSONAL PLEAS INCLUDING PLEAS OF THE CROWN.

Prologue.

King's style and salutation.

EDWARD[a], by the grace of God, king of England, lord of Ireland, and duke of Aquitaine, to all his faithful people and subjects of England and Ireland, peace and grace of salvation.

Object of laws; and of this book.

Desiring peace among the people who by God's permission are under our protection, which peace cannot well be without law, we have caused such laws as have heretofore been used in our realm to be reduced into writing according to that which is here ordained. And we will and command, that throughout

Authority of this book.

[a] Edward I. See Introduction by the Editor.

Stat. de Bigam. (4 Ed.I.) Pream. Glanvil. Prol. Brac. 1, 1 *b*; Fle. 16, 17 (§ 6, 9).

tut[1] Hyrelaunde soint issi usetz et tenuz en touz poyntz, sauve a nous de repeler les et de enoyter et de amenuser et de amender a totes les foiz qe nous verums qe [2]bon serra[2], par le assent de nos Countes et Barouns et autres de noster conseyl, sauve les usages a ceux qe par prescripcioun de tens [3]ount autrement[3] usé en taunt qe lour usages ne soynt mie descordauntz a dreiture.

[4]CHAPITRE I.

De Poer des Justices[4].

Brac. 108; Fle. 18 (§ 16).

1. En primes en dreit de nous mesmes et de nostre Curt avoms issi ordinee, qe[5], pur ceo qe nous ne suffisums mie en nostre propre persone a oyer et terminer totes les[6] quereles del poeple avauntdit, avoms parti noster charge en plusours parties, sicum est issi ordinee[7].

1. tut *om. YE.* 2—2. bien serra *ARM.* bon seit *C.* 3—3. les ont autrement *M.* ou autrement vnt *AR. sim. Y.* 4—4. *om. L.* Cap^m^ primum. Del hostel le Rey *N. sim. D.* C. i. de pouwer des Iustices *M.* 5. *so ARMYECHB.* et *LND.* e *GS. om. F.* 6. les *om. MECFB.* 7. de quel nous sumus vicare dieu a Iustifeer les orgoyllous par redour de dreyt e les humbles par mercy *add. W. sim.* (Iustiser *for* Iustifeer) *E. sim.* (a iustifeer *om.*) *M.*

England and Ireland they be so used and observed in all points, saving to us the power of repealing extending restricting and amending them, whenever we shall see good, by the assent of our earls and barons and others of our Council[b]; saving also to all persons such customs as by prescription of time have been differently used, so far as such customs are not contrary to law.

Legislative power of king with assent of Council.

Local customs.

CHAPTER I.

Of the Authority of Justices.

Jurisdiction of king and his Court, distributed.

1. First, with regard to ourselves and our Court, we have ordained, that, inasmuch as we are not sufficient in our proper person to hear and determine all the complaints of our said people, we have distributed our charge in several portions, as is here ordained.

b 'This Preamble or Prologue is divided into two parts; first, the regal style, where he says, "Edward &c.;" and then the salutation, where he says, "And we will and command &c.;" affirming a prerogative in his person, that what he thinks right ought to be held to be law; according to the saying, "Quod principi placuit pro lege habetur." Because peace cannot be without law, nor law without a king: who can change the laws and establish others, but not without the assent of the Earls and others of his Council: quia ubi voluntas unius in toto dominatur, ratio plurimum succumbit.' (Note in MS. *N.*) This note is cited by Selden as from a MS. in his possession; Diss. ad Flet. p. 468. The passage from the Civil Law, "Quod principi &c." (Inst. lib. i. tit. 2. § 6. Dig. lib. i. tit. 4. l. 1) was imported into English Law by Glanvill, in his Prologue, and was a frequent subject of controversy with subsequent writers. See Bracton f. 107; Fleta 16, 17. See also Selden. Diss. ad Flet. 466.

2. [1]Nous volums qe nostre jurisdiccioun soit sur totes jurisdicciouns en noster reaume; issint qe en totes maneres de felounies trespas et contractz, et en totes maneres de autres accciouns personeles ou reales, eyoms poer a rendre, ou[2] a fere rendre, les jugementz teus cum il afeert[3] sauntz autre proces par la ou nous savoms la certeyne[4] verité cum juge. Et qe le Seneschal de noster hostel tiegne noster leu de eynz la verge de noster hostel, et qe soen office se estende a oyer et terminer les presentementz des chapitres de nostre Coroune quant nous veroms qe bon serra. [1 *b.*]

Brac. 107. Fle. 16 (§ 4), 66 (§ 1, 2).

Fle. 66 (§ 2, 3), 67 (§ 1); Rot. Parl. tom. 1, p. 17 *a*, 93 *a*, 97 *a*.

3. Estre ceo volums nous, qe Justices errauntz soint assignetz de mesmes les chapitres[5] oyer et terminer[6] en chescun counté et en chescune fraunchise de vii. aunz en vii. aunz. Et autel poer volums nous, qe nos chefs Justices eynt de Hyrelaunde et de Cestre.

Brac. 105 *b*, 108; Fle. 66 (§ 10, 11).

4. [7]En dreit des Justices qi sount assignez de nous sure et de tener noster[8] liu ou qe nous seoms en Engleterre, volums nous qe il eynt conisaunce[9] de amender faus jugementz et de terminer apeaus et autres trespas fetz encountre nostre [2.]

Brac. 105 *b*, 108; Fle. 66 (§ 5).

1. C. ii. De Iurisdictioun le Rey *add. N. sim. D.* 2. e *MH.* 3. affierent *H. sim. C.* asserount *ARE.* afferount *M. sim. YB.* 4. dreit *C.* dreite *B.* 5. *so ARMYCHB.* a *add. LNSEF.* 6. determiner *ARYEH.* a terminer *G.* de terminer *F.* 7. C. iii. Des hautz Iustices le Rey *add. N. sim. D.* 8. *so ND. sim. MGSARHCF.* noster *om. L.* 9. conge e conysaunce *H.* conge *F.*

2. We will that our jurisdiction be superior to all jurisdictions in our realm; so that in all kinds of felonies trespasses and contracts, and in all manner of other actions personal or real, we have power to give, or cause to be given, such judgment as the case requires without any other process, whenever we have certain knowledge of the truth, as judge. And the Steward of our household shall take our place within the verge of our household; and his office shall extend to the hearing and determining the presentments of the articles of our Crown, when we shall see good.

Royal jurisdiction.

Jurisdiction of Steward.

3. Further, we will that Justices Itinerant be assigned to hear and determine the same articles in every county and franchise every seven years; and that our Chief Justices of Ireland and Chester have the like power.

Justices Itinerant.

4. With respect to the Justices assigned to follow us and hold our place wheresoever we shall be in England, we will that they have cognizance of amending false judgments, and of determining appeals and other pleas of trespass committed against

Justices of the King's Bench.

pes, et qe lour jurisdiccioun et record se estende solum ceo qe nous [1] les maunderoms [1] par nos brefs.

Fle. 67, 69. 5. [2] Et volums qe le Counte de Norfolk, par ly on par autre chivaler, soit entendaunt a nous et a noster Seneschal, a fere nos commaundementz et les attachementz et les execuciouns de nos jugementz et de noster Seneschal par la verge de noster hostel, taunt cum il tendra la Marchauscie [2].

Fle. 71 (c. 8), 74 (§ 13). Art. sup. Chart. (28 Ed. I.) c. 3. 6. Et en noster hostel soit un Corouner, qi face le mester de la Coroune par mi la verge, par tut ou nous seroms et vienoms en noster reaume; et qe celi mesmes [3] ou autre [3] soit assigné de assaer touz peys et totes mesures par tote nostre verge par mi noster reaume solom nos estaundarz: et ceux deus [4] mestiers ne lesse [4] a fere pur nuli fraunchise, [5] si la fraunchise ne soit [5] graunté en [6] fee ferme ou en aumoyne par nous ou par nos predecessours.

Glan. li. 1, c. 1, 4; li. 8, c. 9. Fle. 94 (c. 43). Post c. 28, s. 1. 7. [7] En chescun counté soit un Viscounte, qi soit entendaunt as comaundemenz de nous et de nos Justices avauntditz, qe des pletz pledez devaunt eux par nos brefs eynt record. Et de

1—1. so *MGE. sim DHC.* le amenderoms *LS.* le manderoms *corr. N.* 2—2. *So LNDGS. This section is placed in ARMEYWCHB. before the preceding.* 3—3. oue autres *M. sim. CHB.* 4—4. ministres ne lessent *CFB.* 5—5. *so MW. sim. GAEF.* [Si *interl.*] ne soit *L.* qe soit *NDY.* ne sait *S.* 6. a *ARMCB.* 7. C. iiii. Des Viscountes *add. N. sim. D.*

our peace, and that their jurisdiction and record shall extend so far as we shall authorise by our writs.

Earl Marshal. 5. We will that the Earl of Norfolk, by himself or another knight, be attendant upon us and upon our Steward, to execute our commands and the attachments and executions of our judgments and those of our Steward throughout the verge of our house, so long as he shall hold the office of Marshal.

Coroner of the household. Weights and measures. 6. In our household let there be a Coroner to execute the business of the Crown throughout the verge and wheresoever we shall be or come within our realm; and let the same person or some other be assigned to assay all weights and measures in every our verge throughout our realm according to our standards; and these two duties he shall not fail to do by reason of any franchise, unless such franchise be granted in fee farm or in alms by us or our predecessors.

Sheriff. Record of County Court. 7. In every county let there be a sheriff who shall be attendant on our commands and those of our Justices; and let him have record of pleas pleaded before him by our writs[c];

c The text may admit of another interpretation. But see c. 28, s. 1, and note there.

suth les viscountes soint hundreders serjaunz et bedaus, qi soint entendauntz as viscountes. Et qe en chescun counté soint corouners esluz a la garde des pletz de nostre pes, solum ceo qe en les chapitres de lour office serra entitlé; et eux eynt record des choses qe touchent lour office. Fle. 29.

8. [1]Estre ceo volums, qe Justices demurgent continuelment[2] a Westmoster, ou aylours la ou nous voderoms ordiner, a pleder communs pletz solum ceo qe nous [3]les maunderoms[3] par nos brefs; qi[4] des paroles dedutes[5] par devaunt eux par nous brefs eynt record. [2 *b*.] Mag. Char. c. 11. Brac. 105 *b*, 108. Fle. 88 (c. 34.)

9. [6]Ausi volums nous, qe a [7]nos Eschekers a Westmoster et aylours eynt nos Thresorers et nos Barouns illucs jurisdiccioun et record des choses qe touchent lour office, et[7] a oyer et terminer totes les causes qe touchent nos dettes et nos feez, et les incidentes choses sauntz les queles tieles choses ne porount estre tryez; et qe il eynt poer a conustre des dettes qe hom deit a nos dettours, parount nous peusoms le plus tost aprocher al nostre. Prov. in Scacc. (Stat. 12 Ed. I.) Fle. 81, 82.

1. C. v. Des Iustices del commun Bank R7. *add. N. sim. D.* 2. comunement *MARE.* 3—3. ordeyncroms *M.* 4. e qe *M.* issint qe *C.* 5. so *M.* *so corr. R.* [de] dites *LN.* dedites *D.* desdites *GS.* dedytes *W.* dites *F.* 6. C. vi. Del Tresorier e des barons del Eschekere R7. *add. N. sim. D.* 7—7. la Eschekere aient noz barons poer *Y.*

and under the sheriffs let there be hundredres serjeants and beadles attendant on the sheriffs. And in every county let there be coroners chosen for keeping the pleas of our peace, as shall be authorised in the chapters concerning their office, and let them have record of things relating to their office. Hundreders, Serjeants &c. Coroner.

8. Moreover our will is, that there be Justices constantly remaining at Westminster, or at such other place as we shall be pleased to ordain, to determine common pleas according as we shall authorise them by our writs; and these Justices shall have record of the proceedings held before them by virtue of our writs. Justices of Common Pleas.

9. Also our will is, that at our Exchequers at Westminster and elsewhere our Treasurers and our Barons there have jurisdiction and record of things which concern their office, and to hear and determine all causes relating to our debts and seignories and things incident thereto, without which such matters could not be tried; and that they have cognizance of debts owing to our debtors, by means whereof we may the more speedily recover our own. Court of Exchequer.

Mag. Char. c. 12. Stat. West. 2. (13 Ed. I.) c. 30. Brac. 105 *b*, 108. Fle. 66 (§ 9.) Stat. Glouc. (6 Ed. I.) c. 9. Fle. 66 (§ 8.)

10. Et volums ausi, qe en chescun countee soint Justices assignez a conustre en les causes qe [1]nous les maunderoms[1] par nos lettres patentes de petites assises et de autres choses, [2]dount nous voloms qe eus eynt[2] record. [3]Et Justices soint ordinez en chescun counté a deliverer les gaoles chescune simeyne pledable une foiz, taunt cum il truvent a fere; et qe il eynt ausi record en les paroles dedutes devaunt eux et[4] en lour Jugementz.

11. [5]Et tut eyoms nous graunté a nos Justices de porter
[3.] record de pletz pledez devant eux, pur ceo ne voloms mie qe lour record lour soit garraunt en lour tort demeyne, ne qe eux peusent lour roudles rere ne amender ne encountre le enroudlement recorder. [6]Et volums qe le poer de nos Justices soit limité en ceste manere, qe il ne pasent mie les pointz de nos brefs, ne des presentementz de jurours, ne des pleintes a eux fetes, sauve ceo qe il eynt la conisaunce des garrauntz vouchez et des autres choses incidentes sauntz les queles les originales

Brac. 108 *b*.

1—1. *so GARM. sim. DF.* nos les demaunderoms *L sim. NSHB.* nos comaunderoms *C.* 2—2. *so M. sim. G.* par nous eynt *L. sim. NDS.* nous voloms qe eus eient lour *ARC. sim. AF.* 3. C. vii. Des Iustices assignez a deliuerer gaoles *add. D. sim.* (gaoles *om.*) *N.* 4. *so E. sim. H.* et *om. LNDSGM.* 5. C. viii. De Recordz *add. N.* C. viii. De Record des Iustices *D.* 6. C. ix. De limitacioun de lour power *add. N. sim. D.* Cap. ii. De poer des Iustices *H.*

Justices of Assise,

10. And we will, that Justices be assigned in every county to have cognizance in such causes of petty assises and other matters, as we shall assign them by our letters patent, of which causes we will that they have record. Let Justices also be appointed to deliver the gaols in every county, once in every pleadable week[d], while they find anything to do; and let them likewise have record of the pleas brought before them and of their judgments.

and gaol delivery.

11. And although we have granted to our Justices to bear record of pleas pleaded before them, yet we will not that their record be any warrant to them in their own wrong, nor that they be permitted to erase their rolls or amend them or record contrary to the enrollment. And we will that the power of our Justices be limited in this manner, that they go not beyond the articles of our writs, or of presentments of jurors, or of plaints before them made, save that they shall have the cognizance of vouchers to warranty, and of other incidental matters without

Record of Justices.

Rolls not to be altered.

Jurisdiction of Justices limited by writs.

[d] The same rule is laid down in c. 12. s. 5, where the expression is *chescune simeyne en tens pledable.* Mr. Kelham interprets this as excluding times prohibited by the church (see book ii. c. 21. s. 1); but the whole passage appears to require further explanation. See Kelham's Britton, p. 8. n. (24.)

causes ne porront mie estre determinez. Et defendoms[1] generalment [2]qe nul hom ne eyt[2] poer [3]de amender nuli faus[3] jugement de nos Justices, sauve[4] les Justices qi suwent nous en nostre Court, qi a ceo sunt de par nous entitlez, ou[5] nous Stat. Marl. mesmes ove[6] noster conseil; car ceo reservoms nous especial- (52 Hen. III.) c. 19. ment a nostre jurisdiccioun.

12. Et defendoms a touz nos Corouners et Justices et a touz Brac. 108 *b*. autres, a qi nous avoms doné auctorité de record, qe nul, sauve noster Seneschal et nos Justices de Hyrelaunde et de Cestre, mette autre en soen liu sauntz nous, pur ren fere dunt il meymes deit fere record; et si ren soit fet devaunt teus substituz, volums nous qe ceo soit [7]de nule force, tut soit de abjúracioun ou de utlagerie.

13. Et volums ausi, qe en counteez et hundrez et en Court [3 *b*.] de chescun fraunc tenaunt, soint les Courtz tenues par les Fle. 66 (§ 12, 13), 112, 115. suytours, et ausi en cyteez et en burgs et en fraunchises, et en tourns[8] des viscountes, et[9] en vewe de fraung plege[10].

1. *so DARMEC. B. sim. F.* defende *LS.* defend[ums] *N.* defendpm nous *G.* 2—2. *so D.* qe hom ne eyt *LS.* qe [nul] hom ne eit *N.* a touz qe nul neit *M. sim. ARCHFN.* a touz qe nuly eit *GE.* 3—3. *so verb. G. sim. HCB.* a demaunder nuli faus *L. sim. S.* a demander riens de nuli saunz *AR.* domaunder [amender *interlin.*] faus *M.* de demaunder nul saunz *E.* 4. *so DHAR.* sauntz *LG. sim. S.* saue *M.* sauf *C.* 5. forqe *M.* 6. ou *DMGEFB.* e od *AR.* od *H.* 7. vein e *add. GCF. sim. MARHB.* 8. *so GE. sim. MC.* court *L.* courtz *DN.* tours *SARHB.* 9. ou *CB. om. H.* 10. e en autres Cours *add. C. sim. HB.*

which the original causes could not be determined. And we forbid, that any have power of amending any false judgment of our Justices, except the Justices who follow us in our Court, who are authorised by us for that purpose, or ourselves, with our Council; for this we specially reserve to our own jurisdiction. Amendment of judgments reserved to King's Court, or Council.

12. We forbid all our Coroners and Justices, and all others to whom we have given authority of record, that any, except our Steward and our Justices of Ireland and of Chester, without our leave substitute another in his place, to do any act of which he himself ought to make record; and if anything be done before such substitutes, we will that it be of no force, though it should be of abjuration or outlawry. Justices cannot in general appoint deputies, but Steward and Justices of Ireland and Chester may.

13. We will also, that in counties and hundreds, and in every freeholder's Court, the Courts be held by the suitors; the like in cities boroughs and franchises, and in sheriffs' Tourns and in view of frankpledge. Courts in which the suitors are judges.

CHAPITRE II. [I.]

Des Corouners[1].

1. Et pur ceo qe nous volums qe Corouners soint en chescun countee principaus gardeyns de nostre pes, a porter record des plez de nostre Coroune et de lour vewes et de abjuraciouns et de utlageries, voloms nous qe il soint esluz solum ceo qe est contenu en [2]noster estatut[2] de lour eleccioun. Et cum[3] il serrunt esluz, volums qe en pleyn Countee facent le serment devaunt le viscounte, qe eux leaument et sauntz lower demaunder frount lour enquestes et les enroudlementz et quant qe al office de Corouner appent.

Stat. West. I. (3 Ed. I.) c. 10. Fle. 20 (§ 1). Stat. West. I. (3 Ed. I.) c. 10, 26.

2. Et voloms qe, cum nule felounie ou mesaventure soit avenue, ou qe tresor soit trové desouth terre mauveisement muscié, ou de rap de femme, ou de brisure[4] de nostre prisoun, ou de homme naufré pres a la mort, ou de autre aventure avenue, qe le Corouner hastivement, si tost cum il le savera, maunde au viscounte et au baillif del leu, qe a certeyn jour face vener devaunt ly, [5]al leu la ou[5] le aventure serra avenue,

Offic. Coron. (Stat. 4 Ed. I.) Stat. Wall. (12 Ed. I.) c. 5. Brac. 121, 121 b. Fle. 36.

1. le Rey *add. N. sim. D.* 2—2. nos estatutz *AB.* 3. so *DN. sim. MGSHARCF.* cum *om. L.* 4. brusure *MGCB.* brusoures *F.* burgosure *A.* 5—5. al leu ou *NGDEKC. sim. AM.* la ou *SF.*

CHAPTER II.

Of Coroners.

Coroners, nature of their office; 1. And because our will is, that coroners shall in every county be the principal guardians of our peace, to bear record of the pleas of our Crown, and of their views, and of abjurations and outlawries, we will that they be chosen according as is contained in our statute concerning their election; and when they shall be chosen, we will that in full County they take the oath before the sheriff, that they will lawfully and without demanding any reward make their inquests and enrollments, and do whatsoever belongs to the office of coroner.

How chosen. Their oath. No reward to be taken by them.

Coroner's Inquest. 2. Also, we will, when any felony or misadventure has happened, or if treasure be found under ground and wickedly concealed, and in case of rape of women, or of the breaking of our prison, or of a man wounded near to death, or of any other accident happening, that the coroner do speedily, as soon as he is informed of it, give notice to the sheriff and the bailiff of the place, that at a certain day he cause to appear before him, les quatre viles[1] proscheynes, et autres si mester soit, par les queles il pora enquere la verité del aventure. Et cum il serra venu, si face les villeez jurer sur Sainctz, qe il verité [4.] dirount des articles qe il lour demaundera de par nous. Et en teus cas, et[2] as tourns de viscountes, et a vewe de fraunc plege, et en office de nos Eschetours, et en presence de nous devaunt noster Seneschal, et en heyre de nos Justices, volums **Stat. Marl. (52 H. III.) c. 22.** nous qe gentz jurent, tut ne veigne[3] noster bref. **Fle. 68 (§ 11).**

3. Et peus auge[4] le Corouner [5]ove les jurez[5] veer le cors [6]et les[6] playes et les coups, [7]et si[7] acun eyt esté estraunglé ou eschaudé ou par autre peyne a mort liveré. Et tauntost **Brit. 121 *b*, 122.** apres cele vewe soint les cors enterrez[8]. Et si le Corouner **Fle. 37 (§ 8).** troeve ceus cors enterrez[9] avaunt tele vewe fete, ceo face enrouler; mes le Corouner jalemeyns ne lese [10]qe il ne face[10] desenfower les cors et [11]veye les apertement et face veer les des viles[11].

4. Et ceux qe averount esté somouns et ne vindrent a teles

1. *So LAM.* villes *DGEC.* vilees *F.* villez *S.* 2. en cas semblables sicom *add. C.* 3. veyent il *DNHFB. sim. AMEC.* vient *G.* 4. voist *AMF. sim. CHB.* deit *E.* 5—5. e les iurez oue li *M. sim. EFH.* e les Iorours od li *A.* 6—6. e bien enserchent les *C.* 7—7. si *ME.* ou si *C.* 8. en seueles *E.* 9. enseuely *E.* 10—10. *om. M.* 11—11. veer les apertement et veer les des viles *L. sim. GS.* les veie apertement et les face veer des villeez *D. sim. AMF. sim. on eras. N.* les veer apertement de villes *CH.*

at the place where the accident happened, the four adjacent **Four adjacent townships to be summoned,** townships and others if need be, whereby he may inquire of the truth of the casualty. And when he is come, let him swear **and sworn.** the townships upon the Holy Evangelists, that they will speak the truth of such articles as he shall demand of them on our behalf. And in this case, and at the sheriffs' tourns, and at **Oath administered without writ.** view of frankpledge, and in the office of escheators, and in our presence before our Steward, and in the eyre of our Justices, we will that people be sworn though our writ come not.

3. Afterwards, let the coroner with the jurors go and view **View of body;** the body, and the wounds and blows, or if any one hath been strangled or scalded[e] or by other violence come to his end; and immediately after the view, let the body be buried. And **burial.** if the coroner find the body buried before such view made, let him make an enrollment thereof; but let him nevertheless not fail to have the body disinterred, and view it openly, and have it viewed by the townships.

4. Those who are summoned, and come not to the coroner's

[e] Perhaps, suffocated,—a sense suggested by Carpentier. Ducange, Gloss. *s. v.* excaldare.

enquestes des Corouners, volums nous que il soint en nostre merci a la venue de nos Justices as premeres assises en cel counté, si soint[1] teles defautes entrez[2] en roule de Corouner; issint qe nos Corouners ne nos eschetours ne simples enquerours ne eynt poer de nuli amercier pur nule defaute.

Stat. Marl. c. 18.

5. Et cum le Corouner avera suffisauntment gentz par queus il pora ses[3] enquestes fere, si enquerge tut al comencement, si tel homme fust occys par felonie ou par mesaventure; et si par felonie, le quel la felonie fust fete de eynz mesoun ou de hors, et si a taverne ou a lute ou a autre assemblé. Et peus soit enquis quels furent al fet, grauntz ou petiz, males ou femeles, et qi sount coupables del fet, et qi del ayde, ou de la force, ou del comaundement, ou del consentment, ou del recettement de ceux felons a escient. Et si le Corouner de la premere enqueste eyt suspecioun de concelement de la verité, ou qe mester soit de plus enquere et par autres, si enquerge plusours foiz, mes qe[4] pur nule contrarieté de verdit ne chaunge ne amenuse soen enroulement en nul point. Et si enquerge de

Offic. Coron. (Stat. 4 Ed. I.) Brac. 121 *b*. Fle. 36, 37.

[4 *b*.]

Fle. 37 (§ 3).

1. soint *om. MECH.* 2. *so NDS.* entre *L.* entres *G.* truuent *M. sim. AE.* troeuent entre *C.* trouuent entrez *H.* 3. celes *DACH.* ce[le]s *N.* teus *E.* tieles *B.* 4. qe *om. AMECFB.*

Defaulters in appearance, amerced.

inquest, shall be in our mercy at the coming of our Justices at the next assises in that county, if such defaults be entered in the roll of the coroner; so that neither our coroners, nor our escheators, nor any mere inquirers, have authority to amerce any one for any default.

Power of amercement.

Articles of the inquest.

5. When the coroner shall have a sufficient number by whom he may make his inquests, let him in the first place inquire, whether such person was killed by felony or misadventure; and if by felony, whether the felony was committed in or out of a house, or whether in a tavern, or at a wrestling-match or other meeting. Then let it be inquired, who were present at the fact, great and small, male and female; and who are guilty of the fact, and who of aid, or of force, or of commandment or consent, or of knowingly receiving such felons. And if the coroner on the first inquiry suspect concealment of the truth, or that there is need of further inquiry, and that by others, let inquiry be made again and again; but let him not for any contrariety in the verdicts alter or curtail his enrollment in any point. And further, he must inquire of the

Second inquest.

Enrollment not to be altered.

la manere del occisioun, et de quel arme, et totes les circumstaunces.

Offic. Coron. Brac. 121 *b* (§ 2). Fle. 37 (§ 4). Stat. Exon. (14 Ed. I.) Offic. Coron. Brac. 121 *b* (§ 6). Fle. 37 (§ 7.)

6. Et touz ceux qi serount enditez face le viscounte hastivement prendre, si il soint trovez. Et si ceo noun, si enquerge le Corouner queus ceux sount, qi se sount sustrez par cele enchesoun; et tauntost face le viscounte seyser lour terres en nostre meyn simplement, sauntz baillifs remuer ou nul i mettre de[1] par nous, deques a[2] taunt qe tiels soynt dampnez par jugement ou purgez de cele felonie. Et puis face seyser touz lour chateus en nostre meyn, et les face priser par bone enqueste, et ausi bien[3] les chateus des vileyns fuiz[4] et mescruz cum de fraunces, et le pris face enrouller en la roule del Corouner, et liverer a la villee[5] pur nous en[6] respoundre, si celi endité defuye de ester a dreit en nostre Court, ou si il soit atteynt [5.] peus pur feloun. Et peus enquerge, si nul des enditez unkes par noster bref de manace [7]al tué[7] trova surté de nostre pes, et les nouns des meynpernours, solom ceo qe il troverunt[8] par le verdit, face enrouler.

Reg. Brev. 88 *b*.

1. so *NDAMGSF.* de *om. L.* 2. so *NDAMGF.* a *om. LS.* 3. so *DAMCB. sim. F.* bien *om. L.* bien *interl. N.* 4. sustretz *add. D. sim. interl. N.* 5. so *NDC.* ville *LB.* vilee *A.* vile *MF.* 6. so *MF.* en *om. LNDGSACHFB.* 7—7. a autre *M.* de tuer *C.* a tiel *B. om. E.* 8. troue *G.* trouera *E.* trouerent *H.*

manner of the killing, and with what weapon, and of all the circumstances.

Persons indicted to be apprehended.

6. And let the sheriff forthwith cause all those who shall be indicted to be taken, if they be found. If they be not found, let the coroner inquire, who they are who have withdrawn themselves on that account; and let the sheriff forthwith seize their lands into our hand simply, without removing bailiffs or putting in any one on our behalf, until the parties are convicted by judgment or cleared of the felony. Next, let him seize all their chattels into our hand, and appraise them by good inquest, and that, whether they be the chattels of villains, who have fled and are suspected, or of freemen, and cause the value to be enrolled in the coroner's roll, and the goods to be delivered to the townships to be answered for to us, in case the person indicted shall either refuse to submit himself to justice in our Court, or be afterwards attainted as a felon. Afterwards let it be inquired, whether any of the persons indicted ever by virtue of our writ of menace found surety of our peace to the person killed; and let the names of the mainpernors be enrolled according as shall be found by the verdict.

Lands of fugitives taken into the king's hand;

and chattels delivered to the township for the king.

Inquiry as to sureties of peace.

Mag. Char. c. 37. Stat. Glouc. (6 Ed. I.) c. 9. Brac. 125. Fle. 40 (§ 5), 48 (§ 9).

7. Et si il i eyt akun qi vodera sure venjaunce de la mort par apel de felonie, plus tost soit resceu le madle qe la femele, de quel age qe il soit, et plus tost le proscheyn del saunc qe le remué. [1]Et si[1] le pleyntif vodera sure soen apel de eynz le an et le jur, si troeffe deus pleges suffisauntz et[2] destreynables al viscounte del pays en qi baillie la felonie avera esté fete, en pleyn counté, qe il soen apel sewera solom ley de terre; et soit a ceo receu. Et peus face le Corouner entrer soen apel et les nouns des pleges. Et peus soit comaundé al serjaunt del pays ou la felonie fust fete, qe il eyt le cors del appelé al proscheyn Counté a respoundre a celi pleyntif.

Brac. 138. Fle. 48 (§ 9), 53 (§ 42).

8. Et si il appele plusours, issi qe akuns del fet, et akuns de la force, ou des fetz accessories, a chescun apel soint entrez[3] deus pleges de sure, et vers chescune persone soit entré le apel severalment. Et si le serjaunt tesmoigne al secund Counté, qe il ne les peut mie trover, dunc soit agardé, qe les principaus [5 *b*.] appelez del fet soint solempnement demaundez qe il veignent a nostre pes de ester a dreit sur tele felonie dunt il sount apelez. Et issi soint demaundez de Counté en Counté jekes au taunt qe

Brac. 125. Fle. 40 (§ 5).

1—1. E quel houre qe *M.* e ke *F.* 2. et *om. AMH.* 3. requis *Y.*

Appeal, to be brought by male, next of blood, within the year and day. Pledges of prosecution.

7. If there be any one who would seek vengeance of the death by appeal of felony, let the male, of what age soever he be, be received before the female; and the next of blood before one more remote. And if the plaintiff is willing to prosecute his appeal within the year and day, let him find in full county two sufficient pledges, distrainable to the sheriff of the county in whose bailiwick the felony was committed, that he will prosecute his appeal according to the law of the land, and thereupon let him be admitted thereto. Then let the coroner enter his appeal and the names of his pledges. Afterwards, let the bailiff of the place where the felony was committed be commanded to have the bodies of the appellees at the next county court to answer to the plaintiff.

Attachment of appellee.

Appeal of principal and accessories. Process of outlawry. Exigent.

8. And if he appeal several, some of the fact and some of the force or accessory facts, to every appeal let two pledges to prosecute be entered; and let the appeal be entered separately against each person. If the bailiff at the second county court testify that he could not find them, then let it be awarded that the principals appealed of the fact be solemnly demanded that they do come to our peace, to take their trial for the felony whereof they are appealed; and let them be so demanded from county

il vengent ou soint utlagez. Et si le pleyntif face defaute a nuli Counté, adunc cessent les exigendes jekes a nostre venue en le pays, ou en heyre des Justices; [1]et si[1] le pleyntif vodera soen apel recomencer, si troeffe autres pleges de sure, et soit a ceo receu, si il ceo prie deynz le an et jour.

9. Et lequel qe les apelez del consentement ou des fetz accessories se retreent ou apergent, ne volums mie qe exigendes courgent sur eux ne qe il soint tenuz a respoundre al pleyntif avaunt jugement pronuncié en le princepal. Mes si li princepal soit utlagez, tauntost courgent les exigendes en les accessories. Et quant nuli sera utlagé ou sustret et mescru, si enquerge le Corouner [2]de qi dixeyne ou[2] de qi meynpast celi futif avera esté, et solum le verdit face l'enroulement; et si enquerge des terres et des chateus a chescun futif, et[3] ou il les avera eu aylours qe en sa baillie. Et si il soint apparuz avaunt la

Stat. West. 1. (3 Ed. I.) c. 14. Brac. 138 (§ 4), 139. Fle. 41, 42.

Brac. 124, 124 b. Fle. 40 (§ 2).

1—1. E si neqedent *AM. sim. F.* issi neqedent si *C.* issi neqedent qe si *B.* 2—2. *so verb. S.* de dixeyne ou *L.* de qui recettement et de dixeyne ou *D.* [de qui recettement e] de deizeyne ou *N.* de qui dozeyne ou *G.* de qi diseyne ou de qi mesnee ou *M.* de ki receuement ou *Y.* de qi meyne ou *B.* 3. et *om. LNAGSECFB.* e *M.*

court to county court until they appear or be outlawed. And if the plaintiff makes default at any county court, then let the exigent[d] stand over till our coming into the county or the Eyre of the Justices; and if the plaintiff will resume his appeal, let him on finding other pledges to prosecute be received thereto, so as he pray it within the year and day.

Default of appellor.

9. But whether those who were appealed of consenting and of accessory facts withdraw themselves or appear, no exigent shall run against them, nor shall they be compelled to answer to the plaintiff before judgment be pronounced in the case of the principal. But if the principal be outlawed, then let exigents be immediately awarded against the accessories. And when any of them is outlawed, or hath withdrawn himself and is suspected, let the coroner inquire of whose tithing or whose mainpast such fugitive was, and make his enrollment according to the verdict; and let him inquire of the lands and chattels of every fugitive, and in what place he has had property elsewhere than in his bailiwick. And if they appear before the outlawry of

Principal to be convicted, or outlawed, before accessories.

Enrollment of fugitives and outlaws, and of their tithings.

d The exigend or exigent is the writ or precept in pursuance of which an absent defendant is *exacted* or required at the county court, with a view to his outlawry. The name and the practice still continue. See Termes de la ley, s. v. Exigent; 3 Blackst. Comm. 283. App. xix.; 4 ib. 319.

utlagerie del princepal, si soint il replevisables; et tauntost apres le princepal utlagé vienent a respoundre al pleyntif.

Offic. Coron. Brac. 121 *b.* (§. 4.) Fle. 37 (§ 6.) [6.]

10. Et si la felonie eyt esté fete hors de mesoun, adunc enquerge le Corouner, qi trova primes le cors, et celui volums nous qe soit pris, ou plusours si il i soint, aussi ben femmes cum hommes, et ausi ben petiz cum grauntz, et lessez[1] par plege jekes a nostre venue en le pays, ou en heyre des Justices; et qe le Corouner face enbrever lour nouns et les nouns des pleges.

Stat. West. 1. (3 Ed. I.) c. 9.

11. Et si defendoms a touz Corouners sur peyne de enprisounement et de greef raunsoun, qe nul face ses enquestes de felonie ou des aventures ne des autres choses qe apendent a soen office par amis procurez, ne qe nul remue jurour par chaleng de nule partie, ne que nul ne prenge rien par ly ne par autre, ne sufre de estre pris par soen clerc ne par nul des soens, pur soen office fere, ne rasture ne chaunge ne nule manere de fraude ne face en ses roules, ne soefre de estre fet.

Stat. West. 1. (3 Ed. I.) c. 10.

Fle. 37 (§ 3.)

Brac. 122. Fle. 37 (§ 4.)

12. Et si il troeve qe aukun avera esté mort par mesa-

1. soyent lessez *D.* *sim.* *M.* [soient] lesse *N.* lesse *GSE.*

the principal, let them be replevisable, and immediately after outlawry of the principal, let them come and answer to the plaintiff.

Dead body found. Finders to be bailed.

10. If the felony was committed out of a dwelling-house, then let the coroner inquire, who first found the body, and let him or them, if there be several, women as well as men, young as well as old, be taken and released by pledges, until our coming into the county or the Eyre of the Justices; and let the coroner cause their names and the names of the pledges to be imbreviated.

Inquests to be taken impartially, and without reward.

11. We forbid every coroner, upon pain of imprisonment and heavy ransom, to make his inquests of felonies accidents or other things belonging to his office, by procurement of friends[e], or to remove a juror on the challenge of any party, or to take anything by himself or other, or suffer anything to be taken by his clerk or any person belonging to him, for the executing of his office; or to erase, or alter, or practise any kind of fraud in his rolls, or suffer it to be done.

Rolls not to be altered.

Death by accident.

12. If he finds that any one has come to his death by acci-

e The meaning appears to be: by procuring friends of the parties implicated to make up the jury.

venture, adunc enquerge par quele mesauenture, si il fust neyez, ou chayt, ou tué saunz autri felonie purpensé, ou feloun de ly mesmes; et si neyez, lequel en mer, ou en braz de mer, ou en ewe douce, ou en puyz, ou en fosse; et par quele enchesoun il se neya, et de quel vessel il chei, et queles choses furent en le vessel, et a qui meyns devindrent, et cum ben valeyent, et qi trova primes le cors. Et si en puyz, adunc soit enquis, a qi le puyz fust. Et si il chayst, lequel de molyn, ou de chival, ou de mesoun, ou de arbre; et si de molin, [6 *b.*]
queles choses furent [1]adunk movauntes en le molin, et a qi fut le molin, et cum ben [2]valeynt les choses[1] leynz[2] adunc movauntes[3]; et ausi des mesouns, des chivaus, des arbres, et des charettes.

13. Et si tuez, adunc soit enquis, ou de homme, ou de beste, ou de autre chose. Et si de homme, lequel par ly meymes ou par autre. Et si par autre, lequel la mesaventure avynt par cas, ou par necessité pur mort eschure. Et si par beste, lequel par cheen ou par autre, et lequel la beste fust aprise [4]a ceo

1—1. *om. ND.* 2—2. *so verb. AF. sim. S.* valeynt leynz *L.* valent les choses leinz *M. sim. C.* valerent les choses *G. sim. E.* 3. el Molyn *add. G. sim. E.* 4—4. *so LS.* e abette a ceo faere *G.* ou affete ou abette a teus maus fere *A. sim. MYEC.*

dent, then let him inquire by what accident, whether he was
drowned, or fell, or whether he was killed without felony
prepensed of any other, or was a felon of himself; and if he
was drowned, whether in the sea, or in an arm of the sea, in [Drowning.]
fresh water, or in a well, or ditch, and by what occasion he
was drowned; also from what vessel he fell, and what things [Inquest of goods in boat or ship.]
were in such vessel, and to whose hands they came, and of
what value they were, and who first found the body. If in a
well, then let it be inquired, whose the well was. If by a fall, [Death by a fall.]
whether it was from a mill, or from a horse, or a house, or a
tree. If from a mill, what things were then moving in the [Inquest of goods in mill or house.]
mill, who owned the mill, and the value of the things therein then moving; and likewise of houses, horses, trees, and carts.

13. If the person was killed, then let it be inquired, whe- [Killing.]
ther it was done by man or beast or any other thing; if by
man, whether by the person himself, or by another; and if by
another, whether the misadventure happened by chance, or from
necessity to avoid death; if by a beast, whether by a dog, or [Man killed by a beast.]
other beast, and whether the beast was set on to do it, and

fere et abbeté a teus maus fere[4], ou noun, et par queus, et issi de totes les circumstaunces.

Brac. 122 (§ 8). 135. Fle. 37 (§ 9). 14. De neyez hors de mer en noster reaume cheuz hors de vessel, volums ausi, qe le vessel et quant qe leynz serra trové soit prisé[1] cum deodande et enroulé par le Corouner, ceo est a saver, quant qe il i avera esté movaunt. Kar si homme se lesse cheyer de nef siglaunt, ren est enchesoun de sa mort for qe soulement la nef, et les choses movauntes porount estre dites cause de la mort; les marchaundises nequedent gisauntes au sounz ne funt mie pur ceo enchesoun de sa mort; et ausi en cas semblables. Et de neyez en fontaynes et en puyz voloms nous ausi cum des autres, qe les Corouners facent mettre par meynprise les troveours et facent enrouler lour nouns et les nouns de lour pleges. Et de ceux qi serount mortz par charettes, ou par molins, ou par arbres, ou en cas
[7.] semblables, face le Corouner ses enquestes et ses enroulementz
Offic. Coron. (Stat. 4 Ed. I.) sicum desus est dit de neyez.

Brac. 135, 135 b. Fle. 46. 15. Et de chescune enqueste qe le Corouner fra des cors des gentz felounousement tuez, face le Corouner vener un parent al mort, ou plusours, de par pere ou de par mere, devaunt sei en

1. pris *M G C.* prisee *S.* preise *E.* *sim. F.*

encouraged to such mischief, or not, and by whom, and so of all the circumstances.

Death by drowning. Deodand. 14. Of such as are drowned within our realm by falling from a vessel not at sea, our will is, that the vessel and whatsoever shall be found therein be appraised as a deodand and enrolled by the coroner, that is to say, whatsoever was moving; for if a man happens to fall from a ship under sail, nothing can be deemed the cause of his death, except the ship itself and the things moving in it; but the merchandise lying at the bottom of the ship, is not presumed to be the occasion of his death, and so in like cases. And of those drowned in fountains and wells, we will, as in the other cases, that the coroners admit to mainprise the first finders, and enroll their names and the names of their pledges; and of those who have come to their death by carts or mills, and in the like cases, let the coroner make his inquests and enrollments as above directed where persons are drowned.

Proof of Englishery. 15. Whenever the coroner takes his inquest on the body of a person feloniously killed, let him cause one or more of kin to the deceased on the side of the father or mother to appear

temoygnaunce de Englescherie solum le usage del pays; et ceux nouns face le Corouner enbrever.

16. Et voloms ausi, qe les Corouners receyvent les reconisaunces de felonies fetes par provours en presence del viscounte; [1]qi nous[1] volums qe soit soen countreroullour[2] [3]en tut[3] soen office; et celes reconisaunces facent enrouller. Et quant hom serra fui al moster, volums nous qe le Corouner, si toust cum il le savera, maunde al bailif del liu, qe a certeyn jour face vener devaunt ly les veysins et les quatre proscheynes viles a cele eglise ou le futif serra, et en lour presence receyve la reconisaunce de la felonie. Et si le futif prie de forjurer noster reaume, tauntost face le Corouner ceo qe a ly apent. Et si noun, si soit liveré a la villee a garder sour lour peril.

Brac. 152. Fle. 56, 57. Stat. West. 1. (3 Ed. I.) c. 10. Brac. 135 b, 136. Fle. 45. Post. c. 13.

17. Et si il deit fere enqueste de rap, si enquerge ententivement de totes les circumstaunces de la force et de la felonie; et les signes presumptives, cum de saunc espaundu, et de robe decyré, face[4] enrouler. Et si de playe, si enquerge de quel [7 b.] arme, et de la loungure et de la parfundesce de la playe. Et

Offic. Coron. (Stat. 4 Ed. I.) Brac. 122. Fle. 38. Brac. 122 b.

1—1. *so DN. sim. GA.* car nous *L.* ke nu, *F.* qi *M.* 2. countre roule *M.* cuntur e enrouleour e *F.* 3—3. de *A.* 4. e ceo face *A.* e face *M.* si facc *C.*

before him in proof of Englishery according to the custom of the country, and enroll their names.

16. We will also that the coroners receive the confessions of felonies made by approvers in the presence of the sheriff, whom we intend to be his controller in every part of his office; and let them cause such confessions to be enrolled. And when any man has fled to church, we will that the coroner as soon as he has notice of it, command the bailiff of the place, that he cause the neighbours and the four nearest townships to appear before him at a certain day at the church where the fugitive shall be; and in their presence he shall receive the confession of the felony; and if the fugitive pray to abjure our realm, let the coroner immediately do what is incumbent on him. But if he does not pray abjuration, let him be delivered to the township to keep at their peril.

Confessions of approvers. Sanctuary. Abjuration.

17. If the coroner be to take an inquest of rape, let him carefully inquire into all the circumstances of the force and of the felony, and make enrollment of the presumptive signs, such as stains of blood, and tearing of clothes. If of a wounding, let him inquire with what weapon, and of the length and depth of the wound. Let him likewise enter in his roll all

Inquest of rape; of wounding.

Post. c. 16. s. 1. ausi face mettre en roule touz les jugementz de mort de homme fetz par autres qe par nos Justices en sa baillie; et en tel cas voloms nous, qe lour roulles portent record. Et ceo qe desus est dit, qe il deyvent fere enroullementz de apels de felonies de mort de homme, soit ausi fet en apels de rap, roberies, larcyns, et de touz autres apels de chescune manere de felonie.

Offic. Coron. (Stat. 4 Ed. I.) Stat. West. 1. (3 Ed. I.) c. 4. Prerog. Reg. (Stat. incert. temp.) c. 13. Brac. 120, 120 *b*, 122. Fle. 38 (c. 35. § 11), 61.

18. Et ausi apent a lour office de enquere de viel tresor trové en terre, et de wrek de meer, et de estorgon et de baleyne, quant hom lour fra de ceo a saver; et de fere prendre et mettre par meynprise les trovours et les alienours, et lour nouns fere enbrever, et [1]teles troveures[1] a nostre oes sauver. Et voloms qe nos viscountes et nos baillifs soint entendauntz a eux et a lour maundementz.

CHAPITRE III. [II.]

Des Heyres [2]*des Justices*[2].

Brac. 115 *b*. Fle. 23.

1. Quant a nos venues [3]et a heyre des[3] Justices voloms nous qe generale crye soit fete solempnement par les marchez cytez

1—1. tels troueours *L. sim. NDMS.* celes troueures *A.* teus troueures *F.* les choses trouez *G.* 2—2. des Justices *om. AMCF.* 3—3. a heyre des *L. sim. NDS.* en eyres des *G.* e a eyre de nos *M. sim. A.* e al heire de nos *F.*

Judgments of death in inferior Courts to be enrolled. Coroner's rolls a record. Enrollment of appeals.

judgments of death given in his bailiwick by any other than our Justices; and in such cases, we will that their rolls be a record. And whereas it is declared above, that coroners ought to make enrollments of appeals of felonies of the death of a man, let them do the like in appeals of rape, robbery, larceny, and in appeals of every other kind of felony.

Treasure-trove. Wreck, &c. Sheriff and bailiffs to assist coroner.

18. It also belongs to their office to inquire of ancient treasure found in the earth, of wreck of the sea, of sturgeons and whales, as soon as they shall have notice thereof; and to attach and let to mainprise those who have found or made away with them, and to enroll their names, and to secure such findings for our use. And we will that our sheriffs and bailiffs be attendant on our coroners, and execute their precepts.

CHAPTER III.

Of Eyres of Justices.

Proclamation of the eyre.

1. With respect to our coming, and the Eyre of our Justices, we will that general proclamation be solemnly made in the

[8.] et bourghs par tut le counté de eynz fraunchise et de hors, qe trestouz les fraunes del counté, et quatre et le provost de chescune vile[1], et touz [2]les meynpernours et[2] les meynpris del counté soint a certeyn jour, qe conteigne xl. jours au meyns, devaunt nous ou teles Justices, qi serrount nometz en noster maundement a heyrer en mesme le counté; et qe touz ceux, qi aucune fraunchise cleyment aver en mesme le counté, soint a teu jour devaunt nous ou devaunt mesmes les Justices, et qe chescun moustre [3]par lettre[3] distinctement queles fraunchises il cleyme; et qe touz ceux, qi pleyndre se voderount de nos ministres ou de nos baillifs ou de autres [4]ou qi qe il soint[4], soint [5]a mesme le jour illoekes[5], a lour pleyntes moustrer et a trover pleges de sure; et qe le viscounte del pays eyt illucs trestouz les brefs qe ajournez ount esté jekes en heyre et trestotes les [6]noveles disseisines, assises[6] de mort de auncestre, de dareyn present, de utrum, et de dowarie, et trestouz les prisouns[7] et les attachementz. Et endementers maunderoms a nos Justices du baunk, qe trestouz les pletz de cel counté

Stat. Glouc. (6 Ed. I.) Pream. Fle. 23.

1. et xii Burgeys de chescon Burgh *add. Z.* 2—2. *om. NSGM.* 3—3. par bref ou par lettre *M. sim. W.* 4—4. queus qe il seent *M.* qi qe unkes seient *C.* oueke qui cunqes seient *A. sim. WF.* od qi qil seient *G. sim. S.* 5—5. *so verb. GMW. sim. F.* amene illoekes le Iour *L.* amenee li iour illucs *N. sim. DS.* 6—6. assises de nouele disseisine de *A. sim. MCF.* 7. presentmentz *M. sim. A.*

markets cities and boroughs throughout the county, as well within franchises as without, that all the freemen of the county, and four men and the provost of every vill, and all the mainpernors and those who have been let to mainprise throughout the county, appear at a certain day, which shall be forty days distant at least, before us, or such Justices as shall be named in our precept to keep the eyre in the same county: and that all those who claim any franchise in the same county be the same day before us or the same Justices, and that every one show distinctly in writing what franchises he claims; and that all those, who have any complaints to make against our ministers or bailiffs or those of others or any persons whatsoever, be there at the same day, to exhibit such complaints and find pledges to prosecute; and that the sheriff of the county have there all such writs as have been adjourned until the eyre, and all the assizes of novel disseisin, mortdancester, darrein presentment, utrum, and of dower, and all the prisoners and attachments. And meantime we will command our Justices of the bench, that they adjourn all the pleas of the county and

Summons of freemen. Provost and four men of vill.

Claim of franchise.

Complaints of king's officers and others.

Assizes.

Pleas of the county to be

ajournent et enveynt devaunt nous ou teles[1] Justices errauntz en cel counté, issint qe il i soint au certeyn jour.

Brac. 115 *b.* Fle. 23. 2. Et quant a la venue de nos Justices, voloms nous, qe [8 *b.*] cum il serrount venuz la ou il deyvent heyrer, qe il moustrent le poer qe il averount de nous par nos lettres patentes, et en audience del poeple les facent lire; et puis qe celui qe primes serra nomé en celes lettres moustre et die al poeple les enchesouns et les profitz de lour venue en cel counté. Et puis receyvent les essoynes de la commune somounse, et tauntost soint jugez et ajournez. Et puis soint recewes les essoynes de play de terre; et ceux soint ajugez, et [2]apres le quart jour ajournez[2].

Stat. Glouc. (6 Ed. I.) Pream. Fle. 23. 3. Et puis soint recewes les lettres par les queles, qikonqe soint, cleyment tener fraunchise en cel counté, et ceux cleyms soint enroullez, et le transescrit de cel enroullement soit liveré au viscounte; et soit comaundé, qe trestotes les fraunchises en soen counté nient clamez prenge en nostre meyn en noun de destresce, et qe le viscounte nous respoigne des issues jekes autaunt qe ceux qi les claymerunt eynt sauvé[3] lour defautes

1. celes *LNDGS.* tiels *M.* ceus *AF.* 2—2. *so DGS. sim. MF.* apres le quart iour apres aiournez *L.* apres le quart [iour] aiournez *N.* aiornez le quart iour *C.* 3. saune (*qu.* saune) *LG.* sauuez *MA.* sane *S.* sanee *D.* salue *Y.*

adjourned from the bench. send them before us or such Justices itinerant in that county, so that they be there at the day named.

Opening of the Eyre. 2. And as to the coming of our Justices, our will is, that as soon as they be come to the place appointed for holding the eyre, they produce the authority they have of us by our letters patent, and cause them to be read in the hearing of the people; and afterwards let him who is first named in the letters, show and declare to the people the occasions and advantages of their coming into that county; this done, let them receive the essoins of the common summons, which shall be immediately determined and adjourned. Then let the essoins of pleas of land be received; and let these be adjudged and the fourth day after adjourned.

Essoins.

Claims of franchises. 3. Next let the letters whereby any persons whatever claim to hold franchises in that county be received, and let their claims be enrolled, and a transcript of the same enrollment be delivered to the sheriff; and as to all such franchises as are not claimed, let the sheriff be commanded to seize them into our hands by way of distress, and be answerable to us for the issues, until those who shall claim them have saved their

de la sursise de la somounse; et puis respoignent par quel garraunt il les averount tenues.

4. Et peus prengent les Justices les verges del viscounte et des seignurs des fraunchises et de touz autres menours[1] baillifs; et puis jure le viscounte, qe il leaument fra les comaundementz de nos Justices en dreiture, et les priveteez et les counseils de lour heyre ben concelera, si ly ayde Deus et les Saintz. Et, le serment fet, ly soit la verge rendue. Et puis presente le viscounte touz ses ministres et ses baillifs, clers et autres, par les queus les comaundemenz des Justices et les execucicouns de lour jugemenz deyvent estre forniz; et trestouz facent autiel serment cum fist le viscounte; et puis lour soint lour verges liverez.

Stat. Sacr. Min. Reg. (inc. temp.)

[9.]

5. Ei si il i ad ercevesk, evask, abbé ou priour, counte ou baroun, ou autre, qe cleyme fraunchise de retour de nos brefs, si facent autel[2] serment cum fist le viscounte; ou prengent lour verges et presentent tels[3] baillifs [4]pur eux, qi[4] facent le serment [5]pur eux, et[5] pur qi fetz il voderunt respoundre quant a ceo qe appendera a lour office; et puis soint les verges

Fle. 23.

1. menuz *MC.* meindres *AF.* 2. ausi le *AM.* 3. lour *M.* 4—4. pur qe *M.* 5—5. So *L.* *sim.* *N.* *om.* *AMCF.*

defaults for not attending the summons; and let them then answer by what warrant they have held them.

4. Afterwards let the Justices take the wands of the sheriff, and of the lords of the franchises, and of all the other inferior bailiffs, and then let the sheriff swear, that he will duly execute the lawful commands of our Justices, and will well conceal the secrets and counsels of their eyre, so help him God and the Saints. And after this oath is taken, let the wand be delivered back to him. Then let the sheriff present all his officers and bailiffs, clerks and others, by whom the precepts of the Justices and executions of their judgments are to be performed; and let them all take the same oath that the sheriff took, and their wands be delivered back to them.

Swearing the sheriff.

Swearing the bailiffs and officers.

5. And if there be any archbishop, bishop, abbot or prior, earl or baron, or other, that claims the franchise of return of our writs, let him take the same oath that the sheriff took; or let them take their wands in their hands, and present such bailiffs in their stead as will take the oath for them, and for whose acts they will be answerable as to that which to their office shall belong: and then let the wands be delivered by

Swearing the lords of liberties or their bailiffs.

Fle. 23. deliverez par tiels seignurs a lour baillifs. Et puis soit crié, qe trestouz tiels de fraunchise voisent en lour pays a lour mesouns, for qe les baillifs, jekes sour somounse et jekes a tiel certeyn jour.

Stat. Sacr. Minis. Reg. (inc. temp.) Brac. 116. Fle. 23.

6. Et peus jurent les baillifs le viscounte, qe eux leaument presenterunt chescun deus[1] ou quatre de sa baillie, ou plus ou meyns, qi poynt ne soint apelez de mauvesté [2]ne de[2] apelours, et teus qi meuz saverunt et voderunt enquere et moustrer les [9 *b*.] privetez qe touchent nostre pes enfrainte. Et puis, quant il averunt teus nouns nomez, si vengent ceux jurer, qe il leaument associerunt a eux tiels par les queux verité meuz apparra. Et puis jurent eux ensemble[3] ovek ceux qe il averount esluz[4] pur les plus suffisauntz, qe des chapitres qe liveré lour serrount en escrit leaument presenterount, et qe ceo pur nul amour ne pur nul haunge ne doute ne doun ne promesse ne lerrount, et qe il les privitez celerount, si lour ayde Deus et les Seyntz.

1. so *NDAMSF*. *sim*. *G*. ii. *C*. de eux *L*. 2—2. par *M*. ne des *AC*. 3. ensemblement *AMCF*. 4. choisiz *AM*. *sim*. *CF*.

those lords to their bailiffs. Afterwards let proclamation be made, that all persons belonging to franchises, except the bailiffs, depart unto their own homes until further summons or until a certain day.

Formation of the inquest or grand jury.

6. Next let the bailiffs of the sheriff swear, that they will truly present two or four[f] of their bailiwick, or more or less, who are not appealed of any crime, nor are appellors, and such as shall best know and will inquire and discover secret acts concerning the breach of our peace. And when the names are given in, let those come and swear, that they will lawfully associate to themselves such others, by whom the truth may best appear. Afterwards, let them, together with those whom they have chosen for the most sufficient, swear, that they will lawful presentment make of such chapters as shall be delivered to them in writing, and that in this they will not fail for any love, hatred, fear, reward, or promise, and that they will conceal the secrets[g], so help them God, and the Saints. And then let

[f] According to the so-called Statute of uncertain date, but probably of the early part of the reign of Edward I, entitled 'de sacramento ministrorum regis,' *two* knights or *prodes homes* were to be chosen by the bailiffs, and twelve knights or *prodes homes* to be chosen of themselves and others of their hundred by the first *two*. According to Bracton and Fleta *four* knights were to be first chosen. Cf. Blackst. Comm. vol. iv. p. 302.

[g] This clause of the oath is not in Bracton or Fleta, nor in the statute 'for oaths of the king's officers.' In MS. *N* a form of oath is given in French nearly resembling that in the text, and concluding, 'mes vostre conseil e de ceste eyre bien e loialmente celeray.'

Et puis lour soint les chapitres luz, et a chescune dozeyne soint les chapitres severaument liverez.

7. Et puis soit crié, qe nul ne soit si hardi de amercier nul homme en court de baroun ne en hundred par defaute qe il[1] face, qi adunc soit par devaunt nous ou nos Justices; et qe nul marché soit tenu aylours, for qe en la vile ou nos Justices serrount, a x. liuwes environ de eux, si la vile ne suffise de trover a ceux qe i demorount suffisaunte vitayle; et [2]qe, si nul i soit venu[2] qi ren i ad a fere, qe il face attorné s' il voile, et s'en voist [3]a sa mesoun[3]. Stat. Sacr. Min. Reg. (inc. temp.) Brac. 116 b, 117 b.

8. Et puis soit comaundé as Corouners, et a lour heyrs, qe il deliverent[4] as Justices lour roules puis le dreyn heyre. Et voloms, qe les Justices les enselent desouth lour seaus, et tauntost sauntz nul examinement les deliverent a eux arere, issi qe il soint chescun jour devaunt eux ove lour clers, taunt cum les Justices averunt de eux a fere. Stat. Exon. (14 Ed. 1.) Fle. 23. [10.]

9. Et peus soint resceus les presentementz sur les chapitres Brac. 116.

1. fra ou *add. M.* 2—2. qe nul i soit venu *L. sim. F.* si nul i soit *N. sim. D.* si nuly seit venue *C.* 3—3. al hostel *M.* 4. liuerunt *M.*

the chapters be read to them, and delivered to every dozen separately[h].

7. Afterwards, let proclamation be made, that none presume to amerce any man for making default in a court baron or hundred, who shall at that time be before us or our Justices; and that no market be kept within ten miles, except in the town where our Justices shall be, if the town is not able to find sufficient provision for such as shall abide there; and that, if any person be come who has no business on hand, he shall make his attorney, if he please, and depart home. Proclamation of freedom from suit at other courts. No market to be held within ten miles. Persons having no business dismissed.

8. Afterwards, let the coroners, or their heirs, be commanded to deliver to the Justices their rolls since the last eyre; and we will that the Justices seal them under their seals, and forthwith without any examination deliver the rolls back to them, so that they be every day with their clerks before the Justices, while they have occasion for them. Coroner's rolls delivered to the Justices.

9. Afterwards, let the presentments upon the chapters deli- Presentments received.

h 'He [*qu.* the Justice] shall then read the articles distinctly *in English*. And that which they shall present, he shall put first in a roll, which shall be their note and shall remain with them. And afterwards of that and the other things, by command and direction of the more prudent of the twelve, he shall make his chief roll.' (Note in MS. *N.*)

deliverez [1]a les[1] dozeynes en escrit, issint qe le escrit soit endenté et qe les Justices eynt la une partie et l'autre partie remayne as presentours. Les chapitres neqedent qe lour deivent estre deliverez ne sunt mie numbrez en certeyn. Car ausi cum les malices de gentz cresent, si covent de acrestre chapitres et autres remedies, dunt partie des chapitres sount de fauseners, de murdres, de aventures[2] et autres, solum les chapitres suawnz.

CHAPITRE IV. [III.]

Des Chapitres[3].

Capit. Itin. (Stat. incert. temp.) Brac. 116, 116 b. Fle. 24 (§ 13).

Al comencement soint enquis oyez et determinez les viels articles[4] presentez en le dreyn heyre en cel counté tochaunt nostre pes enfreynte, qe adunc remistrent a terminer. De nos mortels enemys demorauntz en nostre terre ne put estre nul presentement proprement, mes encusement et appel, sicum apparra entre les apels.

Post. c. 23.

1—1. so *GA*. as *MCF*. a lez *S*. et les *LND*. 2. e de mesauentures *add. A. sim. MF*. 3. en eyre des Iustices *add. D*. 4. chapitres *M*. chapitres e articles *C*.

Chapters or articles of the eyre.

vered to the dozens be received in writing; and let the same be indented, so that the Justices may have one part thereof and the other may remain with the presentors. The chapters which are to be delivered to them are not however of any certain number; for as crimes increase, so must the chapters and other remedies increase. Some of these chapters are concerning counterfeiters, murders, accidents, and other matters, as will appear from the following heads.

CHAPTER IV.

Of the Chapters of the Eyre.

Remanets of last eyre.

In the first place, let the old articles presented in the last eyre in that county touching breaches of our peace, which then remained undetermined, be inquired of, heard, and determined. Of our mortal enemies abiding in our land presentment cannot properly be made[1], but accusation and appeal, as will appear in the chapter of appeals.

King's enemies not prosecuted by presentment.

[1] This appears to be a correction of Fleta 24 (li. 1. cap. 20. sect. 1), who puts treason as the first article of the eyre. It does not appear among the matters enumerated by Bracton, or in the Capitula Itineris (Stat. incert. temp.) But compare post. c. 30. s. 3.

CHAPITRE V. [IV.]

De Fauseners de Seal et de Moneye. [10 *b*.]

1. [1]De fauseners[1] soit enquis, et ne mie soulement de noster seal countrefet, mes de touz ceux qi acune fausine averount fet a noster seal, cum de ceux qi par engyn ount noster seal pendu a acune[2] chartre sauntz congé, ou qi de noster seal emblé ou robbé ou autrement trové eynt selé bref sauntz autre auctorité. Et ausi de ceux fauseners qe ount nostre monee countrefete, ou plus de allay mis a nostre monee qe dreit[3] ne seroit solum la forme et le usage de nostre monee, ou qe en noster royaume eynt fete monee bone ou mauveyse sauntz congé de nous. Et ausi de ceux qi averount nostre monee retoundu ou autrement enpiré; et ausi de ceux qe monee countrefete et aukes semblable a la nostre eynt aporté en noster reaume en despit et damage de nous et de noster poeple. Glan. li. 14, c. 7. Brac. 118 *b*, 119 *b*. Fle. 32. Stat. de Mon. (12 Ed. I.)

2. Sur le presentement de ceste felonie voloms nous, qe trestouz ceux qi en serrunt enditez face le viscounte hastivement prendre et sauvement les cors en prisoun garder; et qe

1—1. De fauseour del seal le Rey e de monee *C*. De fauseours de seal e de Monee *H*. De fauseours *A*. *sim*. *F*. 2. lettre ou *add*. *DM*. *interl*. *N*. 3. meister *C*.

CHAPTER V.

Of counterfeiting the seal and coin; and of the trial of felons.

1. Let inquiry be made of forgers, and not only of such as counterfeit our seal, but of all those who shall have in any way falsified our seal, as those who have fraudulently hung it to any charter without our leave, or when it has been stolen or robbed or otherwise obtained, have sealed writs therewith without other authority. And also of forgers who have counterfeited our coin, or put more alloy in it than according to the form and usage of our mint ought to be put, or that have coined money, whether good or bad, in our realm without our leave. Likewise of those who have clipped our coin or otherwise impaired it. Of those also who have brought into our realm counterfeit money in any way resembling ours in despite and damage of us and our people. Crime of counterfeiting the royal seal or coin. Illegal use of royal seal.

2. Upon presentment of this felony, we will that the sheriff do cause all those who are indicted of it to be instantly taken, and their bodies kept safely in prison; and that they be Presentment of felony. Apprehension of felons.

il soint menez devaunt nous ou devaunt nos Justices. Et pur ceo qe nul ne soit desgarni de respounse, volums de ceux qi sount issi suspris, qe il eynt tens de purveer lour respounse
[11.] de xv. jours a meyns, si il le prient; et endementers soint sauvement gardez. Et cum il vendrount devaunt nous ou devaunt nos Justices en jugement, la soint aresounez par le viscounte ou par autre serjaunt de par nous et encoupez de
Stat. West. 1. (3 Ed. I.) c. 12. Fle. 51 (§ 33). la felonie, solom la manere del presentement. Et si il ne se veulent aquiter, si soint mis a lour penaunce jekes autaunt qe il le prient. La penaunce soit tele, qe il soint deschaucez et sauntz ceynture et sauntz chaperoun [1]en pyr liu de la[1] prisoun sur la nuwe terre assiduelment jour et nuyt, et qe

1—1. so *L. sim. NDGS.* en loor cote en *A. sim. Y.* en pure lour cote en *M. sim. E.* et serrount en lour cote *Z.* en sengle cote *C.* en vne cote solement en *F.*

Time for defence. brought before us or our Justices; and, to the intent that no one may be unprepared with his answer, let those who are so taken have fifteen days at least, if they pray it, to provide their defence, and in the meantime let them be safely kept.
Arraignment. And when they shall appear in judgment before us or before our Justices, let them be there arraigned by the sheriff or other officer on our behalf, and indicted of the felony according
Penance for standing mute. to the nature of the presentment. And if they will not put themselves upon their acquittal[k], let them be put to their penance, until they pray to do it; and let their penance be this, that they be barefooted, ungirt and bareheaded, in the worst place in the prison, upon the bare ground continually night

[k] That is, if they refuse to be tried by an inquest or jury. This sort of trial appears, in theory at least, not to have been considered valid either in criminal or civil causes, without the consent of the parties. Compare liv. ii. c. 20. § 2. So in liv. iii. c. 23. § 4, the consent of the party is extorted by the alternative of a judgment against him. It has been a question, whether the penance here described, which is referred to in Stat. West. I. c. 12, as *prisone forte et dure*, was introduced by that Statute. Coke contends (2 Inst. 178) that it was previously used in cases of appeals, (see post. c. 24. s. 7; Fle. 51, § 33), but was extended by that Statute to indictments at the king's suit. Others have observed that no trace of it is to be found in any authorities anterior to the reign of Edward I; and examples have been cited from earlier records, showing that by the practice of the previous reign, the inquest might be taken by jury without the consent of the prisoner, either voluntary or enforced. (See Hale, Pleas of the Crown, vol. ii. p. 321; Kelham's Britton, p. 35.) This might appear to be in some degree confirmed by the general statement of Glanville, that in cases of treason where there was no appellor, but the prisoner was accused by common fame, the truth was to be inquired by inquests and interrogations before the Justices. (Glan. li. 14. c. 1.) On the other hand, it does not appear to have been observed, that Bracton, although he does not mention the particular means employed, expressly refers to a prisoner on trial for felony being forced to put himself upon the inquest *per patriam.* "Istam vero formam inquisitionis per patriam servabunt justiciarii generaliter in omnibus inquisitionibus quæ faciendæ sunt pro morte hominis, ubi quis se posuerit super inquisitionem sive sponte sive per cautelam inductus sive per necessitatem." Brac. 143 *b.*

il ne mangeusent for qe payn de orge ou de bren, et qe il ne beyvent mie le jour qe il mangerunt [1]et le jour qe il beyvent ne mangerount mie[1], et qe il ne beyvent for qe del ewe[2], et qe il soint en fyrges.

Stat. West. 1. (3 Ed. I.) c. 2. Brac. 123 *b*. Fle. 44, 51.

3. Et si le clerk encoupé de felonie alegge clergie, et il soit tel trové et par ordinarie demaundé, si soit enquis coment il est mescreu. Et s' il ne soit[3] mescru par certeyns resouns, qe les presentours ount puis de luy enquis, si soit ajugé tut quites. Et si il en[4] soit mescru, si soynt ses chateus taxez, et ses terres prises en nostre meyn et soen cors deliveré al ordinarie. Et si le ordinarie ly delivere hors de sa prisoun avaunt due aquitaunce solom purgacioun des clers, ou si il le face si negligaument garder qe il eschape, ou si maliciousement le fet detener qe il ne peuse a sa purgacioun vener, et [5]ceo soit atteynt, en [11 *b*.] chescun poynt soit le ordinarie en nostre merci; et solum ceo

1—1. *om. AC.* 2. cest a sauer le iour qil mangent nient *add. C.* 3. mie *add. G.* nient *M. sim. S.* 4. so *M.* ne *S.* ne *erased LN. om. DGACF.* 5. de *add. M.*

and day, that they eat only bread made of barley or bran, and that they drink not the day they eat, nor eat the day they drink, nor drink anything but water, and that they be put in irons.

Privilege of clergy.

3. If one indicted of felony alleges clergy, and be found to be a clerk and claimed by the ordinary, let it be inquired how he is suspected; and if the presenters upon inquiry find that there are no certain grounds for suspicion, let the judgment be that he be entirely acquitted; and if he is believed to be guilty, let his chattels be appraised, and his lands taken into our hands, and his body delivered to the ordinary[l]; and if the ordinary deliver him out of prison before due acquittance according to the purgation of clerks, or if he keep him so negligently as to let him escape, or out of malice keep him in such a manner as to prevent his coming to his purgation, and be convicted thereof,— in each of these cases let the ordinary be in our mercy[m]. And

Purgation of clerks.

[l] If the principal accused refused to put himself on the country, and claimed clergy, the accessories could not be attainted of felony. A case to this effect is cited in the note in MS. *N.* as having occurred at Lincoln. 'The accessory put himself on the country and by Sir John del Ille was commanded to the gallows. But Sir Elias de Preston said "Repeal that judgment, for the principal never put himself, and is not yet attainted." And he was ordered back to prison and afterwards made his fine for ten pounds.' John del Isle was a baron of the exchequer from 23 Ed. I. to 12 Ed. II. (Foss, Judges, vol. iii. p. 270). Elias de Preston is not mentioned in Mr. Foss's work.

[m] 'The amercement shall be 100*s.* at least; and 100*l.* for an escape from prison.' (Note in MS. *N.*)

qe le ordinarie nous fra a saver del aquitaunce de tels clers, lour [1]from nous fere[1] restitucioun de lour biens, si il ne[2] eynt defuyz nostre pes.

Mag. Char. c. 1. Stat. circum. agat. (13 Ed. I.) Brac. 401, 401 *b*. Fle. 429, 430.

4. Car nous volums qe Sainte Eglise eyt ses fraunchises desblemies, issi qe ele eyt conisaunce a juger de pure espiritualté, de testament et de matrimoine, de bastardie et de bigamie, et en felonies de ses clers, et en correccciouns des pecchez; sauve qe les ordinaries ne prengent nul dener, ne la value, [3]des lays[3], ne de nul[4] dener ne facent jugement for qe de testament et de matrimoine et de pure espiritualté et de amendment de cymiteres et [5]de defautes des eglises[5] et de mortuaries et [6]de dyme[6], sauntz prejudice de nous.

Leg. Hen. I. lvii.9; Stat. de big. (4 Ed. I.) c. 5. Fle. 51 (§ 34).

5. Et si nul ordinarie demaunde, par ly ou par procuratour, tel qe tut est lay ou bigams ou de autre condicioun qe il ne deive la fraunchise de [7]Sainte Eglise[7] joyer, voloms qe tel

1—1. serra fet *A.* serrunt fet *M.* frommes *C.* 2. so *NDAM.* sim. *CF.* ne *om. L.* 3—3. *om. A.* 4. nuly *M.* nuli *CF.* 5—5. so *AF.* sim. *C.* de defautes de sainte eglise *LN.* sim. *D.* de fautes des eglises *M.* 6—6. deuises *C.* 7—7. clergie *AMC.* clerk *F.*

according as the ordinary shall certify us of the acquittance[n] of those clerks, we will cause restitution to be made them of their goods, if they have not fled from our peace[o].

Jurisdiction of Holy Church.

4. For we will that Holy Church retain her liberties unimpaired, so that she have cognizance of judging of mere spirituality, of testaments, of matrimony, of bastardy, of bigamy, and in the felonies of clerks, and in the correction of sins, provided the ordinaries take of the laity no money nor the value thereof, nor give judgment of any property except concerning testament and matrimony and mere spirituality, and of the repairs of churchyards and defects in churches, and of mortuaries, and of tithes, without prejudice to us.

Privilege of clergy, how limited.

5. And if any ordinary, either in person or by his proctor, demands one who is a mere layman, or a bigamist[p], or of such other condition that he ought not to enjoy the privilege of

n 'Et sic habet ordinarius recordum in eodem.' (Note in MS. *N.*)

o 'Hence the inquest may be had, whether the clerk put himself thereupon or not, for two things; namely, to know for what cause he ought to be delivered to the bishop, and also for his chattels, whether he has forfeited them by his flight.' (Note in MS. *N.*)

p *Bigamus* in the canon law is he that has married two or more virgins successively, or that has married a widow. See Coke, Inst. Pt. ii. p. 273; Blackstone, Comm. vol. iv. p. 163. By the Council of Lyons, A. D. 1274, *Bigami* were declared to be 'omni privilegio clericali nudati, et coertioni fori saecularis addicti,' and forbidden under anathema to assume the tonsure. (Sext. Decr. tit. 12.) This was confirmed in England as to benefit of clergy by the Statute 4 Ed. I, thence called Statutum de bigamis.

soit comaundé a la prisoun et soit puni par fin. Et ausi soit de procuratour, qi se profre pur la ordinarie sauntz garrauntie de lettre.

6. Et si aucuns felouns veulent lour mauvesté reconustre et encuser autres et devener provours, si soint mis hors de la penaunce, et hastivement soint lour conusaunces resceues et enroullez par corouner, et tauntost eynt de ceo jour en avaunt chescun jour trois mayles a lour susteynaunce par les viscountes. Brac. 152, 153. [12.]

7. Et cum tiels apelez apparount en jugement, et demaundent jugement, si de fet fet avaunt le autre heyre et nient adunc presenté en cel counté deivent respoundre, pur ceo qe nous ne voloms mie qe les felonies remeynent despuniz, si voloms nous en touz teus cas semblables qe hom respoigne; et si le article ne fut mie presenté en le autre heyre, qe les presentours en le autre heyre del hundred soint en nostre merci pur le concelement, et soint puniz par prisoun et par fin, si nul soit trové en vie. Brac. 116 *b*, 140 *b*, 141. Fle. 49 (§ 6). Brac. 116 *b*. Fle. 30 (§ 138).

8. Et cum les defendauntz se soint mis en pays, et les Brac. 143 *b*. Fle. 52.

Holy Church, we will that he be committed to prison and punished by fine; and so of a proctor who presents himself for the ordinary without warrant in writing.

6. If any felons will confess their crimes and accuse others and become approvers, let them be put out of penance, and let their confessions be presently received and enrolled by the coroner, and from that day forward let them have of the sheriffs three halfpence a day for their support. Approvers.

7. When persons appealed at the eyre shall appear for trial, and demand judgment, whether they ought to answer concerning an act done before the last eyre and not then presented in that county, in all such cases they shall be put to their answer[q], because we will not that felonies remain unpunished; and if the article was not presented in the last eyre, the presenters for that hundred in the former eyre shall be in our mercy for the concealment, and any of them found to be living shall be punished by imprisonment and fine. Plea of act done before last eyre, not allowed. Amercement of presentors for concealment.

8. When the defendants have put themselves upon the Challenge of jurors.

[q] This is mentioned as a valid exception by Bracton, who cites a case of the 9 Hen. III. in affirmance of it. Brac. 116 *b*, 140 *b*, 141; so Fleta 49 (§ 6).

jurours soint venuz en court, si porunt il estre chalengez[1]: Sire, il n' i deit estre, car mei[2] endita, et ay presumpcioun de ly et de touz mes enditours, [3]qe il soint uncore de mesme la volunté vers moi cum [4]a cel houre qe moi[4] enditerent[3]. Et ceste excepcioun voloms nous qe soit allowable en peril de mort. Outre ceo eux porount estre chalengez en plusours maneres, sicum serra dit entre les excepciouns. Et cum il ne saverount ou ne voderount les jurours chalenger, et il i eyt des jurours suffisaument deschalengez jekes a xii., si voisent al livre. Et si n'i eynt mie asez, si soint les chalengs triez[5].
[12 *b.*] Et si les chalengs soint trovez verrays, ensint qe [6]n'i eyt[6] pleynement[7] xii., [8]si soit assis[8] un autre jour; et face le viscounte vener plus.

Brac. 143 *b.* 9. Et quant il deyvent jurer, si jurge le un apres le autre, qe il verité dirrount de ceo qe hom les demaundera de par nous, si Deu lour ayde et les Saintz; ne ja soit [9]fete mensonge a lour escient[9], car en plus haut dreit ne parount il

1. issi *add. ND.* par ceste chaleng general *add. M. sim. GACF.* 2. il moi *N. sim. DCF.* il mesmes moi *A. sim. M.* 3—3. qi uers moi vnt mauueis volunte *A.* 4—4. quant mey *M.* quant il moy *C.* kant il me *F.* 5. par les iurez *add. A.* 6—6. ni ad *LND.* il ni eit mie *A.* il ne eyent mye *M.* il ny eit *C.* il [n]i eit *F.* 7. *om. ND.* 8—8. si remeygne la sise ieques a *M.* 9—9. fete mencioun de lour a escient *L.* fete mencioun de lour escient *N. sim. DARSW.* mencioun fete de lour escient *M.* fet mencōn a lur aescient *G.* fet mension de lour ascient *Y.* fet mensoinge a lor a ecient *F.*

country, and the jurors are come into court, they may be challenged in the following form. Sir, this man ought not to be upon the jury, because he indicted me, and I presume of him and all those who indicted me, that they still bear the same ill will against me as when they indicted me. And we will that, where a man's life is at stake, this exception shall be allowed. They may also be challenged in many other ways besides this, as shall be shown in treating of exceptions. And when the accused either cannot or will not challenge the jurors, or there are jurors enough unchallenged, to the number of twelve, let them go to the book. If there are not sufficient, let the challenges be tried; and if the challenges be found true, so that there are not full twelve remaining, let another day be appointed, and let the sheriff summon more.

Oath of Jurors. 9. When they are to swear, let them swear one after another, that they will speak the truth of what shall be demanded of them on our part, so help them God and the Saints. And let no falsehood be ever knowingly practised; for they

jurer qe de vie et de membre. Et puis soint les jurours chargez de quel fet il deyvent dire verité. Et puis s'en voisent tut par eux parler, et soint gardez par baillif, qe nul ne parouge a eux; et si nul le face, ou si nul [1]i soit qe ne soit mie[1] juré, soit comaundé a la prisoun, et trestouz les autres en la merci pur la fole suffraunce.

10. Et si il ne se porount acorder a une volunté, si soint severez et examinez pur qey il ne [2]poent a unir[2], et si la grande[3] partie de eux sache la verité et partie nient, soit jugé par la ou la greynure partie se tendra. Et si il dient sur lour sermentz qe il ne sevent riens del fet, soint mis autres qi en sevent; et si celi qi se mist en enqueste ne se vodera poynt mettre en autres, si soit comaundé arere a la penaunce jekes autaunt qe il se vodera mettre. Leg. Hen. I. xxxi. 2. Brac. 143, 143 b Fle. 52. Brac. 151, 186.

11. Et voloms, qe chescun qi est acoupé [4]de felonie cum[4] de vie et de membre, et se aparceit, qe le verdit del enqueste, Brac. 143, 143 b. Fle. 52, 53.

1—1. *so N. sim. ACF.* i soit mie *L.* seit troue qe ne seit mye *M.* 2—2. porrount a vnir *L. sim. NGS.* pount accorder *A. sim. F.* poent a vner *M. sim. C.* 3. greniore *A.* greindre *GMF.* greigneure *C.* 4—4. *om. AMCF.*

cannot swear in a matter of greater moment, than in that of life and member. Afterwards let the jurors be charged of what fact they are to speak the truth. And then let them go and confer together, and be kept by a bailiff, so that no one speak to them; and if any one does so, or if there be any one among them who is not sworn, let him be committed to prison, and all the rest amerced for their folly in suffering it. Charge of jury. No person to speak with the jurors.

10. If they cannot all agree in one mind, let them be separated and examined why they cannot agree; and if the greater part of them know the truth and the other part do not, judgment shall be according to the opinion of the greater part. And if they declare upon their oaths, that they know nothing of the fact, let others be called who do know it[r]; and if he who put himself on the first inquest will not put himself on a new jury, let him be remanded back to penance till he consents thereto. Disagreement of jurors. Majority to prevail. Where the jury is ignorant of the facts, new jury called.

11. We will also, that if any man, who is indicted of a crime touching life and limb, and perceives that the verdict of the Allegation of corrupt verdict.

[r] The statements of the text as to receiving the verdict of a majority, and as to impanelling a fresh inquest in criminal cases require to be examined and compared with other authorities. Section 12 appears to be inconsistent. See a learned note by Mr. Kelham upon this passage in his translation of the first book of Britton, and the authors there cited. The question as to the right of the judge in criminal cases to discharge a jury without a verdict, has been discussed in modern times in the case of *Regina* v. *Charlesworth*, 1 Best and Smith, 460.

ou il se avera mis, deyve passer encountre ly, et voile dire qe [13.] aucun des jurours est procuré a ly dampner par soen seignur de qi il tient sa terre pur coveytise del eschete, ou pur autre [1]achesun par aukun autre, qe les Justices sur ceo examinent[1] les jurours ententivement, si nul lour eit fet entendre cel esclaundre estre verité. Et sovent i ad mester de bon examinement; car en tel cas pora hom enquere coment les jurours sevent la verité de lor verdit; ou il dirount, par acun de la cumpaynie, et celi par aventure dirra, qe il le conust[2] pur verité, a la taverne ou aylours, de acun ribaud [3]ou autre[3] a qi hom ne [4]deit ren[4] crere, ou[5] par aventure celi ou ceux par queus les jurours serrount ensensez[6] averount esté priez ou procurez par les seignurs ou[7] par les enemis a le endité pur ly dampner. Et si hom treve ceo, si voloms nous, qe tieus procurours soint pris et puniz par prisoun et par fin.

Art. sup. chart. (28 Ed. I.) c. 10.

Fle. 52 (§ 37).

12. Et si les jurours soint en awer de la chose [8]et nient en certeyn, si soit touz jours en teu[9] cas jugé pur le defendaunt[8].

1—1. resun e sur ceo deiuent les Iustices examiner *A. sim. R.* 2. *so LNDSG* conceust *MCEF.* oit dire *AR.* oyst counter *Z.* 3—3. *om. A.* 4—4. puit nient bien *A.* 5. *so NDAMCF.* et *L.* 6. sensez *NDS.* senses *G.* assensez *AR.* 7. *so GAMCF.* et *LN.* 8—8. mes [seuent] ne mie la pure verite conte dient pur lendite *A.* 9. *so MF.* touz *LNDG. sim. S.*

inquest, on which he has put himself, is likely to pass against him, desires to say that any one of the jurors is suborned to condemn him by the lord, of whom the accused holds his land, through greediness of the escheat, or for other cause by any one else, the Justices thereupon shall carefully examine the jurors, whether they have any reason to think that such slander is true. And often a strict examination is necessary; for in such case inquiry may be made, how the jurors are informed of the truth of their verdict; when they will say, by one of their fellows, and he peradventure will say, that he heard it told for truth at the tavern or elsewhere by some ribald or other person unworthy of credit; or it may happen that he, or they, by whom the jurors have been informed, were intreated or suborned by the lords, or by the enemies of the person indicted, to get him condemned; and if the Justices find this to be the fact, let such suborners be apprehended and punished by imprisonment and fine.

Examination of jury by Justices.

Subornation of jurors.

12. And if the jurors are in doubt of the matter and not certain, the judgment ought always in such case to be for the

Accused to have the benefit of doubt.

Et si les jurours dient, qe il est nient coupable de la felonie, si soit agardé, qe il s'en voist quites, et qe il eyt deliveraunce de ses terres et de touz ses biens. Et si il dient, qe il est coupable, sicum il peccha par treysoun vers nous, si soit trayné et condempné a la mort.

13. En la felonie de fausenerie ne gist nul appel, for qe entre le encusour pur nous et le encusé, et entre provour qi avera la [13 *b.*] felonie reconue et celi [1]qe il[1] avera appelé de sa cumpaynie, et par entre celi qi serra trové seysi et le garraunt qe il avera vouché; car nuli sute ne gist for qe la nostre.

14. En dreit de faus brefs ou brefs desavowez ou brefs de faus jugement trovez en acuni seisine, voloms nous, qe ceux soint arestuz et detenuz en prisoun jekes autaunt qe il [2]soint garrauntiz[2] ou jekes autaunt qe lour garrauntz s'en soint defenduz ou soint utlagez. Et si lour garrauntz soint utlagez, ou qe il eynt vouchez teus qi ne sunt mie conuz en le counté, adunk voloms nous, qe il se aquitent par pays, ou soint mis a la penaunce. Et s' il soint garrauntiz par teus, qi tels brefs ne

Post. l. ii. c. 17. s. 2.

1—1. *so M.* qi il *L.* qi ly *N.* qe luy *D.* qil *A.* qi *R.* 2—2. *so N.* *sim. DARMCF.* [s]eynt garraunt[iz] *L.*

defendant. If they say that he is not guilty of the felony, the award shall be, that he go quit, and that he have restitution of his lands and of all his goods. And if they find that he is guilty, as he hath offended by treason against us, let him be drawn and condemned to death.

Verdict of not guilty.

Verdict of guilty.

Sentence.

13. In felony of counterfeiting there lies no appeal, except between the accuser on our behalf and the accused, and between the approver, who has confessed the felony, and him whom he has appealed as his accomplice, and between a person found in possession and another whom he shall vouch to warrant; for in these cases no suit lies, except ours.

Appeal of counterfeiting.

14. With regard to false writs or writs disavowed or writs of false judgment, found in any person's possession, we will, that such persons be arrested and detained in prison, until they are warranted, or until those whom they have vouched have either put themselves on their defence or are outlawed; and if the vouchees are outlawed, or if they have vouched such as are not known in the county, then we will, that they either acquit themselves by the country or be put to penance. If they are warranted by those who cannot justify those writs according to

False writs, to be warranted.

porount avower solum les leys et les usages de noster reaume, si courge le jugement en[1] les garrauntz. Et si le garraunt desdie garraunter, adunk courge la ley, cum apres serra dit. En dreit de faus deners et de deners retounduz et de deners countrefetz a nostre monee soit fet solum les estatuz de nostre monee, ou solum ceo qe dit est de faus brefs trovez en acuni seisine.

Post. c. 16. s. 3.

Stat. de Moneta (12 Ed. I.).

CHAPITRE VI. [v.]

Dę Homicides[2].

Brac. 120 *b*. Fle. 33.

1. De homicides soit ausi enquis et de murdres. De ceste felonie voloms nous, qe ausi bien soint enditez ceux, qi co-[14.] maundent ou aydent ou counseilent[3] de tuer la gent, cum les principaus fesours. Et pur ceo qe ceste felonie pora estre fete par colour de jugement par male volunté de juge et par autre colour, sicum par faus phisiciens et par mauveys surgiens et par poysoun et en meynte[4] maneres, volom nous, qe trestouz ceux soint enditez, par qi teles covertes[5] felonies ount esté fetes, et ceux ausi qi fausement par louwer ou en autre manere

1. uers *A.* sur *M.* a *F.* 2. et de lour Peynes *add. D. sim. N.* 3. so *S. sim. G.* concelent consentent *L.* consentent *NDAR.* conseilunt *M. sim. F.* concelent *C.* 4. mout de *M.* 5. cointes *A.*

the laws and usages of our realm, let judgment be given against the warrantors; and if the vouchee refuses to warrant, then the course of law is such as shall be afterwards mentioned. And with respect to false and clipped money and money counterfeited like our coin, let proceedings be taken according to the statutes concerning our coin, or according to what is laid down concerning false writs found in any one's possession.

Forgery of money.

CHAPTER VI.

Of Homicides.

Homicide, who may be indicted of.

Accessories.

1. Let inquiry also be made of homicides and murders; and our will is, that those, who command aid or counsel others to kill, be indicted of this felony as well as the principal actors. And inasmuch as this felony may be committed under colour of judgment through malice of the judge, or under some other pretence, as by false physicians and bad surgeons, and by poison and sundry other ways, our pleasure is, that all those who have committed such secret felonies be indicted; and also those who falsely for hire, or in any other manner, have con-

ount[1] nul homme dampné ou fet dampner [2]a la mort par faus serment.

2. Et solum le presentement fet sour ceo chapitre, si soint trestouz les enditez comaundé de prendre. Et si il i ad nul demoraunt hors del counté, et il soit de tel ret mescreu, tauntost soint ses terres seisies et ses chateus preyseez[3] et deliverez a les[4] villez, et puis mis en exigende jekes autaunt qe il veigne ou soit utlagé. Et cum aucuns felouns vendrount en jugement a respoundre de lour felonie, volom nous qe il veignent dechaucez et deceyntz, sauntz coyfe, et a teste descoverte, en [5]pure lour[5] cote, [6]hors de fers et hors de chescune manere de[6] lyens, ensint qe peyne ne lour toulle[7] nule resoun[8], ne qe par force ne lour estovera mie respoundre for qe solum lour fraunche volunté. Et puis, solom ceo qe presenté serra sour eux, soint encoupez.

Glan. li. 14. c. 3; Brac. 121 *b*. Fle. 37 (§ 7).

Brac. 137; Fle. 47.

3. Et si jugement face encountre eux, si lour soit ajugé mort pur mort; et lour biens moebles soint nosz, et lour heyrs

Glan. li. 7. c. 17; Brac. 122 *b*, 137.

1. *so D. sim. GAMCF.* ou *LS.* 2. fausement *add. M.* 3. prisesz *D.* prises *AMCF.* 4. iiij. *add. A.* 5—5. lour peioure *D. so on eras. N.* 6—6. *so LGS.* hors de trop gros fers et hors de trop gros *D. so on eras. N. sim. A.* saunz fers e saunz nule manere de *M.* 7. toille *ND.* face oblier *F.* 8. respouns *M.* manere de resoun *C.*

demned, or caused to be condemned, any man to death by means of a false oath.

2. According to the presentment of this article let it be commanded, that all those who are indicted be apprehended; and if any one suspected of this crime be dwelling out of the county, let his lands be immediately seized, and his chattels appraised and delivered to the townships; and let him afterwards be put in exigent until he appear or be outlawed. And when any felons appear in judgment to answer of their felony, our will is, that they come barefooted, ungirt, uncoifed, and bareheaded, in their coat only, without irons or any kind of bonds[a], so that they may not be deprived of reason by pain, nor be constrained to answer by force, but of their own free will; and then, agreeably to the presentment against them, let them be indicted.

Presentment of homicide; Apprehension of persons presented.

Exigent, and outlawry.

Mode of trial.

3. If the prisoners are found guilty, let their judgment be death for death, and let their movable goods be ours, and

Judgment, death. Forfeiture of goods.

[a] In MS. *N.* the above words, which probably originally stood as in the text, are erased and altered, in the same hand as the notes frequently cited, as follows: "en lour peiore cote hors de trop gros fers e hors de trop gros liens." This may serve to show that the practice was not so indulgent as the rule laid down by our author.

[14 b.] desheritez. Et volums aver de lour tenementz, de qi qe unques soint tenuz, le an et le jour, issint qe lour heritages demurgent un an et un jour en nostre meyn, par issi qe nous ne faceum [1]estreper ne gaster les tenementz ne[1] les boys ne arrer les preez, sicum hom soleit fere en remembraunce de felonies atteintes, for pris les tenementz dunt tiels felouns ne furent vestuz ne seisiz en lour demeyne cum de fee; car des terres qe il averunt tenues a terme de vie ou des aunz, ou par fresche disseisine[2], ou a fee ferme par an rendaunt la veraye value, ou en gage ou par semblables condiciouns, ne voloms rien aver. Et volums, qe lour terres alienez puis lour felonies fetes soint eschetes[3] as seignurages des feez, ensint qe tauntóst apres le jugement rendu list a teus seignurs ceux tenements alienez demaunder par noster bref de eschaete.

Mag. Char. c. 22; Glan. li. 7. c. 17; Brac. 137. Fle. 43.

Glan. li. 7. c. 17; Brac. 29 b, 30, 130 (s. 19); Fle. 43.

Brac. 137, 137 b, 143.

4. Et volums qe si nul homme soit trové occys, et acun soit

1—1. *so verb. D.* estre peri ne gaste[z] le tenementz ne *L.* estrepp[er] ne gastier les tenementz ne *N.* gaster les tenemenz[ne] en *A.* estrep en les tenemens ne gastier *M.* estre par les tenemenz ne gaster *F.* 2. *so DASMCF.* seisine *L.* 3 *so M.* Eschaete *L.* eschete *NDS. sim. F.*

King's year and day, without waste.

their heirs disinherited; we will also have the year and day of their inheritances, of whomsoever they are holden, that they may remain one year and one day in our hands, so that we neither cause the tenements nor the woods to be destroyed or wasted[t], nor the meadows to be ploughed, as was wont to be done in memory of felonies attainted, such tenements being excepted whereof the felons were not invested or seised in their demesne as of fee; for of such lands as they held for term of life or years, or by fresh disseisin, or in fee farm rendering annually the true value, or in mortgage or on like condition, we will take nothing. We will also, that their lands aliened after commission of their felonies, be escheated to the lords of the fees, so that immediately after judgment given it shall be lawful for those lords to demand by our writ of escheat the tenements so aliened.

Escheat.

Homicide taken in the fact.

4. If any man be found killed, and another be found near

[t] It was the opinion of Bracton that the year and day were given to the king in lieu of the right of laying waste the lands of felons. The Great Charter (c. 22) appears implicitly to give up the claim to waste, and to have been so understood by Bracton and the authors of Fleta and Britton (Brac. 129; Fle. liv. i. c. 28, § 6). But both rights were afterwards insisted on (Brac. 129, 129 b; Stat. Prærog. Reg. 17 Ed. II.); and such appears to be the present law in cases of murder. See Hawkins's Pleas of the Crown (8th ed.), vol. ii. p. 638.

trové pres de ly ovek le cotel ou autre armure[1] tot sanglaunte dunt il le eyt occys, qe hom face le Corouner hastivement venir, et en sa presence par le teymonage de ceux qi virent la felonie fete[2] soit jugé a la mort. Et ausi de homme trové en mesoun ou aylours, ou homme serra trové occys, ou celi qi serra trové en vie ne serra naufré ne blescé, [3]ne heu ne cri ne avera levé, ne les felouns avera[4] ne savera encuser[3]. [15.]

Fle. 47 (§ 2).

5. Et volums qe les heyrs as felouns, engendretz avaunt la felonie fete, soint desheritez de chescun heritage qe escheer lour pora de par le saunc al feloun atteynt par jugement; et les heyrs engendrez apres la felonie fete soint forclos de totes maneres de successioun de heritage, ausi ben de par mere cum de par pere. Et voloms qe les femmes as felouns ne tiegnent nule terre en dowayre de nul tenement qe lour fust assignee par teus barouns.

Brac. 130, 130 b; Fle. 43 (§ 4).

Brac. 311; Fle. 347 (§ 6).

1. arme *AMCF*. 2. fete *om*. *NDARCF*. 3—3. ne seit occis seit leue hue e crie e seit sui dekes as iiii. procheins viles mes pur home malment naffre ne seit hu ne crie ia leue *AR*. e il ne sauera les felons encuser ne hue ne crye ne soit leuee soit prys celui qui serra trove pres de lui *Z*. 4. auera *om*. *NDRGSMCF*.

him with the knife or other weapon in his hand all bloody, wherewith he killed him, the coroner shall be presently fetched, and in his presence the felon shall, upon the testimony of those who saw the felony done, be judged to death[t]. The like when a person is found in a house, or other place where one shall be found killed[u], and the person found alive is neither hurt nor wounded, and has not raised the hue and cry, and has not charged any with the felony, and shall not be able to do so.

Judgment before the coroner.

5. We will also, that the heirs of felons, begotten before the felony committed, be disinherited of every inheritance which may fall to them on the part of the blood of the felon attainted by judgment; and heirs begotten after the felony committed, shall be excluded from all manner of succession to the inheritance, as well on the part of the mother as on the part of the father; the wives also of felons shall not hold in dower any tenement assigned them by such husbands.

Corruption of blood.

Extinction of dower.

[u] Bracton (137, 137 *b*) mentions the two instances here given, as cases of presumptive guilt, in which there is no need of proof, *seu per corpus seu per patriam*, either by duel or jury; and this, he says, is an old established law, *antiqua constitutio*. I find no mention either in Bracton or Fleta of judgment of death for homicide before the coroner. Cf. Mag. Char. c. 17. The coroner's presence was required at capital trials in courts of lords. Ante, c. 2. s. 17. In the Year Book 30, 31 Ed. I, app. ii. p. 545, a thief taken with the mainour is adjudged to death, by the custom of Yorkshire, coram quatuor villatis. Compare post. c. 16. s. 1.

CHAPITRE VII. [VI.]

De Murdre.

Leg. Ed. Conf. 15, 16. Leg. Hen. I. xci, xcii. Glan. li. 14. c. 3. Brac. 134 b. Fle. 46. Stat. Winton. (13 Ed. I.) c. 2. Leg. Will. I. 22. Leg. Hen. I. xci, xcii. Brac. 135, 135 b. Fle. 46. [15 b.] (52 Hen. III.) Stat. Marl. c. 26.

Murdre est occisioun de homme desconu, felounosement fete, dunt homme ne peut saver par qi ne par quels. Et volums qe a chescun murdre soit le hundred, ou le murdre serra trové fet, en nostre merci; et si le fet serra trové en deus hundrez, si soint ambideus [1]amerciez solum la quantité qe serreit un hundred. Et volums qe nul murdre soit ajugee par la ou acun parent al mort peuse estre trové, qi peuse moustrer qe il fust Engleys, et issi presenter de ly Englescherie; ne, tut soit il alien, par la ou il avera taunt de espace de vie qe il meymes encuse les felouns; ne ausi ou aukun feloun serra pris pur le fet; ne en cas de aventure ne de mesaventure; ne par la ou akun serra fui a mouster pur la felonie; ne en nul cas ou akun feloun serra conu, par quei la felonie puse estre punie par utlagarie ou en autre manere atteinte; ne la ausi ou deus hommes ou plusours se averount felounosement entretuez, tut soint il desconuz ou [2]de aliene terre[2].

1. les Hundrez *add. MCF.* 2—2. aliens *AMC. sim. F.*

CHAPTER VII.

Of Murder.

Murder. Hundred to be amerced. Presentment of Englishery.

Murder is the felonious killing of a person unknown, whereof it cannot be known by whom it was done. And our will is, that for every murder the hundred in which it shall be committed be amerced[x], and if the act is found to have been done in two hundreds, let both the hundreds be amerced in proportion to the extent of each hundred. And it shall not be adjudged murder, where any of kin to the deceased can be found, who can prove that he was an Englishman and thus make presentment of Englishery; nor, although the person killed was a foreigner, if he lived long enough to accuse the felons himself; nor where any felon shall be apprehended for the fact; nor in case of accident or mischance; nor where any man shall have taken sanctuary for the felony; nor in any case where the felon shall be known, so that the felony may be punished by outlawry or otherwise attainted; nor where two or more persons have feloniously killed each other, although they be unknown or aliens.

x 'At 100 s.' (Note in MS. *N.*)

CHAPITRE VIII. [VII.]

De Aventure.

Aventure est chose qe avent de mort de homme sauntz felonie, sicum des gentz qe sodeynement murgent par akune sodeyne maladie, ou se lesent cheer en le feu ou en ewe, et la demurent jekes autaunt qe il soint mortz esteyntz. Et mes-aventure est sicum des gentz mortz par cheyer des arbres, des nefs, ou des batz, des charettes, ou des chivaus, ou de molins, ou en tels cas semblables, ou nule felonie de homme ne avera esté fete; en les quels[1] ne ad mie mester qe hue ne cri soit levé, ne qe presentement soit fets de parentz ne des villes al proscheyn Counté; mes suffist le office del Corouner. Et en teles aventures soint les causes des mortz jugez a nous pur[2] deodande, sicum desus est dit en le chapitre del office de Corouner. Et en cas, ou homme est feloun de sei meymes, soint les chateus jugez nostres[3] cum chateus de feloun; le heritage neqedent remeyne[4] a les heirs enterement[5]. [16.]

Brac. 120 b, 136 b. Fle. 54.

Ante, c. ii. s. 12, 14.

Brac. 150. Fle. 54.

1. cas *add. M.* 2. so *NDAC. sim. F.* par *L.* 3. les noz *M.* nos *C.* 4. demoerge *A.* 5. enterement *om. AMCF.*

CHAPTER VIII.

Of Accidents.

An accident is that which occasions the death of a man without felony, as where people die suddenly by any sickness, or fall into the fire or into the water, and there lie until they are quite dead. A mischance is where a man is killed by a fall from a tree, ship, boat, cart, horse, or mill, or in the like cases, where no felony is committed, and in which there is no need of raising the hue and cry, or making any presentment by the kindred of the deceased or by the township at the next county court, but the coroner's inquest is sufficient. In such mischances, the things which caused the death shall be adjudged to us as deodands, as is mentioned before in the chapter concerning the office of coroner. And where a man is felon of himself, his chattels shall be adjudged ours, as the chattels of a felon, but his inheritance shall descend entire to his heirs.

Death by accident.

Deodand.

Felo de se; forfeiture of chattels.

CHAPITRE IX. [VIII.]

De Tresouns.

Glan. li. 1. c. 2. Brac. 118, 118 b.

1. Tresun est en[1] chescun damage qe hom fet a escient ou procure de fere a cely a qi hom se fet ami. Et poet estre treysoun graunt et petit; dunt acun demaund jugement de mort, et acun amissioun de membre ou jugement de pillori ou penaunce de prisoun, et aukun plus[2] simple punisement, solum la manere del fet.

Glan. li. 1, c. 2; li. 14. c. 1. Brac. 118 b. Fle. 31. Leg. Hen. I. lxxv. 1.

2. Graunt tresoun est a compasser nostre mort, ou de nous desheriter de noster reaume, ou de fauser noster seal, ou de countrefere nostre monee ou de retoundre. Et si poet hom fere graunt treysoun vers autres persones en moutz des maneres, cum en procuraunt la mort de aukun [3]qi se affiera de luy[3], sicum est de ceux qi enpoysounent lur seignurs ou autres, et de ceux qi meynent les gentz en tel peril ou il perdent vie ou membre ou chateus.

Glan. li. c. 2. Brac. 118 b.

3. Et le jugement [4]de graunt treysoun est[4] de estre trayné, et de suffrer mort pur la felonie. Et mesme le jugement deyvent

1. en *om. M.* 2. plus *om. M.* 3—3. qi en li se affiera si est de li *A.* a qi il se affiera de ly e est de ly *M.* qe fie de luy *C.* est de ly *F.* 4—4. de ceus est *A.* de eus est de graunt traisoun e est *M.*

CHAPTER IX.

Of Treasons.

Treason.

1. Treason consists of any mischief, which a man knowingly does, or procures to be done, to one to whom he pretends to be a friend. And treasons may be either great or little, of which some require judgment of death, some loss of limb, pillory, or imprisonment, and others lighter punishment, according to the nature of the case.

High treason.

2. Great or high treason is to compass our death or to disinherit us of our kingdom, or to falsify our seal, or to counterfeit our coin, or to clip it. A person may likewise commit great treason against others in several ways, as by procuring the death of any one who trusts him; as for instance those who poison their lords or others, and those who lead persons into such perils, that they lose life and member or chattels.

Treason against lords and others.

Judgment in high treason.

3. The judgment in high treason is to be drawn and to suffer death for the felony. The same judgment is incurred

encoure ceux, qi par appels de felonies sunt atteyntz, qe il le seal lour seignur, qi meynpast il sount, ou qi hommes par homage, countrefet ou autrement fausé, ou de avouterie des femmes lour seignurs, [1]ou de purgiser des filles lour seignurs ou des[1] norices de lour enfauntz. Et si nule femme de aukun treysoun soit atteynte, si soit arse. Fle. 54 (c. 37. § 4). [16 *b*.] Brac. 105. Fle. 54.

4. Et si tele manere des fetz soint atteintz a nostre sute, si soint pur le seal[2] fausé[3] [4]jugez al jugement de pillori[4] ou de perdre la orayle, si le fet soit simple; et si le fet soit graunt et led, sicum tochaunt desheritisoun ou perpetuel damage, si soint jugez a la mort. Et del autre pecché eyt Sainte Eglise la correccioun. Brac. 104 *b*, 105, 155. Fle. 63. Stat. circumspecte agatis. (13 Ed. I.)

CHAPITRE X. [IX.]

De Arsouns[5].

Ausi soit enquis de ceux qe felounousement en tens de pes eynt autri blez ou autri mesouns arses; et ceux qi de ceo serount atteyntz soint ars, issint qe eux soint puniz par meymes Glan. ii. 14. c. 4. Brac. 146 *b*. Fle. 54.

1—1. ou depurgeser les *M*. ou des *AF*. 2. lour seignur *add. D. sim A. sim. interl. N.* 3. et pur legiere treisoun *add. D. sim. A. sim. interl. N.* 4—4. so *ND*. [a *interl.*] iugement de pillori soint iugez *L*. si lour seit Iugement de pillori *A*. jugez al pillori *M*. 5. et ardeurs de mesuns *add. N. sim. D*.

by those, who in appeals of felony are attainted of having counterfeited or otherwise falsified the seal of their lord, of whose dependence or homage they are, or of adultery with the wives of their lords, or of violation of the daughters of their lords or the nurses of their children. And if a woman be attainted of any treason, let her be burnt. Judgment in petty treason, upon appeal.

4. Where persons are attainted of crimes of this nature at our suit, let them be sentenced for falsifying a seal, if the act be of small consequence, to judgment of pillory only, or to lose an ear; but if the act be of importance and heinous, as touching disherison or lasting damage, they shall then be judged to death. And of the other offence let Holy Church have correction. Punishment of petty treasons, by the king's suit.

CHAPTER X.

Of Arsons.

Let inquiry also be made of those who feloniously in time of peace have burnt others' corn or houses, and those who are attainted thereof shall be burnt[y], so that they may be punished Arson. Punishment by burning.

y As to this punishment for arson by burning, which is not mentioned in Bracton or Fleta, see a record of 5 Hen. III. cited by Sir Samuel Clarke in his edition of the first

Brac. 123 *b*, 124. Fle. 54. tele chose dunt il peccherent. Et meymes tiel jugement eynt sorciers et sorceresces, et [1]renyez, et[1] somodites, et mescreauntz apertement atteyntz.

CHAPITRE XI. [x.]

[17.]

De Bourgeysours.

Leg. Cnut. 65. Leg. Will. I. 15. Brac. (§ 5). Et soit ausi enquis de burgesours. Et [2]tenoms a[2] burgesours trestouz ceux, qi felounousement en tens de pes brusent eglises, ou autri mesouns, ou murs ou portes de nos citez ou de nos burgs, forpris enfauntz de eynz age, et povers qi par famine entrent pur aukun vitayle de meyndre value de xii. deners, et forpris fous nastres et arragez et autres, qi ne sevent nule felonie fere. Mes ceux, qi aukuns tenementz entrent en noun de seisine pur dreit qe il entendent aver, ne tenoms mie a burgesours. Le jugement de tiels felouns[3] soit la mort.

1—1. *om. AC.* 2—2. seient tenuz *C.* 3. *so NDMC. sim. AF.* felonies *L.*

Sorcery and heresy. in like manner as they have offended. The same sentence shall be passed upon sorcerers, sorceresses, renegades, sodomites, and heretics publicly convicted[z].

CHAPTER XI.

Of Burglars.

Burglary. Let inquiry also be made of burglars. Such we hold to be all those who feloniously in time of peace break churches, or the houses of others, or the walls or gates of our cities or boroughs. Infants under age, and poor people, who through Defence of hunger. hunger enter the house of another for victuals under the value of twelve pence, are excepted; as are also idiots and madmen, and others, who are incapable of felony; and those, who enter into any tenement by way of seisin in respect of some right which they think they have, are not held to be burglars. The punishment of such felons is death.

book of Fleta, c. 18. p. 36 n. (d), and by Mr. Kelham in his notes on the first book of Britton, p. 40.

z It seems that as to these offences, though the king's court was in general ancillary to the ecclesiastical tribunal, it sometimes acted independently. 'Burners of corn and houses, wives guilty of treason against their husbands, sorcerers, sodomites, renegates, and misbelievers, run in a leash (currunt en une leesse) as to their sentence of being burned. But the inquirers of Holy Church shall make their inquests of sorcerers, sodomites, renegates, and misbelievers; and if they find any such, they shall deliver him to the king's court to be put to death. Nevertheless, if the king by inquest find any persons guilty of such horrible sin, he may put them to death, as a good marshall of Christendom (come bon Mareschal de la Chrestieneté).' (Note in MS. *N.*)

CHAPITRE XII. [XI.]

De Prisouns.

1. De ceux qi nostre prisoun eynt debrusé soit ausi enquis. Car de autri prisoun eschaper ne peut hom fere nule felonie. Car nous voloms qe prisoun soit tenue[1] place par [2]nous boundé[2] de eynz certeynes boundes assignez a la garde de cors de homme, les queles boundes nous defendoums sur peril de la mort qe nul ne passe oveske felounesse volounté de eschaper. Et si nul oveskes tiele volunté soit pris, et il de ceo compassement de tiele felounesse volunté soit atteynt, si voloms nous qe il eyt jugement de la mort. Brac. 124. Fle. 24 (§ 12). 39 (§ 4). [17 b.]

2. Et si la prisoun avera esté en acuni garde, qi cleyme la garde en fee, si soit la fraunchise prise en nostre meyn. Et si le prisoun, qi si avera eschapé, soit eschapé hors de la garde de aukun de nos ministres, si soit celi ministre amercié a C. s. en heyre des Justices. Et si celi qi avera esté issi eschapé[3], avera esté provour, si soit le gardeyn reynt a nostre volunté. Et si aukun prisoun avera eschapé[3] hors de la garde de aukune Fle. 29 (§ 110).

1. *so AMCHY.* en *add. LNDGS.* e *F.* 2—2. nos boundes *ND.* noz bundes *M.* 3—3. *so verb. NDAMF. sim. C. om. L.*

CHAPTER XII.

Of Prisoners.

1. Let inquiry also be made of those who have broken our prison; for to escape from the prison of another is no felony. We will that a prison be accounted a place limited by us within certain bounds for the keeping of the bodies of men, which bounds we forbid on pain of death any one to pass with a felonious intent of escaping; and if any one having such intent is taken, and is attainted of compassing that felonious intent, let him receive judgment of death[a]. Breach of prison.

2. If the prisoner was in the custody of any one claiming the wardenship in fee, let the franchise be seized into our hands. And if the prisoner, who made his escape, has escaped from the custody of any one of our officers, let that officer be amerced at 100s. in the eyre of the Justices. And if he who thus escaped was an approver, let the warden be ransomed at our will. If any prisoner escape from the custody of a township, let Allowing the escape of prisoners, how punished.

[a] This passage may serve to assist in ascertaining the age of the present book. By the *Stat. de frangentibus prisonam* (23 Ed. I.) it was enacted that none should undergo sentence of life or limb for breaking of prison only. See Introduction by the Editor.

villee, si soit la villee en nostre merci en heyre des Justices soloum le usage del pays; et si hors de la garde de aukun homme, si soit le gardeyn amercié. Et si aukun gardeyn soit suspect [1]del consent[1] del eschap, si soit pris et encoupé[2] del assent de la felonie. Et si nul soit trové coupable del consent, si soit jugé a la mort.

Brac. 105. 3. Et des prisouns volom nous qe nul ne soit mis en firges, for qe ceux qi serrount pris pur felounie, ou [3]qi serrount en prisoun[3] pur trespas de parcs ou de vivers, ou qi serrount [4]tenuz pur[4] arrerages de acounte; et defendoms qe autrement ne soint penez[5] ne turmentez qe estre ne deyvent; et qe nul soit deseisi de nule rien qe a ly soit, taunt cum il ert en prisoun. Et voloms, qe lour terres et lour biens soint seisiz en nostre meyn sauntz rien oster; et qe les prisouns et lour meysné soint trovez de lour chose demeine, taunt cum il serrount en prisoun; et qe nul baillif ne soit osté ne autre mis. Et quant il se averount leaument aquitez, si reprengent quant qe lour fust; et si rien lour soit en le meen tens alloigné, nous voloms

Fle. 39.
Brac. 123, 136 *b*, 137.
Fle. 38, 39.
[18.]

1—1. de la consuence *M.* 2. so *ACF.* enceppee *L.* acoupe *ND.* encope *M.* 3—3. *om. C.* 4—4. detenuz pur *D.* en *C.* 5. puniz. *AMC.*

the township be in our mercy in the eyre of the Justices, according to the custom of the country; and if from the custody of a private person, let such person be amerced; and if any gaoler be suspected of having consented to the escape, let him be taken and indicted for consenting to the felony; and if he be found guilty of consenting, let him have judgment of death.

Treatment of prisoners. 3. As to prisoners, we will that none be put in irons but such as have been apprehended for felony, or are imprisoned for trespasses committed in parks or vivaries, or detained for arrears of accounts; and we forbid their being put to any pain or torture otherwise than by law they ought[b], or that any person be disseised, while in prison, of anything which shall belong to him. Their lands and goods shall be seized into our hand, but without ousting anything; the prisoners and their families shall be supported out of their own goods as long as they remain in prison, and none of their bailiffs shall be removed, nor others put in. And when they have lawfully acquitted themselves, all that was theirs shall be delivered back

Their lands how to be kept.
On acquittal, property restored.

b 'Note, that for a felon slain in prison judgment of homicide shall be given. For, though he was lawfully condemnable for the felony, yet it is necessary that it pass by judgment. For we ought not to hold them absolutely felons until the law has condemned them.' (Note in MS. *N.*)

en tel cas especialment ayder de le repeler et de punir les trespassours. Et s' il soint jugez a la mort, adunc voloms adeprimes qe nos ministres boutent hors lour femmes et lour baillifs [1]et facent seyser[1] chateus et terres[2] en nostre meyn; et qe par office de Corouner soint lour biens moebles [3]esmez et soint liverez[3] a les villez, issi qe [4]il nous[4] respoignent en heyre des Justices. Ante, c. ii. s. 9.

4. Et si nul homme murge en prisoun, si volom nous, qe le Corouner voise veer le cors, et prenge bone enqueste de sa mort, coment il avera esté mort. Et si hom troeve par enqueste, qe il eyt esté plus pres de la mort et plus loinz de la vie par dure garde de ses gardeyns ou par peyne qe hom ly avera fete outre dreit, adunc soit le cors enseveli et trestouz ceux, qi serount enditez del enchesun de sa mort, hastivement soint pris et detenuz cum felouns homicides. Fle. 39 (§ 5).

5. Et voloms, qe chescune simayne une foiz en tens pledable soint nos gaoles deliverez des prisouns qi serunt deliverables, for qe de ceux qi sauntz nostre comaundement especial ne deyvent mie estre deliverez. Ante, c. i. s. 10. [18 *b.*]

1—1. e seisient *A.* e seisisent lour *M.* e seient *C.* seisent *F.* 2. pris *add. C.* 3—3. esmes et soint liuerez *L.* prises et estimez e seyent liuerez *D.* [prisez e] estmiez et soint liuerez *N.* e muz liuerez *A.* preisez e bailez *M.* enprises e seient liuerez *C.* 4—4. de ceo *M.*

to them; and if anything belonging to them shall in the mean time have been removed, we will in such case afford our especial aid to recover it and to punish the offenders. But if judgment of death pass upon them, we will that then, and not before, our officers put out their wives and their bailiffs, and cause their chattels and lands to be seized into our hand, and that their movable goods be appraised by inquest of office of the coroner, and delivered to the townships, who shall be answerable to us in the eyre of the Justices. On judgment, property forfeited.

4. If any person die in prison, our pleasure is, that the coroner go and view the body and take a true inquest of his death, in what way it has happened. And if the inquest find that his death was hastened by the harsh keeping of his gaolers, or by pain unlawfully inflicted on him, then let the body be buried, and let all those, who are indicted as being the cause of his death, be immediately apprehended and detained as felons homicides. Death in prison.

5. And we will, that in time pleadable our gaols be delivered once in every week of all prisoners deliverable, such being excepted as are not to be delivered without our special command. Gaol delivery.

6. Et voloms, qe touz prisouns soint a touz responables a ceux qi les enplederount taunt cum eux serount en prisoun, et ausi soint autres a eux, et qe essoynes lour soint allowez, sicum as autres del poeple; et voloms qe il perdent rien par nule defaute. Mes les [1]prisounez pur[1] felounie en[2] nule manere voloms suffrer[3] de nul homme enpleder ne de estre empledez, for qe en plus haute[4] felounie, issi qe graunt felonie ne soit mie esteinte ne coverte par meyndre felonie; eynz volums qe tiels prisouns eynt pur excepcioun en chescun meyndre play dunt il serount empledez, qe [5]n'en est[5] la cause pur quei il serount pris, lequel qe le play sera meu vers eux avaunt lour prise ou apres, qe il ne sount[6] mie tenuz a teu play respoundre jekes autaunt qe il soint quites de la plus grosse cause pur quei il sount arrestez.

7. Et defendoms, qe nul prenge pur prisoun receyvere nul dener, ne la value, ne qe nul [7]ne delaye[7] de les receyvere, ne qe nul prenge de prisoun pur sa garde plus qe iiii. deners, sur peyne de raunceun et de fin. De[8] povers ne soit

1—1. prisouns pris et en prisonez pur *D.* prisouns [pris e enprisonez *interl.*] pur *N.* prisuns pur *A.* *sim.* *CF.* prisouns de *M.* 2. E en *M.* 3. les *add.* *M.* 4. *so* *DAMCZF.* aunciene *LG.* *sim.* *S.* haute *on erasure* *N.* 5—5. nest *A.* ceo ne est nyent *M.* 6. *so* *NDAC.* *sim.* *MF.* soint *L.* 7—7. ne de veye *M.* delay ne seit *F.* 8. *so* M. des *C.* de *om.* *LNDAF.*

Actions by and against prisoners.

6. Prisoners shall in general be answerable to such as shall implead them as long as they remain in prison; others shall likewise be answerable to them; and essoins shall be allowed to them, as well as to others, neither shall they lose anything by any default. But prisoners apprehended for felony we will by no means suffer to implead or be impleaded by any one, unless for some greater felony, so that a greater felony be not stifled or covered by a less. But our will is, that such prisoners may allege as an exception in every lesser plea whereof they shall be impleaded, not being the cause for which they have been apprehended, whether the plea be moved against them before their apprehension or after, that they are not bound to answer such pleas, until they are acquitted of the greater cause for which they are detained.

Fees to be taken of prisoners.

7. We forbid any one to take money, or the value thereof, for receiving prisoners, or to delay receiving them, or to take for the keeping any prisoner more than four pence, on pain of ransom and fine. Of the poor let nothing be taken, and let

pris rien, ne ja par defaute de tiel fee ne soit nul prisoun plus detenu[1].

8. Et voloms, qe touz prisouns, qi ne serount mie pris ne detenuz pur felonie, qe quant qe il ferount des contractz en prisoun soit tenu estable, si il ne eynt fetz les contractz par tiele distrese qe conteigne pour de mort ou tourment de cors; et en tel cas voloms qe tiels recleyment lour fet si toust cum il serrount deliverez, et facent a saver la poour as proscheins vesins et au Corouner. Et si il ne recleyment teus fetz par pleynte de eynz le an et le jour, adunc volom nous qe tiels fetz soint[2] estables. [19.] Brac. 16 *b*. Fle. 184.

9. Et defendoms a touz ceux qi cleyment aver garde des prisouns en fee, qe nul ne tiegne provour, qi se avera reconu feloun et apelé autres de la felonie, outre un jour et une nuyt, qe hastivement ne le envoye a nostre prisoun qe serra en nostre meyn demeyne, sur peril de perdre mesme la garde. Et ausi qe nul autre ne tiegne homme en prisoun pris pur felonie outre un jour et une nuyt, qe hastivement ne le envoye a Brac. 122 *b*.

1. so *NDA*. *sim*. *MCF*. tenu *L*. 2. tenuz *add*. *DAMF*. so *interl*. *N*.

no prisoner be longer detained for default in payment of such fees. No prisoner to be detained for non-payment of fees.

8. And we will, that whatever contracts shall be made in prison by prisoners not taken or detained for felony shall be held valid, unless made under such distress as includes fear of death or torture of body; and in such case they shall reclaim their deed, as soon as they are at liberty, and signify the fear they were under to the nearest neighbours and to the coroner; and if they do not reclaim such deeds by plaint within the year and day, the deeds shall be valid. Contracts by prisoners. Duress.

9. Those who claim the custody of any prison in fee shall not detain a prover, who has confessed himself to be a felon and appealed others of the felony, beyond a day and a night, but shall send him forthwith to our prison which is in our own hand, on peril of forfeiting the said custody; and no other person shall keep in prison any one apprehended for felony beyond a day and a night, but shall send him forthwith to our prison[c] on pain of Provers to be sent to the king's prison. Felons not to be detained in private prisons.

[c] This rule was subject to an exception, where there was a franchise of Infangthef or Utfangthef; for the lord might keep those in his prison whom he could judge in his court. Brac. 122 *b*, 123. The abbot of Peterborough in the parliament of 3 Ed. I. established his right to keep in his own prison twenty-nine prisoners of his liberty appealed of homicide in the county court of Northampton. Chron. Petroburg. p. 21.

Brac. 145. Fle. 63 (§ 5). nostre prisoun[1] sur peyne de raunsoun. Et pur ceo, quant a ceo chapitre, soint enquis, qi ad enprisouné autre ou detenu a tort en sa garde, ou en nostre prisoun par colour de jugement par malice et a tort, et ceux qi de ceo serrount atteyntz soint puniz par prisoun et par raunsoun simple ou grave[2] solom le fet.

[19 b.] CHAPITRE XIII. [XII.]

[3]*De Forbaniz*[3].

Brac. 117. Fle. 24 (§ 10). Mag. Char. c. 35. Brac. 124 b. 125. Fle. 40. 1. Puis soit enquis de felouns utlagez et de ceux qi ount forjuré le reaume pur felonie, retournez sauntz congé de nous, et de lour receptours a escient. Et pur ceo qe mester est, qe chescun sache le peril de receptement, voloms nous qe trestouz ceux de xiiii. aunz [4]ou plus[4] nous facent serment, qe il nous serount feaus et leaus, et qe il ne serount felouns ne a felouns assentauntz. Et voloms qe touz soint en dizeyne[5] et pleviz par

Leg. Ed. Conf. 20.

1. *om. M.* 2. graunt *C.* 3—3. De Bannes *M.* des banniz *A.* *sim. C.* Des otlagez e de lor recetturs F. 4—4. en suis *A.* en ceus *M.* 5. duzeyne *M.* dozein *C.*

False imprisonment. ransom. And therefore with respect to this article, let it be inquired, who has imprisoned another or detained him wrongfully in his custody, or in our prison maliciously and wrongfully under colour of judgment; and let such as shall be convicted thereof be punished by imprisonment and by ransom, which shall be greater or less in proportion to the offence.

CHAPTER XIII.

Of Outlaws.

Outlaws returned, and their receivers. 1. In the next place, let inquiry be made of felons outlawed, and of such as have abjured the realm for felony, who have returned without our leave; and of those who knowingly receive them. And because it is needful that every one should know the danger of receiving such persons, our will is, that all who are of the age of fourteen years[d] or upwards shall take an oath to us, that they will be faithful and loyal to us, and will neither be felons nor assenting to felons; and

Oath of fealty.

[d] Bracton (124 *b*) and Fleta (p. 40) mention the age of twelve years as the time of taking the oath; and this is in some degree confirmed by the terms of the Stat. Marl. c. 25. The Mirror, however, as printed (p. 13, 283), agrees with our author in fixing the time at fourteen years. Coke (2 Inst. 121, 147) cites both Britton and the Mirror as naming the age of twelve, and says, that where old books mention sometime fourteen years, it is but misprinted. The mistake, however, if it be one, appears to run through all the manuscripts. Compare Brac. 115 *b*, where the age of fifteen is mentioned as the time for persons of higher station to take a similar oath.

dizeyners[1], save gentz de religioun clercs et chivalers et lour fiz eynznez[2] et[3] femmes. La force de plegage soit tiele, qe, si il ne eynt avaunt lour plevyz de ester a dreit en nostre Court quant mester serra, qe les [4]dizeiners oveke la dizeyne[4] soint en nostre merci. En dreit des clercs et des chivalers et gentz de religioun et femmes, voloms, qe chescun qi meysnee teigne soit responaunt pur ses meynpastz qi ovek luy sount en chef, et ceux respoignent de lour sugetz. En dreit de hostes, voloms qe chescun respoigne pur soen hoste qe il avera herbergé plus de deus nuytz ensemble, issi qe la premere nuyt soit [5]tenu pur estraunge[5] cum *uncouth*, [6]le autre nuyt *geste*, et la terce nuyt *oune hyne*[6].

Leg. Will. I. 20, 25; Cart. Will. I. iii. 14; Leg. Hen. I. viii. 2; Stat. Marl. (52 H. III.) c. 10. Leg. Will. I. 52; Leg. Hen. I. viii. 3. Leg. Ed. Conf. 23; Leg. Will. I. 48; Leg. Hen. I. viii. 5. Brac. 124 b. Fle. 40.

2. Et voloms, pur la pes meyntener, qe touz soint prestz de les felouns sure et arester, solom nos estatuz de Wyncestre, [20.] en chescune felonie oveke la menee des corns et de bouches de vile en vile jekes autaunt qe il soint prys ou suyz[7] jekes

Leg. Will. I. 49, 50; Stat. West. 1. (3 Ed. I.) c. 9; Stat. Winton. (13 Ed. I.) c. 1.

1. douzain *A.* dozeyners *M.* dozainers *C.* 2. demeyne *LND.* *sim.* *SG.* eynez *MC.* ainnes *F.* 3. so *NSAMF.* lour *add.* *L.* *sim.* *G.* 4—4. dozeiners oueke lour dozeins *A.* *sim.* *G.* duzeyners ouesqe lour duzeynes *M.* dozeiners *C.* 5—5. il tenu estraunge *NDSG.* le estraunge tenuz *M.* *sim.* *F.* tenue *C.* 6—6. e lautre nuyte qe il seyt tenuz com kouz *M.* 7. fui au Mouster *C.*

that every one be in some tithing and pledged by their tithingmen, except persons in religion, clerks, knights and their eldest sons, and women; and let the obligation of the pledge be this, that if they do not produce those for whom they are pledged, to be amenable to justice in our Court when required, the tithingmen with the tithings shall be in our mercy. With regard to clerks, knights, persons of religion, and women, our pleasure is that the head of every household be answerable for all his chief domestics, and that they answer for those under them. As to guests, we will that every one answer for his guest that he shall have harboured for more than two nights together, so that the first night he shall be deemed a stranger and uncouth[e], the second night a guest, and the third night a hoghenhine[f].

Tithings. Frank pledge. Uncouth, guest, and hoghenhine.

2. And for the maintaining of peace, we will that when a felony is committed, every one be ready to pursue and arrest the felons, according to our Statutes of Winchester, with the company of horns and voices from township to township, until they are either taken or have been pursued as far as the

Hue and cry.

e Anglo-Saxon, *uncuð*, unknown. f Anglo-Saxon, *agen hina*, his own hind or domestic.

Brac. 115 *b*, 124; Fle. 35. Brac. 128 *b*, 129; Fle. 41 (§ 9).

a la chef vile del counté ou de la fraunchise. Et voloms qe chescun homme defuaunt[1] nostre pes forface ses chateus a nous pur sa fute, si il soit mescru de felonie, tut soit ceo qe il se aquite puis del fet princepal. Et si ceo soit murdre ou autre felonie de mort de homme, si soit cele felonie presenté al proscheyn Countee par une villee ou par plusours, et par le troveour, et[2] les parentz celi qe avera esté occis, ceo est a saver, par un[3] ou par plusours de par pere ou de par mere, solom le usage del pays.

Brac. 135 *b*, 136.

Brac. 125 *b*; Fle. 40, 41 (§ 18).

Leg. Will. I. 48.

3. Et si aukun ou plusours soint appeletz de la mort, dunt aukuns de la force et des fetz accessories, si soint primes demaundez les principals par tres Countez, qe il veingent respoundre de la felonie. Et s'il ne vengent al quart Countee, ne ne soint meynpris de vener al quint, si soint utlagez al quart[4]. Femme neqedent ne peut estre utlagé proprement, pur ceo qe ele ne est mie ordeyné a dizeyne[5], ne a la ley, mes weyvé, qe vaut utlagerie.

Brac. 125 *b*; Fle. 41 (§ 12).

1. *so MC. sim. DGAF.* defuy *LS.* defuy[ant] *N.* 2. et *om. LSG.* e *M.* et par *D. sim. C.* od. *F.* e par *interl. N.* 3. vij. *LF.* seet *GS.* vn *DAMCZ.* vn *on erasure N.* 4. Countee *add. M. sim. F.* 5. duzeyne *M. sim. GCF.*

Fugitive forfeits chattels.

chief town of the county or franchise. We will also, that every one who flies from our peace forfeit his chattels to us for such flight, if he be suspected of felony, although he be afterwards acquitted of the principal fact. And if it be murder or other felony concerning the death of a man, let such felony be presented at the next county court by one or more townships, and by the first finder and the kindred of the person killed, that is to say, by one or more of kin on the part of the father, or on the part of the mother, according to the custom of the country.

Presentment of murders and homicides.

Outlawry of fugitive.

3. If one or more be appealed of the death, and others of the force and accessory facts, let the principals be first demanded at three county courts to come and answer concerning the felony, and if they do not come at the fourth court, and are not mainprised to appear at the fifth, they shall be outlawed at the fourth[g]. A woman however cannot properly be outlawed, because she is not appointed to any tithing or to the law, but she may be waived, which is equivalent to outlawry.

Females not outlawed but waived.

[g] The practice has been to proclaim a fugitive at five county courts, so that he is not adjudged an outlaw until the fifth; and Bracton agrees with this practice. He says, however, that the proceeding at the first court is merely a calling of the fugitive, and is not part of the outlawry, and therefore the fifth court is called the fourth, Brac. 125 *b*.

4. Quant a la peyne des utlagez en lour vies pur lour felonies, soit tiele, qe pur ceo qe il ne voilent ley attendre, si soint il forjugez de chescune ley et hors de nostre pes, et soint responauntz a touz et nul a eux, et soint[1] jugez pur felouns, et touz ceux qi a escient les receyverunt ou compaynie porterunt puis lour utlagerie; et qi les tuera quites soit de lour mort, for qe en cas ou il [2]se voderount rendre[2], et en cas ou il porrunt autrement estre pris; ne en appels ne eynt voiz vers nul homme; et s'il soint pris, qe il soint penduz, si il soint trovez utlagez par record de roule de Corouner; lour chateus soint nostres, et lour heyrs[3] disheritez de tote manere de heritage. Brac. 128 b, 129; Fle. 42, 43. [20 b.] Brac. 130; Fle. 43.

CHAPITRE XIV. [XIII.]

De Inlagerie.

1. Inlagerie deit a plusours estre graunté de dreit, et en aukun cas purra estre graunté de grace. Et en les cas de grace, si ount tels mester de nostre chartre, qe conteigne le reles de Brac. 131; Fle. 42. Brac. 131 b; Fle. 44 (§ 14.)

1. so *N. sim. DSGAMCF.* soint *om. L.* 2—2. voudreyent respoundre *M.* 3. a remenaunt *add. NDSGAC. sim. F.* en remenaunt *add. M.*

4. As to the punishment of outlaws in their lifetime for their felonies, their judgment shall be this, that, since they will not be amenable to the law, they be forejudged from all law, and put out of our peace, and be answerable to all, and none to them, and be judged felons, as shall also all those who knowingly receive them or bear them company after their outlawry; and he who shall kill them shall be acquitted of their death, except in cases where they shall offer to surrender themselves or where they might have been otherwise taken; neither in appeals shall they be heard against any man; and if they are taken, and found to be outlawed by record of the roll of the coroner, they shall be hanged, and their chattels shall be ours, and their heirs disinherited of every kind of inheritance. **Punishment of outlaws.**

CHAPTER XIV.

Of Inlawry, or being restored to law.

1. Inlawry in many cases ought to be granted of right, and in others it may be of favour; and, where of favour, the outlaws ought always to carry about them our charter, containing the **Inlawry by royal pardon.**

la utlagerie en eux avaunt pronuncié, touz jours porter ovekes eux, en aventure qe il ne defaillent de estre garrauntiz de

Brac. 127, 132, 133; Fle. 42 (§ 2). 44 (§ 14). par nous cum il averunt mester. Mes si il eynt esté utlagez a dreit et par lour decert, james neqedent ne lour vaudra tel reles de rien recoverer des terres ou des chateus qe lour furent

[21.] avaunt la utlagerie en eux pronuncié, ne a heritage demaunder ne dettes ne nule manere de dreit de nul tort qe il averount avaunt suffert.

Brac. 127; Fle. 42 (§ 1). 2. De dreit deit estre inlagerie graunté en ceo cas, ou homme ad esté utlagé avaunt le quart Counté, [1]ou sauntz[1] sute, et[2] sauntz comaundement des Justices Eyrauntza pres lour heyre finie, ou sauntz noster bref, ou par interrupcioun des Countez, ou si ne mie en Counté, ou si ne mie en presence de Corouner, ou si le utlagé en tens [3]de utlagerie pronouncié[3] fust de eynz age de xiiii. aunz, ou hors de sen, ou surd, ou muwet, ou folnastre, ou hors de noster reaume, ou detenu en prisoun;

Brac. 133; Fle. 45. ou si la cause de utlagerie soit trové nule, cum si celi, qi dust aver esté occis, soit uncore en pleyne vie, ou si le utlagerie

1—1. od fause *G.* 2. *om. G.* ou *C.* 3—3. del pronunciement de la utlagerie *M. sim. AC.*

release of the outlawry before pronounced against them, that they may not fail to be protected by us, when they shall have occasion. But if they have been legally and deservedly outlawed, such release will not avail them to recover any of the lands or chattels which were theirs before the outlawry pronounced against them, or to demand any inheritance or debts, or any manner of remedy for an injury which they shall before have suffered.

Inlawry of right, where the outlawry was irregular. 2. Inlawry ought of right to be granted in these cases, namely, where a man has been outlawed before the fourth county court, or without suit and without command of the Justices Itinerant after their eyre ended, or without our writ, or where there was not a regular succession of county courts, or if the outlawry was not in the county court, or not in the presence of the coroner; or if the outlaw at the time of pronouncing the outlawry, was under the age of fourteen years[h], or out of his right mind, or deaf, or an idiot, or out of our realm, or detained in prison; or if the cause of outlawry be found null, as if the man who was supposed to have been killed be still alive, or if the outlawry was pronounced in any other

[h] See note to chap. xiii. s. 1. ante, p. 48.

fust pronouncié en autre countee qe par la ou la felonie fust fete, ou si le bani fust en noster service adunc en guerre ou en chastel, ou si la cause ne seit mie trové felonie.

3. Et en tiel cas et en autres semblables, voloms nous qe si les banniz revignent et se rendent a nostre prisoun, et se aquitent du fet princepal, qe Justices [1]le nous[1] facent a saver; et nous tauntost de dreit maunderoms par nos brefs a nos viscountes de cel counté et des countez joingnauntz, qe il facent crier la pes de eux en citez et en burgs et en feyres et en marchez; et qe il facent solempnement pronuncier la cause de lour utlagerie estre trové fause; et qe il soint restituz [2]a lour terres et a lour[2] heritages, sauve a nous lour chateus, si il erunt[3] mescruz pur lour fute[4].

Brac. 127, 132; Fle. 42.

[21 *b.*]

Brac. 128 *b*, 129, 132 *b*, 133.

4. Et voloms, qe ceux qi par graunt malice compassé averunt suy vers aukun homme utlagerie en autre counté qe par la ou la cause principale fu fete, et ceo peuse estre atteynt, qe tels soint exileez [5]de noster reaume pur lour[6] malice.

5. Et tut soit a dreit aukun bani, et par soen decert, uncore

Brac. 127.

1—1. nous *GA.* les nouns *M.* les nous *C.* 2—2. de leur terres e de leur tenemenz e de rentes e des *C.* 3. erent *NDM.* seient *AC.* eyent *F.* 4. defaute *M.* 5. hors *add. GM.* 6. so *DM.* *sim. F.* sa *LSGA* sa[la] *C.* lur *on erasure N.*

county than where the felony was committed, or if the outlaw was then in our service in war or castle, or if it be found that the occasion of the outlawry was not felony.

Process of inlawry.

3. In these and other like cases, if the outlaws return and surrender themselves to our prison, and acquit themselves of the principal fact, the Justices shall certify us thereof; and we will immediately, as of right, command by our writs the sheriff of that county and the counties adjoining, that they cause the peace of such outlaws to be proclaimed in cities and in boroughs, in fairs and in markets, and cause it to be solemnly declared that the cause of the outlawry is found to be false, and that the outlaws be restored to their lands and inheritances, saving to us their chattels, if they shall have given occasion of suspicion by flight.

Fraudulent outlawry.

4. We will that those who by malicious contrivance sue any man to an outlawry in any other county than where the principal fact was committed, and are convicted thereof, shall be banished our realm for their malice.

5. And although a person be rightfully and deservedly

pora estre qe il avera esté mort avaunt la utlagerie en luy pronuncié, en qeu cas voloms nous qe lour heyrs eynt lour heritages, pur ceo qe lour auncestres ne attendirent mie jugement en lour vies.

6. Et si hom troeve teles utlageries estre pronunciez avaunt le tierz Counté, ou qe le Counté eyt autrement erré, si soit le Counté ajugé en nostre merci. Et si trové soit qe utlagerie eit esté pronuncié en absence de Corouner, et defaute soit del[1] Corouner, si soit le Corouner puni par prisoun et par fin; et ausi de abjuracioun fete en sa absence, tut eit il enveyé ses roulles par soen clerk ou par autre nent auctorizé.

[22.] Brac. 130; Fle. 43 (§4). 7. Des terres et des tenementz alienez [2]par felouns atteyntz puis lour felonies fetes[2], voloms nous qe teles alienaunces[3] soint repellables par les chiefs seignurs des feez par nos brefs de Eschaete.

1. trouee en le *M. sim. ACF.* en le *D. so on eras. N.* 2—2. *so verb. GAMCF. sim. ND.* par felonies fetz par felouns atteyntz *L.* 3. alienaciouns *D. sim. MACF. sim. on eras. N.*

No one can be outlawed after his death.

outlawed, yet it may appear that he was dead before the outlawry pronounced against him; in which case his heirs shall enjoy their inheritance, because the ancestor did not live to have judgment passed upon him.

County or coroner amerced for default.

6. If it be found that an outlawry was pronounced before the third county court, or that the proceedings in the county court were in any other manner erroneous, let the county be adjudged in our mercy; and if it be found that the outlawry was pronounced in the absence of the coroner, and that the coroner was in fault, let the coroner be punished by imprisonment and fine. The like of abjurations made in his absence, although he send his rolls by his clerk or other person not properly authorised.

Alienations by felons voidable.

7. As to lands and tenements aliened by felons attainted after commission of their felonies, we will, that such alienations be voidable by the chief lords of the fees by means of our writs of escheat.

CHAPITRE XV. [xiv.]

De Raap[1].

Rap est une felonie de homme de violence fete au cors de femme, quele[2] qe ele soit pucele ou autre; et de tiels felouns soit enquis. De la quele felonie qi qe soit atteynt a la sute de la femme par appel de felonie, ou a[3] la nostre, si soit le jugement tiel cum pur mort de homme, le quel qe ele soit assentue puis la felonie fete ou noun; sicum est contenu en nos estatuz de Westmoster[4].

Glan. li. 14, c. 6; Brac. 147; Fle. 53, 54 (§ 8).

Stat. West. 1. (3 Ed. I.) c. 13; Stat. West. 2. (13 Ed. I.) c. 34.

CHAPITRE XVI. [xv.]

De[5] *Larcyns.*

1. De robbours et de larouns et de semblables mesfesours soit ausi ententivement enquis. Des queux gentz nous volums, qe ceux qe soint trovez robbaunz ou emblauntz autri

Leg. Hen. I. lvii. 4, 7; Brac. 150 *b*. Fle. 24 (§ 5).

1. des femmes *N. sim. D.* 2. lequel *M. sim. F.* le quele *A.* 3. *so SGAMF.* a *om. LND.* de *C.* 4. le secounde *add. C.* 5. Robberies e des *N. sim. D.*

CHAPTER XV.

Of Rape.

Rape is a felony committed by a man by violence on the body of a woman, whether she be a virgin or not. Of such felonies let inquiry be made; and whoever is attainted thereof, either at the suit of the woman by appeal of felony, or at our suit, shall have the same judgment as for the death of a man, whether the woman have consented after commission of the felony or not, as is contained in our Statutes of Westminster.

Rape.

Punishment of rape.

CHAPTER XVI.

Of Larcenies.

1. Let careful inquiry also be made concerning robbers[h], thieves, and such like offenders; as to whom our will is, that if those who rob, or steal the goods of another, amounting

Theft, how punished by fresh suit.

h 'A robber is he who by force in the day or night despoils another of his goods. A thief is he who carries off or steals another's goods in the absence of the owner, or in his presence but without his knowledge.' (Note in MS. *N.*)

Stat. West. 1. (3 Ed. I.) c. 15; Fle. 56. Leg. Will. I. 24, 27; Leg. Hen. I. lviij. 4, 7. Brac. 54 *b*; Fle. 54, 55. 113 (§ 37). [22 *b*.] Ante, c. 2. s. 17; c. 6. s. 4.

biens muntauntz a xii. deners [1]ou de[1] plus, et de ceo soint freschement suiz par ceux a qi les choses serrount, ou par ceux hors de qi garde la chose avera esté emblé ou robbé, et de ceo soint les mesfesours trovez seisiz, qe tauntost soint pris et en la Court le seignur del fee, si il eit la fraunchise de Infangenthef, ou en la nostre en[2] Hundred ou en Counté ou aylours, soint menez en jugement; et puis face hom venir le Corouner hastivement, et en sa presence soit oi le sakebere en sa propre persone, et si il demaunde la chose cum emblé ou robé[3], tels[4] robbeours tauntost soint jugez a la mort, [5]s' il y eyt teymonage de leaus gentz qe ceo temoignent[5].

1—1. e *M.* 2. ou en *MC.* 3. e il eit testmoignes de leles gentz qe ceo testmoignent *add. N. sim. DSGAMC.* 4. larons ou *add. G. sim. SM.* 5—5. *om. NDSGAMC.*

to twelvepence or more[i], be freshly pursued for the same by the owners, or by those out of whose custody the things were stolen or robbed, and the goods are found upon them, they shall be forthwith taken and brought to trial in the court of the lord of the fee, if he has the franchise of infangthief, or in our court in the hundred, or county, or elsewhere; and the coroner shall be fetched forthwith, and in his presence the sakeber[k] shall be heard in his own person, and if he claims the goods as stolen or robbed and there are lawful people as witnesses to prove it, such robbers shall be immediately adjudged to death.

Infangthief.

Sakeber.

[i] In the time of Edward I. the price of a cow varied from 5*s.* to 12*s.*, the price of a sheep from 8*d.* to 3*s.* Wheat varied from 2*s.* to 16*s.* the quarter, and in times of scarcity rose much higher. See Fleetwood's Chronicon Preciosum; and see the provisions as to the assize of bread below, in c. xxxi. Bracton says that stealing a pig is a petty theft (Brac. 105); and we shall see below, in s. 7. p. 61, that stealing a sheaf of corn is so treated. The commentator in MS. *N.* states that three halfpence (iii mailles) a day was a poor living for a man, and gives the following singular reason for 12*d.* being fixed as the limit of petty larceny. 'At three halfpence a day, 12*d.* would be eight days' wages; and as a man going without sustenance for eight days might be expected to die on the ninth, the 12*d.* has regard to the destruction of life, for which offence a man is rightfully put to death.' The same note asserts, that 'in France and many other countries beyond sea, thieves are put to death for less than in England, as for the value of sixpence or one penny.' By the Anglo-Saxon laws no mercy was to be shown to a thief of above the value of 8*d.* (Leg. Athelst. i. 1. Leg. Hen. I. lix. 20.) But by another law of Athelstan the sum is fixed at 12*d.* (Leg. Ath. v. 1.) Spelman points out the increased severity of the law arising from the change in the value of money. In quantam asperitatem ex rerum temporumque vicissitudine lex antiqua abripitur. Quod enim olim 12*d.* venit, hodie sæpe 20*s.*, imo 40, vel pluris est. Nec vita hominis interea carior sed abjectior. (Spelm. Gloss. *s. v.* Laricinium.)

[k] 'Sakbere is he from whom the chattels are stolen, and is so called from *sak* (English) which is *enchesun* in French, and *bere* which is *porteur* in French: as being he who bears the cause to go to the deliverance of the thief.' (Note in MS. *N*). Compare Spelman, Gloss. *s. v. Sacaburth, Sacaber;* Thorpe's Glossary to ancient English laws, *s. v. Sagemannus.* The former part of the word appears to be the A. S. *Sacu,* Germ. *Sache,* a cause or matter of contention, whence the legal term *sak* for jurisdiction. The latter part of the word is variously derived from the A. S. *beran,* to carry, the A. S. *borh,* a pledge or security, and the old Teutonic *Bar* (A. S. *war*) a man, whence the French and English *Baron.*

Brac. 150 b, 151; Fle. 55.

2. Et si[1] tiels ne soint pris freschement sur le fet, tut soint il seisiz, si voloms en teu cas qe il pusent respoundre; et adunc porount il demaunder, coment le pleyntif vodera sure vers eus. Et si il die qe par motz de felonie, adunc soit ly lers envoyez a nostre gaole ou lessé par meynprise jekes au proscheyn Counté, ou jekes a la proscheyne deliveraunce de nostre gaole; et illucs face sa sute par motz de apel sicum de suth[2] serra dit entre les apels. Et si le fet eyt esté fet el foreyn, ou si le seignur ne eyt mie sutiers dunt la enqueste puse estre prise suffisauntment, adunc voloms, qe tiels felouns soint hastivement envoyez a nostre prisoun del counté. Et si le sakebere vodera, si pora bien sure sa chose cum adirree, et adunc ne suira il nul jugement de felonie, mes de simple trespas. Mes del houre qe le sakebere avera sa suite comencé [23.] felounousement, voloms nous aver suite de atteyndre la felonie, si autre ne sue.

Brac. 154 b; Fle. 55 (§ 6).

Brac. 150 b; Fle. 55, 56, 63 b, (§ 5).

3. Ou[3] si le liers eyt garraunt en nostre terre, adunc se pora il defendre par voucher. Et si il vouche a garraunt

Glan. li. 10. c. 15, 17; Brac. 151; Fle. 55.

1. so *NDAMF.* si *om. L.* 2. so *G. sim. SA.* de sus *L.* de suis *N. sim. D.* desus *C.* desuz *F.* 3. Et *D.*

Proceeding where the thief is not taken upon the fact.

2. If they are not taken freshly[1] upon the fact, although the goods are found upon them, they shall be permitted to answer, and then they may demand in what manner the plaintiff intends to proceed against them, and if he answer, 'by words of felony,' then the thief shall be either sent to our gaol or let to mainprise until the next county court, or until the next gaol delivery, and there the plaintiff shall make his suit by words of appeal, as will be explained below in treating of appeals. And if the fact was committed out of the lord's jurisdiction, or if the lord has not suitors sufficient to take the inquest, then such felons shall be forthwith sent to our county gaol. The sakeber, if he pleases, may bring an action for his goods, as lost; and then he shall not sue judgment of felony, but of trespass only; but when the sakeber has begun his suit in the form of felony, if he does not prosecute it, we may ourselves proceed to conviction of the felony.

Plaintiff may sue by appeal of felony or in trespass.

Vouching warrant.

3. If the accused has any warrant within our realm, then he may defend himself by voucher; and if he vouches

[1] The commentator in MS. *N* explains the word *freschement* as denoting that the sakeber must make his suit the same day.

aukun qi ly dona la chose, ou ly vendi, ou autrement lessa, si ly soit jour doné de aver soen garraunt si aver le peut, si adunc ne soit present. Et si il ne le peuse aver, si le face hom venir par ayde de nostre Court; a quel jour si il defaille de aver soen garraunt [1]qe il avera voché, si a soen peril et li avera[1] vouché sauntz ayde de la Court, si soit mis a autre respounse ou a sa penaunce, et la chose soit deliveré au chalengeour. Et cum tieus vocherount a garraunt par ayde de nostre Court, si maunderoms au viscounte, en qi baillie le garraunt pora estre trové, qe il eyt le cors un tiel en tiel liu au tel certeyn jour a garraunter ou a dedire. Et si le viscounte retourne [2]qe nul tiel est conu en sa baillie, si soit adunc le voucheour boté a chef respounse, ou a sa penaunce, si il ne voille respoundre. Et si le viscounte retourne[2] qe [3]le vouché ne est mie[3] trové, adunc voloms nous, qe noster bref yse a mesme celi viscounte, qe il face le vouché demaunder de Counté en Counté jekes autaunt qe il aperge ou qe il soit utlagé.

Glan. li. 10. c. 16; Brac. 151; Fle. 55.

1—1. qe a sun peril lauera *A.* qe il auera *M. sim. CF.* et *om. G.* 2—2. *so verb. NSMF. sim. DGA. om. LC.* 3—3. *so D. sim. NGSMC.* nul tiel vouche est *L.* nul tiel purra estre *A.*

to warrant any person who gave him the thing, or sold it, or otherwise made it over to him, let a day be given him to produce his warrant, if he be not then present; and if he cannot produce him, let him be compelled to appear by the aid of our Court; at which day if he fails to produce his warrant whom he has vouched, where he vouches him at his own peril and without aid of our Court, he shall be obliged to give some other answer, or be put to his penance, and the goods shall be delivered to the person who claims them. And when a person is vouched to warranty by aid of our Court, the sheriff, in whose bailiwick the warrant is expected to be found, shall be commanded to have his body at such a place on a certain day, either to undertake the warranty or to refuse it. If the sheriff returns that no such person is known in his bailiwick, the voucher shall be driven to his answer in chief, or to his penance if he refuse to answer; and if the sheriff returns that the vouchee is not found, then let our writ issue to the same sheriff, to cause him to be demanded from county court to county court until he either appear or be outlawed.

Writ of warranty.

Process against vouchee.

4. Et si le garraunt veigne et entre [1]en la[1] garrauntie pur defendre le voucheour en la possessioun de la chose, si soit le plé del princepal suspendu, et soit comencé vers le garraunt. Et si le garraunt face sa partie bone, si soint jugez quites et [23 *b.*] le voucheur et soen garraunt, et le pleyntif a la prisoun par la resoun qe serra dite el chapitre des appels. Et si jugement [2]face countre[2] le garraunt, adunc soit la chose chalengé ajugé al pleyntif, et le princepal soit encoupé de la felonie a nostre suite pur la presumpcioun de la compaynie du garraunt atteynt de la felonie.

Glan. li. 10. c. 15; Brac. 151; Fle. 55.

Post. c. 23. s. 9.

5. Et si le princepal [3]ne eyt qi voucher[3], si porra il dire qe il achata la chose chalengé tel an tiel jour en tiele feyre, ou en tel marché, en presence de moutz des gentz, et de ceo paya tolun[4] as baillifs. Et si il vouche de ceo testmoynage de mesmes tiels baillifs et de autres adunc en present, et de ceo soit tesmoignee, ou si[5] il se met en pays et sei aquite de la felonie, et celi qi fet la suite eyt mis a voir qe la chose chalengé

Glan. li. 10. c. 17; Brac. 151, 151 *b*; Fle. 55.

1—1. *so NDSACF.* la *L.* en *M.* 2—2. passe encountre *M. sim. F.* se face encountre *C.* 3—3. ne auoit qe voucher *L. sim. SG.* ne eyt qi il vouche *D. so on eras. N.* neit qe voucher *A.* nen eyt qe voucher *M.* neit qi voucher *C. sim. F.* 4. tonu *AM.* tonue *C.* tounu *F.* 5. *so NDAMCF.* qe *L.*

4. If the vouchee comes and enters into the warranty to defend the vouchor in the possession of the thing, let the plea against the principal be suspended, and one commenced against the warrant. And if the warrant makes good his case, then let both the vouchor and his warrant be acquitted, and the plaintiff be adjudged to prison for the reason which shall be given in the chapter of appeals. If judgment be given against the warrant, then the thing challenged shall be adjudged to the plaintiff, and the principal shall be indicted of the felony at our suit, upon presumption of his being an accomplice of the warrant, who is attainted of the felony.

Proceedings upon appearance of vouchee.

5. If the principal has no one to vouch, he may say that he bought the thing challenged in such a year and on such a day, at such a fair or at such a market, in the presence of a great number of people, and paid a toll to the bailiffs for it. And if he vouches the testimony of the said bailiffs and others then present, and evidence is given accordingly, or if he puts himself on the country and is acquitted of the felony, and yet the prosecutor has proved that the thing challenged belonged to

Purchase in market overt, a defence to the felony,

soit la suye, et qe ele ly fust emblé ou hors de sa garde, dunc ly covendra respoundre et de fere le asetz al seignur de la chose, si soit le jugement tiel qe le demaundaunt recovere sa demaunde, et le chalengé voist quites, et perde ceo qe il avera doné pur la chose. Et si il ne soit mie tesmoignee, si se aquite par pays.

Fle. 56. 6. Et si nul soit endité par presentement de robberie, ou de larcyn, ou de couperie des bourses, ou de rescept de felouns, [24.] ou[1] de enchaunteries[2], sicum de ceux qi endorment les gentz, ou de gilours qi mauveise chose vendent pur bone, sicum peutre pur argent ou latoun pur or, ou des autres petites mauvestez semblables, voloms nous qe touz soint pris, ou demaundez, si il ne soint trovez, et qe lour terres et lour chateus soint seysiz en nostre meyn. Et cum il vendrount en jugement, et ne se porunt de tiele felonie aquiter[3] a nostre Brac. 104 *b*; Fle. 56, 63. suite, ou a autri[4], si soint jugez a morir par pendre[5], ou a la perte del orayl, ou a pillori, solom ceo qe lour fetz soint

1. *so NDMF.* et *L.* e *AC.* 2. enchantiers *ND.* chanteries *A.* enchantours *F.* 3. *om. A.* 4. ne eux desauolupier *add. D. sim. interl. N.* desuoluper *add. A.* 5. ou a estre descorche *add. D. sim. interlin. N.*

him, and that it was stolen from him or out of his custody, but does not change the property. in such case he must be answerable to the owner, and make him satisfaction, and the judgment shall be, that the claimant recover the thing demanded, and that the person challenged go quit, and lose what he gave for the thing; and if he can produce no such witnesses, let him acquit himself by the country.

Cutpurses, receivers of felons, wizards, cheats, how punished. 6. If any one be indicted by presentment of robbery, or of larceny, or of cutting of purses, or of receiving of felons, or of enchantment, as those who send people to sleep[m], or of cheating by selling bad things for good, as pewter for silver, or latten for gold, or of other petty offences of the like nature, our will is that such be apprehended; or, if they cannot be found, they shall be demanded, and their lands and chattels be seized into our hands; and if, when they are tried, they cannot acquit themselves of the felony, whether at our suit or another's, let them be condemned to be hanged, or to lose an

[m] This seems to give some support to the conjecture, that the experiments of mesmerism and animal magnetism, which have created so much interest in our times, were not unknown in the 13th century. *Endormeurs de genz* are mentioned as offenders in the *Consuet. S. Genov. f.* 34. *MS.* cited in Ducange, Gloss. *s. v. Dormitabilis.* It is possible however that the effect may have been produced by drugs.

grauntz ou petiz, et solom ceo qe il ount esté acustumez, ou noun.

7. De petiz larouns, cum des garbes en aust, et de autri columbeus ou gelyns, si soit le jugement tiel, qe si il ne soint trovez de autre mauveis ret, et la chose emblé[1] ne vaile mie xii. deners, qe il soint mis au pillori par un houre de jour, et qe mes ne soint receyvables a serment fere en jurez ne enquestes, ne en tesmoignages. Et ausi soit de touz ceux qi [2]tiels juyses, ou juise[2] de tumberel, ou perte de membre averount suffert par jugement. Et si tiels [3]petitz mauveys[3] soint de [4]mauveis ret[4], ou si il averount teles mauveistez fetes par dreite mauvesté et nent par bosoigne, adunc voloms nous, qe le jugement de tiels soit, qe il perdent le orayl et soint [24 *b*.] defamez[5] a touz jours, cum avaunt est dit. Et si autrefoiz de mauvesté soint atteyntz, adunc soit en la descrecioun des Justices de juger les a la mort, ou de fere couper le autre oraille. Et si la terce foiz soint atteyntz de mauvesté graunde ou petite a nostre suite ou a autri, si soint jugez a la mort.

Brac. 105, 151 *b*; Fle. 56.

1. demaundee *M.* *om.* *C.* 2—2. tels Iuises *A.* Iuyses ou Iuyse *M.* cele iuise *C.* 3—3. petitz maufesours *Z.* *om.* *C.* 4—4. male rette *Z.* 5. enfames *M.*

ear, or to the pillory, according to the greatness of their crime, and according as they have been habitual offenders or not.

7. In small thefts, as of sheaves of corn in harvest, or of pigeons or poultry, let the judgment be this, that if the thieves are not found to be otherwise of bad character, and the thing stolen is under the value of twelve pence, they shall be put in the pillory for an hour in the day, and be not admissible to make oath on any jury or inquest, or as witnesses; and the like as to all those who have been sentenced to undergo such punishments or the punishment of the tumbrel, or to lose a limb. And if these petty thieves are persons of bad character, or if they have offended out of mere wickedness, and not through want, then their sentence shall be to lose an ear, and be rendered infamous for ever, as above mentioned; and if they be found guilty of a second offence, then it shall be in the discretion of the Justices, either to judge them to death or order their other ear to be cut off; and if they are convicted a third time, whether it be for a great or a small crime, and whether at our suit or another's, let them receive sentence of death.

Petty larceny.

Fle. 56.

8. Des cyllours des bourses voloms, qe pur[1] bourse coupé, si autre mauvesté n'en eynt fete, eynt jugement de pillori; et si [2]il eyt[2] emblé [3]par le coupour[3] autre chose meyns de xii. deners ou de la value, si perdent le oraylle. Et si la chose passe [4]la value de[4] xii. deners, adunc eint il jugement de la mort.

CHAPITRE XVII. [XVI.]

De Abjuraciouns.

Stat. Wall. (12 Ed. I.) c. 5; Brac. 135 *b*, 136; Fle. 45.

1. De ceux qe s'en fuyent a mousteers pur lour mauvesteez, voloms qe le Corouner del lu voist a eus de enquere et de oyer lour conisaunce[5], pur qei il se tiegnent a mouster. Et s'il ne voillent felonie reconustre ne venir hors de eglise de ester a dreit, si perdent lur chateus pur lour fute, et tauntost face le Corouner seyser lour terres et lour chateus en nostre meyn, et face priser lour chateus et deliverer a la villee; et [6]la reconi-

1. par *L.* pur la *NDA.* pur le *M.* la *C.* por la *F.* 2—2. ly eint *N.* ly eyent *D.* il eient *GA.* *sim.* *SMFY.* 3—3. par le coupor *NDAGSZ.* par le copier *M.* par le coper *F.* *om.* *C.* 4—4. *om.* *AMCF.* 5. reconissaunce *D.* *sim.* *MF.* reconoissaunz *C.* 6. a *add* *CF.*

Cutpurses.

8. As to cutpurses, if they have not been guilty of any other offence, let them be sentenced to the pillory for the cutting of the purse; and if there be anything else stolen by the prisoner under twelve pence or of that value, he shall lose one of his ears, and if the thing exceed the value of twelve pence, then judgment of death shall be passed upon him.

CHAPTER XVII.

Of Abjurations.

Proceedings where a felon flies to sanctuary.

1. Concerning those who fly to churches for their crimes, our will is, that the coroner of the place go to them to inquire wherefore they have taken sanctuary, and hear their confessions; and if they will neither confess felony nor come out of church to be amenable to justice, they shall forfeit their chattels on account of their flight, and the coroner shall immediately cause their lands and their chattels to be seized into our hand, and their chattels to be valued and delivered to the township. The admission which they shall make that they are not willing to appear to answer to our peace, shall be

saunce qe il frount, qe il ne voillent a nostre pes venir [1]si soit entré[1] en roulle, ensint qe mes ne soint de nostre pes, [25.]
jekes autaunt qe il soint aquitez en nostre Court des choses dunt il serrount acoupez. Et mes ne voist le Corouner, si il ne voille, tut voille le futif reconustre felonie et prier grace de abjuracioun.

2. Et s'il demurent outre les xl. jours de cel houre qe le Corouner vient a eux premerement, si soit tut le counté chargé de lour garde, et soint tenuz pur felouns ou sicum gentz hors de noster pes. Et si il reconusent felonie et prient nostre reaume de forjurer, et prient tuycioun del eglise jekes autaunt qe il eynt perveu et ordinee lour[2] aler, adunc voloms nous, qe tiels eynt cele tuycioun par xl. jurz puis le jour de la venue del Corouner iloekes; et tauntost apres la reconisaunce enroullé, si soint liverez a les gardes des villes issint qe il ne les lesent eschaper hors de mouster en le men tens.

Brac. 136; Fle. 45 (§. 2.)

3. Et la abjuracioun soit fete a la porte [3]ou al eschalere[3]

1—1. *so N. sim. DGSMF.* et soit entre *L.* seit entre *A.* seient entreez *C.* 2. de *M.*
3—3. *om. AMCF.*

entered in the roll, to the intent that they may never be under our peace, until they are acquitted in our Court of the crimes wherewith they shall be charged; the coroner however is not obliged to go, unless he pleases, notwithstanding the fugitive is desirous of confessing felony and praying the favour of abjuration.

2. If the fugitives abide in sanctuary above forty days from the time of the coroner's first going to them[n], the whole county shall be charged with their custody, and they accounted as felons or as persons out of our peace. And if they confess felony and pray to abjure our realm, and beg the protection of the church until they have provided for and settled their departure, then our pleasure is, that they have such protection for forty days from the day of the coroner's coming to them; and forthwith after the enrollment of their confession, let them be given in charge to the constables of the townships, that they may not in the meantime be allowed to escape out of sanctuary.

Forty days of sanctuary.

3. Let the abjuration be made at the gate or fence[o] of the

Ceremony of abjuration.

[n] Other authorities seem rather to show that the forty days were to be reckoned from the arrival in the church. See Brac. 136; Fle. 45, and compare Stat. 32 Hen. VIII. c. 12.

[o] *Qu.* Steps. See Ducange Gloss. *s. v.* Scalarium; Roquefort Gloss. *s. v.* Eschallier.

Abjuratio latronum (Stat. inc. temp.); Brac. 136; Fle. 45.

del cymitere en ceste manere. Ceo oyetz, vous Corouner et autres bones gentz, qe jeo tel pur tel fet, qe jeo felounousement fis ou assenti de fere, istrai hors del reaume de Engleterre, ou hors de la terre de Hyrlaunde, et james [1]ne retourneray si noun par coungé le roi de Engleterre ou de ses heirs, si me ayde Deus et les Saintz.

[25 *b.*] Stat. Wall. (12 Ed. I.) c. 5; Brac. 135 *b*; Fle. 45, 46.

4. Et tauntost elise mesmes port de mer ou passage en Escoce hors del reaume, jekes a quel porte ou passage nous receyvoms tiels en nostre proteccioun, si fraude ne facent. Et puis [2]defende hom[2] a tels sur peril de vie et de membre, qe il ne se tournent nule part hors de commun chemyn, jekes autaunt qe il soint del reaume, ou de la terre, issuz[3] a cel port ou passage qe il averount choisi et a nul autre a plus toust qe il porrount, sauntz fraude fere. Et puis s'en voisent, a une croiz de fust en lour meins, deschaucez et desceyntz, a testes descovertes, [4]en lour cotes senglement[4]. Et defendoms sur peril de vie et de membre, [5]qe nuly[5] teus ne oceye taunt

1. leynz *add. NDG. sim. SMACF.* 2—2. *so ND. sim. AMCF.* defendoms *L.* 3. passe *C.* 4—4. en lour pure cote senglement *D.* en lour pure Cote *A.* en pur lour cotes *M. sim. F.* en pur lour cotes soul *C.* 5—5. *so N. sim. DSC. om. L.* qe nul *A.* qe nul homme *MG.*

churchyard, in this manner. Hear this, you coroner and other good people, that I for such an act which I feloniously did, or assented to the doing thereof, will depart from the realm of England, (or the land of Ireland,) and will never return thereto unless by leave of the king of England or his heirs, so help me God and the Saints.

Mode of leaving the kingdom.

4. Immediately after they shall choose for themselves[p] some seaport, or passage into Scotland out of the realm, as far as which port or passage we admit them to our protection, provided they are not guilty of fraud. And then let them be forbidden on peril of life and limb to turn aside anywhere out of the high road, until they have left the kingdom, or country, at that port or passage which they have chosen, and no other, with all possible dispatch and without fraud. Let them then go with a wooden cross in their hands, barefooted, ungirded, and bareheaded, in their coat only. And we forbid any one under peril of life and limb to kill them so long as they are on

[p] There is a note in the Year Book of 30 Ed. I. that he who wishes to abjure the realm shall take the port assigned him by the Coroner and no other. (Year Book 30 and 31 Ed. I. App. i. p. 509.) See also the Statutes of Wales (12 Ed. I.) c. 5. Bracton and Fleta agree with the text.

cum il serount trovez en lour chemyn encheminaunt[1]; et ausi qe nul ne les tue ne autres en fuaunt, si en autre manere hom les peuse prendre.

5. Et si tels futifs se tiegnent a mouster xl. jours apres apparaunce de Corouner, adunc soint forclos de la grace de abjuracioun a remenaunt et tenuz a felouns atteyntz, issint qe il ne pusent autres encuser ne appeler. Et defendoms a touz lays sur forfeture[2] de vie et de membre, et as clers sur peyne[3] de exil de noster reaume a nostre volounté, qe nul a tiels outre les xl. jours avauntditz ne lour doyne a manger ne a boyre ne ovekes eux ne commune en nule manere. [26.] Brac. 136; Fle. 45.

6. Et voloms et grauntoms, qe en cas ou acun avera forjuré noster reaume par poour, et puis peut estre atteynt qe il ne avera mie esté coupable de la felonie qe il avera reconue, qe il peusent sauvement revenir sauve chescuni suite, et qe lour heirs en tel cas ne soint mie desheritez; de[4] lour chateus neqedent soint forjugez pur la fute. Fle. 46.

7. Et voloms qe abjuracioun soit tenue nule et qe ele puse estre dedite et anentye, si ele eit esté fete par aucun qi se

1. cheminaunt *M.* 2. peyne *M.* 3. peril *F.* 4. so *DAMCF.* de *om. L.* de *interl. N.*

their road pursuing their journey; nor shall they, or any other fugitives, be killed, if they can be taken in any other manner.

5. If such fugitives abide in sanctuary forty days after the coroner's coming to them, they shall be debarred thereafter from the favour of abjuration, and deemed as felons convict, so as to have no right of accusing or appealing any others; and we forbid all laymen under forfeiture of life and limb, and clerks under pain of banishment from our kingdom during our pleasure, to give them any meat or drink after the said forty days, or to have any manner of communication with them. Penalty of remaining after the forty days.

6. We will and grant, that whenever any one has abjured our realm through fear, and it can be afterwards proved that he was not guilty of the felony which he confessed, he may safely return, saving to every one his suit; and in such cases the heirs of the fugitives shall not be disinherited, but their chattels shall notwithstanding be forfeited by reason of their flight. Abjuration through fear set aside.

7. And our will is, that all abjurations taken by any one, who shall have meddled with the office of coroner without Abjuration must be before coroner.

avera entremis del office de Corouner et ne avera mie esté a ceo par nous auctorizé[1] ne par nos predecessours; et ausi si Corouner auctorizé ne eit esté en propre persone.

8. Et en abjuracRiouns pur nostre veneysoun, ou pur autre trespas, ne voloms nul estre desherité des terres [2]ne des tenementz for des chateus[2] soulement.

CHAPITRE XVIII. [XVII.]

[3]*De Troveures*[3].

Leg. Ed. Conf. 14; Leg. Hen. I. x. 1; Stat. West. 1. c. 4; Brac. 120; Fle. 61.

1. En dreit de tresor muscee en terre trové, de wrek trové et de weyf a nous apporteynauntz, et de estourgeouns et de baleyns, et de autre chose trové, qe nous sount detenuz, qe nostres dussent estre, soit ausi ententivement enquis, et des nouns des trovours, et a qi meyns teles troveures soint [26 *b.*] devenuz, et cum ben. Car tresor muscee en terre et trové voloms qe soit noster; et si il soit trové en la mer, adunc[4] soit il al troveour. Et volums qe homme qi le trovera en

1. *so M. sim. GAC.* attourne *LN.* attornee ne de coe auctorize *D.* auctorite *F.* 2—2. ne des chateus *AMC.* mes des chateaus *F.* 3—3. De troueours *L.* De troueures de tresor *N.* Des Troueors de Tresor *D.* De tresor troue *A.* De troueurs *CF.* De tresor musce de wrek de chose perdue e de weyf *M.* 4. *so ND. sim. AMCL.* et *L.*

being authorized thereto by us or our predecessors, shall be held void and may be disavowed and annulled; the like, if the coroner, though authorized, he did not attend in his own person.

In abjurations for trespass, no forfeiture of lands.

8. In abjurations made on account of our game, or other trespasses, let none be disinherited of his lands or tenements, but forfeit his chattels only.

CHAPTER XVIII.

Of Treasure-trove, Wrecks, Waifs, and Estrays.

Treasure-trove.

1. Concerning treasure found concealed in the earth, and concerning wrecks and waifs belonging to us, and sturgeons and whales, and other things found, which of right belong to and are detained from us, let careful inquiry be made, and of the names of those who found them, and to whose hands they have come, and to what amount. For treasure hid in the earth and found shall belong to us, but if found in the sea, it shall belong to the finder; and any person who shall find such

terre le face hastivement saver au Corouner del pays ou as baillifs; et le Corouner sauntz delay voist pur enquere si rien en soit aloygné[1], et par qi; et ceo qe pora estre trové soit sauvé a nostre oes, et les aloygneours[2] soint mis par meynprise jekes en heyre des Justices; et adunc voloms nous, [3]qe si[3] nos Justices pusent atteyndre la malice en [4]le esloigner[4], qe les esloigneours[5] soint puniz [6]par prisoun et par fin; et si nule malice ne soit trové, adunc soint puniz[6] par simple amerciement. Brac. 122.

2. De chose perdue et trové sour terre voloms nous, qe, si[7] le seignur de la chose la demaunde de eynz le an et le jour, et la puse prover estre la sue, adunc soit la chose deliveré al demaundaunt; et ausi soit a celi qi le avera perdue si il puse averreer la perte. Et si nul ne eyt suy la chose de eynz le an et le jour, et celi qi le avera trové le eit fet crier et publier as marchez et as eglises proscheynes[8], adunc remeyne la chose al troveour. Leg. Will. I. 6.

3. Et weyf ou estray nent chalengez de eynz le an et le Brac. 120; Fle. 62.

1. aliene *A.* enloignee *M.* 2. eloigneurs *M.* allienours *C.* 3—3. qe [si *interl.*] *A.* qe *LNDM.* si *F.* 4—4. le aloigneur *M.* les alienors *G. sim. AC.* 5. alienours *G. sim. AMC.* en loygnurs *F.* 6—6. so *D. sim. NAMCF. om. L.* 7. so *DAMCF.* si *om. L.* si *interl. N.* 8. parochienes *C. om. A.*

treasure in the earth shall forthwith inform the coroner of the district or the bailiffs thereof; and the coroner shall go without delay and inquire, whether any of it has been carried off, and by whom, and save all that can be found for our use; and those who carried it off shall be held to mainprise until the eyre of the Justices; and if our Justices can convict the eloiners of malice, they shall be punished by imprisonment and fine, but if malice be not found, they shall be punished by amercement only. Duty of coroner.

2. As to things lost and found above ground, if the owner demand them within the year and day, and can prove them to be his property, they shall be delivered to him; so likewise to him who lost the things, provided he can prove the loss; and if the things are not claimed within the year and day, and the finder has caused them to be cried and published in the neighbouring markets and churches, then the finder may keep them. Property found above ground; rights of finder and of owner.

3. Waifs or estrays, not challenged within the year and day,

jour si soit al seignur de la fraunchise[1], si il de cele fraunchise eit esté seysi de dreit. Et si le seignur ne eit fet crier tele
[27.] beste trové solempnenent, cum [2]de sus[2] est dit, adunc ne courge nul tens encountre celi a qi la chose[3] avera esté [4]ou beste[4], qe il ne la puse replever a quel houre qe il vodera. Et si le seignur la avowe pur la sue, si eit le demaundaunt accioun a demaunder [5]cum sa beste[5] adirree en forme de trespas, ou de apeller de[6] larcyn par motz de felonie. Et lequel qe le seignur soit atteynt de torcenuse detenue par la une voie ou l'autre, si perdra il la fraunchise de estray aver a remenaunt.

Leg. Hen. I. x. 1; Stat. West. 1. c. 4; Brac. 120; Fle. 61.

4. En dreit de wrec de mer trové, voloms qe soit fet solum [7]nostre ordinaunce en[7] nos estatuz. De estourgeoun pris en nostre terre voloms nous qe il soint nostres, sauve al troveour ses mises et ses custages renables. De baleynz trovez en noster poer volom nous qe la teste soit nostre et la cowe a nostre cumpayne solom le auncien usage.

1. so *G.* *add.* *L.* *sim.* *SM.* et *ND.* e *AC.* 2—2. de souz *M.* 3. beste *AMCF.* 4—4. *om.* *AMCF.* 5—5. sa beste com *G.* 6. so *NAMCF.* de trespas de *L.* le seignur de *D.* 7—7. ceo qe est ordeyne en *M.* lordinance de *A.*

Estrays; rights of lord and of owner.

shall belong to the lord of the franchise, if he be rightfully seised of such franchise; but if the lord did not cause the beast so found to be publicly cried in manner aforesaid, then no time shall run against the owner of the thing or beast, to bar him from replevying it whenever he pleases; and if the lord avow it to be his own, the person demanding it may either bring an action to recover his beast as lost, in form of trespass, or an appeal of larceny, by words of felony; and if the lord by either proceeding be found guilty of a tortious detaining, he shall lose his franchise of estray for ever after.

Wreck.

4. With regard to wreck of sea found, the ordinance of our statutes shall be observed. Sturgeons taken within our dominions shall belong to us, saving to the persons who took them their reasonable costs and expenses; and of whales caught within our jurisdiction the head shall belong to us and the tail to our consort, according to ancient usage.

Sturgeons and whales.

CHAPITRE XIX. [XVIII.]

De Dreit[1] le Roi.

1. Et quant a nos feez, soit enquis de eglises cathedrales parochieles et religiouses et des mesouns de religioun et des hospitals en cel counté, quels sount de nostre avoweysoun, et queus le deivent estre et ne sount mie, et par queus eux ount esté sustretz, et coment; et queus demeynes nous tenoms en nostre meyn en cel counté, et queus demeynes [2]nous et[2] autres tenoms de auncienes demeynes de nostre Coroune; et queus de eschete et de purchaz, et queus celes terres teignent [3]autres de[3] nous, et cum bien les terres vaillent severaument a la verreye value; et de demeynes qe deyvent estres nostres qe nel sunt mie, coment eles ount esté aloigneez[4] et par queus, et qi les teignent; et ausi des feez, et des avouesouns des eglises. Cap. Escaetriæ (Stat. temp. inc.); Brac. 116 b; Fle. 24 (§ 45, 46, 47). [27 b.]

2. Et des hundrez qe deyvent estre tenuz de nous en chef et ne sount mie, coment il ount esté alienez et par queux, et qi les teignent, et puis quel tens, et de lour verraye value par Brac. 117, 117 b; Fle. 25 (§ 48, 49).

1. feez *MGW*. 2—2. noe *D*. 3—3. *so WF*. autre de *LNDSA*. autres qe *GM*. dautre qe de *C*. 4. alienes *A*.

CHAPTER XIX.

Of the King's Rights.

1. With respect to our seigniories, let inquiry be made of cathedral, parochial, and conventual churches, and of religious houses and hospitals in the county, what are of our advowson; and what ought to be so, but are not; and who has deprived us of them, and how; also what demesnes in the same county we hold in our hands, and what demesnes we and others hold of the ancient demesnes of our crown, and what by escheat and by purchase, and who hold such lands besides ourselves, and what the lands are severally worth according to their true value; and of demesnes which ought to be ours and are not, how they have been aliened, and by whom, and who hold them. So likewise of seigniories, and advowsons of churches. Advowsons of churches, convents, and hospitals. King's demesnes. Ancient demesne.

2. Also of hundreds, which ought to be held of us in chief and are not, inquiry must be made how they have been aliened, and by whom, and who now hold them, and from what Hundreds.

an; et ausi de la verraye value del counté, et cum bien le viscounte nous en rent par an de ferme; et cum bien de hundrez sount en nostre meyn, et cum ben chescun hundred vaut par an, et cum bien les baillifs [1]en rendent[1] a nous, ou as autres.

Brac. 116 b; Fle. 25, 26. 3. Et ausi des custumes[2] et des services dues a nous, s' il eynt esté sustrez et par queus, et cum ben de tens; et ausi de sutes dues a noster Counté, et a nos hundrez, et a nos maners, et a tourns de noster viscounte, et a nos vewes de frauncplege, et a nos molins, si eles eynt esté pleynement fetes, et si noun, coment eles eynt esté sustretes, et de quel tens, et par queux[3], et ausi de touz services dues a nous de dreit.

[28.] Brac. 116 b; Fle. 24 (§ 17). 4. De eschetes qe a nous dusent escheer par la felonie des felouns, ou par la mort de nos tenauntz sauntz heir, ou par acune manere de reversioun, et des terres des Normauntz et de felouns, qi tyndrent de nous en chef, alienez puis[4] lour felonies fetes, qe dusent estre nos eschetes, soit ausi enquis,

1—1. en rendent de ferme *A. sim. MF.* rendent par an de ferme *C.* 2. *Conj.* ausmones *LG.* ausmoynes *N.* ausmeynes *D.* almoignes *A.* aumones *S.* aumoignes *Z.* amounes *M.* aumounes *C.* amoynes *F.* 3. et qi tieles maneres customes et seruices ou autres choses a nous appendantz a eux meismes ont approprie et puis quel temps *add. Z.* 4. so *A. sim. W.* pur *LNDMC.* por *F.*

time, and what is their true value by the year; likewise of the true value of the county, and how much rent the sheriff pays us a year, and how many of the hundreds are in our hands, and what each hundred is worth, and how much the bailiffs annually pay to us or any other for them.

Farm of the county, and hundreds.

Customs, services, and suits. 3. Inquiry must also be made of customs and services due to us, whether they have been withheld, and by whom, and how long. The like with respect to suits due at our county court, our hundreds, and our manors, and at the tourns of our sheriff, and our views of frankpledge, and at our mills, whether they have been fully performed; and if not, how they have been withheld, and from what time, and by whom; and so of all services which of right are due to us.

Escheats. 4. Inquiry shall also be made concerning escheats, which ought to fall to us by the felony of felons, or by the death of our tenants without heirs, or by any kind of reversion; and concerning the lands of Normans, and of felons who held of us in chief, which have been aliened after the commission of

qi les teignent et de quel tens, et cum bien eles vaylent par an en totes issues a la vereye value; et ausi des terres et des tenementz alienez par [1]felouns autri[1] tenauntz[2] puis[3] lour felonie fete, dunt noster gree ne ad mie esté fet del an et del wast.

5. Des countez et des baronies, feez de chivalers, grauntz serjaunties et petites, desmembrez sauntz coungé de nous, coment eles sount tenues, et qi les tenent, et de qi, ou de nous en chef, ou par men; et si ren nous soit arere de nul service ou profit qe noster dust estre de dreit; et si pleynement eyoms eu les gardes et les mariages, homages et relefs, [4]et heireez[4] par tut ou les aver dussoums de dreit, ou si noun, par queus il nous ount esté sustrez, et de quel tens, et cum bien il vaylent par an; des enfauntz madles, damaysels[5] et vedues, qi mariages dusent estre nostres, mariez sauntz coungé de nous, et quant de foiz et a queus, et cum bien lour terres vaillent par an. Cap. Escaet. (Stat. temp. inc.)

1—1. *so verb. MW.* autres felouns *LNDG. sim. S.* feluns as *A.* felouns e autres *C.* felons autres *F.* 2. des autres *add. D. so interl. N.* 3. *so DAC.* pur *LM.* por *WF.* puis *on erasure N.* 4—4. et herietz des heirs *D.* e herietes *G. sim. S.* des heirs *AW.* e heirs *C.* eyrs *F.* 5. femeles *M.*

their felonies, and ought to be our escheats, who hold them, and from what time, and how much a year they are worth with their whole profits at the true value; the like as to lands and tenements held of other lords, and aliened by felons after the commission of their felony, without compounding with us for the year and waste.

5. Also concerning earldoms, baronies, knights' fees, grand and petty serjeanties, dismembered without our leave, inquiry must be made how they are held, and who hold them, and of whom, whether of us in chief, or by mesne. Also whether there be anything in arrear to us for any service or profit which of right belongs to us; and whether we have fully had the wardships, marriages, homages, reliefs, and heriots, wherever we ought to have them of right, and if not, by whom they have been withheld from us, and how long, and what is their yearly value; so of all children, male and female, and widows, whose marriages belong to us, and who have been married without our leave, how often and to whom they have been married, and how much their lands are worth by the year. Baronies and knights' fees, dismembered. Wardships, marriages, reliefs, heriots.

[28 *b*.] Stat. de Big. (4 Ed. I.) c. 4; Glan. li. 9. c. 11; Brac. 116 *b*; Fle. 24 (§ 18).

6. Et ausi soit enquis de totes maneres de purprestures fetes sur nous de terres et de fraunchises; et ceux qi serrount presentez deforceours et purprestours[1] par fresche force puis le heyre crié, si soint somouns de vener a certeyn jour a respoundre de lour tort, et soit le proces cum de play de terre par nos brefs solom[2] la nature del graunt *Cape* et del petit.

7. Et ceux deforceours en les autres articles avauntditz soint ausi somouns. Et cum acun apparra en court, et die qe il trova soen auncestre seisi et ceo puse averrer, si cesse la demaunde sauntz bref, et ceux qi serrount assignez a pursure nos dreitz hastivement maundent[3] quere brefs de dreit, qe sunt appelez *Precipe quod reddat nobis*, sur les defourceours. Et si les brefs seynt purchacez sur acune chose appendaunt a nostre Coroune, cum sount auncienes demeynes, [4]si ne[4] soit nul tens limité en counte countaunt. Et si les tenauntz se voillent mettre en enqueste en fourme de graunt assise, a ceo ne soint point receuz sauntz le assent de nous et de noster conseyl, si[5] nos attournez en tel cas ne sachent les verditz

1. purpresturers *LNDS*. purpresturs *AM*. porprestors *W*. purprestures *GC*. *sim*. *F*.
2. *so NDAGMCW*. par *L*. solum les proces de *F*.
3. *so on erasure N*. *sim*. *A*. demaundent *LGSCF*. facent *M*.
4—4. *so NDAF*. Et si ne *L*. dounc ne *M*. sil *C*.
5. *so NDAMCF*. Et *L*.

Purprestures; proceeding by summons.

6. Let inquiry also be made of all kinds of purprestures made upon us of lands or franchises; and those who shall be presented as deforceors and purprestors by fresh force since proclamation of the eyre, shall be summoned to appear at a certain day to answer for the wrong they have done, and the process against them shall be as in a plea of land by our writs of great and little *Cape*.

Proceedings against deforceors by writ.

7. The deforceors also in the other articles aforesaid shall be summoned. And when any of them appears in court, and pleads that he found his ancestor seised and can prove it, the demand made without our writ shall be stayed, and those who are appointed to prosecute our right, shall immediately apply for a writ of right which is called a *Præcipe quod reddat nobis* against the deforceor; and if the writ be obtained for anything appendant to our crown, such as our ancient demesnes, let no time be limited in the count; and if the tenants desire to put themselves upon an inquest in form of the great assize, let them not be admitted thereto without the consent of us and our council, unless our attorneys in any such case are of opinion

Great assize, where allowed.

passer pur nous. Car nous sumus tenuz de repeler les dreitz de nostre Coroune a tort alienez; en les queus dreitz nul ne se deit eyder par excepcioun de lounge[1] tenure, mes list a chescun de sei ayder par garraunt voucher et par excepciouns [29.] renables, solom ceo qe dit serra entre les excepciouns. Et si brefs soint purchacez pur nous sur eschetes ou terres purchacez alienez, ou de autres choses qe ne soint mie apurteynauntes a la Coroune, en tel cas voloms nous qe hom ne counte mie de plus haut [2]tens qe en[2] bref de dreit, et qe prescripcioun de tens courge encountre nous cum encountre autre del poeple.

8. Nos eschetes defforcez soint demaundez par bref de eschete[3]. Et quant a sutes a nous sustretes, courgent destresces; car taunt de prerogative volums nous aver, pur les grauntz delays qe il i ad en brefs de custumes et de services. Quant a nos feez desmembrez et tenuz de nous par men pus le dreyn heyre, voloms nous qe tels feez soint pris en nostre meyn, et qe le viscounte respoigne des issues, et qe point ne soint renduz sauntz nous. Et quant as gardes et mariages a

Reg. brev. orig. 164 b, 165.

1. noun *C.* 2—2. *so R. sim. D.* tens qe *LNS.* tens qe [en] *A.* tens qe [de] *M.* temps qe de *G.* tens qe par *C.* tens qe le *W.* qe en *F.* 3. dreit *C.*

that a verdict will pass in our favour; for we are bound to recover such rights of our crown as have been wrongfully aliened; in which rights no man ought to aid himself by exception of long tenure, though he may by vouching to warranty, and by reasonable exceptions, as shall be hereafter set forth in treating of exceptions. And if the writ is obtained on our behalf concerning escheats or purchased lands which have been aliened, or other things which are not appurtenant to our crown, in such case the count ought not to go farther back than in a writ of right, and prescription shall run against us as well as against others.

No prescription against the right of the crown.

Otherwise, as to escheats and purchases.

8. Escheats deforced from us, shall be demanded by writ of escheat. And as to suits withheld from us, the proceeding shall be by distress, for this prerogative we claim on account of the great delays which occur in writs of customs and services. With respect to our fees dismembered and held of us by mesne since the last eyre, our will is, that they be taken into our hands, and the sheriff be answerable to us for the issues of them, and they shall not be restored without our leave. And as to wardships and marriages detained from us, we will that

Mode of proceeding in cases of escheat; of subtraction of suits; of dismemberment of fees; of subtraction of wardship or marriage.

Stat. Mert. (20 Hen. 3.) c. 6; Stat. West. 1. (3 Ed. I.) c. 22; Stat. West. 2. (13 Ed. I.) c. 35.

nous detenuz, voloms qe tauntost soint pledez tut sauntz bref, et courge la penaunce encountre les deforceurs solom le ordeynement de nos estatuz.

Glan. li. 7, c. 12; Brac. 88.

9. Et voloms qe chescun sache, qe si homme murge qi avera tenu de nous par fee de chivalerie ou[1] de graunt serjauntie, lequel qe il eyt tenu de auncienes demeynes de la [29 b.] Coroune, ou de eschetes, ou de purchace, qi[2] heritage chete apres sa mort a plusours fyles cum a un heyr, qe de totes les files voloms aver les mariages a totes les foiz qe eles serrount a marier. Et ausi de[3] totes vedues, qi seignurs averount tenu de nous en chief. Et si presenté soit, qe acune soit marié sauntz congé de nous, soit male soit femele, qi mariage a nous apent, tauntost soint seysiz en nostre mein totes lour terres, et les terres lour barouns, et qe le viscounte nous respoigne des issues, et sauntz nous ne lour soint point renduz.

Glan. li. 9. c. 11; Stat. de Big. (4 Ed. I.) c. 4.

10. En dreit de purprestures voloms nous qe les nusauntes[4] soint ostez a coustages [5]de ceux qi le averount fet[5], et les suffrables soint prises en nostre meyn, et la value par an soit

1. *so* *ARM.* et *LN.* e *CF.* 2. *so* *NDARM.* qe *LC.* de *F.* 3. *so* *NDAMF.* des *C.* a *L.* 4. nusaunces *LN.* *sim.* *DAR.* nusantes porprestures *W.* *sim.* *M.* 5—5. des prouours *A.* des fesours *W.* de purpresturs *M.* *sim.* *R.* des purpernours *C.*

proceedings shall be taken immediately without writ, and the penalty provided by our statutes shall be enforced against the deforceors.

Marriage; rights of the king as lord.

9. And we will have it known to all, that if any man dies who held of us by knights' fee, or by grand serjeanty,—whether he held of the ancient demesnes of the crown, or lands escheated, or purchased,—and his inheritance after his death descends among several daughters as one heir, we will have the marriage of all the daughters as often as they shall be to marry; and the like with regard to all widows, whose husbands held of us in chief; and if it be presented that any one, whether male or female, whose marriage belongs to us, has been married without our leave, let all their lands and the lands of their husbands be immediately seized into our hand, and the sheriff shall answer to us for the issues, and they shall not be restored to them without our leave.

Proceedings in case of purprestures.

10. As to purprestures our will is, that such as are nusances shall be removed at the costs of those who have made them, and such as may be permitted to remain shall be taken into

enroullé; et solom la discrecioun [1]des Thresorers[1] et des Barouns [2]de nos Eschekers[2] soint arenteez a fee ferme a ceux qi plus voderunt doner.

CHAPITRE XX. [XIX.]

Des[3] Fraunchises.

1. Soit ausi enquis, quels del counté cleyment retourn de nos brefs, ou garde de nostre gaole, ou la venue des Justices heyrauntz jekes en lour fraunchises, ou Corouner de eus' meismes, ou chateus des felouns, ou vewe de frauncplege, ou fraunchise de infangenthef et de outfangenthef et fourches, ou feires, ou[4] marchez, ou juyse de pillori ou de tumberel, ou de aver wrek de meer, ou de pleder en sa court pletz de vee de naam, ou de aver lestage, ou amerciement de ses tenauntz, ou travers, ou toluen, ou estray, ou murage, ou pontage, ou cheminage[5], ou garreyne en ses demeynes terres ou en autres, ou de estre quites de sute fere a noster Counté ou a tourns de

Brac. 117; Fle. 26.

[30.]

Stat. West. 1. (3 Ed. I.) c. 31; Fle. 26, 27.

1—1. del tresorer *M. sim. G.* 2—2. de nostre eschequere *M. sim. A.* del Eschequere *G.* 3. De claim de *M.* 4. so *DAMF.* ou *om. L.* e *C.* 5. chacentage *M.* kauceage *F.*

our hand, and the yearly value thereof enrolled; and according to the discretion of the treasurers and barons of our exchequers, they shall be let at fee farm to those who will give most for them.

CHAPTER XX.

Of Franchises.

1. Let inquiry also be made, what persons in the county claim to have return of our writs, or custody of our gaol, or that the Justices in eyre shall come into their franchises, or to have their own coroners, or chattels of felons, or view of frankpledge, or the franchise of infangthief and outfangthief and gallows, or fairs, or markets, or the execution of pillory or tumbrel, or to have wreck of sea, or to have pleas *de vetito namio* pleaded in their courts, or to have lestage, or amercements of their tenants, or traverse, or toll, or estray, or murage, or pontage, or cheminage[q], or warren in his demesne lands or in other lands, or to be quit of doing suit at our

Claim of franchises.

q *Murage* was a tax for the repair of town-walls; *pontage*, a toll taken on bridges, or for their repair; *cheminage*, a toll exacted for the use of a way through a forest; *traverse*, a toll paid for passing through the limits of a town or lordship; *lestage* or *lastage*, an impost in fairs and markets, calculated by the last, a measure by which several kinds of solid goods were sold. See Ducange, Glossary; Comyns's Digest, *s. v.* Toll.

viscounte ou a nos vewes de fraunceplege, ou de lestage, ou de murage, ou de pontage, ou autre fraunchise cleyme plus de autre.

2. Dunc nous voloms, qe les presentementz sour ces articles soint pledez en ceste manere; qe hom face venir les cleymauntz primes par renables somounses, [1]sicum dit serra entre

Post. l. 6. c. 5. s. 3.

les somounses[1]. Et puis si·la somounse soit tesmoigné, et il facent defaute, si soit la fraunchise prise en nostre meyn; et le viscounte nous respoigne des issues; et en tele manere demurgent en nostre meyn, jekes autaunt qe [2]ceux qi les cleyment en[2] veignent a respoundre. Et si ceux qi fount de-

[30 *b.*]

Post. c. 27. s. 3, 14.

faute eynt purpris sur nous[3] teles fraunchises de lour tort demeyne, si soint destreyntz, sicum dit serra en le chapitre des attachementz de trespas et de dette. Et cum il vendrount [4]en Court[4], et ne se[5] porount desafoeblir de teus personels torz fetz sur nous en desheritaunce de nous, soit agardé qe nous recoveroms la fraunchise, et il soint desheritez de la value, ou[6] en nostre merci.

3. Et si trové soit par mi lour respouns, qe lour auncestres

1—1. so *verb. DGARMWF om. LC. interl. N.* 2—2. teus cleymauns *M.* 3. so *NDGARMCWF.* par *add. LS.* 4—4. *om. M.* 5. so *NDSGARMCF.* se *om. L.* 6. seent *add. M.*

county court, or at sheriffs' tourns, or at our views of frankpledge, or to be quit of lestage, murage, or pontage, or who claim any kind of liberty more than other people.

Mode of proceeding by presentment, without writ.

2. We will therefore that the presentments upon such articles shall be pleaded in this manner. First, the claimants shall be ordered to appear by reasonable summons, as shall be mentioned in treating of summonses; and then if the summons be attested and they make default, the franchise shall be taken into our hand, the sheriff answering to us for the issues, and so remain in our hand until the claimants appear and answer. And if those who make default have of their own wrong usurped such franchises upon us, they shall be distrained in such manner as shall be mentioned in the chapter concerning attachments in trespass and debt; and when they appear in court, if they cannot clear themselves of the personal wrongs committed against us to our disherison, let it then be awarded, that we recover the franchise, and that they be disinherited of the value thereof, or be in our mercy.

3. But if it be found by their answer, that their ancestors

murirent seisiz, adunc voloms nous qe tiels ne soint mie tenuz a respoundre sauntz nos brefs, si il ne voillent. Mes tauntost facent nos attournez purchacer nos brefs sur eux del *Quo warranto*, par les queus brefs il soint premerement somouns, qe il veignent a respoundre a certeyns jours, a queus jours s' il fount defautes, si soint les fraunchises prises en nostre meyn, cum de sus est dit, et issint remeignent sauntz autre somouns fere jekes a taunt qe nous eyoums autrement ordeyné, ensint nequident qe mes ne eynt tele fraunchise par plevine, si tauntost [1]ne nous en[1] respoignent. Et si en lour respounse aleggent lounge possessioun, ou vouchent a garraunt autres qi alleggent lounge tenure, en tels cas voloms nous qe les jugementz remeignent al ordeynaunce de nous et de noster conseyl, lequel cele respounse soit continuance de tort fet a nostre Coroune, ou title de dreit as tenauntz.

Stat. Glouc. (6 Ed. I.); Stat de quo warr. (18 Ed. I.)

CHAPITRE XXI. [XX.]

[2]*De Plusours Tortz*[2]. [31.]

Cap. Escaet. (Stat. temp. inc.)

1. Puis soit enquis, [3]qi unqe[3] ount fet chastels et forcelettes

1—1. *so verb. F.* ne vous nous *L.* ne nous *NDSGC.* a nous ne *M.* nous en *AR.* a nous ny *W.* 2—2. Des chasteus e des autres forcelez *M.* 3—3. qe vnqe *L.* qonqe *S.* [qui] qe vnques *N.* qi qe vnqes *D.* *sim.* *GC.* qi *ABMCW.* ki *F.*

died seised, then they shall not be obliged to answer without our writs, unless they choose to do so; but our attorneys shall immediately cause our writs of *Quo warranto* to be issued against them. By such writs they shall first be summoned to come and answer at a day certain, at which if they make default, the franchises shall be taken into our hand, as aforesaid, and so remain without any other summons, until we shall otherwise direct; so that they shall never be permitted to replevy such franchise if they do not answer forthwith. If in their answer they allege long possession, or vouch others to warrant who allege long tenure, in such case judgment shall be stayed for the determination of us and our council, whether such answer be a continuance of the wrong done to our crown, or a title of right in the tenants.

Proceeding by writ of *Quo warranto*.

Plea of long possession.

CHAPTER XXI.

Of various wrongs.

1. In the next place let it be inquired what persons have

ou mesouns de pere charnelez et defensables; et[1] ceux qe ensi averount fet soint somouns qe il veignent respoundre et a moustrer si ren eynt de nous ou de nos auncestres par quei il avoynt coungé de teles forcelettes [2]fere ou[2] redrescer. Et si ren ne puisent moustrer del coungé, si soint eles prises en nostre meyn a tener a remanaunt[3] a nostre volunté ou[4] de les abatre.

Cap. Itin. (Stat. temp. inc.) c. 56.

2. Et dounc soit enquis des pountz et des chauceez[5] et des communs chemins brusez, ou autrement mal attirez, qi les dust repariller ou remender; et ceux qi serrount nomez el presentement soint attacheez de venir par personeles destresces. Et si [6]trové soit cum ceux vendrount en Court[6], qe aucun de eux teigne tenement de nous pur teus chemins amender, si soint tiels tenementz pris en nostre meyn, et le viscounte en soit chargé de nous respoundre des issues et de fere amender les defautes. Et en cas ou nul tenement serra tenu de nous pur tiels services fere, voloms nous qe ceux qi serrount a ceo tenuz et ne ount mie fet ceo qe il deyvent, qe

1. *so ND.* ou *L.* e *AMCWF. om. R.* 2—2. *so ND. sim. F.* fere ou *om. LGSMRW.* 3. *so CF.* ou *add. LNDARMW.* 4. *om. F.* 5. *so ND. sim. GAR.* chauceus *L.* chaleres *M.* cauces *C.* chasteaus *F.* 6—6. *so verb. NDGS. sim. AFC.* ceux vendrount en Court et troue soit *L.* troue soit com acun vendra en Court *M.*

Houses fortified without license.

built castles or fortlets or houses of stone, crenellated and defensible; and let those who have so done be summoned to come and answer, and show if they have any license from us or our ancestors for erecting or repairing such fortlets, and if they cannot produce any such license, let them be taken into our hand, either to be held by us or pulled down, according to our pleasure.

Bridges and roads neglected.

2. Afterwards, let inquiry be made of bridges and causeways, and of common highways destroyed, or otherwise in bad repair, who is bound to repair and amend them; and such as are named in the presentment shall be attached to appear by personal distresses. And if it be found on their appearance in court, that any of them hold tenements of us, for the repairing of such ways, let the said tenements be taken into our hand, and the sheriff be charged to answer us for the issues, and to cause the repairs to be done; and where there is no tenement held of us by the performing of such services, our will is, that the persons who are bound to repair the ways, and have not done what they ought, shall be in our mercy, and the

il soint en nostre merci; et soit comaundé au viscounte, qe il les face destreyndre par lour avers et par lour chateus, et les destresces retener, jekes autaunt qe il eynt les defautes amendez a totes les foiz qe mester serra. Reg. brev. orig. 154. [31 *b.*]

3. De ceux qi ount levé puis le premer jour del dreyn heyre fourches pillori ou tumberel soit enquis; et ceux qi de ceo serrount enditez soint maundez de venir a respoundre par destresces. Et cum il vendrount et ne porrunt mie moustrer pur euz suffisaunt garraunt, ne dedire qe ensi nel eynt fet, si soint agardez en nostre merci; et qe les juyses soint abatuz. De ceux ausi, qi ount tenu pletz de felonies et de graunt trespas fet encountre nostre pes, autres qe nos Justices et nos Corouners, soit enquis; et de tels qi ount tenu pletz de vee de naam ou de dette passaunt xl. s. ou de trespas passaunt mesmes la summe sauntz noster bref; et de ceux qi ount fraunchises de vewe de frauncplege et de infangenthef, et ne ount mie juyses appendauntes a teles fraunchises, par ount il ount teles fraunchises desuseez. Cap. Escaet. (Stat. temp. inc.) Mag. Cart. c. 17; Stat. Glouc. (6 Ed. I.) c. 8; Brac. 115 *b*, 116 *b*, 117; Fle. 28 (§ 86, 95.

4. Et queus tienent lour terres en garrennes[1] autres qe il ne

1. garraunteez *LND.* *sim.* *GS.* garenne *AR.* garannes *M.* gareines *C.* *sim.* *F.*

sheriff shall be commanded that he cause them to be distrained by their beasts and chattels, and detain the distresses until they have amended the defects, and this as often as it shall be needful.

3. Let inquiry also be made concerning those, who since the first day of the last eyre have erected any gallows, pillory, or tumbrel; and such persons as are indicted thereof shall be compelled by distress to come and answer; and if on their appearing, they can neither show sufficient warrant for what they have done, nor deny that they have done it, let them be awarded to be in our mercy, and let the instruments be pulled down. Let inquiry also be made concerning those, who, not being our Justices or our coroners, have held pleas of felony and of important trespasses committed against our peace; and concerning those who have held pleas *de vetito namio,* or of debt exceeding forty shillings, or of trespass exceeding the same sum without our writs. And also concerning those who have the franchises of view of frankpledge and of infangthief, and have not the instruments of punishment which belong to such franchises, whereby such franchises have become disused. Usurpation of judicial franchise. Excess of jurisdiction. Disuser of franchise.

4. Let inquiry also be made of those who keep their lands

avoint en lour demeyne cum de fee le jour de la confeccioun [1]de lour chartre de garrenne[1]; ou qe aucune autre fraunchise autrement ou plus largement eyt usee en nul point
[32.] qe solom ceo qe contenu est en sa chartre, par quei il deit tut perdre pur le outrage; et de ceux qi pernent fins pur coungé de beul[2] pleder; et de ceux qe tiegnent pletz de autres [3]qe de teus qe sount de lour[3] jurisdiccioun; et de touz ceux qe le poeple ount grevé par destresces encountre la ordinaunce de nous estatuz. Et ceux qi serrount de ceo encusez face le viscounte venir par destresces; et cum il serount venuz en Court, et ne porount dedire qe ensi nel eynt fet, ne de ceo porount estre garrauntiz, si soit lour court et lour garrennes prises en nostre meyn sauntz replevyr.

Stat. Marl. (52 Hen. III.) c. 11; Stat. West. 1 (3 Ed. I.) c. 8.

Stat. Marl. (52 Hen. III.) c 4; Stat. West. 1. (3 Ed. I.) c. 16; Fle. 28 (§ 88).

5. De[4] ceux ausi qi ount detenuz felouns ou provours en prisoun aylours qe en nostre gaole gardé par nos ministres demeynes outre un jour et une nuyt qe[5] les ount issi detenuz.

Ante, c. 12. s. 9. p. 47.

1—1. *so verb. F.* de lour garrauntie *L. sim. SG.* de lour chartre de garrauntie *NDC.* de lour lettre de garantie *AR.* de la chartre de lor garenne *M.* 2. beal *N.* bel *A.* beau *MCF.* 3—3. qe de lur *G.* qe de sa *M.* 4. *so NDARMCF.* et *L.* 5. *so M.* qi *LNDSARC.* qui *G.*

Excess of warren.

in warrens, other than those lands which they held in their demesne as of fee on the day of granting their charter of warren; or who have used any other franchise otherwise or more largely in any point than is warranted by the tenor of their charter whereby they ought to forfeit the whole for the abuse. Also of those who take fines for leave of beau pleader[r]; and of those who hold pleas of persons not within their jurisdiction, and of all such as have aggrieved the people by distresses contrary to the ordinance of our statutes. Those who are accused thereof, shall be distrained to appear by the sheriff; and if on their appearance in court, they can neither deny the fact, nor justify what they have done, their court and their warrens shall be taken into our hand without replevin.

Abuse of franchise. Fines for beau pleader.

Excessive distresses.

5. Inquiry shall also be made concerning those who have detained felons or provers above a day and a night in prison elsewhere than in our gaol under the custody of our own

Felons detained elsewhere than in king's prison.

r It was forbidden by Stat. Marl. c. 11, (confirmed by Stat. West. 1. c. 8) that arbitrary fines should be imposed in Justices' Eyre, County Court, or Court Baron, *pro pulchre placitando*, that is, for license to amend a defective plea. But when such fines had become settled by custom they were allowed. See Coke Inst. pt. ii. p. 122.

Et si nul, [1]mort en prisoun, eyt[1] esté enterré sauntz vewe del Corouner, adunc sois enquis par queus les enterrementz eynt esté fetz, et de la manere de lour mort. Et ceux qi serrount encusez del premer article et atteyntz si perdent lour feez de la garde; et si plus eynt trespassé, plus soint puniz. Et quant al autre article, soint les villez, ou teus cors ount esté enterrez, en nostre merci. Et si il i out nule felonie, si respoignent ceux qi serrount enditez. Ante, c. 12, s. 4.

6. Puis soit enquis de gorgs levez en ewes communes, et de ewes et chemins estoupez ou destrescez[2] ou en autre manere appropriez, et des cours des ewes trestournez; et de murs et de mesouns ou marlers ou fossez levez pres des communs chemins a nusaunce des passauntz, et [3]des fesours de[3] teles nusaunces; et des chemins nent enlargez; et de ceux qi ount sursis [4]de esveiller[4] solom nostre ordinaunce de nos[5] estatuz de Wyncestre; et de devises et boundes remuez. Et solom le presentement de ces articles soint les defautes redrescez par la vewe des presentours as custages des fesours, Stat. Wall. (13 Ed. I) c 4. [32 *b.*] Stat. Winton. (13 Ed. I.) c. 4. 5; Artic. super. cart. (18 Ed. I.) c. 17; Fle. 35.

1—1. Mort en prisoun et eyt *L.* morust en prisoun et eit *N.* *sim.* *AR.* qe moert en prison eyt *M.* moert en prison e eit *GS.* *sim.* *F.* 2. estraitez *C.* 3—3. *so* *G.* *sim.* *DF.* de fesours et de *L.* *sim.* *ARS.* des fesors e de *M.* 4—4. de veiler *M.* *sim.* *G.* des veilles *C.* 5. *so* *NDAR.* nostres *L.* noz *M.*

officers. And if any one has died in prison and been buried without view of the coroner, then let it be inquired who buried him, and of the manner of his death; and those who are indicted and convicted of the first article shall lose their wardenships in fee, and if their offence extends farther, shall be punished more; and as to the other article, the townships where such bodies were buried shall be in our mercy, and if there be any felony, let those who shall be indicted answer it. Death of prisoners.

6. Afterwards let inquiry be made concerning weirs raised in common waters, and concerning waters and highways stopped or straitened or in other manner appropriated, and concerning watercourses diverted; also of walls, houses, marlpits, or ditches, made near the common road to the nusance of passers by, and of those who are guilty of such nusances; and of highways not widened, and of those who have neglected to watch according to the ordinance of our Statutes of Winchester; and of landmarks and boundaries removed; and according to the presentment of these articles, let the abuses be redressed Weirs, nusances in water-courses, highways, &c.; watch neglected; landmarks removed.

et les fesours soint en nostre merci solom les damages qe il averount fet, et solum les profitz qe il [1]en ount euz[1].

Stat. Marl. (52 Hen. III.) c. 3; Fle. 26 (§ 56), 28 (§ 92).

7. Et ausi de ceux qi le jugement de nostre Court eynt a tort destourbez, qe les execuciouns ne poient estre fetes, ou qi les sequestres de nos ministres a escient eynt bruseez; et ceux soint puniz par prisoun ou[2] par fins.

Mag. Cart. c. 36; Stat de Relig. (7 Ed. I.); Stat. West. 2. (13 Ed. I) c. 32.

8. De terres ausi et de tenementz alienez en morte meyn; et celes terres et ceux tenementz[3] soint prises en nostre meyn sauntz[4] replever [5]a eus[5]; et jalemeyns les purchaceours soint en nostre merci, et chargez des issues puis un an apres le purchaz; et le viscounte soit chargez de nous en[6] respoundre des issues.

Brac. 116 b; Fle. 24 (§ 19, 20); Post. c. 31. s. 6.

9. De faus poys et de fauses mesures soit enquis et fet solom ceo qe serra dit en [7]le chapitre[7] des mesures.

Stat. Circ. ag. (13 Ed. I.); Brac. 402 b.

10. Soit ausi enquis des clers qi teignent pletz des layes gentz de autre chose qe de testament ou de matrimonie ou des

[33.] dimes, ou qi eynt jugez nul lay homme en Court Cristiane a nule contribucioun de argent, [8]ou en nule autre manere ou[8]

Ante, c. 5. s. 4. point qe es pointz avaunt ditz, ou qi ount layes gentz a tort

1—1. so *M.* sim. *FW.* ount de eux *LD.* sim. *NCAB.* 2. e *AMCF.* 3. so *SGAMCF.* alienez en morte meyn *add. LN.* 4. les *add. F.* 5—5. so *LNSG.* *om. AMCF.* 6. so *NM.* a *LAF.* *om. C.* 7—7. so *NAMF.* le *om. L.* les chapitres *C.* 8—8. en nul autre *AMF.* ou nul autre *C.*

by view of the presentors at the cost of the offenders, and let the guilty be amerced in proportion to the damage they have done and the profit they have received therefrom.

Disturbance of executions and sequestrations.

7. Concerning those also who have tortiously disturbed the judgments of our Court, so that execution thereof cannot be made, or have knowingly broken the sequestrations of our officers; and let such be punished by imprisonment or fine.

Mortmain.

8. Also concerning lands and tenements alienated in mortmain; and let such lands and tenements be taken into our hand without replevin; and the purchasers also shall be in our mercy and charged with the issues from one year after the purchase, and the sheriff shall be answerable to us for such issues.

False measures.

9. Let inquiry be made of false weights and measures, and let such order be taken as shall be mentioned in the chapter concerning measures.

Abuses of ecclesiastical courts.

10. Let inquiry also be made of clerks who hold pleas of lay people concerning other matters than wills, marriages, or tithes, or who have adjudged any layman in Court Christian to any pecuniary payment, or in any other manner or case than

excumengez, et a tort fet prendre et enprisouner; et ausi[1] de ceux qi autres ount grevez par [2]billes et autres somouns doubles[2] a un jour en divers leus par malice; et touz ceux soint puniz par prisone et par fin.

Stat. Wall. (12 Ed. I.) c. 4; Visus franc. pleg. (Stat. temp. inc.); Fle. 113 (§ 35). Stat. judic. pill. (temp. incert.); Stat. de pistoribus (temp. incert.)

11. Et puis soit enquis de ceux qi ount pris thefbote; de redobeours de dras demorauntz hors de bourgs et hors de citeez; et ausi de tannours [3]qi se fount tannours et bouchers qi vendent[3] chars par peces; et des blauncheours des quirs des bestes emblez pur ceo qe il ne fuessent mie conuz; et ausi de keus[4] qi quisent chars suceines[5] ou emblez a escient, ou autre manere de chars contraries a saynté de[6]

1. *so ARMF.* autres *LND.* 2—2. *so L.* baill' par double somouns *ND.* billes par double somons *GS.* bulles par doubles somons e *AR.* bulles par doubblez somonses *M. sim. W.* baillifs par dubble somouns *C.* bulles par double somonse *F.*. 3—3. *so verb. D.* et de Bouchers qi vendent *L. sim. GS.* [qui se sunt tannours *interl.*] et bouchiers qe vendent *N.* qi se fount e tannors e bouchers : ou bouchers e cous a vendre *AR.* qe sunt e tannours e buchiers e keus a vendre *M.* ke sunt tannurs. e de bochers e keus a vendre *F.* qe fount enteinz de bouchers qe vendent *C.* 4. *so MF.* ceux *LND.* ceus *AR.* 5. *so D. so corr. N.* sucentes *L.* sorceines *A.* sorseines *R.* s uscenez *G.* sursaneez *M.* sursannez *C.* sossiners *F.* 6. cors de *add. C.*

in the articles aforesaid, or who have excommunicated lay people wrongfully, or wrongfully caused them to be apprehended and imprisoned; of those also who have aggrieved others by maliciously serving them with two bills[s] or summonses for the same day at different places; and let all such be punished by imprisonment and fine.

11. Moreover let inquiry be made of those who have taken thefbote[t], of menders of clothes dwelling out of boroughs or cities[u]; and also of tanners who follow the trade both of a tanner and of a butcher retailing meat[x]; and of those who blanch the skins of beasts which have been stolen, that they may not be known again; also of cooks who Thefbote, &c.

Stale meat.

[s] The text here is doubtful. The mention of abuses of ecclesiastical courts immediately preceding lends some support to the reading *bulles*, which appeared in the former printed editions of Britton. Bracton (f. 402 *b.*) has a form of prohibition issued to an ecclesiastical court from proceeding in a cause concerning an advowson under the authority of a letter of the Pope.

[t] 'Taking thefbote' is explained in a note in MS. *N*, as equivalent to letting thieves escape for reward. In the Statutes of Wales it is thus defined: 'De Thefbote, hoc est de emenda furti capta sine consideratione curiæ Regis.' (Stat. Wall. (12 Ed. 1.) c. 4.) The word appears to have originally signified the legal *bote* or composition for theft; and then to have been applied to the illegal compounding of theft, or taking money to maintain or connive at such offenders. See the Glossaries of Ducange and Spelman; Termes de la ley, *s. v.* Theftbote; Coke, Inst. iii. 134.

[u] 'It is forbidden,' says the commentator in MS. *N*, 'that any redubber of clothes or tanner or bleacher of skins (i. e. *Wyttawiares*), shall dwell elsewhere than in cities or boroughs, to avoid the mischief of receiving stolen goods. For a receiver may be the occasion of great wickedness, as is commonly said: Ne is non thef wythouten rescet.' As to whitetawers see Stat. Wall. (12. Ed. I.) c. 4; Cowel's Interpreter, *s. v.* Whitawarii.

[x] This restriction of trade was at a later time established by Statute. Stat. 1 Jac. I. c. 22. s. 3.

Mag. Cart. c. 21. homme pur vendre par peces; et ausi de forstallours; et de pernours des cariages a noster oes plus qe mester nous serroit, et de touz trespassours encountre la forme de nos estatuz; et [1]des messagers et des autres qi vount grever le poeple pur ceo Stat. West. I. (3 Ed. I.) c. 34. qe il se avowent a tels ovek qi il[1] ne sunt mie; et de ceux qi trevent [2]et countent noveleries et[2] mensonges de nous; et [3]des escorgeours[3] ou toundours des berbiz; et de ceux qi ount Cap. itin. (Stat. temp. inc.) c. 59; Brac. 117 b; Fle. 25 (§ 44). [33 b.] curru en autri garreynes sauntz coungé; et de touz hamsoknes, et de[4] saunc felounosement espaundu puis le dreyn heyre. Et [5]a chescun presentement[5] soit mis hastif remedie ovek[6] punisement de vie ou de autre[7] membre ou de autre peyne.

Brac. 117; Fle. 25 (§ 33). 12. Puis soit enquis de ceux qi ne vindrent pas devaunt nous ou devaunt nos Justices le premer jour del heyre, sicum Cap. itin. nov. (Stat. temp. inc.) c. 30; Fle. 28 (§ 91). il furent summons, et ceux soint en nostre merci; et ceux ausi qi lour tenement alienerent encountre le heyre, qe il ne fussent en jurez ne en enquestes.

13. Puis soit enquis des usages usez en le countee autres qe

1—1. de ceus qi se fount messagers e vnt greuo le poeple qi dient qil sount od granz genz o *AR.* 2—2. controueures e conteks e fount *A.* *sim.* *R.* e countent *HC.* contek e noueleries *F.* 3—3. descorgers *LS.* de escorchers *N.* des corchers *A.* de escorchoures *M.* des escorcheurs *C.* de cheueres *F.* 4. *so G.* de *om.* *LSM.* 5—5. al presentement de chescun article *M.* 6. e neqedent *R.* *sim.* *F.* ouesques due *C.* 7. autre *om.* *AC.*

knowingly cook stale or stolen meat or any kind of flesh hurtful to the health of man for the purpose of retailing it; also of forestallers; and of those who take up more carts for our use than we need; and of all other offenders against the form of our statutes; also concerning messengers and others, who go about aggrieving the people by representing themselves as False news. in the service of those with whom they are not; of those also who invent and report rumours and falsehoods concerning us; of those also who flay or shear sheep; and of those who have coursed in others' warrens without leave; also concerning all Hamsoken. hamsokens, and blood feloniously shed since the last eyre; and upon every such presentment, let a speedy remedy be applied with punishment either of life or limb or other penalty.

Default of appearance at eyre. 12. Further, let inquiry be made concerning those who did not appear before us or before our Justices the first day of the eyre according to their summons, and let such be amerced. Evasion of duties as freeholder. The like concerning those who alienated their tenements against the eyre, that they might not be summoned upon juries or inquests.

13. Let inquiry also be made of customs used in the county

comune ley, queus il sount, et s' il i eyt nul contrariaunt a la commune ley, si soit defendu, s' il ne soit par nous ou par nos predecessours confermez.

CHAPITRE XXII. [XXI.]

De [1]*Ministres*[1].

1. De nos eschetours soit ausi enquis, et de sutheschetours[2], queles terres il eynt seysez en nostre meyn en cel counté puis le dreyn heyre, et de chescune terre issi seysie soit enquis severaument la verreye value del profit qe chescune parcele lour respoundi [3]ou a autre[3] poeit aver respoundu [4]el tens de cele[4] seysine; et ausi del wast par eux fet en parcs et vivers de veneysoun et de pessoun [5]et des coniys[5], et de autre destruccioun par eux fete en garrennes en bois et en totes choses, et de la verreye value; et ausi des chateus trovez en teus tenementz ou aylours par eux seisiz de tut le tens qe teles terres demorerent en lour garde. Cap. Escaetriæ. (Stat. temp. inc.); Cap. itin. nov. (Stat. temp. inc.) c. 32; Fle. 26 (§ 60, 61). [34.]

2. Et ausi soit enquis de toutes lour prises a noster oes, et

1—1. Eschetours *M.* 2. so *D.* *sim.* *ARMCWF.* Suthchetours *LN.* 3—3 so *ND.* ou autre *LAR.* e al autre *M.* e as autres *C.* e aultre *W.* 4—4. sil eust eu la *AR.* 5—5. *om.* *M.* et de conys *ND.* coninz *AR.* e des Conyns *G.* *sim.* *S.* e des coniers *C.* e des coningers *F.*

differing from the common law, and what they are, and if there be any repugnant to the common law, let them be prohibited, unless they have been confirmed by us or our predecessors. Customs contrary to common law.

CHAPTER XXII.

Of our Officers.

1. Let inquiry be made concerning our escheators and under escheators, and what lands they have seized into our hand in the county since the last eyre; and of the several lands so seized let a separate inquiry be made of the true value of the profits which every part returned to them or might have returned to others during the time of their possession; also of waste committed by them in parks and in vivaries, of venison, of fish, and of rabbits, and of other destruction done by them in warrens and woods and in other things, and of the value thereof; and of the chattels found in such tenements or elsewhere and taken by them during the time the lands remained in their custody. Account of lands seized by the king's escheators; of waste done; and of chattels found therein.

2. Inquiry is also to be made of all their receipts to our

Brac. 117, 117 b; Fle. 26 (§ 61–64). a lour, cum bien il eynt pris pur vedues femmes dower ou de suffrer estre dowez, ou suffrer les enfauntz heyrs oveke les meres, et ausi pur terre estendre meyns suffisauntment, ou pur tesmoigner nos gardes et nos mariages estre de meyndre pris de la verreye value, ou de rien conceler qe a profit de nous dust estre[1], ou de procurer ou de suffrer enqueste fausement passer sur les ages de nos gardes, ou en autre chose, en damage de nous. Et ceo qe serra presenté de eux soit enroulé et enveyé al Escheker, et iloekes soint les presentementz determinez. Les jugementz neqedent de lour graunt trespas reservoms a noster ordeynement.

Cap. itin. nov. (Stat. temp. incert.) c. 36.

Stat. Excest. (temp. incert.) 3. [2]Puis soit enquis des prises et des fraudes des Corouners et [3]de lour clers et lour ministres, solom ceo qe contenu est en nos estatuz de Excestre. Et ausi des Viscountes, et de autres ministres, qi pur louwer ou pur priere ou pur amité de nul homme eynt concelé felonies fetes en lour baillies, ou suffertz[4] les prisouns despris, en fraunchises ou dehors, et ount

Fle. 28 (§ 104). [34 b.]

1. *so LGS.* estre [tourne *interl.*] *N.* estre tourne *D.* returner *AR.* turner *M.* tourner *C.* torner *F.* 2. *In M. a new chapter commences here, with a rubric:* De coroners e de viscontes. *sim. in G.* 3. de visconte *add. M.* 4. soffrent *ND.* sustrez *F.*

Of money taken by the king's officers.

use and their own use, how much they have taken for endowing widows, or for suffering them to be endowed, or for permitting heirs being infants to continue with their mothers; and also for making insufficient extents of land, or for certifying our wardships and our marriages to be of less than their real value, or for concealing anything which ought to turn to our profit; or for procuring or suffering false inquests to pass upon the ages of our wards, or in any other thing, to our prejudice; and let such presentments as shall be made concerning these officers be enrolled and transmitted to the exchequer, and there determined. We reserve however the judgments upon great offences committed by them for our own determination.

Frauds and exactions of coroners.

3. In the next place let inquiry be made concerning the fees taken and frauds committed by coroners, their clerks, and officers, according to that which is contained in our Statutes of Exeter. Also of sheriffs and other officers, who for reward or entreaty or out of friendship for any man have concealed felonies committed in their bailiwicks, or suffered prisoners to remain unapprehended, whether within franchises

Misconduct of sheriffs.

lessé les nent plevisables prisouns par meynprise, et les plevisables detenuz. Stat. West. I. (3 Ed. I.) c. 15; Brac. 117 b; Fle. 28 (§ 97, 98).

4. Et ausi cum bien des prisouns ount eschapé de nostre prisoun ou de autri garde en cel counté puis le dreyn heyre, et queus, et hors de qi garde, et queus chateus il avoint, et ou lour chateus sunt devenuz, et en qi meyns lour terres sount devenuz, et cum bien eles vaillent par an, et qi en ad eu les profitz puis lour eschap, et de quel tens; et cum bien des provours eynt esté eschapez, et hors de qi garde, et par qi assent tels prisouns eynt esté eschapez. Et pur chescun eschap hors de la garde le viscounte soit le viscounte amerciez a C. s., et pur eschap de provour soit comaundé a la prisoun[1] a nostre volounté. Et ausi soit enquis de defautes des gaoles, queles defautes il i ad, et qi deit les defautes amender, et par [2]qi defaute[2] tels eschaps eynt esté fetz. Cap. itin. nov. c. 27; Ante, c. 12. s. 2.

5. Et ausi des viscountes et de lour clercs et de lour ministres, qi fausement et malicieusement ount fet provours apeler leales gentz, ou les eynt desturbez de apeler [3]acun coupable[3]; Cap. itin nov. c. 26; Fle. 29 (§ 109.)

1. e reint *add. C.* 2—2. *so AMCF.* qi teles defautes *L. sim. NDS.* queles defautes *G.* 3—3. *so NM. sim. DCF.* les acuns coupables *L.* les coupables *A.*

or without, or have let to mainprise prisoners who were not bailable, and have detained others who were bailable.

4. Likewise, how many prisoners have escaped out of our prison or from the custody of any others in that county since the last eyre, and who they are, and out of whose custody they escaped, what chattels they had, and what is become of their chattels, into whose hands their lands are come, what they are worth a year, and who has received the profits thereof since their escape, and from what time; also how many provers have escaped, and out of whose custody, and by whose consent such prisoners have escaped. And for every escape out of the custody of the sheriff, let the sheriff be amerced one hundred shillings, and for the escape of a prover, let him be committed to prison during our pleasure. Let inquiry also be made concerning the defects of gaols, what they are, and who ought to repair them, and through whose default such escapes have happened. Escape of prisoners. Amercement of sheriff. Defects of gaols.

5. Also concerning sheriffs, their clerks and officers, who have falsely and maliciously made provers appeal innocent people, or hindered them from appealing the guilty; and let Misconduct of sheriffs in appeals.

et touz les coupables soint comaundez a la prisoun a nostre volounté. Et ausi des viscountes qi a escient ount lessé lour hundrez a ferme a gent qi rien ne avoint a trop hautes fermes pur le poeple a tort grever en deverses maneres; et ceux soint amerciez.

[35.] Cap. itin. nov. (Stat. temp. inc.) c. 21; Fle. 29 (§ 108).

Fle. 29 (§ 114). 6. Et ausi des viscountes et des baillifs, qi eynt levé deners des chateus as felouns, ou de eschaps des prisouns, ou des amercimentz pur defautes fetes devaunt Corouners ou eschetours ou autres generaus enquerours, ou pur noun sute des apels de felonie, ou de meynpernours de meynprise trové et faillie en brefs de manace, ou pur noun sute de heu et de crie levé, ou [1]pur tresor ou[1] wrek de meer ou esturgoun ou baleyne trové et aliené; les queus amercimentz ne list a nuli lever sauntz nos brefs de la verte ceire par estretes de noster Escheker; et ceux soint puniz par fyn.

Stat. de militibus (6 Ed. I.); Brac. 117; Fle. 28 (§ 94). 7. Et ausi des viscountes qi eynt pris fins et amerciementz des gentz de lour baillie, qe il ne soint destreintz de estre chivalers; et en cel cas sount amerciables; ou qi eynt meyn-

1—1. so *NDAMC.* *sim. F.* purchasour de *LG.* *sim. S.*

such as are guilty of this offence be imprisoned during our pleasure. Also concerning sheriffs who have knowingly let their hundreds to farm to persons of no substance at too high a rent, to the wrongful oppression of the people in divers manners; and let such be amerced.

Leasing of hundreds to unfit persons.

Misconduct of sheriffs in levying money without authority. 6. Also concerning sheriffs and bailiffs who have levied money of the chattels of felons, or for the escape of prisoners, or from amercements for defaults made before coroners or escheators or other general inquirers, or for non-prosecution in appeals of felony, or from mainpernors who failed in producing the persons delivered to them on writs of menace, or for not pursuing the hue and cry raised, or for treasure or wreck of sea, or sturgeon or whale found and carried away, which amercements no man ought to levy without our writs of green wax by estreats of our exchequer; and let such offenders be punished by fine.

Exactions for evading knighthood. 7. Also concerning sheriffs, who have taken fines and amercements from persons in their bailiwick, that they might not be distrained to become knights[y], in which case the sheriffs are

[y] As to the date attributed in the margin above to the so called Statutum de militibus, which has been commonly ascribed to 1 Ed. II., and the whole subject of compulsory knighthood, see a paper by the Editor in the Archæologia, vol. xxxix. p. 216.

tenu quereles et parties pledauntes, et procuré fauses enquestes par quei dreiture fust arerié; et en ceo cas soint puniz par fyn; ou qi deus foiz ount levé un amerciement, ou de deus hommes portauntz un noun, ou plus levé qe contenu ne fust en les estretes de noster Escheker; ou si nul viscounte eit procuré le remuement de nul Corouner par nos brefs purchaceez par fauses suggestiouns; et en tel cas sunt il amerciables; ou si nul viscounte par malice eyt fet demorer en prisoun aucun qe il dust aver fet venir devaunt[1] nos Justices a la deliveraunce de nostre gaole; et en cest cas sount a punir par prisoun et par fyn.

Cap. itin. (Stat. temp. inc.) c. 50, 51; Brac. 117 b; Fle. 28 (§ 99–101).

[35 b.]

8. Ou si aucun viscounte eyt par malice fet prendre plus des avers pur nostre dette, ou pur autri, qe a la vaillaunce de la dette; ou s' il eyt pris bestes des charues et motouns ou berbez et vessele et mounture ou robes et de eynz mesoun, la ou autre destresce poeit trover suffisauntment [2]et hors de mesoun[2]; et si aucun eyt fet chacer teles destresces hors del fee; ou si il ne voillent suffrer qe teles bestes[3] fuissent puz et sustenues par les serjauntz et a les custages de ceux a qi

Districc. de Scacc. (Stat. temp. inc.); Brac. 217, 217 b; Fle. 28 (§ 88), 103, 104.

Fle. 29 (§ 118).

Fle. 28 (§ 87).

1. nous ou deuaunt *C.* 2—2. de hors *M.* de hors meison *G.* 3. destresces *M.*

amerciable; or that have maintained suits or the parties to actions, and have procured false inquests, whereby justice has been hindered, in which case they shall be punished by fine; or that have levied one amercement twice, or of two persons bearing the same name, or have levied more than was contained in the estreats of our exchequer; or if any sheriff has procured the removal of any coroner by obtaining our writs upon false suggestions, in which case they are amerciable; or if any sheriff through malice has kept any man in prison whom he ought to have brought before our Justices at our gaol delivery, and in this case they are to be punished by fine and imprisonment.

Maintenance.

Amercement twice levied.

Removal of coroner.

Prisoner detained after gaol delivery.

8. Or whether any sheriff through malice has taken more cattle for our debt, or another's, than the amount of the debt, or whether he has distrained beasts of the plough, or wethers, or ewes, or household utensils, or riding-horses, or apparel, or things within doors, when other sufficient distress might have been found, and that without doors; and whether any one has caused such distresses to be driven out of the fee[z], or whether they would not suffer such beasts to be fed and supported

Excessive or improper distress.

z It is possible some words may have been lost in this sentence. The rule was, that distresses were not to be driven out of the *county*, or *taken* elsewhere than in the lord's fee. Stat. Marl. (52 Hen. III.) c. 2, 4, 15, Stat. West. I. (3 Ed. I.) c. 16.

'eles furent,' pur mal des uns et pur gayner des autres; et en ceo cas sunt il amerciables; et qi ount tenu teles destresces[2] enparkez[3] outre xv. jours.

Fle. 28 (§ 89). Prohib. de art. cleri. (Stat. temp. inc.)

9. Et queus ount suffert pleder en Court Cristiene autres pletz qe de testament ou de matrimonie, ou de pure espiritualté sauntz dener prendre de lay homme, ou suffert lay homme jurer devaunt ordinarie.

Cap. itin. nov. c. 19; Fle. 29 (§ 107). [36.] Fle. 28 (§ 93, 105). Stat. West. 2. (13 Ed. I.) c. 38.

10. Et qi ount pris fins pur reddiseisines, ou pur surcharge[4] de pasture, et de purpresture; et qi eynt pris annuels feez ou robes, ou autre guerdoun, pur suffrer aucun tort estre fet a nous. Et ausi des viscountes et des bailliffs qi ount plus de gentz somouns qe mester ne serroit en jureez et en enquestes, pur les uns grever et des autres prendre lower pur suffrer les demorer a lour mesouns, et pur uns remuer hors des panels et autres mettre[5]; et de ceux ausi qi ount mis en jureez et en enquestes gentz malades et crampuz de goute et mahaigneez et passetz le age de lxx. aunz, et gentz nent demorauntz el pays, et gentz loynteins qe[6] meins dusent saver de la verité de

1—1. il yl estoyent *M.* 2. bestes *A.* 3. *So NDS. sim. C.* ou enparkez *L.* en Parkes *MF.* 4. surcarke *M.* surcharger *AF.* 5. mettre leynz *M.* remettre *F.* 6. e ke *F.*

by the servants and at the cost of the owners, to the injury of one party and to the advantage of the other; and in these cases they are amerciable; and who have kept such distresses impounded above fifteen days.

Usurpations of Courts Christian.

9. Of those also who have suffered other pleas to be pleaded in Court Christian besides such as relate to wills, matrimony, and subjects merely spiritual, wherein no money is taken from any of the laity, or have suffered a layman to take oath before the ordinary.

Corruption and bribery of sheriffs and officers. Misconduct of sheriffs respecting juries.

10. It is also to be inquired who have taken fines for redisseisins, or for surcharge of pasture, and for purprestures; and who have accepted annual fees or robes or other bounty for suffering any wrong to be done to us. Also concerning sheriffs or bailiffs, who have summoned more people upon juries and inquests than were necessary, with intent to oppress some of them and take bribes from others for leave to stay at home, or to remove some from the panel and put others thereon; concerning those also who have put persons on juries or inquests who were sick, or disabled by gout, or maimed, or passed seventy years of age, or persons not resident in the county, or persons who live remote and may be supposed to

la chose dunt debat avera estee; et qi ausi ount mis en panels gentz qe meyns tenent de terre qe xl. southe[1] pur travailer hors del counté, ou meyns de xx. southe[2] pur estre en enquestes et en jurez en mesme le counté.

11. Et ausi soit enquis des baillifs fesauntz scotalles pur coiller argent des poveres gentz, et de ceux qi coillent garbes en Aust, agneus et purceus, et issi vount begaunt, et les fount norir en lour baillies al grevaunce del poeple.

Carta de foresta (2 Hen. III.) c. 7; Cap. itin. c. 45; Brac. 117 *b*; Fle. 28 (§ 102, 103), 91 (§ 25).

[36 *b*.]

12. Et ausi soit enquis de viscountes, qi plus de deus foiz par an eynt tenu lour tourns; [3]et de lour Hundreders[3] et des autres, qi plus de deus foiz par an eynt tenuz lour vewes de frauncplege. Et ausi des viscountes meyns de dreit responauntz des issues forfetes; [4]et en teu[4] cas sount amerciables solom la double value del profit qe il ount eu.

Leg. Cnut. l. 18; Leg. Hen. I. vii. 4, viii. 1; Fle. 29 (§ 106.)

13. Et ausi des Justices viscountes hundreders et autres qi ount Courz, et des seneschaus et des baillifs, qi par malice

Fle. 28 (§ 96).

1. *so L.* southes *D.* soudeez *M G. sim. S.* souze *A.* souz *C.* sodeyes *F.* 2. *so L G.* southes *D.* soudeez *MS.* souze *A.* souz *C.* sodeyes *F.* 3—3. *So L N D S. sim. F.* E des Hundreders *G.* e lor hundrez *W.* de lour Hundredez *M.* 4—4. en touz teus *M C. sim. A F.*

have less knowledge of the truth of the matter in dispute; of such also as have put on the panel persons holding land under forty shillings to do duty out of the county, or under twenty shillings to be on inquests and juries in the county.

11. Let inquiry be also made concerning bailiffs who make scotales[a], in order to collect money of poor people, and concerning such as collect sheaves in harvest and lambs and young pigs, and thus go about begging, and have them fed in their bailiwick, to the grievance of the people.

Scotales and exactions of bailiffs.

12. Further let inquiry be made concerning sheriffs who have held their tourn oftener than twice a year; and of their hundreders and others, who have held their views of frankpledge oftener than twice a year[b]; also concerning sheriffs who have answered to us less than they ought for issues forfeited, in which case they are amerciable in double the value of the profit they have made.

Tourns held more than twice a year.

False accounts by sheriffs.

13. The like of Justices, sheriffs, hundreders, and others who have courts, and of the stewards and bailiffs of the same, who through malice have procured suits to be stirred up

Abuses of Courts.

[a] Scotales (*A.S. scot*, payment, *eale*, ale) appear to have been meetings for drinking, which were in some way made the occasion of extortion by foresters and other bailiffs. See Ducange, Gloss, *s. v.* Scotallium; Capitula itineris (printed among the Statutes of the Realm), c. 45. *var. lect.*; Fleta, p. 28 (§ 102).

[b] By the Anglo-Saxon customs hundred courts were held twelve times a year for other business, but twice only for filling up the tithings. (See leg. Hen. I. l. vii. s. 4; l. viii. s. 1.)

eynt procuré pletz estre meuz vers aucun pur ly grever, ou fet purchacer a tort nos brefs de dreit en lour [1]Court, pur lour Court et[1] lour amerciementz encrestre, ou amercié gent par lour taxacioun demeyne, ou autrement qe par lour piers, outre les quantitez des trespas encountre la ordinaunce de la graunt chartre. Et ausi de totes torcenouses prises fetes par nos ministres de travers ou de tolune, sicum pur lestage pontage murage et chauciage[2]; [3]en teus pointz[3] sunt il amerciables al double qe les damages amounterount; des trespas des Justices neqedent ne voloms nous mie qe nul jugement soit ordeyné sauntz nous.

Mag. Cart. c. 14. Brac. 116 b; Fle. 27 (§ 77). Fle. 27 (§ 83, 84).

14. Et ausi des prises fetes par nos chasteleyns, et autres, qi se fount nos pernours de vitayle ou de autre chose, par qi teles prises ount esté fetes, et a quel damage, et de quels gentz; et en tel cas nous voloms qe nul soit garraunti par continuaunce de seysine en damage del poeple, qe gré ne soit

Mag. Cart. c. 19. Stat. West. 1. (3 Ed. I.) c. 7; Brac. 117, 117 b; Fle. 25 (§ 32), 27 (§ 78).

[37.]

1—1. *so verb. CW.* Courts pur lour Courts e *M. sim. F.* Court et pur *LND.* Court e *SG.* Court pur *AR.* 2. cheminage et chauciage *D.* cheminage *F.* 3—3. en ceo cas *M.*

against any to oppress them, or have caused our writs of right to be brought wrongfully in their court, in order to increase their court and the amercements of it; or have amerced people according to their own assessing, or in any other manner than by their peers, beyond the proportion of their offence, contrary to the ordinance of the Great Charter. And of all wrongful payments taken by our officers of traverse or of toll, as of lestage, pontage, murage, or causeage, in which case they are amerciable in double the amount of the damages. But as to trespasses of Justices we will that no judgment shall be given without our order.

Amercements contrary to the Great Charter.

Wrongful toll, &c.

Justices answerable to the king only.

14. Also of prises or seizures made by our castellans, and others who take upon themselves to be our takers of victuals[c] or other things; let it be inquired by whom such prises have been taken, and to what damage, and of what people; and in such case our will is, that none be warranted by continuance of seisin to the damage of the people, but satisfaction be made

Illegal prises by castellans and others.

Purveyance.

[c] It is remarkable that the word 'purveyor,' which was afterwards in such ill repute, does not appear to have been used at this time, although the abuse of purveyance was at its height. No grievance is more frequently mentioned in the ancient statute-book. By a statute of Edward III. (36 Ed. 3, c. 2) it was enacted that the very name of purveyor (le haignous noun de purveour) should be abolished, and the officers called 'buyers' (achetours.) But the name very frequently makes its appearance in the statutes of subsequent reigns.

fet a touz, ne qe nul ne soit pernour de nule manere de prise pur nous, s' il ne eyt de ceo nos lettres qe de ceo facent especiale mencioun.

15. Et ausi des viscountes et de touz nos autres ministres Justices et Corouners et autres, qe gentz de religioum et autres gentz grevent par surcharges de lour venues pur herberger ovekes eux sovent a autri custages oveke trop de frape des gentz, et par sojourner de lour gentz et de lour chivaus et de lour chiens, ou autrement par empromptez de lour chivaus ou de cariage ou de deners, ou par begger[1] merrym ou fustz[2] ou autre chose a eus ou a aukun de lour meyné ou de lour amis; et en cest cas soint puniz par fins.

Stat. West. 1 (3 Ed. I.) c. 1; Fle. 27 (§ 68, 74); 29 (§ 116).

16. Et ausi de nos serjauntz et de nos attornez assignez a nos dreitures pursure et defendre, si par favour ou en acune manere ount lessé et suffert acun graunt seignur del counté ou autre demorer en seysine de acune fraunchise ou de autre chose corporale a nous aporteynaunt de dreit; et ceux soint puniz par fins. Et ausi de ceux qi ount pardoné, ou fet ouster de roulle, ou lessé de mettre en roule, fins et amerciementz

1. beguigner *AB.* 2. so *F.* feez *LGS.* *sim. MW.* fust ou feyn *D.* feins *AB.* busche *Y.* [ou fustz *interl.*] ou feyn *on erasure N.*

to all, nor shall any one make any manner of prises for us, unless he has the authority of our letters making express mention thereof.

15. Of sheriffs also and all other our officers, Justices, coroners, and others, who shall oppress religious communities and other persons, overburdening them by often coming with too great a crowd of people to lodge with them at their cost, or by quartering servants, horses, and dogs upon them, or else by borrowing horses or carts or money of them, or by begging timber or wood or other things for themselves or some of their household or friends; in which case let them be punished by fine.

Abuse of hospitality of convents.

16. Let inquiry also be made concerning our serjeants and our attorneys assigned to prosecute and defend our rights, whether through favour or otherwise they have permitted or suffered any great lord of the county or other to continue in seisin of any franchise, or any corporeal thing belonging of right to us; and let such be punished by fine. Also concerning those who have remitted, or have caused to be put out of the roll, or have omitted inserting in the roll, fines

Frauds of serjeants and attorneys of the king.

Frauds in enrollment of fines.

[37 b.] a nous aporteynauntz; et ceux soint reyntz et oustez hors de la Court a remanaunt, et lour mestres puniz a nostre volunté.

Stat. West. 1. (3 Ed. I.) c. 25, 28; Brac. 117; Fle. 27 (§ 81). 87.

17. Et ausi de nos ministres qi aukun tort ount meyntenu, ou acune eglise ount resceu dount l' avouesoun ad esté en debat en nostre Court; et ceux soint puniz solom les estatuz; ou qi averount nul plé meyntenu a champart ou en autre manere, ou s' il eynt acune dreiture distourbé en nul point; et des feez qe il pernent, et de qi, covertement ou apertement.

Stat. West. 2. (13 Ed. I.) c. 44; Fle. 86, 87.

18. Et ausi des clers de nostre Court de la Chauncelerie et del un baunc et del autre, et des clers del Escheker, qi pernent plus de un dener pur le escripture de un bref, et de cirographers qi plus pernent qe iiii. s. pur le cirographe; et des criours, si nul prenge plus qe le establisement de noster estatut; et ceux soint puniz par fins et ostetz de Court, et si lour sovereyns savoyent de lour utrageouses prises et ne mistrent point de amendement, ceux soint puniz a nostre volountee. Et ausi des clers des Justices eyrauntz, si il pristrent plus qe ii. s. pur deliveraunce de ces chapitres solom la ordey-

Stat. West. 1. (3 Ed. I.) c. 30.

Fle. 27 (§ 82).

and amercements belonging to us; let such be ransomed and from thenceforth removed from the Court, and their superiors punished at our will.

Maintenance and champerty.

17. Also concerning our officers who have maintained any wrong, or have accepted the presentment to any church, of which the advowson was in litigation in our Court, and let such be punished according to the statutes; or who have maintained any plea by champerty or in any other manner; and whether they have hindered justice in any point; and of the fees which they take, and of whom, secretly or openly.

Exactions of clerks of chancery and other courts,

18. Also concerning the clerks of our Court of Chancery, and of the one Bench and the other, and of the Exchequer, who take more than a penny for writing a writ; and of chirographers who take more than four shillings for the chirograph of a fine; and of criers, whether any of them take more than is appointed by our statute; and let such offenders be fined, and expelled the Court, and if their superiors knew of their extortion, and took no measures to correct it, let them be punished at our will. Also concerning the clerks of Justices Itinerant, whether they have taken more than two shillings for delivering the chapters

of criers,

and of clerks of Justices Itinerant.

naunce de nos estatuz, ou si autre outrage eynt[1] fet qe par nos estatuz lour est. defendu a fere, ou si nul enroudlement eyt esté delayé, ou nule manere de damage ou grevaunce fete a aukun pur damages nient graunteez as clers de nos Justices, [38.] queus qe les Justices eynt esté; et ceux soint puniz par fyn, et osteez de Court.

19. Et ausi soit enquis de alliaunces des jurours par entre nos ministres et eux, et par entre veisin et veisin, en arerisement de dreiture; et queus del counté se procurent estre mis en enquestes et en jurez, et queús se voillent parjurer pur louwer ou pur doute de nul; et ceux soint reyntz a nostre volounté, et qe mes ne soint cruz de[2] nul serment.

20. Et ausi soit enquis de dras [3]fetz hors del reaume menez et venduz en cel counté,[3] qe ne furent mie de dreit assise solum le purport de la graunt chartre, et cum bien de[4] Mag. Cart. c. 25; Brac. 115 b; Fle. 24 (§ 21. 22).

1. *so N. sim. DSGAMCF.* soit *L.* 2. en *M.* pur *C.* 3—3. venduz en le Countee e fetz hors de nostre reaume *M.* 4. *so NDSGMCF.* de *om. L.*

of the eyre according to the ordinance of our statutes, or whether they have been guilty of any other excesses prohibited by our statutes, or whether any enrollment has been delayed, or any manner of damage or grievance done to any one, on account of damages not allowed to the clerks of our Justices, whoever the Justices may be; and let them be punished by fine and expelled the Court.

19. Let it be also inquired concerning confederacies between the jurors and any of our officers[d], or between one neighbour and another, to the hinderance of justice; and what persons of the county procure themselves to be put upon inquests and juries, and who are ready to perjure themselves for hire or through fear of any one; and let such persons be ransomed at our pleasure, and their oath never after be admissible. Conspiracies to defeat justice.

20. Let it also be inquired of cloth made out of the realm, brought into the county and sold there, not being of the right assize according to the purport of the Great Charter, what Assize of cloth.

[d] The commentator in MS. *N* gives the following example of an offence coming under this head. 'In the county of Northampton a sheriff named Sir Robert de Veer in the 30th year of King Edward made a confederacy with several others of the county, that some of them should indict persons, and the others save them, for bribes, according as the same sheriff should arrange the panels. These persons were afterwards called 'the company of the pouch' (les queux furent apelez puis : La Compaignie de la pouche).' Sir Robert de Vere here referred to was sheriff of Northampton 29–30 Ed. I., but was not continued in his office as was then usual, possibly on account of the above offence. (See the list of Sheriffs in Bridges' History of Northamptonshire, vol. i. p. 5.)

ceux dras ount esté venduz puis le autre heyre, et par qi, et cum bien les dras ount valu de chescun marchaunt severaulment, et qi fust assigné par nous de seiser tels dras en nostre meyn; et cest article soit terminé a noster Escheker.

Brac. 116 *b*; Fle. 24 (§ 23). 21. Et ausi soit enquis de vins venduz, dunt les tonels ne tindrent mie xii.xx. galouns, queus ceux sount qi issint les ount venduz en gros; et de la prise de vins, cum bien des tonels ount esté pris a noster oes puis le autre heyre, et par qi meyns; et si tels vins eynt esté venduz a autre qe a nous [38 *b*.] sauntz noster comaundement; et cest article soit terminé a noster Escheker.

22. En mesme la manere soit enquis de totes maneres [1]des chars, et de tote manere de pessoun[1], et de tote manere de especerie, de [2]cyre, de cendal[2], de canevaz, de dras, de aver de poys, et de tote manere de prise, qe ount esté pris a noster oes puis le dreyn heyre, et de la value de chescune prise. Et ausi soit enquis de nos custumes des quirs et de

1—1. des pessouns chars *M.* de charrs e de pessons *F.* 2—2. crie [cyre *interlin.* de Co[e]yne *L.* Cire de seye de teylle *D.* cyre [de seye] de ceyne [*corr.* teylle] *N.* Cire *R.* Cire de cendal *M W.* cire de teme *A.* Cire de Teyne *G.* Cyre de ceyne *S.* cire e de toille *C.* cire de ceim *F.*

quantity of such cloth has been sold since the last eyre, and by whom, and what was the value of the cloth so sold by each merchant separately, and who was appointed by us to seize such cloth into our hand; and let this article be determined in our Exchequer.

Assize, and prisage of wines. 21. Let inquiry also be made of wines sold, whereof the tuns did not contain two hundred and forty gallons, and who those are who thus sold them by wholesale; and also of the prisage of wines, how many tuns have been taken to our use since the last eyre, and by whose hands, and whether those wines have been sold to any other than to ourselves without our orders; and let this article also be determined at our Exchequer.

Prisage of spices, silk, &c. 22. In like manner let inquiry be made concerning all sorts of flesh and fish, and of every kind of spice, wax, silk, canvas, cloth, and avoirdupois[e], and of all manner of prises, which have been taken to our use since the last eyre, and of the value of each prise. And let inquiry also be made con-

[e] This word is said to have been applied to all goods sold by weight. See Ducange, Gloss. *s. v.* averium ponderis.

leynes, qi les ount coillez, et cum bien les coillours ount suffert de passer de saccs de leyne saunz payer custume, et cum bien eit valu la custome chescun an en chescune manere de custume a nous aporteynaunte; et ces articles soint terminez [1]a noster Escheker[1] solom la descrecioun [2]del Tresorer et des Barouns[2].

CHAPITRE XXIII. [XXII.]

Des Apels.

1. Dit avoms de partie des articles purveus pur nos heyres, par les queus nous voloms punir les mesfesours et atteyndre[3] les malices des gentz, a nostre sute; ore dirroms coment felonies et malices sount a punir par autri sute, et primes des apels. Appel est pleynte de homme fete sur autre ovek purpos de ly atteyndre de felonie par motz a ceo ordeyneez. Chescun homme neqedent ne peut mie apeler generalment; car homme utlagé, ne cil qi ad noster reaume forjuré, ne [39.]

Brac. 118 b; Fle. 31.

1—1. *om. M.* 2—2. de nos barouns a nostre Eschekere *M.* de nos barouns *CF. sim. RW.* del Escheqer *add. D.* 3. esteyndre *LDW. sim. SGCF.* ateindre *M.* esteyndre [al. atteyndre] *N.* estendre *AR.*

cerning our customs of leather and wool, who have collected them, and how many sacks of wool the collectors have permitted to pass without paying custom, and how much the yearly value of every kind of custom belonging to us amounts to; and let these articles likewise be determined at our Exchequer, according to the discretion of the Treasurer and Barons.

Customs of leather and wool.

CHAPTER XXIII.

Of Appeals.

1. Having in part treated of the articles provided for our eyres, by which we desire to punish evildoers and to convict the wickedness of people at our own suit, we will now set forth how felonies and crimes may be punished at the suit of others; and first of appeals. An appeal is a plaint brought by one person against another in a set form of words with intent to convict him of felony. Not every man however can be an appellor; for neither an outlawed person, nor one who

Appeals.

Who may be appellor.

homme jugé en nostre Court a la mort, ne provour qi avera failli de sa pruve, ne enfaunt de eynz age de xiiii. aunz, ne homme aragé, ne fol nastre, ne muet, ne surd, ne mesel ostee de commune[1] des gentz, ne homme ordeyné de eynz saintz ordres, ne sount mie receyvables en apels, encuser neqedent porunt il nos enemys mortels demorauntz en nostre terre.

Brac. 142 b. 2. Et sount acunes felonies qe touchent nostre sute, et pount estre suiz pur[2] nous et ne mie par[3] nous, sicum devers nos mortels enemys, et de noster seal et de nostre moné fausé; et sount aucunes qe touchent autri sute, et nent la nostre, sicum de treysoun fet par acun a seignur par le purgiser de sa femme ou de sa file ou de la norice de ses enfauntz, ou del seal soen seignur fauser. Et ausi sount aukunes felonies, ou a nostre sute ne ad point de execucioun, for sicum execucioun de trespas, sicum de maheyngs, de playes, et de enprisounement. Et sount autres ou jugement de mort

1. ley *add. M.* 2. par *A.* 3. *so NDRMWF.* pur *LA.*

has abjured our realm, or been sentenced to death in our Court, nor an approver who has failed of his proof, nor an infant under the age of fourteen years, nor a madman, nor an idiot, nor one deaf, or dumb, nor a leper expelled from common society, nor a person in holy orders, is to be admitted in appeals; yet they may accuse our mortal enemies abiding within our dominions.

Felonies concerning the king.

Felonies concerning others.

Some crimes punished by death, only upon appeal.

2. There are some felonies which concern our suit, and may be prosecuted for us and not by us[f], as against our mortal enemies, and for counterfeiting our seal and our coin; and there are some which concern the suit of others and not ourselves, as of treason committed against any lord, by violating his wife or his daughter or the nurse of his children, or of counterfeiting the seal of his lord. There are also some felonies, where no other execution follows at our suit than such as takes place in trespass, as in mayhems, wounds, and imprisonment; and there are others, where judgment of death ensues, as well

[f] I understand this as meaning, that certain crimes affecting the king, as well as certain crimes affecting subjects, may be prosecuted by appeal, but in that case the appeal must be by a subject for the king and not by the king himself. So Bracton says that where, upon failure of an appeal by the death of the appellor, the appellee is brought to trial at the king's suit, he cannot defend himself by his body, but must put himself on the country, because the king does not fight, and has no other champion but the country, and, even if he were allowed to fight, he could not use the words *de visu et auditu* necessary in an appeal. Brac. 142.

suit ausi bien a nostre sute cum a autri, sicum felonies de mort de homme, de rap, de arsouns, de robberies, et autres.

3. En[1] primes fet a dire de apels de felonies qe pount estre fet pur[2] nous et ne mie par[3] nous, sicum de treysoun et de cumpassement purveu vers nostre persone pur nous mettre a mort, ou nostre cumpaigne, ou noster pere, ou nostre mere, ou nos enfauntz, ou de nous desheriter de noster reaume, ou de trayer noster ost, tut ne soit cel cumpassement mis a effect. De quel cumpassement voloms nous qe le encusement soit fet a nous meymes, ou a autre qe saunz delay le nous face a saver; a quel encusement nous voloms qe chescun soit receyvable. Car nul presentment de ceo ne pora estre fet apres loung tens passé, qe les presentours ne se englueroun en partie ou de la consense ou del concelement. Glan. li. 14, c. 1; Brac. 118, 118 b; Fle. 31. [39 b.] Brac. 141, 155 b. Brac. 118 b; Fle. 32, 49 (§ 2).

4. Et cum acun[4] se profra del prover vers un ou vers plusours, feroms hastivement prendre les cors des encusez et mener par devaunt nous. Et cum il vendrunt en jugement, si face[5] le encusour soen apel pur nous en ceste forme par Brac. 119; Fle. 31.

1. Et *D.* *sim. M.* 2. par *C.* 3. *so NDARMF.* pur *LC.* 4. *so MW.* asqune *R.* asqun *interl. A.* *om. LNDC.* 5. *so NDARMC.* fa *L.*

at our suit as at another's, as in felonies of the death of a man, rape, arson, robberies, and others.

3. First we must treat of appeals of felonies which may be brought for us, and not by us; as of treason and a compassing designed against our person, to put us, or our consort, or our father, or our mother, or our children, to death, or to disinherit us of our kingdom, or to betray our host, although such compassing be not put in execution. Of which compassing, our will is, that the accusation be laid before ourselves, or some other who shall without delay inform us thereof; and any person shall be permitted to make such accusation[g]; for no presentment can be made thereof after any great length of time, without the presentors being in some degree implicated either in consent or in concealment. Appeals of treason for the king; to be brought before the king. Danger of delay.

4. When any person shall offer to prove this crime against one or more, we will cause the body of the accused to be immediately apprehended and brought before us. And when they appear for trial, let the accuser make his appeal for us by some serjeant

[g] In case of high treason, a servant or even a bondman might appeal his own lord. This was contrary to the general rule respecting appeals. Brac. 141, 155 b.

acun serjaunt. Johan, qi ci est, apele Peres, qi iloeqes est, [1]de ceo[1] qe, com il fu en certeyn leu a tel certeyn jour a tel an, la oy mesmes cestui Johan purparler tele mort, ou tiel treysoun par entre cestui Peres et un autre, tel par noun, et par tieles alliaunces, et[2] qe cesti Perys issi fist et issint le purparla felounosement cum feloun et traytouressement cum traytre, est cestui Johan prest de prover par soen cors en totes les maneres qe la Court vodera agarder qe prover le deit. Plusours choses sount neqedent qe distourbent batayle en chescune felonie; et la covendra autrement[3] parler. Car si le apelour soit maheyné, ou de eynz le age de xiiii. aunz, ou outre le age de lxx. aunz, ou ordeyné de eynz saintz ordres, ou femme, ou si homme peut estre eydé par record, dunc dirra il issint: est cesti Johan prest de prover en totes les maneres qe la Court vodera agarder qe homme maheyné, ou [4]de tel[4] age ou de tel estat prover le puse et[5] deive; ou: de ceo vouche il record de celi, ou de celi, [6]et de lour[6] roulles[7] a garraunt.

Glan. ii. 14. c. 1.

[40.]

1—1. *om. M.* 2. *so ND* et *om. L.* e *MC.* etc. e *AR.* 3. sauuement *C.* 4—4. *so NDAMC.* del *L.* 5. ou *AMC.* 6—6. ou de ceo vouche il *A.* 7. a record ou *add. C.*

Form of appeal. in this manner. 'John who is here appeals Peter who is there of this, that being in such a place on such a day and year, the same John there heard such a death or such a treason contrived between the same Peter and another, such an one by name, and by such confederacies, and that the said Peter thus acted and thus contrived feloniously as a felon and traitorously as a traitor, he the same John is ready to prove by his body, in any manner the Court shall award that he ought to prove it.' In every felony however battle may be hindered by many circumstances; in which cases it will be necessary to speak otherwise; for if the appellor be maimed, or under the age of fourteen years, or above seventy, or in holy orders, or a woman, or if he can be aided by record, then he shall say thus: 'This the same John is ready to prove, in whatsoever manner the Court shall award that a man, who is maimed, or of such an age, or of such a condition, ought to prove it;' or he may say, 'And of this he vouches record of such or such an one, and of their rolls, to warrant[h].'

Tender of proof. Battle, when disallowed.

Proof by record.

[h] It is not easy to see to what sort of cases this mode of proof refers. Possibly to such a case of manifest homicide or petty treason as is mentioned before, (c. vi. s. 4) where the Coroner's roll may have been held conclusive, no other proof either by battle or by the country being required. See before, p. 37, note; and compare Bracton, 137.

5. Et defendoms qe nul attourné ne soit resceu pur le apelour ne pur les apelez, ne nul essoigne alowé de une part ne de autre, en nul cas de mort. Stat. West. 2. (13 Ed I.) c. 12.

6. Et voloms qe [1]si le apel[1] soit pronuncié par bouche de serjaunt, et le apel soit abatu par mauveyse mustraunce ou autrement par defaute del serjaunt, qi se duist conustre en le mester de counter, qe le serjaunt soit en nostre merci a C. s.; et si manvesté i courge privément et de ceo soit atteynt, si soit il comaundé a la prisoun et suspendu de soen office. Stat. West. 1. c 29; Fle. 87.

7. Et quant a la defensę, si se pora le defendaunt defendre en ceste manere: Pierres, qe ci est, defend totes felonies et totes treysouns, et totes purparlaunces, et cumpassementz de mal envers la persone de tel ou de tel, solom ceo qe serra purposé[2] encountre ly, de mot en mot. Et voloms bien en tels apels, qe le apelour eyt plus de mester de asser les paroles ordineement sauntz omission eynzces qe soen apel estoyse, qe le defendour en sa defense; et grauntoms al defendour de chescune felonie qe il defende les motz de la felonie en gros sauntz estre noun[3] defendu, issint qe pur defaute de mot ou Brac. 138 b; Fle. 31. [40 *b*.]

1—1. *so ND. sim. AC.* le apel si *L.* si apel *M.* 2 *so NABMC. sim. DW.* purpense *L.* 3. *so DM.* noun *om. LSGA.* non *interl. N.*

5. We forbid any attorneys to be received either for the appellor or for the appellees, or any essoin to be allowed on one side or the other, in any cases of death. No attorney or essoin, in capital cases.

6. And our will is, that if the appeal be pronounced by the mouth of a serjeant, and be abated on account of its being ill set forth, or through other default of the serjeant, who ought to understand the art of pleading, the serjeant himself shall be amerced one hundred shillings; and if there was secret malice in the act, and he be convicted thereof, then let him be sent to prison, and suspended from his office. False pleading by serjeant.

7. And as to the defence, the appellee may defend himself in this manner. 'Peter who is here defendeth all the felonies, and all the treasons, and contrivances, and compassings of mischief against the person' of such an one, or such an one, according as he is charged, word by word. And we will that in these appeals, it shall be more necessary for the appellor to set forth the words orderly without any omission, that his appeal may stand, than for the defendant in his defence; and in every felony we allow the defendant to defend the words of the felony generally, Form of defence.

de sillabe ne soit il mie ajugé pur noun defendu, eynz suffise al defendaunt, qe il die qe de cele felonie ne est mie coupable, sicum le apelour ly met sour, et prest est qe il se defende vers ly par soen cors solum ceo qe la Court agardera qe
Fle. 51 (§ 33). fere le deyve, ou par pays. Nul neqedent ne soit tenu atteynt pur ceo qe il est noun defendu en cas de mort, mes soit mis a la penaunce, jekes autaunt qe il soit purveu de meuz respoundre, s' il eit pronuncié la defense par mi sa bouche; et si par mi bouche de serjaunt, et le serjaunt soit avowé, si soit
Ante, s. 6. le serjaunt en la merci cum de sus est dit, et s' il soit disavowé, si soit puni par prisoun et par fin, et il se purveye de meillour serjaunt.

Brac. 139 b; Fle. 31, 49. 8. Et cum il avera suffisauntment defendu le[1] gros del apel, si se pora il eyder par excepciouns: et primes de la juris-
[41.] diccioun le juge, et puis a la persone le apelour, et puis a sa propre persone, et puis a le apel, et puis al accioun, sicum
Brac. 400; Fle. 427, 428. serra dit entre les excepciouns. Et quant a la jurisdiccioun put il dire, qe il n'est mie tenu a respoundre en place ou le juge est partie, desicum nul jugement ne se put fere de

1. so *GABSMC.* les *LND.*

General words sufficient. without treating him as undefended, so that for default of a word or syllable he be not adjudged undefended, but it shall
Not guilty. be sufficient for him to say, that he is not guilty of such felony as the appellor lays to his charge, and that he is ready to defend the same against him by his body, in such manner as the Court shall award that he ought to do it, or by the country.
Appellee compelled to plead by penance. And in cases of death none shall be held convicted for being undefended, but he shall be put to penance, until he be prepared to answer better, if he has spoken his defence by his own mouth; and if by a serjeant, who is avowed by the appellee, let the serjeant be amerced as above directed, and if he be disavowed, let him be punished by imprisonment and fine, and let the defendant provide himself with a better serjeant.

Exceptions, or pleas. 8. The appellee, having sufficiently defended the substance of the appeal, may then aid himself by exceptions, and first to the jurisdiction of the judge, afterwards to the person of the appellor, then to his own person, and next to the appeal, and lastly to the action, as shall be mentioned amongst exceptions.
Exception to the jurisdiction. With respect to the jurisdiction, he may say, that he is not bound to answer in a place where the judge is a party, since

meyns qe de iii. persones, ceo est a saver de un juge, de un pleyntif, et de un defendaunt; et en cas ou nous sumus partie, voloms nous qe nostre Court soit juge, sicum countes et barouns en tens de parlement. Et confermé la jurisdiccioun del juge, se avise s'il se pora point ayder par acune excepcioun quant a la persone le pleyntif, ou sa persone demeyne; et puis al apel abatre; qe pora venir en moutz des cas, sicum par omissioun de nomer en le apel an ou jour ou liu, ou en nomaunt un noun pur un autre, ou moustraunt le apel issi, ceo vous mostre Johan, ou il dust dire, Johan apele, ou cloaunt soen apel par cestes paroles, et ceo voil jeo averrer, la ou il dust dire, ceo profre jeo a prover; ou par variaunce[1] en soen appel devaunt Justices en une forme et en roulle del Corouner en autre fourme.

Brac. 138, 141; Fle. 49 (§ 4), 50 (§ 15).

Brac. 137, 139 *b*, 140; Fle. 49 (§ 2).

9. Et si par acune excepcioun peuse abatre le apel, adunc voloms nous, qe il soit jugé quites quant devers cel apelour, et le apelour soit comaundé a la prisoun pur ceo qe il avera failli de prover ceo a quei se obligea; et issi soit en touz apels de felonie, et ausi la ou le apelour se avera retret de [41 *b*.]

Stat. West. 2 (13 Ed. I.) c. 12; Fle. 32 (§ 9), 41 (§ 15).

1. variacioun *NDAM*.

in every judgment there ought not to be less than three persons, to wit, a judge, a plaintiff, and a defendant; and in cases where we are party, our pleasure is, that our Court, to wit, the earls and barons in time of parliament, shall be judges. The jurisdiction of the judge being established, he should consider whether he can aid himself by excepting either to the person of the plaintiff or to his own person; and next in abatement of the appeal, which may occur in many cases, as by omitting to name in the appeal the year, day, or place, or naming one name instead of another, or setting forth the appeal thus, 'This showeth unto you John,' where he ought to say, 'John appeals'; or by closing his appeal by these words, 'and this I will aver,' instead of saying, 'this I offer to prove,' or for variance, the appeal being made before the Justices in one form, and in the coroner's roll in another.

Court of Parliament.

Exception to the person of the plaintiff or defendant.

Abatement of appeal.

9. If he can by any exception abate the appeal, then our will is that he be acquitted as against this appellor, and the appellor shall be committed to prison, because he has failed to prove that he bound himself to prove; and so it shall be in all appeals of felony, and also where the appellor withdraws him-

Appellee succeeding by exception is acquitted against appellor, and the appellor imprisoned.

soen apel sauntz jugement, et jalemeyns ses pleges de sure soint en nostre merci pur ceo qe il averount faili de plegage.

Brac. 142 (§ 7); Fle. 51 (§ 32). Mes en tel cas voloms nous, qe mitigacioun soit fete, pur ceo qe tiels se profrent a cumbatre pur nostre pes meyntener.

Brac. 137, 142 *b*; Fle. 41 (§ 15), 52 (§ 38). 10. Et tut soit qe les apelez soint issi agardez[1] quites quant envers le pleyntif, pur ceo ne remeigne mie qe il ne soint coupables de ceo qe lour est mis sur; [2]pur quei[2] en tel cas volom nous qe tauntost maunde[3] hom a tieus de par nous, coment il se voderount aquiter de tel esclaundre. Et s' il dient par pays, soint [4]mis arere[4] a la prisoun jekes a un certeyn jour, et en le men tens soit [5]maundé le pays[5], et solom le veyrdit del pays sur ceo chargé soint jugez.

Brac. 137; Fle. 47. 11. Et si le defendaunt ne puse abatre le apel, adunc soit en sa eleccioun a sei defendre par soen cors ou par pays. Et

1. *so M. sim. F.* garde *L.* gardee *ND.* gardes *ARC.* 2—2. *om.* A. pur ceo *M.* 3. *so LM. sim. SG.* demande *Z. sim. interl. N.* 4—4. comaunde a rere *M.* remis *A.* 5—5. *so GM. sim. C* garde pays et maunde *L. sim NDS.* maunde pays *AR. sim. F.*

self from his appeal before judgment[i]; and his pledges to prosecute shall also be in our mercy, because they have failed in their engagement. But in these cases we will that moderation be used, inasmuch as such persons proffer themselves to fight in maintenance of our peace.

Appellee may be put upon his trial at the king's suit. 10. But though it happen that the appellees are thus acquitted as against the plaintiff, it does not therefore follow that they are not guilty of what is laid to their charge; wherefore in such case let it be immediately demanded of them on our behalf, how they will acquit themselves of such slander; and if they say, by the country, then they shall be remanded to prison until a certain day, and in the meantime the country shall be summoned, and according to the verdict of the country charged thereon, judgment shall be given.

Mode of trial in election of appellee. 11. If the defendant cannot abate the appeal, then it shall be in his election[k], whether he will defend himself by his body

[i] In later times an appellor could by release discharge an appeal. (Hale, Pl. Cr. vol. i. p. 9); and Blackstone is of opinion that the chief object of an appeal *at all times* was to compel the defendant to make a pecuniary compensation; and that when the verdict in the appeal was given in favour of the appellor, he might insist upon what terms he pleased as the ransom of the defendant's life, or for a commutation of the sentence. (Blackst. Comm. vol. iv. p. 316.) It will be seen that this opinion, so far as regards appeals for minor offences, is confirmed by our author. See below, ch. xxvi. s. 2.

[k] In Glanvill's time, the appellee of felony appears to have been bound to defend himself by battle, unless he was excused for age or infirmity, in which case the trial was by ordeal. (Glan. li. 14. c. 1.) The beneficent change which gave the accused the election of purging himself by the country was introduced between the time of Glanvill and Bracton.

ausi soit en totes felonies quant a autri sute, hors pris cas especials, sicum femmes et maheynez et autres qe ne pount ne ne deyvent cumbatre. Et si par soen cors, et ceo soit cas de autri[1] felonie, adunc soit la cause examiné eynz qe la batayle se joygne, lequel la cause soit trespas ou felonie, et si trespas, si soit le apel abatu par office des Justices; et si felonie, adunc doune le defendour gage a sey defendre, et le apelour gage pur la cause desreyner[2]. Lors lour soit jour doné pur eux attirer de armures[3]; et le defendour en le men tens remeygne en prisoun.

Glan. li. 14. c. 1. Brac. 137 (§ 3); Fle. 50 (§ 12, 28). [42] Brac. 141 b; Fle. 50 (§ 28).

12. Et cum il vendrount armez en Court, si comence le pleyntif soen apel mot pur mot cum il fist avaunt, et le defendour se defende cum devaunt. Et puis prenge le un le autre par la meyn, et jurge premer le defendaunt en ceste manere, [4]et puis apres jurge l'apelour cum apres serra plus

Brac. 141 b; Fle. 50 (§ 28, 29).

1. *so F. sim. W.* autre *LNDARGS.* 2. reseruer *LA.* desrener *G.* desresner *S.* de reseruer *N.* de reuerser *D.* reseruer [desrenier *in marg*] *R.* de reignier *M.* de reseruer *C.* dresner *W.* 3. armes *C.* 4—4. *so LN. sim. D. om. AMC.*

or by the country, and so in all felonies prosecuted by private persons, except in special cases, as of women, persons maimed,[1] and others who neither can nor ought to wage battle[m]. And if he says by his body, and it be in the case of felony at the prosecution of another, then let the matter be examined before battle is joined, whether the cause be trespass or felony, and if trespass, let the appeal be abated by the Justices *ex officio*. But if felony, then let the defendant give security to defend himself, and the appellor security to prove the cause; next let a day be given them to provide themselves with arms, and let the defendant in the meantime remain in prison.

Battle, when disallowed.

Trial by battle not allowed in trespass.

12. When they appear armed in Court, let the plaintiff repeat his appeal word for word as he did before, and the defendant defend himself as before; and afterwards let them take each other by the hand, and let the defendant swear first in this manner, and the appellor afterwards as shall be

Proceedings in trial by battle.

[1] The commentator in MS. *N.* adds, that if the appellee, not being actually maimed, is otherwise 'in so poor a state' that his inability to fight is evident, the Court ought not to allow him to be wantonly destroyed; and that lepers are not permitted to wage battle, lest their disease should be communicated to the other combatant. See before, s. 1.

[m] It was one of the privileges of the citizens of London, that they should not be obliged to wage battle. See the Charter of Henry I in Ancient English Laws, p. 217, and the Charters of Richard I, Henry III, and Edward II, in Liber Custumarum, p. 248, 252, 259. The same immunity was claimed by the citizens of Lincoln (Kelham's Britton, p. 153, note), and the burgesses of Bury. Cron. Joc. de Brakelonda, p. 74.

pleynement dit[4]. Ceo oyez, vous homme qe jeo tieng par la meyn, qe vous fetes apeler Johan par noun de baptesme, qe jeo Pierres [1]ne en[1] tel an ne a tel jour ne en tel leu la mort avaundite ne compassay ne purparlay, nc a tele felonie ne assenti, sicum vous me avet mis sur, si Deu mei ayde et les Saintz. Et puis jurge le apelour issi. Ceo oyez, vous homme qe jeo tieng par la meyn, qe vous fetes [2]estre apelé[2] Pierres par noun de baptesme, qe vous estes parjurs, [3]et pur ceo parjurs[3], car a tel jour en tiel an et en tel lu purparlastes vous tel traysoun ou tele mort, solom ceo qe dit ay vers vous en le apel, si [4]me ayde Deus[4] et les Saintz.

Brac. 141 *b*, 142; Fle. 50, 51.

[42 *b*.] 13. Puis soint ambedeus amenez en certeyne place, ou ambedeus jurgent issi. Ceo oyetz, vous Justices, qe jeo Johan, ou Pierres, nent ay mangé ne bu, ne autre chose fet, ne fet fere pur moi, par quei la ley Deu soit abessé et la ley del diable [5]avauncé ou enhauncé[5]. Et issi soit fet en totes les

1—1. *so M.* au *LGW.* a *NDSARC.* 2—2. apeler *AMC.* 3—3. *om. AMC.* 4—4. me aye deus *L.* deu mei eyde *N.* *sim. AMC.* 5—5. enhauce *ARMC.*

Oath of parties in Court.

presently more fully set forth. 'Hear this, you man whom I hold by the hand, who call yourself John by your name of baptism, that I, Peter, did not in such a year, nor on such a day, nor in such a place, compass or propose the death aforesaid, nor did assent to such felony as you have charged me with, so help me God and the Saints.' Afterwards the appellor shall swear thus. 'Hear this, you man whom I hold by the hand, who call yourself Peter by your name of baptism, that you are perjured, inasmuch as on such a day, in such a year, and in such a place, you did propose such a treason or such a death as I have said against you in the appeal, so help me God and the Saints[n].'

Proceedings on the field. Oath against enchantments.

13. Then let them both be brought to a place appointed for that purpose, where they must swear thus. 'Hear this, ye Justices, that I John (or I Peter) have neither eaten nor drunk anything, nor done or caused to be done for me any other thing, whereby the law of God may be abased, and the law of the devil advanced or exalted.' And thus let it be done

[n] Selden observes, that in these oaths the clause *de visu et auditu*, which occurs in Bracton (141 *b*), is omitted, and that this is in analogy to the rule established in civil trials by the Statute of Westminster the first, c. 41. Selden's Duello, c. vii. See below, p. 109, note; and compare s. 5. p. 100.

batayles de felonies. Et tauntost soit crié, qe nul ne soit si hardi, autre qe les combatours, qele chose qe il veye ou oye, qe il se muve ne haute voiz pronouncie, par quei destourbaunce puse surdre a la batayle. Et voloms qe qi qe face encountre la crye, qe il eyt la prisoun par[1] un an et un jour.

14. Puis voisent combatre, armez sauntz feer et sauntz linge[2] armure, a testes descovertes, et a meyns nues, [3]et a peez[3], oveke deus bastouns cornuz de une loungure, et chescun de eux ove[4] un escu a iiii. corners, sauntz autre armure dunt nul ne peut autre grever; et si nul eyt autre armure sur ly muscee, et de ceo eit grevé soen adversarie, ou[5] profert de grever, si soit cum serra dit entre les batayles de pletz de terre.

15. Et si le defendour se peuse defendre jekes autaunt qe homme puse ver les esteyles el firmament, et demaunde jugement si plus deyve combatre, si voloms qe pur le defendaunt Brac. 142; Fle. 51.

1. par *om. M.* de *GC.* 2. so *LNSGAM.* lynge *HKZ.* lunge *C.* 3—3. a pee *SGK.* e piez *MZ.* e a pee *A.* 4 so *DM.* ou *LN.* od *SG.* *om. ARC.* eyt *W.* 5. so *Z.* et *LND.* e *GSABMCW.*

in all battles in appeals of felony. And let proclamation be immediately made, that no one, except the combatants, whatever thing he see or hear, be so bold as to stir, or cry aloud, whereby the battle may be disturbed; and whosoever disobeys the proclamation shall be imprisoned a year and a day.

14. Next, let them go to combat, armed without iron and without the slightest armour[o], their heads uncovered, their hands and feet bare, with two staves tipped with horn of equal length, and each of them a target of four corners, without any other arms, whereby either of them may annoy the other; and if either of them have any other arms concealed about him, and therewith annoy or offer to annoy his adversary, let it be done as shall be mentioned in treating of battle in a plea of land.[p] Arms of combatants.

15. If the defendant can defend himself until the stars can be seen in the firmament, and demands judgment whether he ought to combat any longer, our will is, that judgment pass Defendant must defend himself until nightfall.

[o] These particulars as to the armour and weapons of the combatants in an appeal are not found in Bracton or Fleta. Leather armour appears according to most authorities to have been allowed. Other notices of this curious subject are to be found in Dugdale, Orig. Juridic. 68; Dyer, Rep. 301; Y. B. 1 Hen. VI. 7 *a*; Selden's Duello, c. viii; Archæologia, vol. xxxii. p. 287.

[p] The passage here referred to is not to be found in the work as it exists at present. See Introduction by the Editor.

Stat. West. 2. (13 Ed. I.) c. 12.

se passe jugement; et ausi en totes batayles de champiouns; et le apelour en felonie soit comaundé a la prisoun. Et si le defendaunt voile la felonie reconustre avaunt ceo qe il soit [43] autrement atteynt, et apeler autres de la consense, voloms bien qe il soit a ceo resceu.

Brac. 142 (§ 6); Fle. 51.

16. Et si le defendaunt soit vencu, si soit le jugement tiel, qe il soit traynez et pendu, ou autrement tourmenté a la mort a nostre volounté, et qe touz ses biens moebles soint nostres, et ses heirs desheritez; et lour fitz james ne teignent terre en noster reaume. Ne nul ne soit tel de prier pur eux, s'il ne voille mesmes estre tenuz[1] suspect de la felonie. Et le encusour qe freschement avera ceste felonie suye a bone fin, eyt de nous graunt guerdoun. Et de fausine de noster seal et de nostre monee pora hom sure apels pur nous en mesme la manere; et ausi del purgiser nostre cumpayne, ou de nos files, ou des[2] norices de nos enfaunz; en queus cas sunt jugementz de estre traygnez et[3] pendu, lequel qe hom soit atteynt par enditement a nostre seute, ou par apel de autre homme pur nous.

1. tenuz *om. C.* 2. *so K.* de nos *LM.* de *GS.* 3. *so N.* ou *L.* e *AMC.*

for the defendant, and so in all battles between champions; and in the case of felony the appellor shall be committed to prison. And if the defendant will confess the felony before he is otherwise attainted, and appeal others of consenting to the same, we allow him to be admitted thereto.

Appellee may be admitted to appeal accomplices.

Judgment in appeal of treason.

16. And if the defendant be vanquished, let the judgment be this, that he be drawn and hanged, or put to such other painful death as we shall direct, and that all his movable goods be ours, and his heirs disinherited; and his children shall be incapable of ever holding land in our realm. And let not any, unless they would be suspected themselves of the felony, presume to intercede for him; and let the accuser, who without delay shall prosecute such felony with good effect, receive from us a notable reward. Appeals may likewise be sued for us in the same manner for counterfeiting our seal and our coin, and also for violating our consort, or our daughters, or the nurses of our children; and in such cases, the judgment is, to be drawn and hanged, whether the conviction be upon an indictment at our suit or upon an appeal by another person for us.

Reward of appellor.

CHAPITRE XXIV. [XXIII.]

De Apels de Homicides.

1. De homicides voloms nous, qe chescun [1]a qi il affera si suwe, c'est a saver le proscheyn[1] madle de saunc del parenté celi qi felounousement avera esté tué, ou autre qi ly avera fet homage, ou qi avera esté de soen mesnage, issi qe lour accioun dure un an et un jour; et qe chescun comence soen appel el[2] counté ou la felonie fust fet, issint qe au premer Counté qe le pleyntif se vodera pleyndre truyse deus pleges de sure et

Glan. li. 14. c. 3; Brac. 125; Fle. 47, 48.

[43 *b*.]

Stat. Glouc. (6 Ed. I.) c. 9.

1—1. sue a qi il affiera cest asauer le prochein *M.* *sim.* *CW.* suie qi prochein serra *AR.* 2. *so G.* en *L.* en le *SMK.*

CHAPTER XXIV.

Of Appeals of Homicide.

1. Concerning homicides, our will is, that those shall prosecute whom it concerns, to wit, the male nearest in blood of the kindred of him who has been feloniously killed, or one who has done homage to him or been of his household [q]. And their right of action shall last a year and a day. Every man must commence his appeal in the county where the felony was committed, and the plaintiff at the first county court,

Appeal of homicide, by next of blood, or homager, within year and day of death.

Mode of proceeding in county court.

[q] A woman might bring an appeal of the death of her husband. Mag. Cart. c. 34. Glan. li. 14. c. 3; Brac. 125. (s. 3.) A godson might appeal the slayer of his sponsor. (*Post*, s. 3.) The appellor in earlier times was required to be one who had been actually present at the homicide. (Glan. li. 14. c. 3. Brac. 125, 138, 141, 141 *b*) There is no intimation in our author that this was considered necessary in his time; and in later times, when appeals were allowed only by the wife or the heir male, it was not required. Staundford Plac. Cor. 59 *b*; Blackst. Comm. vol. iv. p. 314. Coke treats the change as a consequence of the Statute of Gloucester, c. 9. which provided that appeals should not be so lightly abated as they had previously been. Coke, Inst. ii. 317. The case of the champion in civil actions was analogous, the oath *de visu et auditu* (See Glan. li. 2. c. 3.) being abolished by Stat. West. 1. c. 41, on the ground that it only led to perjury. The expression used by the older authors as to the wife's appeal for the death of her husband, 'killed between her arms,' (Bracton, 125, 148 *b*; Fleta 53; Britton, *post*, s. 7.) which implied the necessity of the wife being present at the killing (see Glan. li. 14. c. 3.); was in later times explained to mean, that the wife was 'in seisin' of her husband as his lawful wife at the time of his death. See Coke, Inst. ii. 68, 317; and compare Mirror, c. 3. s. 18. There is another observable change in the law of appeal, probably connected with the change already noticed. In the time of Glanvill and Bracton it would seem that any kinsman was admitted to appeal, although of several appellors the nearer in blood was preferred. (Glan. li. 14. c. 3. Brac. 125.) In our author's time the appeal appears to have been abatable, if there was any person nearer in blood than the appellor, who might have appealed though he did not actually do so. See below, s. 3. But the author of the Mirror states this ground of exception in accordance with the older practice; Sir, cest actor n' avera nule accioun, de sicome il y ad un autre pluis prochein de sank que ad attamé son appeal. (Mirr. c. 3. s. 18.)

face entrer soen apel en roulle del Corouner, et puis face continuance de Counté en Counté sauntz interrupcioun. Et si hom[1] face tort al pleyntif ou as apellez, voloms bien qe il peussent remuer le apel par renable enchesoun hors del Counté par devaunt nous, par bref de nostre Chauncelerie, ou qe nous seums en Engleterre.

West. I. (3 Ed. I.) c. 14, 15; Brac. 128 (§ 13), 139; Fle. 41, 42, 48 (§ 8); Ante, c. 2. s. 9.

2. Et defendoms qe nul ne soit detenu en prisoun pur le fet accessorie, s'il puse trover meynpernours a respoundre, jekes apres le fet atteynt; ne qe nul Justice ne acoupe les apelez de la force ou des causes[2] accessories eynz qe le princepal fet soit atteynt ou [3]qe les apelez del princepal soint banyz [4]pur lour contumace[4]. Et si le princepal apelé soit aquité del fet, si voloms nous, qe ceux, qi serrunt apelez de la force et del recet et del comaundement et des autres accessories, soint de ceo quites par mesme le jugement.

Brac. 138, 138 *b*; Fle. 49.

3. Et cum les parties vendrount en jugement, si moustre le pleyntif soen apel; et le defendaunt defende la felonie, par

1. so *NM.* *sim. ARC.* *om. L.* 2. fez *C.* 3. dekes a taunt *add. AR.* apres ceo *add. M.* a ceo *add. C.* 4—4. so *S.* *sim. NGAR.* pur lour continuaunce *L.* par contumace *M.*

when he wishes to bring his plaint, must find two pledges to prosecute, and cause his appeal to be entered in the roll of the coroner, and then continue the same from county court to county court without interruption; and if justice be not done either to the plaintiff or to the appellees, we will that upon reasonable occasion they may by writ out of our Chancery remove the appeal out of the county court before us wheresoever we shall be in England.

How removed *coram rege.*

Accessories how proceeded against.

2. We forbid that any person be detained in prison for an accessory fact, if he can find mainpernors to answer for him, until conviction of the principal fact, or that any Justice proceed against the persons appealed of the force or accessory causes before conviction of the principal fact, or until those who are appealed of the principal fact are outlawed for their contumacy. And if the person appealed as principal be acquitted of the fact, our will is, that those who are indicted or appealed of the force, or of the receipt, or of commanding, or of other accessory facts, shall be cleared thereof by the same judgment.

Exceptions to appeal.

3. When the parties appear in judgment, let the plaintiff set forth his appeal; and let the defendant defend the felony,

motz de la Court, et puis se eyde par excepciouns, cum en cas ou le apelour est utlagé ou jugé a la mort pur sa felonie ou forjuré le reaume; en les queus cas [1]ne voloms mie, qe il soint tenuz a respoundre a ceux apellours. Le apel pora il abatre en plusours maneres, cum si le apel ne fu mie comencé de eynz le an et le jour ou nent comencé el Counté ou la felonie dust aver esté fete; ou par variacioun[2] del apel fet illoeqes et en les roulles [3]del Corouner[3]; ou s'il i ad autre madle plus proscheyn de saung, qi meillour accioun averoit de apeler; ou si rien afert al pleyntif de apeler, puis qe il ne est de soen saung, ne soen homme ne fu, ne soen nurri, ne soen meynpast, ne par ly ne fu levé de founz de baptesme; ou s'il y ad uncore homage duraunt entre le pleyntif et le defendaunt; ou si la cause ne soit mie felonie; et ausi par omissioun, cum si nule felonie ou treysoun ne soit nomé en le apel; et ausi pur le omissioun de nostre pes enfreynte, ou pur[4] omissioun de autre parole de la substaunce del apel, sicum de sus est dit; et ausi par errour, cum si il noume en soen apel Reyner pur Reynald, sicum dit serra entre les excepciouns.

Brac. 141; Fle. 31 (§ 6). [44.]

Glan. ii. 14. c. 3; Brac. 125.

Brac. 141 b.

Brac. 141; Fle. 49. (§ 7). Fle. 50 (§ 11, 12). Stat. Glouc. (6 Ed. I.). c. 9; Brac. 140, 141, 141 b; Fle. 50 (§ 20, 21). Brac. 141; Fle. 50 (§ 15).

1. auerrez *add. AMC.* sil soient auerrez *interl. N.* 2. variaunce *C.* 3—3. so *NM..* de Corouners *L.* de Corouner *A.* *sim. C.* 4. so *ARM.* de *LN.* par *C.*

in words agreeable to the form of the Court, and then aid himself by exceptions, as where the appellor is outlawed, or adjudged to death for felony, or has abjured the realm; for in these cases they shall not be bound to answer such appellors. He may likewise abate the appeal several ways, as where the appeal was not commenced within the year and day, or not in the county where the felony appears to have been committed, or for variance between the appeal made there and in the roll of the coroner, or if there is any other male nearer of blood, who has a better right to bring the appeal, or if the plaintiff is not concerned to appeal, not being of the blood of the dead man, nor having been of his homage, nor his fosterchild, nor his mainpast, nor by him lifted from the baptismal font; or if there is homage still subsisting between the plaintiff and defendant; or if the fact alleged is not felony; it may likewise be abated for omission, as if no felony or treason is named in the appeal, or if the breaking of our peace, or other words of the substance of the appeal are omitted, as above mentioned; so likewise for error, as if the name of Reyner is used for Reginald, as will be noticed in treating of exceptions.

Appeal abated.

Brac. 141; Fle. 41 (§ 15), 50 (§ 16), 51 (§ 32).

4. Et ausi par la noun sute del pleyntif, cum s'il eit sui en Counté par deus Countez et failli au tierz, et ceo puse averreer par roule del Corouner, en queu cas nous voloms qe si le defendaunt puse averreer la noun sute le pleyntif el Counté fete avaunt la date de noster bref de remuer le apel, qe nos Justices comaundent[1] le pleyntif a la prisoun pur sa noun sute et ses pleges en la merci. Et voloms, qe si le apelour murge ou [2]grevement soit enmaladi[2], par ount il ne pora sure, qe en teus cas ne soint mie les pleges amerciez pur la noun sute; et en ceo cas grauntoms nous, [3]qe autre, qe deit et poet, puse[3] resusciter la suite et sure jekes autaunt qe les apelez soint aquitez ou condempnez. Et si nul des apelez se profre avaunt utlagerie, ou le apelour fet defaute, si soit il lessé par bayl[4] jekes a la premere deliveraunce de la gaole, quant a nostre suite, par la ou il serra plevisable; [5]et coment qe il aquita quant a nostre sute[5], ja pur ceo ne perise nuli suite qi suyr vodera de eynz le an et le jour.

[44 b.] Brac. 139; (§ 10), 142 b; Fle. 52. (§ 38).

Brac. 125 b (§ 6), 142 b; Fle. 40, 41.

5. Et quant al accioun put le defendaunt respoundre par

1. aiugent *M.* aioignent C. 2—2. suppris par maladie *C.* 3—3. *so verb. M. sim. G.* qe quatre foiz pusent *L. sim. N.* quatre foiz passent *S.* qe autre qi ad dreit puisse *AB.* a autre qe poet e deit *C.* 4. meinprise *C.* 5—5. *om. C.*

Nonsuit.

4. The appeal may also be abated for want of prosecution by the plaintiff, as when he has sued in the county at two courts, and made default at the third, and this can be proved by the coroner's roll; in which case our will is, that if the defendant can prove the nonsuit in the county to have been made before the date of our writ to remove the appeal, our Justices shall commit the plaintiff to prison for his nonsuit, and his pledges shall be in mercy. But if the appellor die or fall so grievously sick that he cannot carry on his suit, in such case the pledges shall not be amerced for the nonsuit, and we allow that some other person, whose duty it is and who is capable of doing it, shall be permitted to revive the suit and prosecute it until the appellees are either acquitted or condemned. And if any of the appellees surrenders himself before he is outlawed, where the appellor makes default, let him be admitted to bail, as to our suit, until the first gaol delivery, in cases where he is bailable. And although he acquit himself as to our suit, yet the suit of any other, who will prosecute within the year and day, is not thereby taken away.

Appellee, on default of appellor, may be indicted.

Person acquitted on indictment may be afterwards appealed.

Exceptions to the action.

5. The defendant may also answer by exception to the action

excepciouns en plusours maneres. Car il pora dire, qe autre foiz i avoit apel en nostre Court par entre mesmes les persones de mesme la felonie, dount il passa quites devaunt tels Justices; et s'il vouche de ceo record a[1] garraunt, et le record passe pur ly, si soit il agardé quites, et le pleyntif a la prisoun. Ou il pora dire, qe tut feist il le fet, neqedent ne le fist il mie par felonie purpensé, mes par necessité, defendaunt sei ou sa femme ou sa mesoun ou sa meyné ou soen seignur ou sa dame, de la mort; ou il pora dire qe il ly tua en defendaunt[2] nostre pes, ou par mescheaunce[3] [4]en akune manere et[4] sauntz felonie penser[5]; les queus cas averreez voloms qe touz teus voisent quites par jugement. [45.]

Brac. 140 b (§ 5); Fle. 49 (§ 5).
Brac. 120 b; Fle. 49 (§ 8).
Stat. Marl. (52 Hen. III.) c. 26; Stat. Glouc. (6 Ed. I.) c. 9.

6. Et cum le defendaunt ne se pura eyder par nule excepcioun; si soit en sa eleccioun a defendre la felonie par soen cors, si le pleyntif soit able a combatre, ou par pays; et s'il ne voille, soit mis a la penaunce jekes autaunt qe il [6]le prie[6]. Et solom la aventure[7] de la batayle, ou del verdit del pays, soit rendu jugement. La peyne des felouns homicides soit la

Brac. 137; Fle. 50.
Ante c. 5. s. 2; Fle. 51 (§ 33).
Brac. 137; Fle. 51 (§ 32).

1. so *G.* et *L.* e *SM.* 2. so *NABMCF.* defuaunt *L.* 3. mesauenture *AC.* 4—4. *om.* *C.* 5. purpense *C.* 6—6. prie eyde *C.* 7. nature *AC.*

in several ways; for he may say that at another time there was an appeal in our Court between the same persons for the same felony, and that he was acquitted thereof before such Justices; and if he avouches this by warrant of record, and the record passes in his favour, he shall be awarded quit, and the plaintiff to prison. Or he may say, that although he committed the act, yet he did not do it by felony prepense, but by necessity, in defending himself, or his wife, or his house, or his family, or his lord, or his lady, from death; or that he killed the man in defence of our peace, or by some mischance, without any thought of felony; in all which cases, if proved, the appellees shall have judgment of acquittal.

Autrefois acquit.
Self defence.
Accident.

6. If the defendant cannot aid himself by any exception, let it be in his election to defend the felony by his body, if the plaintiff be able to fight, or by the country; and if he will not put himself on his defence, let him be put to penance until he prays to do it. And according to the event of the battle, or of the verdict of the country, judgment shall be given. The punishment of felons who have committed homicide shall be

Election of mode of trial.
Penance.
Sentence.

mort ovek desheritesouns des heyrs, ovek [1]plus de[1] peyne, si [2]la cause[2] le demaunde.

Mag. Cart. c 34; Brac. 125, 148 b; Fle. 53.

7. Des femmes voloms nous qe nule ne puse apeler de felonie de mort de homme, for qe de la mórt soen baroun tué entre ses bras de eynz le an et le jour. De enfaunt occys de eynz soen ventre ne poet ele mie apeler; car nul n'i est tenu a respoundre a apel de felonie, ou [3]le pleyntif ne set nomer[3] le noun a qi la felonie avera esté fete. En dreit de apel de rap, voloms, qe chescune femme, pucele ou autre, eyt sa accioun a sure la venjaunce de la felonie par apel en Countee de eynz xl. jours; apres quel tens ele perd sa sute; en quel cas si le defendaunt graunte le fet, et die qe ele conceust de ly enfaunt en mesme le tens, et ceo puse averreer, voloms nous qe en [4]ceo cas[4] ne soit nule felonie ajugé, pur ceo qe nule femme ne peut conceyvre, si ele ne se assente.

Stat. West. 1 (3 Ed. I.) c. 13; Stat. West. 2 (13 Ed. I.) c. 34; Glan. c. 14. s. 6; Brac. 147; Fle. 54.

Fle. 54.

[45 b.]

1—1. greigneur *C.* 2—2. le trespas *C.* 3—3. de pleintyf si ne soit nome *M.* 4—4. cas *om. LS. interl. N.* teu cas *M.* teus feez *G.* *sim. ABC.*

death, with disherison of their heirs, with further punishment if the occasion requires it.

Appeals by women.

7. As to women, our will is, that no woman shall bring an appeal of felony for the death of any man, except for the death of her husband killed within her arms[r], within the year and day. For an infant killed within her womb[s], she may not bring any appeal, no one being bound to answer to an appeal of felony, where the plaintiff cannot set forth the name of the person against whom the felony was committed. With regard to an appeal of rape, our pleasure is, that every woman, whether virgin or not, shall have a right to sue vengeance for the felony by appeal in the county court within forty days, but after that time she shall lose her suit; in which case, if the defendant confesses the fact, but says that the woman at the same time conceived by him, and can prove it, then our will is, that it be adjudged no felony, because no woman can conceive if she does not consent.

Appeal of rape.

[r] As to the interpretation of this phrase, see note above, p. 109.

[s] Although neither Glanvill nor Bracton specifically mention an appeal by a woman for the death of her unborn child, the expressions used by them, 'injuria corpori suo inflicta' (Glan. li. 14. c. 3.) 'injuria et violentia corpori suo illata' (Brac. 148 b.), may include this crime as well as rape. And it is clear from ancient records of the time of John and Henry III, that such an appeal was anciently allowed. (See Sir Sam. Clarke's Note on Fleta, li. i. c. 35 Kelham's Britton, p. 152.) Fleta expressly admits it, and gives the form of accusation (Fle. 53, 54.); and the statement in the text may have been intended as a correction of that author. Possibly it was considered that the right of appeal in this case was abolished by Magna Carta, s. 24.

CHAPITRE XXV. [XXIV.]

De Apels de Robberies et de Larcins.

1. De robberies et de larcins voloms nous [1]autri sutes durer[1], qi appeler voderount et sure venjaunce des felonies, par un an et un jour, et qe les apels soint comenceez en Countez ou les felonies averount esté fetes. Les apels porount estre fetz en ceste manere. Johan, qi ci est, apele Piers qi illucs est, qe, cum mesmes cesti Johan a tel jour tiel an out tel chyval qe cestui Johan[2] tent en soen estable ou aylours en tel certeyn leu, la vint mesme cesti Piers et mesmes cest chival felounousement cum feloun le embla et prist et amena encountre la pes, et qe ceo mauveysement fist offre cesti Johan de prover par soen cors, sicum la Court agardera qe fere le deyve. Et si le chival fust emblé hors de sa garde, ou s'il fust de ceo robbé, si chaunge les motz de soen apel, solum ceo qe affera. Et ausi si le pleyntif soit maheygné, ou de autre condicioun par quei batayle ne sei deit joyndre.

Stat. Glouc. (6 Ed. I) c. 9.

Brac. 146; Fle. 58.

1—1. autres sutes doner *C*. 2. Piers *LG*. *sim*. *NMSCF*. I. *AR*.

CHAPTER XXV.

Of Appeals of Robberies and Larcenies.

1. With respect to robberies and larcenies, our will is, that if other persons desire to bring an appeal and sue for revenge of such felonies, their right of prosecution shall continue a year and a day, and that appeals be commenced in the counties where the felonies were committed. The appeals may be made in this manner. 'John who is here appeals Peter who is there, that whereas the same John on such a day in such a year had such a horse, which he kept in his stable' or elsewhere in such certain place, 'the same Peter there came, and the same horse feloniously as a felon stole from him, and took and led away against the peace, and that this he wickedly did, the same John offers to prove by his body as the Court shall award that he ought to do it.' And if the horse was stolen out of his custody, or if he was robbed of it, let him change the words of his appeal according to the sense required; so if the plaintiff be maimed, or in such other condition that battle ought not to be joined.

Appeal of larceny.

Form of appeal.

2. Et adunc respoigne Piers et defende la felonie par motz defensables. Dunc[1] il se pora defendre par excepcioun, ou par [46.] soen cors, si nule condicioun ne desturbe[2] la batayle, ou par pays, ou voucher a garraunt, si il eyt qi. Et si il die qe le chival fu soen, et cum soen le prist, et cum soen chatel adirré[3], et ceo puse averrer, si chete le apel hors de felonie jekes en nature de trespas. En queu cas soit l'agard tel, qe il perde soen chival a remenaunt; et ausi de totes usurpaciouns en cas semblables, pur ceo qe nous voloms qe chescun overe plus par jugement qe par force.

Brac. 151; Fle. 55.

3. Et si le defendaunt vouche a garraunt par eyde de nostre Court, et le vouché veigne par [4]le eyde[4] de nostre Court, ou sauntz eyde, et entre en la garrauntie, adunc cesse le principal plé, et comence le apel de novel vers le garraunt, et solom sa defense soit jugé.

Brac. 151; Fle. 55.

4. Et si le garraunt ne vodera mie garraunter, adunc pora le voucheour dire issi. Piers, qi ci est, dit qe Thomas, qe la est, a tort ne ly garraunte cest chival devers Johan, qe illucs est, qi le chalenge pur soen, et pur ceo a tort, qe mesmes

1. dount *M.* 2. defende *M.* 3. amena *C.* 4—4. lordenaunce *C.*

Defence.

2. Next let Peter answer and defend the felony by words proper for defence; and then he may either defend himself by exceptions, or by his body if there are no circumstances to prevent the battle, or by the country, or vouch to warranty, if he has any one to call. And if he pleads that the horse was his own, and that he took him as his own and as his chattel lost out of his possession, and can prove it, the appeal shall be changed from felony to the nature of a trespass. In this case let it be awarded that the defendant lose his horse for ever; and the like of all usurpations in similar cases, because our will is that every one proceed rather by course of law than by force.

Claim of chattel as property of appellee.

Voucher of warrant.

3. If the defendant vouches to warranty by aid of our Court, and the vouchee comes by aid of our Court, or without such aid, and enters into warranty, the principal plea shall cease, and the appeal begin anew against the warrant, and according to his defence let judgment be given.

New plea against warrant.

Refusal to warrant; proceeding thereon.

4. If the vouchee will not enter into warranty, the vouchor may say thus. 'Peter who is here, says that Thomas who is there, wrongfully refuses to warrant the same horse against John who is there, who challenges it as his own; and herein

cesti Thomas mesme cest chival a mesme cesti Piers vendi, ou dona, ou autrement lessa, tel jour tel an en tel lu; et qe issi le fist, se profre mesmes cesti Piers del prover par soen cors, sicom la Court agardera qe prover le deyve. En cel cas covendra il, qe le vouché defende cel contract par soen cors, ou par pays, issi qe [1]del vencu[1] soit fet jugement de mort; et del[2] [46 *b.*]
vencour soit [3]agardé de aler[3] quites, et la chose chalengé soit deliveré al chalengeour, s'il eyt bien fet sa suite; et si noun, si remeigne ove[4] nous.

5. Et si fraude soit en la garrauntie, cum si[5] le apelé Brac. 151 *b*; Fle. 55, 56.
vouche a garraunt un chaumpiun par collusioun ou un autre fort homme, ou clerc, qe maliciousement pur louwer entre en garrauntie, et le demaundaunt[6] prie a mettre a voir la fraude et la malice pur fere sei sustrere de la batayle pur pour de la Fle. 56.
force del chaumpiun, ou pur la surté de la clergie en antencioun de sei purger en Cristiene Court, tut soit atteynt en la [7]laye Court[7], si soit a ceo resceu; et si la malice soit atteynte,

1—1. del vn *C.* 2. le *AC.* 3—3. agarde qe il aile *M.* iuge de aler *A.* *sim.* *C.* 4. a *AMC.* 5. so *MABC.* si *om.* *L.* 6. so *NMC.* *sim.* *AB.* demaundie *L.* 7—7. ley [Court *interlin.*] *M.* lei *AB.* ley *CF.*

wrongfully, inasmuch as the same Thomas sold (or gave or lent) the same horse to him the said Peter on such a day and year, in such a place; and that he did so, the same Peter offers to prove by his body, in such a manner as the Court shall award he ought to prove it.' And in this case it behoves the vouchee to defend such contract, either by his body, or by the country, so that judgment of death may pass upon the one who is defeated, and the successful party be allowed to go quit; and the thing challenged shall be delivered to him who challenged it, if he properly prosecuted his suit, otherwise it shall belong to us.

5. And if there be any fraud in the warranty, as if the Fraudulent voucher of champion or clerk.
appellee by collusion vouches to warrant some champion or other strong man, or a clerk, who maliciously and for hire enters into warranty, and the demandant prays leave to lay open the fraud and the malice, as done to make him withdraw himself from the battle for fear of the might of the champion, or for the privilege of the clergy, inasmuch as the vouchee being a clerk intends to purge himself in Court Christian, should he be attainted by the lay Court, let him be admitted thereto; and if the malice be proved, both the

si soit le jugement tiel, qe le garraunti et le garraunt eynt la mort, et le demaundaunt recovere sa demaunde.

Brac. 150 b; Fle. 54, 55. 6. De larcyns et de robberies fetes en tens de pes, dunt les maufesours ne averount mie esté freschement suyz voloms nous, qe ceux a qi les choses averount esté eynt lour sute par apels de felonie de eynz le an et le jour, sicum en autres felonies; apres quel tens cesse lour sute et soit[1] la sute nostre. Et issi serra jalemeyns de eynz le an et le jour, si autre sute ne courge, et ausi en totes maneres de felonies. Et si les[2] demaundauntz facent sute en fourme de trespas, si soint oyz, si il [47.] ne eynt avaunt comencez a sure en fourme de felonie, en quel cas il ne porount mie sei retrere de sure, qe nostre sute ne remeyne. Mes en cas ou il averount sui en fourme de trespas, tut eyt nostre pes esté enfreynte, ne voloms ja sute aver.

7. Et si nul apelé [3]se retree[3], soit demaundé de Counté en Counté, jekes autaunt qe il aperge ou soit utlagé. Et cum[4] serra venuz en Court, et le apelour le avera apelé par motz de

1. so *NM*. *sim*. *ARC*. soit *om*. *L*. 2. autres *add*. *C*. 3—3. so *LNS*. se retret *GA*. se retre[t]e *M*. seit retret *C*. 4. acun *add*. *NM*. *sim*. *ARC*.

warrantee and the warrant shall have judgment of death[t], and the demandant shall recover his demand.

After year and day, the king's suit only remains. 6. As to larcenies and robberies committed in time of peace, where the offenders were not freshly pursued; the owners of the things shall have their suit by appeal of felony within the year and day as in other felonies; but after that time their right of appeal shall cease, and the suit shall be ours. It is equally so within the year and day, if no other suit is commenced, and so in all manner of felonies. If the demandant sues in trespass, no indictment for felony. And if the demandants bring their suit in form of trespass, they shall be heard, if they have not before commenced their suit in form of felony, in which case they cannot, by withdrawing from their suit, deprive us of ours. But where they have sued in form of trespass, although our peace may have been broken, we will not prosecute.

Appearance, how compelled. 7. If any appellee has withdrawn himself, let him be demanded from county court to county court, till he either appears or is outlawed. And when he shall have come into

[t] By this clause a severer punishment is imposed upon the colluding vouchee than was before in use. According to Bracton and Fleta, the hireling champion was to lose a foot and hand. And according to Fleta, the clerk was to be imprisoned and ransomed. (Brac. 151 *b*; Fle. 55, 56.)

felonie, et le apelé se avera defendu par motz defensables, en primes deit il [1]veer s'il se pora eyder par excepciouns generales, sicum de la persone al juge, cum s'il ne eyt mie poer de oyer et de terminer cel apel, la quele excepcioun pora estre veyre en plusours maneres, cum [2]si le fet[2] dount il avera esté acoupé ne fu mie fet en soen poer, et cele excepcioun tient leu en Countez; ou si le juge ne eit mie comaundement de ceo de nous par bref; ou de la persone le apelour, qe pora estre en moutz des maneres; ou de sa persone demeyne. Ou[3] confermeez les persones, adunc deit il veer, s'il se pora eyder par excepciouns generales pur abatre le apel. Et cum il ne le pora abatre, si se eyde par excepciouns al accioun, cum si la chose chalengé ne vaille mie xii. deners; et autres poent estre plusours. Et si nule excepcioun ne ly pora valer, ne garraunt ne avera, si se pora [4]il defendre[4] par soen cors, ou par pays. Et s'il soit atteynt, soit jugé a la mort. [47 *b.*]

Brac. 140 *b*, 141; Fle. 31 (§ 6), 49 (§ 7, 9).

Brac. 146 *b*; Fle. 58 (c. 39. § 2).

8. Et puis pora le apelour sure vers les receptours et les

1. *so NARMC* venir et *add. L.* 2—2. *so AM.* cil le fet de nuyt *L.* cil le fet *NS.* 3. *so C.* en *LA.* e *M.* e *on eras. R.* 4—4. eyder *C.*

Court, and the appellor shall have appealed him by words of felony, and the appellee defended himself by proper words of defence, let him in the first place consider whether he can aid himself by general exceptions, as to the person of the judge, that he has not authority to hear and determine the appeal, which exception may be true in many ways, as if the act wherewith the defendant is charged was not done within his jurisdiction, and this exception holds good in counties, or where the judge is not authorised thereto by our writ. Or he may except to the person of the appellor, which may also be in sundry ways; or to his own person. If no objection lies against any of the persons, then let him see whether he can aid himself by general exceptions to abate the appeal; and if he cannot, let him then aid himself by exceptions to the action, as that the thing challenged is not of the value of twelve pence; and many other exceptions may be used. If he cannot avail himself of any exception, and has no warrant to vouch, he may lastly defend himself by his body, or by the country. And if he be attainted, let him have judgment of death.

Exception to jurisdiction.

Other exceptions.

Trial, by battle or by the country.

Sentence.

8. The appellor may afterwards proceed against the receivers

Appeal of accessories.

Brac. 153; Fle. 57 (§ 20). autres de eyde et de la consense, qi qe il unqes soint. Et cum un soit de plusours apelé, ou plusours de un, et batayles deyvent estre, si ne soint mie les batayles a une foiz, mes a
Brac. 151 b; Fle. 56 (§ 1–14). deverses. La femme neqedent au feloun pora dire, qe tut savoit ele de la mauvesté soen baroun, pur ceo ne le poeit ele mie encuser, ne devoit, taunt cum ele fu de ly coverte, le quel respouns ne voloms mie qe soit alowé trop generalment a teles femmes, qe eles ne se aquitent del fet et de la consense par pays, car les femmes as felouns sovent porount tener[1] les hommes taunt cum lour barouns les occient, et en tel cas sount ambedeus coupables de la felonie. Et des femmes concubines ne voloms en nule manere qe eles pusent se[2] coveryr
Brac. 151 b, 152; Fle. 56 (§ 15). par les felouns. [3]Si avenge[3] qe acune, jugé a la mort en ceste felonie ou en autre, soit enceynte de enfaunt, adunc voloms qe la execucioun del jugement soit delayé jekes a taunt qe l'enfaunt soit nee.

Brac. 152; Fle. 56, 57. 9. En ceste felonie, sicum en totes autres, porount les felouns aver compaignouns et receptours et fautours, les queus

1. *so N. sim. ARMC.* tener *om. L.* 2. *so N. sim. AMC.* se *om. LR.* 3—3. E si il auient *M.*

Separate battles. and the others for aiding and consenting, whosoever they are. And when one man is appealed by several, or several by one, and battles are to ensue, the battles shall not take place
Feme covert, when guilty as accomplice. at one time, but at different times. Nevertheless the felon's wife may plead, that although she was privy to the crime of her husband, yet she neither could nor ought to accuse him as long as she was under coverture; but this answer must not be allowed in too general a manner to such wives to excuse them from acquitting themselves of the fact, and of the consent, by the country; for it may often happen that the wives of felons hold the persons attacked whilst their husbands kill them, and in such case both of them are guilty of the felony; and as to the concubines of felons, they shall in no wise be allowed to
Execution of pregnant women delayed till delivery. excuse themselves by coverture. If it appears that any woman who is adjudged to death for this or any other felony be big with child, then execution of the judgment shall be delayed until the child be born[u].

Provers. 9. Felons, in this as in all other felonies, may have accomplices, receivers, and abettors, whom they may appeal for the

[u] Bracton derives this rule of humanity from the Roman Law, citing a passage in Dig. lib. 48, tit. 19. l. 3.

il poroune apeler et purloigner[1] lour vies; et si il voillent [48.]
devener provours, adunc voloms nous, qe les Corouners voisent a eux pur oyer lour reconisaunces de lour propres felonies, et celes reconisaunces facent enrouler, et ausi lour apels et les nouns des apelez. Et si les provours mettent a veir lour apels, et en nul point ne eynt mentuz, adunc voloms fere grace a eux de vie et de membre par la ou nous veroms qe bon seit, pur ceo qe il averount combatu pur nostre pes. Et voloms, qe qel houre qe nul tel provour eyt faili de soen apel, qe mes ne soit oi vers nul autre, qe il avera appelé, eynz seynt touz autres par ly apelez jugez quites quant a soen apel, et [2]le provour[2] a la mort; et s'il soint suspectz, si respoignent a nostre sute pur le esclaundre purger. Et si tels apelez soint de bone fame, adunc grauntoms qe tels soint lessez par bone meynprise quant a nostre sute, jekes en heyre des Justices, ou jekes autaunt qe nous voderoms de ceo parler vers eus. Et ausi le

Brac. 152, 153 *b*; Fle. 56, 7.

Brac. 153; Fle. 57.

1. aloigner *M*. 2—2. il *M*.

sake of prolonging their own lives; and if they will become provers, then let the coroner go to them, and hear the confession of their own felonies, and cause such confessions to be enrolled, and also their appeals, together with their names and the names of the appellees. And if the provers make the justice of their appeals appear, and have lied in no particular, then they shall have our pardon of life and limb where we shall see meet, because they have fought for our peace[x]. But our will is, that from the time any such prover has failed of his appeal, he shall be no more heard against any other whom he has appealed, but all others appealed by him shall be adjudged quit as to his appeal, and the prover shall be condemned to death; and if the persons appealed are suspected, let them answer at our suit, and clear themselves of the slander; but if they are of good fame, then we permit them to be let out by sufficient mainprise as to our suit until the eyre of the Justices, or until we shall take proceedings against them. The like liberty shall be granted to those who

Successful prover, pardoned.

Consequence of failure of appeal of prover.

Writ *De odio et atia*.

x The commentator in MS. *N*. states that it was considered that an approver had not merited pardon until he had made good his appeal by battle against seven accomplices; and that by some the number was put at nine; and that even then he was not to be permitted to remain in the country, but to be exiled, or to take the cross in the Holy Land. The latter point is confirmed by Bracton: 'Vitam habeat et membra, sed in regno remanere non poterit, etiam si velit plegios invenire.' Brac. 153 *b*.

Mag. Cart. c. 26; Stat. West. 1. (3 Ed. I.) c. 11; Stat. West. 2. (13 Ed. I) c. 29; Brac. 121 b, 123; Fle. 39. Stat. West. 1. (3 Ed. I.) c. 20; Fle. 58 (§ 26). [48 b.] Brac. 144; Fle. 59 (c. 41. § 3).

grauntoums nous, de ceux, qi enditez sount de acune felonie par hayne et par procurement des enemys, la quele hayne nous poroms atteyndre par enqueste fete par noster bref *de odio et atya*, sauve chescuni[1] sute.

10. Des coloumbs pessouns [2]ne de ees ne[2] de autre sauvageyne [3]trové en lour sauvagine[3] ne voloms qe nul ne porte jugement de mort, s'il ne seint felounousement emblez hors de mesoun, ou damasche beste hors de parc; ne qe nul apel se tiegne de meyns de xii. deners de damage; ne en nul cas qe plus serra par[4] examinement des Justices trové trespas qe felonie, sicum brusure ou riffiure, la ou le apel serra fet de playe.

CHAPITRE XXVI. [xxv.]

De Apels de Maheygns.

Brac. 144 b; Fle. 58.

1. De Maheygns volom nous bien, qe les maheignez suent par apels de felonie vers teus felouns. Et si akun apelé serra de tele felonie atteynt et[5] attende jugement, si soit le juge-

1. chescune *L N F.* chesquni *A.* *sim. M.* *so corr. R.* 2—2. nyds oefs e *M.* 3—3. *om. C.* 4. *so N A R M F.* qe *L.* 5. et *om. L C.* e *M.* e *interl. N.*

are indicted of any felony through hatred, and by procurement of their enemies; which hatred shall be convicted by inquest by virtue of our writ *De odio et atia*, saving to every one his suit.

No appeal lies for wild animals,

10. As to pigeons, fish, bees, or other wild animals, found in a wild condition, we ordain that no man have judgment of death on account of them; but otherwise if they have been feloniously stolen out of houses, or if they are tame beasts, out of parks.

nor for petty larceny,

And no appeal shall lie where the damage is under twelve pence, nor in any case which shall be found by examination of the Justices to be rather trespass than felony;

nor mere trespass.

as where the appeal is made of a wound, and it appears to be only a bruise or scratch.

CHAPTER XXVI.

Of Appeals of Mayhem.

Appeal for mayhem.

1. Concerning mayhems, we are content that the maimed shall sue by appeals of felony against the offenders; and when any appellee is convicted of such felony, and brought up for

ment[1], qe il perdra autel membre cum il avera tolet al pleyntif. Et si[2] la pleynte soit fete de femme, qe ele avera tolu a homme ses membres, en tel cas perdera la femme la une meyn par jugement, com le membre dunt ele avera trespassé. En ceste felonie ne voloms nule sute aver, quant a jugement de perte pur perte; mes en cas ou le apel serra abatu, voloms nous qe les felouns respoignent de tieles felonies[3]; et s'il soint atteyntz a nostre sute, si soint il agardez a la prisoun, et de illucs soint reyntz pur nostre pes enfreynte. Et voloms qe nul maheyn ne soit tenu fors qe de membre tolet dunt homme est plus feble a combatre, sicum del oyl, ou de la meyn, ou del piee, ou del os de la teste brusé, ou des dentz devaunt. De dentz moellers ne del orayle ne del nees [4]n'en est counté[4] nul maheyn, mes blemure del cors.

Fle. 59.

Glan. li. 14. c. 1; Brac. 145; Fle. 58.

[49.]

2. Des playes et de enprisounement de fraunces hommes, et de chescun led trespas porount estre fetz ausi apels de felonie. Mes pur eschure la perilouse aventure de batayles, meutz vaut fere la sute par nos brefs de trespas qe par appels. Car si

Brac. 145 b; Fle. 59, 60.

1. tiel *add. NAR. sim. MC.* 2. so *NARMC.* si *om. L.* 3. fetes *add. GARM.* fez *C.* 4—4. so *G.* nen est contenu *LNS.* ne est counte *AR. sim. MF.* nest *C.*

judgment, let the judgment be this, that he lose the like member as he has destroyed of the plaintiff; and if the plaint be made against a woman who has deprived a man of his members, she shall have judgment to lose a hand, being the member wherewith she committed the offence. In this felony no prosecution shall lie at our suit with a view to the judgment of loss for loss; but if the appeal be abated, the felons shall answer for such felonies, and if they are attainted at our suit, they shall be awarded to prison, and ransomed thence for breaking our peace. And our will is, that nothing be deemed a mayhem unless a member be lost, whereby a man is rendered less able to fight; as the loss of an eye, a hand, or a foot, or fracture of the skull bone, or loss of the fore teeth; but the loss of the molar teeth, or of an ear, or of the nose, is not accounted a mayhem, but a disfigurement only.

Judgment.

Mayhem, how punished at the king's suit.

What injury amounts to mayhem.

2. Appeals of felony may also be brought for wounds, and for imprisonment of freemen, and for every other enormous trespass; but for avoiding the perilous risk of battle, it is better to proceed by our writs of trespass than by appeals; for

Appeals for wounds and false imprisonment,

how discouraged.

variaunce soit trové del apel en roulle del Corouner et en sa mustraunce autre foiz el Counté, ou qe omissioun soit fete, ou interrupcioun des Countez, ou autre vice, si serra le pleyntif comaundé a la prisoun, pur ceo qe il ne avera mie parfourni ceo a quei se obligea, et fra[1] gré al defendaunt et puis a nous. Mes si le apel estoise, et le defendaunt se eyt mis de ben et de mal el pays, et le pays die qe il soit coupable, si avera mesme le jugement qe il averoit s'il fust vencu par batayle, ceo est a saver playe pur playe, et enprisounement pur enprisounement, et trespas pur trespas. Mes en tel cas voloms qe teles mitigaciouns soint, qe les apelez soynt comaundez a la prisoun, et la demurgent en fers, [2]ci la qe[2] satisfaccioun soit fete as pleyntifs, et [3]puis soint puniz[3] pur nostre pes enfreynte.

Fle. 60 (c. 42, § 7).

[49 *b.*] 3. Et mesme le jugement voloms qe soit[4] issaunt de noster bref de trespas. Aucuns trespas sount neqedent plus punisables, sicum trespas fetz en tens de pes as chivalers ou as autres gentz honourables par ribaudz et par autres viles persones,

1. *so ARMCF.* fere *LGS.* 2—2. *so G.* si la qe la *L.* ci la qe la *S.* si la qe *M.* 3—3. plus seent reinz *M.* puis seient reinz *AC.* *sim. F.* 4. *so NM.* *sim. C.* soit *om. L.*

if variance be found between the appeal as entered in the roll of the coroner and as set forth in the county court, or if there has been any omission, or any interruption of the county courts, or other error, the plaintiff shall be commanded to prison for not having performed what he bound himself to do, and shall make satisfaction to the defendant, and afterwards to us. But if the appeal be maintained, and the defendant have put himself for good or ill on the country, and the jury say that he is guilty, the same judgment shall be given against him, as would have been in case he had been vanquished in battle, to wit, wound for wound, imprisonment for imprisonment, and trespass for trespass. But in such cases our will is, that the execution of the judgment be so far mitigated, that the appellees be sent to prison, and there remain in irons till they have made satisfaction to the plaintiffs; and they shall afterwards be punished for breach of our peace.

Judgment upon such appeal.

Lex talionis, how mitigated in practice.

3. The like judgment shall result where the proceeding is by our writ of trespass. But some trespasses deserve a greater punishment, as trespasses committed in time of peace against knights or other honourable persons by ribalds or other

Punishment in trespass.

en queus cas nous voloms, qe si ribaud soit atteynt a la sute de aucun chivaler, qe il ly eit feru par felonie sauntz deceert le chivaler, qe le ribaud perde le poyng dount il trespassa; et avoms dit en tens de pes, car de trespas fetz en tournementz ne as justes, ne en tels fetz semblables a guerre, ne voloms rien entremettre, si nous mesmes n'i[1] eyoms esté.

4. Et voloms ausi, qe les [2]pointz et les[2] peynes ordeynez par nous et par noster Conseil, [3]et crieez[3] a fere pur gentz estraunges a durer jekes a certeyn tens, soint tenues et rendues solom lour[4] ordinaunces. Mag. Cart. c. 30.

CHAPITRE XXVII. [XXVI.]

De Attachementz.

1. Dit avoms avaunt la forme de atteyndre nostre pes enfreynte par apels et par presentementz; ore fet a dire, coment nostre pes enfreynte fet atteyndre par forme de trespas. Et primes cum aucun avera purchacé noster bref

1. so *NAR.* *sim. M.* ne *LC.* 2—2. so *L.* *om. NARGSMCF.* 3—3. a criees *L.* encriees *NF.* en criez *GS.* encrieez *M.* e criez *ARC.* 4. les *MC.*

worthless people; in which case our pleasure is, that if a ribald be attainted at the suit of any knight of having feloniously struck him without any provocation from the knight, the ribald shall lose the hand wherewith he offended. We have said, in time of peace, because as to injuries done at tournaments and jousts, or such warlike feats, we will not interpose, unless the acts be done in our presence. Punishment for striking a knight. Injuries at tournaments.

4. Our will also is, that the articles and penalties ordained by us and our council, and proclaimed to be put in force for a certain time with regard to strangers, be observed and executed according to such ordinances. Protection to strangers.

CHAPTER XXVII.

Of Attachments, and other proceedings in actions of trespass; and of the conclusion of the Eyre.

1. We have already treated of the manner of convicting offenders for breach of our peace by appeals and presentments; we must now show how the breach of our peace is to be convicted by way of trespass. In the first place, when any Form of proceeding in action of trespass.

[50.] de trespas sur maheyng ou enprisounment ou playe, ou sour chose emblé [1]ou robbé[1] ou [2]autrement malement[3] enporté et[2] detenu, ou de brusure[4] de parcs ou de baterie, ou sour autre chose fete encountre nostre pes, ou sur serjaunt fuaunt del acounte rendre a soen seignur, al comencement delivere soen bref al viscounte; et puis ly truysse deus pleges destreynables a ly de sure sa pleynte; et le viscounte face destreyndre les trespasours par lour avers et par lour chateus, et puis les ajourne qe il soint en nostre Court, solom ceo qe contenu serra en noster bref, a respoundre a tels pleyntifs des trespas contenu es brefs; issi qe chescun defendaunt soit garni de la entencioun de soen adversarie.

Brac. 442; Fle. 150.

2. Et si les brefs soint retournables en fraunchise, et les baillifs ne voillent mie fere solom noster maundement, si[5] les pleyntifs ne lour truissent pleges destreynables a eus, en tel cas list al viscounte de retourner en nostre Court, qe il maunderent as baillifs celi qi ad la fraunchise de retour des brefs, qe il feissent la execucioun, qi rien ne firent; et nous tauntost

1—1. *so ARMC. om. LS. interlin. N.* 2—2. *om. AR.* 3. maueisement *M. om. C.* 4. *so GMR. sim. C.* brusours *L.* brusour *N.* 5. *so NARMC.* et *L.*

one has obtained our writ of trespass for a mayhem, imprisonment, or wound, or for anything stolen or robbed or in any other manner wrongfully carried away or detained, or for breaking parks, or for battery, or for other things committed against our peace, or against a bailiff for refusing to render account to his lord, let him begin by delivering his writ to the sheriff; and afterwards let him find two pledges distrainable to the sheriff to prosecute his plaint. And let the sheriff cause the trespassers to be distrained by their cattle or by their chattels, and afterwards adjourn them to be in our Court at the day prefixed according as shall be contained in our writs, to answer to the plaintiffs for the trespasses contained in the writs; so that every defendant may have notice of his adversary's case.

Delivery of writ to sheriff. Pledges to prosecute. Process for compelling appearance.

Nature of the trespass to be specified in the writ.

2. And if the writs are returnable in a franchise, and the bailiffs will not execute our precept unless the plaintiff will find them pledges distrainable to them, in such case the sheriff may make a return in our Court, that he sent to the bailiffs of the person having the franchise of return of writs to do execution, but that they have nothing done; and we will

Although the writ be returnable in a franchise, the pledges may be distrainable to the sheriff.

maunderoms as viscountes, qe il ne lessent [1]pur la fraunchise qe il ne entrent et facent execucioun[1]. Et si le pleyntif voille, si pora il sure vers le baillif de recoverer ses damages. Car suffrable chose serroit, qe les pleyntifs eussent trové surtee de sure lour pleyntes en nostre Chauncelerie sauntz nuli prejudice, par quei peert qe la surté trové al viscounte suffist a chescun bref.

3. Et si les defendauntz suffrent les destresces en meyns des viscountes, si porount les viscountes respoundre, qe il les ount destreynt par tels avers et par teus chateus. Et si les defendauntz ne veignent dunc en Court, dunc fet a saver lequel en nostre Court ou aylours, sicum en Counté ou en court de baroun ou de autre fraunc homme; et si en nostre Court devaunt nous ou devaunt nos Justices, dunc voloms nous qe nule defaute soit ajugé jekes apres le quart jour en nul play. Et s'il ne veignent de eynz le quart jour ne ne seynt essoygniez, et la partie pleyntive se profre et demaund jugement de la defaute, si soit agardé la graunt destresce, et le viscounte soit chargé de respoundre des issues de la premere destresce, et qe il ajourne[2] le defendaunt de estre en Court a [50 *b*.] Brac. 439, 440; Fle. ii. 2. c. 65. s. 8–12. Stat West. 1. (3 Ed. I.), c. 45.

1—1. la execucion pur franchise qil ne la face *R. sim. A.* lexecucion *C.* 2. eniourne *M.*

immediately command the sheriff that he omit not by reason of the franchise to enter and do execution. And the plaintiff, if he will, may proceed against the bailiffs to recover his damages; for it would have been allowable for the plaintiffs to have found sureties to prosecute their plaints in our Chancery without prejudice to any one; wherefore the surety found to the sheriff on every writ is sufficient.

Process in the king's court, if the defendant fails to appear after distress.

3. If the defendants suffer distresses to be taken into the hands of the sheriffs, the sheriffs may return that they have distrained them by such cattle or by such chattels; and if the defendants do not thereupon come into court, then it must be distinguished whether the plaint is in our Court, or elsewhere, as in the county, or in a court baron or other freeholder's court; and if in our Court before us or before our Justices, then we will that no default be adjudged in any plea until after the fourth day. If they do not come within the fourth day, and are not essoined, and the plaintiff offers himself and demands judgment for the default, the great distress shall be awarded, and the sheriff shall be charged to answer unto us for the issues of the first distress; and the Justice shall adjourn the

un autre jour; a quel jour nul essoygne ne ly soit allouwé, car nous defendoms, qe en nul cas ne soit essoigne allouwé [1]apres defaute, ci la qe la defaute soit sané[1] en nostre Court; a quel jour si les defendauntz facent defaute, si soint les issues forfetes a nous, et le viscounte de nous en respoundre soit chargé; et celes destresces courgent de jour en jour jekes a taunt qe il veignent respoundre.

4. Et si le play soit aylours qe en nostre Court, et les de- [51.] fendauntz ne veignent, ne se eynt fet essonier, si ne voloms nous mie qe les jugementz [2]soint delayez[2] jekes al quart jour; mes tauntost le premer jour soit agardé par les sutiers, qe cele destresce soit retenue, et qe hom prenge plus, et issi de Court en Court. Et si le viscounte, ou le baillif, ne eyt fet le comaundement, si soit en la merci.

Stat. West. 1. (3 Ed. I.) c. 45.

5. Et mesme le proces en destresces soit agardé en defautes fetes apres essoines en bref de trespas fet encountre nostre pes. Mes en attachementz de felonie ne courge nule destresce for qe par le cors, si hom le puse trover. Et si le viscounte

Brac. 439, 444 *b*; Fle. 141, 142, 145.

Brac. 441; Fle. 144 (§18).

1—1. apres ci la qe la defaute soit sane *L.* apres [defaute] si la qe la defaute soit sanee *N.* apres ci e la qe la defaute seit sauue *G.* *sim. S.* apres defaute ieqes ataunt qe la defaute seit sauue *AR.* apres defaute sauue *M.* apres defaute seit sauue *C.* *sim. F.* apres qe defaute seyt saune en nostre Court *W.* apres defaute eynz ceo qe la defaute soit sanee *Z.*
2—2. se delaeynt *N.* *sim. ARMC.*

defendant to be in court on another day; at which day no essoin shall be allowed him, for we forbid the allowing of an essoin in any case after default, until such default be cleared in our Court. And if upon this day the defendants make default, the issues shall be forfeited to us, and the sheriff shall be charged to answer unto us for the same, and these distresses shall be continued from day to day until they appear and answer.

Process in county court or court baron in like case.

4. If the plea be in any other court than ours, and the defendants have neither appeared nor caused themselves to be essoined, we will not that judgment be delayed until the fourth day; but immediately on the first day let it be awarded by the suitors, that such distresses be detained, and more be seized, and so from court to court. If the sheriff or the bailiff has not executed the precept, let him be in mercy.

Process in trespass *contra pacem*; in felony.

5. The same process of distress is to be awarded in defaults after essoins in a writ of trespass committed against our peace; but in an attachment of felony no distress runs excepting against the body, if it can be found. And if in the above cases

retourne en les avauntditz cas, qe les trespasours ne ount rien en sa baillie par quei il pusent estre attachez, si soit agardé, qe le viscounte preyne les cors. Et s'il retourne, qe les cors ne sount mie trovez en sa baillie, si soit remaundé[1] par noster bref de jugement, qe il soint demaundez de Counté en Counté jekes a taunt qe il soint utlagez s'il ne veignent.

6. Et cum aucun qi serra destreynt vendra en Court et ne peuse sa defaute saner[2], tauntost soit ajugé en nostre merci pur sa defaute. Et si plusours defautes soint, plusours soint les amerciementz. Et si acun soit attaché par pleges et eyt fet defaute, si soint les pleges somouns de oyer lour jugement, pur quei il ne avoint en Court celi qe il plevirent; a [51 *b*.] quel jour s'il ne veignent, ne ne pusent dedire la plevine, [3]si soint ausi en la merci[3]; et s'il voillent dedire la plevine, si soit le toyl entre eux et le viscounte.

Brac. 440, 440 *b*; Fle. 144.

7. Et cum les defendauntz vendrount en Court et averount oiz les pleyntifs counter vers eus, si se porrount eus eyder par excepciouns generales et especiales, quant il se averount de-

1. apres le tierce Cape *add. Wingate in corrections.* 2. so *LNS.* sauuer *GMK.* 3—3. *so verb. W.* ausi en la merci *LS.* soint ausi en la merci *N.* *sim. AR.* si seent ausi en nostre mercy *M.* ausi seient amerciez *C.*

the sheriff return, that the trespassers have nothing in his bailiwick whereby they may be attached, it shall be awarded that he take their bodies; and if he return that the bodies are not found in his bailiwick, then let it be ordered by our writ of judgment, that they be demanded from county court to county court until they be outlawed, if they do not appear.

Process, if no distress be found. *Capias.* Outlawry.

6. And when any person who has been distrained shall come into court, and cannot clear his default, let him be straightway adjudged in our mercy for his default; and if there be several defaults, let there be several amercements. And if any one be attached by pledges and make default, let the pledges be summoned to hear their judgment, for not having him in court for whom they were pledged. At which day if they do not appear, or cannot deny their being pledged, they also shall be in our mercy; but if they will deny the plevin, the debate shall be between them and the sheriff.

Amercement, for default of appearance, of defendant and his pledges.

7. When the defendants have appeared in court, and heard the plaintiffs count against them, and have defended themselves by proper words of defence, they may then aid them-

Dilatory pleas or exceptions of defendant.

fenduz par motz defensables. Et premerement par excepciouns devers le juge, et puis par excepciouns de[1] la persone al pleyntif ou de[2] lour persone demeyne, sicum dit serra entre les excepciouns de bref de dreit; et par [3]excepciouns al[3] bref, cum si le bref soit purchacé en autre counté qe par la ou le fet dust estre fet, ou par vice, ou par errour, ou par omissioun.

8. Et s'il ne eyt[4] excepcioun dilatorie, si respoignent al accioun; ou il porount dire, [5]de mesme ceo trespas qe[5] il passerent quites eynz ces houres par jugement vers mesmes le pleyntif; et si ceo soit averré par record, solom ceo sei[6] face jugement. Ou il porount dire qe de cel trespas furent il accordez; et si le pleyntif le dedie, si soit la verité enquise par pays; et si le pleyntif ne le voille, si [7]soint les defendauntz agardez[7] de aler quites, et les pleyntifs en la merci.

9. En dreit de receptours de trespasours, de comaundours[8] et de accessories, n'en est nule peyne uncore ordinee for qe

1. deuers *M.* 2. deuers *M.* 3—3. *so M.* excepcioun de *LN.* excepcion du *AR.* 4. eent *M.* *sim. C.* 5—5. qe de mesme cel trespas *N.* *sim. SGAMC.* 6. si *L.* se *NM.* *om. C.* 7—7. *so verb. GK.* *sim. C.* soint les defenduz agardez *LN.* *sim. S.* seient les defendanz Iugez *AR.* soit le defendaunt iugee *M.* 8. e des assentours *add. GSM.* *sim. AH.*

selves by exceptions general or special; and first, by exceptions to the judge; afterwards to the person of the plaintiff or to their own person, as shall be mentioned amongst exceptions in the writ of right[n]; or they may except to the writ, as where a writ is sued out into any other county than where the fact is alleged to have been committed, or for a fault, error, or omission therein.

Plea of defendant; as judgment in his favour in former action,

8. If there be no dilatory exception, let them answer to the action; to which they may say that they were previously acquitted of the same trespass, as against the same plaintiff; and if this be verified by record, let judgment be given accordingly. Or the defendants may say that the parties made accord of this trespass; and if the plaintiff deny it, let the truth be inquired by the country. And if the plaintiffs will not agree to the accord, let the defendants be awarded quit, and the plaintiffs in mercy.

or accord.

Accessories in trespass.

9. With regard to receivers of trespassers, commanders, and accessories, there is not as yet any punishment ordained,

[n] The proposed chapter on Exceptions in the Writ of Right is not contained in the Treatise as it now exists; but some further observations upon exceptions to the person may be found in book ii. chap. 18.

soulement vers les persones de principals trespasours. Et si [52.]
le pleyntif se pleigne de damage fet a ly et a ses hommes, ou Brac. 155, 155 b.
soulement pur ses hommes, la porount les defendauntz[1] dire, qe chescun homme[2] ad severale accioun; en quel cas nous voloms qe tels pleyntifs ne recoverent rien par lour pleyntes for qe solement les damages qe il porount renablement moustrer, qe il averount euz par defaute de service de lour hommes batuz ou enprisounez ou autrement si atterez[3] qe il ne pusent server, et qe lour accioun coṁence apres qe le trespas serra atteynt fet as serjauntz.

10. Et si le viscounte retourne, qe le defendaunt soit[4] clerc Brac. 442 b, 443; Fle. 153.
et se ne veut justicer a ly, ne qe il ne ad nul lay fee en sa baillie ou il le puse destreyndre, si soit maundé par noster bref a soen ordinarie, sicum Archevak ou Evak, q'il face venir un tel soen clerc. Et si le Evak nel eyt al jour nomé[5] en noster bref, si soit le Evak somouns a respoundre pur quei il nel out a noster maundement. Et si le Evak sursece nostre

1. *so verb. PZ. so corr. A.* pleyntifs *L. sim. SGMH.* 2. e chesqune femme *add. CH.* 3. attyrez *N. sim. ABMC.* attirreez *S.* 4. est *AMK.* 5. *so MG. sim. SNAB.* mene nome *L.* assigne *C.*

How far a master may recover for damage done to his servant.

except only against the principal trespassers. And if the plaintiff complains of a damage done to himself and to his men, or only on behalf of his men, the defendant may say that every man has a separate action; and in such cases we will that the plaintiffs recover nothing by their plaints beyond the damages which they can reasonably show they have sustained by the loss of the services of their men, who have been beaten or imprisoned, or so treated as to be incapable of service. And their action shall not be brought until after conviction of the trespass committed against the servants[o].

Process against a clerk.

10. If the sheriff return that the defendant is a clerk, and refuses to submit to his jurisdiction, and that he has no lay fee in his bailiwick whereby he can be distrained, let his ordinary, as the archbishop or bishop, be commanded by our writ that he cause such a one his clerk to appear. And if he does not produce him at the day named in our writ, let the bishop be summoned to answer why he did not produce him at our

[o] According to Bracton, an action might be brought by the master for the insult and disgrace inflicted upon him in the person of his servant, although no loss of service followed; and even though the servant withdrew from his action, or refused to prosecute, the master might himself sue. (Brac. 115.) The change of law is indicative of an increase of personal independence.

Stat. West. 1. (3 Ed. I.) c. 45. somouns, si soit ataché de venir par destresce; et s'il ne veigne a la premere destresce, si courge [1]sour ly[1] la graunt destresce, cum de sus est dit, jekes aut auntqe il veigne; et cum il serra venuz en Court, et ne puse saner[2] ses defautes, si soit amercié.

[52 *b.*] Brac. 439, 444; Fle. 141 (§ 4), 142 (§ 10), 154 (§ 9). 11. Plusours accionns sount neqedent de trespas, en les queus covendra plus haster, cum de trespas fet a nous, ou a nostre compaigne, ou a nos enfauntz, ou a gentz estraunges, com a solempnes messagers ou a nos amis aliens, ou a nos ministres, ou a marchaunz, et sicum a gentz croizez; en les queus cas ne voloms nule solempneté de attachement estre fete, mes tauntost soint les attachementz fetz par les cors, issi qe le viscounte eit les cors a respoundre al premer jour.

Glan. II. 10. c. 2; Fle. 142. 12. Et sount acunes accioùns pledables par mesmes teles destresces cum en trespas, en les queles nule utlagerie ne seut[3], et qe sount plus dilatories par un jour, et qe comencent par somouns, sicum play de dette, et de covenaunt, et en cas de garrauntie de chartre, et de wast, et de vente, et de[4] destruccioun des mees et des boys ou de autre fraunc tenement, et des pletz de naifté, et de plusours autres.

1—1. *so N. sim. SGARMC. om. L.* 2. *so LNS.* sauuer *GMK.* 3. fust *LF.* fust [siust *corr.*] *N.* suit *AR.* suyt *W.* fu fete *M.* feust *C.* 4. *so SG.* de *om. LM.*

precept. And if the bishop neglect our summons, let him be attached to come by distress; and if he does not come at the first distress, let the great distress, as above said, proceed against him until he shall come; and when he has appeared in court, if he cannot clear his default, let him be amerced.

Expeditious process used in special cases of trespass. 11. There are however several actions of trespass which require greater expedition, as trespasses committed against us or our consort, or our children, or against foreign persons, as solemn ambassadors or alien friends, or against our officers, or against merchants, or against those who have taken the cross; in which cases no formality of attachment shall be required, but the bodies of the defendants shall be immediately attached, so that the sheriff shall have them to answer on the first day.

Process in actions of debt, covenant, &c. 12. There are some actions also pleadable by like distresses as in trespass, where no outlawry ensues, and which are more dilatory by a day, and commence by summons; as a plea of debt, of covenant, in case of warranty of charter, waste, sale, destruction of houses or woods or other freehold, and pleas of naifty, and several others.

13. Et en heyre des Justices pount estre pledez quant qe pouent estre pledez en Counté, sicum de plé de vee de naam, et de dette, et de naifté, de gardes, et de mariages, et les presentementz fetz en tourns de viscounte et en vewe de fraunc-plege, et ausi les pletz de faus pois et de fauses mesures, et autres plusours[1] par devaunt nos Justices assignez as assises prendre en countez, et les brefs pledables par devaunt nos Justices [2]du baunc a Westmouster[2]. Brac. 108 b, 109 b; Fle. 23. [53.]

14. Et si acun presentement des articles de nostre Coroune remeyne desatamé et desterminé[3], adunc soint les Justices punisables a nostre volunté, s'il ne eynt [4]pur eus[4] bone et renable excusacioun. Et cum les presentementz sour les chapitres deliverez[5] soint determinez, tauntost soint les pletz de terre ajournez par devaunt eux jekes en un autre counté. Mes s'il ne deyvent plus heyrer, si soint ajournez en baunc en presence des parties. Et tauntost soint les amerciementz taxez, et les estretes enveez a noster Escheker, et ausi de fins, Fle. 63, 64.

1. so *LGSM.* qe sunt pledables *interl. N.* 2—2. so *LM.* *sim. N.* au baunk *AR.* en Baunk *C.* a banc a Westm. *W.* 3. determinez *MC.* *sim. RW.* 4—4. *om. ABC.* 5. del Eire *AB.* *sim. MC.* [del Eyre] deliuerez *N.*

13. Whatever may be pleaded in the county court may also be pleaded in the eyre of the Justices; as pleas *de vetito namio*, of debt, of naifty, of wards, and marriages; also presentments made in the sheriffs' tourns and in views of frank-pledge; and also pleas concerning false weights and measures, and many others, which are pleadable before our Justices assigned to take assises in the county, and writs pleadable before our Justices of the Bench at Westminster. Concurrent jurisdiction of Justices in eyre with county court and Justices of assise, and of the Bench.

14. If any presentment upon the articles of our Crown remain uncommenced or undetermined, then let the Justices, unless they have a good and reasonable excuse, be punishable at our discretion. When the presentments on the articles of the eyre are determined, the pleas of land shall be immediately adjourned before them to another county; or if the eyre is not to be continued, they shall be adjourned into the Bench, in the presence of the parties. The amercements are immediately to be assessed[p], and the estreats sent to our Exchequer; the like as to fines and the chattels of felons and fugitives; and Crown business to be concluded at the eyre. Conclusion of the eyre.

p See before, c. ii. s. 4.

et des chateus de felouns et de futifs; et les nouns des futifs soint enroullez en deus roulles dount le un remeygne as Corouners et al viscounte du pays suth le seal la Justice pendaunt; et ceux nouns soint [1]demaundez al[1] premer Counté apres le heyre, qe il veignent ester a dreit en nostre Court, et issi de Counté en Counté jekes autaunt qe il veignent ou soint utlagez. Et le autre roulle ensemblement ovek touz les roulles del heyre soint enveez a noster Escheker, et sauvement gardez en nostre Tresorie.

[53 *b.*] 15. Et si les sutiers del counté soint atteyntz de faus jugement, ou autrement eynt erree de[2] usage de la ley, si soit le counté en nostre merci; et ausi les hundrez pur les defautes les sutiers, et les villes pur plusours defautes; et ceux amerciementz soint assis solom la fourme de nos estatuz de Westmoster. Et puis soit comaundé qe le viscounte soit en eyde as presentours, qe les veysins lour facent renables contribuciouns de lour despenses.

Mag. Cart. c. 14; Stat. West. 1. (3 Ed. I.) c. 18; Brac. 116 *b*; Fle. 63.

1—1. *so NM. sim. GS.* maundez a *L.* maundez al *ABC.* 2. en *NGAM.* e *S.* ou *C.*

Coroner's rolls and rolls of the eyre.

the names of the fugitives shall be enrolled in two rolls, whereof one shall remain with the coroners and the sheriff of the county under the seal of the Justices thereto attached, and such persons are to be demanded by their names at the first county court after the eyre, to come and submit to justice in our Court, and so from county court to county court, until they appear or be outlawed. The other roll, together with all the rolls of the eyre, shall be transmitted to our Exchequer, and safely kept in our Treasury.

Amercements.

15. If the suitors of the county be attainted of false judgment, or have made any other error in the usage of the law, the county shall be in our mercy. The hundreds also for the defaults of the suitors, and the townships for divers defaults; and the amercements shall be assessed according to our Statutes of Westminster. And afterwards let the sheriff be commanded to aid the presentors by causing the neighbours to raise reasonable contributions towards their expenses.

Expenses of presentors.

CHAPITRE XXVIII. [XXVII.]

De Prises de Avers.

1. En countez avoms nous double Court: une des pletz de nostre pes, la quele tenent nos Corouners et les sutiers, et dount les Corouners soulement [1]portent record[1]. Et si avoms Court ausi, cum court de baroun, dunt les sutiers sount chargez des jugementz, et ne ount point de record hors de lour court, for qe par assent des parties. Car en lour courtz ne pora nul desdire ceo qe il avera avaunt pledé; mes si la parole soit remué hors des courtz de tels sutiers, si pora une des parties dedire le record; mes a ceo covent il, qe il eit prest en meyn sute, ceo est a saver, un soen fraunc homme, qi adounc fust en cele court, qe veist et oist, qe issi fu le plé pledé, qi prest soit del prover par soen cors en totes les maneres qe la Court agardera qe prover le deit. Et avoms

Stat. Glouc. (6 Ed. I.) c. 8; Fle. 94, 115.

Brac. 156 b; Fle. 115.

1—1. recordent *C.*

CHAPTER XXVIII.

Of Distresses.

1. In counties we have a twofold court[q]; one of the pleas of our peace, which is held by our coroners and the suitors, and of which the coroners only have record; we have also a court of the nature of a court baron, in which the suitors are judges, and have no record out of their court, except by consent of the parties. For in their courts neither party may deny what he has before pleaded; but if the plea be removed out of the court of such suitors, either of the parties may deny the record. But for that purpose he must have suit ready at hand, to wit, such a one his free man who was present at such court, and saw and heard that the plea was so pleaded, which he is ready to prove by his body, in whatever manner the Court shall award that he ought to

Various courts of the King in counties. Crown Court; Civil Court;

The record of the suitors may be traversed, how.

[q] This description of the several branches of the county court is somewhat obscure. The twofold division probably applies to the original or ordinary jurisdiction of the county court on the one hand, and the derivative jurisdiction by virtue of the King's writ on the other. The first is again subdivided into the criminal jurisdiction, in which the coroner took part, and the jurisdiction in civil actions commenced by plaint, where the process was similar to that in courts baron. (See *post*, s. 20, and c. 29. s. 1.)

Glan. li. 10. c. 9; Brac. 105 *b*; Fle. 94. [54.]

ausi nostre Court illucs, [1]et noster Justice le viscounte[1] del pays, a totes les foiz qe nous maunderoms[2] a nos viscountes par nos brefs, qe il a dreit facent dedure[3] akune querele devaunt eux, et dunt le viscounte ove les sutiers portent record.

Stat. Marl. (52 Hen. III.) c. 21; Brac. 155 *b*; Fle. 94.

2. Et cum[4] plusours brefs lour porount estre maundez a terminer, en primes voloms nous, qe il sachent la nature del plé de prise des avers; le quel plé nous ne grauntoms mie a nul de terminer sauntz noster bref. Mes pur qe bestes et autres destresces ne soint mie trop loungement detenues enparkez[5], avoms graunté, pur[6] plus de damage eschure, qe le viscounte par simple pleyntes et par pleges deliverent teles destresces et determinent les prises sauntz rien parler del vé et de la torcenouse detenue, si la parole ne soit remué par noster bref jekes au[7] baunc, pur ceo qe [8]le vé[8] est un article de nostre pes enfreynte. En deus choses remeynt tote la force

Stat. West. 2. (13 Ed. I.) c. 2.

1—1. et noster Iustice del viscount *LN*. *sim*. *GABS*. e nostre Iustice le viscounte *M*. e nostre Iustice de visnee *C*. 2. *so NAC*. *sim*. *M*. demaunderoms *L*. 3. *so AM*. *om*. *LN*. dire *C*. 4. ticus *M*. issi *AC*. 5. *so G*. sim. *N*. en parkez *LS*. en Parks *M*. *sim*. *AF*. 6. *so NAMC*. pur *om*. *L*. 7. en *AMC*. 8—8. ceo *M*.

Sheriff's court.

prove it. We have also our court there, with the sheriff of the county for our Justice, whensoever we command our sheriffs by our writs, that for purposes of justice they cause any plaint to be brought before them, whereof the sheriff with the suitors bears record[r].

Nature of the sheriff's jurisdiction in replevin.

2. And whereas they may be entrusted with the determination of several kinds of writs, in the first place we will that they understand the nature of the plea of distress; which plea we do not allow any one to determine without our writ. But to the intent that beasts and other distresses may not be too long detained or impounded, and to avoid further damage, we have granted that the sheriff by simple plaints and by pledges may deliver such distresses, and determine the taking without regard to the *vee*[s] and tortious detaining, if the plea is not removed by our writ into the Bench, because *vee* is an article of the breach of our peace. The substance of this plea

[r] The sheriff, when sitting by virtue of the King's writ, is treated by our Author as the King's Justiciary, and as having the power of record incident to that office. See before, c. 1. s. 7; and farther on, li. ii. c. 30. s. 8. See also Brac. 117. Hengham Mag. c. iv. pp. 20, 21. It was decided in later times, that the county court, though sitting by virtue of the King's writ of *Justicies*, or *De Nativo habendo*, had not the powers of a court of record. Y. B. 2 H. IV. 24; Brooke, Abr. *Faux Imprisonment*, 30; Dalton, Offic. Vicecom. p. 158 *b*; Jentleman's Case, 6 Coke, Rep. 11.

[s] The *vee* (from the old French *vier* or *véer*, Latin *vetare*) was the refusal to deliver the distress upon offer of surety. See below, s. 6.

de ceo play, ceo est a saver, en la prise et en la detenue; et pur ceo qe un poit prendre et un autre detener, mester est qe ambideus soint en noster bref nomez. Et pur ceo qe cil fet plus de tort qi a tort detent, qe cil qi a tort prent, voloms nous qe les detenours soint chargez en ceo cas del [1]gros del respouns[1]. Naam si est un general noun a avers et a chateus et a totes choses moebles qe hom put prendre en noun de destresce.

3. Et cum acun qe se sentera grevé par torcenouse detenue de ses avers ou de ses chateus avera noster bref purchacé a soen viscounte, et li[2] eit trové pleges de sure sa pleinte, tauntost voist le viscounte, ou envoie acun baillif conu [3]a ly[3], ou le pleyntif dirra[4] la distresce estre detenue. Et si le viscounte ou soen baillif veigne illucs, si demaunde la vewe des bestes ou des chateus dount la pleinte est fete. Et si[5] il ne peuse la vewe aver pur disturbaunce de acun detenour ou de autre, par quei[6] il ne put fere ceo qe a soen office apent, tauntost leve la menee de corn et de bouche, et face prendre touz les

Brac. 157, 157 *b*; Fle. 98 (§ 9).
[54 *b*.]
Stat. West. 2. (13 Ed. I.) c. 37.
Brac. 157; Fle. 98 (§ 9).

1—1. *so ARCW.* gros respouns *LN. sim. GS.* gros del trespas *M.* 2. *so ARM.* il i *L.* il *N.* cely *C.* 3—3. *so LS. sim. G.* [al liu e] a ly *N.* od li *AR.* oue ly *M.* 4. *so NARMC.* *om. L.* 5. *so NM. sim. GAR.* si *om. LS.* 6. *so AR.* qi *LS.* qui G. q̃i *N.* quey *M.*

consists in two things, to wit, in the taking and in the detaining; and forasmuch as one may take, and another detain, it is necessary that both be named in our writ. And because he who wrongfully detains, does a greater injury than he who wrongfully takes, the principal burden of the answer shall in such case fall upon the detainers. *Naam*[t] is a general term for cattle, chattels, and for all other movable things which may be taken by way of distress.

Naam.

3. When any one, finding himself aggrieved by a wrongful detaining of his cattle or of his chattels, shall have obtained our writ to his sheriff, and found pledges to prosecute his plaint, let the sheriff immediately go or send some known bailiff to the place where the plaintiff says the distress is detained; and when the sheriff or his bailiff come there, let him demand a view of the beasts or chattels whereof the plaint is made. And if he cannot have a view by reason of disturbance from any detainer, or other person, whereby he cannot discharge the duty of his office, let him immediately raise the hue and cry, and cause all the disturbers to be apprehended and

First proceedings in replevin.
View of distress.
Disturbance of view, how punished.

t *Naam* (Anglo-Saxon, *name*, from *niman*, German, *nehmen*, to take), a seizure, or taking.

destourbours et sauvement en prisoun garder, issint qe ne soint deliverez sauntz nous, pur la distourbaunce de nostre pes. Et si les bestes soint encloses de eynz mesoun ou de eynz park, ou si eles soint chacez hors del counté, ou si le baillif autre desturbaunce troeffe, tauntost face prendre des bestes del deforceour a la double value cum wythernam, et cele destresce teigne saunt lesser par plevine, jekes a taunt qe la destresce esloigné soit remené.

Stat. West. 1. (3 Ed. I.) c. 16, 17; Brac. 157; Fle. 97, 98. Fle. 98 (§ 10).

4. Et si le pernour, ou le detenour, face la vewe al baillif, et avowe la destresce sue propre, issi qe le pleyntif rien ne eit, adunc cesse le poer le viscounte et del baillif. Et si[1] le pleyntif [2]ne soit vileyn al deforceour[2], tauntost leve heu et cry, et al premer Counté sue soen chatel cum de ly robbé par apel de felonie, si il quide bien fere.

[55.] Brac. 157 b; Fle. 100.

5. Et cum le viscounte [3]ou le baillif eyt[3] eu la vewe de la destresce sauntz disturbaunce, tauntost soit la destresce deliveré al pleyntif; et le viscounte ou le serjaunt done jour as parties al proscheyn Counté; a quel jour nul essoine ne soit

1. so *ARMCW.* om. *LSG.* interl. *N.* 2—2. so verb. *MCW.* sim. *AR.* om. *LSG.* interl. *N.* 3—3. et le baillif eynt *LN.* sim. *SAR.* ou le bailif eent *M.* sim. *GW.* et les baillifs eient *C.*

kept safely in prison, so that they may not be set at liberty without our leave, for the disturbance of our peace. And if the beasts are shut up within a house or within pound, or if they are driven out of the county, or if the bailiff meet with other disturbance, let him immediately cause beasts of the deforcer to be taken to the extent of double the value by way of withernam[u], and keep that distress without permitting it to be replevied, until the distress eloined be brought back.

Withernam.

Claim of property by distrainor.

4. If the taker or detainer admit the bailiff to view, and avow the thing distrained to be his property, so that the plaintiff has nothing therein, then the jurisdiction of the sheriff and bailiff ceases. And if the plaintiff is not a villain of the deforcer, let him immediately raise the hue and cry; and at the first county court let him sue for his chattel, as being robbed from him, by appeal of felony, if he thinks fit to do so.

Redelivery of goods.

Day given for appearance.

5. When the sheriff and the bailiffs have had the view of the distress without disturbance, the distress shall be delivered to the plaintiff; and the sheriff or bailiff shall give a day to the parties at the next county court. At which day no essoin shall

[u] Withernam, Anglo-Saxon, *wiðer-name*, a counterdistress.

alouwé encountre le pleyntif, cum ceo soit play mout annex a robberie, ausi cum disseysine. Et si le defendaunt face defaute, si soit la destresce ajugé au pleyntif, et le destreynour en la merci. Et si le pleyntif ne veigne au jour ne se face essonier, et le defendaunt se profre et demaunde jugement de la noun suit le pleyntif, soit agardé qe le defendaunt eit retour de la destresce, et le pleyntif et ses pleges de sure en la merci.

6. Et cum ambideus apparount en Court, lors die le pleyntif sa pleinte, qe com il out ses bestes, nomément deus boefs, [1]ou deus vaches, ou deus chivaus[1], ou tels chateus solom la manere de la destresce, tel jour, tel an de noster regne, en tele vile, ou en tel certeyn leu, la vint tel detenour, et[2] mesmes les bestes illucs trovez prist, et prendre fist par un tel, ou par autres gentz desconuz, et les enchacea, et[3] les fist enchacer, de mesme cel leu jekes a un autre leu; lors vint le pleyntif et demaunda ses avers quites, et aver ne les pout, puis ly tendi gage en noun de pes, et offri pleges de venir en sa court ou [55 *b.*]

1—1. [deus vaches] ou deus cheuals *N.* ou deus vaches *M.* ou deus chiuaus *F.* *sim.* *C.* *om.* *AR.* 2. so *N.* e *AM.* ou *L.* ouo *C.* 3. ou *G.*

be allowed against the plaintiff, since this suit, like disseisin, is nearly connected with robbery; but if the defendant makes default, the distress shall be adjudged to the plaintiff, and the distrainor in mercy. If the plaintiff does not come at the day, nor cause himself to be essoined, and the defendant offers himself and demands judgment of the nonsuit of the plaintiff, let it be awarded that the defendant have the distress returned, and that the plaintiff and his pledges to prosecute be in mercy.

Effect of default of appearance of defendant; of plaintiff.

6. When both parties appear in court, the plaintiff shall set forth his plaint, that 'whereas he had his beasts, to wit two oxen,' or two cows, or two horses, or such chattels, according to the nature of the distress, 'on such a day in such a year of our reign, in such a township,' or in such a certain place, 'there came such an one (the detainer) and took the same beasts there found,' or 'caused them to be taken by such a one,' or 'by other persons unknown, and drove them away,' or 'caused them to be driven away, from the same place, to another place, and there came the plaintiff, and demanded to have his cattle quietly, and could not have them, and afterwards tendered security for the sake of peace, and offered

Count of plaintiff.

aylours de ester a dreit, si ren ly savereit[1] demaunder, il jalemeyns encountre gage et plege a tort les detynt, et detener fist, jekes a taunt qe mesmes les bestes furent deliverez par le viscounte; cest tort ly fist il, et ceste destresce encountre gage et plege a tort ly via, et si[2] autres grevaunces ly fist, si les assigne, a ses damages de C. s., ou de plus ou de meyns, solom ceo qe il avera suffert, encountre la pes, et si il le dedie, il ad sute bone.

7. Adounc respoigne le defendaunt, et defende tort et force et la pes enfreynte, et la torcenouse prise et la torcenouse detenue et le vé des bestes avauntdites, et les damages de C. s., ou de plus ou de meyns, solom ceo qe le pleyntif avera counté vers ly, et defendera ou et quant devera.

8. Et cum il se avera si defendu, si veye, s'il puse sei eyder par excepciouns vers le juge, cum si la detenue ne fu mie fete en le poer le juge; et puis par excepciouns vers la persone le pleyntif; et puis de sa persone demeyne; et puis al bref, cum

1. *so GAMC.* sauera *LNS.* 2. *so AMC.* si *om. LNSG.*

pledges to appear in his court or elsewhere to stand to justice, if he had any demand to make against him, and yet he wrongfully against gage and pledge detained them, or caused them to be detained, until the same beasts were delivered by the sheriff; this wrong did he to him, and this distress against gage and pledge wrongfully him refused,'—and if he did him any other injury, it should be assigned,—'to his damages of a hundred shillings,'—or more or less, according to what he shall have suffered,—'against the peace, and if the defendant do deny the same, he has good suit.'

Answer of defendant.

7. Then let the defendant answer, and defend 'the wrong and force, and the breaking of the peace, and the tortious taking, and the tortious detaining, and the refusal of the beasts aforesaid, and the damage of a hundred shillings,' or more or less as the plaintiff shall have counted against him, 'and this he will defend where and when he ought so to do.'

Exceptions.

8. When he has thus defended himself, let him try if he can aid himself by exception against the judge; as for example, if the detaining was not done in the jurisdiction of the judge, and afterwards by exception against the person of the plaintiff, and afterwards against his own person, and then to the writ,

si le bref fust purchacé avaunt le jour de la prise contenu en sa pleynte. Et s'il i ad plusours pleyntifs en commun nomez en le bref, et se soint pleynz en commun de accioun severale, si chete le bref. Et puis se eyde par excepciouns al accioun. Et pora respoundre a la prise par plusours respounses; et le vé [56.] pora il defendre par sa ley. Mes si la parole soit remué hors Brac. 156; Fle. 94, 95. del Counté, adunk ne voloms mie, qe cele resoun soit alouwable al defendaunt; eynz voloms qe, tut puse il defere[1] la prise, qe jalemeyns ne respoigne al vee et a la torcenouse detenue, qe est un article fet encountre nostre pes, de quei nul ne se pora aquiter par sa[2] ley[3]. Car refuser gage et Fle. 102 (§ 30). pleges est tut outrement refus de nostre pes.

9. Ou il pora avouwer la prise et la detenue pur dreiturele[4], Brac. 158; Fle. 101 (§ 25). car mesmes le jour trova il mesmes les bestes en soen pree, ou en ses blez, ou aylours en soen damage, en tele vile, ou il solom la ley et les usages del reaume celes bestes fist chacer jekes a sa mesoun en mesme la vile, et illucs les detint, jekes autaunt qe dues amendes ly fusent fetes des damages avaunt-

1. defere [al. defendre *interl.*] *N.* 2. la *M.* 3. *so ABC.* de la prise *add. LNSGMFW.* 4. *so ARMC. sim. W. so corr. N.* dreiture *L.*

as, if the writ was obtained before the day of the taking mentioned in his plaint. Also, if there are several plaintiffs, who are named together in the writ, and they have complained in common where the cause of action is several, the writ fails. He may afterwards aid himself by exceptions to the action; and he may answer to the taking in several ways, and may defend the *vee* by his law; but if the plea is removed out of the county court, this proceeding shall not be allowed to the defendant; but although he can justify the taking, nevertheless he shall answer concerning the *vee* and the tortious detainer, which is an article committed against our peace, of which none may acquit himself by his law, for to refuse gage and pledge is a total renunciation of our peace.

The *vee* may be defended by wager of law in the county court, but not in the King's Court.

9. Or he may avow the taking and detaining as rightful, 'for that on the same day he found the said beasts in his meadow,' or in his corn or elsewhere, 'to his damage, in such a vill, and he according to the law and custom of the realm caused those beasts to be driven to his house in the same vill, and there detained them until due amends should be made him for the damage aforesaid, or until pledges should be

Avowry of distress, *damage fesant.*

ditz, ou qe pleges ly fusent tenduz de renable satisfaccioun, issi qe unkes les bestes autrement ne ly via, et de[1] ceo pora il [2]tendre averrement par pays[2].

Brac. 158; Fle. 101 (§ 25). [56 b.] 10. A quel[3] le pleyntif pora respoundre par replicacioun, et dire qe il ly tendi pleges de satisfaccioun et de vener en sa court, et de fere dues amendes par taxacioun des veysins, ou il resoun refusaunt et dreyture, ly vea ses bestes cum avaunt ad dit en sa pleynte. A quei le defendaunt purra respoundre en triplicaunt, et[4] graunter qe il ly tendi pleges mes nient destreinables a ly. Et si le pleyntif ne puse averrer le contrarie, si soit la destresce agardé arere al defendaunt et le pleyntif en la merci pur sa torcenouse pleynte.

Brac. 158; Fle. 101 (§ 26). 11. Et ausi a ceo qe le defendaunt dit, qe il prist les bestes en soen damage, put estre respoundu par le pleyntif, qe il ly tendi pleges de ses damages amender, mes quant ceo vint a damages moustrer, le defendaunt ne savoit nul damage moustrer ne assigner, et de ceo pora il tendre averrement; ou il pora dire qe sur les amendes[5] de ceux damages se mistrent il

1. de *om.* *AR.* 2—2. *so verb.* *M.* *sim.* *FW.* *sim. corr.* *N.* descendre autrement en pays et averrer *L.* *sim.* *GS.* auerrer par pais *AR.* autrement tendre par pais *C.* 3. *so LS.* quei *AR.* *sim.* *GMC.* ki *F.* 4. a *LNSARMF.* e *GC.* 5. amendemenz *M.*

tendered to him for a reasonable satisfaction, so that he never refused him the beasts in any other manner;' and of this he may tender averment by the county.

Replication, stating tender of pledges of satisfaction. 10. To this the plaintiff may answer by way of replication, and say that he 'tendered him pledges to make satisfaction, and to appear in his court, and to make him due amends by the award of neighbours; but he not complying with reason and right, refused him the beasts, as he hath before alleged in his plaint.' To this the defendant may answer by way of triplication, and admit that the plaintiff tendered him pledges, but not distrainable to him; and if the plaintiff cannot prove the contrary, let the distress be awarded back to the defendant, and the plaintiff in mercy for his wrongful plaint.

Triplication, that the pledges were not distrainable to the defendant.

Other modes of replication. 11. And also as to what the defendant says, that he took the beasts doing him damage, it may be answered by the plaintiff, that he tendered pledges to make amends for his damages, but when the damage was to have been shown, the defendant could not show or assign any damage, and thereof he may tender averment; or he may say that concerning satisfaction for those damages, they referred themselves to the en[1] arbitrement de tel et tel, [2]et qe il[2] arbitrerent qe il ne avoit nul damage fet; ou qe pur les damages amender ly fist aukunes amendes certeynes, et de ceo ad trové pleges, et sur ceo pora il tendre averrement; et solom ceo qe trové serra, soit jugé pur le un ou pur le autre.

12. Et cum la prise et la detenue de teles destresces soint fetes par baillifs autres qe par les nosz[3], et le pleyntif se eyt purchacé soen bref en commun sur les baillifs et sur le seignur ovekes, en tel cas list a seignurs de avouwer le fet de lour serjauntz ou desavouwer; et solom ceo soit le plé pledé. Et si le bref soit purchacé sur les baillifs soulement, en tel cas voloms qe chescun respoigne pur soen fet, si le fet eyt esté fet en la absence de les seignurs. Mes si les seignurs veignent avaunt jugement, et voillent garraunter de lour[4] gré les fetz de lour baillifs, si seynt les seignurs chargeez des fetz lour baillifs, et les baillifs deschargez. Brac. 158 b; Fle. 102. [57.]

13. Ou il pora issi respoundre et avouwer la prise et la detenue bone et dreiturele, pur ceo qe le pleyntif est soen tenaunt, et del tenement qe il tient de ly est arere de relef, Brac. 157 b, Fle. 101 (§ 27).

1. sur *M.* en le *C.* *sim. G.* 2—2. qe il *LN.* *sim. CF.* e qe il *M.* e *A.* 3. so *N.* *sim. AMCF.* nosz *om. L.* 4. lour *om. AMC.*

arbitration of such and such persons, who awarded that no damage was done; or that he made him some settled amends for the damages, and thereof found pledges, and thereupon he may tender averment. And according as the truth shall be found, judgment shall be given for the one or other.

12. When the taking and detaining are made by other bailiffs than ours, and the plaintiff has obtained his writ against the bailiffs jointly with the lords, in such case the lords may either avow or disavow the act of their servants; and the plea shall be pleaded accordingly. If the writ be obtained against the bailiffs only, in such case we will that each shall answer for his own act, if the act was done in the absence of the lords; but if the lords come before judgment, and are willing of their own accord to warrant the acts of their bailiffs, the lords shall be charged with the acts of their bailiffs, and the bailiffs discharged. Joint action against lord and bailiff.

13. Another answer of the defendant may be by avowing the taking and detaining as 'good and rightful, inasmuch as the plaintiff is his tenant and is in arrear for relief,' or suit Avowry of distress for service in arrear.

ou de sute due a sa court, ou de autre service, si qe, quel houre qe le pleyntif ly vousist aver fet ceo qe il devoit par resoun, ou de ceo trové renable surté par pleges, il ly eust
Fle. 104. deliveré ses aveers. A[1] quei le pleyntif respoigne[2], qe en chescune prise et detenue pur services, covendra il assigner treis[3] choses, a ceo qe la prise soit resounable, ceo est a saver, certeyn leu dount le service dut isser, certeyne cause pur quei la prise fust fete, et certeyne seysine, si le destreignour ne puse moustrer certeyn fet, qe il puse destreyndre par mi et par tut ou ly plera quant sa rente ly serra arere, tut ne eit il nul fee. Et si le defendaunt en soen defens eit fet omissioun
[57 *b.*] de acun des treys poyntz, et le pleyntif demaunde jugement
Brac. 157 *b*, Fle. 95 (§ 5). de ly, cum de noun defendu, si soit jugee pur le pleyntif. Et si le defendaunt counte de acune seisine, et le pleyntif la dedie, si courge de ceo l'averrement par pays, et solom le verdit soit rendu le jugement.

14. Ou issi, par la ou le defendaunt assigne la prise et la detenue dreiturele pur service qe arrere ly est, et noméme nt

1. de *M.* 2. *so LSG.* porra respondre *A.* *sim. MC.* 3. teles treis *M.*

at his court or other service, 'for the tenement which he holds of him, so that whenever the plaintiff would have performed to him what was in reason due, or to that end would have found reasonable security by pledges, he would have deli-
Replication. vered to him his cattle.' To which the plaintiff may reply, that for every taking and detaining for service, three things ought to be assigned in order to render the taking reasonable,
Conditions of a legal distress. to wit, a certain place, out of which the service ought to issue, a certain cause for which the taking was made, and a certain seisin, unless the distrainor can show a deed warranting him to distrain *per my et per tout* wheresoever he please, when his rent shall be in arrear, although he have no fee. If the defendant in his defence has omitted any of these three points, and the plaintiff demands judgment against him as being undefended, judgment shall be given for the plaintiff. And if the defendant counts of any seisin, and the plaintiff denies it, the point shall be verified by the country, and judgment be given according to the verdict.

Plea of homage tendered and refused. 14. Where the defendant assigns the taking and detaining to be rightful on account of service in arrear, and in

pur relef, la pora il respoundre, qe il ly tendi soen homage, et il ne le vout adounc prendre, par quei il pora demaunder jugement, si il ly fust tenu a fere nul service, ou reconustre pur seignur, einz ces qe il eust soen homage pris, et reconu pur soen homme. Et si le pleyntif puse ceo averrer, soit jugé encountre le defendaunt. Car relef et autres services dues de acun tenement tenu par fee de chivalerie sount accessories choses al homage, qe est princepal, [1]et, cessaunt le princepal[1], de dreit deyvent cesser les accessories.

15. Ou le defendaunt purra respoundre, et avouwer la prise et la detenue pur dreiturele, et purra assigner [2]pur renable[2] eyde a soen fiz eynzné fere chivaler, ou sa fille eynznee marier. A quei le pleyntif pourra respoundre, et dire qe cel assignement ne ly deit valer; car ly mesmes ne est mie chivaler, ou[3] pur ceo qe il n'ad nul fiz ou nule file, ou pur ceo qe le un ne l'autre ne est mie uncore de age pur ordre de chivaler receyvre, ou a baroun assenter, ou pur ceo qe autre foiz paya le pleyntif sa renable contribucioun de tel eyde a mesme cely [58.]

Fle. 104 (c. 49. § 3).

Stat. West. 1. (3 Ed. I.) c. 36.

1—1. so *N.* *sim.* *SGARM.* *om.* *LC.* 2—2. renable enchesoun de *M.* 3. so *NARMC.* et *L.*

particular for relief, the plaintiff may answer that he tendered him his homage, and that he would not then take it; whereupon he may demand judgment whether he was obliged to perform any service to him, or to acknowledge him for his lord, until he had taken his homage and accepted him as his man. And if the plaintiff can aver it, let it be adjudged against the defendant. For relief and other services due from any tenement held by knight's fee, are things accessory to homage, which is the principal, and, the principal ceasing, the accessories ought of right to cease.

15. Another answer of the defendant may be by avowing the taking and detaining as rightful, and assigning it to be for reasonable aid, to make his eldest son a knight, or to marry his eldest daughter. To which the plaintiff may reply, and say, that what he has assigned ought not to avail him, inasmuch as he is not a knight himself, or inasmuch as he has no son or no daughter; or inasmuch as the one or the other is not yet of age to receive the order of knighthood, or to consent to a husband; or inasmuch as the plaintiff did before pay his reasonable contribution towards such aid to the same lord.

Avowry of distress for aid *pur faire fitz chivaler* or *pur file marier.*

seignur; et les queles resouns averresz, une ou plusours, si soit jugee pur le pleyntif, si le defendaunt ne puse averreer le contrarie.

Brac. 156, 156 *b*; Fle. 95, 104 (§ 9).

16. Et cum les defendauntz avouwent les destresces et les detenues estre fetes sur les pleyntifs cum sur les[1] tenauntz pur arrerage de rente ou des autres services, et les pleyntifs les desavowent pur seignurs, si soit agardé qe les seignurs en tiel cas soint en la merci, et qe les pleyntifs eynt lour aveers quites, et recoverent lour damages; et les seignurs eynt accioun a recoverir les tenementz en demeyne, solum ceo qe dit serra el chapitre des homages.

Post, II. iii. c. 4. s. 16.

Brac. 84; Fle. 106.

17. Et si les seignurs assignent les prises et les detenues estre fetes pur arrerages de aukun service issaunt de aukun tenement qe les pleyntifs tiegnent, et ceux pleyntifs soint feffez par aukun[2] a tener de eux, qe sount meens entre eux et les chefs[3] seignurs, adounc covendra a ceux tenauntz qe les meens, qe sount lour seignurs, les veignent aquiter devers les chiefs seignurs destreynauntz, solom ceo qe eux sount obligez par lour chartres de feffement. Et si ne les voillent aquiter

1. ses *M.* lour *R.* 2. so *LS.* *sim. M.* ascuns *G.* 3. chefs *om. M.*

And if one or more of these answers be averred, it shall be adjudged for the plaintiff, unless the defendant can prove the contrary.

Answer to avowry of distress for rent, by denial of lord's title.

16. When the defendants avow the distresses and detainings to be made upon the plaintiffs as upon tenants for arrears of rent or other services, and the plaintiffs disavow them for their lords, let it be awarded that the lords in such case be in mercy, and that the plaintiffs have their cattle quietly delivered to them and recover their damages; and the lords shall have their action to recover the tenements in demesne, according as shall be mentioned in the chapter upon Homage.

Forfeiture.

Acquittance of tenant by mesne lord.

17. And if the lords assign that the taking and detaining was for the arrears of some service issuing out of a tenement which the plaintiffs hold, and the plaintiffs be enfeoffed by any to hold of those who are mesne between them and the chief lords, the tenants will then have the right to be acquitted by the mesne tenants, who are their lords, as against the chief lords distraining, according as such mesne tenants are bound by their charters of feoffment. And if they will not acquit

de lour gré, si soint les pleyntifs eydez par nos brefs de garrauntie de chartre, et de meen, et par proclamaciouns solom la ordinaunce de nos estatuz. Stat. West. 2 (13 Ed. I.) c. 9.

18. Et cum les meens vendrount en Court, et entrent en garrauntie et en aquitaunce devers les seignurs, adounc cessent [58 *b.*] les pletz originals, et comencent les pletz de garrauntie. Ou les meens porount respoundre en plusours maneres, car il pourrount desavouwer tener de eus, ou il porunt dire qe les tenementz ou il firent les destresces ne sount mie de lour fee, les queus respouns averreez, soit jugé pur les premers pleyntifs encountre les seignurs.

19. Et ausi se porount les meens soi eyder par excepciouns Fle. 107, 108. [1]vers lour[1] tenauntz, car il porount demaunder, s'il eynt riens par quei il soint tenuz et obligez al aquitaunce; et si les pleyntifs [2]ne eynt la chartres ou escritz[2] qe les obligent, soit jugé encountre les pleyntifs. Mes si les pletz fusent remuez hors del Counté[3] par devaunt nos Justices, et[4] lour chartres fusent arses ou robbeez, et ceo deissent en Court cum[5] pur

1—1. encountre les *M.* vers les *AC.* 2—2. veyent la chartre ou escrit *L.* ne eynt chartre ou escrit *N. sim. SMCF.* ne eient chartres ne escriz *AR. sim. G.* 3. iekes *add. NAC. sim. MF.* 4. ou *L.* e *AMCF.* ou [Mes ke] *N.* 5. cum *om. M.*

them of their own accord, let the plaintiffs be aided by our writs of Warranty of Charter, and of Mesne, and by proclamations, according to the ordinance of our statutes. Writ of warranty of charter. Writ of mesne.

18. When the mesne tenants shall appear in court and enter into warranty and acquittance against the lords, then let the original pleas cease, and the pleas of warranty commence; wherein the mesnes may answer several ways. For they may disavow holding of them, or say that the tenements where they took the distresses are not of their fee; which answers being verified, let it be adjudged for the first plaintiffs against the lords. Plea of warranty.

19. The mesnes may also aid themselves by exceptions against the tenants; for they may demand whether the plaintiffs have anything whereby they are held and bound to acquittance. And if the plaintiffs cannot produce charter or writing binding them, let it be adjudged against the plaintiffs. But if the pleas were removed out of the county, so as to be before our justices, and their charters have been burned or stolen, and they allege the same in court by way of exception, the truth shall Exceptions by mesne against tenant. Loss of charters.

excepcioun, si serra de ceo verité enquise par pays, et solom le verdit del enqueste, passereit jugement pur les meens, ou pur les pleyntifs. Ou si acun bref de meen soit purchacé sur un parcener, qe dust estre purchacé sur touz les parceners, ou touz sunt obligez al aquitaunce cum un heyr par lour commun auncestre, si est le bref abatable pur errour del purchatz; et

Fle. 108. ausi de touz pletz reals. Et ausi purra acun meen dire pur

[59.] excepcioun, qe il ne est mie tenu de aquiter soen tenaunt, pur ceo qe mesme celi tenaunt ne ly fist unques [1]homage, feuté ne autre service[1], et si ceo soit averree, et qe la defaute eyt esté en le tenaunt, soit jugé encountre le pleyntif.

Brac. 158 *b*; Fle. 101, 102.

20. Ou le defendaunt pora avouwer la prise et la detenue dreiturele, et assigner qe par jugement de sa court, et de ceo pora voucher sa court a garraunt, et nomément pur pleynte fete de ly par un soen veysin qi trova surté de sure sa pleynte, a la quele pleynte cest pleyntif fu somouns a respoundre a tel certeyn jour, a quel jour il ne vint ne essonié ne fust, par quei la court agarda a la seute le pleyntif, qe

1—1. seruice hommage ne suite *AR.* *sim. C.* autre *om. M.*

be inquired by the country, and according to the verdict of the inquest, judgment shall pass in favour of the mesnes or of the

Error in defect of parties.

plaintiffs. Or if any writ of Mesne is obtained against one parcener which ought to be sued out against all the parceners, where all are bound to acquittance as one heir by their common ancestor, the writ is abatable for error in the

Non-performance of homage or fealty.

obtaining of it, and so in all real pleas. And also any mesne may say by way of exception, that he is not bound to acquit his tenant, because the same tenant never performed to him homage, fealty, or other service; and if this be verified, and that the default was in the tenant, it shall be adjudged against the plaintiff.

Avowry of distress by judgment in the lord's court.

Process in court baron.

20. Again, the defendant may avow the taking and detaining to be rightful, and assign that he did it by judgment of his court,—and thereof he may vouch his court to warranty,—and in particular for a plaint made against the plaintiff by such an one his neighbour, who found security to prosecute his plaint, to which plaint this same plaintiff was summoned to answer at a certain day, at which day he neither came nor was essoined, wherefore the court awarded at the suit of the plaintiff, that he who now is plaintiff should be distrained to

cestui qe ore est pleyntif fust destreynt de venir al autre court, jekes autaunt qe il se vousist justicer par ley. Et si le pleyntif se voille de ceo mettre en record de la court, le defendaunt [1]si face[1] venir le record en[2] Court. Et si le record face pur le defendaunt, si ly soit agardé le retourn des avers, et le pleyntif en la merci pur sa fause pleinte. Et si le record face pur le pleyntif, [3]eyt le pleyntif[3] sa destresce quite, et[4] recovere ses damages, et le defendaunt en la merci. Et si faus jugement ou faus proces soit trové en le record, et la parole soit en Counté, de ceo ne voloms nous mie qe le viscounte ne les sutiers eynt conisaunce, mes pleyne sei qi grevé se sentera, et face venir par noster bref le proces et le record devaunt nos Justices [5]du baunc a Westmouster[5], et illucs soit redrescé le errour si poynt i soit trové.

Brac. 157 *b*; Fle. 100 (§ 20).

Stat. Marl. (52 Hen. III.) c. 20.

[59 *b*.]

21. Et si le pleyntif reconusce la destresce estre fete par agard de la court al defendaunt, en taunt graunte il la prise estre dreiturele; mes si il die outre, qe quant il ly tendi pleges

1—1. *so NG.* se face *L.* face *F.* si face lem. *AMC.* 2. de la *G.* 3—3. si soit agarde qe le pleintif eit *AM.* *sim. C.* *sim. corr. N.* 4. qe il *add. MC.* *sim. A.* 5—5. en baunk *A.* *sim. C.*

come to the next court, until he would submit himself to justice by law. If the plaintiff, as to the matter alleged, is willing to put himself upon the record of the court, the defendant shall cause the record thereof to be brought into court, and if the record make for the defendant, a return of the cattle shall be awarded to him, and the plaintiff in mercy for his false plaint. But if the record make for the plaintiff, let it be awarded that the plaintiff have his distress free, and recover his damages, and the defendant be in mercy. And if false judgment or erroneous proceedings be found in the record, and the action be in the county, we will not that the sheriff or suitors have cognizance thereof; but he who shall find himself aggrieved shall make his complaint, and cause the proceedings and the record to be brought by our writ before our justices of the Bench at Westminster, and the error shall be there redressed, if any be found therein.

Record of court baron.

False judgment in court baron, remedied in the king's court.

21. If the plaintiff acknowledge the distress to be made by award of the court of the defendant, he so far admits the taking to be legal; but if he further say that, when he tendered him pledges to appear in his court, and there to submit

Plea in bar of avowry by award of court.

de venir en sa court et de ester illucs a dreit [1]solum ley[1], il[2] cele plevyne refusa, et ly vya la destresce par plevine, si le defendaunt ceo denie, si courge le averrement; et solom le verdit soit jugé pur le un ou pur le autre.

Brac. 156 *b*; Fle. 98 (§ 5, 6). 22. Et si le pleyntif se pleynt de un soul, et ly eyt fet pernour et detenour par sa pleynte, et a ceo meyne sute, en tel cas pora le defendaunt dedire la prise; et si en[3] la seute soit trové descordaunce[4] par examinement, soit jugee pur le defendaunt, et le pleyntif en la merci pur sa fause seute; et si [5]il i soit trové bone acordaunce[5], adunc pora il defendre la prise par sa ley encountre ly et encountre sa seute. Et s'il tende sa ley al pleyntif, et il la refuse, soit jugé encountre le pleyntif; et ausi la reverse. Et s'il la receyve, si soit doné jour al defendaunt, qe il veigne a un autre jour a parfere sa ley [6]ove sa duzime meyn[6]. A quel jour il se pora fere essonier de sa ley fere, et le pleyntif ausi. Et si aucun face defaute, soit jugé encountre le absent. Et si le defendaunt ne eyt

1—1. *om.* *AC.* 2. *conj.* et il *LN.* e il *ASGRMCF.* 3. en *om.* *AMF.* 4. desacordaunte *M.* *sim.* *F.* descordaunt *A.* *sim.* *C.* 5—5. ele soit troue bien acordaunte *AM.* *sim.* *CF.* 6—6. ou sa xij. demeyn *L.* ou sa xij. Meyn *N.* sey xij. de Meyn *S.* od sa xij. main *G.* sei duzyme [en] meyn *M.* oue sa xii. mein *AC.* sey doxime main *F.*

to justice according to law', the defendant rejected such plevin, and refused to permit him to replevy the distress, and if the defendant deny it, averment shall be made, and according to the verdict, it shall be adjudged for one party or the other.

The question of taking may be tried by wager of law. 22. If the plaintiff complain only against one, and has by his plaint made him both taker and detainer, and in evidence of this produces suit; in such case the defendant may deny the taking, and if the suit on examination be found to disagree, let it be adjudged for the defendant, and the plaintiff be in mercy for his false suit. If the suit be found to agree, then the defendant may defend the taking by his law against the plaintiff and his suit; and if he tenders his law to the plaintiff and he refuses it, it shall be adjudged against the plaintiff, and so in the reverse case. If the plaintiff accepts it, a day shall be given to the defendant, that he come that other day to perfect his law with his twelve co-jurors; at which day he may be essoined from making his law, and the plaintiff may also be essoined. But if either make default, it shall be adjudged against the absent party. If the defendant has not fully twelve

Proceedings in wager of law.

pleynement xii. conjuratours, ou qe acun soit refusable par [60.]
verreye excepcioun, cum par excepcioun de vileyn, ou de Glan. li. 5. c. 5.
escomengé, ou de atteynt de faus serment, ou de juise, adounc soit jugé pur le pleyntif, et le defendaunt soit en la merci, pur ceo qe il defailli de sa ley fere.

23. Et si le pleyntif die, qe le defendaunt se absenta, et a escient, pur ceo qe il ne dust estre trové ou hom ly poreit pleges tendre, ou s'il die qe il tendi pleges a soen baillif, tel par noun, et il ne les vout deliverer, pur ceo qe soen seignur avoit defendu la deliveraunce, en ambideus les cases gist defense par ley, si le pleyntif eyt de ceo seute acordaunte; [1]ou s'il ne ad point de seute, ou seute nent acordaunte[1], adounc ne serra mie mester al defendaunt de gager la ley encountre sa soule voiz, eynz soit jugé encountre le pleyntif. Car nous voloms, qe nul ne soit tenu a gager ley a autre sauntz renable[2] seute a ceo amené[3]. Et si le pleyntif se vodera pleyndre del Brac. 158 *b*, 159; Fle. 102, 103.
baillif del vee, soit le toil entre le pleyntif et le baillif.

24. Et si le defendaunt avowe la prise et la detenue re-

1—1. *om. M.* 2. couenable *ARMCF.* 3. menee *NARMC. sim. F.*

co-jurors, or any of them are refusable upon good exception, as by the exception that he is a villain, or excommunicated, or has been attainted of perjury, or condemned to the pillory, let it be adjudged for the plaintiff, and the defendant in mercy, inasmuch as he has failed in performing his law.

23. If the plaintiff say that the defendant designedly absented himself, in order not to be found where pledges might be tendered to him; or if he say that he tendered pledges to his bailiff, such a one by name, and he would not deliver them, because his lord had forbidden the deliverance; in both these cases defence by law lies, if the plaintiff has his suit agreeing therein. But if he has no suit, or such as do not agree, then it will be unnecessary for the defendant to wage law against the sole word of the plaintiff; but it shall be adjudged against the plaintiff. For we will that none be obliged to wage law against another without proper suit produced upon the point. And if the plaintiff would complain of the bailiff in respect of the refusal, the contest shall be between the plaintiff and the bailiff.

Evasion of replevin tried by wager of law.

Wager of law by defendant not required, unless the plaintiff has sufficient suit.

24. Where the defendant avows the taking and detaining

Brac. 156, 156 *b*, 158; Fle. 100, 101.

sounable pur service qe arere ly fust de un tenement en tele vile, qe mesme celi pleyntif tient, et dount il fust seysi, ou autre auncestre, par mi la meyn le pleyntif, ou de autre [60 *b*.] certeyn tenaunt, puis le tens limité en assise de novele disseisine, si le pleyntif ne peuse dedire la seysine, soit jugé pur le defendaunt. Car lequel sa seisine eyt esté dreiturele ou torcenouse, ne voloms nous mie qe par tel bref soit detrié; mes se purchace le tenaunt par noster bref, qe soen seignur ne ly demaunde autres services ne autres custumes qe fere ne ly deit de dreit; issi qe s'il soit grevé en la possessioun, dunc voloms nous, qe il se purchace remedie en le dreit, et qe chescun bref eyt sa propre nature, et qe nul ne soit pledé par[1] autre.

Mag. Cart. c. 10; Glan. li. 12. c. 10.

Brac. 158; Fle. 101 (§ 23, 24).

25. Ou le defendaunt pora dire, qe il prist et detint les aveers a dreit, et par la resoun de un soil qe est soen several, en le quel il trova mesmes ces avers pesaunts plusours foiz, dunt il ly[2] avoit sovent amonesté[3] qe il les ostast, et il jalemeyns autre foiz les enveea encountre soen defens, et apparillé fu totes houres a les deliverer, si il se vousit estre retret

1. so *LNSGAFC.* pur *M.* 2. ly *om. AMC.* 3. mesmes celi pleintif *add. M. sim. GACF.*

Avowry by allegation of seisin.

to be justifiable on account of service which was in arrear for a tenement in such a vill, which the same plaintiff holds, and whereof he was himself seised or some other his ancestor by the hands of the plaintiff or other certain tenant, since the time limited in assise of novel disseisin, if the plaintiff cannot deny the seisin, let it be adjudged for the defendant. For we will not have it tried by such writ, whether the seisin has been rightful or tortious; but the tenant may procure by our writ, that his lord do not demand of him other services or other customs than he ought of right to do to him; so that if he is aggrieved by the possession, it is our will that he shall procure his remedy in the right; and that every writ shall have its proper nature, and one shall not be pleaded by means of another.

Right of seisin not to be tried in action of replevin.

Distinction of writs to be observed.

Avowry by allegation of trespass upon defendant's land.

25. Another plea of the defendant may be, 'that he took and detained the cattle rightfully, and by reason of a soil which was his several, in the which he found the same cattle feeding several times, and from the which he had often warned the plaintiff to turn them out, and he nevertheless sent them in another time contrary to his prohibition, and he was always ready to deliver them, if the plaintiff had been willing to

de tiels tortz fere et de ceo aver trovee surté, ou le pleyntif onkes nel voleit. A quei le pleyntif purra dire, qe a tort les prist le defendaunt et a tort les detynt, pur ceo qe la pasture [1]de mesmes[1] le soil est sa commune, et sa commune estre deit, ou ly et ses auncestres touz jours ount communé[2], et ceo est il prest de averrer ou et quant devera. Et pur ceo qe il ne voleyt ses bestes deliverer quites, si le pleyntif purroit[3] par cas par mi ceo bref recoverer title de commune et de fraunc tenement, ou unques par aventure dreit n'en out de communer, si enqueste feist[4] pur ly; en tiel cas voloms nous qe les avers remeygnent al pleyntif, et le defendaunt en la merci; et si le pleyntif mes voille communer en cleymaunt fraunc tenement de commune, si eit le defendaunt recoverer et remedie par noster bref de novele disseisine, si il quide ben fere. [61.]

1—1. demeyne e *C.* 2. eu commune *A.* *sim. C.* communee *S.* *sim. G.* 3. so *N.* *sim. AM.* pora *N.* 4. seit *AC.*

abstain from doing those wrongs, and thereof to have found surety, whereas the plaintiff never would do so.' To this the plaintiff may reply, that 'the defendant wrongfully took them and wrongfully detained them, because the pasture of the same soil is his common, and his common ought to be where he and his ancestors have always had common, and this he is ready to verify, where and when he ought.' And because he would not deliver the beasts quit, the plaintiff might by means of this writ recover title of common and freehold, where peradventure he had never any right of common, if an inquest were to decide in his favour[x]; in such case it is our will that the cattle remain with the plaintiff, and the defendant be in mercy; and if the plaintiff will still be a commoner and claim a freehold of common, the defendant shall have his remedy by our writ of Novel Disseisin if he thinks fit to pursue it.

Plea of common.

Defendant's remedy by assise of novel disseisin.

[x] This passage is obscurely expressed. If we understand it as implying that the inquest upon the title to common is taken in the action of replevin, it is contrary to the general rule, that a title to freehold is not to be tried in such an action (see before, s. 24); and is contradicted by the parallel place in Fleta, where it is expressly said, that the sheriff upon such a plea has no power to proceed further. (Fle. 101. § 24.) Yet this construction appears to be adopted by the commentator in MS. *N*, who says: 'par cas poet il recoverir title de franc tenement parmi verdyt en le replegiari, tot seit ceo a tort.' I should rather suppose that the sense of *pur ceo qe* in the beginning of the sentence ought to be repeated, and that the true translation would be, 'And because, on account of the non-delivery of the beasts, the plaintiff might recover title of freehold, &c.; therefore it is our will in such case, &c.'

Fle. 100 (§ 17).

26. Et voloms qe ceux qi serrount atteyntz de destresce fete par eux outre la value de la demaunde, tut eynt il averree[1] la cause de la destresce estre dreiturele, qe jalemeyns ne soint en la merci pur le outrage. Et si acun eyt fet double destresce pur une demaunde, et noméement apres la deliveraunce de la premere destresce pendaunt le play de la premere prise, voloms en teus cas qe la pleyntif eit de nous bref a fere deliverer ses aveers et qe le destreignaunt soit mis par gages et par pleges de estre devaunt nous ou devaunt nos Justices a certeyn jour a respoundre de cel trespas fet encountre nostre pes. Et qi de ceo serra atteynt, en primes soint les damages agardez al pleyntif, et puis soit le distreignour puni par prisoun et par fin; ou nous maunderoms[2] en tiel cas a nos viscountes, [61 b.] qe si il troevent tiel trespas estre fet encountre nostre pes, qe hastivement facent[3] tiels punisementz par enprisounement des cors de tiels trespassours et par grevous amerciementz, qe autres par ensample de eux soint chastiez en cas semblables.

Brac. 159; Fle. 103.

1. auowe *AC.* 2. so *MR.* sim. *A.* demaunderoms *LNC.* sim. *GS.* 3. so *ARMC.* facent om. *L.* interl. *N.*

Punishment of illegal and excessive distresses.

26. Such as shall be convicted of taking a distress beyond the value of their demand, although they have avowed the cause of their distress to be legal, shall nevertheless be in mercy for the excess. And if any one has made a double distress for one demand, and in particular, after the deliverance of the first distress, pending the plea concerning the first taking, in such case the plaintiff shall be entitled to our writ, to cause his cattle to be delivered, and the distrainor shall be bound by gage and pledge to be before us or our justices at a certain day to answer for such trespass committed against our peace. Whosoever shall be convicted of this offence, damages shall be first awarded to the plaintiff, and afterwards the distrainor shall be punished by imprisonment and fine; or in such cases we will command our sheriffs, that if they find such trespasses to be committed against our peace, they shall speedily inflict such punishment by imprisonment of the trespassers and by heavy amercements, that others by their example may be corrected in like cases.

CHAPITRE XXIX. [XXVIII.]

[1]*De Dette.*[1]

1. En Countez ausi par devaunt nos viscountes et les sutiers, et en hundrez et en courtz des fraunes hommes poent estre pledez sauntz nos brefs par gage et pleges simplement pletz de trespas et de dettes, issi qe les biens enportez en[2] les trespas, ne les dettes demaundez ne passent mie xl. s., save trespas de maheign et des playes et de enprisounement et de bateries fetes encountre nostre pes, dount nous ne voloms qe nul ne eyt la conisaunce ne poer de teles quereles pleder, ne autres trespas des biens enportez outre la value de xl. s. ne des dettes passantz mesme la summe, sauntz nos brefs; les queus brefs nous voloms acune foiz qe soint pledez en Countez et en fraunchises, si il ne soint de illucs remuez [3]par nos [4]comaunde- Fle. 133 (§ 19, 20.) Stat. Glouc. (6 Ed. 1.) c. 8.

1—1. Des pleez des dettes *S.* *sim. R.* 2. so *NABC.* et *L.* ne *MF.* 3—3. *om. C.* 4. brefs e noz *add. M.*

CHAPTER XXIX.

Of Debt.

1. In county courts also before our sheriffs and the suitors, and in hundred courts, and in courts of freemen, pleas of trespass and debt may be pleaded without our writs[y], simply by gage and pledge, provided that neither the goods carried away in trespass nor the debt demanded exceed forty shillings; except trespass of mayhems and wounds, and imprisonment, and batteries committed against our peace. For we will that no one have cognizance or jurisdiction to hold pleas of such complaints, nor of other trespasses for goods carried away beyond the value of forty shillings, or of debts exceeding the same sum, without our writs; which writs shall sometimes be pleaded in the county court, and in franchises, unless removed therefrom Jurisdiction of county court and other courts in trespass and debt.

[y] The following note explains some of the disadvantages of proceeding in the inferior courts: 'In pleas commenced by plaint, issue cannot be taken by averment of the country, but only by suit or proof. And although there may be jurisdiction in the county court or in the court of a liberty, extending to ten, twenty, or thirty pounds, still it is more advantageous to plead in Bank by the *præcipe quod reddat*, on account of the *fieri facias* which follows by statute. But the sheriff or bailiff has no power to levy the debt out of the lands and chattels, though he has power to distrain by virtue of execution of judgment.' (Note in *MS. N.*)

mentz, et acune foiz aylours[3] par devaunt nos Justices. Et les grauntz trespas volom nous qe soint pledez devaunt nous mesmes.

Just. Inst. li. 3. ti. 14; Brac. 99; Fle. 120.

2. [1]Obligacioun est lyen de dreit dunt acun est lié a doner ou a fere acune chose, et si est mere de play, et prent sa nesaunce de aukun precedent trespas ou contract. Par contract nest ele en plusours maneres par l'unité de assent des parties,

[62.] qe acune foiz est nue et sauntz garnement, et acune foiz vestue. Mes de[2] obligacioun nue n'encrest nulli plee, si noun par commun assent; et pur ceo iert mester en chescune obligacioun qe ele soit vestue. Obligacioun deit estre vestue de[3] v. maneres de garnisementz[4], de chose, de parole, de escrit, de unité de bone[5] volounté, de bayl, et[6] de joynture.

Just. Inst. li. 3. ti. 15; Brac. 99; Fle. 120.

3. Par[7] chose est ele vestue, quant acune chose est presté et apromté de rendre a certeyn jour; et par tels empromtz sunt les dettours obligez as creaunceours de mesmes les choses apromtez rendre en ausi bon point[8] ou en meillour qe il les

1. *In MG. a new chapter commences here, with the rubrical heading,* **De obligacioun.**
2. *so NMSGC.* de *om. L. interl. A.* 3. par *M.* en *AC.* 4. garnementz *NG. sim. ASMCF.* 5. bone *om. NSGAHMF.* 6. et *om. AH.* 7. De *M.*
8. estat *C.*

by our precept, and sometimes elsewhere before our justices; and we will that great trespasses be pleaded before ourselves.

Nature of a legal obligation.

2. An obligation is a legal bond, whereby a person is bound to give or do anything, and thus it is the parent of an action, and takes its origin from some precedent trespass or contract.

Obligations, *ex contractu, ex delicto.*

An obligation by contract may arise in many ways by the united consent of the parties; which consent is sometimes

Nudum pactum.

naked and without clothing, and sometimes clothed. From a naked obligation no action arises, except by common assent;

Requisites of a legal obligation.

it is necessary therefore in every obligation that it be clothed. An obligation should be clothed by five incidents, by a material thing, by words, by writing, by unity of will, by delivery, by relation[z].

Contract of borrowing.

3. It is clothed by a material thing, when anything is lent and borrowed, to be restored on a certain day; and by such loans the debtors are bound to restore to the creditors the things borrowed in as good or better condition than they received

z Our author gives no explanation of the meaning of *joynture*. The word is borrowed from Bracton, where it appears to be used to denote the connection of several contracts relating to the same subject matter. (Brac. 99, 100 *b*; Fle. 128, c. 60. § 2.)

resceurent, ou le pris, si par aventure de feu ou de ewe ou de robberie ou de larcyne ne les eynt perdues. Car encountre teles [1]aventures de choses perdues[1] ne deit nul respoundre, si noun par sa coupe ou par sa negligence. Mes si acun dettour porte sur ly deners, et il les moustre folement entre larouns, et il en soit robbeé, ja par taunt ne remeyndra qe il ne ert tenu al creaunceour, pur ceo qe il ne mist mie sa diligence [2]de les garder, car meuz les pout[2] aver gardé.

4. Le autre garnement est des paroles courrauntes entre le creaunceour et le dettour, par les queles il [3]deveignent de un assent[3] par offres et par demandes. Just. Inst. li. 3. ti. 16; Brac. 99 *b*; Fle. 121.

5. Le autre garnement est escrit; et dunt il iert pur et simple et sauntz jour et saunz condicioun, et dounc pora le creaunceour demaunder sa chose meyntenaunt, ou quel houre qe il vodera. Et si jour de soute soit mis en le escrit, [4]avaunt le jour ne ert le dettour point obligé de rendre. Et quant le jour vendra[4], suffist si aucun houre de jour face la Brac. 100, 100*b*; Fle. 122 (§ 20). [62 *b*.]

1—1. *so R.* auentures perdues *LGE.* *sim. S.* auentures des [choses *interl.*] perduz *N.* auentures [de choses] perdues *A.* auenturis de celes perdues *M.* auentures *F.* 2—2. qe il poeit de les garder car autrement les pout meuz auer gardee *N.* *sim. M.* qi poet le deners garder qar autre les poeit meuz auer garde *R.* *sim. C.* ke il pust de les garder. Car autres les puet meuz garder *F.* 3—3. *so verb. GS.* deyuent de un assent *LN.* veignent de un asent *M.* donassent *ARC.* 4—4. *om. C.*

them, or else their value, unless by accident of fire, water, robbery, or larceny, they have lost them; for against such accidents no one ought to answer for things lost, unless they happened by his own fault or negligence. But if a debtor carries money about him, and foolishly shows it among thieves, and is robbed of it, it does not follow that he is not bound to the creditor; because he did not use his diligence to keep the money, for he might have taken better care of it.

4. The second kind of clothing is by words passing between the creditor and debtor, by which they come to an agreement by offers and stipulations. Words.

5. The next incident is by writing, which may be pure and simple, and without day or condition; in which case the creditor may demand the thing presently or whenever he pleases. But if a day of payment be specified in the writing, the debtor is not bound to pay before the day, and when the day arrives, it is sufficient if he makes the payment any time of the day, for the debtor has the whole day; and likewise it is with Writing. Time of performance of contracts.

soute; car tut le jour [1]est al[1] dettour. Et en mesme la manere est de certeyn an ou de certeyn meys nomé en le escrit, si nul jour certeyn i soit especefié. Et ausi pora le escrit estre condicionel; et vaudra ou ne vaudra solom ceo qe [2]sera dit de eynz de[2] purchaz condicionels. Mes queles qe les condiciouns soint, nul escrit ne nule obligacioun [3]ne lyera, qe soit condicionel[3], si la condicioun soit inpossible ou descovenable; inpossible sicum en ceo cas: si tu me facis aver la lune, jeo tei [4]doray x.[4]; descovenable issi: si tu ocyes cel homme, jeo tei doray x. En la negative neqedent tendreit bien lu obligacioun condicionele, issi: si tu ne[5] me facis point aver la lune, ou si tu ne ocies un tiel, jeo tei doray x. Et si le dettour se obligea a acune peyne suffrable et honeste, si tiegne la peyne; car le dettour le voleit quant il se obligea a ceo, et encountre sa volunté ne ly fist hom nul tort.

Brac. 99 b; Fle. 121 (§ 10).

Brac. 100; Fle. 122.

6. Le autre garnement est unité de volunté et consentement; et ceo est dit pur eux qe ne sevent ne ne poent consenter, sicum les surdz, et les arragez, et les pur sotz, et en-

Brac. 100; Fle. 102 (§ 19).

1—1. so *MSC.* *sim. GA.* al *L.* ad le *N.* 2—2. sera dit de eynz et de *L.* *sim. GS.* serra dit de deinz [desous] et de *N.* dit serra de denz de *M.* serra escrit de deinz e des *ARC.* *sim. H.* sera dit dedenz e de *F.* 3—3. condicionele ne liera *A.* *sim. M.* condicionel ne luy eydra *C.* 4—4. fray auer x. *M.* 5. so *M.* ne *om. LC.* *interl. N.*

regard to a certain year, or a certain month, named in the writing, if no certain day be specified. Also, the writing may be conditional, and will or will not take effect, according as shall be mentioned below concerning conditional purchases. But whatever the conditions may be, no writing or obligation shall be binding as a conditional contract, if the condition be impossible or unlawful. Impossible, as in this case, if you will procure me the moon, I will give you ten shillings. Unlawful, thus, if you kill such a man, I will give you ten shillings. Yet in the negative such conditional obligations would hold good, thus, if you do not procure me the moon, or if you do not kill such a man, I will give you ten shillings. And if the debtor binds himself in any allowable and innocent penalty, the penalty shall stand, for the debtor was willing when he bound himself thereto, and no injury is done him against his will.

Conditional contracts.

Contracts under penalty.

6. The next incident is unity of will and consent; and this is mentioned with reference to those who know not how or are not able to consent, as the deaf,[a] and the mad, and mere idiots,

Consent.

Incapacity of consent.

[a] Bracton admits, that a deaf man may contract by writing; so also Fleta. See the passages referred to in the margin above.

faunz en lour tendre age, et les lunatics et frenetycs en lour rage, [1]ne femmes espousez, ne gentz de religioun remuables par les[2] sovereyns de mesme la religioun, ne ceux qe sount afforcez de eux obliger, ne purs vileyns; ovesqe cestes gentz ne tiegnent nul contract ne nule obligacioun. [63.] Brac. 336 *b.*

7. L'autre garnement est bayl, ceo est induccioun [3]de la chose en[3] seisine par la volunté le creaunceour, sicum dit serra de teles induccions en purchaz apres douns[4]. Brac. 100 *b.* Post, l. 2. c. 9.

8. Et cum aucun se vodera pleyndre de acune dette de eynz la summe de xl. s. ou de acun petit trespas, en primes truysse pleges de sure sa pleynte al viscounte, si il vodera pleder en le Counté, ou a acun baillif, solom ceo qe il vodera pleder en hundredz ou en courtz des fraunes hommes; et le dettour soit somouns qe il soit a la procheyne court a respoundre al Fle. 134. (§ 3).

1. ne mutes genz *add. M.* ne nul degeetz *G.* ne endegez nuls *ARC. sim. F.* 2. lour *AR. sim. GCF.* 3-3. *conj.* en la chose en *L.* en la *NSGARMF.* par la *C.* 4. douns *om. M.*

and infants in their tender age, and lunatics and frantic persons during their fury, and married women, and persons in religion removable by their superiors of the same order[b], and those who are compelled to bind themselves, and pure villains[c]. With such persons no contract or obligation is binding. Monks. Villains.

7. The next incident is delivery, which is an induction of the thing into possession with the consent of the creditor, as shall be mentioned concerning such inductions in treating of purchases after gifts. Delivery.

8. When any one will sue for a debt within the sum of forty shillings, or for any small trespass, first, let him find security to the sheriff to prosecute his plaint, if he will proceed in the county court, or to some bailiff, according as he chooses to proceed in the hundred court, or in a freeholders' court. And let the debtor be summoned to be at the next court to answer the Action of debt or trespass in county or hundred court, or court baron. Process by plaint and summons.

[b] Among the statutes of the Benedictine order, confirmed at a council of the heads of the order in England, A. D. 1249, is the following: "Nullus monachus obedientiarius vel claustralis det aliquid vel suscipiat absque licentia sui superioris." (Matth. Paris. Addit. p. 1096.) By the same regulations no prior or other officer or obedientiary was to be appointed for life, but all were to be subject to removal. (ib. 1096, 1098.) See Littleton, Ten. s. 200.

[c] A villain might acquire property real or personal, and his acquisitions enured to the benefit of his lord, if the latter chose to take them; but the villain while in possession could make a good title to a stranger. See li. ii. c. 7. s. 1; Brac. 25 *b.* It follows from s. 25, below, p. 168, that debts and executory contracts could not be enforced against a villain pleading his own villenage. But no reason appears why a contract should not have been enforcedby a villain against a third party, if the rule generally held, that an exception of villenage against the person of the plaintiff could only be pleaded by his lord. Compare below, li. ii. c. 18. ss. 2, 5; Brac. 193 *b*, 196 *b*, 197; Hengham P. c. 8. p. 103; Littleton, Ten. s. 189.

pleyntif sur tele demaunde qe il ly fet, issi qe il soit renablement garni de respoundre a la demaunde le pleyntif.

Fle. 134, 135. 9. [1]A quel jour ambideus poent estre essoniez[1]. Et si le dettour face defaute, ou autre sur ky acune pleynte de trespas serra fete saunz noster bref, lequel qe il facent defaute avaunt le essoigne ou apres, soit agardé qe il soint destreyntz par lour avers et par lour chateus, qe il soint al autre court. Et si autre foiz facent defaute, soit agardé qe la premere destresce [63 *b.*] soit retenue, et qe hom prenge plus, et issi de court en court, [2]et qe il ne eynt mie les bestes par plevine[2], jekes a taunt qe il trevent pleges a respoundre al pleyntif. [3]As pleyntes[3] de trespas ne soit nule somunse fete, eynz soint destreyntz le premer jour. Et si la parole soit remué jekes par devaunt nos Justices, si courge la graunt destresce, et le viscounte soit chargé de respoundre des issues, sicum de sus est dit en le chapitre de attachemenz. Ante, c. 27. s. 3.

10. Et cum les defendauntz vendrount lour destresces deliverer, si truysent pleges de respoundre a la proscheyne court,

1—1. *so verb. M. sim. ARCF. om. LNSG.* 2—2. *so verb. MC. sim. AR. om. LNGS.* 3—3. En pleyntes neqedent *ARM. sim. C.*

plaintiff upon such demand as he has made against him, so that he have reasonable warning to answer the demand of the plaintiff.

Process, in default of appearance, by distress.

9. Upon the day named in the summons both parties may be essoined; but if the debtors or any persons against whom a plaint of trespass is brought without our writ shall make default, whether such default be before essoin or after, it shall be awarded that they be distrained by their cattle or by their chattels to be at the next court. And if they make default another time, it shall be awarded that the first distress be retained, and a fresh one taken, and so from court to court, and that they may not replevy the beasts, until they find pledges to answer the plaintiff. In plaints of trespass no summons shall be made, but they shall be distrained on the first day. And if the plea be removed before our justices, the grand distress shall take place, and the sheriff be charged to answer for the issues, as above mentioned in the chapter of Attachments.

In trespass, the first process is by distress.

Defendant after distress must find pledges to appear.

10. And when the defendants come to have their distresses delivered, let them find pledges to answer at the next court,

et de retourner les destresces si il ne veignent; et issint soint les destresces deliverez. A quel jour si il ne veignent, soit agardé qe les pleges soint sumouns de estre a la proscheyn court, a moustrer pur quei il ne avoyent avaunt ceux q'il plevirent, sicum il pristrent a meyn. Et lequel qe il veignent au jour qe il serount somouns ou noun, soint en la merci; et eux eynt lour recoverer vers ceux qe il plevirent de ceo qe il ne les aquiterent de plegeage, sicum fere deyvent[1]; et les defendauntz soint destreyntz autre foiz de venir a respoundre as pleyntifs, et celes destresces remeignent nent plevisables jekes autaunt q'il eynt respoundu.

11. Et cum acun defendaunt serra trové en court puis qe il avera esté attaché, tauntost respoigne, ou remeigne noun defendu, lequel qe il avera avaunt fet defaute ou noun. Et cum il avera respoundu, dunc a primes ly soit sa destresce deliveree; et ceo soit fet pur la presumcioun de sa malice, qe il ne se voleit avaunt justicer par pleges. [64.]

12. Et cum les parties serount venuz [2]en court[2], adounc moustre le pleyntif sa pleynte, et die qe le defendaunt a tort

1. *so L. sim. NGH.* deueient *A. sim. M. sim. corr. S.* 2—2. *so NARSGMC. sim. F. om. L.*

and to return the distresses if they do not appear, and then let the distresses be delivered. At which day, if they do not appear, let it be awarded that the pledges be summoned to be at the next court, to show why they did not produce those for whom they were pledged according to their undertaking; and whether they come on the day on which they are summoned or not, let them be amerced; and they shall have their recovery against those whom they pledged, for not acquitting them of their suretyship, as they ought to have done. The defendants shall then be distrained again to come and answer to the plaintiff, and these distresses shall remain irreplevisable until they have answered.

Second distress.

11. When any defendant shall be found in court, after he has been attached, let him immediately answer, or be treated as undefended, whether he has before made default or not; and when he has answered, then and not before let the distress be delivered to him. This shall be done upon presumption of his malice, in that he was not willing before to find pledges to be amenable to justice.

Defendant appearing after attachment must answer immediately.

12. When the parties shall have appeared in court, then let the plaintiff open his plaint, and say, that 'the defendant

Count of plaintiff.

ly detent et point ne ly rent xx. s. les queus il ly presta tel jour en tel an en tele vile en deners countaunz, et les queus deners il ly dut aver rendu a tel jour suant en mesme le an, [1]icels deners point[1] ne rendi, eynz les ly detynt a tort et a ses damages de x. s., et s'il le voille dedire, si pora le pleyntif tendre sute.

13. A quei le defendaunt covendra[2] respoundre et defendre tort et force et la dette et les damages. Et sicum la obligacioun se fet en plusours maneres, ausi se defend; et dunc les dettours se porunt eyder par excepciouns en moutz des maneres; et pur ceo se eyde le defendaunt par excepciouns, si point en eyt Fle. 132 (§ 2). pur ly qe valer ly pusent. Et entre les autres pora il demaunder, si il ad rien de[3] ly par quei il soit obligé a cele dette rendre. Et s'il tende tayle ou seute, et la seute soit trové acordaunte, adounc pora il defendre la dette par sa ley; et adunc soit fet cum devaunt est dit en le chapitre de prises de avers.

Fle. 132 (§ 3, 4). [64 b.] 14. [4]Et s'il moustre escrit, a ceo pora il respoundre en plusours maneres[4]. Car il pora dedire le escrit et tendre

1—1. i ceus point *M.* il point ses deniers *C.* 2. purra *C.* 3. pur *M.* 4—4. *om. C.*

wrongfully detains from him and does not render to him twenty shillings, which he lent him on such a day in such a year in such a town, in ready money, and which money he ought to have rendered to him on such a day following in the same year, and the said money did not render, but detained the same wrongfully and to his damage of ten shillings, and if he will deny it,' then the plaintiff may tender suit.

Answer of defendant. 13. To this the defendant must answer and defend the wrong and force, and the debt, and the damages. And as an obligation is contracted in divers ways, so likewise it may be Exceptions. defended; hence the debtors may aid themselves in many ways by exceptions. Wherefore let the defendant aid himself by exceptions, if there be any which can avail him. Among the rest, he may demand whether the plaintiff has anything from him, whereby he has bound himself to render that debt; and if he produces a tally, or a suit, and the suit is found to Wager of law. agree, then he may deny the debt by his law, and in that case the proceedings are the same as are before mentioned in the chapter on Distress.

Defences to action upon a deed. 14. If the plaintiff produces a writing, the defendant may answer thereto in several ways; for he may deny the writing,

averrement par pays, qe ceo n'est mie soen fet; et si le pleyntif prie le averrement, soit adunc enquise la verité par tesmoignes nomez en le escrit [1]qe il ad[1], ou par pays.

15. Ou, si le escrit soit le fet soen auncestre[2], si pora il demaunder jugement del escrit, s'il est tenu a respoundre a cel escrit pur la dette soen auncestre, puys qe nule mencioun ne est fete en le escrit, qe il soit obligé a la soute; en queu cas nous ne voloms mie, qe acun soit tenu a rendre la dette soen auncestre, qi heir il est, a autre qe a nous, si il ne soit a ceo par le fet soen auncestre especialment obligé. Fle. 135 (§ 10).

16. Ou il pora dire, qe le escrit ne ly deit grever, car quant il fit le escrit, il fust de eynz le age de x.[3] aunz. Et si ceo soit averree, soit jugé encountre le pleyntif. Fle. 133.

17. Ou il pora dire, qe cel escrit ne ly deit grever, car en tens de la confeccioun avoit il perdu soen seal, et ceo fist il crier et puplier par eglises et par marchez, [4]issi qe si riens[4]

1—1. qe il y ad *M.* *om. AC.* 2. *so LSG.* e il ne soit mye obligez par le fet son auncestre *add. M.* e il ne seit Mie oblige par sun auncestre *add. A.* *sim. RF.* *sim. interl. N.* 3. *so LNMSACF.* xj. *G.* 4—4. *so M.* si qe si *AR.* si qe rien ne *L.* *sim. C.* si qe [si] rien en *N.* si qe riens *G.* *sim S.*

and tender averment by the country that the same is not his deed. And if the plaintiff prays the averment, then let the truth be inquired by means of the witnesses named in the writing, when there are any, or by the country. Plea of *non est factum.*

15. Or, if the writing be the deed of his ancestor, he may demand judgment of the writing, whether he is bound to answer to that writing for the debt of his ancestor, whereas there is no mention made in the writing of his being obliged to the payment thereof. For in this case we will that none be bound to pay the debt of his ancestor, whose heir he is, to any other but to us, unless he be thereto especially bound by the deed of his ancestor. Heirs not bound by deed of ancestor unless expressly named.

16. Or he may say that the writing ought not to affect him, for when he made it he was under the age of ten years[d]; and if this be verified, let it be adjudged against the plaintiff. Plea of infancy.

17. Or he may plead, that this writing ought not to affect him, for at the time of its being made he had lost his seal, and caused it to be cried and published at the churches and markets, so that if anything was made under that seal after a Plea of loss and misuse of seal.

d The age under ten years appears to be selected merely as an example of pleading in a particular instance, with no reference to any especial disability connected with that age.

fu fet par cel seal puis tel certeyn jour qe il fust perdu, ceo ne ly deit grever; et en tele manere pora il dedire le fet; et sur ceo soit enquise la verité par le visnee ou le fet dust estre fet, et solom le verdit du pays soit celi qe serra trové mentour jugé a la prisoun et puni par fin.

[66.] 18. Et si le fet ne fu mie fet en noster poer, si qe la verité ne pora estre enquise par nous, soit la pruve abaundoné au pleyntif, issi qe s'il puse averreer par bons tesmoignes le contract [1]estre fet[1], soit jugé pur le pleyntif. Et cestes excepciouns eynt leu en nostre Court par devaunt nos Justices; car en Countez ne en tels autres petiz courtz ne put hom nul foreyn contract prover, si il soit dedit.

Brac. 398 b; Fle. 426 (§ 5). 19. Ou s'il y eyt en le escrit rasture en [2]le noumbre, ou en propres nouns[2], ou en la date[3], ou en le jour de la soute, ou

1—1. *om.* *AM.* dette *LA.* 2—2. les nouns ou en le proces *C.* 3. *so* *NSGMC.*

certain day on which it was lost, it ought not to affect him; and in such manner he may deny the deed[e], and thereupon let the truth be inquired by the neighbourhood where the deed is supposed to have been made, and according to the verdict of the country, let him who shall be found to have been guilty of falsehood be adjudged to prison, and punished by fine.

Foreign deed, how proved. 18. And if the deed was not made within our jurisdiction, so that the truth cannot be inquired by us, the proof shall be left to the plaintiff, so that if he can prove the contract by good witnesses, it shall be adjudged in his favour. These exceptions shall have place in our court and before our justices; for in county courts and other petty courts no one can prove a foreign contract, if it is denied.

Defective deed, presumed fraudulent 19. If there is in the writing any erasure in the number, or in proper names, or in the date, or day of payment, or if there

e There is an entry in MS. *M.* of an assise of novel disseisin concerning land at Thorley, between William de Gerburg and William de Clifford and others, which appears to belong to the end of the reign of Henry III or the beginning of Edward I, in which this defence is set up against the deed of Arnald de Thorley under which the demandant claimed. The jury found, 'quod prædictus Arnaldus amisit sigillum suum, et si aliqua carta vel scriptum ab illa hora in posterum proferatur sigillatum prædicto sigillo, quod pro nullo haberetur. Et dicit, quod prædicta carta et scriptum facta fuerunt tempore quo prædictus A. amiserat prædictum sigillum; unde dicit præcise quod licet prædicta carta et scriptum signatum fuit de sigillo suo, unquam de voluntate prædicti Arnaldi facta fuerunt.' Fortunately the demandant had also pleaded an acknowledgment of the deed by Arnald de Thorley before Gilbert de Preston and his companions Justices Itinerant in the county of Hertford, 39 Hen. III, and as to this fact had vouched the rolls of the said Iter. 'And because the said William had put himself as well upon the rolls of the said Iter as upon the assise, the trial was adjourned.' Upon the subsequent day the acknowledgment of Arnald was found upon the rolls, and the plaintiff obtained judgment.

s'il y eyt autre fausine, sicum deverseté de meyn ou de enke en la escripture, ou si le seal put estre osté et remis par engyn[1], adunc pora le defendaunt demander jugement, si il soit tenu a respoundre a tiel escrit vicious; en quel cas nous voloms qe les jugementz se facent encountre les pleyntifs pur la graunt presumpcioun de malice.

20. Ou il pora dire qe le escrit ne ly deit grever, pur ceo qe le escrit fu fet en tens qe le defendaunt fust en prisoun; le quel respouns voloms qe soit alowé [2]ou desalowé[2], solom ceo qe pour ou force ly fu fet en la prisoun, sicum de sus est dit en le chapitre des prisouns. Ou il pora dire, qe le fet ne ly deit grever par la resoun qe il le fist quant il ne fu mie en soen dreit sen; la quele excepcioun nous voloms qe teigne leu en arragez et ceux qi ount perdu memorie par maladie ou par autre peyne, et ne mie en les yvronkes, n'en les somilleus, tut ne soint il acune foiz en lour dreit sen. [66 *b.*]

Fle 133, 424; Ante, c. 12. s. 8.

21. Ou il pora dire qe le fet ne ly deit grever, car en acun tens fu le pleyntif soen seneschal ou soen chaumberleyn, ou

Fle. 424, 426.

1. so *NS.* *sim.* *ABMGC.* meyns *L.* 2—2. so *NMG.* *sim.* *in marg.* *R.* om *LA.* ou deuisable *C.*

be other signs of falsification in it, as diversity of hands or of ink in the writing, or if the seal be so attached that it may be taken off and put on again by contrivance, then the defendant may demand judgment whether he is bound to answer to such a defective deed; in which case we will that judgment be given against the plaintiff for the great presumption of fraud.

Plea of duress.

20. Or he may say that the writing ought not to affect him, because it was made at a time when the defendant was in prison; which answer must either be allowed or disallowed, according as fear or force was used against him in prison, as above mentioned in the chapter upon prisoners. Or he may say that the writing ought not to affect him, by reason that he executed it when he was not in his right senses. This exception shall hold in the case of madmen and those who have lost their memory by sickness or any other pain; but not in the case of drunkards, or of such as are light-headed, although they may sometimes not be in their right mind.

Plea of insanity.

Plea of abuse of confidence in use of seal.

21. Or he may say, that the deed ought not to affect him, because the plaintiff was once his steward, or his chamberlain,

en autre service ovek ly, et pur la graunt affiaunce qe il aveit a ly, ly bailla il soen seal a garder, et taunt cum il [1]le out en[1] garde fit il fere cest escrit sauntz soen sceu; et pur ceo qe il ad conu le fet estre soen en partie, soit agardé pur le pleyntif, et se purveye autre foiz le defendaunt de meillour gardeyn; et le defendaunt eit sa accioun vers le pleyntif de treysoun par apel de felonie s'il voille; la quele accioun soit suye[2] un an et un jour de[3] cel jour qe il savoit primes de cel escrit; et si il ne vodera sure par apel de felonie, eit sa sute par fourme de trespas. Car si la excepcioun fu trié par enqueste et feist countre le pleyntif, si sereit il puni cum en fourme de trespas, et la felonie remeyndreit despunie.

Fle. 132, 133. 22. Ou il pora dire qe le fet[4] ne ly deit grever, car il [5]li fust fet[5] par condicioun, issi qe si[6] le pleyntif ust fet solom la condicioun, adounc ly fust il tenuz. Mes de ceo covendra moustrer lettre del pleyntif, ou enroullement de court qe porte record; et si noun, si pora le pleyntif defendre la con-

1—1. en out la *NSFM.* *sim. G.* 2. sue *NSGAMCF.* 3. apres *M.* 4. escrit *M.* 5—5. ly fist *M.* *sim S.* le fist *NAC.* *sim. G.* 6. so *SGAMC.* si *om. L.* *interl. N.*

or in other service with him, and on account of the great confidence which he had in him, he delivered him his seal to keep, and while he had it in his custody he caused the said deed to be made without his privity. Inasmuch as he thus in part acknowledges the deed to be his, it shall be awarded for the plaintiff; and let the defendant provide himself for the future with one who will keep his seal safer. And he shall have his action of treason against the plaintiff by appeal of felony, if he pleases; which action must be prosecuted within a year and a day from the time when he first knew of that writing; or if he will not sue by appeal of felony, he may bring his suit in form of trespass. For if the exception were tried by an inquest, and given against the plaintiff, he would be punished as in form of trespass, and the felony would remain unpunished.

This plea is no defence to the action.

But defendant may take proceedings to punish the treason.

Plea of condition not performed.

22. Or he may say that the deed ought not to affect him, because it was made on condition, so that if the plaintiff had performed the condition, then he would have been bound to him. But in proof of this he must show some writing of the plaintiff or enrollment in court of record, in default of which

dicioun par sa ley, et recoverer sa demaunde vers le dettour. Et s'il moustre escrit de condicioun, le quel le pleyntif ne pora dedire, soit trycé lequel le pleyntif ad fet assetz a la condicioun ou noun, et ne mie par reddour de dreit mes par eyde de excepcioun; et solom ceo qe trové serra de la satisfaccioun de la condicioun soit jugé pur [1]le un ou[1] pur le autre. Car reddour de ley veut qe nule accioun soit detrié par autre, sicum nule questioun[2] estre asoutz[3] par autre. Mes si la condicioun soit contenue en le escrit qe le pleyntif profre, en tiel cas ne avera mie double accioun. [67.]

23. Ou il pora aleger soute, et moustrer quiteclamaunce.

Brac. 101; Fle. 128, 129 (§ 5, 11), 132 (§ 11). Stat. Acton Burnel. (2 Ed. I.); Fle. 136, 137.

24. Ou, si la dette soit demaundé vers ly cum vers plege, et il demaunde jugement si il deyve a la dette respoundre taunt cum le principal dettour suffit, si la cause soit verreye, soit alouwé la excepcioun al defendaunt. Mes si le principal dettour[4] et les pleges soint obligez chescun pur le tut severalment, adunc ne soit mie la excepcioun alouable, mes soit jugé

1—1. so M. sim. GACF. ly et L. li e S. le vn et N. 2. puit *add.* N. 3. aforce *AH.* 4. ne suffyse *add.* M.

the plaintiff may defend the condition by his law, and recover the demand against the debtor. And if he produce a writing containing the condition, which the plaintiff cannot deny, it shall be tried, whether the plaintiff has performed the condition or not, and this not by rigour of law, but by means of the exception, and according as shall be found concerning the satisfaction of the condition it shall be adjudged for one or the other. For rigour of law would require that one action should not be tried by another, any more than one question can be resolved by another. But if the condition is contained in the writing produced by the plaintiff, in such case there shall not be two causes of action.

23. Or the defendant may allege payment, and show an acquittance. Plea of payment.

24. Or, if the debt is demanded against him as a surety, and he demands judgment, whether he ought to answer for the debt so long as the principal debtor is capable of doing so, this exception shall be allowed to the defendant, if the cause be true. But if the principal debtor and the pledges are bound each for the whole severally, then the exception shall not be

Plea of surety, that he is bound to answer only for default of principal.

Joint and several obligation.

pur le pleyntif, et le plege eit sa accioun et soen recoverer vers le princepal dettour. Et si les pleges seynt obligez en commun, et la [1]demaunde soit fete[1] severalment vers un, cum[2] plusours [3]i ad[3], et cestui plege demaunt jugement si il deyve severalment respoundre de commune obligacioun de plusours, soit la excepcioun alouwable, si la cause soit verreye, et soit agardé qe le plege voist sauntz jour, et le pleyntif en la merci.

[67 *b*.] 25. Ou il pora dire, qe cel fet ne ly deit grever, car il est vileyn un tiel par la resoun de soen saunc et de soen tenement, et de tiel estat fust quant il li fist le escrit, et quant qe il ad si est a soen seignur, si qe il ne ad rien propre, et demaunde jugement si il deyve a tel contract respoundre sauntz soen seignur; et si le pleyntif ceo ne puse dedire, soit agardé qe le pleyntif ne prenge rien pur sa pleynte, eynz soit en la merci, et le vileyn sauntz jour. Et si le pleyntif se pleyne del seignur, et [4]le seignur[4] demaunt jugement si soen vileyn ly[5] puse obliger, ou s'il soit tenu a respoundre del personel fet

1. dette demaunde fet soit *M*. 2. vers *add. A*. 3—3. il seent *M. om. A*.
4—4. *so verb. AR. sim. interl. N.* son seygnur *M. om. LSG*. 5. se *MC*.

allowed, but judgment shall go for the plaintiff, and the surety shall have his action and his recovery over against the principal debtor. And if pledges are jointly bound, and the demand is made severally against one, when there are more than one, and this pledge demands judgment whether he ought to answer severally for the joint obligation, this exception shall be allowed, if the cause be true, and it shall be awarded that the pledge do go without day, and the plaintiff in mercy.

Joint obligation.

25. Or he may say that this deed ought not to affect him, because he is the villain of such a one, by reason of his blood and of his tenement, and was of that condition when he made the writing, and whatsoever he has belongs to his lord, so that he has nothing of his own; and he may demand judgment whether he ought to answer to such contract without his lord. And if the plaintiff cannot deny this, it shall be awarded that the plaintiff take nothing by his plaint, but be in mercy, and the villain without day. And if the plaintiff brings his plaint against the lord, and the lord demands judgment whether his villain can bind him, or whether he is bound to answer for the personal act of his villain, it shall also be adjudged against the

Plea of villenage of defendant.

soen vileyn, soit ausi ajugee encountre le pleyntif. Et ausi en cas ou femme coverte de baroun soit obligé; car nous ne voloms mie qe femme puse obliger soen baroun, ne vileyn soen seignur, [1]ne autre soen chef[1], ne persone sa eglise, pur le mal qe poroit avener, sauntz le Evesque ou le pateroun. Fle. 133 (§ 16).

26. Ou il pora dire, qe il est enpledé ou apelé de felonie, et s'il demaunde jugement si il deyve respoundre [2]a nule dette[2] eynz qe il soit aquité de la felonie, et si la cause soit veraye, et la felonie cause de mort, adounc voloms nous qe la excepcioun soit alouwable.

27. Ou il pora dire, qe autre foiz fu il enpledé de mesme cele dette et de mesme la persone en nostre court ou en autre, ou il passa quites par jugement, et le pleyntif en la merci; et si le pleyntif ceo ne puse dedire, ou si les parties descendent [68] en averrement de record, soit jugé solom le record pur le un ou pur le autre.

28. Ou il pora dire, qe il ne deit illucs de cele dette respoundre, car il i ad plee pendaunt de mesme la dette

1—1. *conj.* autre qe le chef *L.* *sim.* *NSGARCF.* ne autre qe le chef *M.* 2—2. *so* *GF.* *sim.* *ARC.* a nule *LS.* de acune dette *M.*

plaintiff. And the like, in case where a married woman is bound; for we will not that a wife shall have power to bind her husband, or a villain his lord, or any other his superior, or a parson his church without the bishop and patron, on account of the mischief which might arise therefrom. **Feme covert.** **Parson.**

26. Or he may say, that he is impleaded or appealed of felony, and if he demands judgment whether he ought to answer in a plea of debt until he is acquitted of the felony, and if the cause be true, and the felony be capital, then we will that the exception be allowed. **Plea of appeal of felony pending.**

27. Or he may say, that he was formerly impleaded for the same debt and by the same person in our court, or in another, where he was acquitted by judgment, and the plaintiff in mercy. And if the plaintiff cannot deny this, or if the parties put themselves upon proof by the record, let it be adjudged according to the record for one or the other. **Plea of *autrefois acquit.***

28. Or he may plead, that he ought not there to answer concerning this debt, because there is a plea depending concerning the same debt between the same persons in a superior court, **Plea of action pending for the same matter.**

entre. mesmes les persones en plus haute court, ou aylours en nostre court; et si le pleyntif ceo ne peuse dedire, si chete de sa pleynte.

Fle. 132 (§ 9). 29. Ou si la dette soit issaunte de acun tenement cum annuele rente due par an al meyns a terme de vie, et le dettour demaunde jugement, si il de fraunc tenement deyve respoundre a pleynte ou a bref de dette sauntz autre bref, en tiel cas voloms nous qe le pleyntif ne prenge rien, eynz se purchace par bref de annuele rente ou par destresces.

Fle. 131 (§ 33), 132, 133. 30. Et si la pleynte soit par devaunt nous ou devaunt noster Seneschal, [1]dounc voloms qe chescun dettour respoigne de chescune dette de la quele il [2]serra trové[2] obligé al pleyntif [3]a la destresce[3] et a la jurisdiccioun du Seneschal de noster hostel, ou qe le contract eit esté fet, en noster reaume ou de hors, lequel qe la dette soit graunde ou petite, sauve qe la dette ne touche mie fraunc tenement. Fle. 131 (§ 33). Et voloms qe les pleyntifs suent lour pleyntes devaunt noster Seneschal de tele manere de dettes sauntz nos brefs soulement par pleynte et par seurté trover de seure les pleyntes. Et ausi de trespas

1. de nostre hostel *add. M.* 2—2. so *M.* *sim. N.* troue *L.* serra *GSARC.* 3—3. *om. AHC.*

or elsewhere in our court. And if the plaintiff cannot deny it, he loses his plaint.

Plea of frank tenement. 29. Or, if the debt be issuing out of any tenement as an annual rent payable yearly for term of life at least, and the debtor demand judgment whether he ought to answer concerning frank tenement to a plaint or writ of debt without other writ, in such case we will that the plaintiff take nothing, but proceed by writ of annual rent, or by distress.

Jurisdiction of the Steward of the King's household. 30. If the plaint is before us or before our Steward, then we will that the debtor answer concerning every debt for which he shall be found bound to the plaintiff under the distress and jurisdiction of the Steward of our household, wherever the contract was made, whether within our realm or without, and whether the debt be great or small, so as it does not concern frank tenement. Process in the Steward's court. And we will that plaintiffs prosecute their plaints before our Steward for such debts without our writs, but by simple plaint only, and by finding surety to prosecute the plaints; and the like of trespasses and felonies committed

et de felonies fetes de eynz la verge de noster hostel, ou qe nous seoms en noster reaume; la quele verge nous voloms qe contiegne a la rounde entour nous xii. leuwes. [68 *b.*]

31. Et cum acun serra attaché, et soit venu en court devaunt noster Seneschal, et soit en querele de dette, et ne puse sei de la dette defendre, soit agardé qe le pleyntif recovere sa dette et ses damages par taxacioun de la court, et le dettour soit [1]liveré al[1] Mareschal a garder a soen peril, jekes autaunt qe satisfaccioun soit fete al pleyntif, et a nous del amerciement pur la torcenouse detenue. Et si acun dettour soit plevi al comencement del attachement ou apres, et le dettour ne aquite mie ses pleges en la manere qe il est[2] plevi, tauntost soint destreyntz a la satisfaccioun del pleyntif. Countes et Barouns neqedent de eynz nostre verge trovez et nos serjauntz de noster hostel soint avaunt somouns pur dettes qe destreyntz ou attachez par les cors; les uns pur reverence de lour persones, les autres pur favour[3] de nostre service[4]. Et voloms qe par la ou le Mareschal deyve fere ses attachementz, et ne Fle. 131 (§ 36).

1—1. liuere a *L.* deliuere al *NSMC.* sim. *G.* 2. so *NSGAMC.* est *om. L.*
3. reuerence *C.* 4. Court *A.*

within the verge of our household, wheresoever we shall be in our realm; which verge shall comprise a circumference of twelve miles around our dwelling. Verge.

31. When any one shall be attached and shall appear in court before our Steward, being impleaded of a debt, which debt he cannot deny, let it be awarded that the plaintiff recover his debt, and damages by taxation of the court; and let the debtor be delivered to the Marshal, to be kept at his peril, until satisfaction be made of the plaintiff's demand and of the amercement due to us for the wrongful detainer. And if any debtor is bound by pledges at the commencement of the attachment, or after, and the debtor does not acquit his pledges according as they are bound for him, let the pledges be immediately distrained to satisfy the plaintiff. Nevertheless let earls and barons found within our verge, and the servants of our household, be summoned for debts, before they are distrained or attached by their bodies, the first out of respect for their persons, and the others out of regard for our service. And wherever the Marshal is to execute his attachments, and does

Judgment in the Steward's court. Execution by Marshal. Process against pledges. Privilege of peers and king's servants. Attachment by the person.

troeve mie suffisaunte destresce a la vaillaunce de la demaunde le pleyntif, qe il face les attachementz par les cors, lequel qe les defendauntz soint clers ou lays, et sauvement garde les cors jekes autaunt qe il se lessent justicer par ley, lequel qe
[69.] les pleyntes soint de dette ou de trespas ou de felonie.

Fle. 131 (§ 33). 32. Et voloms qe nul ne soit attaché par noster Mareschal for qe par la ou les dettours sount[1] obligez especialment par lour escrit a la jurisdiccioun de noster Seneschal. Et voloms nous, qe de ceux qi se sustreent[2] hors de nostre verge [3]qe il ne soint attachables[3] par noster Mareschal, qe[4] ou qe il soint autre foiz trovez de eynz nostre verge, qe il soint responauntz[5] de lour trespas ou de lour felonies fetes de eynz nostre verge
Fle. 132 (§ 7, 8). aylours qe par la ou eux serrount trovez. Et si acuns encoupez devaunt noster Seneschal de[6] lour trespas ou lour felonie pusent averrer qe le fet ne fu mie fet de eynz nostre verge, ou qe il ne [7]furent mie trovez[7] de eynz nostre verge quant il [8]furent attachez,[8] en tel cas voloms qe teles excepciouns soint
Ante, c.1. s.5. alouwables a tels defendauntz. Et voloms qe les execuciouns des jugementz noster Seneschal et les attachementz de eynz

1. se soint *N.* se sunt *M.* *sim.* *SGC.* 2. sount remuez *M.* 3—3. qil seient attachez *C.* 4. mes *M.* 5. responables *C.* 6. *so* *AM* et *L.* e *SG.* *om.* *C.* 7—7. *so* *C.* fu mie troue *L.* *sim.* *NM.* 8—8. *so* *AC.* fust attache *L.* *sim.* *M.*

not find sufficient distress to the value of the demand of the plaintiff, he shall execute the attachments by the bodies, whether the defendants be clerks or laymen, and safely keep the bodies until they submit to the determination of the law, whether the plaints are for debt, or trespass, or felony.

32. And we will that none be attached by our marshal, except where the debtors are especially bound by their writing to the jurisdiction of our steward. Such as withdraw themselves out of our verge to avoid being attachable by our marshal, shall, wheresoever they are again found within our verge, be answerable for their trespasses or felonies committed within our verge, though not in the same place where they are
Limit of the Steward's jurisdiction. found. If any one, accused before our steward of a trespass or felony, can prove that the fact was not committed within our verge, or that he was not found within our verge when he was attached, in such cases we will that such exceptions be allowed to the defendant. Execution of the judgments of our steward, and attachments within our verge shall be made by

nostre verge soint fetz par noster Mareschal, et de hors la verge par nos viscountes[1] et par nos brefs.

33. En plusours autres maneres put homme dever qe par enpromtz de deners, sicum par propre reconisaunce ou de auncestre qi avera reconu en nostre court sei [2]dever a autre[2] acune certeyne soume de deners a rendre a certeyn jour, et eit[3] graunté, s'il ne face, qe le viscounte le face lever[4] de ses terres et de ses chateus; et par teles reconisaunces fetes en nostre court voloms nous qe [5]les terres et les heyrs[5] [6]de reconisours[6] remeygnent obligez, lequel qe les heyrs soint obligez en les reconisaunces especialment ou noun; et ne mie soulement les heirs, mes les terres et les tenementz de reconisours, en qi meyn qe il deveignent. Fle. 130 (§ 25). 135 (§ 8). [69 *b*.]

34. Et ausi cum homme put dever pur deners apromtez, ausi put hom dever pur chescune chose moeble apromté et nient rendue al jour, et des queles choses covendra demaunder le pris et les damages. Glan. li. 10. c. 13; Brac. 102 *b*; Fle. 127, 129, 130.

35. Et ceo qe hom ne put demaunder as dettours pur la

1. *so NAGSMC.* et par nos baillifs *add. L.* 2—2. estre tenuz a autre en *M.* 3. soit *M.* 4. leuer *om. AMC.* 5—5. *so verb. GF.* ces terres et ces heyrs *L.* ses terres et ses heirs *N.* *sim. SA.* les terres e les bens heyrs *M.* ses terres e ces chateus e les terres *C.* *sim. H.* 6—6. *om. A.*

our marshal, and without the verge by our sheriffs and by virtue of our writs.

33. A person may be indebted several other ways besides by money borrowed, as by his own recognizance, or by that of his ancestor, who has acknowledged in our court that he was indebted to another in a certain sum of money to be paid at a certain day, and granted that if he should not pay it, the sheriff should levy it out of his lands and chattels. And by virtue of such recognizances made in our court, we will that the lands and heirs of the recognizors remain bound, whether the heirs are especially mentioned as bound in the recognizances or not; and not only the heirs, but the lands and tenements of the recognizors, into whosesoever hands they come. Debt upon recognizance.

34. Also, as a person may be indebted for money borrowed, so he may likewise be indebted by reason of any movable thing borrowed and not returned at the day; and of such things the value and damages should be demanded. Action for chattels borrowed.

35. And what a person cannot demand of his debtors by

Glan. li. 7. c. 5, 6; Brac 60; Fle 123, 124, 125.

Glan. li. 7. c. 8, 18; Fle. 126.

mort, soit demaundé vers les[1] executours. Et ne covendra mie en touz[2] cas demaunder vers touz[3] les executours for qe soulement devers les administrours des biens et des chateus as mortz. Acunes dettes sount neqedent dues, les queles nous ne voloms mie qe soint pledez en nostre court, ne en nule court laye, sicum de testament, et de matrimoine, ceo est a saver des chateus lessez en la seysine del testatour, et des chateus donez pur mariage. Mes des chateus as mortz dunt il ne furent mie en possessioun le jour de la confeccioun de lour testament, sicum des dettes qe hom lour deveit[4], et des autres[5] chateus en autri meyns, et ausi des chateus dues et promis pur mariage, voloms nous aver la conisaunce en nostre

1. lour *M.* 2. *so LNSGACF.* teu *M.* 3. *so AMSGO. om. L.* 4. *so CHF. sim. M.* deyuent *LN.* deueynt *S. sim. G.* deit *AR.* 5. autres *om. ARCH.*

Remedy against executors of deceased debtor.

Jurisdiction of ecclesiastical courts as to legacies and marriage contracts.

reason of their deaths, shall be demanded against their executors; which demand need not in every case be made against all the executors, but only against such as administer the goods and chattels of the deceased. There are however some debts, which shall not be pleaded in our court, or in any lay court. as those arising from testament and marriage, that is to say, concerning chattels left in the possession of the testator[f], and chattels given as a marriage portion. But as to chattels of the deceased of which he was not possessed on the day of making his will, such as debts owing to him, and chattels in the hands of others, and also chattels promised and due on account of marriage, of these the cognizance shall belong to

Intestacy.

our court. And if any debtor die without making any testa-

[f] The annotator in MS. *N.* observes upon this, that will and intention not carried into act are spiritual matters; and that the will and conscience of a testator are so obscure and secret that no earthly judge can be certified thereof. For that the law of this land determines nothing that is not open and certain, as where an intention is carried into effect by an act. 'But the king,' he adds, 'hath sometimes cognizance of devises, not of movable chattels, but of tenements purchased in an enfranchised town, as London or Northampton, which may be devised in like manner as movable chattels, because burgesses being in trade generally employ (enplaient) the half, or more, of their goods in their houses (herbergage), the purchase whereof they may devise, but not their inheritance. The king hath therefore of necessity cognizance thereof as of a thing annexed to freehold. For though the spiritual judge had cognizance of such tenements so devised, he would have no power of execution, inasmuch as such tenements savour more of freehold, yea and of fee and seigniory (oyl e de fee e de sr'), and testament in such case is in lieu of charter. Wherefore such testaments ought to be solemnly proved in the boroughs, as is customarily done in London, not by proof of the testament, but by proof that the testament hath been proved in court christian, on account of the disherison done by false testaments.' The writer then gives the form of a writ, addressed to the king's bailiffs of Northampton, which differs little from the writ *Ex gravi querela*, which may be seen in Reg. Brev. Orig. 244 *b*; Vet. Nat. Brev. 85 *b*; Fitzh. Nat. Brev. 199.

court. Et si acun dettour murge sauntz testament fere[1], [70.]
respoignent ceux[2] pur [3]les dettes al mort[3] a[4] qi meyns les Stat. West. 2.
biens al mort devindrent, sicum dit est en nos estatuz de (13 Ed. I.) c. 19;
Westmoster. Mes si acun mort simplement sauntz acune[5] Fle. 124 (§ 10).
especialté eit mis[6] sa dreyne volunté en[7] la distribucioun de
touz ses biens moebles en la ordinaunce de acun ami, et cele Fle. 125 (§ 12).
dreyne volunté peuse estre prové, en tel cas volom nous qe
ceo suffise pur testament.

36. Et cum acune dette soit recoverie en nostre court, soit Stat. Marl. (52 Hen. III.) c. 23;
le jugement et la execucioun fete solom la ordinaunce de nos Stat West. 2.
estatuz, et de cely, qi rien ne avera, rien ne soit recoverie. (13 Ed. I.) c. 11.

37. Et si ad une manere de dette due as gentz par lour Stat. Marl.
serjauntz qi lour detenent lour aver, et de ceo [8]fuyent de (52 Hen. III.) c. 23;
rendre acounte[8]; en queus cas nous voloms qe les [9] pleyntifs Stat. West. 2. (13 Ed. I.)
eynt remedie solom la ordinaunce de nos estatuz. Et si acun c. 11. Fle. 154,
serjaunt die pur excepcioun, qe il ad rendu acounte a soen 155 (§ 11).
seignur ou a soen attourné, [10]et qe soen seignur ou soen attourné ad[10] ses roulles et ses autres monumentz dunt il dust

1. e les biens cely mort deuindrent a les ordiners *add. C.* 2. cil *LNAGSMH.* eus *C.* 3—3. *so M.* le mort al dettour *LN.* la mort al dettour *SG.* le mort *C.* 4. *so NGSCH. om. L.* en *M.* as *AF.* 5. acun *L. sim. H.* autre *NSGAM.* 6. en *add. AM.* 7. e *SGCH.* a *A.* en *om. M.* 8—8. deuent acounte rendre *M.* defuent de rendre acounte *N. sim. AC.* 9. seygnurs *add. M.* 10—10. qad *C.* qe ad *H.*

ment, let those into whose hands the goods of the deceased shall come be answerable for his debts, as is laid down in our statutes of Westminster. But if any person who dies shall simply and without any specialty commit his last will respecting the distribution of all his movables to the disposal of some friend, and such last will can be proved, this shall be a sufficient testament. Nuncupative will.

36. When any debt is recovered in our court, judgment and execution shall be had according to the ordinance of our statutes, and from him who has nothing, nothing shall be recovered. Execution of judgment.

37. There is also a kind of debt due to persons from their servants who detain from them their property, and refuse to give an account thereof; in which case the plaintiffs shall have remedy according to the ordinance of our statutes. And if any servant allege, by way of exception, that he has given in his accounts to his lord, or to his lord's attorney, and that the lord or the attorney has his rolls and other memoranda Action of account against bailiffs, &c.

acounte rendre, en tel cas volom nous qe, s'il puse averrer ses excepciouns, qe eles ly soint alouwez, for qe en cas ou le seignur [1]ly rebaut[1] ses roulles de suth le[2] seal al serjaunt[3]. Et en cas ou la parole est remué jekes en nostre court pur

[70 *b.*] le tort des premers auditours, voloms qe quant qe fu primes alouwé devaunt les premers auditours, remeygne alouwé devaunt les secounds, issi qe il ne covendra as auditours en nostre court rien del acounte[4] terminer[5] for soulement le tort qe les premers auditours averount fet al serjaunt. Et voloms qe nul soit tenu de rendre acounte a soen seignur autre qe a nous, for qe el visnee ou il avera esté [6]serjaunt soen seignur[6].

Glan. li. 12. c. 9; Brac. 105 *b.*

38. Et sunt autres personeles acciouns, pledables par viscountes par nos brefs [7]de *Justicies*[7], des tortz fetz en contractz, cum est de acun covenaunt enfreynt, ou de acounte, ou de fere aver renable eyde [8]a fiz[8] fere chivaler ou a file marier, ou de ewe prendre en autri puyz, ou de aver fraunc tor ou fraunc sengler, ou de communer a un abevrour ovek

1—1. *so M. sim. ARF.* le ribaud ad *L.* le rybaud ad *N.* ly Ribaut *G.* le Ribaud *S.* luy robbast *CH.* 2. *so LNGSARHCF.* son *M.* 3. seignour *AR.* 4. accion *A.* 5. determiner *NAMCH.* 6—6. soen serjaunt *N. sim. SGARHC.* sergaunt au seygnur *M.* 7—7. *so SGAC.* des Iustices *LM.* de Iustic[i]es *NR.* 8—8. au fiz eyne *M.*

relating to the matters whereof he should render account; in such case if he can verify his exception, it shall be allowed, unless the lord redeliver to him his rolls under the servant's seal.

Proceedings in error upon actions of account.

In cases where the action is removed into our court on account of an alleged wrong of the first auditors, we will that whatsoever was allowed before the first auditors shall remain allowed before the second, so that it shall not be the duty of the auditors in our court to determine anything relating to the account, except as to the wrong which the first auditors may have done to the servant. And we will that no one shall be obliged to render an account to any lord, except ourselves, elsewhere than in the neighbourhood where he was his bailiff.

Jurisdiction of sheriff by writ of *Justicies*.

38. There are also other personal actions of which sheriffs may take cognizance by virtue of our writs of *Justicies*, concerning torts in contracts, as where a covenant is broken, or concerning account, or to enforce a reasonable aid for knighting the lord's son, or marrying his daughter, or a right to take water at another's well, or to have a free bull, or free

[1]ses aveers[1], ou de renables estovers, ou de chemin aver, ou de commune pescherie, ou de aquitaunce fere, ou de gage enpiree ou nent rendu, et [2]de chartres, et de seutes[2] detenues, et de molyn a tort levé, et de mesoun, et de faude, et de teles autres nusaunces, [3]et autres[3] plusours, qe voillent estre pledez par destresces de chateus et par damages, et terminez par[4] jureez.

CHAPITRE XXX. [XXIX.]

De Tourns de Viscounte. [71.]

1. Et sount acuns articles, tochauntz nostre Coroune et nostre pes enfreynte, pledables par viscountes autres foiz qe a jour des Countez et aylours qe par la ou les pletz des Countez sount tenuz, les queus pletz sount apelez tourns de viscounte; qi deus foiz par an les deit tener par mi chescun hundred de soen counté. Et ceo qe est apelé devaunt les viscountes tour

Brac. 154 b, 155; Fle. 112. Mag. Cart. c. 35.

1—1. les soens *C.* 2—2. *so verb. M. sim. H.* des chartres et seutes *L. sim. GARC.* des chartres [e escris *on erasure*] *N.* 3—3. *om. CH.* 4. *so NARMC.* et *L.*

boar, or to have common at a watering-place for his cattle, or to take reasonable estovers, or to have a way, or common of fishery, or to enforce an acquittance, or concerning gages damaged or not returned, or charters, or concerning suits detained, or mills wrongfully erected, or houses or folds, or other such nusances; and many other actions, wherein the proceeding is by distress of chattels, and by damages, and the trial is by juries.

CHAPTER XXX.

Of the Sheriff's Tourns.

1. There are some articles concerning our Crown and the breach of our peace of which sheriffs may hold plea at other times than on the county days, and in a different place from that where the pleas of the county are held. These pleas are called the tourns of the sheriff, who ought to hold them twice in the year, within every hundred of his county. And that which before the sheriff is called the sheriff's tourn, is in

The sheriff's tourn.

de viscounte est apelé en court de fraunc homme et en fraunchises [1]et en nos hundredz[1] veuwe de fraunc plege, [2]et la[2] enquert hom especialment de ceux qi sount hors de dizeynes, plus qe homme ne fet en tour des viscountes.

Stat. Marl. (52 Hen. III.) c. 10. Fle. 113 (§ 36).

2. A queus tours touz les fraunes[3] del hundred et autres terres[4] tenauntz a [5]ceo somouns[5] communement deyvent venir, hors pris clers gentz de religioun et femmes. A quel jour le viscounte face trier xii. des plus sages et plus leaus et les plus suffisauntz de tut le hundred; et ceux face jurer, qe eux verité presenterunt des articles suth escritz. Et puis soint [6]touz les[6] autres jurez par dozeines et par villeez, qe eux leal presentement frount as premers xii. jorours sur les articles dunt il serount chargez par eus. Et puis lour soit enjoynt, qe, si il trevent akun mesfesour dunt peril soit de vie et de membre, qe soen noun soit privément[7] presenté. Et puis

[71 b.] soint liverez ces articles as premers xii. jorours, a queus soit enjoynt sur lour sermentz, qe les tortz et les mesfetz, qe il

1—1. *om. A.* 2—2. e la *M.* *om. L.* ou *ACH.* 3. hommes *add. M.* 4. terres *om. M.* 5—5. *conj.* cele somounse *LNH.* *sim. SF.* cele somouns *AR.* *sim. G.* teles somounses *M.* tel somouns *C.* 6—6. deus *M.* 7. primerement *ARCH.*

Views of frankpledge, in hundred courts and courts baron.

the court of a freeman and in franchises, and in our hundreds, called view of frankpledge, where a more special inquiry is made concerning those who are not in any tithing, than is done in the sheriff's tourn.

Proceedings at sheriff's tourns.

2. At these tourns all the freemen of the hundred and other landholders being summoned, ought in general to appear, except clerks, persons in religion, and women. At which day

Juries of presentors.

let the sheriff cause twelve of the most sage, lawful, and sufficient men out of the whole hundred to be chosen, and to swear they will present the truth of the articles hereinafter mentioned. Afterwards the rest shall be sworn by dozens, and by townships, that they will make lawful presentment to the first twelve jurors upon the articles wherewith they shall be charged by them. Next it shall be enjoined them, that if they find any offender, from whom there may be any danger of life or limb, the name of such offender be secretly presented.

Charge of the jurors.

Afterwards the following articles shall be delivered to the twelve first jurors, who are to be charged upon their oaths that they will lawfully present the wrongs and offences which

porount enquere des villeez[1] par mi ces articles, leaument presenteround.

3. Des enemys mortels le Roi ou la Reyne ou de lour enfauntz, et de lour consentours; des fauseners de seal le Roi et de sa monee; de homicides et de murdrisours; de ardours de autri mesouns ou bleez felounesement; de burgesours; de robbeours; de larouns; de brusours de la prisoun le Roi; de ravisours de femmes; de utlagez [2]et de[2] forjurours del reaume retournez; de sorciers et de sorceresses; de renyez et mescreauntz; de touz traytres; de enpuysounours; de cillours de bourses; de usurers; de mascecreefs[3] achatauntz et vendauntz a escient chars emblez; de ceux qi enblaunchisent quirs a escient des bestes emblez; de redubbours [4]achatauntz a escient[4] dras emblez, et les attirent en autre fourme; de tresor muscé en terre et trové; de huteys[5] a tort levé, et a dreit levé et nent suiz; de ewes estopez ou estrescees ou trestournez; de chemins estopez estrescez ou trestournez; de devises ostez ou a tort chaungez; de murs, mesouns, portes, marleres, ou fossez, ou autres destourbaunces levez ou fetes Fle. 112, 113.

1. so *NSGA*. viles *L*. vilees *M*. villes *C*. 2—2. e de *M*. Des *L*. des *NR*. de *C*. 3. so *LN*. Macecrefs *M*. Mascres *AR*. Massegrefs *G*. macegrefs *CH*. 4—4. qe a escient akatent *C*. 5. huthes *M*. fourches *C*. houches *H*.

they shall find upon inquiry from the townships by means of these articles.

3. Of mortal enemies of the king or queen, or their children, and of those consenting to them; of counterfeiters of the king's seal and of his money; of homicides and murderers; of those who feloniously set fire to the houses or corn of others; of burglars, robbers, and thieves; of breakers of the king's prison; of ravishers of women; of outlaws and abjurors of the realm who are returned; of sorcerers and sorceresses; of apostates and heretics; of traitors; of poisoners; of cutpurses; of usurers; of salesmen knowingly buying and selling stolen meat; of those who knowingly bleach skins of stolen beasts; and of menders of clothes knowingly buying stolen clothes and turning them into other shapes; of treasure hidden and found in the earth; of hue and cry wrongfully raised, or duly raised and not pursued; of waters stopped or narrowed or turned from their course; of roads stopped, narrowed, or turned; of boundaries removed or wrongfully altered; of walls, houses, gates, marl-pits, ditches, or other Articles of the tourn.

sur acun chemin commun a la nusaunce de mesme le chemin en peril de trespasauntz; de petitz larouns qi toundent ou [72.] escorgent motouns ou autres bestes nutauntre pur embler la pel; de ceux qi pernent thefbote; de ceux qi ount fet prisoun en lour mesouns, ou hamsokne, ou pountbreche; de maufesours [1]de parcs e de[1] vivers; de pernours de autri columbs; de assise de payn et de cerveyse enfreinte; de ceux qi achatent et vendent par poys et par mesures hors de assise; de mellifs[2], et de conteckours, et de saunc espaundu; de veilles nent gardez; de chemins reals nient enlargeez; de ceux qi ount retenu pruvours en autri prisoun qe en nostre garde, ou autre feloun aylours qe en nostre prisoun outre un jour et une nuyt; de noveles fraunchises et custumes, ou juises, levez puis le autre tour en euwe ou en terre; de weyf et de wrek de meer trové et retenu; de pountz et de chauceez[3] debruseez, et qi les deit appariler; de dreitz au Roy appendauntz sustrez, sicum[4] des gardes, mariages, relefs, demeynes, avouwesons des eglises, et de totes maneres de seutes; et de ceux qi cleyment

Ante, c. 21. s. 11. p. 83.

Stat. Winton. (13 Ed. I.) c. 4, 5.

Ante, c. 12. s. 9. p. 47.

1—1. *so N.* de parcs de *L.* *sim. CH.* en parks ou en *M.* *sim. AR.* 2. medlifs *NACH.* *sim. M.* 3. *so N.* chaucies *LS.* chauces *G.* chaleres *M.* 4. *so NARMCH.* des gages *add. L.*

Articles of the tourn.

nusances raised or made in any common way to the annoyance of the same way and to the danger of passengers; of petty thieves, who shear or flay sheep or other cattle in the night to steal their skins; of those who take thefbote; and of those who have made a prison in their houses; or committed hamsoken, or breach of pound; and of offenders in parks or in vivaries; of takers of others' pigeons; of breach of the assise of bread and beer, and of those who buy and sell by weights and measures not according to the assise; of affrays, of brawlers, and of bloodshed; of watches not kept; of the king's highways not widened; of those who have detained approvers in any other prison than in our custody, or other felons elsewhere than in our prison above a day and night; of new franchises, customs, or instruments of correction[f], set up since the last tourn, in water or land; of waif, or wreck of sea found and retained; of bridges and highways broken, and who ought to repair them; of rights belonging to the king withheld, as wards, marriages, reliefs, demesnes, advowsons of churches, and all kinds of suits; and of those who claim

[f] 'Gallows, pillory, tumbrel, or the like.' (Note in MS. *N.*)

fraunchises et juises reals; de ceux de xii. aunz [1]et de plus[1] [2]del hundred[2] qi ne sount mie venuz au tour.

4. Et de touz ces articles soit enquis en[3] veuwe de fraunc plege; et ceux articles outre; si touz les chefs[4] pleges soint venuz a la veuwe; et si il eynt touz lour dizeynes entieres; de ceux [5]de xii. aunz et en sus[5], hors pris les clers, et chivalers et lour enfauntz, et femmes, qi ne sount mie en dizeyne, et de lour receptours, et qi meynpast il sount; de wakerours[6] par pays, qi ne sunt de nuly meynpast, de qi suspecioun est de mal. Fle. 112 (§ 4–7). [72 *b*.]

5. Et cum les villeez[7] averount dit lour verdit as premers jurours et eus soint certifiez de la verité, tauntost voisent les premers jurours rendre sus lour presentement tel cum il Fle. 113.

1—1. en suis *A*. en fuiz *H*. enfreinz *C*. 2—2. *so GAMCH*. *sim. E*. *om. LNS*. 3. *so NARM*. de *LCH*. 4. *so ARM*. *sim. CH*. *om. L*. chiefs *interl. N*. 5—5. *so verb. M*. qi xij. aunz en sus *L*. [qi sunt] de xij. aunz et de plus qi ne sount mie venuz al tour ne suis *N*. de dozze anz en suz *S*. *sim. H*. de dozze aunz e plus *G*. de xij. anz e sus *F*. 6. waucrours *M*. wacreours *C*. waskerours *F*. 7. *so NG*. villes *LC*. vilees *SM*.

royal franchises and powers of punishment; and of those of twelve years old and upwards in the hundred who have not come to the tourn.

4. All these articles shall also be inquired of at the view of frankpledge; and the following articles besides; whether all the headboroughs are come to the view, and whether they have their tithings complete; of those of twelve years old or upwards, excepts clerks, and knights and their children, and women, who are not in tithings, and of their receivers, and of whose mainpast they are[g]; of vagrants through the country who are not of any one's mainpast, and are of suspicious character. Articles of the view of frankpledge. Tithings. Vagrants.

5. When the townships have given in their verdict to the first jurors, and they are certified of the truth, let the first jurors immediately go and deliver up their presentment to the Presentments how made.

g The annotator in MS. *N* observes here, that frankpledge was so called, 'because villains and naifs ought not to be in tithings, *secundum quosdam*.' It is not improbable that the term frank, or free, pledge arose from a misinterpretation of the Saxon Friðborh, or pledge of peace. It is true however that the Anglo-Saxon tithings were composed of 'freemen;' (Leg. Cnut. 20; Cart. Will. I. de stat. 14); but the churl was in Saxon nomenclature 'free.' In the laws of William I. it is provided that 'all the villains shall be in frankpledge.' Leg. Will. I. 20. There can be no doubt that the peasants were the principal subjects of this regulation when in its vigour, the military tenants, the *liberi homines* of Norman law, being exempt. See Bracton 124 *b*; Fleta 62 (§ 10). The doubt above mentioned as to the admission of villains seems to show that at the time when it was entertained either the institution of frankpledge was already in decay, or the peasants were in a great measure enfranchised.

voderount avouer as viscountes sauntz estre enchesounez[1]; et les presentementz de felonies moustrent privément, et les autres presentementz apertement.

Fle. 113. 6. Et si acun soit present endité de felonie, tauntost soit Brac. 150 b, 154 b; Fle. 54. pris et envoyé a nostre gaole, si il ne soit acun laroun ou robbeour seisi de soen larcyn handhabbynde et bacberinde, et sakebere soit present fesaunt la seute, en queu cas soit le Ante, c. 16. s. 1, 7. p. 56, 61. tesmonage examiné, et soit fete juyse de ly, si le sakebere aveyre la chose [2]sue ou[2] hors de sa garde emblé ou robbé, dount la juyse soit solom la quantité de la chose emblé, sicum Fle. 113 (§ 38. s. 39). avaunt est dit. Et des enditez qi ne serrount mie trovez [3]en present[3] soint les presentementz enselez de suth les seaus des xii. presentours; les queus le viscounte face prendre, et eux[4] nent replevisables sauvement en prisoun tener jekes a la pre- [73.] mere deliveraunce de la gaole, et les plevisables soint jekes Stat. West. 1. (3 Ed. 1.) c. 15; mesme le tens repleviz.

Glan. li. 14. c. 3; Brac. 123, 154; Fle. 114. 7. Et les queus sount replevisables et queus noun, [5]dit est[5] en nos estatuz; et estre ceo ne sount mie replevisables enditez ou apelez de compassement de nostre mort, sicum de sus est

1. so *N.* sim. *GARM.* en chesoune *L.* 2—2. sui de *A.* 3—3. en presentz *L.* presentz *NG.* sim. *SM.* present *C.* 4. les *MC.* retigne les *on eras.* *N.* 5—5. auoms dit *AC.*

sheriff, such as they will abide by without being questioned, and let them exhibit the presentments for felony privately, and the other presentments openly.

Persons presented as trespassers to be apprehended. Thief *hand-habbende* and *bacberende* to be tried on the spot.

6. If any person indicted of felony be present, he shall be immediately apprehended and carried to our gaol, unless it be any thief or robber in possession of his theft 'handhaving and backbearing,' and the sakeber be present to make his suit, in which case let the evidence be examined, and judgment executed upon him, if the sakeber verifies the thing as his own, or as stolen or robbed out of his custody; and let the punishment be according to the quantity of the thing stolen as before is mentioned. As to such of the persons indicted as shall not be found present, let the presentment be sealed under the seals of the twelve presentors. And the sheriff shall cause them to be apprehended, and keep such as are not bailable safe in prison until the first gaol delivery, and bail those who are bailable until the same time.

What prisoners are not bailable.

7. What persons are bailable and what not, is mentioned in our statutes. Besides, those persons are not bailable, who are indicted or appealed of compassing our death, as is above said;

dit; ne ceux qi sount pris par jugement de nos Justices, sicum ceux qi sount atteintz de aperte deceyte fete en nostre court; ne ceux qi sount pris pur reddesseisine; ne ceux qi par jugement de nostre court sount comaundez a la prisoun pur arrerage de acounte, ne ceux qi sount pris [1]pur rap de femme ou par estatutz de marchaunz; ne ceux qi sount[1] atteyntz de trespas [2]de parcs et de[2] vivers, ou de destourbaunce fete encountre la execucioun de jugementz de nostre court; ne ceux qi averount amené femmes de religioun de lour covent; ne ceux qi ount amené enfauntz de autri mariage.

8. Kaunt as presentementz fetz sur devises remuez, chemins et euwes estopez, et de tiels autres personels trespas, tauntost respoignent les trespasours, si il soint presentz. Et s'il ne voillent, ou s'il ne soint mie presentz, adounc soit comaundé as xii. presentours qe tauntost voisent redrescer tels tortz solom le dreit usage, s'il eynt esté fetz puis le autre tourn[3]. Et si ceux jurours en absence de acun eynt acun homme grevé a tort par lour presentement, en tel cas voloms nous, qe les [73 *b*.] grevez eynt accioun a recoverer lour estat par pleyntes en

1—1. so *N.* *sim. MACH.* *om. L.* 2—2. fet en Parks ou en *M.* en parks e en *A.* 3. so *MC.* cort *A.* tour *G.* *om. L.*

nor those who are apprehended by the judgment of our justices, as persons convicted of open deceit committed in our court, nor those who are apprehended for redisseisin, nor those who by judgment of our court are committed to prison for arrears of accounts, nor those who are taken for rape of women, or by statute merchant, nor those who are convicted of trespassing in parks and vivaries, or of impeding the execution of judgments of our court, nor those who have carried off religious women from their convent, nor those who have carried off infants whose marriages belong to others.

8. As to the presentments made of boundaries removed, ways and waters obstructed, and such other personal trespasses, let the trespassers, if they are present, immediately answer thereto; and if they will not, or if they are not present, then let the twelve presentors be commanded immediately to go and remedy such nusances, if they have been done since the last tourn, by restoring matters to their lawful and usual state. And if such jurors have wrongfully aggrieved any persons in their absence by their presentment, in such case the persons aggrieved shall have an action to be reinstated, by

Nusances, how remedied.

Countez, ou par nos brefs, si mester soit, lequel qe il voillent en commun sur touz les xii. presentours ou sur acun de eux en several. Et si les pleyntifs ne pusent averrer lour pleyntes, adounc recoverent les defendauntz lour damage, et les pleyntifs en la merci.

Stat. Marl. (52 Hen. III.) c. 10.

Fle. 114 (§ 48).

9. Puis soint amerciez touz ceux qi sount nomez trespassours par les presentementz, et ceux ausi de xii. aunz en sus qi ne sount mie venuz, hors pris Prelatz, Countes et Barouns, gentz de religioun, et femmes, et hors pris ausi ceux qi ne sount mie conversauntz et continuelment demorauntz en les hundrez, tut eynt il manauntises. De assises enfreyntes soit fet solom ceo qe dit serra en le proscheyn chapitre. En vewes de fraunc plege soint les chef[1] pleges amerciez qi ne averount mie lour dizeynes entieres illucs en present, s'il ne peusent estre excusez par la mort de acun ou de plusours. Et ausi soint amerciez ceux qi ount xii. aunz et plus, qi devereynt estre en dizeyne et ne eynt mie esté, [2]et ceux ausi qi maynpast il [3]sount et[3] ount esté[2]. Et si acun soit en dizeyne aylours, ceo suffise.

1. chiefs *NSGMC.* 2—2. *om. AR.* 3—3. *om. MCH.* sount ou *N.*

plaint in the county court, or by our writ, if necessary, either against all the twelve presentors jointly, or against any of them severally. And if the plaintiffs cannot make good their plaints, then let the defendants recover their damage, and the plaintiffs be in mercy.

Amercements of trespassers and defaulters.

Amercements in views of frankpledge.

9. Afterwards let all those be amerced who shall be named as trespassers by the presentments, and those also of twelve years and upwards who have not appeared, except prelates, earls, barons, persons of religion, and women, and except also those who are not living or constantly resident in the hundreds, although they may have dwellings there. As to breach of assises, let the proceedings be as mentioned in the next chapter. In views of frankpledge, let the headboroughs be amerced, who shall not have their tithings complete, there present, unless they are excusable by reason of the death of any one or more. Also let those be amerced who are twelve years old and upwards, and who ought to be in a tithing and have not been, and those also of whose mainpast they are and have been; but if any person be elsewhere in a tithing, it is sufficient.

10. Et cum akun deit [1]estre entré[1] en dizeyne, en primes truisse pleges a nos baillifs, qe il serra prest de ester a dreit en nostre court quant mester serra; et face le serment de feuté a nous et a nos heyrs, et soit liveré a ses pleges; et adounc soit enroullé soen noun et les nouns de ses pleges. Fle. 114 (§ 47). [74.]

11. La feuté soit juré par cestes paroles. Ceo oyez vous N. baillif, qe jeo P. de ceo jur en avaunt serray feal et leal a noster seignur E. Roi de Engleterre et a ses heirs, et foy et leauté lour porteray de vie et de membre [2]de cors et de chateus[2] et de terrien honur, et qe jeo lour mal ne lour damage ne saveray ne oyray qe jeo ne le defenderay a moen poer, si me ayd Deu et les Sainctz.

CHAPITRE XXXI. [xxx.]

De Mesures[3].

Mag. Cart. c. 25; Stat. de Pistoribus (Stat incert. temp.) c. 8, 9; Fle. 71.

1. Nous voloms qe nul ne eyt mesure en noster reaume for qe nous, mes qe chescun prenge ses mesures et ses peyz de

1—1. entrer *NSGARMH.* 2—2. *om. C.* 3. e de poiz e de veuwe de fraunc-plege *add. M. sim. F.*

10. When any one is to be admitted into a tithing, first he shall find pledges to our bailiffs, that he will be amenable to justice in our court as often as there shall be occasion, and shall take the oath of fealty to us and to our heirs; and let him be delivered to his pledges, and let his name and the names of his pledges be enrolled. Mode of admittance into tithing.

11. Fealty shall be sworn in these words: Hear this you, N., bailiff, that I, P., from this day forward will be faithful and loyal to our lord E. king of England and his heirs, and will bear unto them faith and loyalty of life and limb, of body and chattels, and of earthly honour, and will neither know nor hear of their hurt or damage, but I will oppose it to the best of my power; so help me God and the Saints. Formula of fealty.

CHAPTER XXXI.

Of Measures.

1. We will that no one have measures in our realm except ourselves, but that every one take his measures and his weights Royal standard of weights and measures.

nos estaundardz, sicum de bussels, galouns, lyveres, et aunes, et teles autres mesures.

Assisa panis (Stat. incert. temp.); Fle. 71, 72.

2. Et voloms qe assise de payn soit gardé en ceste fourme; qe quant le quarter de furment est vendu a xii. deners, qe le gastel de ferling blaunc et bien quit poyse vi. li. et xvi. s.; payn de coket de mesme le blé et de mesme le bultel peyse plus qe le gastel de deus south; payn de meyndre value del coket et de un autre bultel peyse plus qe le gastel de v. s.; le [74 b.] payn de symenel peyse meyns del gastel de ii. s. pur ceo qe il serra deus foiz quit; le payn de ferling de furment entier peyse coket et demi; le payn de trayt peyse deus gastels; et le payn de touz blez poise dus cokettes[1]. Quaunt le quarter de furment se vent pur xviii. deners, adunc poise gastel de ferling iiii. li. x. s. viii. d. Quaunt a ii. s. dounc soit le poys de lxviii. s. Quaunt a ii. s. vi. d. dunc soit le poys liiii. s. iiii. d. [2]mayle ferling[2]. Quaunt a iii. s. dunc soit le poys xlviii. s. Quaunt a iii. s. vi. d. soit le poys xlii. s. Quaunt a

1. le payn cribre peyse un gastel et demy. le payns fraunceys peyse meyns del gastel xij. deners. *add. B.* 2—2. ob. ferlyng *M.* ob. q̃. *CB.*

from our standards, as of bushels, gallons, pounds, ells, and other such measures[h].

Assise of bread.

2. And we will that the assise of bread be observed in this manner[i]. When the quarter of wheat is sold for twelvepence, the farthing loaf of wastel bread white and well baked shall weigh 6lb. 16*s.*; coket bread of the same corn and the same bolter shall weigh more than wastel by two shillings; bread of a lower price than coket and of another bolter shall weigh more than the wastel by 5*s.*; simnel bread shall weigh less than the wastel bread by 2*s.*, because it shall be twice baked; the farthing loaf of entire wheat shall weigh one and a half of coket; bread of trayt shall weigh two wastels; bread of all corn shall weigh two cokets. When wheat is sold for 18*d.* the quarter, then the farthing loaf of wastel shall weigh 4lb. 10*s.* 8*d.*; when for 2*s.*, it shall weigh 68*s.*; when for 2*s.* 6*d.*, the weight shall be 54*s.* 4¾*d.*; when for 3*s.*, the weight shall be 48*s.*; when for 3*s.* 6*d.*, the weight shall be 42*s.*;

h As to the measures used in England in the thirteenth century, and their respective quantities, see Assisa de Ponderibus (Stat. incert. temp.), Flet. 72, 73.

i It should be observed, that the same standard of weight is used for bread and money. The *solidus*, or shilling (*s.*), is the 20th, and the *denarius*, penny or pennyweight (*d.*), the 240th part of a pound. See below, s. 5.

iiii. s. [1]dounc soit le poys xxxiiii. s. Quaunt a iiii. s. vi. d.[1] dounc soit le poys xxx. s. Quaunt pur v. s. dounc soit le poys xxvii. s. [2]ii. d. mayle[2]. Quaunt a v. s. vi. d. dunc soit le poys xxiiii. s. viii. d. ferling. Quaunt pur vi. s. [3]dunc soit le poys xxi. s. viii. d. ferling. Quaunt a vi. s. vi. d.[3] dunc soit le poys xx. s. xi. d. Quaunt pur vii. s. dounc soit le poys xix. s. i. d. Quaunt pur vii. s. vi. d. dunc soit le poys xviii. s. i. d. mayle[4]. Quaunt pur viii. s. dounc soit le poys xvii. s. Quaunt pur viii. s. vi. d. dounc soit le poys xvi. s. Quaunt a ix. s. dounc soit le poys xv. s. ferling. Quaunt a ix. s. vi. d. dounc soit le poys xiiii. s. iiii. d. mayle[5]. Quaunt a x. s. dounc soit le poys [75.] xiii. s. [6]viii. d.[6] Quaunt a x. s. vi. d. dounc soit le poys xii. s. xi. d. ferling. Quaunt pur xi. s. dounc soit le poys xii. s. iiii. d. Quaunt a xi. s. vi. d. dounc soit le poys xi. s. x. d. Quaunt a xii. s. dounc soit [7]le poys xi. s. iiii. d.; issi qe le poys del payn acrese ou[7] amenuse pur vi. d. accressaunt ou amenusaunt en chescun quarter.

3. Et uncore pora le pestour gayner de chescun quarter de forment iii. d. et le bren et deus payns del pris de deus

Ass. panis (Stat. incert. temp.) c. 2; Fle. 72.

1—1. so *AC.* om. *LSM.* 2—2. ij. d. ob. *MB.* iiij. d. *C.* 3—3. so *N.* sim. *SAMH.* om. *L.* 4. ob. *MCB.* 5. ob. *AMHCB.* 6—6. so *LSMC.* vij. d. *G.* vij. d. q̄. *B.* 7—7. om. *HC.* le peys xj. s. iiij. d. e quant un quarter de furment est vendu at xj. s. e un altre a xj. s. vj. d. dunke seit le peys *B.*

when for 4*s.*, the weight shall be 34*s.*; when for 4*s.* 6*d.*, then 30*s.*; when for 5*s.*, the weight shall be 27*s.* 2½*d.*; when for 5*s.* 6*d.*, it shall be 24*s.* 8¼*d.*; when for 6*s.*, the weight shall be 21*s.* 8¼*d.*; when for 6*s.* 6*d.*, it shall be 20*s.* 11*d.*; when for 7*s.*, the weight shall be 19*s.* 1*d.*; when for 7*s.* 6*d.*, the weight shall be 18*s.* 1½*d.*; when for 8*s.*, the weight shall be 17*s.*; when for 8*s.* 6*d.*, the weight shall be 16*s.*; when for 9*s.*, then 15*s.* 0¼*d.*; when for 9*s.* 6*d.*, the weight shall be 14*s.* 4½*d.*; when for 10*s.*, then 13*s.* 8*d.*; when for 10*s.* 6*d.*, the weight shall be 12*s.* 11¼*d.*; when for 11*s.*, then it shall be 12*s.* 4*d.*; when for 11*s.* 6*d.*, then the weight shall be 11*s.* 10*d.*; when for 12*s.*, the weight shall be 11*s.* 4*d.*; so that the weight of the loaf shall be changed for every 6*d.* rising or falling in the quarter of corn.

3. The baker may still gain out of every quarter of wheat threepence, and the bran and two loaves of the value of two

The baker's profit.

Stat. de pistoribus, c. 2.

esterlings al fornage, et iii. mayles pur les gages de ses treys serjauntz, et mayle pur les gages de deus garceouns, [1]et mayle a sel et bultel[1]. Et voloms qe, si le pestour soit atteynt de faus poys [2]issi qe[2] pur la defaute del poys de un ferling[3] trové en le peys de ii. s. en tel cas soit il amerciable, et en chescun exces[4] soit il mis a la juyse.

[75 *b*.]

Ass. panis (Stat. incert. temp.) c. 2; Fle. 72.

4. Et voloms qe assise de cerveyse soit gardé en ceste manere; qe cum le quarter de forment vaudra iii. s. ou xl. d. et le quarter de orge xx. d. ou ii. s. et le quarter de aveyne xvi. d., adounc soint venduz ii. galouns de cerveyse a un dener en bourgs et en citeez, et iii. galouns de cerveyse a un dener en viles champestres. Et quaunt en citez[5] serrount venduz iii. galouns de cerveyse a un dener, adounc soint venduz de hors iiii. a dener. Et quaunt le quarter de orge soit vendu pur ii. s. dounc vailent iii.[6] galouns de cerveyse un dener; et

1—1. e Maile a seel e maile a bulters *AR.* *sim. CH.* a sel ob. e a gest ob. en chaundeille ferling en busche iij. deners e a bulter ob. *B.* 2—2. ou ke il neyt mie tenu les assises auauntdites une foez deus foez e la tierce foez seyt amercie solom la quantite de sun trespas. E si il eyt greuement trespasse e plusurs foez qe *B.* 3. esterling *GCB.* 4. si il passe le noumbre de ij. s. en le peys de payn de ferling *add. B.* 5. e en Burgh. *add. M.* *sim. CB.* *sim. interl. N.* 6. *so LA.* iiij. *NGFH.*

sterlings[k] for his oven, three halfpence for the wages of his three servants, and one halfpenny for the wages of two boys, and one halfpenny for salt and for the bolter. We will that if a baker be convicted of false weight[l], where there is found a deficiency of the weight of one farthing in the weight of two shillings, he shall be amerciable; and for any greater default he shall be set in the pillory.

Punishment of baker transgressing the assise.

Assise of beer.

4. The assise of beer shall be observed in this manner. When a quarter of wheat is worth from three shillings to forty pence, and a quarter of barley from twenty pence to two shillings, and a quarter of oats sixteen pence, then two gallons of beer shall be sold in cities and boroughs for one penny, and in country places three gallons of beer for one penny; and when three gallons are sold in cities and boroughs for one penny, then four shall be sold without for a penny; and when the quarter of barley shall be sold for two shillings, three gallons

[k] A sterling appears to be the same as a penny. 'Denarius Anglicanus, qui vocatur sterlingus, rotundus et sine tonsura, ponderabit xxxii. grana frumenti in medio spice.' Assisa de ponderibus. (Stat. incert. temp.); Fleta 72, 73.

[l] Similar varieties of readings to those mentioned in the note above are also found in the several copies of the Latin Assisa panis, (Stat. incert. temp.) See Statutes of the Realm, (Rec. Com.) p. 200. See also Fleta 72. The Assisa panis was formerly printed as a statute of the 51st year of Henry III.

issi accrese et descrese le marché de cerveyse solom le foer coraunt de blee.

5. Et cum nous eyoms les estaundartz et les essaumplaries de nos poys et de nos mesures baylé[1] a garder a akun de nos ministres, voloms qe cely ministre eyt le poer et la conisaunce de faus poys et des fauses mesures par tote nostre verge, ou qe nous seoms en nostre terre de eynz fraunchises et de hors, et de arder quaunt[2] il trovera de fauses, [3]et de amercier ou autrement punir ceux qi teles[3] mesures ou tels poys ount usez. Et ly avoms assigné a deliverer estaundartz a ceux qi aver les voderount; dount la livre poyse xx. s. en deners countauntz; le aune de deus coutes et deus pouz; et le bussel content CC. livres de deners; et le galoun xxv. livres. Les marchauntz neqedent eynt lour pois, [4]quant a aver de pois[4], solom lour usages. [76.]

Fle. 71; Ante c. 1. s. 6.

6. Et quant le ministre des mesures deit fere soen office, si le face en ceste manere. En primes voist ovekes ses

Fle. 74.

1. et bayle *L.* et bayllee *N.* baillez *A.* e seient baille *G.* e baile *MCH.* baille *B.* 2. kaunqe *M.* quant qe *CH.* *sim. A.* quant [qe] *N.* 3—3. *so verb. G.* *sim. ARMSCB.* *om. L.* e de eus qi les deueint amercier e de autrement punir ceus qi tiels *A.* *sim. interl. N.* 4—4. *so verb. NM.* *sim. S.* quant auoir de pois *L.* come auer deiuent *G.* qaunt al auer del pois *A.* *om. C.* quant aver deivent de peys *B.*

of beer shall be worth a penny; thus the market of beer shall rise and fall according to the current price of corn.

5. And whereas we have entrusted one of our officers with the custody of the standards and samples of our weights and measures, we will that this officer shall have jurisdiction and cognizance of false weights and measures throughout our verge, wheresoever we be in our territory, within franchise and without, and to burn such as he shall find false, and to amerce and otherwise punish those who have made use of such weights or measures. We have also appointed him to deliver standards to all those who require them, whereof the pound shall weigh twenty shillings of current money; the ell shall be two cubits and two inches; a bushel shall contain two hundred pounds in pence, and a gallon twenty-five pounds. Merchants nevertheless shall have their weights as far as regards avoirdupois[m] according to their customs.

King's officer having custody of weights and measures. His jurisdiction in the verge.

Standards of weight and measure.

6. When the officer of the measures is to perform his office, let him do it in this manner. First let him go with his

Inquests of weights and measures.

[m] See above, c. xxii. s. 22, and note there, p. 96.

estaundartz de marché en marché, en[1] quant qe il trovera de marchez de eynz la verge; et tauntost face venir les baillifs devaunt ly a fere ceo qe il lour enjoyndra de par nous. Et s'il ne voillent venir, ou s'il vengent et ne voillent mie estre entendauntz a ly, soit prise la fraunchise del marché en nostre meyn, si autre de nous la tiegne; et s'il soint nos[2] baillifs, soint puniz par prisoun et par fins. Et si les bayllifs veignent solom ceo qe fere deyvent, adunc lour soit enjoynt, qe il facent venir devaunt ly touz les bussels demi-bussels et quartz et galouns et demi-galouns et totes les autres mesures dount hom eit achaté ou vendu en ceste vile, et de chescun pestour un payn de chescune manere[3], et trestouz les pestours et totes les braceresces de la vile, et les taverners [4]et trestouz ceux a qi le mesures sount[4], et autres bones gentz de la vile par queux il pora enquere verité sur les articles de soen office. Et ceux qi serrount sommons et ne viegnent mie, si lour somounse soit tesmoigné, soint en la merci. Et cum il serrount venuz devaunt ly, tauntost face jurer xii. des [5]plus leaus

1. *so G.* et *L.* *sim. S.* de *AMCB.* 2. *so ARMCB.* nos *om. L.* *interl. N.* 3. *so ARMCB.* manere *om. L.* manere de ble *interl. N.* 4—4. *om. ARCHB.* 5—5. pluis sages homes *AR.* plus prodes hommes *M.* plus purdes hommes *CH.*

standards from market to market, wherever he shall find any within the verge, and immediately summon the bailiffs to come before him to perform what he shall enjoin them on our behalf. And if they will not come, or if they come and will not be obedient to him, let the franchise of the market be taken into our hand, if it is held by any other than by us; and if they are our bailiffs, let them be punished by imprisonment and fine. If the bailiffs appear as they ought to do, then let them be commanded that they cause to be brought before him all the bushels and half bushels, and quarts, gallons, and half gallons, and all other measures whereby people have bought or sold in the town, and from every baker a loaf of every sort, and all the bakers and brewers of the town, and the taverners, and all those to whom the measures belong, and other good people of the town, by whom he may inquire the truth concerning the articles of his office. And those who are summoned and do not come, if the summons be proved, shall be in mercy.

Jury in inquests of market.

When they are come before him, he shall immediately cause twelve of the most lawful householders to be sworn, that they

prudeshommes[5] qe eux verité presenterount des articles dount eux serrount chargez de par nous. [76 *b.*]

7. Les articles soint tels; si le seignur de la fraunchise eit illucs levé marché par soen poer demeyne, ou par garraunt de nous; et si par nostre chartre, s'il eyt la fraunchise de vewe de frauncplege, ou noun; et s'il eyt les amendes de assise enfreynte de payn et de cerveyse; et s'il eit les juyses qe a celes fraunchises appendent, sicum fourches, pillori et tumberel. Et si trové soit qe il ne ad nul marché, ne nule autre fraunchise par garraunt de nous, soit prise la fraunchise en nostre meyn; et le viscounte del lu soit chargee de nous respoundre des issues. Et si il eit la fraunchise de la vewe, et ne eit point des fourches, ausi soit la vewe prise en nostre meyn, et ausi les amendes de assise enfreynte, par defaute de autre juyse. Fle. 74 (§ 18, 19).

8. Et puis soit enquis de pestours et de braceresces qi ount fornié et brascé hors de dreite assise; quaunt de foiz il ount Fle. 74 (§ 20, 21).

will present the truth of the articles wherewith they shall be charged on our behalf.

7. The articles shall be these: whether the lord of the franchise hath set up a market there of his own authority, or by our warrant, and if by our charter, whether he hath the franchise of view of frankpledge or not, and whether he has the correction of the breach of assise of bread and beer, and whether he has the instruments of punishment appendant to such franchises, as gallows, pillory, and tumbrel. And if it be found that he has no market or franchise by our warrant, the franchise shall be seised into our hand, and the sheriff of the place shall be responsible to us for the issues. Likewise if he has the franchise of view, but no gallows, the view shall be seised into our hands, and also the correction of breach of assise, for want of other instruments of punishment[n]. Articles of the inquest. Jurisdiction of the lord of the market.

8. Afterwards let inquiry be made concerning bakers and brewers[o], who have baked and brewed out of the right assise, Bakers and brewers amerced for transgression of the assise.

[n] This passage is obscure, and possibly corrupt. The *fourches* or gallows would only be required where the lord had jurisdiction of infangthief.

[o] It will be observed, that the word in the original implies that the trade was carried on by females. So in the Latin Assisa panis (Stat. inc. temp.) the word is *braciatrix*.

esté amerciez, et [1]quaunt de foiz jugez [2]a la[2] juyse, et pur queles quantitez de trespas il ount esté amerciez ou[1] mis a la juyse; et pur chescun desleal jugement soit la fraunchise prise

Fle. 75 (§ 23). en nostre meyn. Et puis soit enquis, si nul homme ou nule femme eyt esté peri par defaute et par febleesce de juyses; et si tele defaute soit trové, soit la fraunchise prise en nostre meyn; et si nos baillifs soint trovez en defaute, soint puniz par prisoun, et par fins.

Fle. 75 (§ 24). 9. Et puis soit enquis de taverners, qi ount vendu vins en-
[77.] countre la dreite assise puis la dreyne heyre en cel counté, et cum bien lour gayng amounte hors de dreite assise; et ceux soint puniz, s'il soint trovez en vie, par juyse de pillori, et par fin mountaunt a la double value de lour gayn. Puis soit enquis

Fle. 75 (§ 25, 26). de ceux qi achatent par une manere de mesure, et vendent par une meyndre mesure fause; et ceux soint puniz cum vendours des vins; et ausi ceux qi serrount atteyntz de fauses

Fle. 75 (§ 27, 28). aunes et de faus pois; et ausi les mascecrefs et les queus, qi de usage vendent as trespassauntz mauveises viaundes corrumpues ou waucrues et autrement perilouses a saunté de homme; et

1—1. *om. ARCHB.* 2—2. *so M.* al assise de *LN.*

Illegal judgment. how many times they have been amerced, and how many times sentenced to the pillory, and for what amount of offence they were amerced or put in the pillory; and for every illegal judg-

Condition of pillory, &c. ment let the franchise be seised into our hands. Let inquiry afterwards be made whether any man or woman has been destroyed in consequence of the instruments of punishment being faulty or out of repair, and if such default be found, the franchise shall be seised into our hands; and if our bailiffs are in fault, they shall be punished by imprisonment and fine.

Taverners transgressing the assise of wine. 9. Afterwards let it be inquired concerning taverners, who since the last eyre in the county have sold wine contrary to the legal assise, and how much their profit above the right assise amounts to; and if they are living, let them be punished

False measures. by pillory and fined in double the value of their gain. Afterwards let inquiry be made concerning those who buy by one kind of measure, and sell by a false measure of less quantity; and let them be punished as the sellers of wines; and likewise those who shall be convicted of false ells and of false weights;

Unwholesome food. also salesmen and cooks, who make a practice of selling to passers-by bad meat, tainted or diseased, or otherwise danles forstallours ausi, qi acherisent[1] les foers de vitayle vendable par lour traverser qe il fount de hors les marchez.

10. Pris soint examinez les pois et les mesures severalment, Fle. 75 (§ 31). et les bones soint deliverez a ceux [2]qi eles[2] deverount, et les fauses mesures soint arses. Et les pestours et les braceresces atteyntz del assise enfreynte soint puniz solom ceo qe il averount trespassé par amerciement ou par juyses; et les estretes et l'enroullement de soen office face noster ministre des mesures sauntz delay deliverer al Seneschal de noster hostel, qi hastivement face lever celes estretes par le Mareschal, ou par somounse de noster Escheker.

[3]Icy finist la pure personalté[3], [4]et comence de condicioun de vileyns[4].

1. acressent *CB.* 2—2. qi les *N.* a qi il les *M.* *sim. S.* qe les *GACHB.* 3—3. *so N.* Icy finist le liure de personels pleez *L.* *sim. MARCHB.* 4—4. *so verb. N.* *om. LGSM.* e comence les Reaus pleez *C.* e comence le liure de Naifte *HB.* e comence le liure des disseisines *AR.*

gerous to the health of man. Likewise forestallers, who raise the market price of victuals by their dealings outside the market. Forestallers.

10. Afterwards let the weights and measures be severally examined, and the good ones be restored to the owners, and the false ones burned. And let the bakers and brewers convicted of breaking the assise be punished in proportion to their offence either by amercements or pillory. And let our officer of measures without delay cause the estreats and the enrollment of his proceedings to be delivered to the Steward of our household, who shall speedily cause such estreats to be levied by the marshal, or by summons out of our Exchequer. Examination of weights and measures. Termination of the inquest. Amercements, how levied.

Here ends the subject of pure personalty, and begins that of the condition of villains.

CHAPITRE XXXII. [XXXI.]

[77 b.]

[1]De nayfté[1].

Glan. ii. 5; Brac. 4 b, 5; Fle. 1, 2.

1. Dit avoms de sus en partie de dreit des fraunches gentz; ore fet a dire de la condicioun des vileyns. La quele condicioun fust chaungé hors de fraunchise jekes en servage [2]en graunt antiquité[2] par constitucioun des gentz, et ne mie par ley naturele, sicum del tens del deluvie et avaunt, en le quel tens totes choses furent communes a touz, et touz hommes outrement[3] fraunes, et vesquirent en ley naturele; et par multiplicacioun des gentz et appropriement des biens qe avaunt furent communs, surdirent batayles par divers luys el mound, et pur eschure effusiouns de saunc et les perilouses aventures des batayles fust adounc ordeyné par constitucioun des gentz, qe nul ne tuast autre, mes qi autre pout prendre en batayle qe cil qi fust pris demorast serf a soen pernour a touz jours mes, a fere de ly et de tote sa seute, qe de ly vendroit, tote sa volunté, ausi cum de sa beste ou de soen autre chatel, a doner

1—1. so LM. om. NGS. De condicon de vileins AR. 2—2. de graunt antiquite M. en antiquite C. en grant iniquite F. 3. entierment AR. sim. GCHB. ouwelement M.

CHAPTER XXXII.

Of Villenage.

Naifty or bondage, its origin.

1. We have above in part treated of the law of free persons; we must now treat of the condition of villains. This condition was of ancient time changed from freedom to bondage by the constitution of nations, and not by the law of nature, as it stood at the time of the flood and earlier, when all things were common to every one, and all men were entirely free, and lived according to the law of nature. But from the increase of mankind and the appropriation of goods which before were common, battles arose in divers places in the world, and to avoid bloodshed and the perilous chances of battle, it was then ordained by the constitution of nations that men should not kill one another, but whenever one could take another in battle, that the person taken should for ever remain a bondman to him who took him, to do with him and all his issue that should proceed from him whatsoever he would, as with his beast or chattel, to give, to sell, and to kill. After-

Bondage by captivity.

ou a vendre et a tuer[1]. Et puis fust ordeyné pur la cruelté des acuns seignurs, qe nul ne les ocist, et qe vie et membre de eus ausi cum des fraunes hommes fusent en meyns de rois et [2]de princes; dount[2] le ley est ceo: qi qe unque tue[3] soen vileyn, qe il porte jugement ausi cum [4]pur un[4] homme fraunc. Brac. 6; Fle. 2 (§ 6).

2. Une autre[5] manere de nayfs sount, qi ne sount mie nayfs de vyelle[6] nacioun, et sount proprement vileyns, sicum fraunes hommes qi se sount conuz vileyns en nostre court, ou en acune manere par plee de noster bref de nayfté eynt esté atteyntz pur vileyns. Et nient plus de maneres de vileyns ne sount. Brac. 5; Fle. 1. [78.]

1. tenir *M.* 2—2. dount adeprimes *C.* 3. occist *C.* 4—4. de vn *M.* vn autre *CH.* 5. autre *om. CH.* 6. so *L.* *sim. NSM.* vile *GAHF.* ville *C.*

wards it was ordained, on account of the cruelty of some lords, that no one should kill them, but that their lives and limbs, as well as those of free men, should be under the protection of kings and princes[p]. Whence the law is this, that whosoever kills his villain, shall bear the same judgment as if he had killed a free man. Life of bondmen protected by law.

2. There is another kind of naifs who are not naifs by ancient birth, but are properly villains[q], such as free men who have acknowledged themselves in our court to be villains, or who have been in any manner convicted as villains by plea under our writ of Naifty. Beside those mentioned, there are no other kinds of villains. Villains by recognizance or judgment of law.

[p] 'Although the property of villains is in their lord, yet he may not kill them, inasmuch as life and limb belong to the king, who has in every subject a sort of remote fee by title of seignory (qi ad en chescun homme auxi come un fee sutyl en noun de seignurie). The lord is therefore in the position of a mesne between his bondsman (serf) and the king, and ought to treat his villain in due manner as for his employment, and not for his destruction (pur lui enprower e ne mie dampnier).' Note in MS. *N.*

[q] The annotator in MS. *N.* distinguishes between naifs, villains, and serfs in the following way: 'Naif is he that is come of such lineage that they have been in servitude for several generations (qe tote voirs de eve e de treve unt esté en servage). Villain is he that is come afresh into servitude, from which he cannot depart though he be of a free stock. Serf is he who is not absolutely a villain, nor absolutely free, but is *de facto* in servitude, as a freeman who marries a nief and enters into the villain tenement, and does to his wife's lord the villain customs which belong to the land held in villenage. Wherefore this freeman and the issue he has by the nief, are serfs *de facto* and freemen *de jure*, and are called serfs for the servitude in which they are. Wherefore if the issue of this freeman remains in servitude, and his issue the same all their lives, and so on to the fourth degree, the fourth will be a villain for ever, and those who come of him.' I do not know any other authority for this last statement, which is inconsistent with the text of Britton, (see below, ss. 3, 19.) but may probably have agreed well with the earlier practice. (See note on sect. 4.) The whole passage, as compared with the other authorities, shows the uncertain and fluctuating condition both of the law on this subject, and of the meaning of the terms employed.

Brac. 4 *b*, 195; Fle. 1 (c. 1. § 2), 193, 238.

3. En dreit de ceux qe par la resoun de acun tenement eynt fet redempcioun de saunc, ou autres vileyns services, tut les eynt eus et lour auncestres [1]fetz de eve et de treve[1], et acun qi soit venu de tiel cep defuaunt de soen seignur [2]soit demaundé par soen seignur[2] cum soen vileyn, et celi futif puse averrer soen cep fraunc par bone enqueste del visnee, et qe le seignur pleyntif ne fu mie seysi de luy et de ses auncestres cum de ses vileyns par la resoun des cors, mes par la resoun del tenement qe il tyndrent de ly en villenage,—en tel cas voloms nous qe jugement face[3] encountre les seignurs; car dreit ne suffre mie qe villenage pur nule lounge seysine de servage puse aserver nul fraunc homme, nient plus qe lounge seysine de fraunc tenement puse chaunger la condicioun de vileyn jekes en fraunc estat; si qe nul ne poet estre vileyn for de aunciene nativité ou par reconisaunce; ne nul ne poet

1—1. feez de oeue e de treue *M.* *sim. H.* fez de neue e de treue *F.* 2—2. so *verb. GARMC.* *sim. interl. N.* *om. LS.* 3. passe *M.* se face *ARC.*

Villain tenure does not make a villain.

3. With respect to those who by reason of any tenement have made redemption of blood[r] or done other villain services, although they and their ancestors have performed such services from one generation to another[s], if any one sprung from such a stock has fled from his lord, and is demanded by him as his villain, and such fugitive can prove his stock to be free by good inquest of the neighbourhood, and that the lord claiming him was not seised of him and his ancestors as his villains by reason of their bodies, but by reason of the tenement which they held of him in villenage; in such case judgment shall be given against the lords. For justice will not allow that villenage, by any long seisin of a servile tenement, shall make any freeman a bondman; nor, on the other hand, that long seisin of a free tenement shall change the condition of a villain into free estate. So that none can be a villain except by birth, or by recognizance. Nor can one be more a villain than

Nor free tenure a freeman.

[r] 'Redemption of blood' is the same as *mercheta* or *merchetum*, called in Fleta, *merchetum sanguinis* (Fle. 193), a customary payment made by a tenant for license to give his daughter in marriage. This custom was considered a special mark of tenure in villenage. (Brac. 26, 195, 208 *b*; Littleton, Tenures, ss. 174, 209).

[s] The annotator in MS. *N*, in a note upon Bracton, c. 11, has the following explanation of the expression of the text: 'Unum est genus hominum, qui dicuntur villici sive rustici et nativi ex avo et tritavo; unde Gallice dicitur, vileyn de eyve e de treyve; quia villici sunt personaliter.' It will be seen that the annotator himself uses the phrase in the note last cited. Coke has a different explanation. See Coke Lit. 25 *b*. The same expression is found in the Year Books, Hil. 1 Edw. II. p. 4; Pasch. 15 Edw. II. p. 464.

estre plus vileyn de autre, car [1]touz sount de ouwele condicioun[1],—qi qe unques est serf, il est ausi pur serf cum nul autre[2]. Brac. 5; Fle. 1 (c. 3. § 3), 239 (§ 22); Glan. li. 5. c. 6; Brac. 5; Fle. 1, 2.

4. Touz ceux neqedent qi sount de vileyns engendrez ne sount mie serfs; car nul engendré de homme serf hors de matrimonie de fraunche femme n'est serf, tut aveigne qe tele engendrure soit nee puis de eynz matrimonie; ne celi ausi ne serra mie serf, qi serra engendré de une serve en matrimonie mes qe le piere soit fraunc. [78 *b.*]

5. Et cum akun serra nee serf, il[3] serra purement le chatel soen seignur a doner et a vendre a sa volunté; mes pur ceo qe serfs sount annex al fraunc tenement le seignur, ne sount

1—1. *om. SGARMCF.* 2. car touz sunt de owele condicioun *add. M.* *sim. SGCHF.* qar touz sont de vile condicion *AR.* 3. *so NM.* et *L.* e *SG.* *om. C.*

another; for they are all of equal condition,—whosoever is a bondman, is as absolutely a bondman as any other[t]. **Villains and bondmen are all of equal condition.**

4. Nevertheless all who are begotten by villains are not bondmen, for no one begotten by a bondman of a free woman out of matrimony is a bondman, although it happen that the issue be afterwards born within matrimony. Nor shall he be a bondman who was begotten on a bondwoman in matrimony, so as the father be free[u]. **Naifty or bondage by birth**

5. Where any one is by birth a bondman, he shall be merely the chattel of his lord to give and sell at his pleasure. But as bondmen are annexed to the freehold of the lord[x], **Naifs may be aliened *inter vivos*;**

[t] The doctrine that there is no distinction of condition among those not accounted free, appears to have been imported by Bracton or his predecessors from the civil law. 'In servorum conditione nulla est differentia.' (Justin. Inst. li. 1. tit. 3. § 5.) In Anglo-Saxon and early Norman times nothing is more remarkable than the gradations of servitude among the peasants. In Domesday Book the various classes inferior to the liberi homines (villani, bordarii, cotseti, &c.) are clearly distinguished from the bondmen or slaves (servi). In Glanvill (li. 5. s. 4.) the word *servitus* is used as equivalent to *villenagium* or *nativitas*, but I think that the term *servus* is not employed, the various expressions being *in villenagium positus*, *nativus* (li. 5 *passim*), and *rusticus* (li. 14. c. 1). In Bracton and Fleta *servus*, *nativus*, and *villanus* appear to be synonymous. This confusion of ancient distinctions was pointed out in the fourteenth century by Andrew Horne in the Mirror of Justices. (Mirror, c. 2. s. 28. p. 169; c. 5. s. 1. pp. 291, 295.)

[u] In Glanvill's time the children followed the status of the mother, according to the rule of the civil law: 'Servi sunt qui ex ancillis nostris nascuntur;' (Dig. li. 1. tit. 5. l. 5.) and the free husband, if he adopted his wife's estate, and lived upon a tenement held by her in villenage, forfeited 'his law.' (Glan. li. 5. c. 6.) In the time of Bracton, if the father was a freeholder, and the children were born *in libero toro*, they were free; but if the husband adopted his wife's estate, and the children were born *in villenagio*, they followed their mother's condition. (Brac. 5, 193 *b.*) The more liberal rule stated in the text prevailed in later times. (Littleton, Tenures, s. 187.)

[x] It should not pass without notice, that there is no mention in Britton or in the other earlier authors (so far as I am aware) of the class of bondman described by Littleton as

il mie devisables en testament, et pur ceo ne poet Sainte Eglise en Court Cristiene aver nule conisaunce, tut soint il devisez en testament.

Brac. 194 b; Fle. 193.

6. En plusours maneres porra[1] recoverer estat de fraunchise[2], cum si soen seignur le feffe de acun tenement a ly et a ses heyrs, lequel qe il prenge soen homage, ou noun; car puis qe [3]il veut qe son serf[3] eit heirs propres autres del seignur, et voet qe ses heirs eynt successioun en soen heritage, bien semble qe il voet qe soen serf eit estat de fraunc homme. Et ausi devient[4] serf fraunc s'il espouse sa dame, ausi cum de[5] nayve quant le seignur la espouse. Car autrement suereit si graunt inconvenience, qe le heir seroit soen vileyn demeyne, et qe la terre serroit eschaete al chief seignur, qi tendreit le heyr pur soen vileyn, qi unques nel fu par aventure ne nul del linage. Mes si le vileyn eit espousé fraunche femme qe ad terre en fee, lour fiz nee en matrimonie

1. *so LSG.* vilein *add. AR.* il *M.* lem *C.* 2. ou de fraunc homme *add. M.* 3—3. son seigneur voet qil *C.* 4. *so RM.* *sim. SGC.* deit *L.* 5. de *om. SGMC.*

but being annexed to freehold cannot be devised.

they are not devisable by testament; and therefore Holy Church can take no cognizance of them in Court Christian, although devised in a testament.

Enfranchisement by feoffment.

6. A villain may recover his freedom several ways, as if his lord enfeoff him of any tenement to him and his heirs, whether he receive his homage or not; for since it is the lord's pleasure that his bondman shall have heirs of his own other than the lord, and that his heirs shall succeed to his inheritance, it sufficiently appears that he intends his bondman to have the status of a freeman.

Enfranchisement by marriage.

A bondman also becomes free if he marries his lady, as well as a nief when her lord marries her; for otherwise so great inconvenience would ensue, that the heir should be villain to himself, and the land should escheat to the chief lord, who would hold the heir as his villain, when perhaps neither he nor any of his lineage were ever so[y]. But if a villain espouses a free woman who has land in fee, their son born in matrimony is a villain, and his lord shall acquire

villains in gross. (Littleton, Tenures, s. 181.) Examples may be found of villains being transferred in the thirteenth century from one lord to another without the soil on which they lived; but they were probably held to become annexed to the new manor upon which they were settled. The Mirror agrees with our author in treating villains as always annexed to the freehold. (Mirror, c. 2. s. 28. p. 166.) Servitude, as a personal relation, appears to have been then unknown in England.

[y] That is, they were not the villains of *that lord*.

est vileyn, et soen seignur conquerra la terre la mere par sa propre intrusioun ou par mi soen nayf heyr sa mere par assise de mort de auncestre, si ele ne le assigne en sa vie, et si le fiz la survive, et si ele ne eyt autre fraunche engendrure. Et pur ceo voloms nous, qe puis qe acun serf ou acune serfve soit une foiz fraunc ou enfraunchi par fraunc lit de soen seignur ou de autre, qe eus et lour issue, des[1] dounc a touz jours mes, seynt tenuz pur fraunes pur favour de fraunchise et de matrimonie, et qe les hommes joysent a tener par la ley de Engleterre et les femmes eynt dowaries. [79.] Brac 5; Fle. 1, 2.

7. Et voloms qe en chescune accioun soint vileyns responables vers totes gentz[2], et totes gentz a eux, si qe excepcioun de villenage ne [3]tiegne point de leu for qe par entre le [4]seignur et soen[4] vileyn, et[5] dount le seignur est en fresche possessioun de ly et de sa seute, ou au meyns eyt esté seisi de ly cum de soen vileyn de eynz le an et le jour[5]. Brac. 190 (c. 21. § 3); Fle. 111 (§ 15).

1. de *N.* *om. M.* 2. si noun en uers sun seignour *add. AR.* *sim. in margin N.* 3—3. chesce en nuli bouche si noun en la bouche son seignour qil ne est a chesqun responable qe par excepcion de vilnage ia ne serra par autre de sun seignour rebote de accion *AR.* *sim. in margin N.* 4—4. *so verb. MG.* seignur et autri *LN.* seingnur e autre *S.* luy e autri *C.* luy e autre *H.* 5. demeine *G.*

the land of the mother either by his own entry or by means of his villain, heir to his mother, by assise of Mortdancester, if she does not assign it over in her lifetime, and the son survives her, and she has no other issue which is free. Wherefore when any bondman or bondwoman once becomes free, or is enfranchised by the free bed of his lord or of any other, we ordain in favour of freedom and of matrimony that they and their issue shall for ever be held free, and the husbands be entitled to hold by the courtesy of England, and the wives to dower. An enfranchised bondman has the rights of a freeman. The law favours freedom, and marriage.

7. We will that villains in all actions be answerable to every one, and every one to them, so that the exception of villenage shall only hold good between the lord and his villain[z], and that only when the lord has been in recent possession of him and of his suit, or at the least has been seised of him as his villain within a year and a day. Actions by and against villains. Exception of villenage.

[z] The principle here stated was of gradual introduction. According to Glanvill a stranger might in some cases except to the competency of a naif to take part in certain legal proceedings even after his enfranchisement. For the lord could make him free as against himself, but not as against third parties. (Glan. li. 5. c. 5.) Compare before, c. 29. s. 6, p. 159, and the note there.

Brac. 194; Fle. 239 (§ 15). 8. Ausi poet serf enfraunchi estre par la reconisaunce soen seignur, cum si[1] soen seignur ly eit reconu fraunc en court Brac. 8 b; Fle. 174, 175; Post, liv. 2. c. 2. s. 3. qe porte record; et ausi si il soit weyvé par le seignur, [2]cum si le seignur ly eit deguerpi; et ausi par escrit del seignur[2], Glan. li. 5. c. 5; cum si soen seignur eit quiteclamé a ly et a ses heyrs pur ly Brac. 194 b; Fle. 3, 239 (§ 17). et pur ses heyrs tote manere de dreit qe il avoit, ou aver porroit, en la persone al neyf par la resoun del servage de soen [79 b.] saunc. Et ausi porrount recoverer estat de fraunchise par la Brac. 7, 197 b; Fle. 3. negligence del seignur, cum si acun soeffre soen vileyn estre soen futif par prescripcioun de tens limité en noster bref de Glan. li. 5. c. 5; mort de auncestre, ou a demorer en nos demeynes par un an Brac. 190 b; Fle. 235 (§ 2). et un jour sauntz chaleng, qe en acun tens nous fust comunement graunté pur noster profit et pur emendement de nos villes; et ausi, s'il soeffre soen neyf estre ordeyné a clerc ou a chivaler, au meyns jekes autaunt qe il soint desgradez de lour ordres; et ausi de sa neyve s'il la soeffre estre esposé

1. so *SGARMC.* si *om. L.* *interl. N.* 2—2. issi qe le seygnur le eyt guerpy e ausi par escrit son seygnur *M.* *sim. SGAR.* *om. CH.*

Enfranchisement by recognizance; 8. A bondman may be enfranchised also by the recognizance of his lord, as if his lord has acknowledged him to be free in a by waiver; court of record. So also if he be waived by the lord, as where by deed. the lord has abandoned him. Likewise, by writing of his lord, as if his lord has for himself and his heirs quitclaimed to the bondman and his heirs all manner of right which he had or might have in the person of the naif by reason of the bondage Enfranchisement by prescription. of his blood. Villains may also recover their freedom by the negligence of their lords, as if any lord suffer his villain to be fugitive for time of prescription limited in our writ of Mort-Privilege of the royal demesne. dancester; or to abide within our demesnes without challenge for a year and a day,—a privilege which was heretofore granted to us by common allowance for our profit and for the Enfranchisement by ordination, knighthood, marriage. improvement of our towns. Likewise, if he permit his naif[a] to be ordained clerk, or created a knight, at least until they be degraded from their orders; and so in the case of his neif,

[a] 'The lord who permits his villain to be on the level of a freeman (a foer de franc homme) loses the right to his service; or if he suffers him to be his attorney, or juror on an assise (ou assis[r]) or clerk, or knight, or burgess, and in other cases where the sufferance of the lord shows his intention that the villain should have any reverence out of servitude.' (Note in MS. *N.*)

a fraunc homme, en tel cas serrount ele et tote sa issue de fraunc estat a touz jours mes, sicum avaunt est dit.

9. Et cum aucun neyf defuyra soen seignur, en tiel cas voloms qe le seignur le puse sure cum soen chatel, a prendre et a remener en soen fee, ou qe il le troeve, de eynz le an et le jour; apres quel tens nous voloms qe il soint tenuz fr…auncs, taunt cum il [1]voderount, jekes qe[1] les seignurs les pusent recoverer par jugement de nostre court. Et si ne covendra mie qe chescun seignur garde soen vileyn cum en prisoun, mes suffist qe les seignurs soint en possessioun de lour services, issint qe des uns preignent services des tenementz, et de les autres, qi rien ne tiegnent en villenage, un dener par an de chefage et un jour en aust de service, ou autre petit service ou graunt solom lour poer; issi qe accioun le seignur de quere soen neyf futif comence quant soen nayf cessera de fere tels services et de ly reconustre pur seignur. Brac. 6 *b*; Fle. 3. [80.]

10. Et si le seignur ne ly puse trover en soen fee ne justicer de eynz le an et le jour, si maunderoms al viscounte del leu, en qi baillie le vileyn serra demoraunt, qe a dreit et Glan. II. 5. c. 1; Fle. 110.

1—1. vendrount ieqes ataunt qe *M.* *sim. A.* viuerount *C.*

if he suffer her to be married to a freeman, she and all her issue shall for ever after be of free estate, as before is said.

9. Where any naif flies from his lord, his lord may pursue him as his chattel, to apprehend and bring him back into his fee wheresoever he shall find him within the year and day. But after that time they shall be deemed free as much as they please, until the lords can recover them by judgment of our court. It is not however necessary for every lord to keep his villain as a prisoner; but it is sufficient if the lords are in possession of their services, so as to take of some the services due from their tenements, and from others, who hold nothing in villenage, a penny a year for chevage and one day's work in harvest, or other service, small or great, according to their ability. So that the lord's right of action to recover his fugitive naif commences when the naif ceases to perform such services and to acknowledge him for his lord. Fugitive villains may be followed within a year and day. How the lord may retain seisin of his villains. Right of action commences for cesser of service.

10. If the lord cannot find the fugitive in his fee, nor bring him to justice within the year and day, we will command the sheriff of the place in whose bailiwick the villain shall be re- Writ *De nativo habendo.*

Glan. li. 5. c. 3.

sauntz delay face aver a tel pleyntif un tel soen nayf et soen futif oveke touz ses chateus et tote sa sute. En ceo plé ne gist nule somounse, mes tauntost destresce et retener la premere et prendre plus, si le plee soit en Counté, jekes a taunt q'il aperge ou se attache par pleges.

Glan. li. 1. c. 2; li. 5. c. 1; Fle. 110 (§ 2, 3), 111 (§ 13).

11. Et pur ceo qe cely futif pora alegger fraunchise, la quele le viscounte ne ad mie poer de pleder, avoms graunté pur tels futifs en favour de fraunchise, cum il se senterount grevez par tels pletz de lour seignurs, q'il eynt pes de celes grevaunces jekes en heyre de nos Justices en cel counté, et qe il de ceo eynt nos brefs, quant il les voderount purchacer, issi qe il truyssent pleges al viscounte de lour fraunchises prover en le heyre avauntdit, et en le meen tens eynt pes.

12. Ceo bref de pes est appelé bref de fraunchise, et[1] en favor de fraunchise il[2] est plus tost pledable qe n'est bref de [80 *b.*] naifté, si le purchaceour ne se absente, par quei ly et ses pleges soint [3]et la merci[3] pur sa noun suite. Mes si il sue soen bref, et le seignur face defaute, et la somounse de[4] ly

1. *om. MC.* 2. e il *M.* e ceo *C.* 3—3. amerciez *M.* 4. so *SGAMH.* de *om. L.*

siding, that he 'justly and without delay cause such a one the plaintiff to have such a one his naif and fugitive with all his chattels and all his suit.' In this plaint no summons lies, but the first process is distress, and the first distress is retained and others taken, if the plea be in the county court, until the defendant appears or is attached by pledges.

Process in action of naifty.

11. And because the fugitive may allege freedom, a matter which the sheriff has not jurisdiction to try, we have, in favour of freedom, granted to such fugitives that whenever they find themselves aggrieved by such proceedings of their lords, they shall have peace from such grievances until the eyre of our justices in that county, and that they shall have our writs for that purpose, whenever they wish to obtain them, upon finding pledges to the sheriffs to prove their freedom in the eyre aforesaid; and that in the meantime they shall have peace.

If the defendant allege freedom, the plea may be reserved for the eyre, by writ De libertate probanda.

12. This writ of peace is called the writ *De libertate,* and in favour of freedom the pleadings are sooner dispatched than in a writ *De nativo*, unless the person who purchased the writ fail to appear, upon which he and his pledges shall be in mercy for his nonsuit. If, on the other hand, he prosecutes his suit, and the lord makes default, and the summons be in evidence,

Proceedings in the writ De libertate, upon default of either party.

soit testmoyné, soit agardé, qe il remeigne [1]fraunc et le seignur en la merci, de ceo qe il[1] ly ad[2] a tort grevé; et soit comaundé al viscounte, qe il ne soeffre mes qe le seignur le greve. Et si le seignur perge, adounc gist la pruve al serf a prover sa fraunchise; et ceo pora il fere en plusours maneres, sicum par les articles apeert contenuz en ceo chapitre. Glan. li. 5. c. 4.

13. En le plee de nayfté ne est nul essoygne alouwable al defendaunt jekes apres apparaunce, ne en ces pletz, *replegiari facias*, ne en *venire facias*, ne en semblables. Et si le seignur se profre et le futif[3] face defaute, soit agardé pur la defaute, qe le futif et ses pleges soint en la merci, et qe le pleyntif par la defaute le futif face la pruve de nayfté vers le futif, issi qe le futif mes ne soit resceu en nostre court a la pruve de sa fraunchise, et qe il soit destreynt par la graunt destresce jekes a taunt qe il veigne. Fle. 112 (§ 19).

14. Et si acun seignur eit purchacé de remuer la parole par *Pone* jekes a plus haute court, eynzces qe nule parole du bref original soit entamé[4] el Counté, par taunt [5]est le *Pone*[5] abat- Fle. 111 (§ 10, 11).

1—1. en cel vers le seygnur qi de ceo *M.* frank en ceo qe le seignur *C.* *sim. H.* 2. *so SGAMCH.* ad *om. LN.* 3. *so GAMCH.* pleyntif *LN.* 4. attamee *NA.* atame *M.* atteint *C.* *sim. H.* 5—5. *so M.* enchesoun est pone *L.* enchesoun est le Pone *N.* est chescun Pone *GS.* serra le pone *ARCH.*

let it be awarded that he be free, and the lord in mercy, because he has wrongfully aggrieved him, and let the sheriff be commanded not to permit the lord to aggrieve him for the future. If the lord appears, it then lies on the bondman to prove his freedom, which he may do in divers ways, as appears by the several points, which have been stated in this chapter. Proceedings in the same writ upon appearance.

13. In a plea of naifty (as also in pleas of *Replegiari facias*, *Venire facias*, and the like) no essoin is to be allowed to the defendant until after appearance. And if the lord offers himself, and the fugitive makes default, let it be awarded on account of his default, that the fugitive and his pledges be in mercy, and that the plaintiff by the default of the fugitive do make proof of his naifty against the fugitive, so that the fugitive be never afterwards admitted in our court to prove his freedom, and that he be distrained by the grand distress until he appear. In action of naifty no essoin allowed. Effect of non-appearance of defendant.

14. If any lord has obtained a writ to remove the plaints by *Pone* to a higher court, before any plaint upon the original writ is commenced in the county court, the *Pone* shall thereby Writ of *Pone*, when allowed.

able pur la fause suggestion leynz contenue, qe suppose parole [81.] estre el Counté, ou nule somounse unqe ne fust fete. Car avaunt somonse, ou attachement, ou apparaunce, n'est james parole en court; et porra estre averree par la date del ***Pone***, et par le jour de la somunse.

15. Et cum il serra venuz en court, adounc counte le pleyntif vers ly, [1]par ly mesmes ou par serjaunt[1], en ceste manere: Ceo vous moustre Johan, qi cy est, qe Piers, qi illucs est, a tort ly defut, et pur ceo a tort, qe il est soen vileyn [2]et de sa terre fuy puis le terme[2], et de qi il fu seysi, sicum de soen vileyn jekes a tel an, qe il ly[3] defuy. Et pur ceo qe la force de ceo bref est a detrier[4] la possession sicum de chatel, ne deit hom mie counter en ceo play par descente ne par resource[5], ne rien attamer del dreit, puis qe nule mencioun n'est fet en le bref. Car issi avereyt il variaunce en le bref et en la demoustraunce, et issi serroit le bref abatable. Et estre ceo si [6]hom pout issi counter[6], par taunt porreit[7] le

1—1. *om. CH.* 2—2. de Eiue e de treiue *AR.* e de sa tere fuy ou fu nee puis le terme *M.* e de sa terre fust nee *H.* *sim. C.* 3. *so M.* *sim. SGCH.* ly *om. LA.* 4. destrure *C.* *sim. H.* 5. resort *AM.* recours *CH.* 6—6. si hom pout conuerter *L.* *sim. MA.* si poet em isci counter *CH.* si lem i pout conuerser *G.* *sim. S.* 7. *so M.* *sim. HC.* pora *L.* *sim. AR.*

be abatable, on account of the false suggestion therein contained, which supposes a plaint to be in the county court, where in fact no summons was ever made. For before summons or attachment or appearance, a plaint is never in court. And this may be verified by the date of the *Pone* and the day of the summons.

Declaration of the plaintiff. 15. And when he is in court, let the plaintiff count against him by himself or his serjeant in this manner: 'John who is here declareth this to you, that Peter who is there wrongfully fled from him, and herein wrongfully, that he is his villain who fled from his land within the term, &c., and of whom he was seised as of his villain until such a year when he fled from him.' Forasmuch as the effect of this writ is to determine the possession as of a chattel, it is not proper to count in this plea by descent nor by resort, nor to touch at all upon the right[b], no mention being made thereof in the writ. For then there would be a variance between the writ and the declaration, and so the writ would be abatable. And besides, if one could so

Plea of naifty, a possessory action.

[b] The property, as distinguished from the possession.

defendaunt defendre le dreit par batayle ou par graunt assise, et ceo seroit graunt inconvenience al seignur. Et pur ceo qe la pruve de nayfté neest de la seute, si fet a dire issi : et s'il ceo dedie, a tort le dedit, car il en ad sute bone et suffisaunte. Glan. li. 5. c. 4. ad fin.

16. Et tauntost soit examiné la sute, ne soulement mie a prendre reconisaunces s'il soint vileyns al pleyntif, mes si celi, de qi la pleynte est fete, fust unques[1] en la terre le pleyntif, et coment il fu seysi[2] de ly. Et si sute soit trové desacordaunte, par taunt est ele viciouse et defective; et perira la pleynte. [81 *b*.]

17. Et si acordaunte, adounc respoigne le defendaunt issi : Tort et force defend Peres, qi ci est, et la fute[3] de la terre Johan et la nayfté [4] defendera ou et quant devera.

18. Et puis se eyde par excepciouns vers le juge, et puis vers la persone le pleyntif, et puis [5]de sa persone[5] demeyne et puis par excepcioun al bref, s'il ad vice ou errour, et puis

1. futif *A.* adonk *C.* *sim. H.* 2. disseysi *L.* seisi *GAMCH.* 3. *so M.* sute *LCH.* *sim. A.* 4. e *add. MFH.* *interl. N.* 5—5. vers sa persone *M.* vers sun cors *A.* *sim. C.*

count, the defendant might then defend the right by battle, or by the great assise, which would be a great inconvenience to the lord. And because proof of naifty is made by suit, he must add thus, 'and if he denies this, he denies it wrongfully, for the plaintiff hath thereof suit good and sufficient.' Naifty not to be tried by battle or great assise. Count concludes by proffer of suit.

16. And immediately let the suit be examined, not only by taking their acknowledgments whether they are villains to the plaintiff, but whether he against whom the plaint is prosecuted was ever upon the land of the plaintiff, and in what manner the plaintiff was seised of him. And if the suit be found to disagree, in so much is it bad and defective, and the plaint shall be lost. Examination of the plaintiff's suit.

17. But if the suit agrees, then let the defendant answer thus : 'Peter who is here defends the wrong and force, and the flight from the land of John and the naifty, and will defend the same where and when he ought.' Answer of defendant.

18. Afterwards he shall aid himself by exceptions to the judge, and then to the person of the plaintiff, and afterwards to his own person ; and next by exception to the writ if there s any defect or error ; and afterwards to the declaration, if Order of exceptions or pleas.

al counte, si il i ad vice omissioun ou variacioun; et a la fin al accioun.

19. Ou il pora dire qe il est fraunc, et qe Robert soen pere fu fraunc, et ceux de la seute furent fruancs jekes autaunt qe il se reconusent pur vileyns, car en tens le roi Richard[1], ou autre roi, avint qe un tiel chivaler engendra un Thebaud besael mesmes cestui Pieres, le quel Thebaud esposa la neyve le auncestre mesme cestui Johan, la quele tynt terre de ly en villenage, le quel Theobaud fist les services villeyns qe [2]al villenage[2] appendeyent a tote sa vie, et en mesme le villenage morust,—de Theobaud vint Philip, de Phelipe William, de William Symon, de Symon Robert, de Robert Piers, qi ci est, dount touz firent les services avauntditz par la resoun del
[82.] vilnage et ne mie par la resoun des persones, jekes en le tens Robert, pere meymes cestui Piers. Et si ceo puse averrer par enqueste, soit jugé countre le pleyntif.

Fle. 111 (§16), 112 (§ 20). 20. Et ausi se pora le defendaunt eyder par excepciouns encountre la seute,—qe, quant al un de sa parenté pora il

1. Ion *A.* Estefne *M. sim. CH.* 2—2. so *S.* a villinage *L. sim. ABCH.* a tiel villenage *G.* au tenement *M.*

there is any defect, omission, or variance in it; and lastly to the action.

Plea in bar to the action.

19. Thus he may say that 'he is a freeman, and Robert his father was free, and those of the suit were free, until they acknowledged themselves villains; for in the reign of king Richard,' or of some other king, 'it came to pass that a certain knight begot one Theobald, great-grandfather of this same Peter, which Theobald married the nief of the ancestor of the same John, who held land of him in villenage, which Theobald as long as he lived performed the villain services to the tenement appertaining, and died in the same villenage; that from Theobald came Philip, from Philip William, from William Simon, from Simon Robert, from Robert Peter who is here, all of whom performed the services aforesaid by reason of the villain tenement, and not by reason of their persons, until the time of Robert, father of this same Peter.' And if he can prove this by inquest, it shall be adjudged against the plaintiff.

Exceptions to the suit.

20. The defendant may also aid himself by exceptions against the suit, for he may say that as to one of his kindred

dire qe il ne est mie recevable a la pruve, car s'il [1]i erent[1] treys parentz madles et [2]v. femeles[2], ou plus ou meyns, et il puse averrer del un parent, qe il fust engendré hors de matrimonie de fraunche femme, et qe le autre parent, qi se profre pur seute, fust engendré de fraunc homme en matrimonie tut fu sa mere nayve, tut ne sache il mettre excepcioun encountre le tierz parent de la seute, voloms nous qe, s'il demaunde jugement s'il deyve respoundre a la seute del un homme, qe en tel cas soit jugé encountre le pleyntif, de sicum saunc de homme ne peut, ne deit, estre tryé par femmes, ne un madle sauntz plus[3] n'est mie receivable pur suffisaunte sute.

21. Ou il pora dire qe il ad fet soen seignur homage pur[4] tenement; ou qe soen seignur ly ad quiteclamé totes accions; ou qe il esposa sa dame, ou fu esposé a soen seignur, ou a autre fraunc homme; ou par autres excepciouns paremptories pora il estre eydé, sicum [5]de sus[5] est dit. Fle. 193, 239 (§ 18, 19, 24).

22. Et si akun die qe il est clerc ou chivaler, en tel cas voloms nous qe jugement se face encountre le pleyntif; et Brac. 190 *b*, 198 *b*; Fle. 110, 1:1. [82 *b*.]

1—1. vrent *G.* y vrent *M.* i eurent *CH.* ameneit *A.* 2—2. L. femmes *M.* *sim. ARL.* femmeles *C.* *sim. H.* 3. plusours *AMC.* 4. *so AMC.* le *add. LSG.* 5—5. de souz *M.* desuz *C.*

he is not admissible in evidence. For if there were three of his male kindred, and five females, or more or less, and he can aver of one of the kinsmen that he was begotten out of matrimony of a free woman, and that the second kinsman who offers himself for suit was begotten in marriage by a freeman although his mother was a nief, notwithstanding he has no exception to make against the third kinsman of the suit, we will that if he demands judgment whether he ought to answer to the suit of a single man, it shall in such case be adjudged against the plaintiff; because the blood of a man cannot nor ought to be tried by means of women, neither is one male alone without more to be admitted as sufficient suit. The suit must be of male kindred of defendant.

21. Or he may plead that he has done homage to his lord for a tenement; or that his lord has released him from all actions; or that he married his lady; or (if the defendant is a woman) that she was married to her lord or to another freeman. Or he may be aided by other peremptory exceptions, as above is mentioned. Plea of homage received. Release. Enfranchisement by marriage.

22. If any one pleads that he is a clerk or knight, in such case judgment shall be given against the plaintiff, who must Plea of orders or of knighthood.

[1]ceo rette[1] a sa negligence demeyne. Et si le clerc ou le[2] chivaler ou[3] lour ordinarie n'en eyt eu congé de tiel seignur de estre ordinee a tiel ordre, ou de eus ordiner, adounc eyt le seignur accioun de recoverer de ceux qi lour ordeynerent as chivalers ou as clers lour damages qe il porrount renablement assigner.
Fle. 111. Et si tiels clers ou tels chivalers ne voillent honestes services, qe a eux [4]apent a fere, plus tost abandoner[4] a tiels seignours naturels, qe as autres, [5]ou autrement[5] soint a eus desnaturels, en tiel cas voloms nous qe il soint degradez, et s'il ne pusent estre, qe satisfaccioun soit fete a lour seignurs de lour chateus, et si les chateus ne suffisent, si respoignent ceux, par qi il furent ordeynez.

23. Ou pora dire le defendaunt, qe il ne deit estre respondu, de sicum ceo est une accioun limité de eynz certeyn
Brac. 314 *b.* terme, sicum autres accious sount, et de sicum ly ne nul de ses auncestres ne furent unques seysiz de ly ne de [6]nul de ses auncestres[6], [7]cum de lour vileyns[7], pora demaunder jugement si il soit tenu ore a ly respoundre. Et si ceo soit averree, le

1—1. so *GMCH.* ce rette *L.* ceo est rette *AR.* 2. so *SGAMCH.* le *om. L.* 3. so *M.* de *LSG.* ne *ACHF.* 4—4. apendent fere plus tost e abaundoner *M.* 5—5. qe en autre manere *M.* 6—6. so *ASMCHF.* ces auncestres nul *LN.* ses Auncestres *G.* 7—7. *om. ARCHF.*

Action against persons conferring orders or knighthood. impute it to his own negligence. And if the clerk or the knight had not leave from the lord to take upon him such order, or those who ordained them to confer the same upon them, then the lord shall have his action to recover against those who ordained them to be knights or clerks such damages as he can reasonably assign. And if such knights or clerks refuse to perform honourable services becoming their station more readily and cheerfully to such natural lords than to others, or behave in any other manner unnaturally to
Degradation. them, in such cases we will that they be degraded; and if this cannot be done, that satisfaction be made to their lords out of their chattels; and if their chattels are not sufficient, let those who ordained them be answerable.

Plea of limitation. 23. Or the defendant may say that the plaintiff is not entitled to an answer, inasmuch as this is an action limited within a certain term (as other actions are), and inasmuch as neither he nor any of his ancestors were ever within the term seised of him or any of his ancestors, as their villains, he may demand judgment whether he is at this time bound to answer to him. And if this be proved, the plaintiff shall

pleyntif iert atteynt de fause pleynte. Mes a ceo pora il replicer[1], sicum en totes autres accioun s, qe ceo ne ly deit point valer; car par diligentes impetraciouns ad il esté autre- [83.] foiz demaundé, et ses auncestres autresi, par ly et par ses auncestres par autres brefs semblables, [2]si qe par[2] mort de auncestres et de[3] rois[4] se abatirent les brefs.

24. [5]Ou issi, qe il[5] ad demoré en nos demeynes terres ou aylours en acune de nos villes ou de nos citeez par un an et un jour sauntz chaleng del pleyntif, et s'il demaunde jugement s'il deyve en tiel cas respoundre, et cele excepcioun porra averrer, en tiel cas soit le seignur forsjugé de accioun pur sa negligence; et ausi ou le defendaunt porra averrer par record de nostre court, qe soen seignur le ad soeffert a escient en jurez et en enquestes en nostre court cum fraunc homme; et ausi s'il puse averreer par record, qe il recoveri fraunc tenement de ly par jugement de nostre court, ou le pleyntif ne aleggea nule excepcioun de nayfté encountre ly.

Glan. li. 5. c. 5; Brac. 190 b; Fle. 111, 235; Ante, s. 8.

Fle. 112 (§ 18).

Brac. 7, 25 b, 191; Fle. 194, 236, 237.

25. Ou il pora dire qe le pleyntif ne deit estre respoundu

1. repleder *CH.* respondre *F.* 2—2. si com par *AR.* sicom par bref de *CH.* 3. par *CH.* 4. Naifte *AR.* 5—5. Ou si il *M.*

Replication of continual claim.

be convicted of false plaint. But to this, as in all other actions, he may reply that such plea ought not to avail the defendant, for that by continual claims he has been theretofore demanded and his ancestors likewise, by him and his ancestors by other like writs, but by the death of his ancestors or by the king's death those writs abated.

Plea of residence in king's demesne or in a city or borough;

24. Or the defendant may plead that he has resided upon our demesne lands or elsewhere in any of our towns or cities for a year and a day without having been claimed by the plaintiff, and if he demands judgment whether in such case he ought to answer, and can verify this exception, the lord shall be forejudged of his action for his negligence. So also, where the defendant can prove by record of our court that the lord has knowingly suffered him to be upon juries and inquests in our court as a freeman. So, if he can verify by record that he has recovered frank tenement against him by judgment of our court, wherein the plaintiff did not allege any exception of villenage against him.

service on juries;

recovery of free tenement against lord.

Defendant may decline to answer

25. Or he may say that the plaintiff ought not to be

eynzces qe il eyt pleynement rendu quant qe il [1]tient del soen, ou tynt[1] puis ceo qe il clama fraunc estat, le quel dit nous voloms qe soit alouwable pur les paroles contenues en noster bref, qe dit, ovek touz ses chateus et tote sa seute, dount le pleyntif en soen purchaz demeyne suppose qe il n'en est de rien seysi.

26. Et cum jugement se fra pur le pleyntif, soit agardé qe le pleyntif ly recovere cum soen vileyn ovek tote sa sute et
[83 *b.*] touz ses chateus et tut soen purchaz, et qe le vileyn mes ne eyt heyr autre qe le seignur, et le vileyn demurge en nostre merci.

[2]Ici finist le livre de plez personels, et comencent les plez reals[2].

1—1. li deueit de soen e teint *A.* il detint de soen e tint *H.* *sim.* *C.* 2—2. *so verb.* *N.* Ici finist le liure de la condicioun de vileyns *L.* *sim.* *M.* *om.* *GSR.*

While plaintiff detains his goods. answered until he has fully restored to him whatever goods of his he detains from him, or hath detained since he claimed free estate; which plea shall be allowable by reason of the words contained in our writ, which says, 'with all his chattels and all his suit,' so that the plaintiff in his own writ supposes himself not to be seised of any of the chattels.

Form of judgment for plaintiff. 26. If judgment is given for the plaintiff, let it be awarded that the plaintiff recover him as his villain with all his suit and all his chattels and all his acquisitions, and that the villain have no heir other than the lord, and the villain shall remain in our mercy.

Here ends the book of personal pleas, and begins that of real pleas.

BRITTON.

LIVRE II.

CHAPITRE I. [XXXII.]

[1] Terre pledable par attachement [1].

PASSÉ la fourme et la manere de pleder personels pletz pledables par attachementz de cors ou par destresces des biens moebles, ore fet a dire de terre pledable par attachementz de mesmes les choses demaundez; et primes des pletz qe plus touchent nostre pes enfreynte par fresche force, sicum est de homme a tort engitté ou desturbé de la peysible possessioun de soen fraunc tenement.

Glan. li. 13; Brac. 159 *b*; Fle. 213.

1—1. De disseisines *N.* *sim. SARCH.* De Purchaz *M G.*

BOOK II.

OF DISSEISINS AND THEIR REMEDIES.

CHAPTER I.

Of Suits concerning Land, pleadable by Attachment.

HAVING gone through the form and manner of pleading personal pleas pleadable by attachments of the body or by distresses of movable goods, we must now treat of pleas concerning land, in which the process is by attachment of the very thing demanded. And first, of those pleas which more nearly concern the breach of our peace by fresh force, as when a person is wrongfully ejected or disturbed in the

Process in real actions.

Disseisin, what. Fresh force.

Brac. 161. Et cele violence est apelé disseisine et fresche force. Et en favour des pleyntifs est ordeyné a pleder disseysines par petites assises en countez mesmes, ausi bien en absence des trespassours, cum en lour presence.

Brac. 26 b, 27; Fle. 192 (§ 6). 2. Nule disseisine put estre fete for qe de fraunc tenement. Fraunc tenement est une possessioun de soyl, ou de service de soil issaunt, [1]de fraunc homme qi tient[1] en fee a ly et a ses heyrs, ou a meyns a terme de vie, coment qe le soil soit Brac. 160; Fle. 213 (§ 2). chargé de fraunes services ou de autres. Fee est un dreit reposaunt en la persone le verrey heyr, ou de autre, qi par dreit title le ad purchacé, qi qe unqe soit seysi del fraunc [84.] tenement; et ceo est la propreté, et dount un ad plus et un autre meyns, sicum le heyr de disseisour ad une manere de fee et de propreté, mes le disseisi en ad plus. Mes pur ceo qe nul ne peut estre disseisi [2]si eynz ne eyt esté[2] seisi, si voloms nous, eynzces qe nous ayloms as pletz, moustrer en quele manere hom put purchacer seysine.

1—1. qe fraunc home purchace *A.* qe fraunc homme tient *M.* *sim. H.* dasqun fraunc tenaunt *C.* 2—2. einz ceo qe il soit *M.*

Trial in actions of disseisin by petty assise. peaceable possession of his freehold, which act of violence is called disseisin, and fresh force. And in favour of complainants it is ordained that disseisins may be pleaded by petty assises in the counties where the lands lie, in the absence as well as in the presence of the offenders.

Definition of freehold. 2. There can be no disseisin except of a freehold[a]. A freehold is a possession of soil or of services issuing out of the soil by a freeman holding in fee to him and his heirs, or at the least for term of life, whether the soil be charged with free or Definition of fee and property. other services. Fee is a right vested in the person of the true heir, or of any other who hath acquired it by lawful title, whoever may be seised of the freehold. And this is the property, whereof one may have more and another less, as the heir of the disseisor has one kind of fee and of property, but the disseisee has a greater. But inasmuch as no one can be disseised unless he be first seised, we will therefore, before we proceed to pleas, show in what manner seisin may be acquired.

[a] 'Note that there is a difference between seisin and possession, for one supposes a term of life, and the other a term of years.' Note in MS. *N.*

CHAPITRE II. [xxxiii.]

De Purchaz.

1. Aucunes choses sount corporeles, sicum celes qe hom peut taster; et aucunes nient corporeles, sicum sount propretez, et dreitz, et feez, et servages de tenementz; et aucunes communes, sicum la mer, et le heyr, et le rivage de la mer, et sicum dreit de pescher en flodz et en la mer et en communes ewes et rivers; et acunes meyns communes, [1]sicum communes[1] [2]a acunes communaltez[2], sicum les moers et les portes de citez et de bourgs; et aucunes plus especiaument communes, sicum terres et rentes et autres possessiouns et dreitures[3] donez a commun profit de la communauté; et dount nule singulere pleynte ne porra estre fete par estraunge persone, qe ne serra nient de la communauté, ne nule singulere persone ne porra teus tenementz mener en jugement sauntz la communauté, ne enpleder ne estre enpledé par nul estraunge; car membre ne put mie respoundre pur tut le cors si cum attourné noun.

Brac. 7 *b*. 8; Fle. 174.

[84 *b*.]

1—1. *om. NHF.* 2—2. et acunes communaltez *L. sim. S.* en ascunes comunaltez *G.* [en *corr.*] acunes communautes *N.* e communautes *M. sim. AH.* e [a *corr.*] comunalte *R.* 3. communes *M.*

CHAPTER II.

Of Purchase.

1. Some things are corporeal, as those which one may touch; others incorporeal, as properties, rights, fees, and easements of tenements. Some things are common, as the sea, the air, and the sea shore, and as the right of fishing in tidal waters and in the sea, and in common waters and rivers; and some things are common in a less degree, as being common to certain communities, as the walls and gates of cities and boroughs; others are common in a more special manner, as lands, rents, and other possessions and rights granted for the common advantage of a community, for which no single plaint can be made by a stranger who is not of the community, nor can any single person bring such tenements in judgment, in the absence of the community, or plead or be impleaded by any stranger; for a member cannot answer for the whole body, except as an attorney.

Objects of property, corporeal and incorporeal. Things common.

Degree of community.

Brac. 8; Fle. 174. 2. Et acunes choses sount, qe ne sount a nuli, sicum les choses sacreez et dediez a Deu par prelatz de Sainte Eglise, sicum sount cimeteres et sepultures, eglises, chapeles, et autres places dediez, lequel qe eles soint edifiez ou noun. Car devine chose a humeins us ne deit point estre assigné. Et si eles soint edifiez et les edifices checent, uncore remeynt la place seynte. Et ausi sount acunes choses en nuli biens, qe sount seyntefiez el noun Deu en Sainte Eglise, sicum sount chaliz et encensers, croiz et vestementz, et teles autres choses, qe sount defenduz de vendre doner ou aliener, si noun pur rechater esclaves Cristiens des meyns de payens.

Brac. 8, 8 *b*; Fle. 174, 175. 3. Et ausi sunt acunes choses en nuli biens naturelement, dount nul homme ne put fere douns, sicum oyseus, cerfs, deyms, et autres bestes sauvages, et pessouns, et sicum est terre ou autre heritage dount nul n'est en seysine, et sicum sount fraunces hommes, et vileyns deguerpiz et engitez par lour seignurs, qi tauntost sount fraunes; et ausi de tote autre chose
[85.] guerpie, demoraunt hors de chescuni[1] seysine, des queles choses homme se pora purchacer par ocupacioun.

1. *so N. sim. A R.* chescune *L S G.* autri *H.*

Consecrated places and things, the property of no one. 2. There are some things which are no one's property, as things sacred and dedicated to God by prelates of holy church, such as are churchyards, burial-places, churches, chapels, and other consecrated places, whether they are built upon or not. For things divine ought not to be appropriated to human purposes. And if they have been built upon, although the structure fall down, the place still remains sacred. There are also some things which are not the goods of any person, and which are consecrated in the name of God in holy church, such as chalices, censers, crosses, vestments, and other like things, which are forbidden to be sold, given away, or alienated, except for ransoming Christian slaves from the hands of pagans.

Things not the objects of property. Animals *feræ naturæ*. 3. There are also some things which in their natural state are no one's property, and whereof none can make a gift, as birds, stags, does, and other wild beasts, and fishes. So likewise land or other hereditament whereof no person is in seisin. So likewise freemen; and villains deserted and ejected by their lords, who immediately become free; and all other things abandoned and remaining out of the possession of any one, but

Title by occupancy. in which things a property may be acquired by occupancy.

4. Purchaz pora estre en plusours maneres. Car de chose sauvage prise hors de place defendue et [1]de garenne[1] est la chose a celi qi la prendra taunt cum il la tendra. Mes si ele ly eschape et repreygne la sauvagine et[2] soen naturel estat, [3]si qe est nule esperaunce[3] de soen retourn, [4]des adounc iert autre foiz ne mie a celi qi la pora feryr[4], [5]mes solement a qi qe unques[5] la pora prendre. Et ausi pora hom purchacer par enclousture de pessouns et de autre sauvagine, sicum de ees. Car si ees [6]se jettent[6] en aucun arbre, pur ceo ne sount mie a celi qi deit le arbre, jekes autaunt qe il les eyt enclos en sa rusche, nent plus qe les oyseus qe averount fet lour ny sur le arbre; car si autres les preissent, si sereynt eus soens. Mes si le seignur del arbre prenge [7]autri ees[7] en soen arbre, et il sache a qi il sount, il iert tenuz de les rendre, ou de garder les a chaumpart pur la moyté des issues taunt cum eus dourrount.

Brac. 8 *b*; Fle. 175.

Brac. 8 *b*, 9; Fle. 175.

1—1. *so M.* en garne *L.* en garreyne *N.* *sim. SGHF.* garenne *A.* 2. en *AMH.* 3—3. si est nule esperaunce *L.* si qe nule esperaunce [ne soit *int.*] *N.* issi qe nule esperaunce ne seit *AR.* issi qe nul esperaunce ne est *M.* *sim. H.* si qe nule esperance est *G.* si nul esperaunce nest *S.* 4—4. e puis autre la fere si nest point vncore a li *AR.* E si puis alcun autre la siwe si ne est ele poynt uncore a luy. '*alia lectura*' *in marg. N.* 5—5. mes qe *M.* 6—6. sen[sie]cent *M.* seient *AH.* 7—7. *so AH.* *so corr. N.* autres ees *L.* les ees de autri *M.*

4. Acquisition or purchase may be in divers ways; for wild creatures taken elsewhere than in a forbidden place or a warren, belong to the taker so long as he keeps them. But if the creature escapes, and resumes its wildness and its natural state, so that there is no likelihood of its return, it will afterwards belong, not to him who can wound it, but only to him who can take it[b]. One may also acquire a property by inclosing of fish and other wild creatures, as bees. For though bees settle upon a tree, yet the bees do not belong to the owner of the tree, until he has inclosed them in his hive; no more than birds which have built their nest on a tree, for if another takes them, they are his. But if the owner of the tree takes another person's bees in his tree, and knows whose they are, he will be bound to restore them, or to keep them upon terms of divided enjoyment for half the profit which they shall produce. No person can detain

Purchase in various ways.

By taking beasts *feræ naturæ*.

Law of bees.

[b] This passage appears obscure. The sense is borrowed from Bracton, who observes that the mere pursuit of a wild animal, even though the pursuer succeeds in so wounding it as to make it possible to take it, will not make it his property, but it will belong to the first person who secures it. Brac. 8 *b*.

Ante, li. 1. c. 18. s. 3. Des oyseus, ne des bestes [1]fetes domesches qe furent sauvages[1], ne poet nul detener a autre qe il ne ly face robberie ou trespas apert encountre nostre pes, si due seute soit de ceo fete de eynz le an et le jour, si qe nul ne puse clamer estray.

[85 *b.*] Fle. 61, 62. 5. Et ausi purchace hom par fraunchises grauntez par nous des choses trovez en nuli bens, sicum wrek de mer et bestes estrayauntes et conys et leveres et pessons et fesauntz et perdriz et autres bestes sauvages, par fraunchises de aver wrek de mer trové en soen soil, et weif et estray trové en soen fee, Brac. 9; Fle. 175. et garrennes en ses demeynes terres. Et ausi purchace hom par engendrure et par issues des bestes et de autres choses vives qe sount a la gent; et par troveure [2]de gemmes et des peres[2] en la gravele de la mer ou aylours en communes places; et ausi par pescher et par autre travail ausi bien en mer cum Brac. 120, 120 *b.* en terre. Et si [3]acune idle soit trové[3] en la mer[4] qe ne seit en nuly biens, quant qe [5]la eynz ert trové[5] soit al troveour taunt cum il la tendra [6]en sa meyn et[6] en sa possessioun.

1—1. sauuages fetes damaches *AM.* 2—2. de gamez et des peres *L.* *sim. S.* degamez et des peres *N.* sicom des gemmes e des peres *AB.* des gemmes e des piers *G.* de gemmes e de preciouses pieres *M.* de gemmes e des pierres *F.* 3—3. acun idle soit troue *L.* *sim. N.* acun nef issi seit troue *M.* asqun i seit *AHB.* *sim. GS.* aukuni troeue ryen *F.* alcun y soit qui troeue '*alia lectura*' *in marg. N.* 4. chose *add. in marg. N.* 5—5. il troeue *in marg. N.* 6—6. *om. AMH.*

Domesticated animals may be claimed within a year and day. from another birds or beasts *feræ naturæ*, which have been domesticated, without being guilty of robbery or of open trespass against our peace, if due pursuit be made thereof within the year and day, to prevent their being claimed as estrays.

Title by franchise of wreck, waif, estray, warren. 5. Property may also be acquired by virtue of franchises granted by us concerning things found, which do not belong to anybody, as wreck of sea, beasts estray, rabbits, hares, fish, pheasants, partridges, and other wild creatures; that is to say, by a franchise to have wreck of sea found on his soil, waifs and estrays found in his fee, and warrens in his demesne lands. Title by generation; Property may likewise be acquired by the increase and produce of beasts and other animals belonging to people; and also by finding; by the finding of gems and precious stones on the sea beach by fishing and other labour. or elsewhere in places common to all; so by fishing and by Discovery of island. other labour as well at sea as on land. And if any island is found in the sea which is not any one's property, whatever is found therein shall belong to the finder as long as he shall keep it in his hands or in his possession.

6. Et ausi encrest purchaz par autri fraude et par autri folie, sicum est de ceux qe de lour propre merym edefient par malice ou par nounsachaunce[1] en autri soil, et de ceux qi plauntent arbres ou graffes, et de ceuz qi lour blé sement en autri terre sauntz coungé le seignur del soil; en ceo cas serrount les [2]edifiez et les plauntez et les semez[2] al seignur del soil pur la presumpcioun[3] de doun. Car graunt presumcioun[4] est en teus cas, qe teus edifiours plauntours ou semours voillent qe ces[5] edefices [6]et plauntez et semez[6] fuessent a ceux qi deyvent le soil, et nomément si les edifices soint fermez par clous et les [7]plauntez et les semez[7] soint enracinez. Mes si acun se aperceyve de sa folie, et hastivement, eynz ceo qe nostre prohibicioun ly viegne qe il ne le remue, et enceis qe le merime soit affermé par clous, ou les arbres soint enracinez, oste soen merim ou ses arbres, bien le pora[8] de dreit.

Brac. 9 *b*, 10; Fle. 176, 177.

[86.]

7. Des choses nient moebles communes en nuli possessioun trovez purchace hom ausi en plusours maneres; une manere,

Brac. 9; Fle. 175.

1. *so MH. sim. interl. N.* nusaunce *LN.* noun sauaunce *A.* 2—2. edifices les plauntes e les semences *M. sim. AF.* 3. *so A. so on eras. N.* pretripcioun *L.* prescripcioun *M. sim. FH.* 4. prescription *F.* 5. ses *M.* 6 plauntes e semences *AM. sim. F.* 7—7. semences e les plauntes *M.* plantes e semences *AF.* 8. fere *add. AMH.*

6. A purchase or acquisition may also accrue from the fraud and folly of another, as where persons by malice or ignorance build with their own timber on another's soil, or where they plant or engraft trees or sow their grain in another's land, without the leave of the owner of the soil. In such cases what is built, planted, and sown shall belong to the owner of the soil, upon the presumption of a gift; for there is a great presumption that such builders, planters, or sowers intend that what is so built, planted, or sown should belong to the owners of the soil, especially if such structures are fixed with nails, or the plants or seeds have taken root. But if any one becomes aware of his folly, and speedily removes his timber or his trees, before our prohibition comes against his removing them, and before the timber is fastened with nails, or the trees have taken root, he may lawfully do so.

Title by folly of one building or planting upon another's land.

7. With regard to immovable things of common right, found in the possession of no one, a property may be pur-

Title by gradual addition of soil by water.

sicum par subtraccioun de ewe, dount [1]acuni soil encrest[1] par petit et par petit, si les terres ne soint mie boundez entre veisins. Mes issi ne sereit ceo mie en hastif encrez; car si la force[2] de acun flod toille al un vesin partye de soen soil par quei le soil le autre veysin encrest de autre part del ewe, en tel hastif encrez ne put hom rien perdre, si la rivere ne soit braz de mer, qe le soil ne soit recoveri par ceste assise, si le verrei possessour soit deforcé, si sa negligence ne ly destourbe. Mes si le encrez eit esté si sutil qe nul ne pout veer ne aparceyvre cel encrez, et q'il eit esté encru par proces del tens, sicum en plusours aunz, et ne mie en un jour ne en un an, et[3] qe la chanele et le cours del ewe se remue devers le perdaunt, en tiel cas remeynt tel encrez le purchaz [86 *b.*] et le fee et le fraunc tenement al purchaceour, si certeynes boundes n' i soint trovez; et par le encres des demeynes encressent les seignuries et les feez des seignurs, et porount les seignurs destreyndre en teus encres ausi bien cum aylours en lour feez sauntz tort fere.

1—1. *so verb. M. sim. on eras. N.* acun I. soleit et crest *L.* ascuny soleit auer encreu *G.* acuny soleit encrestre *S.* asqun soil acrest *A. sim. H.* 2. *so GAMH.* founce *L.* founce [force *int.*] *N.* 3. en *L.* e *AMH.*

chased in many ways. One way is by a subtraction of water whereby any one's soil is increased by little and little, provided the lands are not bounded between neighbours. But it would be otherwise in case of a sudden increase; for if one neighbour by the violence of a flood is deprived of part of his soil, whereby the soil of his neighbour on the other side of the water is increased, by such a sudden increase nothing shall be lost, unless the river be an arm of the sea; but the soil may be recovered by this assise, if the true possessor be deforced, unless he be barred by negligence. But if the increase has been so gradual, that no one could discover or see it, and has been added by length of time, as in a course of many years, and not in one day or in one year, and the channel and course of the water is itself moving towards the loser, in that case such addition remains the purchase and the fee and freehold of the purchaser, if certain bounds are not found. And by increase of the demesne the seigniories and fees of the lords increase, and the lords may distrain as well in such additions as elsewhere in their fees without doing a wrong.

Such additions accrue to the seigniory.

8. Et si acune idle crest de novel en l'ewe, a celi iert le idle a qi soil [1]ele soit joynte[1] plus pres, en tut ou en partie, solom ceo qe ele crest en le mi leu ou [2]devers le costié[2] del ewe. Et si ele crest en la mer, cely soit seignur qi serra trové possessour. Mes issi ne ert il mie de idle fete par la mer en acuni[3] soil, eynz soit le idle al seignur del fee et[4] del soil; et s'il en soit deforcé, soit eydé par ceste assise. Brac. 9; Fle. 176.

9. Et si il i ad verrey title, qe est appelé successioun, sicum de [5]verrey heir en soen heritage, et sicum successour en le dreit de sa eglise, dount soen predecessour morut seisi. Et coment heritage decent, et as queus, serra dit el livre de dreit el chapitre de successiouns. Et si ad une manere de title, qe est aukes semblable a successioun, sicum par accres; et ceo est en cas ou acune purpartie, par la mort de aucun parcener sauntz heir de sei, acrest a autres parceners. Brac. 62 b; Fle. 370. Post II. 6. c. 3.

10. Et des choses [6]qe ne sount[6] en autri seysine purra

1—1. e le fee i ioint *M.* lile si ioint *A.* 2—2. deuers le couste *N.* *sim.* *GS.* uers le cost *A.* par une coste *M.* deuers le coste *HF.* 3. *so N.* *sim. M.* aucun *L.* *sim. AHF.* 4. et *om. M.* 5. *so AMH.* de *om. L.* 6—6. *so LGMFH.* *om. S.* ne *eras. N.*

8. If a new island is formed in the water, the island shall belong to him whose soil is nearest adjoining to it, in whole or in part according as it rises in the middle or towards one bank of the water. If an island grows up in the sea, it shall belong to the person who shall be found in possession of it. It is otherwise however of an island made by the sea in any one's soil, for the island shall belong to the owner of the fee and of the soil; and if he be deforced, he shall be aided by this assise. Islands formed in rivers; and in the sea.

9. There is also a good title, called succession, as that of the right heir to his inheritance, and of a successor to the rights of his church, whereof his predecessor died seised. How an inheritance descends, and to whom, shall be explained in the book concerning Right in the chapter concerning Successions. There is also a kind of title which has some resemblance to succession, namely, title by accruer. This is where by the death of one parcener without heir his share accrues to the other parceners. Title by succession. Title by accruer.

10. Things which are not in the seisin of another may be

Brac. 10 b; Fle. 177 (§ 17).

[87.] [1]hom purchacer[1] par title de doun et de feffement, et ausi par successioun, et par eschaete, et par reversioun, et par assignement de dowarie, et par louwage, et par empromt, et par title de testament, et par engendrure [2]de creysurz[2] fraunc tenement par une especialté graunté pur ley en Engleterre et en Hyrelaunde, et en plusours autres maneres; et dount al purchaz des choses corporeles ne suffit nul doun sauntz le bayl de la seysine.

CHAPITRE III. [XXXIV.]

De Douns.

Brac. 11; Fle. 177.

1. Doun est institucioun de acune chose qe de fraunche volunté est translaté de verrey possessour a autre persone, oveke entere volunté [3]qe la chose mes ne retourne al donour, et oveke entere volunté[3] del receyvour de retenir la chose enterement cum sue propre sauntz rendre la al donour. Car autrement ne poit doun estre fet proprement, si la chose doné

1—1. le purcharceour *L.* lẽ purchacyer *corr. N.* lem purchacer *GSMR.* *sim. FH.* [lem] purchacer *A.* 2—2. *so LN.* de creisurs *S.* descressours *G.* des cressours de *AR.* des croysurs *M.* de Croysours *H.* de croisur[s] *F.* 3—3. *so verb. NARMH.* *om. L.*

Various modes of transfer of title.

purchased by title of gift, and of feoffment, and also by succession, escheat, reversion, assignment of dower, hiring, borrowing, and by title of testament. A freehold may also be acquired by being the father of issue born alive, by a special privilege which has the force of law in England and Ireland, and in many other ways. And with regard to the purchase of corporeal things, no gift is sufficient without delivery of seisin.

Necessity of delivery to complete a transfer.

CHAPTER III.

Of Gifts.

Gift, what.

1. A gift is an act whereby anything is voluntarily transferred from the true possessor to another person, with the full intention that the thing shall not return to the donor, and with full intention on the part of the receiver to retain the thing entirely as his own without restoring it to the giver. For a gift cannot be properly made, if the thing given does not so belong to the receiver, that the two rights, of pro-

In a proper gift both the possession and the property is transferred.

ne soit al recevour, issi qe les deus dreitz de propreté et de possessioun se joynent en sa persone, issi qe le doun ne put estre repelé par le donour, ne destruit par autre[1] en qi persone soit remise la dreite propreté, sicum est de douns et de feffementz de disseisours, et autres douns semblables en prejudice de autri dreit. Doun est un noun general plus qe n'est feffement; car doun est general a totes choses moebles et nient moebles, et feffement n'est de rien for qe de soil, et dount [87 *b.*] hom purra recoverer seysine par ceste assise, si [2]hom soit a tort engetté[2].

2. Et fet a saver, qe acuns porrount doner et acuns nient; Brac. 11 *b*; Fle. 178. car nul ne put atteignaument doner fors qe cil en qi persone repose la possessioun et la propreté, et aukunes foiz ceux en qi persones [3]ne reposent nient[3] for qe le fee et la propreté, sicum par assignement et par reconisaunces en nostre court; et totes maneres de autres douns sount repellables.

3. Rois ausi ne porrount rien[4] aliener les dreitz de lour Brac. 14; Fle. 3, 4, 183. coroune ne de lour reauté, qe ne soit repellable par lour successours. Soeffrable chose est neqedent qe baronies et autres

1. *so SGMH.* autri *LN.* 2—2. acun soit engette *M.* lem fuit a tort deforce *A.* 3—3. ne repose riens *M.* repose nient *A.* *sim. H.* 4. rien *om. M.*

perty and of possession, are united in his person, so that the gift cannot be revoked by the donor, or made void by another, in whom the lawful property is vested; as may be done in the case of donations and feoffments by disseisors, and other like gifts in prejudice of the right of another. Gift is a more Feoffment, of what. general term than feoffment; for gift is applicable to all things movable and immovable, and feoffment is only of soil, whereof a person, being wrongfully ejected, may recover seisin by this assise.

2. It should be known, that some persons have power to Who may give. give, and others not. For no one can effectually give but he in whose person the possession and the property are vested, and sometimes those who have nothing but the fee and the property, as by assignments and recognizances in our court; all other manner of gifts are revocable.

3. Kings also may not so alien the rights of their crown or King's power of alienation limited. of their royalty as not to be revocable by their successors. It is nevertheless allowable for kings to grant baronies and Gifts in almoign. other demesnes, and franchises, sometimes in alms, at other

demeynes et fraunchises soint par rois grauntez, en un cas par[1] aumoyne, et en autre cas pur aver les prelatz et les autres sages gentz del reaume del conseil, issi qe il soint as rois somounables et justizables, et en autre cas a fee ferme sicum citez et bourgs et autres demeynes, et en autres cas pur le poeple tener en amour, et en autre cas pur haster dreiture, sicum est des plusours fraunchises grauntez, sicum de infangenthef, et de aver poer de pleder bref de dreit, et de autres fraunchises.

Brac. 12, 14; Fle. 178 (§ 10). [88.] Fle. 178 (§ 11).

4. Ne prelatz de Saincte Eglise les dreitz de lour eglises, ne Templers ne Hospitelers ne autres gentz de religioun, qe les douns ne soint repellables par les donours. Ne countes ne barouns ne chivalers ne serjauntz, qi tenent en chief de nous, ne porrount mie desmembrer nos feez sauntz congé de nous, qe nous ne pusoms par dreit engiter les purchaceours; ne en tiel cas ne lour vaudra nule lounge seisine alegger, de si qe nul tens est limité quant a nos dreitz repurchacer.

Brac. 12 *b*; Fle. 178 (§ 11). Post, ii. 3. c. 16. s. 3.

5. Ne felouns porrount rien aliener puis lour felonie fete, qe la alienacioun ne soit repellable par les seignurs del fee, par noster bref de Entré et de Eschete. Ne bastardz feffez a

1. pur *AM.*

Baronies.

times to have the prelates and other sage persons of the realm of their council, so as they be summonable by the king and amenable to his justice; and in other cases in fee farm, as cities, boroughs, and other demesnes; and in other cases to retain the love of their people; and in other cases for dispatch of justice, for which several franchises are granted, as that of infangthef, and the power of holding plea in a writ of right, and other franchises.

Gifts of boroughs in fee farm.

Alienation by bishops, &c. revocable.

4. Neither can prelates of holy church so alien the rights of their churches, nor templars, hospitallers, or other persons in religion, as that their gifts shall not be revocable by the donors. Neither can earls, barons, knights, or serjeants, who hold in chief of us, so dismember our fees without our leave as that we may not lawfully eject the purchasers; nor in such case will it avail to allege length of seisin, inasmuch as no time is limited for the recovery of our rights.

Tenants *in capite* cannot alien without license.

Nullum tempus occurrit regi.

Restrictions upon alienation; by felons;

5. Felons cannot after the commission of their felony make any alienation, which may not be revoked by the lords of the fee by our writs of Entry and Escheat. And bastards enfeoffed

eus et a lour heyrs, ou assignez ne sount mie especifiez en les feffementz, ne porount rien aliener qe les seignurs des feez n'en eynt les terres alienez cum lour eschete. Ne enfauntz de eynz age, ne fols nastres, ne gentz arragez, ne sourdz, [1]ne mutz[1], ne mesels mis hors de commune de poeple, ne vileyns, ne sokemans lour socage. Brac. 11 *b*, 12; Fle. 178 (§ 10).

6. Ne femmes espouses sauntz lour barouns, ne les barouns sauntz lour femmes ne porrunt rien doner del heritage lour femmes, qe les douns ne soint repellables par les femmes si eles survivent lour barouns, ne uncore oveke lour barouns[2] en prejudice de ceux, en qi persones le fee et la proprete repose par fourme de doun, sicum en feez taillez; ne les barouns [88 *b*.] porrount rien doner a lour femmes ne la reverse puis le contract de matrimonie. Brac. 29. Brac. 12 *b*, 29; Fle. 178 (§ 12).

7. Ne ceux ausi ne porrunt mie atteignaument doner, qi par pour de mort dounent, par qei qe hastivement voillent lour fetz repeller apres ceo qe il eschaperount de prisoun. Mes si pour de la mort ne courge, bien porra chescun doner en prisoun ausi bien cum de hors. Et ausi porrount lunatics et Brac. 16 *b*, 17; Fle. 178 (§ 10), 184.

1—1. ne ranetez ne mutz *M*. ne ranetez *AF*. *sim*. *H*. 2. *so LNGS*. en dues estresces *add*. *M*. en deus estrifs *add*. *F*. en deus escriz *add*. *A*. *sim*. *H*.

to themselves and their heirs (where assigns are not specified in the feoffment) cannot alien so as to prevent the lords of the fees from having the lands aliened as their escheat. Nor may infants within age, nor natural fools, nor madmen, nor deaf persons, nor dumb, nor lepers removed from the society of people, nor villains, make any alienation, nor sokemen of their socage. **bastards enfeoffed to them and their *heirs*; infants and incapable persons; villains and sokemen.**

6. Neither can married women alien without their husbands; nor can husbands without their wives make such a gift of any part of the inheritance of their wives as shall not be revocable by the wives if they survive their husbands; nor yet wives with their husbands in prejudice of those in whose persons the fee and property are vested by form of the gift, as in fees tail; nor may husbands give anything to their wives, nor the reverse, after the contract of marriage. **Alienation by husband and wife, of the wife's land.**

7. Those also cannot effectually give who do so through fear of death, provided they will revoke their deeds as soon as they escape from prison. But unless fear of death can be alleged, any one may give as well in prison as without. Likewise lunatics and frenzied persons may give and alien, **Gifts under duress are void. Gifts of lunatics in lucid intervals, valid.**

Brac. 15; Fle. 178 (§8). frenetics doner et aliener, mes nient en lour rage. Et gentz de religioun avaunt lour professioun porrount doner; et mesels avaunt qe il soint[1] hors de commune [2]des gentz saynes[2]; et ausi les fouls, mes qe il soint neez fous.

Stat. de Big. (4 Ed. I.) c. 6. 8. Mes coment qe douns soint fetz a dreit ou a tort, et[3] le purchaceour soit del doun chalengé en sa seisine, si ert le donour tenuz de garrauntir soen doun, taunt cum il vivera, tut ne soit il a ceo obligé par especiaulté de escrit, tut face le purchaceour de ceo homage a autre qe al donour, sicum al chief seignur; et s'il eit obligé ses heyrs a la garrauntie, et il soit enpledé, james ne perdra le doun qe les heirs ne ly facent a la value, s'il ne le porount defendre en sa seysine, s'il eynt dount, si le purchaceour overe a dreit. Mes si la garrauntie
[89.] soit forprise, adounc covendra overer solom ceo qe fust entre eux acovenu. Teus purchaceours porrount overer folement, et defere lour dreit en ceste manere et en cas semblables. A. engette B. de soen fraunc tenement, et le doune a C.; B. se purchace par ceste assise; A. doute la assise et engette C., et

1. so *LSG*. engettez *add. ABH*. degez ceo est einz qil soient getez *add. M*. de genz ce est einz ceis ke il seyent engettez *F*. 2—2. del poeple *G*. 3. ou *S*.

So, of monks before profession, and of lepers before expulsion from society. but not during their madness. And persons in religion may give before they are professed, and lepers before they are put out of the society of healthy people; fools also, so as they are not fools born.

A donor is bound to warrant his gift. 8. But whether a gift be lawful or wrongful, if the purchaser be challenged in his seisin it becomes the duty of the donor to warrant his gift as long as he lives, although he be not bound thereto by any special clause in a deed, and although the purchaser do homage for the same to another than the donor, as to the chief lord. Heirs of donor, when bound to warranty. And if the donor has bound his heirs to warranty, and the purchaser is impleaded, he shall never be deprived of the gift without the heirs making it up to him in value, supposing they have wherewith to do so, if they cannot defend him in his seisin, and the purchaser proceeds according to law. But if warranty is excepted, then he must proceed according as it was covenanted between them. How a person disseised may lose his title. Such purchasers may act foolishly, and defeat their own right in this manner, and in like cases. A. ejects B. of his freehold, and gives it to C.; B. proceeds by this assise; A., doubting the result of the assise, ejects C., and restores the

le rend a B., qi le receit cum soen fraunc tenement rendu, et nient de doun. Si C. se purchace par ceste assise, il engittera par jugement B.; ei issi perdra B. la possessioun par sa folie.

9. Et sount autres maneres de douns, qe ne sount mie purement douns, eynz sount [1]meuz les[1] et dimissiouns a terme ou en fee, et dount homme espeire reversioun, ou aucun annuel service; et des queus douns aucuns sount condicionels et dount le fee est taylé et [2]en pendaunt[2] jekes autaunt qe la chose aveigne ou cele[3], sicum apres serra dit, et aucuns par enchesoun, sicum par enchesoun de matrimonie, et par plusours autres. Et acuns douns sount purs et larges, et acuns sount estreitz et en fourme, sicum as certeyns heyrs nomez es douns, et sicum de certeynes gentz forpris ens[4] douns. Et acuns porrount estre al comencement purs et puis porrount il estre estrescez par ceste clause, si qe le purchaceour ne peuse le doun aliener a certeynes persones, ou for qe as certeynes, ou a nul homme. Et sount acuns douns parfectz[5] ou les deus [89 *b.*]

Brac. 17; Fle. 178, 185.

Brac. 11 *b*; Fle. 178 (§ 5).

1—1. *so L. sim. NS.* melz les *G.* meins lees *AR. sim. M.* menuz leys *H.* meins leys *F.* 2—2. en *om. N.* dependaunt *M.* 3. *so LNSGM.* 4. *so LN.* es *GS.* en *MH.* 5. purchacez *ARMH.*

land to B., who receives it as his freehold restored, and not by gift. If C. proceeds by this assise, he shall have judgment to eject B., and so B. will lose the possession through his own folly[c].

9. There are other kinds of gifts, which are not absolute gifts, but are rather leases and demises for a term, or in fee, and whereout a man looks for the reversion or some annual service. Of which gifts some are conditional, and in such the fee is cut down and in suspense until a certain thing happens, as shall be afterwards mentioned; and some are made for a particular purpose, as on occasion of marriage, and for several other causes. Some gifts are absolute and large, others are restrained and in special form, as to some certain heirs named in the gifts, or where certain persons are excepted in the gifts. Some gifts may be absolute at the beginning, and afterwards restrained by this clause, so that the purchaser shall not have power to alien the gift to certain persons, or except to certain persons, or to any one. Some gifts are complete, where both

Gifts for a term.

Conditional gifts.

Gifts in marriage.

Gifts restricted to a certain kind of heirs.

Condition in restraint of alienation.

Complete and incomplete gifts.

c B. will be put to his proprietary action or writ of right, his last possession having been wrongful.

dreitz se joygnent en le purchaceour, et aucuns comencez et nent parfetz, et tiels titles sount mauveys, sicum est de douns grauntez, dount nul bail de seisine ne seut.

10. Et aucuns sount el comencement febles, qe puis sount enforcez par confermement de ceux qi ount la proprété, sicum est de douns fetz par enfauntz de eynz age et par ceux qe ren ne ount de la proprété, coment qe il [1]eynt estez venuz[1] a la possessioun. Mes coment qe purchaz soit fet de teles possessiouns, s'il eynt purchacé autre estat qe de dreit ne lour pusent lour feffours fere, si tauntost seynt tiels purchaceours engettez par ceus en qi persones [2]remeygne la proprete ou repose[2], les engettez ne recovrount james par ceste assise pur la viciouse entré; et si tauntost ne soint tels purchaceours engittez, si porount il puis estre engitez par jugement de nostre court, par la vertue de ceste assise et de[3] nos brefs de entré et de[4] autres brefs. En acun cas nequident covendra le remedie de teles desheritables alienaciouns remeyndre jekes apres le deces des alienours, sicum en cas ou les alienours averount tenu a terme de lour vies; et en cas des alienaunces[5] fetes par ceux

1—1. seyent auenuz *S.* *sim. M.* seient venuz *GAH.* 2—2. la proprete repose *MA.* 3. par *M.* *sim. F.* 4. des *LNSA.* dez *S.* par *M.* 5. alienacions *GASMH.*

rights unite in the purchaser; others are begun, but not completed; and such titles are bad, as in case of gifts granted, whereof no livery of seisin follows.

Invalid gifts. Confirmation.

10. Some are weak in their commencement, but are afterwards strengthened by the confirmation of those who have the property, as in the case of gifts made by infants under age, and by those who have no property in the thing, in whatever way they may have come into possession of it. But however such possessions be acquired, where the purchasers have purchased an estate other than their feoffors could legally convey to them, if such purchasers be presently ejected by those in whose persons the property remains or rests, the ejected shall never recover by this assise, on account of the defective entry. And if such purchasers are not presently ejected, they may be afterwards ejected by judgment of our court by virtue of this assise, and of our writs of Entry, and other writs. In some cases, however, the remedy for such disheritable alienations must be delayed until after the decease of the alienors, as in case where the alienors held for the term

Remedies in case of tortious feoffments by persons in possession. Entry.

Writ of Entry, &c.

Feoffment by tenant for life.

qe [1]pir estat[1] avoynt, tendra leu ceste assise devers les feffours et devers les feffez joyntement. [90.]

11. Et ausi sount acuns, qi ne pount mie purchacer for qe moeble sauntz noster coungé, sicum gentz de religioun. Ne nul baroun put purchacer for qe moeble de sa femme, ne la reverse, puis le matrimonie entre eux celebré. Neqedent quant qe est a la femme est a soen baroun, et nent la reverse. Car dreit le defend pur deus resouns. Une est pur presumpcioun[2] de delit de peché; l'autre est, pur ceo qe le donour ne remeigne povere et besoygnous par tiele debonereté. Ne enfauntz de eynz age, ne nul autre, ne purchace rien ou le donour remeynt en seisine del doun, lequel qe il retiegne la seysine cum seignur ou cum tutour. Ne mesels degez, ne arragez, ne fous, ne ceux qi ne sevent assenter al purchaz, ne porount rien purchacer sauntz gardeyns.

Mag. Cart. c 36; Stat. Mortm. (7 Ed. I.); Fle. 180, 181. Brac. 12 b, 29; Fle. 178, 179. Brac. 29; Fle. 178, 179 (§ 12–16). Brac. 12 b; 13; Fle. 179 (§ 17).

12. Et si acun voille doner a enfauntz de eynz age, et jalemeyns retener a terme de sa vie, en primes face plenerement

Fle. 179 (§ 17).

1—1. *so AMH. sim. F.* pur estat qe il. *L.* peur estat qe il *N.* pur estat *G.* pur estat i *S.* 2. *so GARM.* prescripcioun *LN. sim. FH.*

of their lives. And in case of alienations made by those who had an inferior estate, this assise shall be maintained against the feoffors and feoffees jointly.

Feoffment by termor.

11. There are some also who cannot without our leave purchase anything but movables, as persons in religion. Neither can a husband purchase more than the movables of his wife, nor the reverse, after marriage celebrated between them; nevertheless whatsoever is the wife's is the husband's, and not the reverse. For the law forbids gifts between husband and wife for two reasons; first, from a presumption of excessive fondness; secondly, lest the donor should through such good-nature remain poor and necessitous. Neither can an infant under age, nor any other person whatsoever, purchase anything where the donor remains in seisin, whether he retain the possession as owner or as guardian. Nor can lepers expelled society, nor madmen, nor idiots, nor such as are incapable of consenting to a purchase, acquire anything without guardians.

Convents incapable of purchasing land without license. Disabilities of husband and wife. Modified incapacity to purchase of infants, lunatics, &c.

12. If any one would make a gift to an infant under age, and yet retain an estate for the term of his life, let him first

Gift to an infant reserving a life estate; mode of conveyance.

le doun et mette l'enfaunt en seysine, et [1]ly baille aucun[1] estraunge tutour, et quant il avera eu peysible seysine, si engette l'enfaunt, et cum il avera esté graunt pece en seisine, adounc se face engeter par l'enfaunt, si qe le donour repurchase sa seisine par ceste assise et par atteynte en clamaunt fraunc tenement par title de terme de vie. Mes a ceo co-
[90 b.] vendra les assenz [2]del enfaunt[2] et del tutour.

Brac. 39 b; 52 b; Fle. 177 (§ 18).

13. Et sount acuns purchaz qe rien ne vaillent si enduccioun en la seisine ne sue, sicum des choses corporeles, et aucuns qe vaylent sauntz institucioun fere de seysine meyntenaunt sour le doun, sicum des choses nent corporeles, sicum sount fraunchises et servages de soil, et dount ceste assise tient leu ausi ben devaunt la seisine cum apres, sicum de chemin aver en autri soil, ou commune pur acune annuele rente. Car le affeccioun [3]en l'unité[3] des voluntez, et le bail des escritz de veisin a autre suffist pur seysine, sicum piert par la fraunchise de infangenthef[4]; car sovent avent qe nous graunt[o]ms as acunes gentz, qe il eynt la fraunchise de outfan-

Brac. 154 b; Fle. 62.

1—1. si le baylle a acun *W*. *sim*. *F*. 2—2. so *NARM*. *sim*. *FH*. *om*. *LS*.
3—3. est limite *LNARGSFH*. en la vnite *M*. 4. so *LNSGM*. *sim*. *AFH*.

make a complete gift, and put the infant in seisin, and give him some stranger as his guardian; and when the infant has been in peaceable seisin, let him eject him, and after the donor has been a considerable time in seisin, let him procure himself to be ejected by the infant, so that the donor may recover his seisin by this assise and by conviction, claiming a freehold by title of term of life. But for this proceeding the assent of the infant and guardian will be necessary.

Purchases of incorporeal tenements, good without seisin.

Such rights may be recovered in an assise by persons never actually seised.

13. There are some purchases which are invalid, unless induction into seisin follows, as of corporeal things; others which are good without institution of seisin made immediately on the gift, as of things incorporeal, such as franchises, and easements relating to land, for which this assise lies as well before seisin as after, as to have a way in another's soil, or common for a certain annual rent. For the act of the mind in the union of wills, and the delivery of the writings from one neighbour to another, are sufficient for seisin, as appears by the franchise of infangthef[d]; for it often happens that we grant to persons the franchise of outfangthef, that is to say,

Example of franchise of outfangthef.

[d] The above reading is found in all the MSS. which I have consulted, though the context seems to require 'outfangenthef.'

genthef, ceo est a dire, qe eux eynt les juises de lour gentz et de lour tenauntz, ou q'il soint pris hors de lour feez, [1]jugez a pendre[1], qe il les pusent apres jugement rendu prendre et remener en lour fraunchise et fere les pendre illucs sur lour fourches[2] demeyne; de la quele fraunchise nul a qi nous avoms graunté [3]la fraunchise tele[3], ne deit estre desturbé, tut ne eit il esté de ceo avaunt seisi; car bien pora avenir qe de eynz x. aunz ne vendra la aventure; par quei bien piert qe homme pora estre seisi de purchaz nient corporeus sauntz institutioun de hastive seysine. Brac. 226 b.

14. Et sount aucunes choses nient corporeles, qe hom ne pora mie bien purchacer sauntz eyde de nostre court, sicum feez et propretez, et dount par acord del purchaceour et del donour covendra lever fin en nostre court, par mi la quele [91.] Mod. lev. fin. (Stat. 18 Ed. I.) Glan. ii. 8; Brac. 256.

1—1. *so SGAM. sim. H.* iugement aprendre *L. sim. N.* 2. fraunchise *M.* 3—3. tele franchise *SGM.* title de franchise *AH.*

to have the punishment of their people and tenants, wheresoever they may be apprehended out of their fee, and adjudged to be hanged, so that after such judgment given, they may take them and bring them back into their franchise, and cause them to be hanged upon their own gallows[e]. In such a franchise, no one to whom we have granted the franchise in that form ought to be disturbed, although he has not hitherto been seised thereof. For it may well happen, that such a chance may not occur within ten years. Whereby it plainly appears that a man may be seised of incorporeal purchases without institution of speedy seisin.

14. There are some incorporeal things which cannot be well purchased without the aid of our court; as fees and properties[f]; of which by agreement of the purchaser and the donor a fine should be levied in our court, by means whereof this Conveyance by fine.

[e] Bracton defines outfangthef to be the right of trying thieves coming from other parts, and taken within the limits of the lord's jurisdiction; and says expressly that this franchise does not authorise the lord to bring back into his liberty and try one who has left his jurisdiction and been taken elsewhere. (Brac. 154 *b.*) Fleta follows Bracton, but adds, that though the lord cannot try his own man taken elsewhere, yet when convicted, he has a right to hang him on his own gallows. (Fle. 62.) Later authors, following the 'Termes de la ley,' have explained outfangthef to be the right of the lord to call to judgment in his court one of his own men apprehended for felony out of his fee. See Ducange, Gloss.; Tomline's Law Dict.; Wharton's Law Lexicon.

[f] The word *fee* is here used for seignory; the word *property* for a proprietary right not accompanied by possession.

teles maneres de purchaz prendrount effect et estableté. Acuns feez sount neqedent, qe totes gentz ne poent mie bien purchacer sauntz meens[1]; car les barouns ne pount mie bien purchacer les feez des douwaries lour femmes, pur le service qe ne put [2]estre attourné[2] de la femme a soen baroun; et pur ceo vailent en tel cas quiteclamaunces de ceux a qi apent la reversioun.

15. Et acune foiz avent qe cil, a qi reversioun apent de dreit par fourme de doun, ne peut mie doner soen dreit a chescun del poeple jekes autaunt qe il soit seisi; sicum est de ceux heirs a qi accrest heritage apres le deces des purchaceours qi en furent seisiz a terme de lour vies; mes les tenauntz porrount deliverer lour seysines a celi a qi la reversioun apent, et cil les pora refeffer [3]ou autres[3], et dounc n'est mie soulement doné le fee, mes la possessioun [4]ensemblement ove[4] le fee et le fraunc tenement joyntement.

1. *so MW. sim. ARF.* mireus *L.* mireus [al meens *interl.*] *N.* meen *G.* 2—2. atourner *M.* 3—3. *so ARMW.* a autres *LS.* cum autres *N.* e autres *G.* un autre *F.* 4—4. soulement ou *LSHF.* solement oueke *N.* soulement od *G.* ensemblement e *M.* ouekes *AR.* ensemblement ou *W.*

Purchase by husband of the seignory of his wife's dower.

kind of purchase derives effect and stability[g]. Nevertheless there are some fees which are not to be purchased by certain persons without a mesne. For husbands cannot purchase the fees of their wives' dowers[h], by reason of the service which cannot be attorned from the wife to the husband. Hence the use in such cases of quitclaims from those to whom the reversion belongs.

Conveyance by reversioner upon a freehold.

15. Sometimes it happens that he to whom the reversion legally belongs by the form of the gift, cannot give his right to any person he may choose until he is himself seised, as in case of those heirs to whom an inheritance accrues after the decease of the purchasers who were seised for the term of their lives. But the tenants may deliver their seisin to the person to whom the reversion belongs, and he may reenfeoff them or others; and then not only the fee is granted, but the possession at the same time, together with the fee and the freehold.

g 'The right which is severed from the possession is sometimes not vested in the purchaser without recognizance in the King's Court, and then by a judicial writ, called *Quid juris clamat;* sometimes it is vested by quitclaim, and sometimes the two rights must be united, that is, the possession and the property, before the right can be aliened.' (Note in MS. *N.*) As to the writ of *Quid juris clamat*, see Reg. Brev. Judic. 36 *b*.

h That is, the immediate seignory of the tenements held by the wife by title of dower under a former marriage.

CHAPITRE IV. [xxxv.]

De communs purchaz.

1. Et ausi cum un pora fere several purchaz, ausi porount plusours purchacer en commun, a eus et a lour heyrs et a lour assignez, ou a certeyns heirs par feffement estrescié[1], [2]et acune foiz a engendrure apparaunte et[2] [3]acune foiz[3] a engendrure a nestre, et dount ne porra nul estre autri heyr, sicum est de douns qe acunes gentz fount a lour amies con- Brac. 13; Fle. 179. [91 b.] Brac. 13; Fle. 179, 180.

1. estreciez *M.* estreite *F.* 2—2. *om. A.* 3—3. *om. MHF.*

CHAPTER IV.

Of joint purchases[i].

1. As one person may make a separate purchase, so may many purchase in common, to them and their heirs and assigns, or to certain heirs by a limited feoffment, and sometimes to issue born, and sometimes to issue to be born, where one can not be heir to the other. It is thus with the gifts which persons make to their mistresses or concubines[k],—to have and Gift to several persons. Gift to A, and her bastard issue: a jointenancy.

[i] It should be observed that throughout this chapter, and elsewhere, the word *commun* is used of jointenancy. No reference is made to tenancy in common, which appears to have been of later growth.

[k] With respect to the supposed gift to a concubine and her children born and to be born, (an example which is borrowed from Bracton,) the annotator in MS. *N.* observes as follows:—'To that it is said that a concubine can purchase to her and her children born and to be born, I do not at all agree, (Je ne m'y acord poynt.) For, suppose the concubine to have two children at the time of the purchase, and the deed to speak thus: Sciant &c. quod ego dedi Beatriciæ et Clementi et David pueris suis et omnibus aliis pueris de me procreatis ex eadem Beatricia nascituris, habendum et tenendum prædictis B. C. et D. et eorum hæredibus et assignatis;—if Beatrice have afterwards children who claim estate by this feoffment, and are kept out by the first purchasers, and bring assise; being driven to state their title, they must claim either by title of purchase or of succession. And by purchase they can demand nothing, because they are not named by name in the feoffment, and were no parties to the livery of seisin. For in feoffments it behoveth to name certain donor, certain purchaser, and certain tenement; and those who were not *in rerum natura* at the time of the translation cannot claim part in the thing transferred, the nature of the translation being, that when the thing transferred becomes vested in the purchasers, it is extinct in the donors, and the reverse. But in this feoffment everything is extinct in the donor, and is vested in those purchasers who were parties to the induction of seisin, and in none other. Therefore it appears that the word *nascituris* is vain and ineffectual. And if the concubine be pregnant, and the donor say, Dedi Beatriciæ et Clementi filio suo; and order that the child which shall be born be called Clement; although this happen accordingly, and the child remain ten or twelve years with his mother, as it were continuing his seisin, if he be afterwards ejected by his mother, he shall not recover by the assise, as some say. For the alienation gave forthwith a new tenant to the lord; and if the mother had committed

cubines, a aver et a tener a la concubine et a ses enfauntz engendrez [1]et a engendrer[1] et a lour heyrs, des queus nul pora estre autri heyr; et dounc si la mere seit engeté, tut [2]ne eynt les[2] enfauntz [3]eu seysine, la mere et les[3] enfauntz neqedent recoverount[4] par ceste assise par la seysine qe la mere out[5] en lour noun. Et si la mere soit morte, uncore recoverount les enfauntz par ceste assise pur mesme [6]la seisine,[6] pur ceo qe ele prist seysine pur luy et pur ses enfauntz cum lour gardeyne. Car cist est seisi, pur[7] qi et en qi noun hom prent la seisine, sicum est de purchaz de vileyns al oes lour seignur.

Brac. 13, 262; Fle. 180.

2. Et si un neqedent se lesse morer seysi de sa partie avaunt la devisioun, sa partie acrest a ses parceners et a lour

1—1. *so N.* et engendrer *L.* ou a engendrer *M.* *om. HF.* 2—2. neit ele *A.* *sim. H.* 3—3. eu la seisine la miere les *M.* en la seisine les *A.* en la ceisine la mere les *H.* 4. *so AM.* *sim. FH.* ne courrount *L.* ne recoueront pas *N.* 5. prist *M.* 6—6. *so NAGMH.* le assise *LS.* 7. *so G.* par *LNAMSHF.*

to hold to the concubine and her children begotten and to be begotten and their heirs; none of which children can be heir to the others. And if the mother be ejected, although the children have not had seisin, yet the mother and children shall recover by this assise, by reason of the seisin which the mother had in their name. And if the mother be dead, again the children shall recover by this assise by virtue of the same seisin, because she took the seisin for herself and her children as their guardian. For that person is seised, for whom and in whose name the seisin is taken; as is the case with the purchases of villains to the use of their lords.

Seisin of mother operates as seisin of infant jointenant.

2. Nevertheless if one of them allows himself to die seised of his part before division, it accrues to his parceners, and to

Accruer by survivorship before severance.

felony and been attainted, although execution had been delayed until the infant's birth, yet the right of the lord to have the escheat would have accrued immediately; which right cannot be extinguished by him who could claim no estate at the time of the felony committed, for —jus semper in aliquo sibi vindicat locum, nec in loco vacuo requiescere potest.' This latter opinion is upon a point respecting which there is little authority in our common law. By the civil law children in the womb were treated as capable of acquiring property, (see Dig. li. 1. t. 5. l. 26.); and this law was followed in our courts having cognizance of wills and administrations. (See Beale *v.* Beale, 1 P. Will. 244. Doe *v.* Lancashire, 5 Term Rep. 49.) This however was not the case at common law, for it seems to have been the general opinion that if a remainder was limited to a child, who was *in ventre sa mere* at the determination of the particular estate, the remainder failed, the child not being considered to be in *esse*. The contrary rule was finally laid down by Statute 10 and 11 Will. III. c. 16. See Reeve *v.* Long, 1 Salk. 227; Coke Lit. 298 a. (note by Butler); Coke Lit. 390 a.; Blackstone, Comm. vol. i. p. 130.

heirs, et issi de trestouz jekes au dreyn. Et si le dreyn murge sauntz heyr et sauntz assigné, adounc serra le heritage au seignur. Et si acun hom se purchace a ly et a ses heirs, issint qe assignez ne soint nomez en le doun, cel purchaceour ne pora rien aliener ne fere assigné, s'il ne eit heyrs; mes s'il eit heyrs loynteyns ou proscheyns qi pusent le doun garrauntir, en tiel cas porount il vendre et doner et fere assignez; et si n'i ad nul heyr, adounc serra le tenement eschaete al seignur del fee. Brac. 17, 17b; Fle. 191 (c. 12). [92.]

3. Et cum teus purchaceours tenauntz en commun soint de teus purchaz engettez, trestouz joyntement recoverount lour seisine a tener en commun par ceste assise, qi qe soit disseisour[1], estraunge persone ou acun des parceners.

4. Mes si acun murge seisi de sa partie en severauté sauntz heir de sei, et sauntz assigné fere, cele partie ne accrestera mie as parceners puis la devisioun, eynz serra eschete au seignur. Et si le seignur se mette en seisine hastivement apres le deces tiel tenaunt par soulement mettre le pié, suffist sa seisine; et s'il soit engetté ou deforcé, il recovera par ceste assise.

1. so *M.* disseisi sur *LSG.* sim. *N.*

their heirs, and so on to all the rest until the last. And if the last die without heirs and without assign, the inheritance shall escheat to the lord. And if any man purchase to himself and his heirs, without assigns being named in the gift, such purchaser, if he has no heirs, cannot alien or make an assign; but if he has heirs either near or remote, who can warrant the gift, he may in such case give, sell, and make assigns: but if there be no heir, then the tenement will escheat to the lord of the fee. **Escheat.** **Effect of conveyance to one and his heirs (without mention of assigns).**

3. If purchasers holding in common be ejected out of such purchase, they shall all jointly recover their seisin to hold in common, by this assise, whether the disseisor be a stranger or one of the parceners. **Recovery of joint purchase by assise of novel disseisin.**

4. But if any one die seised of his part in severalty without an heir, and without having created assigns, that part shall not accrue to the parceners after the division, but shall escheat to the lord. And if the lord immediately after the decease of the tenant put himself in seisin by merely setting his foot thereon, it is a sufficient seisin; and if he be ejected or deforced, he shall recover by this assise. **Effect of severance.** **Escheat of share.** **Recovery of lord by assise.**

Brac. 13, 13*b*; Fle. 180 (§ 6).

5. Et sount acuns purchaz qe vaillent as acuns purchaceours, et a[1] acuns [2]ne vaillent nient, sicum des douns fetz de barouns a lour femmes et a lour enfauntz communs, ou[3] as enfauntz la femme, puis le matrimonie, ne vaudra nient[2] le doun pur les femmes, mes[4] pur les enfauntz [5]si tendreit bien[5].

Fle. 180 (§ 7).

6. Et si ii. freres se purchacent en commun a eus et a lour heyrs, le eynzné pora estre tutour et gardeyn de le puysnee, si le puysnee seit de eynz age et le eynznee de plener age; et si ambideus soint muyllirez, le un serra le autri heyr[6], s'il ne
[92 *b*.] eynt heyrs de eus mesmes, [7]ne ne[7] eynt fetz assignez, leqel qe la devisioun eit esté fete entre eus ou noun. Et si le un soit engetté ou deforcé apres le autri desces, et apres le soul mettre del pié en noun de seisine de soen heritage, si recovera par ceste assise. Et si l'assise soit porté sur le chief seignur, et cil die par cas, qe il ne cleyme rien si garde noun, cum de la partie le frere qi mort est, ne vaylle rien ceo, tut eyt le frere mort fiz ou autre heyr apparaunt de eynz age,

1. *so M.* a *om. LNAH.* 2—2. qi meins valent: com femme qe purchace de sun barun apres lalliaunce tut seit ceo deuant esposailles ne vaut pas *AR.* 3. *so M.* et *LN.* e *H.* 4. bon est *add. AR.* 5—5. se tendra bien *MF.* si tendra *H.* *om. AR.* 6. *so MH.* et *add. L.* et *N.* e *ARGSF.* 7—7. nen *L.* ne [ne *interl.*] *N.* ou ne *M.* ne *AR.* e ne *H.*

Effect of conveyance by a husband to his wife and another person.

5. There are some purchases which are valid as to some of the purchasers, and not as to others; as, where gifts are made by a husband after marriage to his wife and their common children, or to the wife and the wife's children, such gifts will not avail the wife, but will stand good as to the children.

Joint purchase by brothers.

6. If two brothers purchase jointly to them and their heirs, the elder may be tutor and guardian to the younger, if the younger is under age and the elder of full age; and if both are legitimate, one shall be the other's heir, if he has no heirs of his own body, and has not made assigns, whether partition was made between them or not. And if one be deforced or ejected after the other's decease, and after having merely set his foot upon the land in the name of seisin of his inheritance, he shall recover by this assise.

Right of accruer prevails over the claim of descent.

And if the assise be brought against the chief lord, and he plead that he claims only wardship in respect of the share of the deceased brother, this defence shall not prevail, although the deceased's brother have left a son or other heir apparent under age, inasmuch

[1]de sicum[1] nul ne savoit unques nule severauté en le tenement.

CHAPITRE V. [XXXVI.]

De purchaz Condicionels.

1. Et tut soit qe heyrs seynt nomez en purchaz, ja pur ceo ne accrest as heyrs nul purchaz; eynz fet a entendre, qe la ou acun se purchace a ly et a ses heyrs, il se purchace a ly et a ses heyrs proscheyns et loyngteyns, a aver et tener de heyr en heyr ausi bien a les engendrez cum a ceux qi sount a engendrer. Brac. 17, 17 b; Fle. 185 (c. 8).

2. Et ausi cum heyrs par manere de purchaz se porount purchacer es purchaz lour auncestres, ausi bien porunt acuns estre forclos de purchaz par la manere del contract fet entre les donours et les purchaceours. Car covenaunt desturbe acune foiz successioun, et solom le contract et la volunté des donours covendra overer, sicum en ceo cas et en cas semblables. Si acun se purchace a ly et a sa femme et al issue de eux engendré en leal matrimoygnie, en tiel purchaz ne accrest Brac. 17 b; Fle. 185 (c. 9). Stat. West. 2. (13 Ed. I.) c. 1. [93.]

1—1. si com *M.*

as no separate property was ever recognised in the tenement.

CHAPTER V.

Of conditional purchases.

1. Notwithstanding heirs are named in a purchase, yet no purchase thereby accrues to the heirs. And it must be understood that where any one purchases to himself and his heirs, he purchases to himself and his heirs near or remote, and to have and to hold from heir to heir, as well to those begotten as to those which are to be begotten. Heirs cannot purchase except through their ancestors.

2. And as heirs may by the form of the purchase acquire a property in the purchase of their ancestor, so may they by the form of the contract between the donors and the purchasers be excluded from the purchase. For a covenant sometimes bars succession, and effect must be given to the contract and the will of the donors, as in the following and like cases. If any one purchase to himself and his wife and their issue begotten in lawful matrimony; by such a purchase the purchasers Right of heirs limited by the form of the gift. Conveyance to A. and his wife and their issue.

rien as purchaceours for qe fraunc tenement a lour deus vies, et fee acrest a lour issue si point i ad apparaunt; et si point n'i ad, adounc remeynt le fee en la persone le donour jekes a taunt qe il eynt issue, et revertera le purchaz al donour, si le purchaceours ne eynt poynt de issue, ou s'il eynt issue qe defaylle. Et si le un purchaceour murge, le autre retendra le purchaz a terme de vie; et si nul issue[1] viegne de eus, etle tenaunt face felonie, le donour avera la reversioun, et le chief[2] seignur ne avera nule eschete; et si le donour eit mis le pié en noun de seisine, et il soit engetté ou deforcé, il recovera par ceste assise.

Fle. 185 (c. 9. § 3). 3. Condicioun pora estre fete en plusours maneres, en une manere al profit le purchaceour, par la condicioun qe il ne doigne ne aliene; et acune foiz a soen damage, sicum par la

1. ne *add. NS. interl. M.* 2. *om. M.*

have only a freehold for their two lives, and the fee accrues to their issue if there be any already born; and if not, then the fee remains in the person of the donor until they have issue[1]; and in case the purchasers have no issue, or have issue which fails, the purchase will revert to the donor. And if one of the purchasers die, the other shall retain the purchase for the term of his life. And if they have no issue, and the tenant commits felony, the donor shall have the reversion, and the chief lord shall have no escheat. And if the donor has set his foot on the land in name of seisin, and is ejected or deforced, he shall recover by this assise.

Condition. 3. A condition may be made in many ways; in one way to the advantage of the purchaser, as upon condition that he does not give or alien, and sometimes to his prejudice, as upon

[1] The treatise of Britton appears to have been compiled after the date of the statute *De donis conditionalibus*, 13 Edw. I., and even of the statute *Quia emptores terrarum*, 18 Edw. I., (see the Editor's Introduction); but before the effect of these statutes upon the law had become apparent. The observations of the annotator in MS. *N.* further illustrate this change of law. 'Before the statute [*Quia emptores*] the donor could charge or discharge the tenements at his will, and put one or more conditions in the charter. But since the statute no charter or gift was conditional save gift in fee tail, because every tenant by force of the statute must hold of his chief without mesne. Wherefore some of our companions (les uns de nos compaignons) say that this chapter [of Britton] is vain and antiquated (veyn e antiquité). But let them say what they will (dient lur talent); for it is said 'covenant conquers law,' as, if any one desires that any of these conditions may hold, he may give the tenement in fee simple, and then make indentures containing the conditions at his will; and thus by these collateral covenants (covenans de en costé) one may recover the land either by his own force or by force of law as by writ of covenant. So that, although the charter was not conditional, the conditional writings defeat the charter.' See some further observations on sections 4, 5, and 6.

condicioun qe il ne tiegne en fee ou for qe a terme. Et dount quatre condiciouns sount principalment suffrables en douns et en autres contracts, nomément cestes: jeo tei doigne par issi qe tu mei[1] doignes: jeo faz par si qe tu facz[2]: jeo faz par si qe tu [3]doignes: jeo[4] doign par si qe tu facz[5]. Cestes condiciouns obligent les parties par lour contractz, issint qe chescun se[6] est obligé a autre en tele manere, qe si le un doigne ou face, le autre est tenuz et obligez a fere le countrepan solom le contract, et en mesme la manere en la negative, qe si le un ne face, qe le autre ne soit mie tenuz a fere. Et si le un eit fet et le autre ne voille fere, si list al donour a reprendre soen doun; et s'il en soit deforcé, soit aydé par ceste assise.

Brac. 18 *b*; Fle. 185, 186.

[93 *b*.]

Brac. 19; Fle. 185, 186.

4. Et en mesme la manere soit del purchaceour, [7]qi certeyne terre ly soit[7] promise, et dount escritz sount fetz par si qe le purchaceour espouse soer ou file, et le purchaceour la espouse eynz ceo qe il soit mis en seisine de la terre par le donour; si le purchaceour veye qe le donour ne ly veut tener

1. ne *M*. 2. ne faz *M*. me faces *A*. 3. mei *add*. *N*. ne *add*. *M*. 4. tei *add*. *N*. 5. ne faces *M*. 6. se *om*. *AM*. 7—7. a qi certeyne ly soit *N*. a qi certeine terre seit *M*. qe certeine terre luy seit *G*. *sim*. *S*. ke certaine terme seyt a ly *F*.

condition that he do not hold in fee, but only for a term. There are four principal heads of conditions which are allowable in gifts and other contracts, namely these: I give to thee, so that thou give to me: I do, so that thou do: I do, so that thou give: I give, so that thou do. These conditions so bind the parties by their contracts, that each is bound to the other in such a manner, that if the one gives or does such a thing, the other is bound and obliged to do the counterpart according to the contract; so, in the negative, that if the one does not do such a thing, the other is not bound to do such a thing. And if the one does the act, and the other will not do the act, it is lawful for the donor to take back his gift; and if he is deforced thereof, he shall be aided by this assise.

Negative conditions.

4. A purchaser shall also have the like remedy, where certain lands are promised to him, and writings made thereof, on condition that he marry the sister or daughter of the donor, and the purchaser marries her before the donor puts him in seisin of the lands. If the purchaser, seeing that the

Gift on condition of marriage.

le covenaunt, et le purchaceour se mette en seisine de la terre par ly ou par autre qi le face en soen noun, et il soit engetté ou deforcé, soit aydé par ceste assise. Et si le donour face en partie et en partie nient, en tel cas soit le purchaceour eydé par bref de covenaunt; ou de eschaete par detenue de la sute de deus aunz;—qe fu purveu a Gloucestre.

Fle. 184 (§ 4); Stat. Glouc. (6 Ed. I) c. 4.

Fle. 186 (§ 5).

5. Et si le donour die issi: jeo tei doing taunt de terre ove les apurtenaunces a aver et a tener a tei et a tes heyrs, si tu eys heyrs de toen cors engendrez, en tiels douns ne ad le purchaceour rien purchacé for qe fraunc tenement; mes s'il face engendrure, adounc primes crest[1] fee et dreit, issi qe il pora
[94.] la terre doner et aliener, tut faille l'engendrure, pur la satisfaccioun de la condicioun; et les freres al purchaceour ou les autres heyrs loyngteyns serrount heyrs le purchaceour [2]de cel[2] purchaz.

1. li encrest *M*. 2—2. en teu *M*.

donor will not keep his covenant with him, puts himself in seisin of the land, in person or by another who takes possession in his name, and he is ejected or deforced, he shall be aided by this assise[m]. And if the donor performs his contract in part, and in part not, in such case the purchaser shall be aided by our writ of covenant; or of escheat by detainer of the services for two years, as was provided at Gloucester[n].

Gift to A. and his heirs, if he have heirs of his body.

5. If the donor says thus: I give thee so much land with the appurtenances, to have and to hold to thee and thy heirs if thou have heirs of thy body begotten: in such gifts the purchaser purchaseth only a freehold, but if he has issue, the fee and the right then first accrue to him, so that he will be able to give and alien the land, although the issue fail, because the condition is satisfied[o]; and the brothers of the purchasers or their other remote heirs shall inherit such a purchase.

[m] 'That which is said, that the purchaser may thrust himself into seisin upon the marriage, is not well said as to the present law (quant a ore). For if he can aid himself by writ of covenant, well; if not, let him provide better another time.' Note in MS. *N*.

[n] The conclusion of this sentence is obscure; and probably the text is corrupt. The reference appears to be to the fourth chapter of the Statute of Gloucester (6 Ed. I.), by which a remedy was provided to a donor or lessor to recover the land in case of the non-payment for two years of a fee-farm rent or other service reserved amounting to a fourth part of the value of the land. The writ by which this remedy was enforced was called *Cessavit per biennium*. (Vet. Nat. Brev. 138.) This statute is cited in the corresponding passage of Fleta, as furnishing a remedy for a breach of a condition.

[o] 'This is all void; for the gift is [*qu.* treated in the text as] a conditional gift, and not in fee tail.' Note in MS. *N*.

6. Et si le donour die issint, jeo tei doyn cele terre pur ceo qe tu me as bien servi, tut soit le cause fause, ja pur ceo ne remeynt qe le doun n'est bon. Et ausi en cest cas iert le doun bon et estable, lequel la cause soit verreye ou fause: jeo tei doyn ceste terre [1]pur ceo qe tu me serviras bien. Mes si le donour die issi: jeo te doyn ceste terre[1], si tu bien me serves, en tel cas est le doun daungerous et [2]en pendaunt[2] jekes autaunt qe satisfaccioun soit fete a la condicioun. Brac. 19 b; Fle. 186 (§ 6, 7).

7. Et si doun soit fet par condicioun de chose a venir, et la condicioun soit possible, en tel cas iert le doun delayable deques a la satisfaccioun de la condicioun; et si le purchaceour se pleyne, le donour avera excepcioun pur ly, qe accioun ne pleynte ne ly peut acrestre jekes apres la satisfaccioun [3]del covenaunt[3], cum si acun doyne par si qe il doyne x. Mes si la condicioun soit inpossible, adounc n'est le doun de nule vertue ne de nule force, cum si la condicioun soit tele: jeo tei doyn par si qe tu me facis aver la lune. Brac. 19 (§ 2); Fle. 187 (§ 10).

1—1. *so verb M. sim. AB. om. LN.* 2—2. dependant *M.* pendant *F.* 3—3. de la condicioun *AM. sim. H.*

6. If the donor say, I give thee this land because thou hast served me well: although the cause may be false, it does not follow that the gift is not good. And in the following case also the gift shall be good and firm, whether the cause be true or false: I give thee this land, because thou wilt serve me well. But if the donor say, I give thee this land if thou wilt serve me well, the gift here is doubtful and in suspense until the condition is satisfied [p]. Mistaken consideration does not vitiate a gift. Distinction between cause and condition.

7. Where a gift is made upon condition of something in future, and the condition is possible, there the gift will be deferred until satisfaction of the condition; and if the purchaser brings any plaint, the donor may plead this exception, that no action or plaint can accrue to him until after satisfaction of the condition; as where a gift is made to another on condition that he give 10*l.* But if the condition be impossible, then the gift is of no virtue or force, as if the condition be thus: I give to thee, upon condition thou procure me the moon. Possible condition. Impossible condition.

p 'What is here said of gifts made for a certain cause, and also of gifts depending upon the will of another or upon chance, is bad in law, (rien ne valt.) For it matters not (il ne me chaud) for what cause you give, so you put me in seisin to have and to hold to me and my heirs of the chief lord.' Note in MS. *N.*

Brac. 19, 19 b; Fle. 187 (§ 11). [94 b.] Brac. 19; Fle. 187 (§ 12).

8. Et acuns douns sount [1]en pendaunt par[1] autri volounté, sicum en cest cas: jeo tei doyn, si Johan le voille; en tiel cas ne vaut rien le purchaz si Johan ne se assente. Et acuns purchaz sount aventurous, sicum en cest cas: jeo tei doyn a tener, si jeo soye fet evesqe.

Brac. 19; Fle. 187 (§ 12).

9. Et si acun doun soit fet par plusours condiciouns, si satisfaccioun soit fet a une de ces condiciouns, adounc iert le doun estable, si les condiciouns soint severales. Mes si eles soint joyntes, adounc covendra fere [2]le asset de[2] totes, a ceo qe le purchaz soit estable. Car n'est mie tut un a dire, jeo tei doyn si tu me faz cele chose ou cele, et a dire, si tu faces cele chose et cele joyntement; car en le un cas suffist la satisfaccioun del une des condiciouns, et en le autre cas ne suffist mie, si satisfaccioun ne soit fete a totes les condiciouns.

Brac. 19; (§ 13). Fle. 18 (§ 13).

10. Et acune condicioun est negative et suffrable en les douns, sicum en cas ou le doun est fet al fiz puysnee ou a autre estraunge persone, a aver et a tener a ly et a ses heyrs, si le frere eynzné ne eit point de issue de ly mesmes, ou point de issue de tele femme; et ausi cum en cas ou le doun est fet al purchaceour a aver et tenir a ly et a ses heyrs

1—1. dependant de *M.* 2—2. lassez a *M.* assez a *A.*

Condition depending upon the will of a third party. Casual condition.

8. Some gifts depend upon the will of another, as in the following case: I give to thee, if John is willing; here the purchase is of no avail, unless John assents to it. Some purchases are casual, as in this case: I give to thee to hold, if I shall be made a bishop.

Condition copulative and disjunctive.

9. If a gift be made upon more conditions than one, and one of the conditions is satisfied, the gift will be valid, if the conditions are several; but if they are joint, then all must be fulfilled to make the purchase effectual. For it is not the same thing to say, I give to thee, if thou do such a thing or such a thing, and to say, I give if thou do such a thing and such a thing, jointly. For in one case, satisfaction of one of the conditions is sufficient, and in the other it is not sufficient unless all the conditions are satisfied.

Condition in the negative.

10. Another kind of condition which is permissible in gifts is negative, as where a gift is made to the youngest son, or to a stranger, to have and to hold to him and his heirs, if the elder brother shall have no issue of his own, or no issue by such a wife. So, where the gift is made to the purchaser, to

de soen cors engendrez, et si point de engendrure ne eyt, adounc revertisse le doun al donour, ou as autres certeynes persones, a tenir en commun ou en severauté, et[1] le un apres le autre.

11. Et autres maneres de condiciouns sount doubles, sicum en cas ou le donour dist, si tu ne eys point des heirs de toen cors engendrez, ou si tu les eys et il defaillent, adounc revertisse le doun a moi et a mes heirs, ou issi, qe si tele chose ne[2] aviegne, qe tu adounc eys la terre a touz jours. Et ausi porount douns estre fetz par plusours condiciouns, sicum en cest cas: a aver et a tener, si tu teles choses [3]faces ou[3] ne faces, [4]ou si tu faces[4] qe le doun mei retourne; ou issi: a aver et a tenir par si qe ne faces tele chose, une ou plusours, sauntz moen coungé, et si tu faces, qe adounc me puse[5] mettre en seysine del doun, et retener la seisine a touz jours.

Brac. 19, 19 b; Fle. 187 (§ 15). [95.] Brac. 19 b; Fle. 187 (§ 18).

12. Et dounc si le purchaceour ne face solom le covenaunt, et le donour se plunge en seisine, il retendra; et s'il en soit

1. ou *MG.* 2. ne *om. M.* 3—3 *om. G.* 4—4. so *G.* *om. LNMS.* 5. ieo *add. ABMH.*

have and to hold to him and the heirs of his body begotten, and if he shall have no issue, that then the gift shall revert to the donor, or to certain other persons, to hold jointly, or severally, one after the other.

Double condition.

11. There are other kinds of conditions, which are double; as where the donor says, if thou shalt have no heirs of thy body begotten, or if thou shalt have heirs and they shall fail, then the gift shall revert to me and my heirs: or thus, if such a thing do not happen, then thou shalt have the land for ever [q]. Gifts may also be made upon several conditions, as in this example: to have and to hold, so thou do, or so thou do not such and such things, and if thou do, the gift shall return to me; or thus, to have and to hold so thou do not do such a thing, or several things, without my leave, and if thou so do, then it shall be lawful for me to put myself in seisin of the gift and retain it for ever.

Remedies for breach of condition.

12. If the purchaser do not in such case according to the covenant, and the donor throw himself into seisin, he shall

[q] This example appears imperfect. Possibly some words are lost out of the text.

engitté ou deforcé, [1]si avera recoverer[1] pas ceste assise. Mes si en nule manere ne se peuse mettre en seysine, adounc li vaudra noster bref de covenaunt, qe serra pledé par le graunt *Cape*, et par le petit, sicum accioun reale. Et si les chartres, ou les escritz del premer contract soint dediz en jugement, si ne vaudra nient de prover les escritz, si prové ne soit ovek[2], qe satisfaccioun[3] soit fete a la condicioun. Car cestes deus choses porount estre ensemble, qe le escrit [4]bon seit[4], et qe nule satisfaccioun ne est fete a la condicioun.

Brac. 19 *b*; Fle. 187 (§ 18).

13. Condicioun destourbe a la foiz decente de heritage a dreitz heyrs, sicum en ceste manere: jeo tei doyn ceste terre a certeyn terme, et si jeo moerge de eynz cel terme, adounc remeigne cele terre a tei et a tes heirs, ou a terme de vie, ou a autre terme. Et acune foiz fet condicioun de terme fraunc tenement, et la reverse, sicum est en ceo cas: jeo tei doyn a aver et a tener a terme de la vie le purchaceour et taunt de tens outre, et si tu devies de eynz cel terme, adounc voil jeo qe tes heirs et tes executours tiegnent le doun deques a mesme le terme. As chiefs seignurs neqedent ne pora rien perir[5].

Brac. 19 *b* (§ 4); Fle. 187, 188. [95 *b*.] Brac. 19 *b*, 20; Fle. 188 (§ 21). Stat. Marl. (52 Hen. III.) c. 6; Post, c. 33. s. 4.

1—1. il recouera *M.* *sim. H.* 2. auaunt *M.* 3. ne *add. M.* 4—4. soit loial *M.* 5. deperir *M.* departir *H.*

keep it; and if he be thereof ejected or deforced, he shall recover by this assise. But if he cannot in any way put himself in seisin, then he may avail himself of our writ of covenant, in which the process is by the great and little *Cape*, as in a real action. And if the charters or writings of the original contract are denied in judgment, it will not avail to prove the deeds without making proof withal of the condition being satisfied. For these two things may well stand together, that the deeds may be legal, and that the condition may not have been satisfied.

Estates restricted or enlarged upon condition.

13. A condition sometimes bars the descent of an inheritance to the right heirs; as in this manner: I give thee such land for a certain term; and if I die within that time, then the land shall remain to thee and thine heirs, or for term of life, or for other term. Sometimes a condition makes a freehold of a term, and the reverse; as in this case: I give thee, to have and to hold during the life of the purchaser, and for such a time over; and if thou die within that term, then I will that thy heirs or thy executors shall hold the gift for the same term. The chief lords however cannot be deprived of anything; for

Provisions for rights of lords.

Car terme ne toust mie garde mes delaye a certeyn tens; si le heir ne soit fol nastre, et en tiel cas perd le seignur la garde, et le fermer soen terme, jekes autaunt qe autre chose en soit ordeyné, al meyns a tote la vie le soot; pur la purveaunce Robert Wallraunt, et par commun assent des grauntz seignurs del reaume, et en qi heyr le estatut prit primes effect et en le heir de soen heir.

14. Et si doun soit fet par tele condicioun, qe si le donour rende taunt a certeins jours [1]et leu[1], qe le doun soit retourné al donour, et, si noun, qe la terre remeyne al creaunceour en fee a ly et a ses heyrs, tut soit issi noté[2] en la chartre del feffement, si[3] le creaunceour moerge avaunt le jour [4]qe la soute soit fete, ses[4] heirs ne porount rien demaunder avaunt le jour, sicum serra dit entre les excepciouns de mort de auncestre. [96.]

15. Et issi pora acrestre fee hors de terme, ausi cum est de pelryn, qi baud sa terre a terme des aunz par tele condicioun, Brac. 20; Fle. 188 (§ 23).

1—1. so *L.* *sim. NSG.* a luy *M.* en lu *A.* 2. mote *M.* 3. qe *M.*
4—4. de la soute ne ses *M.* de sa soute ses *G.* *sim. SABH.*

a term does not take away wardship, but only delays it until a certain time; unless the heir is an idiot, in which case the lord loses his wardship and the farmer his term, until it be otherwise ordained, at least during the life of the idiot. This rule was laid down by the common assent of the great lords of the realm and by the provision of Robert Walrand, in whose heir and the heir of his heir the statute first took effect[r]. Statute of Marlbridge, c. 6, drawn by Robert Walrand.

14. If a gift is made on condition that if the donor shall pay so much at certain days and at a certain place, the gift shall return to the donor, and if not, the land shall remain to the creditor in fee, to him and his heirs; now although it be so expressed in the charter of feoffment, if the creditor dies before the day when the payment should be made, his heirs can demand nothing before the day; as shall be mentioned among the exceptions in Mortdancester. Mortgage. Construction of condition in mortgage.

15. A fee may be made to arise out of a term; as is the case where one going a pilgrimage leases his land for a term of years with this condition, that if he does not return, the Condition to enlarge a term of years to a fee, is valid.

[r] See Coke, Inst. pt. 2. p. 109. Robert Walrand was a Justiciary of the latter part of the reign of Henry III. (Foss, Judges of England, vol. iii. p. 503.)

qe, s'il ne retourne, qe [1]la terre[1] remeigne en fee au termer; tiele condicioun serra touz jours barre al accioun le heyr al pelryn. Et issi peert qe feffement et purchaz porunt estre condicionels ausi bien cum purs et sauntz condicioun.

CHAPITRE VI. [XXXVII.]

De [2]Reversiouns des Eschetes[2].

Brac. 23; Fle 191.

1. Acune foiz retourne purchace al donour, sicum de doun fet pur mariage pur defaute de heyrs, et ausi par fourme de douns; et acune foiz par defaute des heyrs [3]des assignez[3], [4]et ausi par defaute des assignez des assignez[4]. Et pur ceo est mester en chescun bon purchaz, qe le feffement soit fet a aver et a tener al purchaceour et a ses heyrs et a ses assignez et as heyrs [5]et as assignez[5] de ses heyrs et as heyrs et as assignez des assignez. Car si nule mencioun ne soit fete de acuns de ceux, et alienacioun en soit puis fete encountre la fourme del [6]doun, le[6] donour pora aver accioun a la reversioun. Et ausi retourne terre al feffour ou a ses heirs, ou

1—1. *so GMH. sim AR.* le terme *LNS.* 2—2. Reuersiouns *N.* reuersion de eschetes *M. sim. GF.* reuersions e des eschetes *A. sim. HR.* 3—3. *om. AH.* 4—4. *so verb. M. om. NS.* des assignez *om. LGAR.* 5—5. *om M.* 6—6. *so M. so interl. N. om. LAS.* doun au donour le *G.*

land shall remain in fee to the termor; such a condition shall always be a bar to the action of the heir of the pilgrim. And thus it appears that feoffments and purchases may be conditional as well as simple and without condition.

CHAPTER VI.

Of Reversions and Escheats.

Reversion; *per formam doni.*

1. A purchase sometimes reverts to the donor; as is the case with a gift made in marriage, for default of heirs. So likewise by form of gift; and sometimes for want of the words 'heirs of assigns,' and for want of 'assigns of assigns.' It is therefore necessary in every good purchase that the feoffment be made to have and to hold to the purchaser, his heirs and assigns, and to the heirs and assigns of his heirs, and to the heirs and assigns of his assigns. For if no mention is made of any of these, and alienation is afterwards made contrary to the form of the gift, the donor may have his action for the

Proper form of limitation of fee simple.

a ses assignez par fin fete en nostre court, qe ad esté lessé a terme de vie ou des aunz, tut eyt esté le terme mout loung.

2. Et aucun purchaz devient eschete al [1]seignur del fee[1], sicum en cas ou le purchaceour fet felonie dount il soeffre jugement; et ausi ou les purchaceours morgent sauntz heirs; et ausi ou les tenauntz weyvent lour tenementz; en queus cas si les seignurs i mettent les piez en noun de seisine, asset suffit a eus pur seysine pur la proprete qe est a eus descendu, si lour negligence par trop de domure ne les desturbe. Mes s'il se mettent en seysine taunt cum le fee est vacaunt, ou de eynz les iiii. jours apres la vacacioun, s'il soint demorauntz pres, ou de eynz les xv. jours, s'il soint demorauntz loynz, ou plus de terme [2]sicum est dit[2] de suth[3], ou acun autre le face en lour noun, et il en soint puis engitez ou deforcez, il averount recoverer par ceste assise. Et s'il demoerent trop, adounc lour pora le plus grever de engitter les tenauntz, qe de overer par jugement de nostre court. Et pur ceo meuz lour vaut de repurchacer lour dreit par bref de eschaete.

[96 *b*.]

Brac. 23, 23 *b*; Fle. 189.

Brac. 23 *b*; Fle. 192 (§ 2).

Post, c. 13.

1—1. chef seignour *A*. *sim*. *MH*. 2—2. solom ceo qe dit est *AM*. *sim*. *H*. 3. *conj*. sus *LSGM*.

reversion. Land also returns to the feoffor or his heirs, or to his assigns by virtue of a fine levied in our court, when it has been leased for term of life or for years, however long the term may be.

Reversion upon term of life or years.

2. Some purchases escheat to the lord of the fee, as where the purchaser is guilty of felony and undergoes judgment. So also, when the purchasers die without heirs. So, when the tenants abandon their tenements. In these cases, if the lords do but set their foot upon the land in name of seisin, they are sufficiently seised in respect of the proprietary right which descended to them, unless they are barred by negligence on account of too long a delay. But if they put themselves in seisin as soon as the fee is vacant, or within four days after the vacancy, if they are resident near, or within fifteen days if they live at a distance, or within a still longer time as is mentioned below, or any other person does so in their names, and they are afterwards ejected or deforced, they shall have their recovery by this assise. But if they delay too long, it may then be more troublesome to eject the tenants than to proceed by judgment of our court. It is therefore their better course to recover their right by writ of escheat.

Escheat for felony; for default of heirs; by waiver of tenement. Escheats recovered by entry. Laches.

Recovery by writ of escheat.

Brac. 26, 26b; Fle. 192 (§ 5). 3. Et si vileyn ou sokeman face doun et[1] feffement del villenage lour seignurs, ou le baillif le seignur, ou soen fermer, ou autre en qi persone ne se joignent mie les deus dreitz, face doun de autri, ou si femme espousé sa propre chose doigne
[97.] sauntz soen baroun, en mesme la manere pora il reprendre sa seysine, qi qe unques soit tenaunt, deseysour ou soen fitz tut seit il de eynz age, s'il le face par tens; et si noun, adounc ly vaut plus de overer par jugement de noster bref de entré qe par propre force.

CHAPITRE VII. [XXXVIII.]

De Purchaz de Vileyns.

Brac. 24, 25; Fle. 193, 194. 1. Ausi bien se porount vileyns purchaser en cas, cum fraunes hommes. Mes quant qe vileyn neqedent honestement purchace, si il le purchace al oes soen seignur, si il ne face le purchaz de soen seignur, taunt cum soen seignur est en seisine de ly et de ses chateus et de sa sute; issi qe le seignur porra seyser le purchaz soen vileyn tard ou tempre quant il vodera; car nul tens en cel cas ne ly put encoure; et dounc les vileyns

1. ou *AM.*

Gift by person having possession, but not property; 3. If a villain or a sokeman make a gift or feoffment of the villenage of their lords, or if the lord's bailiff or farmer, or other in whose person both rights are not united, make a
or by married woman without her husband. gift of what belongs to another, or if a married woman disposes of her own property without her husband, the seisin
Remedy by entry, may in the same manner be taken back, whoever be tenant, whether the disseisor or his son, and although the latter may be under age, provided it be done in time; but, if not, it is
or writ of entry. then better for him to proceed by judgment of our writ of entry than by his own force.

CHAPTER VII.

Of Purchases by Villains.

Purchase by villain enures to the use of lord. 1. Villains may purchase as well as freemen; but nevertheless whatsoever a villain fairly purchases, he purchases to the use of his lord, unless the purchase be made of the lord, provided that the lord is in seisin of him and of his chattels and of his suit; so that the lord may enter upon the purchase of his villain, later or sooner, as he pleases. For in this case no time runs against him. Villains, therefore, ejected by their

par lour seignurs engettez, de qi fee qe le purchaz soit, ne averount encountre lour seignurs nul recoverer par ceste assise, ne nul autre remedie. Le seignur neqedent pora, apres ceo qe il avera esté seisi del purchaz et de la chartre soen vileyn, doner a soen vilein autre terre a la vaillaunce, ou cele mesmes, a tener en villenage, ou tener la en demeyne [97 *b*.] a remenaunt. Mes adounc iert il tenuz a fere les services [1]qe dues sount al chef seignur[1] del purchaz.

2. Mes si le vileyn face acun purchaz de terre ou de autre tenement de soen seignur meismes, qi li feffe a aver et a tener a ly et a ses heyrs, lequel qe le purchaz soit doné a estre tenu par fraunes services ou par vileins custumes, tut deyve estre fet [2]marché ou[2] redempcioun de char et de saunc pur le tenement, si le seignur engette soen vileyn puis de cel purchaz ou de autre, le purchaceour recovera sa seisine par ceste assise. Car puis qe le seignur voleit en soen feffement qe le vileyn eit heirs, par taunt renuncia il a chescune excepcioun de villenage pur les vileyns services de ceo issauntz, ceo ne ly vaille rien. Car n'est mie tut un a tener fraunchement

Brac. 24; Fle 193.

Ante, l. i. c. 32. s. 3. p. 196.

Brac. 24 *b*; Fle. 193.

1—1. al chief seignur qe duwes sunt *M.* *sim. FH.* 2—2. au marche *M.* *om. FH.* marche[t] e *R.*

lords, in whosesoever fee the purchase may be, shall not recover against their lords by this assise, or have any other remedy. The lord however, after he has been seised of the purchase, and of the charter of his villain, may give to his villain other land to the value, or the same land, to hold of him in villenage, or may thenceforth hold it in demesne. But in this case the lord will be bound to perform the services which are due to the chief lord in respect of such purchase.

Lord may enter and regrant it to villain to hold in villenage.

In that case the lord becomes liable to the chief lord.

2. But if the villain purchases any land or other tenement from his lord himself, who enfeoffs him to have and to hold to him and his heirs, whether the purchase is given to be held by free services or by villain customs, and though there is to be merchet or redemption of flesh and blood for the tenement, yet if the lord afterwards ejects the villain from that or any other purchase, the purchaser shall recover his seisin by this assise. For since the lord intended in his feoffment that the villain should have heirs, he thereby renounced every exception of villenage on account of the villain services issuing therefrom, so that this will avail him nothing. For it is not the

Villain enfeoffed by his lord, to hold to him and his heirs, becomes free, although villain services and even merchet be reserved.

et a tener par fauncs services; car qi qe unqes tiegne a ly et a ses heirs, tut ne tiegne il par fraunc service, ja par taunt ne remeynt qe il ne tiegne fraunchement, ceo est a dire en manere de fraunc homme; et par tel feffement ert le vileyn fraunc, lequel qe homage soit motee[1] ou noun.

Brac. 25; Fle. 194; Hengh. P. c. 8, p. 103.
[98.]
3. Et si aucun vileyn [2]face purchaz[2] a ly et a ses heirs de autre qe soen seignur, et autre del seignur le engitte puis, le vileyn recovera par ceste assise encountre totes gentz for qe vers soen seignur, si le seignur ne soit seisi de ly et de ses chateus et de sa seute, cum est de vileyn defuaunt[3] soen seignur en clamaunt fraunchise par acun title, sicum par clergie ou lounge demure en fraunc estat sauntz cleym de soen seignur, ou par autre title, sicum dit avoms en le chapitre de nayfté. Et dounc si tels vileins moergent [4]en tel estat[4], et [5]lour seignurs deboutent lour heyrs[5], les heirs recoverount[6] par[7] assise de mort de auncestre; car ou assise de novele disseisine se tient en le pere, la assise de mort de auncestre se tendra en soen heyr.

Ante, l. i. c. 32.

1. *so LS.* motie *M.* notee *G.* resceu *AR.* note *H.* 2—2. purchaz tenemenz *M, sim. H.* 3. *so M.* defuaunt *om. LNGS.* deuaunt *AH. sim. RF.* 4—4. *om. F.* 5—5. les seignurs se boutent enz *M.* les seignurs engertent les heirs *G.* lour seignours se botereint en le tenement *AR.* lor seygnors en tel estat les deboutent *F.* les seignurs les deboutent *H.* 6. *so N. sim. AMHF.* recourent *L.* 7. *so AMF.* ceste *add. LN.*

same thing to hold freely, and to hold by free services. For whosoever holds to him and his heirs, although he does not hold by free services, yet it follows not that he does not hold freely, that is, as a freeman. And by such feoffment the villain becomes a freeman, whether homage be expressed or not.

Fugitive villain disseised by stranger may recover by assise.

3. And if a villain purchase tenements to himself and his heirs of any other than his lord, and some other than his lord eject him, the villain may recover by this assise against any person except his lord[a], if the lord be not seised of him, his chattels, and his suit, as in the case of a villain fugitive from his lord, and claiming freedom by any title, as by clergy, or long continuance in a free condition without being claimed by his lord, or by any other title, as has been said in the chapter concerning Naifty. And therefore if such villains die in that condition, and the lords put out their heirs, they shall recover by assise of Mortdancester. For where assise of Novel Disseisin holds in the case of the father, there assise of Mortdancester will lie for his heir.

[a] Some words equivalent to 'and even against his lord' have probably slipped from the text here. See above, l. i. c. 32. s. 7. p. 199; and below, c. 18. s. 2, 3.

4. Et si acun qi soit vileyn a plusours face purchaz a ly et a ses heirs, [1]touz jours tient la seisine, qi qe[1] de ses seignurs primes [2]ly en chacera[2]. Et si touz les seignurs seisisent le purchaz le vileyn a une foiz, adounc soit lour a tenir en commun jekes autaunt qe il eynt departi. Brac. 25 *b*; Fle. 194.

5. Et si le vilein vende en fee le purchaz, qe il avera achaté en fee, eynz ceo qe soen seignur le eit pris et seisi, si le seignur engette le fraunc purchaceour puis sa peysible seisine euwe par le doun le vileyn, le engetté recovera sa seisine par ceste assise, et le seignur ert barree a remenaunt de accioun par sa negligence. Brac. 26 *b*; Fle 194 (§ 3).

6. Et cum acun vileyn defuyaunt soen seignur face purchaz, le seignur ne pora a cel purchaz [3]nule accioun aver, ne nul cleym mettre[3], eynz qe le seignur eit recoveré le vilein et disreyné pur soen; et si rien ly eit tolet, james le vilein a ly respoundra eynz ceo qe il ly eit rendu plenerement terres et chateus trovez hors de soen fee, les queus le seignur ly avera Brac 25 *b*, 26; Fle. 194 (§ 3) [98 *b*.]

1—1. cist iour la seisine qe *M.* *sim. F.* 2—2. les achatera *AR.* le achatera *M.* *sim. F.* le attachera *H.* ly engettera *in a later hand N.* 3—3. nul cleim ne nule accion auer *M.*

4. If one who is villain to more than one lord purchases to himself and his heirs, whichever of his lords shall first oust him may retain the seisin for ever[1]; and if all the lords seize the purchase of the villain at the same time, then let it be theirs to hold in common, until they have divided it. Purchase by villain of more than one lord.

5. If the villain sells in fee the purchase which he has bought in fee, before the lord shall have taken and seized it, and the lord ejects the free purchaser after he has had peaceable seisin of the gift of the villain, the person ejected shall recover his seisin by this assise; and the lord will be for ever after barred of his action by his negligence. Villain can convey a good title to a purchaser.

6. When any villain who is a fugitive from his lord makes a purchase, the lord cannot have any action or set up any claim against this purchase, until he has recovered and established his right to the villain. And if he has taken anything from him, the villain need never answer his demand, until he has fully restored to him the land and the chattels found out of his fee, Lord must recover a fugitive villain before recovering his land; and must restore him his property be-

[1] 'When several parceners are seised of a villain, if he purchase in the name of one parcener, the property accrues to that parcener; if in the name of all, to all; if in his own name, the one who enters may hold it, and the others are without recovery. For if the purchase of a villain be aliened before the entry of the lord, no advantage can accrue to him.' (Note in MS. *N.*) The several cases are similarly distinguished by Bracton, f. 25 *b*.

tolet, pur les paroles qe sount el bref, ovek ses chateus et tote sa sute. Car si le vileyn ne fust plenerement restoré et seisi, si sereynt les paroles del bref weyveez et noster comaundement veyn, de maunder a fere aver a un homme chose dount il est mesmes seisi. Mes cum il avera disreyné le cors, adounc pora il par jugement et par dreit seiser terres et chateus et tut le purchaz soen vileyn.

CHAPITRE VIII. [xxxix.]

De Chartres.

Ante, li. i. c. 29.

1. Dit est de sus [1]de dette en soen chapitre[1] qe v.[2] garnemenz ount mester en les obligaciouns; et mesmes les garnemenz ount mester en douns et en purchaz. Et quant al garnement de escrit, qe hom apele chartre, fet a saver qe en moutz des maneres sount chartres, sicum chartres [3]des rois, et chartre de privé persone[3]; et des chartres des rois sount acuns simples, acuns de communauté, et acuns de universeté.

Brac. 33 *b*; Fle. 195.

1—1. so *LN*. el chapitre de dette *GS*. *sim*. *MHF*. en le chapitre de plee de dette *AR*. 2. so *G*. cink *M*. eynz qe *LN*. *sim*. *AF*. *om*. *SH*. 3—3. de Reis e de princes e chartres de autres persones *M*.

fore recovering him by writ.

which his lord has taken from him. This is by reason of the words in writ, 'with his chattels and all his suit.' For if the villain was not fully reinstated, and put in possession of the same, the words of the writ would be thrown away, and our precept would be vain, in commanding a man to be put in possession of a thing of which he is himself seised. But when he has proved his title to the person, then he may by judgment and by law seize the lands and chattels and all the purchase of his villain.

CHAPTER VIII.

Of Charters.

Charters, royal and private.

1. It has been said above in the chapter concerning Debt that it is necessary for an obligation to be clothed in five different ways. The same clothing is also necessary for gifts and purchases. And as to that clothing by writing, which is called Charter, it must be understood that there are several kinds of charters, as charters of kings and charters of private persons; and of the king's charters some are single, some common, some

Et des chartres simples sount acuns de peur feffement et simple, et acuns de feffement condicionel, acuns de con- [99.] fermement, et acuns de quiteclemaunce.

2. Les chartres simples de peur feffement sauntz condicioun deyvent demorer oveke les purchaceours et lour heyrs; et les condicioneles deyvent estre doubles ou trebles endenteez; si qe la une partie remeigne al donour enselé par[1] le purchaceour, et la autre partie deit demorer [2]ove le[2] purchaceour et a ses heirs enselé del seal le donour, et la terce partie soit mis en owele meyn, issi qe nul par proces de tens demaunde dreit en acune chose par fourme de doun et par condicioun for qe nostre court puse estre certifié de la fourme par la chartre. Car nule accioun ne nule excepcioun ne vaut, si ele ne peuse estre prové; ne[3] de prier [4]de la court qe la[4] adverse partie soit aforcé de moustrer escrit ne vaut rien; car nul n'est tenu de armer soen adversarie. Brac. 33 *b*; Fle. 196.

3. Les chartres des rois, lequel qe eles soint alowables ou Brac. 34; Fle. 196 (§ 4).

1. del seal le *A.* *sim. M.* 2—2. al *AM.* 3. ne *om. M.* 4—4. so *G.* qe la Court del *LNAM.* *sim. HF.*

universal. Of simple charters, some are of pure feoffment and single, others of conditional feoffment; some are charters of confirmation, and some of quitclaim[u].

2. Single charters of pure feoffment without condition ought to remain with the purchasers and their heirs. Conditional charters ought to be indented in two or three parts, so that one part sealed by the purchaser may remain with the donor, and another part sealed with the seal of the donor may remain with the purchaser and his heirs, and the third part be put into an impartial hand[x], so that no one may afterwards demand a right in anything by form of gift or by condition, but that our court may be certified of the form by the charter. For no action or exception avails unless it can be proved, and it is useless to pray the court that the adverse party may be compelled to produce a deed, because no one is obliged to arm his adversary. Single charters, and charters indented. Custody of charters. A party to an action not compelled to produce his deed.

3. As to royal charters, whether they are allowable, or Adjudication of royal char-

u This is from Bracton; but there is some confusion arising from the equivocal use of the word *simple*. The word *privata* is similarly employed in Bracton to denote, on the one hand, a charter made by a private person; and on the other, one granted by the king to an individual, in distinction from one granted to a community or to the entire kingdom.

x Bracton advises, that the deed should be either in two parts, or, if in one, should be deposited *in æqua manu*. Bracton, f. 33 *b*. So Fleta, 196 (§ 2).

fauses [1]ou doutouses[1], nul ne put juger for qe nous. Car a celi est respoundre et de juger qi en fu auctour; et pur ceo voloms qe a nous[2] soint les dotaunces et[3] les deloyaunces moustrez[4], et qe par nous soint fetes les interpretisouns.

Brac. 34 b; Fle. 196 (§ 5). [99 b.]

4. Et suffit en les douns simples a taunt dire. Sachent touz ceux qi sount et[5] a venir sount, qe jeo Johan ay doné a Pieres taunt de terre ove les apurteynaunces en tiele ville; et bon est de especefier par entre queles devises; et ne covendra mie a dire a Pierres et a ses heirs, si Pieres voille purchacer a ly fee et fraunc tenement, mes les heirs serount especifiez apres, issi: a aver et a tener a mesme celi Pieres et a ses heirs; et ausi ne covendra [6]mie a dire, graunte et conferme[6], tut le eit hom en usage a dire issint; ne ja ne covendra dire, pur homage [7]ne pur[7] service, si le contract ne le voille. Car coment qe homage ou service soit noté en la chartre, ja pur ceo ne deperira riens al chief seignur del fee. Acune gent neqedent le porrount fere en [8]eschaunge de[8] feez, sicum [9]en feffaunt[9] par feffement de usage[10] de chivalerie, et en tiel

Stat. West. 3. (18 Ed I.), c. 1; Fle. 198 (§ 9).

1—1. *so M.* *so corr. R.* ou dount *LNA.* *sim. S.* desconuz *H.* *om. G.* 2. nul ne *M.* 3. ne *M.* 4. forqe a nous *add. M.* 5. qi *add. NA* ceus qe *add. M.* *sim. H.* 6—6. *so verb. MH.* *sim. GA.* mie grauntee et confermee *LN.* 7—7. e *M.* 8—8. *so LNG.* chalenge des *ARH.* chaunge dez *M.* change de *SF.* 9—9. *om. H.* en fesaunt *G.* 10. homage *G.*

ters belongs to the king.

false or doubtful, can be adjudged by none but ourselves. For it is the office of the author to determine and judge concerning them. Wherefore we will that such doubts and illegalities be referred to none but ourselves, and that all interpretations be made by us.

Common form of a gift of land.

4. In single gifts it is sufficient to say thus: 'Know all men present and to come that I, John, have given to Peter so much land with the appurtenances in such a town;' and it is proper to specify between what boundaries. And it is not necessary to say, 'to Peter and his heirs,' where Peter intends to purchase fee and frank tenement, but the heirs will be specified afterwards, thus: 'To have and to hold to the same Peter and his heirs.' Neither is it necessary to say, 'grants and confirms,' though it is usual to do so; nor is there occasion to say, 'for homage,' nor 'for service,' if it is not intended by the contract; for however homage or service are expressed in the charter, yet the chief lord of the fee shall not lose anything. Some persons however may do so in an exchange of

Parcels. Habendum. Reservation of homage.

cas fet bien a especifier le homage en les feffementz. Les apurteynaunces sount nomez ausi bien pur corporeles choses, sicum hameletz apurteynauntz as chiefs maners, ou commune de pasture ou de turberie ou de pescherie, ou autres, sicum choses nient corporeles, cum sount fraunchises et servages de tenementz. Et puis issi: a aver et a tener la avauntdite terre ove les apurtenaunces a mesme celi Pieres et a ses heirs, fesaunt de ceo as chiefs seignurs del fee les services qe apent[1]. Et fet a saver qe mout necessarie clause est a especefier les services, en noumbre, et en quantité, et en qualité, et a queles persones il sount duwes, issi qe les seignurs del fee ne autres ne pusent demaunder for qe dreit, qe les feffours ne soint especiaument obligez a aquiter et a defendre les purchaceours. Et dounc issi: pur touz services custumes et demaundes. Et si le doun soit fet a terme de vie ou a terme des aunz outre, ou en mariage, ou par fee taillee, ou par condicioun, adounc soit la condicioun especifié en la chartre endenté, sicum de sus est dit.

Fle. 199 (§ 11). Brac. 35; Fle. 197 (§ 7). [100.] Fle. 197 (§ 7).

1. apendent *AM.* *sim.* *GH.*

seigniories[y], as in making a feoffment by custom of knight's service; and in such case it is proper to specify the homage in the feoffment. Appurtenances are named to include both corporeal things, such as hamlets appurtenant to chief manors, and common of pasture, turbary, fishery, or the like; and things incorporeal, as franchises, and servitudes of tenements. Then follows: 'to have and to hold the aforesaid land with the appurtenances, to the same Peter and his heirs, doing therefore to the chief lords of the fee the services thereto belonging.' And it should be understood, that it is a very necessary clause to specify the service by number, quality, and quantity, and to what persons they are due, so that neither the lords of the fee nor any other may demand more than right, without the feoffors being specially obliged to acquit and defend the purchasers. Then follows: 'for all services, customs, and demands.' And if the gift is made for term of life, or for term of years over, or in marriage, or in fee tail, or upon condition, the condition shall be specified in the charter indented, as above mentioned.

Homage, when specified. **Appurtenances, what.** **Habendum.** **Services by which land is held should be specified.** **Limitation a condition.**

y There is a difficulty in the interpretation of this passage, which I confess I cannot clear up. The full effect of the statute *Quia emptores terrarum*, recently passed at the time when this book was composed, does not appear to have been understood. See p. 236, note.

Stat. West. 3. (18 Ed.I.) c.1.

5. Et ne covendra mie en les purs feffementz a dire, a tener del donur et de ses heirs; car ja par taunt ne remeyndra qe le purchaceour n'iert tenaunt le seignur del fee en chief sauntz meen. Et estre ceo ne covendra mie a dire, fraunchement quitement[1] bien et en pes; car celes paroles sount plus del [2]bon estre[2] qe de la substaunce de la besoygne; neqedent, tut i seynt celes paroles mises, eles ne grevent nient. En dreit de tenement doné pur mariage assetz suffit la fourme et la issue pur chartre; chartre neqedent ne greve rien.

Brac. 35; Fle. 197 (§ 5).

Brac. 37 b; Fle 197 (§ 6).

6. Et a la foiz put homme enlarger le doun et acune foiz estrescer[3]. Enlarger en ceste manere: a aver et a tenir al avauntdit Pieres et a ses heirs et a ses assignez; et acune foiz plus, issi: et as heirs et as assignez des assignez; estrescer,
[100 b.] issi: de tener jekes autaunt qe jeo [4]ly rende x. ou jekes a taunt qe jeo[4] ou mes heirs ly rendoms x.; ou issi: jekes autaunt qe jeo ou mes heirs ou mes assignez rendoms a Pieres ou a ses heirs ou a ses assignez; et en autre manere issi: a tener a ly et a ses heirs sauntz fere alienacioun, ou sauntz

1. so *GS*. qe il tiegnent *L*. *sim*. *NM*. tenir *AR*. 2—2. bien estre *M*. 3. so *NG*. especifier [estrescer *interlin. contemp.*] *L*. especifier *SAR*. *sim*. *MH*. 4—4. so *N*. *sim*. *GAMF*. *om*. *LS*.

Tenendum of the donor and his heirs, void in a gift in fee.

5. In absolute feoffments it is not proper to say, 'to hold of the donor and of his heirs;' for whatever be said, it will not follow but that the purchaser will become tenant to the lord of the fee, in chief without mesne. And beyond this there is no occasion to say, 'freely, quietly, well, and in peace.' For these words belong rather to the form than to the substance of the business; but if such words are put in, they are harmless. With respect to tenements given in marriage, the form and issue supply the place of a charter; nevertheless a charter does no harm.

For gift in marriage, no charter necessary.

Qualified gifts.

6. Sometimes a gift may be enlarged, sometimes restricted. It may be enlarged in this manner: 'to have and to hold to the aforesaid Peter, his heirs, and assigns;' and sometimes further thus: 'and to the heirs and assigns of his assigns.' It may be restricted as follows: 'to hold until I pay him ten pounds,' or 'until I or my heirs pay him ten pounds,' or 'until I or my heirs or assigns pay Peter or his heirs or assigns.' In another way thus: 'to hold to him and his heirs without making alienation,' or 'without making alienation to such a

Alienation restrained.

fere alienacioun a celi, ou for qe a celui; ou issi a tener a tote la vie Pieres, et apres soen desces revertise le doun a Thomas et a ses heirs issauntz de luy, et s'il ne eit point de teus heirs, adounc retourne la chose a Theobaud et a ses heirs et a ses assignez. [1]Et en touz teus cas voloms nous qe les voluntez as donours soient tenuz taunt avaunt cum ley et dreit le pora suffrer. Stat. West. 2. (13 Ed.I.)c.1.

7. Et fet a saver qe nul feffour n'est tenu de aquiter soen fee de contribucioun fere del fiz eynzné le seignur fere chivaler ne de sa fille eynzné marier, ne de eyde de viscounte, ne de communs amerciementz ou fins del counté ne de hundred, ne de sutes dues al Counté ne al Hundred ou aylours, par la generale clause de acquitaunce. Chescun neqedent se pora obliger de aquiter soen purchaceour de trestouz ces services par especiale clause, et en teles obligaciouns vaillent les brefs de meen. Brac. 36b, 37; Fle. 198 (§ 9).

8. Et puis i ad: et jeo et mes heirs garraunterom le tenement ove les apurteynaunces acquiteroms et defenderoms al avauntdit Pieres et a ses heyrs et a ses assignez[1] a touz jours. Et ceste clause de warrauntie pora estre plus large Brac. 37 (§ 10); Fle. 197 (§ 6), 199 (§ 10, 11).

1—1. *The whole of this passage is omitted in HB. and in the printed copies.*

one,' or 'except to such a one,' or thus, 'to hold during the life of Peter, and after his decease that the gift revert to Thomas and the heirs issuing from him, and if he has no such heirs, then return to Theobald, his heirs and assigns.' And in all these cases we will that the intention of the donor be observed, so far forth as law and right will allow. **Remainders.** **Intention of donor to be observed.**

7. It must be understood that no feoffor is bound by the general clause of acquittance to acquit the fee from making contribution for the knighting of the lord's eldest son, or the marrying of his eldest daughter, nor from sheriff's aid, nor from common amercements or fines of the county or hundred, nor from suits due to the county or hundred court or elsewhere. Any one, however, may by a special clause bind himself to acquit his purchaser from all these services, and such obligations are enforced by writs of mesne. **General clause of acquittance, its construction.** **Writ of Mesne.**

8. Then there is the clause, 'And I and my heirs will warrant the tenement with the appurtenances, and will acquit and defend the same to the aforesaid Peter, his heirs and assigns for ever.' And this clause of warranty may be more full thus: 'his heirs **Clause of warranty, and acquittance.**

issi : a ses heirs et a ses assignez [1]et as assignez[1] des assignez. Et pur ceo vaillent en plusours cas as purchaceours de prendre vers eus les chartres[2] de lour feffours, issint qe si[3] lour feffours ne eynt rien dount il porrount garraunter si mester soit, qe les purchaceours par les chartres lour feffours pusent voucher a garraunt les feffours de lour feffours; a queus[4] voucher nous voloms qe il soint resceuz par quei qe trové soit qe la garrauntie des premers feffours se estende a la garrauntie sauntz meen. Aquitaunce et defense i sount mis pur ceo qe celuy de qi le purchaceour deit tenir en chief ly soit obligé de aquiter et a defendre, si nul seignur, sovereyn ou autre, ly voille demaunder autre service [5]qe le
[101.] purchaceour ne devera[5] al seignur de qi le purchaceour tient en chief.

Fle.204(§17). 9. Quant a chartre de confermement et de quiteclemaunce, voloms qe chescun sache qe tieles chartres fetes hors

1—1. *so NAR.* *om. LGMHF.* 2. *so NARMF.* chapitres *L.* 3. *so NMF.* si *om. LAR.* 4. quel *NG.* *sim. ARM.* 5—5. *so verb. NR.* qe purchaz ne dorra *L.* *sim. F.* qe le purchaz ne deuera *MH.* *sim. GS.* qe le purchaz[ceor] ne deuera *A.*

Warranty by feoffors of feoffors. and assigns and the assigns of his assigns.' And by reason of this clause it is useful in many cases for purchasers to take to themselves the charters of their feoffors, so that if the feoffors have nothing whereby they can warrant if need be, then the purchasers by virtue of the charters of their feoffors may vouch to warrant the feoffors of their feoffors, to which voucher they shall be admitted wheresoever it is found that the warranty of the first feoffors extends to warranty without mesne. Object of the clause of acquittance. Acquittance and defence are inserted to the intent that the person of whom the purchaser is to hold in chief may be obliged to acquit and defend him[z], in case any lord paramount or other should demand of him other services than the purchaser shall owe to the lord, of whom the purchaser holds in chief.

Charters of confirmation and quitclaim. 9. As to charters of confirmation and of quitclaim, let every one know that such charters made between persons out of

[z] This sentence appears to imply that the purchaser will hold of the donor, who promises to acquit and defend him, and therefore to be inapplicable to the law as altered by the statute *Quia emptores terrarum.* (18 Ed. I. c. 1.)

de possessioun de acun dreit rien ne vaillent, si qe les [1]auctours soint severez[1] del dreit de la possessioun ou del dreit de la propreté. Et pur ceo est bone cautele pur ceux qi fount fere chartres, qe date soit mise[2] del leu et del an.

10. Et puis soint apelez tesmoignes de fraunces veisins en qi presence la chartre soit leuwe et enselé, et les nouns des tesmoignes soint[3] escritz en la chartre. Et bone cautele serroit de procurer qe les seals des testmoignes fuissent mis ove[4] le seal le seignur del fee, ou en presence des parties de fere enrouller la chartre en court qe porte record. Et tut ne soint mie les testmoignes appellez, suffit neqedent si le fet soit puis devaunt eus recordé et graunté. Et si le feffour ne eit point de seal, assetz suffist un seal de apromt. Et plusours purchaz sount ou nule chartre ne ad mester, sicum dreit jugement de nostre court, par rendre, [5]par relesser et quiteclamer[5], et par

Brac. 38; Fle. 199 (§13).

Brac. 38; Fle. 200.

Brac. 33 *b*, (§1).

1—1. *so verb. ARMF.* attournez soint surz *L.* autres [actions *interl.*] soint seuerez *N.* attournez seient formez *G.* atturneez seyent surry *S.* 2. del iour *add. NAM. sim. F.* 3. luz e *add. MF. sim. H.* 4. e *MF.* 5—5. *so verb. M.* relessour et quiteclameour *L. sim. SARF.* relees ou par quitclamer *N.* relesse par quiteclamaunce *G.*

seisin of any right are of no avail, where the parties to them are divested of the right of possession or the right of property[a]. Therefore it is a good precaution for those who are having charters prepared, to take care that the date of the place and of the year be inserted.

Date.

10. Afterwards let some of the neighbours who are freemen be called as witnesses, in whose presence the charter should be read and sealed, and the names of the witnesses should be written in the charter. It would also be a good precaution to procure the seals of the witnesses to be affixed, together with the seal of the lord of the fee; or in the presence of the parties to have the charter enrolled in a court of record. And although the witnesses be not called, it is sufficient if the deed be afterwards recorded and acknowledged before them. If the feoffor has no seal of his own, a borrowed seal will be sufficient. There are many modes of purchase in which no charter is required; as by lawful judgment of our court; by surrender;

Witnesses.

Execution.

Concurrence of lord of the fee.

Enrollment of deed.

Borrowed seal.

Conveyance without charter.

a This passage appears to be taken from Fleta, where, however, the text is scarcely less obscure. I understand the meaning to be, that, in order to give validity to a charter of confirmation, the confirmee must be in possession, and the confirmor must have the right of property.

defaute, et par assignement de dowarie, et par engendrure[1] par la ley de Engleterre, et en plusours autres maneres.

Brac. 38, 38 *b*; Fle. 200. 11. Et pur ceo qe, tut soit chartre fete et testmoignes appelez, et enselé en lour presence, ne vaut uncore rien quant qe [2]en est[2] fet et purparlé, si bail de la seysine ne soit fet par

[101 *b*.] le donour al purchaceour, fet[3] un poi a dire de induccioun de seysine, coment hom deit seysine deliverer, et coment les purchaceours la deyvent receyvere, et de queles choses hom peut tauntost mettre homme en seisine, et de queles nule enduccioun de seisine ne est ja mester.

CHAPITRE IX. [XL.]

De Seisines[4].

Brac. 38 *b*; Fle. 200. 1. Pur ceo qe le graunter ne le otreyer del donour ne suffist mie generaulment as purchaceours, si la possessioun ne sue, des possessiouns fet[5] a saver, qe possessioun proprement est seisine et tenir[6] de acune chose par cors et par volunté oveke

1. *so MF.* et *add. L.* *sim. NR.* 2—2. *so NS.* est en *L.* est *GARMH.* 3. *so GMS.* Ceo est *L.* E fet *NH.* *sim. AR.* 4. e des possessions *add. AR.* 5. *so NARMH.* fet *om. L.* 6. tenaunce *N.* tenour *R.*

by release and quitclaim; by default; by assignment of dower;

Estate by the curtesy. by having issue by the law of England; and by several other ways.

Necessity of livery of seisin. 11. But inasmuch as, although a charter is made, witnesses called, and the deed sealed in their presence, yet whatever has been done and said avails nothing unless livery of seisin be

Subject of the next chapter. made by the donor to the purchaser, we must therefore say somewhat concerning induction into seisin, how seisin ought to be delivered, and how purchasers ought to receive it, of what things a man may be put into seisin immediately, and of what not until a certain time; and of what things induction into seisin is unnecessary.

CHAPTER IX.

Of Seisins.

Definition of seisin or possession. 1. Forasmuch as the mere grant and authorization of the donor is not in general sufficient for purchasers, unless possession follows, with respect to possessions it must be understood, that possession is properly the seisin and holding of

la propreté[1]. De totes choses[2] neqedent ne put hom mie communement retenir possessioun ne seisine. Car des choses nient corporeles ne put estre fet nul bail, ne nule seisine proprement sauntz chose corporele; usage neqedent par prescripcioun de tens done [3]acune foiz[3] title de dreit.

2. Bail et induccioun de seisine est greable translacioun Brac. 39 b, 40; Fle. 200, 201. de chose corporele propre ou autri de la seisine le verrey seignur jekes en la persone del purchaceour, lequel qe le seignur face la translacioun en sa propre persone ou [4] autre de par ly par lettres patentes le seignur a cest atourné et Fle. 201. assigné; les queles lettres ount mester de estre doubles, dount [102.] la une remeigne au procuratour et le autre au purchaceour.

3. Et cum acun bail de seysine deit estre fet, en primes Brac. 41 b; Fle. 201, 202. covendra al donour remuer totes ses choses moebles qe il ad en le tenement, [5]et femme et enfauntz et sa meyné tote, si qe il ne eit rien[5], qe le soen soit, qe il ne eit remué ou vendu ou lessé a ferme, issi qe nule presumpcioun[6] puse estre [7]qe le

1. des cors *add. N.* del cors *add. F.* 2. so *NARM.* choses *om. LH.* 3—3. e le fiez *M.* *sim. H.* acune foiz suffisaunt *N.* *sim. AR.* 4. par *add. AMH.* 5—5. femme ne enfaunz ne rien de sa meignee issi qe riens ne i soit *M.* 6. prescripcioun *MGS.* *sim. F.* 7—7. so *N.* qe le donour vouche *LGSAR.* e si le donour voile *M.* e ke le donour vouche *F.*

anything in fact and in intention, together with the property. There are some things however of which one cannot commonly Of what things seisin is possible. retain possession or seisin; for of things incorporeal there can be no delivery; nor any proper seisin without a corporeal substance. But usage by long prescription supplies in time a legal title.

2. Livery and induction of seisin is a voluntary translation Livery of seisin; of a corporeal thing belonging to the person transferring it or to another, from the seisin of the true owner to the person of the purchaser, whether the owner transfers it in person, or by livery by attorney. another on his behalf attorned and appointed by his letters patent. Such letters should be in duplicate, one to remain with the attorney, the other with the purchaser.

3. When any livery of seisin is to be made, the donor should Vacation of possession by donor. first remove all his movable things which he has in the tenement, and his wife and children and all his family, so that there be nothing of his which he has not either removed or sold or let to farm, so that there may be no presumption that the donor

donour voille[7] rien retener; [1]car taunt cum il ad volunté de retener[1], ne crest james fraunc tenement al purchaceour.

Brac. 41 *b*; Fle. 202. 4. Mes si le donour voide le tenement de cors et de volunté et [2]baud la seisine al purchaceour, qi la receit[2] de cors et de volunté et issi la retient, tauntost acrest al purchaceour fraunc tenement, et fee, si en fee le eit purchacé, par soulement mettre le pié el tenement par le dreit [3]et la unité les[3] voluntez, [4]qe se joignent[4], del verrei seignur, en qi persone furent joyntz les deus dreitz et la seisine, et del purchaceour, qi les deus dreitz et la seisine receit. Dunc, si acun engettast le purchaceour tauntost apres le doun, si recovereit par ceste assise cum soen fraunc tenement, tut ne en eust il pris point espleiz par la seisine. (Brac. 40; Fle. 201.) Car ne us ne espleiz ne sount mie de la substaunce del doun, eynz countrevalent a la declaracioun et al testmoinage de la seisine. Et cum le purchaceour avera issi ewe la seisine par cors et par volunté,

[102 *b*.] mes sauntz les deus [5]ne la pora perdre[5] qe il [6]ne la[6] recovere.

1—1. *om. M.* 2—2. quant le purchaceour auera resceu la seisine *NAR.* quant a seisine le purchasur qe la receit *M.* 3—3. a la vente les *LS.* e la vnite e les *M.* e la vente les *GF.* *sim. AR.* 4—4. *so verb. MW.* qi ceo iugement *L.* qe vient *N.* ke si iugement *F.* *om. AR.* 5—5. *so verb. S.* ne le pora prendre *L.* ne les purra perdre *NAR.* *sim. M.* dreitz purra il perdre *H.* dreiz ne porra perdre *F.* 6—6. nelles *M.*

intends to retain anything. For as long as he has any intention of retaining, no freehold ever accrues to the purchaser.

Effect of a valid livery of seisin. 4. But if the donor vacates the tenement in fact and in intention, and delivers the seisin thereof to the purchaser, who receives it in fact and in intention, and so keeps it, a freehold, and fee (if the purchase be in fee) immediately accrue to the purchaser, by only setting his foot in the tenement, by virtue of the right, and of the union of wills which are joined, to wit, of the true owner in whose person both the right and the seisin were united, and of the purchaser who receives both the right and the seisin. Therefore, if any one ejected the purchaser from the land immediately after the gift, he should recover it by this assise as his freehold, although he had not taken any esplees, by virtue of the seisin. (Esplees are only evidence of seisin.) For neither user nor esplees are of the substance of the gift, but are equivalent to a declaration and evidence of seisin. And whereas the purchaser will thus have had the seisin in deed and in intention, so without both act and intention he can never so lose it, as not to be able to recover it.

5. Mes si acun fermer eit terme en tele terre, qi n'en soit point engetté, ne attourné au purchaceour, si le donour[1] pendaunt cel terme devie, soen heir recovera [2]la terre par la continuaunce[2] de la seisine le termer, qi occupa la seisine en noun del donour. Et pur ceo ne put nule seisine estre a dreit liveré, si noun par jugement de nostre court, ou taunt cum la seisine seit voide. Et ausi recovera le heir en cas ou le fermer ad usé seisine oveke le purchaceour, pur ceo qe le purchaceour ne out onques pesible seisine en la vie del donour. Mes si le fermer se tourne al purchaceour, tut teigne il avaunt soen terme, mes qe il [3]eit regehi a tener[3] del purchaceour, ja par taunt [4]dounc n'est[4] le doun meyns vaillant; car en tel cas poent[5] bien estre ensemble feffement et terme en diverses persones. Brac. 41, 41 b.

6. Et cum le donour rien ne eit en le tenement, et le tenement soit princepal maner ou mies, adounc suffit al donour en presence de frauncs veisins testmoignauntz[6] et de tenauntz a deliverer al purchaceour la seisine par le haspe [7]ou par le anel[7] del uihs, ou par encousture[8] de la porte, et Brac. 40; Fle. 201 (§ 5).

1. *so NAMHF.* donaunt *L.* 2—2. *so NAMHF.* sa terre pur la conisaunce *L.* 3—3. *conj.* eit reguhe *L.* renie a tener *N.* le ereguhe *S.* recouere *G.* le reioie a tenir *AR.* le teigne *MH.* *sim. W.* tiene *F.* 4—4. nen est *M.* dunke est *A.* nest *SGH.* 5. *so N.* *sim. AR.* poeint *L.* poet *M.* purra *H.* 6. temoignes *M.* 7—7. *om. ARW.* 8. enclosture *NARHW.* encusture *M.*

5. But where any farmer has a term in the land, and is neither ejected nor attorns to the purchaser, if the donor dies during that term, his heir may recover the land by reason of the continuance of the seisin of the termor, who occupied it in the name of the donor. Wherefore no seisin can be legally delivered, except by judgment of our court, unless while the seisin be vacant. The heir also shall recover seisin in case the seisin of the farmer has continued with that of the purchaser, inasmuch as the purchaser never had peaceable seisin in the lifetime of the donor. But if the farmer attorns to the purchaser, although he continues to hold his term, provided he has admitted that he holds of the purchaser, the gift is not thereby of less validity; for in such case the feoffment and term may well exist together in different persons.

Effect of retention of possession by farmer without attornment.

Attornment by farmer.

6. Where there is nothing of the donor's in the tenement, and the tenement is a principal manor or mansion, there it is enough for the donor in the presence of some free neighbours as witnesses, and of some of the tenants, to deliver seisin to the purchaser by the hasp or ring of the door, or by

Livery of seisin of capital manor, or mansion.

par taunt n'iert mie le purchaceour soulement seisi del mies mes de quant qe est nomé en la chartre qe fust proprement al donour annex al mies, sicum demeynes, et rentes, et boys, et
[103] preez, et pastures, et autres fraunes tenementz. Mes si acun vileyn eit fet fraunc purchaz, dount le donour ne eit mie esté seisi, de teu purchaz n'en est mie le purchaceour tauntost
Brac. 40; Fle. 201 (§ 5.) seisi. Et si la seisine deive estre fete de tenement ou nul mies ne est, adounc suffit le bail par une verge ou par un gaunt par bon tesmoignage.

Brac. 41 *b*; Fle. 202 (§ 9). 7. Et fet a saver, qe le fraunc tenement ne [1]se porroit james valer[1] al purchaceour eynz ceo qe il [2]soit esteins el[2] donour, for qe par lounge et peisible seysine; [3]ne rien[3] ne porra destourber qe le fraunc tenement ne remeygne en une des deus persones; dount en la persone le donour porra le fraunc tenement demorer par cas, tut voille le donour qe le fraunc tenement et le dreit soit translaté jekes en la persone
Brac. 42; Fle. 202 (§ 10). le purchaceour, et tut ly eit le donour mis de ceo en seisine, sicum par sa meyné et par chateus, qe demurent el tenement,

1—1. se prent iames *NARMHW*. *sim. F.* perist iames *G.* ceo pit̃ iammes *S.* 2—2. soit esteynt en le *N.* *sim. AR.* seit esters̃ al *M.* seit al *F.* 3—3. *so NA. sim. RMF.* *om. L.*

shutting the gate; and thereby the purchaser becomes seised not only of the mansion, but of whatsoever was named in the charter and was properly the donor's, annexed to the mansion, as demesnes, rents, woods, meadows, pastures, and other frank
Purchase of villain does not pass without seisin. tenements. But if a villain of the donor has made a free purchase, of which the donor has never been seised, the purchaser does not immediately become seised of such purchase.
Livery of seisin by rod or glove. If seisin is to be made of a tenement where there is no house, then sufficient livery is made by a rod or by a glove in the presence of good witnesses.

The donor must entirely part with the seisin. 7. It is to be understood, that the freehold never validly attaches to the purchaser until it is extinct in the donor, except by long and peaceable seisin. Nor can anything prevent the freehold from remaining in one of the two persons, and it may happen to remain in the person of the donor, although the donor may intend that the freehold and right should be transferred to the person of the purchaser, and
Presumption arising from persons or things left in the tenement. although he may put the purchaser in seisin thereof,—as by his family or chattels remaining in the tenement, which

par quei presumpcioun overe pur les heirs le donour en tel cas, qe le donour retient le fee et le fraunc tenement en volunté, coment qe il moustra autrement par colour de fet; et en quel cas, si le purchaceour soit engitté par le heir le donour, il ne recovera mie par ceste assise, par la resoun qe le donour ne se demist pas pleynement en sa vie, et pur ceo qe le purchaceour trova le tenement pleyn et le donour tous jours en seisine par ses chateus et par sa meyné; car par la continuaunce de la seisine piert bien qe le donour ne voleit mie [103 *b*.] departer del fraunc tenement. Mes si [1]les chateus i soint emblez[1] [2]ou autrement perduz[2], et comaundé soit as baillifs le donour et as serjauntz par le donour, qe de cel jour en avaunt mes ne demurent[3] qe il ne soint entendauntz al purchaceour cum al seignur del tenement, en tiel cas ne ad nule presumpcioun, qe le donour eit rien en volunté de retener. Et ausi si le donour ne eit mie [4]a gré estable[4], qe acun de sa meyné ne ren de soen chatel remeigne en le tenement en soen noun.

Brac. 42; Fle. 202 (§ 10, 11).

1—1. *conj.* le purchaceour si li soint [chateus *interlin.*] embles *L.* les chatels le purchaceour soint embleez *N.* *sim. A R.* le purchasour se seit mis en seisine par *G.* le purchaceour se seint emblez *S.* le purchasur si i soent emblez *M.* le porchasours si seyent embles *F.* les biens le porchaceor seyent emblez *W.* les chateux del donour seient emblees *var. read. in Wingate.* 2—2. *om. G.* 3. so *ARMH.* et *add. LN.* 4—4. a gre ne estable *NSGARMH.*

creates a presumption in favour of the heirs of the donor, that the donor retained the fee and freehold in intention, although he made it otherwise appear by colour of deed. And in such case if the purchaser be ejected by the heir of the donor, he shall not recover by this assise, by reason that the donor did not wholly divest himself in his lifetime, but the purchaser found the tenement full, and the donor always in seisin by his chattels and family; for by the continuance of the seisin it appears that the donor did not intend to part with the freehold. But if the chattels be stolen or otherwise lost upon the tenement, and the bailiffs and servants of the donor are ordered by him from that day forward not to remain there, unless to wait upon the purchaser as owner of the tenement, in such case there is no presumption that the donor meant to retain anything. So if it was not by the donor's consent or allowance that any of his family or of his chattels remained in the tenement in his name.

How this presumption may be rebutted.

Brac. 44; Fle. 203.

8. Mes si un homme ou une beste demure de part le donour en le tenement doné, assetz par taunt retient il la seysine ausi bien cum par plusours; sicum est del feffour, qi doune commune de pasture qe il ad, et jalemeyns fet pestre la commune par une beste, car par cele une beste retient le donour tote la commune; ausi [1]cum cist retient[1] [2]la rente[2] par mi la meyn de un tenaunt, dount plusours tenauntz sount tenuz a rendre en commun, et la quele rente le seignur ad vendue, et jalemeyns [3]receit le seignur[3] de un des parceners, sicum avaunt est dit. (Fle. 202 (§ 11).) Et pur ceo qe teles presumpciouns sount prejudicieles, covent qe en chescun dreit baill soit la possessioun purement voide ences qe le fraunc tenement se puse aherdre al purchaceour par le baill.

[104.] Brac. 42 b; Fle. 202 (§ 11).

9. Et cum le dreit bail de seisine voide soit fet par solempneté de testmoignes, si qe le donour s'en soit de soen gré osté de seisine, et le purchaceour mis la eynz, mes ne pora le donour sei de ceo repenter. Car si tauntost retournast apres soen departir et engettast le purchaceour, ly engetez recoverast par ceste assise.

1—1. *so S.* cum cist [receit *on eras.*] *L.* bien cum si il resceit *N.* com cil retint *G.* com il resceit *AR.* com cist retint *M.* com si il retent *H.* cum il tyent *W.* 2—2. *om. H.* 3—3. retient *AR.* *sim. MW.*

Seisin may be retained by a single person or beast left in the tenement. So common of pasture by a single beast. And a rent by payment of one of several joint tenants.

8. If a single person or a single beast abides on the part of the donor in the tenement given, the donor thereby retains the seisin as well as by several; as in the case of a feoffor who having given his common of pasture still causes the common to be fed by one beast; for by that one beast the donor retains all the common. So a lord may retain a rent by the hand of one tenant, where several tenants are jointly bound to pay the rent, and the lord has sold it and yet retains the rent, as above said, by means of one of the parceners. And because such presumptions are prejudicial, it is proper that in every regular livery of seisin the possession be absolutely vacant before the freehold can attach to the purchaser by the livery.

Livery of seisin cannot be revoked.

9. When a lawful livery of vacant seisin has been made with the solemnity of witnesses, so that the donor is voluntarily ousted of the seisin and the purchaser put therein, the donor may not afterwards repent thereof. For if he should return immediately after his departure, and eject the purchaser, the ejected would recover by this assise.

10. Et si le donour par cas[1] retourne apres tele seisine fete al purchaceour et prie de estre resceu en le tenement cum homme estraunge, tut murge le donour en le tenement, ja par tele demure ne par tele seisine ne accrest rien de dreit as heirs le donour, s'il ne pusent averrer, qe il meynovera en le tenement cum seignur, ausi cum avaunt avoit fet, et ne mie cum bailif ou serjaunt le purchaceour. Mes pur totes dotaunces ouster, meutz vaut qe les donours facent aylours demure qe en tenementz par eus donez. Et si acun donour soit en tel tenement resceu apres le doun par la deboneretè le purchaceour, et il puse aparcever qe le donour ly voille engetter ou destourber de sa seisine, ou meynoverer sicum en soen demeyne, tauntost se purchace par ceste assise, ou sauntz jugement le engette, s'il quide par ceo meuz fere. Et si la assise passe pur le purchaceour, par taunt est soen estat affermé. Brac. 42 b; Fle. 202 (§ 11). Fle. 202 (§ 12). Fle. 202 (§ 13).

11. Et si le donour ou le purchaceour devie avaunt le bail de la seisine, rien accrest par tiel doun as heirs le purchaceour ne rien ne deperist as heirs le donour. Et si le purchaceour Brac. 43; Fle. 202 (§ 14). [104 *b.*]

1. tens *M.*

10. If the donor perchance return after such seisin made to the purchaser, and pray to be admitted into the tenement as a stranger, although the donor die in the tenement, yet by such abode and such seisin no right accrues to his heirs, unless they can prove that the donor conducted himself in the tenement as owner in the same way as he had before done, and not as bailiff or servant of the purchaser. But to remove all disputes, it is better for donors to make their abode elsewhere than in tenements of their own gift. And if any donor by the good nature of the purchaser is after the gift admitted into the tenement, and the purchaser perceives that the donor intends to eject or disturb him in his seisin, or to act as if in his own property, let him immediately proceed by this assise, or if he thinks it better, eject him without judgment. And if the assise pass in favour of the purchaser his estate is so far confirmed. Effect of reception of donor in the tenement. Danger of donor continuing on the tenement.

11. If the donor or the purchaser dies before livery of seisin, nothing accrues by the gift to the heirs of the purchaser, nor is anything lost to the heirs of the donor; and if Death of donor or purchaser, before livery, avoids gift.

[1]se bote eynz[1] apres le desces le donour, ja pur ceo ne lesse le heir le donour de sei mettre eynz[2]; et s'il soit engeté ou destourbé, si recovera par ceste assise; et si sa negligence ly destourbe en ceste assise, si recovera par assise de mort de auncestre, ou par autre bref solom la cause.

Brac. 426, 43; Fle. 203.

12. Et si acun eit purchacé en autri noun, et issi se tiegne en seisine, et cist en qi noun le purchaz est fet disavowe le fet et le purchaz, et acun estraunge engette le procuratour, ly engettez ne recovera point par ceste assise, pur ceo qe il ne se tint[3] mie en seisine en soen noun demeyne; ne cely en qi noun le purchaz fust fet ne recovera point, car il ne fust unques en seisine par cors ne par volunté; et puis qe le fraunc tenement n'est mie as heirs le purchaceour, adounc remeynt uncore en le donour, et en tel cas recovera le donour par ceste assise. Enfaunt neqedent de eynz age, ne ceux qi ne ount point de descrecioun, ne porount mie disavower le purchaz en damage de eus; car lour estat put estre amendé et nient enpiré communement.

1—1. soit bote [einz *interlin*] *L.* se boute einz *NM.* se boute *G.* *sim. AR.* sait bote *S.* 2. enz *M.* *om. RGSAW.* en seisine *interl. N.* *so in marg. R.* 3. *so M.* tient *LNR.* *sim. W.*

the purchaser thrust himself in after the decease of the donor, the heir of the donor is not to be prevented from putting himself in; and if he be ejected or disturbed, he shall recover by this assise. And if by his own negligence he cannot avail himself of this assise, he shall recover by assise of Mortdancestor, or by other writ according to the occasion.

Purchaser in another's name, if ejected, cannot recover.

12. If any person has made a purchase in another's name, and by virtue thereof keeps himself in seisin, and he in whose name the purchase is made disavows the deed and the purchase, and some stranger ejects the procurator, the ejected shall not recover by this assise, because he did not hold the seisin in his own name, neither shall he in whose name the purchase was made recover, since he never was in seisin either in deed or in intention. Therefore, as the freehold is not in the heirs of the purchaser, it still remains in the donor, and in such case the donor shall recover by this assise. Children however under age, and such as want discretion, cannot to their own detriment disavow a purchase; for, as a general rule, their estate may be rendered better but not worse.

Disclaimer by infant, void.

13. Et si acun donour assigne serjaunt ou ami de mettre le purchaceour en seisine si qe le bail de sa seysine soit fet al purchaceour vivaunt le feffour, le feffement iert bon; et ausi si le bail soit fet freschement apres la mort le feffour, eynz ceo qe le purchaceour sache de la mort. Mes si le heir le feffour apres la mort mesme celi feffour defende la seisine eynz ceo qe le bail soit fet al purchaceour, le doun iert cassé, et le heir recovera le tenement, pur ceo qe soen auncestre morut seisi. Brac 44: Fle. 203, 204. [105.]

14. Avowesouns de eglises ne pount mie estre donez ne purchacez simplement sauntz autre chose corporele ajoynte[1], sicum soil ou rente ou autre chose issaunt del soil. Et tut[2] pusent il estre si alienez, les purchaceours neqedent en plenere seisine ne porount estre des avowesouns, eynz ceo qe il eynt a teles eglises presentez, et qe lour presentez soint resceus et institutz par les Evesques. Car si le purchaceour vende la avowesoun, einz ceo q'il eit esté issi seisi par soen clerc, et celi qi la eit achaté en soit de autre enpledé, par ount il vouche soen feffour a garraunt, le feffour pora dire, qe il n'est mie tenu a garraunter par la resoun qe il del avowe- Brac. 53 b, 246; Fle. 204. Post l. 5. c. 4. s. 1, 2, 3.

1. annexe *NAR.* 2. so *N.* ne *add. LGSAFHW.* ne *eras. M.*

13. If any donor appoints a servant or friend to put the purchaser in seisin, and livery of seisin is accordingly made to the purchaser in the lifetime of the feoffor, the feofment shall be good. So likewise, if livery be made soon after the death of the feoffor, before the purchaser knows of his death. But if the heir of the feoffor after his death prohibits the seisin, before livery is made to the purchaser, the gift will be annulled, and the heir shall recover the tenements, because his ancestor died seised. Livery by attorney. Livery by attorney after donor's death. Appointment of attorney may be set aside by heir before livery.

14. Advowsons of churches cannot be given or purchased simply without some corporeal thing annexed, as soil, rent, or other thing issuing out of the soil. And even if they should be so aliened, yet purchasers cannot be in full seisin of the advowsons until they have presented to the churches, and their presentees have been admitted and instituted by the bishop. For if the purchaser sell the advowson before he has been so seised by his clerk, and the buyer be impleaded by another, and thereupon vouches his feoffor to warranty, the feoffor may plead that he is not bound to warranty, by Advowsons cannot be conveyed in gross. Seisin of advowson by presentee. Sale of advowson before presentation.

soun ne fust unques seisi, de sicum la eglise ne fust unque voide, eynz est uncore la seisine demoré en la persone le premer donour par la resoun qe ele ne [1]se esprist[1] unques uncore[2] en autre[3] persone; et serroit la resoun alouwable, pur ceo qe nul ne poit doner ceo qe il ne ad nient, tut fu le feffour ou le purchaceour pleynement seisi del maner ovekes totes les apurteynaunces.

[105 *b.*] Brac. 55; Fle. 204. 15. Et fet a entendre qe en[4] cas pora avowesoun[5] estre des apurteynaunces, et en cas nient. Car cist qi doune le maner ovekes les apurteynaunces sauntz rien retener[6] soit especefié en le doun, et[7] avowesoun de une eglise ou de plusours appendent[8], en tiel cas purchace le purchaceour les avowesouns de souz le mot des apurtenaunces. Mes si le donour doigne le maner enterement ou par parceles, ou en chescun [9]doun soint[9] notez les apurteynaunces, si le donour neqedent retiegne vers lui mesmes acune parcele de [10]tut entiere[10] oveke les apurteynaunces, en tiel cas remeynt la avowesoun en la parcele forprise, si la avowesoun ne soit

1—1. sespreit *M.* se espreist *S.* se prist *NACH.* se preist *G.* 2. *om. NM.* 3. autri *NM.* 4. *so NM.* ceo *add. L.* 5. des eglises *add. M.* de eglise *ACH.* 6. e *interl. N.* 7. et [si] *L.* *om. N.* e *SG.* e la *M.* e a *C.* 8. appendaunt *N.* dependent *MF.* 9—9. *so verb. MCHF.* dount sereint *L.* 10—10. tut entier *LS.* tut le entier *NM.* *sim. ARHF.* tote lentere *C.*

reason that he never was seised of the advowson, the church not having been void, but the seisin still remains in the first donor by reason that it never took effect in the person of another. And this reason would be allowable, inasmuch as no one can give that which he hath not,—although the feoffor or the purchaser was fully seised of the manor with all the appurtenances.

Advowson, when included in appurtenances. 15. It is to be understood, that in some cases an advowson may be included in appurtenances, and in some not. For if one give a manor with all the appurtenances without any reservation being specified in the gift, and the advowson of one or more churches is appendant thereto, in such a case the purchaser purchases the advowsons under the word appurtenances. But where the donor gives the manor entirely or by parcels, and in each gift the appurtenances are expressed, yet if the donor reserves to himself any parcel of the whole, entire with the appurtenances, in such case the advowson remains in this

especefié en la alienacioun. Et ausi si le maner soit aliené par parceles a diverses gentz, si qe al donour n'en soit rien remis, et chescune parcele soit aliené oveke les apurteinaunces sauntz la avowesoun especifier, si remeyndra la avowesoun al dreyn purchaceour.

CHAPITRE X. [XLI.]

De Purchaz de Rente.

1. Uncore i ad une manere de purchaz qe hom purchace par attornement de rente ou de autre service bon gré ou maugré les tenauntz, cum qi attornast soen tenaunt [1]de achater a un autre[1] estraunge persone de ses services issauntz de acun tenement. Et en tele manere sount purchacéz seignuries qe acune foiz deveynent en demeyne par forfeture ou par defaute de saunc. Mes a ceo qe acun deive estre attorné maugré soen, covendra eyde de nostre court parmi fin levé. [106.]

Brac. 81 b, 169; Fle. 209 (§ 36).

2. Et une autre manere de purchaz est qe home fet de

1. so *LS*. a cheuer a autri *N*. a cheuir a autre *AR*. de escheuer a vn autre *G*. a tenir de autre *M*.

parcel, unless the advowson is specified in the alienation. So if the manor be aliened in parcels to divers persons, without anything being reserved to the donor, and each parcel be aliened with the appurtenances without specifying the advowson, the advowson shall belong to the last purchaser.

CHAPTER X.

Of Purchase of Rent.

1. There still remains another kind of purchase, which is made by attornment of rent or other service, with or without the consent of the tenants; as where one attorns his tenant to become subject to a stranger, as concerning his services issuing out of some tenement. In this manner are purchased seigniories, which sometimes by forfeiture or default of blood fall into demesne. But in order that a tenant may be attorned without his consent, it will be necessary to have the aid of our court by levying a fine.

Purchase by attornment.

A tenant may be attorned against his will by fine.

2. There is likewise another kind of purchase, which is made

annuel fee de deners ou de autre chose en fee ou a terme de vie, qe est doné pur guerdon de service, ou pur eschaunge de terre ou de autre chose; a quei le donour porra charger soen tenement a la destresce, si rien en soit arere, al purchaceour, ou par la reconisaunce le donour en nostre court, ou par sa chartre; qe tiele pora estre.

3. A touz ceux qi ceste lettre verrount ou orrount I. de B. salutz. Sachetz moi aver doné a P. pur le bon service qe il me ad fet, ou pur autre certeyne chose, C. livres de annuele rente en N. et en S. issi que des maners auauntditz prenge la avauntdite rente de an en an al iour de Saint Michel, en qi qe unqes meyns les maners devynent, a tote la vie mesmes celi P., ou en fee a ly et a ses heirs et ses assignez, et dount en noun de seisine jeo ly ay baillé C. sous devaunt meyn, et qe le avauntdit fee ne ly soit detenu, et qe ceo doun soit estable, jeo oblige les avauntditz maners a la destresce mesme celi P., (ou a P. et ses heirs et a ses assignez) issint qe il les[1] pusent
[106 *b.*] destreyndre en qi meyns qe il [2]devinent ataunt avaunt cum[2] jeo mesmes fere poray, [3]et ataunt[3] qe ils sereint parpayez del

1. so *M.* ly *L.* om. *NDACH.* 2—2. deueigne autaunt cum *N.* sim. *D.* 3—3. iekes ataunt *NC* sim. *DAMH.*

Purchase of rent charge by recognisance or charter.

of an annual fee, in money or other things, in fee or for term of life, given in reward of service or for exchange of land, or other thing, and for which the donor may charge his tenement with distress if any part thereof be in arrear to the purchaser, either by recognizance in our court or by charter. The charter may be in the following form.

Form of grant of annuity or rent-charge.

3. 'To all who shall see or hear this letter I, J. of B., send greeting. Know that I have given to P. for the service which he has done me (or for some other thing certain) £100 of annual rent in N. and in S., so that out of the manors aforesaid he may take the aforesaid rent from year to year on the day of St. Michael, in whosesoever hands the manors shall come, during the life of the same P. (or in fee to him his heirs and assigns), and whereof in the name of seisin I have

Seisin of annuity.

delivered to him 100*s*. beforehand, and to the intent that the aforesaid fee may not be detained from him, and that this grant may be firm, I bind the aforesaid manors to the distress of the same P. (or to P. his heirs and assigns), so that they may distrain in whosesoever hands they come, so far forth as I myself might do, until they are fully paid the principal fee

princepal fee et de lour damages. Et jeo Johan et mes heirs garranteroms le avauntdit fee al avauntdit P. et a ses heirs et a ses assignez a touz jours. De date et des testmoignes soit fet cum [1]dit est[1] en le chapitre des chartres. Ante, c. 8. s. 9, 10. p. 257.

4. Et dounc si rien soit arere a tel purchaceour, si pora destreindre les tenementz chargez. Et s'il soit de ceo desturbee, si avera remedie par ceste assise, si les escritz soint atteyntz pur verreys.

CHAPITRE XI. [XLII.]

De Disseisines.

1. Petite[2] assise est reconisaunce de xii. jurours del dreit le pleyntif sur la possessioun, et pur ceo est ele appelé petite a la difference de la graunt, outre quele assise ne ad james accioun ne remedie; qe ne est mie en la petite. Car tut perde Glan. l. 13; Brac. 164 b; Fle. 213 (§ 7).

1. so *MC.* *sim.* *DHF.* deit estre *L.* 2. so *NDAMHF.* Ceste *L.*

and their damages. And I and my heirs will warrant the aforesaid fee to the aforesaid P. his heirs and assigns for ever.' As to the date and the witnesses, let that be done which is mentioned in the chapter concerning Charters.

4. Therefore, if there be any arrear of the annuity due to such a purchaser, he may distrain the tenements charged, and if he be disturbed therein, he shall have remedy by this assise, provided the writings are proved to be genuine. Remedies of annuitant by assise, if disturbed of his distress.

CHAPTER XI.

Of Disseisins.

1. Petty assise is the recognizance of twelve jurors concerning the plaintiff's right upon the possession; and it is called petty to distinguish it from the great assise, after which there is no action or remedy[b]. This is not the case with the petty Petty assise, determines the possession; Great assise, the property.

b 'There is no remedy beyond the great assise, on account of the solemn dignity of the knights, who are as it were the king's companions: for a knight cannot be attainted of falsehood but by battle and by his peers. Therefore it is not to be supposed that so noble persons will perjure themselves for any consideration (a nul foer).' Note in MS. *N.*

hom en la petite, uncore pora hom recoverer par atteynte, ou par bref de dreit en la proprete.

Brac. 161 *b*; Fle. 213 (§ 8).

2. En plusours maneres porra hom estre disseisi. Car cestui est proprement disseisi qi a tort est engetté de acun tenement qe il avera peisiblement tenu, et en qi persone eynt esté joynt le dreit de proprete de fee, et le dreit de la possessioun de fraunc tenement et la seisine. [107.]

Brac. 39, 43.

3. Totes seisines [1]ne dounent mie communement title[1] de fraunc tenement. Car plus toust ad le dreit heir fraunc tenement qe celi qe nul dreit ad. Car la seisine de chescun dreit heir est si tendre qe le mettre del pié soulement en le chief mies de soen heritage suffit pur title de fraunc tenement, si en noun de seisine eit mis le pié en tens de vacacioun del heritage, si qe il ne eit nul autre trové en seisine; et la resoun est pur la conjunccioun del dreit possessorie[2] au dreit de la proprete; et ausi de chescune seisine prise a soen oes. Et pur ceo si teus heirs, issi seisiz par eus [3]ou par procuratours ou par baillifs ou autres qi en lour noun[3] serount mis en seisine,

1—1. *so* S. ne deyuent mie communement title *L.* ne sount mie [ne] ne deyuent communement estre title *N.* *sim. D.* ne dounent mye comunalment title *G.* ne sount pas owelment title *P.* ne deiuent mie comunement title auer *A.* ne vnt mie comunement title *M.* *sim. CHT.* ne deyuent mie comunement estre title *W.* ne ont mye title *F.* 2. possessioun *L.* *sim. S G.* de la possessioun *N D.* possessori *A.* possessore *M.* possessour *CH.* 3—3. *so verb. D.* *sim. NAMCH.* ou procuratours ou baillifs ou autres en lour noun *L.*

assise; for though the cause is lost in the petty assise, yet the plaintiff may recover by attaint, or by writ of right, in respect of property.

Disseisin, what.

2. A person may be disseised in many ways. For one is properly said to be disseised who is wrongfully ejected out of any tenement which he peaceably held, and in whose person the right of property in the fee, and the right of possession of the freehold, and the seisin were united.

Distinction of seisins. What seisin constitutes a freehold title in an heir.

3. All seisins do not equally give a freehold title. For the right heir hath sooner a freehold than he who hath no right; for the seisin of every right heir is so tender, that the mere setting of his foot in the capital mansion of his inheritance is sufficient for title of freehold, if it is done in the name of seisin, and while the inheritance is vacant, no other person being found in seisin. And the reason is on account of the conjunction of the right of possession with the right of property. So likewise of every seisin taken to his use. Wherefore if such heirs so seised by themselves, or by their procurators or

soint engettez par autre qe par nous, de quel age qe il soint, voloms nous qe il recoverent par ceste assise. Et ausi, si eus soint de eynz age et eynt esté en la garde lour seignurs et resceus cum heirs, si les seignurs puis ne les conusent[1] mie pur heirs, tantost seint teus heirs succours par ceste assise, [2]qi qe unqe[2] soit trové tenaunt, seignur ou noun seignur.

4. Et si acun seignur troeve soen fé vacaunt apres la mort soen tenaunt, et se tiegne en seisine de soen fee clamaunt fraunc tenement en le fee par defaute de apparence de heir, si[3] par acun noun heir soit engetté, soit eydé par ceste assise [107 *b.*] a recoverer sa possessioun sauve chescuni dreit.

5. Si acun puisnee frere troeve le heritage soen auncestre vacaunt, et entre, et se fet heir clamaunt fee et fraunc tenement, si le dreit heir ou autre le engette hors de sa seisine pessible, ly disseisi recovera soen estat par ceste assise. Car le dreit de la proscheineté[4], qi est plus proschein de autre, ne pora mie estre detrié for qe par bref de dreit, si le tenaunt ne voille. Mes si le [5]dreit heir engette[5] soen frere bastard ou

1. *so MC.* conisseient *L.* conisent *DH.* conuissent *A.* 2—2. *so NDAM. sim. CH.* si vnqe *L.* 3. *so NDAMH.* sicum *L.* 4. *so CH. sim. NDAM.* progenite *L.* 5—5. *so NDAMC.* dreit heritage *L.*

bailiffs or others who may be put in seisin in their name, be ejected by any but ourselves, we will that, of what age soever they be, they shall recover by this assise. Also, if they be under age, and have been in their lords' ward and admitted as heirs, and their lord afterwards refuse to acknowledge them as heirs, such heirs shall be forthwith aided by this assise, whether the lord or any other be found tenant.

Assise by infant against lord.

4. And if any lord after the death of his tenant finds his fee vacant, and holds possession thereof, claiming a freehold in the fee for default of appearance of the heir, and is ejected by one who is not heir, he shall be aided to recover the possession by this assise, saving to every one his right.

Lord, after entry in his vacant fee, may recover it by assise.

5. Where any younger brother finding the inheritance of his ancestor vacant, enters and sets himself up for heir, claiming fee and freehold, if he be ejected by the right heir or another out of his peaceable seisin, the disseisee shall recover his estate by this assise. For the right of proximity, or which of them is the nearest heir, cannot be tried but by writ of right only, unless by consent of the tenant. But if the right heir

Younger brother after entry may recover the possession against the heir,

puisnee, ou autre, de eynz les xv. jours de lour entré, teus engettez[1] ne recoverent james par ceste assise. Mes si ils eint eu pessible seisine par taunt de tens qe il pusent le heritage aver aliené a acun plus estraunge persone, et cel purchaceour eust usé sa seisine, si qe accioun [2]ly put acrestre de recoverer[2] sa seisine par ceste [3]assise, sil fust engetté, cum taunt de tens et meyns suffit[3] de dreit en la persone del privé del saunc le dreit heir qe en plus estraunge, bien est resoun qe teus qi porunt clamer par mesme la descente en assise de mort de auncestre eint recoverer par ceste assise, s'il soint engettez de lour seisine, encountre les dreitz heirs et touz autres, ausi bien cum serreit un plus estraunge feffé en le
[108.] meen tens par [4]teus intrusours[4], s'il fusent de lour purchaz engettez.

Brac. 165; Fle. 216, 217.

6. Et cist[5] est disseisi en qi persone eynt esté joyntz le dreit de la possessioun del fraunc tenement [6]et la[6] seisine, dount il est engetté, tut remeigne le fee en la persone le dis-

1. *so MC. sim. NDA.* engettent *L.* 2—2. ly purra crestre si recouera *ND.* 3—3. *so verb. W.* assise sil fust engettez cum taunt de tens meyns suffit *L.* *sim. NGSA.* assise si il fust engettee cum taunt de tenps [ou *inserted*] meyns suffit *D.* assise par tant de tens si i fust engete meinz suffist *M.* *sim. F.* assise sil feust eniette par taunt de tens meins suffit *C.* *sim. H.* 4—4. teus intrusiouns *LM.* *sim. GS.* teles intrusions *C.* teles intrusours *E.* 5. *so M.* cist qe *L.* cyl qe *N.* cil qi *A.* sil *C.* cil *H.* 6—6. a la *L.* e de la *NC.* e la *MH.*

unless ejected within fifteen days.

ejects his bastard or younger brother, or other person, within fifteen days after their entry, the ejected shall never recover by this assise. But if they have had peaceable seisin so long that they might have aliened the inheritance to a stranger, and such purchaser might have enjoyed his seisin so that an action would lie to recover his seisin by this assise if he was ejected,—inasmuch as the same time, and less, suffices to constitute a right in the person of one privy in blood to the right heir, than in a stranger,—it is reasonable that those who might claim by the same descent in an assise of Mortdancester, should, if they are ejected from their seisin, recover by this assise against the right heirs and all others, as well as a stranger enfeoffed in the meantime by such intruders might do, if he were ejected from his purchase.

Disseisin may be by the person entitled to the fee.

6. He, in whose person were united the right of possession of the freehold and the seisin from which he was ejected, is considered as disseised, although the fee be all the while in

seisour ou en autri persone. Et ne mie soulement est cestui disseisi, qi est engitté de soen fraunc tenement en sa propre persone, eynz est disseisi, si sa femme ou soen baillif ou soen attourné ou soen fermer soit engetté, tut ne soit il en present. Estre ceo n'est mie soulement disseisi, qi est engitté de soen fraunc tenement, eynz est disseisi quel houre qe il retourne del marché ou del pellerinage ou de aillours et troeve acun autre en soen fraunc tenement, qe ly ne veut soeffrer de entrer en le tenement, ou al meyns se[1] tient einz oveke le dreit seignur clamaunt fraunc tenement en le demeyne le verrei seignur. Et ausi est home disseisi quel houre qe ly ou sa meyné soit destourbé de user sa peissible seisine par autre [2]qi i[2] cleyme fraunc tenement par teles destourbaunces, en le tut ou en la partie, ou en le cors ou en les apurteynaunces. Brac. 161 *b*; Fle. 213 (§ 8).

7. Et aussi est cil disseisi, qi est destourbé si qe il ne puse fraunchement entrer en soen fee et destreindre pur arrerages de services dues del tenement, dount celi seignur avera esté seisi. Ausi, cum le tenaunt eit fet destourbaunce par mur ou par fossé ou par haye, ou en chace ses avers en autri fee, ou [108 *b*.] Fle. 214 (§ 13).

1. so *NDC*. le *LMH*. se *interl*. *A*. qi *AC*. 2—2. qe il *L*. qe *N*. qe i *M*.

the person of the desseisor or in another. And not only is he disseised who is ejected from his freehold in his proper person, but he is disseised if his wife, bailiff, attorney, or farmer, be ejected, although he is not himself present. Moreover, not only he who is ejected from his freehold is disseised, but he also who, at what time he returns from market, or pilgrimage, or elsewhere, finds any one else in his freehold who will not suffer him to enter the tenement, or at least keeps himself therein together with the right owner, claiming a freehold in the demesne of the true owner. A person is likewise disseised from the time that he or his family is disturbed in the enjoyment of his peaceable seisin by another, who by such disturbances claims freehold therein, either as to the whole or part, and either in the principal or in the appurtenances.

Disseisin in the person of agent.

Disseisin by entry in absence of owner.

Disseisin by disturbance, where disturber claims freehold.

7. So likewise is he disseised, who is disturbed in such a manner that he cannot freely enter into his fee and distrain for arrears of services due from the tenement, of which services the lord has been seised. Likewise if the tenant has impeded his distress by a wall, ditch, or hedge, or by driving

A lord is disseised if he is disturbed of his distress;

si nul destresce ne i soit trové, ou en autre manere [1]si qe le seignur ne puse[1] entrer et isser a sa volunté sicum il soleit. [2]Et ausi est cist disseisi, a qi destresce renable est viee[3], et rescouse[4] par le tenaunt, dount le seignur avera esté seisi[2]. Et ausi, si le tenaunt a tort replevise la destresce fete sur ly par le seignur pur arrerages des services dount le seignur avera esté seisi.

Brac. 165 *b*; Fle 214 (§10), 217 (§12).

8. Et ausi est cist disseisi, qi est engitté de soen fraunc tenement par jugement qe rien ne lye, ausi cum par jugement rendu sauntz noster bref original.

Brac. 166; Fle. 214 (§14); 216 (§4).

9. Et ausi sount acuns disseisiz qi tiegnent a [5]termes de lour vies demeynes, ou a terme de[5] vie de ceux qi n'avoint for fraunc tenement. Mes si cestui, en qi reposent les ii. dreitz, lesse sa terre a terme de la vie le lessour, par taunt ne accrest al purchaceour nul fraunc tenement, tut soit le les de la terre fet al purchaceour et a ses heirs a aver et a tener a tote la vie le donour; et dounc, si le purchaceour ou ses heirs soint engettez, si ne lour vaudra rien ceste assise. Et ausi sount

Fle. 214 (§15).

1—1. *so verb. NDMCHW. sim. A.* si le seignur qe ne puse *L.* 2—2. *om. ND.* 3. deuee *M.* due *CH.* 4. refuse *C.* recusez *W.* 5—5. terme sicum a terme de *N. sim. DA.* termes de lur *M.* terme si cum a terme de vye ou a terme de *W.*

his cattle into another's fee; or if no distress is found therein, or any other act has been done, so that the lord cannot go in and out at his pleasure as he was wont to do. Also he is disseised to whom reasonable distress is refused, or rescued by the tenant, where the lord has been seised thereof. Also if the tenant wrongfully replevies the distress made upon him by the lord for arrears of services, whereof the lord has been seised.

or if distress is refused or rescued, or wrongfully replevied.

Disseisin by invalid judgment.

8. So likewise is he disseised who is ejected from his freehold by a judgment which is not binding, as by a judgment given without our original writ.

Tenant for his own life, or his donee, has a freehold, and may be disseised. But lessee for life of lessor has not.

9. Some persons also are disseised who hold for terms of their own life or of the lives of those who had only a freehold. But if he in whom both rights rest leases his land for the term of the lessor's life, no freehold thereby accrues to the purchaser, although the lease of the land be made to the purchaser and his heirs to have and to hold for all the life of the donor; and therefore if the purchaser or his heirs should be ejected, this assise will not avail them. Those also are disseised

teus disseisiz, qi sount engittez des tenementz qe ils averount tenuz par jugement de nostre court, et sauntz jugement, jekes tele chose soit fete ou tele, ou [1]a terme coluerè sicum en gage, ou par[1] feffement condicionel. Brac. 166.

10. Et ne mie soulement n'est disseisine fete des terres et des tenementz, eynz est de rentes et de estovers et de totes maneres de annuels profitz dues au terme de la vie del disseisi, dount vewe put estre fete de acun certeyn leu [2]dount teus profitz[2] deyvent surdre. Stat. West. 2 (13 Ed. I.) c. 25; Glan. l. 13. c. 37; Brac. 164 b. (§ 2); Fle. 214 (§ 15, 16). [109.]

11. Et ausi est home disseisi quel houre qe home ly [3]destourbe et deforce[3] soen fraunc tenement outre noster comaundement a deliverer le tenement et point ne le delivere. Et ausi est home disseisi quel houre qe la seisine de soen heritage ly soit vié par le chief seignur soen gardeyn, a qi il avera fet homage, ou[4] en qi garde il avera esté pur mesme le heritage, tut [5]ne eit[5] il esté en garde[6] par mot poi de tens, et ceo puse averrer. Fle. 214 (§ 11).

12. Et tut seint plusours disseisours, deus neqedent suffisent, ou un en cas ou une persone serra trové disseisour et tenaunt. Car touz jours covendra al meyns nomer en la pleynte un

1—1. a terme colore ou *CH.* 2—2. *so verb. NA.* ou tens dount profitz *L.* ou teus profiz *M.* *sim. CF.* 3—3. detient *M.* detiegne ou deforce *A.* *sim. CH.* 4. *so NDAMCHW.* ou *om. L.* 5—5. ne *om. M.* 6. fors qe *add. G.*

who are ejected from tenements which they held by judgment of our court, or without judgment, until such or such a thing be done, or for a qualified term, as in gage or by conditional feoffments. Disseisin of tenant by statute or mortgage.

10. Disseisin is not only made of lands and tenements, but also of rents, estovers, and all kinds of annual profits due for the term of the life of the disseisee, where view can be given of any certain place from whence these profits are to arise. Disseisin of freehold rents and easements.

11. A person is also disseised at what time another disturbs and deforces him of his freehold, and does not deliver it up after our command to deliver it. One is likewise disseised when the seisin of his inheritance is denied him by the chief lord his guardian, to whom he has done homage, and in whose ward he has been for the same inheritance, so as he can prove the same, although he was in ward but a very short time. Disseisin by holding on after adverse judgment. Disseisin by guardian after homage received.

12. Although there be several disseisors, it is sufficient to name two, or one, where the same person is found to be both disseisor and tenant. For one disseisor and one tenant at least The disseisor and tenant must be named in the plaint.

disseisour et un tenaunt. Et si plusours[1] disseisours soint nomez qi tort et force ount fet, ne greve nent. Mes en cas de jugement qe nient ne lie, covendra nomer les nouns des suetiers, si en court de fraunc home, ou en Counté, ou en hundred, ou en fraunchise, sauntz noster bref soit home jugee et engettee hors de la seisine de soen fraunc tenement, [2]et le noun del baillif et le noun del tenaunt[2]. Et si en nostre
[109 *b*.] court devaunt nos Justices, adounc covendra nomer le noun de la Justice, qi rendi le jugement, et le noun del viscounte et del bailliff et des tenauntz.

Stat. West. 2. (13 Ed. I.) c. 25; Brac. 161 *b*; Fle. 214, 215 (§ 16, 18).

13. Et ausi est disseisine fete par eus qi fount as autres fraunc tenement, ou eus mesmes point ne ount; et la covendra nomer le donour ausi cum le disseisour. Mes en totes les disseisines si cheet[3] le bref de novele disseisine par la mort le disseisour ou del tenaunt, et tient leu bref de entré[4] en le secound degré.

Glan. li. 13. c. 34; Brac. 161 *b*; Fle. 215 (§ 17, 19).

14. Et sount plusours nusaunces qe porount estre pledez par ceste assise, ne mie nequedent a recoverer fraunc tenement

1. so *NDAMC.* plus *L.* 2—2. so *D.* *sim.* *NAW.* el noun del baillif et el noun del tenaunt *L.* en noun del baillif e en noun del tenaunt *MC.* 3. so *ND.* *sim.* *MCW.* gist *L.* 4. foundee sour disseisine *add. D.* *interl. N.*

must always be named in the plaint. And if several disseisors are named as having done the wrong and force, it does not hurt. But in case of disseisin by a judgment which is not binding, where a person is ejected from seisin of his freehold by judgment in a freeman's court, or in the county or hundred, or in any franchise without our writ, the names of the suitors, together with those of the bailiff and tenant, must be mentioned; but if in our court before our Justices, then it will be proper to mention the name of the Justice who pronounced the judgment, and the name of the sheriff, and of the bailiff, and of the tenants.

And in case of disseisin by illegal judgment, the suitors and bailiff, or the Justice and sheriff and bailiff.

13. A disseisin is also done by those who convey a freehold to others, where they themselves have none; and in such case the donor as well as the disseisor should be named. But in all disseisins if the writ of novel disseisin falls by the death of the disseisor, or of the tenant, a writ of entry in the second degree takes its place.

Where a freehold has been wrongfully made, the donors should be named. Writ fails by death of disseisor or tenant.

14. There are several nusances, which may be prosecuted by this assise, and yet not to recover a freehold, but to

What nusances or trespasses may be remedied by assise.

mes a remuer[1] torcenouses nusaunces, cum de cours de ewe ou de chemin a tort trestourné[2] ou enlargi ou destrescé, ou de fossé ou de mesoun ou de mur ou de haye ou de marché a tort levé[3], ou de estaung a tort levé[4] ou abatu a nusaunce de soen veisyn. Acunes nusaunces sount neqedent termina- Fle. 215 (§ 20). bles en Countez par viscountes et ne mie par assises, sicum [5]de encres[5] de curtilage sour commune, ou de waycur, et de enbeverer as bestes, ou de [6]porte levee[6], ou faude, ou vacherie, ou molyn [7]ventresce, ou four, ou bercherie[7].

15. Et si ad une autre manere de disseisine, sicum de Brac. 161 b; pescherie. Car nul ne pora aver garrenne en autri[8] demeynes Fle. 215 (§ 21). [9]si noun par especiauté de fet[9]; einz est la pescherie a li qi terre se joynt a la rivere de une part et del autre; et si for qe de une part, adounc est la pescherie sue jekes au fil del mi leu [110.] del ewe, si la pescherie ne soit commune. Et dounc si acun estraunge vodera destourber tiel a peschier en droit de soen soil en clamaunt fraunc tenement en la pescherie, il fet Brac. 161 b.

1. recouerer les *ND.* *sim. A.* 2. *so C.* *sim. M.* retourne *L.* *sim. AW.* retournee [al. trestournee *int.*] *D.* *sim. N.* 3. e enhaunce *add. W.* 4. ou enhaunce *add. D.* *sim. N.* 5—5. *so G.* *sim. M.* des entrez *LD.* *sim. SW.* 6—6. *so NDMWF.* *sim. AH.* porter le ewe *L.* 7—7. ventresce ou gorz ou fere bercherie *ND.* ventrice ou de gorz ou de fouour [ou] bercherie *A.* venterez ou furn ou estank ou gorz ou bercherie *M.* venteresce ou goinz ou estaunc forn ou bercherie *W.* ventresce ou fumer ou bercherie *C.* *sim. H.* 8. *so MNDACW.* autres *L.* 9—9. *so verb. NDAMCW.* sicum par especiaute des fiez *L.*

remove wrongful nusances, as if a watercourse or way is wrongfully turned or enlarged or straightened, or a ditch, house, wall, hedge, or market wrongfully set up, or a pond wrongfully raised or lowered to the annoyance of his neighbour. Some nusances however are determinable by sheriffs in county courts and not by assises, as in the case of encroachments of curtilage upon common, weirs, watering-places for cattle, erection of gates, folds, cowhouses, windmills, ovens, or sheepcotes.

15. There is another kind of disseisin, as of a fishery. For Fishery. none can have a warren in other's demesnes, except by special deed; but the fishery belongs to him whose land adjoins the river on both sides. And if it adjoins on one side only, then the fishery is his as far as the line of mid-stream, unless it be a common fishery. Therefore where a stranger disturbs such Disseisin of fishery. an owner for fishing in right of his soil, claiming a freehold in the fishery, he commits manifest disseisin of the owner of the

Fle. 215 (§ 21). Stat. West. 2. (13 Ed. I.) c. 25.

aperte disseisine au seignur del soil, s'il eit esté seisi de la pescherie. Et ausi a femme a qei tele pescherie serra assigné en noun de dowarrie. Et ausi porra disseisine estre fete de conreiz et de baillies et de plusours autres profitz, sicum dit est en nos estatutz.

Fle. 217 (§ 10); cf. Brac. 166 b. Stat. West. 2. (13 Ed. I.) c. 34.

16. Et ausi a baroun en cas encountre sa femme, quant apres qe[1] ele avera defuy[2] soen baroun pur[3] avouterie, [4]sauntz coungé del baroun, et sauntz agarde de Cristiene court, se vodera a force tener en le fraunc tenement soen baroun, [5]ou el soen demeyne[5], cum par soen peché eit tut forfet a lour deus vies; et ausi en touz[6] cas ou la femme disseisist[7] soen baroun.

Fle. 217 (§ 12).

17. Et ausi tient ceste assise leu, par entre seignur de acun fee encountre touz autres a tort destreynaunt ses tenauntz, et encountre les tenauntz ausi en commun oveke les torcenous[8] destreynauntz, si les tenauntz achevent a eus de nul torcenous service pur enserver le fee plus qe dreit ne serreit, pur disheritesoun[9] et pur damage qe porroit accrestre

1. *so MW.* quant *L.* [ceo]qe *N.* ceo qe *C.* *sim. D.* 2. desceu *NA.* 3. par *N.* 4. *so ND.* et *add. L.* *sim. AMGW.* 5. *so N.* *sim. DGACW.* ou *M.* et *om. L.* 5—5. *so S* *sim. MW.* ou ele soit demene *L.* ou ele fust demoree *N.* ou ele fust demorree [dowe *in marg.*] *D.* ou en soen demeine *G.* ou ele fuit dowaree *A.* ouuesqe son demein *C.* ouekes son demeine *F.* 6. tiel *NDW.* teu *S.* 7. *so M.* deseisiste *L.* disseise *ND.* disseisie *A.* deseysit *W.* defuist *C.* defui *H.* 8. *so ND.* *sim. AM.* tenementz *L.* 9. *so ND.* *sim. AMC.* desheritesouns *L.* *sim. W.*

soil, if he has had seisin of the fishery. The like of a woman to whom such a fishery has been assigned in right of dower. Disseisin may also be made of corrodies, and of bailiwicks, and of many other profits, as is said in our statutes.

Disseisin of corrody, bailiwick, &c.

Disseisin of husband by wife.

16. Assise of disseisin will also lie in some cases for a husband against his wife, when after having left her husband for adultery, she attempts without his leave, and without any award of court Christian, to keep herself by force in her husband's freehold or in her own, whereas she has forfeited everything for their two lives by her offence. So in all cases where the wife disseises her husband.

Assise by lord against persons wrongfully burdening his fee with services.

17. This assise lies also for the lord of any fee against all persons wrongfully distraining his tenants, and also against the tenants jointly with the wrongful distrainers, if the tenants subject themselves to any wrongful services, to impose on the fee a greater service than it ought to bear, on account

al seignur si le fee devenist en sa meyn par eschete [1]en acune[1] manere.

18. Et si acun dedie soen service, et disavowe tener de soen seignur, en tel cas ne gist point destresce si noun en cas ou destreyndre et disavouer porrount estre ensemble, eynz tient leu ceste assise, sicum en le cas ou le tenaunt replevist destresce resounable hors de la meyn soen seignur, par le quel contek il se fit pier a soen seignur et en taunt dedist il [2]la seignurie[2], tut le face il [3]en teisaunt[3], et par cele perice[4] tient leu ceste assise en le un cas ou[5] en le autre. Brac. 169. [110 b.]

19. Et ausi tient leu ceste assise en la persone del vileyn et de sa femme franche envers le seignur le vileyn, ausi cum en ceo[6] cas ou le vileyn, qi rien ne tient en villenage, espouse franche femme a fraunc tenement, ou le vileyn et sa femme demurgent, si le seignur les engette apres le an et le jour, eus recoverount par ceste assise, tut le put le seignur prover soen[7] vileyn par seute de ses parens; et ausi a fiz de vileyn engetté Brac. 166, 168 b; Fle. 217 (§ 12). Post. c. 26. s. 1. Fle. 217, 218 (§ 13).

1—1. ou en acune autre *N.* *sim. D.* 2—2. le seruice *NDA.* 3—3. enteusaunt *L.* enteisaunt [cessaunt *interl.*] *ND.* enteysaunt *W.* *sim. CH.* entesant *M.* 4. peresce *ND.* partie *M.* *sim. W.* perte folie *C.* 5. et *ND.* e *MW.* 6. ceo *om. AMCF.* 7. so *N.* *sim. AMC.* le *L.*

of the disherison and damage which may accrue to the lord, if the fee should by any means fall into his hands by escheat.

18. If any one denies his service and disavows holding of his lord, in such cases distress does not lie, except where distraining and disavowing are compatible, but this assise takes place, as in the case where the tenant replevies reasonable distress out of the hands of the lord, by which contest he makes himself a peer to his lord, and so far denies the seigniory, although he does it tacitly; and by reason of this assertion of equality this assise holds in both cases. Assise by lord against tenant disavowing his seigniory, or replevying a reasonable distress.

19. This assise lies also in the person of a villain and his free wife against the lord of the villain, as in case where a villain, holding nothing in villenage, marries a free woman, having a free tenement where the villain and his wife dwell, if the lord eject them after the year and day, they shall recover by this assise although the lord can prove him his villain by suit of his kindred. The son likewise of a villain ejected from the purchase of his father, who died in a free estate, may Assise by villain against lord, for his wife's tenement.

del purchaz soen piere qi morut en fraunc estat, ausi bien encountre son seignur cum encountre plus estraunge.

20. Et ausi tient leu ceste assise a ceux qi sount engettez par faus garauntz, sicum en cest cas et en cas semblables. Johan porte[1] assise de mort de auncestre a tort sour P. et P. vient en court et vouche[2] de ceo a garaunt Theobaud, et Theobaud fet defaute, par quei la assise est issi agardé par sa defaute, qe tut veigne il a un autre jour ja pur ceo ne serra oy de rien dire par quei la assise remeigne a prendre; et pur [111.] acun enchesoun est doné un autre jour, sicum par defaute des jurours ou par autre resoun. Si Thebaud[3] veigne al autre jour, et die issi: jeo garrauntis a P., et reng[4] le tenement [5]a Johan[5], si les Justices seint si desavisez qe il recievent cele garrauntie, P. recovera par ceste assise, et serrount disseisours les Justices et [6]le viscounte ou le bailliff[6] qi delivera la seisine, [7]et le tenaunt[7]. Car il ne avoint nul garraunt de rien conustre qe thouche a Thebaud, de sicum il ne avoit

1. *so MC.* porta la *L.* *sim. SG.* porta *AW.* purchacea la *ND.* 2. *so SGMC.* voucha *LNADW.* 3. ne *add. ND.* 4. *so NDSW.* rents *L.* renk *A.* rend *MG.* rende *CHF.* 5—5. par counge a Johan *ND.* *om. MCHF.* 6—6. *so NDAM.* les viscountes ou les baillifs *L.* le vicounte e le baillif *CW.* 7—7. *so verb. MC.* et le tenement *L.* *sim. AH.* del tenement *ND.* al tenaunt *W.*

recover by this assise as well against his lord as against a stranger.

Disseisin by irregular warranty.

20. This assise also takes place in favour of those who are ejected by false warranties, as in the following and like cases. John brings an assise of Mortdancester wrongfully against Peter. Peter comes into court and vouches to warrant Theobald. Theobald makes default, whereupon the assise is thus awarded for his default, that although he come another day, yet he shall not be heard to allege any cause wherefore the assise should remain to be taken. Suppose that for some cause another day is given, as for default of jurors or for any other reason, if Theobald comes at the second day, and says thus, I warrant to Peter, and surrender the tenement to John, if the Justices are so unadvised as to admit such warranty, Peter shall recover by this assise. And the Justices and the sheriff or bailiff, who delivered seisin of the tenement, will be disseisors as well as the tenant; for they had no warrant to take cognizance of anything concerning Theobald, inasmuch as he had then no day. And if Theobald has given

adounc nul jour. Et si Thebaud eit fet les eschaunges a Johan, james ne avera de ceo recoverir, pur ceo qe il le fit de soen gré sauntz autre agard. Car nul ne vouche autre a garraunt pur estre par ly disseisi, mes par ly pur estre defendu en sa possessioun.

21. [1]Si acun[1] homme preigne seisine [2]de tenement[2] par colour de feffement, et ne soit [3]mie mis[3] en seisine par le feffour, si par le feffour soit freschement[4] engetté, le feffé ne recovera mie par ceste assise. Mes si deus ou plus se soint ploungez en seisine par colour de feffement, et contek [5]et toyl[5] soit entre eux qi avera la seisine severale, cely avera meillour recoverer qi seisine le donour avera establé. Et si contek[6] soit entre les feffez qi rien de dreit ount for qe soulement une nue[7] colour de feffement, a celi vaudra ceste assise encountre cestui qi rien de dreit out del engetter, qi avera esté de pessible seisine engetté, pur le dreit possessorie qe il out la ou le disseisour nule manere de dreit ne out de ly engetter. Et si deus ou plusours conteckent pur un tenement, [111 *b.*]

Brac. 40; Fle 201 (§ 7) 218 (§ 15).

Brac. 166; Fle. 288 (§ 15).

Brac. 265; Fle. 218 (§ 15).

1—1. sicum acun *L.* 2—2. *so NDMCW.* del tenement *L.* 3—3. *so AC. sim. W.* meymes *L.* mie mesmes mis *ND.* mie de ceo mis *M.* 4 *so NDAMW.* fraunchment *L.* 5—5. *om. NDMAWC.* 6. ou toyl *add. ND.* e toil *add. AMW.* 7. mene *ND.* meme *A.*

land in exchange to John, he shall never recover it, because he did it of his own accord without another judgment. For no one vouches another to warrant in order to be disseised by him, but to be defended by him in his possession.

21. If any man takes seisin of a tenement under colour of feoffment, but is not put into seisin by the feoffor, if the feoffee be presently ejected by the feoffor, he shall not recover by this assise. But if two or more thrust themselves into seisin under colour of feoffment, and a contest or dispute arises between them which shall have the seisin in several, he whose seisin is ratified by the donor shall have the best right to recover. And if there is a contest between feoffees who have no right beyond a naked colour of feoffment, this assise shall assist the one who has been ejected from peaceable seisin, against the other who had no right to eject him, by reason of the possessory right which he had, whereas the disseisor had no sort of right to eject him. And if two or more contend about a tenement to which

Feoffee taking seisin without feoffor has no assise against feoffor;

but may have assise against others.

So bastard, against all but right heir.

Brac. 166; Fle. 218 (§ 15).

des queus nul ad dreit, cum si ambideus soint bastardz, a cely vaudra ceste assise, qi primes fust en seisine, et avera la seisine jekes autaunt qe cil, qe plus de dreit [1]avera, la recovere [1].

Brac. 166 *b*; Fle. 218 (§ 17).

22. Et sicum pora estre un disseisi de soen propre tenement qe il avera tenu en demeyne et en severalté, ausi porrount plusours estre disseisiz del tenement qe il tienent en commun, sicum est de baroun et de sa femme; et des queus nul ne serra eydé par ceste assise ne oy sauntz autre, hors pris en cas del avouterie la femme defuaunt soen baroun. Et ausi cum est des boundes et devises entre veisins dount ambideus sount disseisiz, adunc a nul vaudra a porter ceste assise severalment par sei, de sicum teles devises ne furent unques tenues en severalté; eynz covendra joyndre ambideus les veisins ou plusours en commun en la pleynte solom ceo [2]qe eles furent tenues[2], si teles devises [3]serrount arrez remuez ou oustez[3] par estraunges[4] en appropriaunt le soil cum soen fraunc tenement. Car sicum la rivere est a cely au meyns jekes al fil del mi leu del ewe, qi soil se joynt al ewe, hors pris commune

Fle. 217 (§ 10). Brac. 166 *b*, 167; Fle. 218 (§ 17).

1—1. eu auera le recouerer *ND*. en aura la recouere *M*. *sim*. *A*. en ad auera le recouerer *W*. 2—2. *so NDA sim. MCW*. qe eles porrunt *L*. 3—3. seent remuez ou ostez. *M*. seient arrez remuez en fee *C*. 4. *so LSM*. estraunge *G*.

neither of them has any right, as if both of them are bastards, he who was first in seisin may avail himself of this assise, and shall retain the seisin, until it is recovered by him who has a better right.

Jointenants disseised, assise must be brought by all.

22. And as one may be disseised of his own proper tenement which he held in demesne and in severalty, so several persons may be disseised of a tenement which they hold jointly, as in the case of a husband and his wife, neither of whom shall be aided by this assise or heard without the other, except in the case of adultery, where the wife has eloped from her husband. It is the same with respect to boundaries and landmarks between neighbours whereof both are disseised; for then neither shall be assisted by bringing this assise separately by himself, since such boundaries were never held in severalty; but if such boundaries are ploughed up, moved, or taken away, by any stranger appropriating the soil as his own freehold, the two neighbours or more according as the boundaries were held must be joined in the plaint. For as a river, unless it be a common river dividing counties or

Disseisin of boundaries.

rivere, qe devise countez ou[1] hundredz, ausi est de devises de terre, hors pris commun chemin qe nul ne porra trestourner ne estrescer, et autres devises semblables. Et si devise entre veisins soit arree par un des veisins, adounc tient leu ceste assise a fere redrescer les devises jekes a lour dreit estat. Ewe corraunte neqedent n'est plus loungement devise for qe taunt cum ele tendra soen dreit cours; mes si toust cum ele chaunge soen chanel en[2] soen cours, mes ne serra devise entre veisins. [112.]

23. Et ausi porra commune disseisine estre fete as parceners et as autres qi tienent en commun, issi qe nul ne savoit unques soen several; ou tut i out il en acun tens severalté, [3]si de la commune volunté des parceners soit[3] puis assigné a acun commun oes, si lour vaudra ceste assise, si il en serrount puis engittez ou destourbez. Et si acun parcener soit engetté ou destourbé de sa seisine par ses autres parceners, un ou plusours, al disseisi vaudra ceste assise par severale pleynte sur ses parceners, et recovera; mes ne mie a

Brac. 167; Fle. 218 (§ 18).

1. *so ND.* *om. L.* e *AM.* de *W.* 2. *so LS.* e *NDAMCH.* 3—3. *so verb. NDAM.* de la commune volunte des parceners et soit *L.* *sim. CH.*

hundreds, belongs, as far as the line of mid-water, to him whose soil joins the water, so it is with boundaries of land, except in case of a common way, which none may turn or narrow, and other such like boundaries. And if a boundary between neighbours be ploughed up by one of the neighbours, then this assise lies to have the boundaries restored to their proper state. Running water however is no longer a boundary than whilst it continues its proper course; but as soon as it changes its channel in its course, it shall no longer be a boundary between neighbours.

23. Parceners and others holding in common, so that none can distinguish his several, may suffer a common disseisin; or, although there has been at one time a severalty, if by the common consent of the parceners the tenement has been afterwards assigned to some common use, they may avail themselves of this assise if they be afterwards ejected or disturbed. And if one of the parceners be ejected or disturbed of his seisin, by one or more of his co-parceners, the disseisee may have recourse to this assise by a several plaint against his co-parceners, and shall recover; but not to hold in

Disseisin of jointenement.

Disseisin of one parcener by another.

tenir en severalté mes en commun soloum ceo qe avaunt [1]le fit[1]. Et si deus parceners ou plusours soint disseisiz par les autres parceners, chescun parcener avera sa [2]assise severale[2] et recoveroumt a tenir en commun. Et tut ansi[3] serra jugé en touz autres brefs de possessioun entre parceners avaunt ceo qe la communauté soit severé. Mes cum lour tenement serra [112 *b.*] severé et chescun savera sa porcioun, et le un parcener soit puis disseisi par le autre, adounc tiegne leu ceste assise entre eus cum entre estraunges tenauntz en severaltez, et autel jugement eit un parcener disseisi ou plusours vers lour parceners disseisours cum vers estraunges persones. Et de plusours disseisines soint plusours assises arramez, et chescun disseisour, parcener ou autre, respoundera de soen tort demeyne. Et ceo qe avoms dit des parceners tenauntz en commun cum un heir pur la unité [4]del dreit de touz[4], soit en mesme la manere entendu entre veisins estraunges parceners qi tiegnent en commun par manere de feffement et en cas semblables.

1—1. les fist *M.* le soleit *C.* 2—2. so *MA.* seisine seuerale *LN.* *sim. D.* seisine en seueraute *CH.* 3. ensi *M.* issi *NDCH.* ausi *A.* 4—4. del dreit ausi *A.* del dreit detrie *M.* de dreit de tot *C.* *sim. H.* de dreit douent *N.* *sim. D.*

severalty but in common, as he did before. And if two or more parceners are disseised by the other parceners, each parcener shall have his several assise, and they shall recover to hold in common. And like judgment shall be given in all other possessory writs between parceners before the jointenancy is severed. But when their tenements have been severed, so that each knows his own part, and one of the parceners is afterward disseised by the other, then this assise lies between them as between strangers holding in severalty; and one or more parceners disseised shall have the like judgment against their coparceners, disseisors, as against strangers. Where there are several disseisins, several assises shall be instituted, and each disseisor, whether parcener or other, shall answer for his own wrong. What we have said of parceners holding jointly as one heir, by reason of the unity of right of them all, shall be equally understood of neighbours, who though strangers in blood, jointly hold as parceners, by feoffment, and in like cases.

Judgment,—to hold jointly as before.

Not so after severance.

For several disseisins the assises must be several.

CHAPITRE XII. [XLIII.]

Ou assise [1]*ne gist*[1].

1. Tote gent ne ount mie accioun uniement a recoverer par ceste assise. Car a nuly est remedie graunté par ceste assise, qi avera esté engetté de possessioun qe il avera tenu en autri noun; sicum baillif, gardeyn, ou attourné; ou fermer, qi avera tenu [2]a terme[2] [3]des aunz; et ceus qi tienent acunes demeynes[3] par vileyns custumes sauntz title de doun ou de feffement; ne homme de religioun ne autre qi avera purchacé de autri fee en morte meyn, si par les seignurs des feez soint engettez solom le ordeinement de [4]noster estatut[4]. Ne vileyn ne pora[5] james recoverer encountre soen seignur de qi le seignur ad esté seisi cum de soen vileyn de eynz le an et le [113.]

Brac. 167 b; Fle. 219. Brac. 168 b; Fle. 220 (§ 4). Stat. Mortm. (7 Ed. I.); Stat. West. 2. (13 Ed. I.) c. 32. Brac. 166, 168; Fle. 217 (§ 8), 220 (§ 4).

1—1. ne gist point *NAH*. *sim*. *DMC*. 2—2. *om*. *G*. 3—3. de auncienes demeynes *L*. [ou] des auncien[e]s demeynes *N*. ou des auncienes demeynes *D*. *sim A*. des ancienes demaynes *SG*. dez aunz e ceus qe tiegnent acuns demeynes *M*. des aunz tenuz de demeines *C*. des aunz teus demeines *H*. des anz dens demeynes *F*. 4—4. noz estatuz *M*. 5. auera *ND*.

CHAPTER XII.

Where an assise does not lie.

1. All persons have not equally a right of action to recover by this assise. For this remedy shall not be granted to any person ejected from a possession which he held in another's name, as bailiff, guardian, or attorney, or to a farmer holding for term of years, or to those who hold any demesnes by villain customs without title of gift or feoffment [c], or to persons in religion or others who shall have purchased land of another's fee in mortmain, if they be ejected by the lords of the fee, according to the ordinance of our statute. A villain, of whom his lord has been seised within a year and day as his

No assise can be brought by tenant *alieno jure*, or by termor, or by customary tenant, or for lands purchased in mortmain, or by villain against lord,

[c] 'Note, that he who holds ancient demesnes without charter, if he enfeoff a stranger, is as a disseisor. And the proof is this. He who makes a higher estate to another than he himself had, as he who makes frank tenement, where he hath none himself, is a disseisor. And the tenant in ancient demesne hath not frank tenement, for he who hath frank tenement can recover by assise, which the sokeman cannot do. And the lord of the manor hath the freehold, wherefore by such alienation he is disseised. And as soon as the sokeman withholds his services, the lord may take the tenement in his hand, and if he were tenant, then the lord would need to recover by way of distress or by *cessavit*.' (Note in MS, *N*.) See Judge Blackstone's argument as to the status of a tenant in ancient demesne, Considerations on Copyholders, Blackstone's Tracts, p. 199–237. See also Bracton, 165 *b*, 166, 168.

Brac. 169 b; Fle. 220 (§ 6). Brac. 168; Fle. 220 (§ 3).

jour, ne fraunc homme qi se avera conu pur vileyn [1]le disseisour[1] en nostre court. [2]Ne intrusour ne pora[2] james recoverer, si freschement par le verrei heir de eynz le an [3]et le jour[3] seit engetté.

Brac. 168; Fle. 220(§ 7); Ante, c 2. s. 6, p. 217.

2. Ne cist recovera mie par ceste assise, de qi soil sount edifices remuez, par autri ignoraunce la einz plauntez, et puis enportez quant le edifiour s'en apercevera de la folie. [4]Mes si[4] le seignur del soil eit porté al edefiour nostre prohibicioun qe il ne les remue, [5]ou si il[5] eit edifié encountre la defense le seignur del soil, ou en male fei, et ne mie par ignoraunce, ou si par ignoraunce soit acune chose semé ou plaunté en autri soil et [6]cel plaunceoun remeigne[6] taunt qe il soit raciné[7], si le edifiour ou le plauntour puis le ad enporté sauntz jugement, le seignur del soil recovera [8]damages autretaunt[8] avaunt cum [9]de soen edefier ou de soen plaunter[9] demeyne.

1—1. *om. M.* 2—2. Ne disseisour ne intrusor ne purrunt *M.* 3—3. *om. NDMF.* 4—4. *so NDMC.* ou qe si *L.* 5—5. *so M.* ou il *LNDA.* ou sil *C.* 6—6. tele plaunte ou teu semence i remaigne *M.* 7. enracine *M.* remue *C.* 8—8. damage autre taunt *L.* damage auxi taunt *N.* damage auxi *D.* damages autretant *M.* damages luy vers autretaunt *C.* 9—9. de soen edifice ou de soen plaunceoun *N.* de sun edifice ou plante *A.* de ces edifices ou de ces plauntes *M.* de son edifiour ou de son plantour *C.*

villain, can never recover against his lord; nor a freeman who has in our court acknowledged himself to be the villain of the disseisor. Nor can an intruder ever recover if he be presently ejected by the true heir, within the year and day [d].

or by intruder ejected without delay.

Law concerning buildings raised on another's land.

2. Nor shall he recover by this assise, from whose soil buildings are removed, which were erected thereon through the ignorance of another and afterwards taken away as soon as the builder perceived his folly. But if the owner of the soil shall carry to the builder our prohibition against his removing them, or if he built them contrary to the forbiddance of the owner of the soil, or in ill faith, and not through ignorance, or where anything is sown or planted in another's soil through ignorance, and that plant remain till it has taken root, if the builder or planter afterwards carry it away without judgment, the owner of the soil shall recover damages as much as if they had been of his own building or planting.

[d] 'To that he saith, that an intruder shall not recover if he be ejected within the year, I do not agree (ne m'i acorde je mie); because it seemeth that he should not be in a worse condition than the disseisor would be.' (Note in MS. *N.*) In Bracton and Fleta the time is not even limited to a year; non competit [assisa] intrusori, nisi tempus habuerit longum et pacificum, quod sufficere possit pro titulo (Brac. 168). A comparison of those statements shows the rapidly growing inclination on the part of the king's court to repress the practice of recovering possession without judgment.

3. Ne teus ne porount james recoverer par ceste assise encountre les verreis heirs, qi serrount engittez de tenementz, qe eus cleimerount tener par la ley de Engleterre, freschement apres ceo qe la prove serra fete, qe les enfauntz, en qi nouns il covendra[1] tenir, serrount provez bastardz ou teus qe il ne porrount estre heirs, ou la ou il ount eu nule engendrure de lour femmes; ou si il ne eynt mie esté les premers barouns tut eyent il eu engendrure. Brac. 168; Fle. 220 (§ 8, 17). [113 *b.*] Fle. 220 (§18); cf. Brac. 169 *b.*

4. Ne les purchaceours, ovek queus les donours se averount tenuz touz jours en seisine deques a lour mort, si teus purchaceours soint freschement engettez par les verreis heirs. [2]Ne les barouns sauntz lour femmes, ne la reverse, del fraunc tenement de femmes[2]. Ne les barouns, ou[3] les femmes jointement [4]seynt feffez[4] del fraunc tenement [5]ove les[5] barouns. Ne teus ne recoverount james par ceste assise, qi par lour gré averount esté engettez, [6]la quele volunté pora estre moustré ou averré[6] par escrit de covenaunt ou par pays. Ne cist ne Brac. 168; Fle. 220 (§ 9). Brac. 166 *b*, 169; Fle. 220 (§10). Brac. 169 *b*; Fle. 220 (§11). Brac. 169; Fle. 220 (§12).

1. voudra *MC.* 2—2. so *verb. MCH.* sim. *G.* om. *LNDSA.* 3. oue *GA.* 4—4. so *L.* sim. *M.* om. *NSGA.* 5—5. so *M.* des *LNDSAC.* lur *G.* 6—6. si lur volente puise estre moustre e auerre *M.*

3. Neither shall those persons ever recover against the true heirs by this assise, who shall be ejected from tenements which they claim to hold by the law of England presently after proof made that the children in whose name they must hold were bastards, or such as cannot be heirs, or where they had no issue by their wives, or were not the first husbands, even if they had issue[e]. Curtesy of England can only be claimed when children were born capable of inheriting; and only by first husband.

4. Purchasers with whom the donors have all along continued in seisin until their death, shall not recover if such purchasers are presently ejected by the right heirs. Nor can a husband recover his wife's freehold without the wife, nor the wife without the husband; nor the husband alone where the wife is jointly enfeoffed of the freehold with the husband. Nor shall those ever recover by this assise who have been ejected by their own consent, where such consent can be shown and verified by deed of covenant or by the country. Nor shall he recover Demandant in assise must have had complete seisin. Husband and wife sue together. Consent of disseisee is an answer to the assise.

[e] The opinion, that tenancy by the curtesy is a privilege of a first husband only, is supported by Fleta, but not by Bracton. (See the passages referred to above.) The contrary appears to be implied by the statute *De donis* (13 Ed. I.), which enacted, that for the future the second husband should not have any estate *per legem Angliæ* in a tenement of which his wife had been enfeoffed in frank-marriage with her first husband. And in a case in the Cornish Iter, 30 Edw. I, an estate by the curtesy was allowed to a second husband, of land which had been given in frank-marriage with the first before the statute *De donis*, upon the ground of this implication. (Year-book, 30 Edw. I. p. 126.)

recovera james par ceste assise, qi est destourbé de user sa seisine par la resoun de gast fet par le tenaunt deques autaunt qe[1] amendes soint fetes del gast[2] et de la destruccioun[3]. Brac. 169; Fle. 220 (§13). Ne seignur ne recovera mie par ceste assise, s'il se pleynt qe soen tenaunt ly avera disseisi, avaunt ceo qe ly avera destreynt pur arrerages des services[4], ou eynz ceo qe il eit esté destourbé a destreyndre en acune manere.

Stat. West. 2. c. 25; Brac. 169, 169 *b*; Fle. 220 (§14). 5. Ne a cely ne vaudra mes ceste assise qi autre foiz se avera[5] retret en mesme le accioun del assise del bref encountre mesme la persone, si ceo puse estre averré par record des roulles des Justices. Brac. 169 *b*; Fle. 220 (§16). Ne ausi a femme engetté de soen dowarie, de qi est prové en Cristiene court, qe ele ne fust unques par leal matrimonie joynte al baroun de qui assignement [114.] ele cleyme estre dowé, si par le verrey heir soit engetté. Brac. 170; Fle. 220 (§18). Ne a ceux ne vaudra ceste assise, [6]qi gré serra fet[6] del tort fet a eus par quiteclemaunce ou par eschaunge ou en autre manere. Ne Brac. 170; Fle. 220 (§19). a celi, qi par bref de eyné date de mesme la assise se soit avaunt

1. dues *add. M.* 2. fet e de la disseisine par la reson del gast fet *add. M.* 3. fete des tenementz *add. ND.* 4. dues al seignur *add. N.* *sim. DAMCH.* 5. *so NMGCH.* aueroit *L.* auereit *SA.* 6—6. a queus serra gre fet *M.*

Caption for waste. by this assise who is prevented from using his seisin by reason of waste committed by the tenant, until satisfaction be made for the waste and destruction[f]. No disseisin of service, so long as the lord can distrain. Nor shall the lord recover by this assise, when he complains that the tenant has disseised him, before he has distrained for his arrears of service, or until he has been in some way prevented from distraining.

Former writ abandoned is an answer to a new assise. 5. Nor will this assise assist one who has before withdrawn himself in the same action of assise from his writ against the same person, if it can be proved by record of the rolls of the Justices. Disseisin of dower; plea of never married. Nor a wife ejected from her dower, of whom it is proved in court Christian that she was never joined in lawful matrimony to the husband by whose assignment she claims to be endowed, if she be ejected by the right heir. Accord and satisfaction. Nor those who by quitclaim, exchange, or in some other manner, have made accord of the wrong done them. Plea of earlier or higher writ pending. Nor one who by another writ of earlier date has brought his plaint for the

[f] It appears to follow from this and the parallel passages in Bracton and Fleta, that when waste had been committed by the freeholder, the reversioner might enter without judgment upon the tenement, and hold it until satisfaction had been made for the waste; and further (according to Bracton), until security had been given against future destruction.

pleynt, et dount le bref soit pendaunt de mesmes les tenementz entre mesmes les persones par bref de plus haute nature.

6. Ne a celi ne vaut nient ceste assise, qi fust feffé par condicioun aperte especifié en lettre, ou privé qe porra estre averré par pays, s'il seit engetté par le feffour puis qe le feffé ne vodera tenir le covenaunt; cum si Johan donast a Pieres par si qe Pieres prist a femme la parente Johan ou autre, ou la reverse, si le feffé chaunge sa volunté et prenge autre femme et le feffour le engitte puis del tenement, al disseisi ne vaudra nient ceste assise. Brac. 169.

7. Ne a celi ne vaudra nient ceste assise, qi serra engetté solom le agard de nostre court, sicum est en ceo cas, et en cas semblables. Acun pusnee frere par defaute de plus proscheyn heir recovere acun heritage par agard de nostre court par tiel jugement, qe si le dreit heir vigne, qe il puse freschement apres sa venue engetter qi qe unques troeve tenaunt, cely qi recovere[1] apres [2]le desces soen auncestre[2] ou autre estraunge feffé. Et si il ne puse engeter le tenaunt, et il puse averrer [114 *b.*] Ante, c. 11. s. 5; Post, l. iii. c. 6. s. 4.

1. recouera *M.* 2—2. *so verb. D.* le decess le auncestre *N.* soen desces *L. sim. MGASOWFR.*

same assise, or where an action is pending for the same tenement between the same persons by a writ of higher nature.

6. Nor can he avail himself of this assise, who was enfeoffed upon an express condition specified in writing, or a tacit condition which can be proved by the country, if he be ejected by the feoffor after he has failed to perform the covenant. Thus, if John gave land to Peter upon condition that Peter took to wife one of the kindred of John, or some other, or the reverse; if the feoffee changes his mind and takes another wife, and the feoffor afterwards ejects him from the tenement, this assise will not avail the disseisee. Feoffee upon condition, ejected for non-performance of condition.

7. Nor will this assise avail him who shall have been ejected pursuant to a judgment of our court, as in the following and similar cases. A younger brother, by default of the next heir, recovers an inheritance by award of our court by judgment in this form, that if the right heir appear, he may presently after his appearance eject whomsoever he may find tenant, whether it be he who so recovers upon the decease of his ancestor or a stranger feoffee; and in that case if the heir is not able to eject the tenant, yet, where he is known to be Disseisin pursuant to judgment. Judgment for younger brother until appearance of the right heir.

le mettre de soen pié en le mies en noun de seisine, s'il soit deboté[1], adounk soit eidé par ceste assise, si il soit conu[2] pur plus proscheyn heir.

Ante, c. 11. s. 4; Post, l. iii. c. 1. s. 5; c. 6. s. 1, 3.

8. Ne a celi, qi serra engetté par le chef seignur qi soit en seisine de soen fee freshement apres la mort soen tenaunt, ou[3] acun qi a tort se dist estre le plus proscheyn heir[4] engette le chief seignur, et le chief seignur autre foiz ly, une foiz[5] ou sovent; si teus faus heirs portent ceste assise vers les seignurs, rien ne lour vaudra, pur ceo qe il ne troevent nient le fee vacaunt. Mes si ils eussent trové le fee vacaunt, et fusent entrez cum heirs, si il fusent puis par le seignur ou par autre engettez de lour pesible seisine, en tiel cas lour vaudreit ceste assise.

9. Ne a celi ne vaut rien ceste assise, [6]qi est destourbé a destreyndre[6] pur rente nient[7] issaunt del soil. Ne a celi, qi est destreint solom ceo qe il est obligé.

Brac. 170 b; Fle. 220 (§ 20).

10. De cimiteres, de communs chemins, de murs des burges ou des citez, ne de choses semblables a touz gentz communes

1. *so GM. sim. ND.* enbote *LS.* 2. tenue *C.* 3. *so SGA.* en [corr. ne] *L.* E si *ND.* de *M.* e *CH.* 4. e *add. M.* qe *interl. L.* 5. *so NSC. sim. DAM.* foiz *om. L.* 6—6. qe est destreint *M.* 7. nient *om. MCH.*

the next heir, if he can prove the setting of his foot in the house in the name of seisin, and he is thrust out, he shall be aided by this assise.

Lord entering on his vacant fee, and ejected by a pretended heir, may re-enter.

8. This assise does not lie for a person ejected by the chief lord, who put himself in seisin of his fee presently after the death of his tenant, where some one who wrongfully pretends to be the next heir ejects the chief lord, and the chief lord again ejects him, once or oftener; and if such pretended heirs bring this assise against the lord, it shall avail them nothing, because they did not find the fee vacant. But if they had found the fee vacant, and had entered as heirs, and had been afterwards ejected by the lord, or any other, from their peaceable seisin, in such case this assise would have availed them.

But person claiming as heir and finding the fee vacant, cannot be ejected by lord.

No disseisin of rent not issuing out of land; nor by lawful distress.

9. Nor does this assise help him who is disturbed from distraining for a rent not issuing out of land; nor one who is distrained in accordance with his liability.

When a common right

10. This assise does not take place in respect to churchyards, common ways, walls of boroughs or cities, or of like

ne tient leu ceste assise, pur ceo qe nule singulere persone ne pora en tieles communes choses nule propreté ne severauté demaunder; et pour ceo [1]tient leu en cel cas pleynte de trespas[1].

CHAPITRE XIII. [XLIV.]

De Remedie [2]de Disseisines[2].

1. Le premer remedie pur disseisine est au disseisi de recoiller amis et force, et sauntz nul delay fere, apres ceo qe il le pora [3]saver, de engetter[3] les disseisours. Et si plus ne puse, au meyns se tiegne en sa possessioun ovek les disseisours, et si use sa seisine en quant qe il porra; et si james ne avera le disseisour fraunc tenement si par le gré noun le verrei seignur. [115.] Brac. 162 *b*, 163; Fle. 215.

2. Mes si les disseisours eint esté en pesible seisine par loung tens en presence le disseisi, adounc ne list point al disseisi de engitter le disseisour saunt[4] jugement; et [5]puis list[5] a enquere, ou le disseisi fust en tens de la disseisine[6]. Car Brac. 163 *b*; Fle. 216.

1—1. tient lu ceste assise as pleintifs de trespas *M*. ne tent leu ceste assise en teu cas einz pleinte de trespas *C*. 2—2. de Assyses *M*. 3—3. *so MG*. sauuer et engetter *L*. sauer engette *N*. saver e eniettre *C*. sauer engettre *SH*. 4. qe le disseisour ne recouere par *G*. 5—5. pur ceo list *N*. *sim. DA*. pur ceo fet *MGC*. *sim. W*. 6. seisine *MC*. disseisine fete *ND*.

things common to everybody, because no single person can claim any property or severalty in such common things; and therefore in such cases the remedy is by plaint of trespass. is disturbed, the remedy is in trespass.

CHAPTER XIII.

Of Remedies in Disseisin.

1. The first remedy in disseisin is for the disseisee to gather friends and force, and without any delay after he may have knowledge of the disseisin to eject the disseisors. And if he can do no more, he should at least keep himself in possession with the disseisors, and make such use of his seisin as he can; in this way the disseisor will never gain a freehold without the consent of the true owner. Remedy by entry.

2. But if the disseisors have been for a long time in peaceable seisin in the presence of the disseisee, then it is not lawful for the disseisee to eject the disseisors without judgment. In such case inquiry may be made, where the Entry should be without delay.

s'il eit esté en present et [1]a sa escient[1] ad suffert le disseisour joyr[2] sa pesible seisine, apres loung tens ne list il point al disseisi engeter le disseisour qe le disseisour ne recovere par ceste assise et ses damages. Car presumptive resoun est en teu cas, qe les disseisiz voillent qe les tenementz as disseisours seient, quant il suffrent lour dreit si loungement dormir[3].

Brac. 163; Fle. 216. 3. Mes si ly disseisi fust en loynteyne pays en tens de la disseisine[4] fete, adounc [5]soit avisé ou jugee[5] de eynz cum bien de tens sa meyné renablement ly poeit aver fet a saver de la disseisine et en cum bien de tens il poeit [6]estre retourné[6] de [115 b.] coiller ses amis et engetter les disseisours. Et qe volunté ne regne mie en teus avisementz, voloms nous qe teus soint

1—1. en sa presence *M.* 2. *so MW.* *sim. GH.* joyr *om. LNDA.* 3. *so DSGA.* demorer *L.* dormer *N.* endormir *M.* 4. *so NDC.* *sim. W.* seisine *L.* [dis]seisine *M.* 5—5. deyt hom auiser e iuger *D.* *sim. NW.* deit auiser e iuger *A.* dreit est de auerrer et a iuger *M.* est dreit de auerrer e iogger *C.* 6—6. auer retorne *M.*

disseisee was at the time of the disseisin[g]; for if he was present, and knowingly suffered the disseisor to enjoy his peaceable seisin, the disseisee has no such right after a long space of time to eject the disseisor, but that the latter may recover his seisin by this assise, with his damages; for in such case it may reasonably be presumed that the disseisees were willing that the tenements should belong to the disseisors; inasmuch as they suffered their right to lie so long dormant.

Time allowed where disseisee is abroad. 3. But if the disseisee was in a distant country at the time when the disseisin was committed, then it is proper to consider and determine within what time his family might have reasonably given him intelligence of the disseisin, and in what time he might have returned to assemble his friends and eject the disseisors. And that such determinations may not be arbitrary, we will that they be adjudged according to the

g The time allowed for re-ejectment is not very clearly stated in the text; and the readings in several of the MSS vary. The following note is from MS. *N.* 'Where the disseisin is done in presence of the disseisee, the disseisor must be ejected within five days; because the law of ancient time granted that the disseisee should go one day to the east, the second day to the west, the third day to the south, and the fourth day to the north, to seek succour of his friends all the country round. If he be disseised in his absence, then if he was out of the district in any other place within the realm, let him be warned forthwith by his household, and let his reasonable days of journey (ses resnables journees) be allowed, and then four days. If beyond sea in pilgrimage, he shall have forty days, two floods and an ebb, and fifteen days to come from the sea to his house, and then four days. If beyond the sea of Greece in simple pilgrimage, he shall have a year, and two floods and an ebb, and fifteen days, and four days. If beyond the sea of Greece in a general passage, then let three years, two floods, one ebb, fifteen days, and four days be allowed.' This statement of the law agrees with Bracton. As to the time allowed in essoins, see below, book vi. c. 7.

jugez solom le tens des essoignes, issi qe si il fust alé en la terre de Jerusalem en general passage et soit retourné[1], et eit engetté le disseisour, ou autre qe avera esté par aventure feffé par le disseisour, lequel qe il troeve leynz enfauntz de eynz age ou autre, bien list a ly de engetter de eynz [2]le quart jour[2] qe il serra retourné en pays, issi qe iiii.[3] jours soint allouwez en armes et amis coiller et force. Et tut porte ly engetté ceste assise sur tiel engettour, pur ceo ne recovere il point de fraunc tenement; car nous ne voloms mie qe la absence de teus lour soit si[4] prejudiciale par quei ils soint de rien endamagez[5]. Et si acun disseisi eit esté en la Terre Sainte en simple[6] pelrinage, adounc soit acounté[7] un an[8], et un ebbe et un flod pur les delays de la mer, et xv. jours pur soen venir en la terre, et [9]iiii. jours[9] pur force coiller. Et si de eynz taunt de tens eit engetté qi qe unques soit[10] trové en soen tenement, tel engetté ne ad ja recoverer par ceste assise, tut morut soen auncestre de ceo seisi. Et si decea la mer

Fle. 216 (§ 3); Post, l. vi. c. 7. s. 3.

1. so *verb. NDMAWC.* trestourne *L.* 2—2. so *M.* *sim. CHW.* les xl. iours *LNDGA.* les quarante iours *S.* 3. so *NDSCHW.* iij. *L.* quatre *MG.* 4. si *om. NMDC.* 5. so *MDA.* en damages *LN.* en damage *SGC.* damages *W.* 6. simple *om. C.* 7. alowe *M.* 8. e un iour *add. C.* 9—9. so *DNCH.* *sim. MW.* xl. iours *LGA.* quarante iours *S.* 10. eit *N.* *sim. D.*

periods allowed in essoins; so that if the disseisee be gone in a general passage to the land of Jerusalem, and after his return he eject the disseisor, or any other who may have been enfeoffed by the disseisor, it is lawful for him so to do, whether it be an infant within age or any other whom he find therein, so as it be done within the fourth day from his return into the country, three days being allowed him to collect arms, friends, and forces; and although the person so ejected brings this assise against the ejector, yet he shall not recover any freehold; for we will not that the absence of such persons be so prejudicial that they be in any way damaged thereby. If the disseisee went on a simple pilgrimage to the holy land, then let there be reckoned a year and a day, and one ebb and flow for delays at sea, and fifteen days for his journey to the land, and four days for assembling his force; and if he has within such time ejected whosoever was found in his tenement, the person ejected shall not recover the land by this assise, even though his ancestor died seised thereof. And if the pilgrimage of the disseisee was on this side of the Grecian sea, the reckon-

Same time allowed as in essoins.

de Grece, adounc soint acountez [1]xl. jours[1] et un flod et un ebbe et xv. jours et iiii. jours. Et si en Engleterre, adounc soint acountez xv. jours[2]. Apres quel tens si les disseisiz
[116.] [3]saunt jugement[3] engettent les disseisours, [4]en ceo qe[4] il averount pesible seisine[5] as escienz les disseisiz par taunt de tens ou plus, si eint les disseisours recoverer de lour estat par ceste assise; car nous voloms qe totes gentz usent plus jugement qe force, outre tens defendu et limité; et mes ne soint les premers disseisiz [6]eidez par[6] ceste assise. Car a tort apele eyde de la ley, qi a la ley est contrarie.

Brac. 165; Fle. 216, 217.

4. Et sicum teus disseisours ount [7]accioun apres certeyn tens et terme encountre les disseisiz, ausi ount il[7] accioun a recoverer par ceste assise encountre touz autres disseisours, qi nuly dreit ne ount de les engetter, avaunt tel tens issi limité. Car la ou deus sount qi nul dreit ne ount, plus de dreit ad le disseisi, qe le disseisour. [8]Et tut recovere le premer disseisour[8] par jugement de nostre court, pur ceo ne voloms nous mie, qe rien del dreit perist al verrei seignur,

1—1. *conj.* iiij. iours *LNDACH.* *sim. S.* quatre iours *G.* iiij. moys *M.* quatres aunz *W.* 2. e iiij. iours *add. MWF.* 3—3. *om. AR.* 4—4. *so B.* eynz qe *LS.* *sim. MGF.* einz ceo qe *NDC.* 5. *so LSGMARCFB.* les disseisours ne recouerount mie par ceste assise. Mes si il soeffre *add. N.* *sim. D.* 6—6. *so MA.* *sim. NDW.* de par *L.* 7—7. *om. MC.* et terme *om. NDSGARW.* 8—8. *so N.* *sim. DMCFW.* *om. LSA.* a recouerir *G.*

ing shall be four months, one ebb and flow, fifteen days, and four days; if in England, fifteen days. And if the disseisee after that time eject the disseisors without judgment, inasmuch as they have been all that time or longer in peaceable seisin with the knowledge of the disseisees, the disseisors shall have recovery of their estate by this assise; for we will that all persons after the prescribed time of limitation proceed rather by judgment than force; and the first disseisees shall not be afterwards aided by this assise; for he who acts in opposition to the law has no right to claim aid of the law.

Disseisors may recover possession against third parties by assise.

4. And as such disseisors have after a certain time and term a right of action to recover against the disseisees by this assise, so they have also before the time so limited a right of action to recover by this assise against all other disseisors having no right to eject them. For where neither of two persons has any right, the disseisee has a greater right than the disseisor. And although the original disseisor may thus recover by judgment of our court, yet the true owner shall not lose anything

quant il se vodra pleyndre. [1]Ou si en tens del engettement[1] ausi[2] sauntz eide de nous ne puse recoverer sa seisine, adounc soit graunté noster bref deques [3]en heire[3] de nos Justices, [4]ou nous ly graunteroms Justices[4] de oyer et terminer la querele solom le cas.

5. Et si femme disseisie soit et prenge puis baroun, si il voderount puis purchacer[5] ceste assise, adounc serra issi dit en le bref: Pleynt se sount a nous Johan et Perounele sa femme qe Pieres a tort ad disseisi la avaunt dite Perounele. Et si le baroun se bye purchacer sur la femme, adounc issi: Pleint se sount a nous Johan et Perounele sa femme qe Perounele de tele vile ad disseisi la avaunt dite Perounele; issi qe ele soit pleyntive tut soit ele deseiseresce, mes qe le surnoun soit chaungé eynz ceo qe ele soit nomé disseiseresce.

Brac. 202 *b*; Fle. 240.

[116 *b*.]

Brac. 202 *b*, 203; Fle. 240; Ante, c. 11. s. 16; Post, c. 16. s. 3.

1—1. ou si en temps de Iugement *G*. *sim*. *S*. sur ceus de eniettre *C*. *om*. *W*. 2. so *M*. et si *LGS*. *sim*. *ARWC*. e auxi *ND*. *sim*. *F*. 3—3. a nostre venue ou a heire *M*. en eyre de nous ou *W*. *sim*. *R*. 4—4. e nous le grauntoms as Iustices *N*. *sim*. *D*. *om*. *MW*. 5. par *add*. *M*.

of the right when he shall choose to bring his plaint. So also, if during the time limited for ejectment he cannot recover his seisin without our aid, our writ shall be granted to him returnable at the eyre of our Justices, or we will assign him Justices to hear and determine the plaint according to the case.

If disseisee cannot enter, —his remedy.

5. Where a woman is disseised, and afterwards takes a husband, if they will afterwards proceed by this assise, the form of the writ shall be thus: 'John and Peronel his wife have complained to us that Peter has wrongfully disseised the aforesaid Peronel.' And if the husband desires to purchase a writ against his wife, then thus: 'John and Peronel his wife have complained to us that Peronel of such a town has disseised the aforesaid Peronel': so that the wife is plaintiff although she is disseisor; but the surname is altered before she is named as disseisor.

Form of writ for husband and wife.

CHAPITRE XIV. [XLV.]

De vewes en Disseisines.

Glan. ii. 13. c. 33; Brac. 179; Fle. 222.

1. Et si le engetté ou ne puse ou ne deyve engetter soen disseisour, ou le tenaunt [1]destourbe ly[1] de user sa seisine ovek luy, adounc ly covendra de sei pleyndre a nous, et nous ly froms[2] sur ceo noster bref al viscounte del pays, en qi baillie le tenement est; en quel bref serount contenuz les nouns de les disseisours et des tenauntz et de ceux qi vindrent en force et en eyde ovek les disseisours [3]et le[3] noun del pleyntif. Mes garde sei chescun qe il ne mette en sa pleynte nul autre qe nul tort avera fet; car pur chescun noun en le bref qi se pora acquiter del tort aver fet, si cherra le pleyntyf en nostre merci pur sa fause pleynte.

2. Et cum acun avera nos brefs purchacez, et eit purchacé lettres de nos Justices al viscounte pur le certefier del jour [4]et del leu[4] de lour cessioun, tauntost serrount[5] le bref
[117.] original et la lettre les Justices portez al viscounte; et le

1—1. ne destourbe ly *L.* *sim. SGAC.* ly destourbe *N.* *sim. M.* 2. dreit e *add. C.* 3—3. *so N.* *sim. SGAM.* el *L.* en le *CH.* 4—4. e de lu e *N.* del leu *om. MCF.* 5. *so A.* *sim. M.* serreit *LS.* soint *N.* serra *G.* se retret *H.* se retent *F.*

CHAPTER XIV.

Of Views in Disseisin.

Proceeding by assise.

1. If the person ejected cannot or ought not to eject his disseisor, or if the tenant hinders him from using his seisin together with him, he must then complain to us, and we will thereupon grant him our writ to the sheriff of the county in whose bailiwick the tenement is; which writ shall contain the names of the disseisors, of the tenants, and of those who come with force and aid to help the disseisors, and the name of the plaintiff. But let every plaintiff beware of putting in his plaint any who were not wrongdoers, because for every one named in the writ who can acquit himself of the wrong the plaintiff shall be in mercy for his false plaint.

Writ should name the disseisor, his aiders, and the tenant.

Writ to be delivered to sheriff.

Justices' letter.

2. When any one has purchased our writs, and also letters from our Justices to the sheriff to inform him of the day and place of their session; the original writ and the Justices' letter shall be immediately taken to the sheriff; and the plaintiff

pleyntyf retiegne nos lettres patentes vers luy jekes au Jour del play, et adounc les delivere sus as Justices pur lour garraunt; car sauntz garraunt general ou especial ne porount[1] rien terminer.

Fle. 226 (§ 8).

3. Et dounc appent al viscounte a receyvere pleges [2]del pleyntif[2] destreynables [3]a luy au meyns deus qe le pleyntif[3] seura sa pleynte, si[4] pur sa poverté ne[5] luy eoms [6]ottreyé par sa[6] surté [7]de sa plevine[7] de sa fei a sure sa pleynte; et[8] dounc ne trovera il point autre surté al viscounte. Et [9]s'il va sauntz eide de nous et[9] ne puse recoverer sa seisine, adounc ly soit graunté noster bref jekes [10]en heyre de nous ou[10] de nos Justices, ou nous ly graunteroms Justices de oyer la querele solom le cas. Et cum aucun avera trové au viscounte ou a nous en nostre Chauncelerie pleges a sure, dount deus pleges suffisent a un bref tut i eynt plusours pleyntifs, mes [11]ne voloms[11] qe teus pleyntifs truissent autre surté, tut deyve[12] le retourn estre fet deques en fraunchise[13].

Brac. 179, 179 *b*; Fle. 222 (§ 2).

1. *so G.* pora *L.* *sim SACH.* purra il *N.* purrount i *M.* 2—2. *so LG.* *om. NDAMCH.* 3—3. a luy au meyns taunt cum le pleyntif *L.* *sim. AS.* al meyns de taunt cum le pleyntif *N.* *sim. D.* a li a mains deus tant com il *M.* a luy al meins deaus qil *G.* *sim. W.* a ly mesmes qil *I.* a luy mesmes ieqes ataunt qil *C.* *sim. H.* 4. e si *N.* 5. ne *om. N.* 6—6. grauntee pur la *N.* grantee par sa *A.* 7—7. *om. N.* de sa pleuine e *M.* 8. et *om. N.* 9—9. si sanz eide de nous *M.* 10—10. a nostre venue ou en eyre *M.* 11—11. *so NDW.* *sim. M.* nous voloms *LACH.* 12. *so ND.* *om. L.* deit *AMH.* *sim. W.* 13. *so NM.* franchises *L.* la franchise *C.*

shall keep our letters patent by him until the day of the plea, and then he shall deliver them up to the Justices to be their warrant; for without either a general or special warrant they cannot determine anything.

Letters patent appointing special Justices.

3. In the next place it is the sheriff's duty to take pledges, two at least, distrainable to himself, that the plaintiff will prosecute his plaint, except where on account of his poverty we have permitted him to sue his plaint upon the pledge of his promise only; and then he shall find no other security to the sheriff. And if he goes without our aid, and is unable to recover his seisin, he may then obtain our writ, returnable at our eyre or that of our Justices, or we will grant him Justices to hear and determine the plaint according to the case. When pledges to prosecute are found to the sheriff, or to us in our Chancery, whereof two pledges are sufficient though there are several plaintiffs in one writ, the plaintiffs are not to be required to find any other security, although the return is to be made in a franchise.

Pledges for prosecution.

Pauper's suit without pledges.

No further security to be found in franchises.

Brac. 179 *b*; Fle. 222 (§ 4), 223 (§ 10).

4. Et receue la surté si le bref le voille, tantost soit enjoynt a deus fraunc hommes del visné terre tenauntz qe il voisent somundre les veisins a estre a un certeyn [1]jour et leu[1] devant nos Justices a reconustre sur lour sermentz, si le pleyntif soit disseisi, sicum il se pleynt, de soen fraunc tenement en tel certeyn leu ou noun, et qe en le meen tens veyent le tenement en ceste manere, lequel la disseisine soit fete de terre ou de rente[2] ou de propre chose ou de commune, ou si commune, lequel commune a totes gentz ou a certeyn noumbre de gentz, et ausi cum bien [3]en quantité[3] amounte la chose dount la pleynte est fete, issi qe il se pusent aviser de certeyne respounse quant il de ceo serount apposez[4], lequel le pleyntif [5]i ad mis[5] trop en sa pleynte ou trop poi. Et ausi deyvent il veer lequel tut le tenement soit en ceo counté et la vile nomé el bref ou noun. Et la vewe lour deit fere ne mie le viscounte ne les baillifs mes le pleyntif, [6]qi lour[6] deit enseigner[7] entre queus boundes et queus devises les tenementz nomez en sa pleynte gisent.

Brac. 179 *b*, 180; Fle. 224, 225.

[117 *b*.]

1—1. iour eslu *L*. iour e lu *NDSGAM*. *sim*. *CW*. 2. ou de pree *add*. *ND*. 3—3. en annuelte *M*. e quant, *C*. 4. opposez *MC*. 5—5. *so M*. mettra *LNCHDASG*. 6—6. *so A*. quel pleyntif qe lour *L*. qe lour *NDM*. qe les *C*. qi *W*. 7. assigner *CH*.

Summons of jurors.

4. Security being thus taken if the writ require it, let two freeholders of the neighbourhood be immediately enjoined to summon the neighbours to be at a certain day and place before our Justices to make recognizance upon their oaths, whether the plaintiff has been disseised, as he complains, of his freehold, in such a certain place or not, and that in the meantime they view the tenements in this manner, whether the disseisin be made of land or of rent, of private property or of common; and if of common, whether common to everybody, or only to a certain number of people; also to how much in quantity the thing whereof the plaint is made amounts, so that they may be prepared with a certain answer when they shall be asked whether the plaintiff hath put too much or too little in his plaint. They ought also to see whether all the tenement is situate in the county and in the vill named in the writ or not. It is not the sheriff's or bailiff's office to give them the view, but the plaintiff's, who is bound to inform them within what boundaries and divisions the tenements named in the plaint lie.

View of tenements by jurors.

The view is made by the direction of the plaintiff.

5. Et si la pleynte soit fete de conreiz[1] ou de estovers ou de liveresoun de blé par an ou de autre vitaile ou des autres necessaries [2]ou des baillies ou des gardeyns[2] ou [3]des gardes de parks[3] ou de porte, ou de autre manere de office annuel, ou de commune de pasture, ou de turbarie, ou de pescherie, ou de autres servages, adounc est mester qe les jurours facent la veuwe des tenementz dount teus servages ou estovers sourdent, ou au meyns de ceus tenementz ou tieles annueles necessaries sount accustumez de estre liverez ou sount assignez de estre receuz.

Stat. West. 2 (13 Ed. I.) c. 25; Brac. 180; Fle. 224.

6. Ei si la pleynte soit fete de rente, adounc covendra as jurours de veer le soil dount la rente sourd; et ne mie soulement le soil, mes la chose ausi pur quei la rente est [4]doné, sicum en ceo cas et en[4] cas semblables: cum si acune rente soit graunté [5]a veisin de autre pur chace aver[5] par mi acun tenement, ou si rente issaunt de acun tenement soit en [118.] partie ou en tut relessé pur acun servage aver en autri soil. Car tut [6]ne voille il mes de servage[6], pur ceo ne pora il mie

Brac. 180; Fle. 225 (§ 4).

Brac. 181; Fle. 225 (§ 4).

1. coniers *LG.* *sim. S.* curreis *ND.* correes *M.* conreis *A.* conier *CH.* *sim. F.* 2—2. *so L.* *sim. NDS.* ou de vitailles ou de gardeins *MF.* ou gardeins *C.* 3—3. des gardes ou de parks *L.* de gardes des parks *N.* *sim. SGAMC.* 4—4. done en soen cas cum en ceo cas et en *LN.* done si com en cest cas e en *M.* *sim. A.* done en son cas com en *C.* done en soun *H.* 5—5. *so verb. AS.* au veisin de autri purchaz auer *L.* *sim. NDGCW.* de veisin a autre purchaz auer *M.* 6—6. vouche il mes estre chargee de seruage *ND.*

5. If the plaint be made of corrodies or estovers, or of the delivery of corn yearly, or other provision or necessaries, or of bailiwicks or wardenships, or of the keepership of a park, or the ward of gates, or other kind of annual office, or of common of pasture, turbary, fishery, or other easements, then the jurors are required to make view of the tenement from whence the easements or estovers arise, or at least of those tenements where the annual necessaries are accustomed to be delivered or are assigned to be received.

Nature of the view, in disseisin of corrodies, bailiwicks, easements, &c.

6. And if the plaint be made of rent, then the jurors must view the soil from which the rent issues; and not only the soil, but the thing also for which the rent is paid; as in the following and like cases, where rent is granted by one neighbour to another to have a right of driving cattle through any tenement, or where a rent issuing out of any tenement is partly or wholly released on condition of having an easement in another soil. For although the one party does not require the easement, yet he

View in disseisin of rent.

Where a rent is granted in consideration of an easement, neither party can be released without consent of the other.

retrere qe il ne doigne la rente et qe le covenaunt ne sei tiegne vers cely qe tener se vodera; ne james ne pora cel contract estre defet, for qe par commun assent, sicum primes fust fet par commun assent. Et pur ceo tut ne voille cil, qi ad doné rente en fee ou a terme de vie, et dount le purchaceour eit esté en seisine, mes [1]aver chace[1] ou autre servage en soil de soen veisin[2], pur ceo ne se pora il mie retrere a doner la rente solom ceo qe entre eus acoveint[3], qe cil a qi la rente est due ne puse destreyndre pur les arrerages de la rente, et si il ne troeve destresce, ou s'il soit destourbé a destreyndre, qe il ne recovera par ceste assise, si il puse moustrer qe acun soil soit a la rente obligé; et si noun, assetz suffist [4]de veer le tenement al pleyntif[4] pur quei la rente fust doné.

Brac. 181; Fle. 225 (§ 5). 7. Et[5] si la pleynte soit[6] fet de nusaunce, adounc veent ceste nusaunce, si ceo soit mur fosse ou haye ou marché, ou estaung enhaucé ou abatu ou autrement nusaunt, et en tel cas ne suffit mie soulement de veer la nusaunce, eynz covendra veer le [7]tenement a quel[7] la nusaunce est fete. Et ausi

1—1. so *A.* *sim. MW.* auer chose *LND.* eschete *CH.* 2. so *NM.* *sim. DW.* vileyn *L.* *sim. ACH.* 3. conuient *ND.* a conueint *S.* aconuint *AM.* a conuenist *G.* est couenaunte *C.* 4—4. al pleintif de veer le tenement *M.* 5. *conj.* Car *LSGMACEWF.* qe *ND.* 6. fut. *L.* fust *N* seit *AMCF.* 7—7. tenement soulement a quel *LNSF.* *sim. A.* tenement al quel *M.* tenement a quoi *G.*

cannot refuse to pay the rent, or prevent the covenant from being binding in relation to him who is willing to keep it; and the contract shall never be dissolved but by common assent as it was at first made; and therefore, although the person who has granted a rent in fee or for term of life whereof the purchaser has been seised, does not wish to have the driftway or other easement in the soil of his neighbour, yet if he refuse to pay the rent according as it was covenanted between them, he to whom the rent is due may distrain for the arrears of the rent; and if he cannot find anything to distrain, or if he be hindered from distraining, he shall recover by this assise, if he can show that any soil is charged with the rent; and if not, it is sufficient to view the tenement for which the rent was given.

Nature of view in case of nusance.

7. If the plaint is made of a nusance, then let them view the nusance, whether it be a wall, ditch, hedge, or market, or a pond raised or lowered, or otherwise injurious; and in such case it is not sufficient to view the nusance only, but they must also view the tenement to which the annoyance is done.

en le cas devaunt, si la [1]disseisine soit desturbaunce de[1] servages, [2]ausi cum de[2] aver commune en autri soil, ou chace, ou chemin, ou ewe en autri pus, [3]ou autres servages semblables[3], de veer le tenement ne suffit mie [4]en soi[4] soulement, eynz covendra veer le tenement a quel la pasture apent. [118 *b.*]

8. Et si les parties voillent estre a la vewe et mettre lour chalenges en jurours, si le facent; et les nouns de ceux en les quex il se assenterount soint enbrevez, si[5] les parties[6] se soint assentuz en jurours, pur deliverer [7]as Justices[7] al jour de plee. Brac. 184 *b*, 185; Fle. 229.

9. Et puis soit le tenaunt attaché et mis par pleges, et touz les disseisours ausi, ou lour baillifs, si eus ne soint trovez, qe il soint au jour de plee a oyer la reconisaunce des jurours sur cele pleynte, issint qe il sachent de quel trespas il deyvent estre acoupez. Brac. 182 (§ 10); Fle. 226.

1—1. seisine est destourbee de autri *ND.* 2—2. ausi de *L.* cum de *ND.* *sim. C.* ausi com de *SGM.* *sim. AF.* 3—3. *so DAMSW.* *sim. N.* ou autres servages ausi cum de aver teus semblables *L.* 4—4. *om. N.* 5. *conj.* et si *L.* *sim. NDSGAMR.* 6. *so ND.* ne *add. LSGAMR.* 7—7. suys as Iustices a oyer la reconisaunce de les Iurours *ND.*

And in the preceding case also, if the disseisin be by a disturbance of an easement, such as having common in another's soil, or right of drift or way, or water at another's well, or other like easement, it is not sufficient to view the tenement subject to the easement, but the tenement to which the pasture belongs must likewise be viewed.

8. The parties, if they please, may be present at the view, and challenge the jurors; and if the parties agree upon jurors, the names of those upon whom they have agreed shall be imbreviated, to be presented to the Justices at the day of plea. Challenge of jurors.

9. Afterwards let the tenant and all the disseisors, or their bailiffs if they cannot themselves be found, be attached, and required to find pledges to be present at the day of the plea to hear the recognizance of the jurors upon the plaint, so that they may know of what offence they are to be accused. Process to compel appearance of disseisors and tenant.

CHAPITRE XV. [XLVI.]

De Proces en Assises.

Brac. 182; Fle. 226.

1. Et cum les Justices soint venuz, tauntost receyvent les essoignes, et puis les ajournent; et si le pleyntif[1] en ceste assise ne venge ne se eit fet essonier, tauntost soit le bref pris hors de la meyn le viscounte, et les nouns des Jurours, et le pleyntif soit apelé. Et s'il face defaute, si soit il et ses
[119.] pleges de seure en nostre merci. Puis soit demaundé le tenaunt ou soen baillif et les autres disseisours; et ceux qi
Glan. l. xiii. c. 38. fount defaute ou se fount essoiner (cum nul essoine ne lour vaut en ceste assise), et testmoigné soit par le viscounte qe ils furent attachez par pleges, adounc soint les pleges en la merci pur ceo que il ne les avoynt mie en court sicum il les plevirent. Et puis soint demaundez les jurours de la assise solom le panel par lour nouns. Et ceux qi ne serrount mie venuz, sicum il furent somouns, soint en nostre merci.

1. so *NDAMF.* soit apele *add. L.*

CHAPTER XV.

Of the Proceedings in Assises.

Effect of non-appearance of parties.

1. When the Justices are come, they shall forthwith receive the essoins, and afterwards adjourn them. And if the plaintiff in this assise neither appears nor causes himself to be essoined, the writ shall be immediately taken out of the hands of the sheriff, and the names of the jurors presented; and the plaintiff shall be called. And if he makes default, let him and his pledges to prosecute be in mercy. Then let the tenant or his bailiff and the rest of the disseisors be demanded, and if they make default, or cause themselves to be essoined, (since in this assise no essoin avails them,) and it be proved by the sheriff that they were attached by pledges, then their pledges shall be in mercy, because they have not produced them in court according to their engagement. Afterwards let the jurors of the assise, according to the panel, be required to answer to their names; and let such as do not appear according as they have been summoned be in our mercy.

No essoin allowed to disseisor.

2. Et si le pleyntif veigne, ou se fet essonier, et le tenaunt ne soen baillif ne soen attourné ne veignent, tauntost seynt les pleges en la merci, sicum avaunt est dit, et en despit de lour defaute soit agardé qe mes ne pusent rien dire par quei la assise remeigne a prendre, et qe l'assise soit prise par lour defaute. Brac. 182, 183; Fle. 226.

3. Et fet a saver qe en ceste assise et en nule autre pura chescun disseisour par ly mesmes respoundre ou par attourné ou par baillif. Chescun neqedent ne ad mie uniement poer; car baillif ne put mie quant qe soen seignur put. Car baillif ne pora conustre ne graunter la disseisine estre fete par soen seignur, qe la reconisaunce au meyns soit prise, sicum le disseisur poreit s'il fust present. Estre ceo ne poreit mie le baillif acorder, ne [1]fere rien estre parti[1], ne ne mettre le dreit soen seignur en nul hochepot, par quei le seignur perdist[2] [3]nul fraunc tenement[3] sauntz reconisaunce del assise. Encountre la assise pora neqedent le baillif dire, par quei ele ne deit james passer, ou [4]pur debarrer[4] la assise par excepciouns [5]dilatories ou[5] peremptories autaunt avaunt cum le Brac. 182; Fle. 226. [119 *b*.]

1—1. fere en partie *M*. 2. so *M*. perdeit *L*. perde *ND*. 3—3. *om*. *ND*. 4—4. pur delayer *NM*. *sim*. *AH*. 5—5. so *ND*. *sim*. *SGAMFH*. *om*. *L*.

2. If the plaintiff appears, or causes himself to be essoined, and neither the tenant, nor his bailiff, nor his attorney, is present, the pledges as before mentioned shall be immediately amerced, and by way of punishment for the default of the parties it shall be awarded that they be not afterwards allowed to allege any reason for staying the assise, and that the assise be taken by their default. If tenant makes default, assise taken in his absence.

3. And it should be known that in this and in no other assise every disseisor may answer either in person or by attorney, or by bailiff. Yet they have not all an equal power; for a bailiff cannot do all that his lord can. For a bailiff cannot acknowledge or grant that the disseisin was committed by his lord, so as to prevent the necessity of taking the recognizance, as the disseisor might himself do, if present. Moreover the bailiff cannot make any accord or partition, nor put the right of his lord into hotchpot, whereby the lord might lose any freehold without the recognizance of the assise. Yet the bailiff may, as well as his master, allege any objection, wherefore the assise ought not to pass, or for the purpose of barring the assise by Tenant may be represented by bailiff. Authority of bailiff.

seignur meymes, sicum par excepcioun encountre le juge, et encountre le pleyntif, et encountre les jurours, et encountre le bref, et par totes autres excepciouns et replicatiouns autaunt avaunt cum le seignur meymes.

Fle. 226.

4. Et[1] attourné put taunt cum le seignur put for qe apeser[2]; car si toust cum le plee et la parole finist en la court, tauntost finist le poer del attourné, et en recreaunt [3]la pes[3] comence une autre manere de parole, qe avaunt ne fust mie[4] en court quant il fust fet attourné en[5] la parole soulement qe adounc fust en court. Et ceo fet a entendre des atturnez especiaus. Mes des generaus attournez est autrement; car general attourné put taunt cum soen client del comencement del play jekes al finiement.

Brac. 182 *b*; Fle. 226.

5. Et cum le pleyntif et les defendauntz soint venuz en court, et le pleyntif die qe il ne vodera mie seure soen bref, en quel play qe ceo soit, mes [6]ne puse resorter a semblable,
[120.] einz[6] remeyndra en nostre merci, et ses pleges de sure ausi. Et si [7]il se·retret[7] del accioun, a touz jours mes soit barré de accioun. Mes si il eit coungé de quere meillour bref, et en

1. Car *L.* *ENDMRF.* 2. aposer *M.* *sim. H.* a poser *F.* 3—3. *so MF. sim. H.* la pes et *L.* poeit apres *ND.* le poer *A.* 4. nomee *ND.* 5. *so NDMH.* et en *L.* 6—6. ne pora a ceo resortir einz *M.* 7—7. *so NAMH.* il retret *L.*

dilatory or peremptory exceptions, as by an exception against the judge, or the plaintiff, or the jurors, or against the writ, and by all other exceptions and replications.

Authority of attorney.

4. An attorney may do all that his lord can, except make accord, for as soon as the proceeding in court is ended, the power of the attorney ceases, and in making the accord another proceeding is begun, which was not before in court, when he was appointed attorney only in the proceeding then in court.

Attorney general and special.

This however must be understood of special, not of general attorneys. For a general attorney can do as much as his client from the commencement to the end of the suit.

Plaintiff abandoning his writ, is barred of his action,

5. When both the plaintiff and the defendants are in court, if the plaintiff declares that he will not further prosecute his writ, in whatever suit this may occur, he shall not afterwards resort to another like writ, but both he and his pledges to prosecute shall remain in our mercy. And if he withdraws himself from the action, he shall be barred of his action for ever; but if he has leave to seek a better writ, or if the writ

meyme la manere si le bref soit abatu pur errour ou pur [1]autre vice[1], et ausi si le play soit meu[2], et [3]en plé pledaunt[3] soit le bref trové vicious, tut die le pleyntif en tel cas, qe il ne vodera mes sure ceo bref, ja pur ceo ne soit barré qe il ne puse resorter a[4] meillour bref semblable[5], pur ceo qe [6]nule parole[6] n'est uncore attamé sur accioun, mes tut al bref, par quei la accioun remeynt entere. Mes [7]si acun se retret de soen bref[7] apres accioun attamé, james ne pora mes resortir al bref semblable de mesmes les persones et de mesmes les tenementz, qe le bref ne soit abatable, si par excepcioun soit averrié. Mes si par replicacioun puse estre averrié qe le tenaunt, sur qi le premer bref fust purchacé, ne fust mie tenaunt del tenement quaunt le bref fust abatu, et qe il purchacea en acune manere [8]puis cel tens par purchaz ou par successioun ou par eschete, en tel cas porra hom resortir a autre bref semblable, et se tendra le bref pur la accioun qe comencea puis le bref abatu.

Brac. 182 b; Fle. 227.

1—1. autre ou par defaute *N.* autre vice ou pur autre defaute *A.* autre vice ou defaute *MH.* 2. taunt auaunt menee *N.* 3—3. en le play pendaunt *N.* en pledant *M.* 4. so *NAMH.* au *L.* 5. de mesmes la persone et mesme le tenement *add. N.* 6—6. nul play *NMH.* *sim. A.* 7—7. si i se retret del accioun de son bref *M.* 8. la seisine *add. NA.* seisine *MH.*

be abated for error or for other fault, and likewise if the plea be opened, and in the course of pleading the writ be found defective, although the plaintiff in such case say that he will not further prosecute that writ, yet he shall not thereby be barred from resorting to a better writ of the like kind, because no proceeding is as yet commenced upon the action, but the whole is to the writ, whereby the action remains entire. But if any one withdraw himself from his writ after the action is opened, he shall never resort to the like writ against the same persons for the same tenement, but the writ shall be liable to abate, if the fact be averred by exception. But if upon replication it can be averred that the tenant against whom the first writ was brought was not tenant of the tenement when the writ was abated, and that he obtained it by some means since that time by purchase, succession, or escheat, in such case the plaintiff may resort to another like writ, and the writ shall hold good, in respect of the right of action which commenced after the writ abated.

unless he has leave to purchase a better writ, or his writ is abated for error.

Brac. 182 *b*, 183; Fle. 227. [120 *b*.] 6. Et si acun attaché[1] die en court qe il ne ad rien en le tenement ne rien ne cleyme, sauntz fere nule forprise, et cele confessioun soit entré en roulles, par taunt iert forclos a touz jours mes de chescun dreit qe il avera eu jekes a cel jour en cel tenement, si par cele excepcioun soit encountré.

Brac. 183 *b*; Fle. 227 (§ 2). 7. Et cum les parties soint venuz en jugement et le pleyntif ne ad mie nostre [2]patente lettre[2] de sa justicerie, les Justices ne averount nul poer de oyer rien ne de rien terminer. Et si le tenaunt entre neqedent en respounse et perde, uncore pora il sa partie recoverer, et tut serra tenu [3]en veyn et a nient[3] quaunt qe les Justices ferount en cel cas. Mes si le pleyntif eit la patente, tauntost soit leu en audience; et si doute soit, par taunt pora le tenaunt aver excepcioun dilatorie a targer la assise. Et puis soit oy le bref clos. Et tauntost soit demaundé al pleyntif de quel fraunc tenement il fet sa pleynte, [4]et la

1. *om. NH.* enplede *M.* 2—2. patente *ND.* bref ou lettre patente *M.* *sim. H.* 3—3. a vein e anenti *M.* en vein *A.* 4—4. *so verb. A.* *sim. NM.* et a la quantite et a la qualite *L.*

Disclaimer bars future claim. 6. If any person attached declare in court that he has nothing in the tenement nor claims anything, without making any reservation, and such confession be recorded, he will be thereby for ever after foreclosed of every right which he may have had until that time in the tenement, if this exception be used against him[h].

Trial without patent is null. 7. If when the parties are come to trial the plaintiff has not our letter patent for trial of his suit, the Justices have no power to hear or determine anything. And if the tenant enter nevertheless into his defence, and lose, he may still recover his former position, and whatsoever the Justices shall do in such case shall be held entirely null and void. But if the plaintiff has the patent, let it be immediately read in audience, and if any doubt arises thereon, the tenant may have on that account a dilatory exception to ward off the assise[i]. Afterwards let oyer be had of the writ close. And let it be immediately demanded of the plaintiff of what freehold he makes his plaint,

Patent to be read. Oyer of writ; Plaintiff's demand stated.

h 'Suppose A to bring a writ of novel disseisin against B, who is tenant. B disclaims. The writ abates. A desires to enter. B will not suffer him. What remedy shall A have? *qu.*' Note in MS. *N.*

i 'Note, that if the Justice takes cognizance of any plea without or beyond their warrant or otherwise, recovery may be had upon them by bill to the king's parliament.' Note in MS. *N.*

quantité et la qualité[4] del tenement soit enbrevé. Et puis soit examiné par nos Justices, coment le pleyntif i out fraunc tenement, et par quel title. Car en nule[1] demaunde [2]ne suffist[2] a soulement demaunder, si le demaundaunt ne moustre par quel dreit, et nient plus en demaunde des choses moebles, qe de nient moebles, ne nient plus en la possessioun qe en le dreit; et qi ne le vodera moustrer ne soit nient respoundu. Brac. 183 *b*; Fle. 227 (§ 2).

CHAPITRE XVI. [XLVII.]

De Title de Fraunc Tenement.

1. Title de fraunc tenement pora hom aver en plusours maneres; sicum par successioun [3]de heritage[3], ou par feffement ou par confermement, ou par quiteclemaunce, [4]ou par [121.] Brac. 183 *b*; Fle. 227, 228.

1. nul manere *ND*. 2—2. so *NDM*. *sim AH*. om. *L*. 3—3. de heritage om. *MH*. 4—4. so *NAH*. *sim*. *MGS*. om *L*.

and let the quality and quantity be imbreviated. Next let our Justices examine how and by what title the plaintiff had a freehold therein; for in every demand it is not sufficient merely to demand, but the plaintiff must show by what right he demands; and this rule applies not only to things movable, but to things immovable, and not only to claims of possession, but to claims of right. And whoever will not make that appear, is not entitled to be answered. Examination of plaintiff's title.

CHAPTER XVI.

Of Title to Freehold.

1. A title of freehold may be acquired several ways[k], as by succession of inheritance, by feoffment, confirmation, quitclaim, recognizance of gift in court of record, chirograph, Several modes of acquiring freehold.

[k] 'Note, that albeit the first part of this chapter saith, that there are sundry titles of frank-tenement, John de Longeville of Northampton tells you shortly (Johan de Longeville de Northampton vus dist curtement) that there are but two and no more, to wit, inheritance and purchase, which are principals, and all the rest are accessories and comprised in the two. For recognizance and judgment of court are sometimes given by reason of purchase, sometimes of inheritance. But confirmation, quitclaim, action of dower and of curtesy of England, and in all other cases, (except inheritance and its accessories, as reversion and escheat,) are comprised in purchase. Seignory purchased also gives rise to escheat. And if the lordship descend before the escheat happens, this is rather inheritance than purchase; for purchase is the acquisition (conqueste) of some right to which the purchaser before was entirely a stranger.' (Note in MS. *N*.) I have extracted this note, principally on account of the light which it may throw on the origin of the whole series of notes of which I have made such frequent use. See the Introduction by the Editor.

reconisaunce[4] de doun en court qe porte record, ou par cirograph, ou par jugement de nostre court, ou par eschete, ou par reversioun, ou par douwarie, ou par ley de Engleterre, ou par fee taylé, ou en gage, ou par condicioun, ou jekes autaunt qe taunt soit levé par jugement de nostre court, ou par simple feffement ou par pesible seisine apres viciouse entré, ou par les autres cas avaunt ditz; et dount le pleyntif ad mester, si il voille estre respoundu, qe il die soen title, ou au meyns qe il fust en seysine pesible taunt[1] de tens qe il ne dust mie sauntz jugement estre disseisi, [2]si qe[2] fraunc tenement luy fust accru[3] par la suffraunce et la negligence le verrei patroun[4] quel qe le entré fust, [5]et cele seisine continua jekes[5] autaunt qe le tenaunt et les autres nomez disseisours en le bref a tort et sauntz jugement le disseisirent, et de ceo prie la assise.

Fle. 227, 228. 2. Et si il die[6] par successioun de heritage, dounc fet a enquere si il trova le fee vacaunt ou noun. Car s'il trova nul autre en seisine, et il soit plus proschein heir le auncestre qi heir il se dit estre, le simple mettre del pié en le chef mees de soen heritage suffit assetz pur aver seisine, qi qe unqes soit

1. par taunt *NAMCH.* 2—2. a quel *N.* si le *M.* si qe autri *C.* 3. encru *M.* 4. possessour *MCH.* 5—5. en cele seisine ieques *M.* en tele seisine iekes *C.* 6. *so NMCH.* dedie *L.* le dedie *A.*

judgment of our court, escheat, reversion, dower, curtesy of England, fee-tail, in mortgage, or by condition, or until so much money be levied by judgment of our court, or by simple feoffment, or by peaceable seisin after a wrongful entry, or by the other cases aforesaid; in which it is necessary for the plaintiff, if he expects to be answered, to set forth his title, or at least to say that he was in peaceable seisin so long a time, that he ought not to have been disseised without judgment, so that a freehold had accrued to him by the sufferance and negligence of the true owner, whatever his entry may have been, and that this seisin continued until the tenant and the other disseisors named in the writ wrongfully and without judgment disseised him, and thereof he prays the assise.

Plaintiff must state his title.

Title by mere possession.

What seisin is sufficient for heir.

2. If the plaintiff states his title by succession of inheritance, then it must be inquired whether he found the fee vacant or not. For if he found no other person in seisin, and he is next heir to the ancestor whose inheritance he claims, the bare setting his foot in the capital messuage of his inheritance is

deforceour, frere ou estraunge, et ne mie soulement del mees, mes de taunt qe al mees [1]apent del heritage[1] dount soen auncestre morust seisi, pur les deus dreitz qe se joynent, ceo est a saver, la possessioun ovesk la propreté. Et en mesme la manere est del dreit de eschete et de reversioun et de la fourme de doun, et en touz autres cas ou la possessioun se joynt verrément[2] ovek la propreté. [121 *b*.]

3. Mes issi n'est mie la ou les[3] deus dreitz ne se joynent mie tauntost en une persone, sicum est de entrusours et des bastardz et des faus heirs, et des autres qi rien ne ount del dreit de propreté for qe soulement la nue possessioun; et sicum est de acuns purchaceours sicum de ceux qi par colour de feffement se boutent en acun tenement, dount les feffours ne les mistrent unques si avaunt de ceo en seisine, si[4] qe les feffours mesmes ne en morrirent seisiz; et sicum est de ceux [5]qi sount excepez en[5] feffementz, [6]sicum Jues ou[6] gent de religioun[7] ou autre persone forprise et defendue; et sicum est de ceux qi entrent par disseisine ou par disseisours, et de Fle. 228.

1—1. *so M.* apent et al heritage *L.* *sim. NA.* apent al heritage *C.* *sim. H.* 2. vniement *M.* 3. *so NMCH.* les *om. LA.* 4. si *om. AMCH.* 5—5. qe exces de *ND.* fount excepciouns en *C.* 6—6. sicum gentz ou *L.* sicum *ND.* sicom *AG.* si com si nous ou *MCH.* si con Ieus e *S.* si cume nus ou *F.* 7. ou Iues *add. NDA.*

enough to give him a seisin, whoever may be the deforceor, whether brother or stranger, and that not only of the messuage but of as much of the inheritance whereof his ancestor died seised as belongs to the messuage, by reason of both rights being united in him, that is to say, the possession and the property. In like manner it is with respect to a right by escheat, reversion, or formedon, and in all cases where the possession is actually united with the property. Possession and property united.

3. It is otherwise where both rights are not immediately united in one person, as in the case of intruders, bastards, pretended heirs, and others who have no right of property but only the naked possession. The same is true of some purchasers, as those who under colour of feoffment thrust themselves into any tenement, whereof the feoffors never so far put them in seisin but that they themselves died seised thereof. So it is of those who are excepted in feoffments, as Jews, persons in religion, and other excluded or prohibited persons. So of those who enter by disseisin or through dis- Feehold by wrong not easily acquired.

autres qi entrent en acuni[1] prejudice et damage. Car ceux qi [2]entrent en acun[2] tenement par teus qe point de dreit ne ount dė doner ne de aliener, sicum par fermers [3]ou par termers[3] ou par condicioun ou par baillif ou gardein ou
[122.] vileyns ou par autres nent verreys seignurs, ceux ne porunt nul fraunc tenement aver for qe par pesible seisine et par[4] continuaunce de tens, ou jekes autaunt qe satisfaccioun soit fete a la condicioun, si alienacioun soit condicionele. Ne teus ausi qi entrent par ceux qi averunt fet felonie, de quel il
Ante, c. 3. s. 5. sount puis atteyntz. Ne ceux qi entrent par feffemenz de bastardz, dount les bastardz ne furent mie feffez a lour assignez; car pur favour de bastardz furent primes assignez [5]trovez pur[5] mettre en feffementz.

4. Et cum le pleyntif avera moustré sa entente et soen title, adounc covent al tenaunt a drescer ses resouns, s'il put,
Cf. Fle. 229 (c. 7. § 6). et moustrer quel dreit il out de ly engitter ou destourber. Et si le tenaunt moustre [6]chartre del[6] pleyntif pur soen title,

1. acun. *L.* *sim.* *AH.* acuny *M.* asqune *C.* acun tenement en *N.* 2—2. so *N.* *sim.* *CH.* entrent acun *L.* *sim.* *A.* entrent en acuny *M.* 3—3. *om.* *AMCH.* 4. lounge *add.* *N.* *sim.* *AMCH.* 5—5. trouez par *L.* graunteez pur *ND.* *sim.* *AGS.* grauntez a *M.* *sim.* *F.* garaunz a *C.* 6—6. lettre de *N.* *sim.* *CF.* lentre le *M.*

seisors, and of all others who enter to the damage or prejudice of any one. For those who enter into any tenement by such as have no right to give or alienate the same, as by farmers or termors, or by those who hold under condition, or by bailiff, guardian, villains, or others not being the true owners, can have no freehold unless by peaceable seisin and lapse of time, or where the alienation was conditional, until the condition be satisfied. Neither can such as enter by those who have committed felony of which they are afterwards attainted. Nor those who enter by virtue of feoffments made by bastards, where the bastards were not themselves enfeoffed to them and

'Assigns,' why inserted in feoffments.

their assigns; for it was in favour of bastards that the word assigns was first devised to be inserted in feoffments.

Defence of tenant.

4. When the plaintiff shall have set forth his intent and title, it then behoves the tenant to make out his defence, if he can, and to show what right he had to eject or disturb

Charter ineffectual without livery.

the plaintiff. And if the tenant in support of his title produces a charter of the plaintiff, that shall not avail him,

ceo ne ly vaille rien, si de la volunté le donour ne ly fut fet le bayl de la seisine.

5. Et si le tenaunt die qe rien ad ne rien ne cleyme, ja pur taunt ne remeigne qe enquis ne soit par la assise, si il ly fist disseisine a tort ou noun, et si as armes [1]ou a force[1] ou nutauntre ou de jour; [2]et des damages et[2] des autres circumstaunces solom le verdit [3]se face[3] le jugement, sicum apres serra dit. Brac. 183, 186 *b*, 187; Fle. 229 (c. 7. § 6). Post, c. 22. s. 4, 8.

CHAPITRE XVII. [XLVIII.]

De Excepciouns al Bref. [122 *b*.]

1. En plusours maneres est ceste assise destourbé qe ele ne soit tauntost prise, sicum par excepcioun peremptorie, sicum sount excepciouns [4]de naifté ou de villenage, condicioun[4], covenaunt, quiteclemaunce, confermement, reles [5], difficulté Brac. 187 *b*; Fle. 233.

1—1. *so NACH.* ou fource *L.* e a force *M.* 2—2. *so verb. GA.* ou de damages ou *L.* des damages et *M.* e de damages ou *S.* 3—3. *so SGAMCH.* ceo face *L.* face *N.* 4—4. de vilenage ou de vileine condicioun *M.* 5. *so NAM.* relef *L.* relefs *CH.*

unless livery of seisin was made to him by the free will of the donor.

5. And if the tenant say that he has no title and claims none, still it does not follow but that inquisition be made by the assise, whether he disseised the plaintiff tortiously or not, and whether with arms or by force, and whether in the night or by day. And concerning the damages and the other circumstances, let judgment be given as shall be hereafter mentioned, according to the verdict. Disclaimer does not prevent inquest as to act of disseisin.

CHAPTER XVII.

Of exceptions to the writ.

1. The immediate taking of this assise is prevented in many ways, as by peremptory exceptions, such as exceptions of naifty or villenage, of condition, covenant, quitclaim, confirmation, release, difficulty of judgment [1], fine and chirograph, lapse Exceptions peremptory and dilatory.

[1] 'Difficulty of judgment is a shameful reason for delay (un delay mult honteus); because the king, who ought to govern the people by the law, ought not to be ignorant of it (la mesconustre); nor his Justices, unless it be in some outrageous and perplexed case (cas horrible e deguisé,) then common counsel is better than private haste.' Note in MS. *N.*

de jugement, fin et cirograph, cours de tens et autres; et par excepciouns dilatories, sicum sount[1] excepciouns pur bref abatre, excepciouns al juge, et a la persone le pleyntif, et [2]a persone[2] demeene, issi qe les excepciouns al bref abatre soint purposez avaunt la excepcioun a la persone le pleyntif.

Brac. 188; Fle. 233.

2. Et confermé la persone la Justice, adounc se pora le tenaunt eyder par excepcioun al bref abatre, sicum par vice trové en le bref, sicum par rasure en leu suspect, ou si le bref ne fust unques selé de noster seal, ou si le ordinaunce ou le estil de nostre Chauncelerie ne soit point contenu; et ausi par defaute de date est le bref abatable et vicious, et ausi par [3]vice de[3] escripture, cum [4]de deverses[4] meyns ou deverses enkes, et de brusure, cum si le bref soit rout[5] ou dampné ou chauncelé; et ausi par vise de la patente[6] cum[7] par vise de rasure, et pur le seal pendu par engyn. Mes en totes les fausines trovez en nos brefs, voloms nous qe les suspecciouns[8] soint purgez[9] et[10]

Ante, l. i. c. 5. s. 14.

1. par *MCH* 2—2. a sa persone *NGAM.* 3—3. *so NAMCH.* vne *L.* 4—4. *so A.* deuerses *LN.* de deus *NCH.* 5. roynt *N.* esquache *M.* rumpu *CH.* 6. parchemin *C.* *sim. H.* 7. e *M.* ou *CH.* 8 *so LH.* *sim. SGM.* suspetious *ND.* suspeteouses *C.* 9. *conj.* puniz *LSNDA.* punis *G.* punit rez *M.* pures *CH.* purs *F.* 10. et *om. SG.*

of time and others; and also by dilatory exceptions, as by exceptions to abate the writ, exceptions to the judge, and to the person of the plaintiff, and to the tenant's own person; but exceptions to abate the writ must be proposed before the exception to the person of the plaintiff.

Exception to the judge.

Exception in abatement of writ.

2. Supposing the jurisdiction of the Justice to be confirmed, the tenant may then aid himself by exceptions in abatement of the writ, as for a defect found in the writ, as by an erasure in a suspicious place, or if the writ was never sealed with our seal, or if the ordinance or style of our Chancery is not observed. The writ is also abatable and defective for want of date; likewise for a defect in the writing, as being written in two hands, or with different inks; and for damage to the writ, as if it be torn, marred, or cancelled; likewise for defect of the patent, as on account of an erasure, or by reason of the seal being fraudulently attached thereto. And in all cases of falsification of our writs, we will that such suspicions be cleared up, and the like as to illegal distresses[m]; but these cases shall be

Falsification of writs to be subject of special trial.

m The text in this passage seems to be corrupt, and the true reading is not recoverable with certainty. I have ventured to introduce the word *purgez* (perhaps originally

les[1] mauveises destresces, et determinez[1] nequedent par Justices a ceo entitlez. Mes les suspectz[2] soint tauntost[3] attachez.

3. Et a ceo qe il dist en le bref, Pleynt se[4] est a nous, pora mettre excepcioun de abatre le bref par defaute de autre qi ad autaunt de dreit a pleindre ou plus qe ne ad le pleyntif; sicum del fraunc tenement la femme, ou le baroun est soul nomé en la pleynte, et en autres cas semblables, [5]ou le bref dust dire: Pleynt se sount a nous[5]. Brac. 202; Fle 240. [123.]

4. Et ausi est le bref abatable, si le bref fust purchacé avaunt la disseisine; et ausi si la cause cessa, tut fust la disseisine fete, sicum si le disseisour eit rendu le tenement al disseisi, qi de soen gré le avera repris par soen rendre. Mes s'il le eust repris par sa propre force, adounc serroit pys[6] pur le pleyntif. Et ausi si le pleyntif soit[7] autre foiz suttret[8] de Fle. 233 (§ 5). Brac. 188; Fle. 233 (§ 5, 6).

1—1. et *om.* *NDSG.* mauueises *om.* *AR.* mauueis desteces e determinez *M.* mauueis determinez *C.* *sim.* *HF.* 2. suspetious *ND.* 3. tauntost *om.* *MCH.* 4. so *NAMH.* ceo *L.* se *om.* *C.* 5—5. *so verb.* *M.* *sim.* *NA.* *om.* *LCH.* 6. piz *N.* pir *M.* pris *C.* prise *H.* 7. se soit *N.* *sim.* *DAR.* 8. sustret *NDACH.*

determined only by Justices thereto authorised. The suspected persons however shall be forthwith attached.

3. The words in the writ, 'has complained to us,' may furnish ground for an exception to abate the writ for want of another who has as much or more right to complain than the plaintiff; as where the plaint is of the wife's freehold, and the husband only is named[n], and in other like cases, where the writ ought to run, 'have complained to us,' &c. Abatement for want of parties.

4. The writ is also abatable if purchased before the disseisin, and also if the cause of action has ceased though the disseisin was in fact committed, as if the disseisor has restored the tenement to the disseisee, who has consented to take it back by such surrender. But if he had retaken it by his own force, then it should be worse for the plaintiff. Also if the plaintiff Various causes of abatement.

written *puriez*), of which there appear to be traces in the various readings. I think the whole may possibly have stood as follows: 'qe les suspecciouns soint puriez et les mauueis brefs detenus et determinez,' &c.; 'that the suspicions be cleared up, and the forged or suspected writs impounded.' The verb *purger* is similarly used in l. i. c. 2. s. 6, ante, p. 11.

n The annotator in MS. *N.* discusses the law here laid down at some length, and distinguishes as follows: 'If the husband has had issue and consequently action to hold by the curtesy, he shall be answered; otherwise not. For the husband detained by his wife out of the wife's right, whereof an estate by the curtesy has accrued to him, shall recover against the wife by the assise, much more against a stranger. So likewise of their common purchase, and of the several right of the husband. But suppose the wife to keep out her husband from the wife's right, *quæro* whether he shall recover.' See above, c. 11. s. 16, c. 13. s. 5, and below, c. 18. s. 9.

[1]mesme tel[1] bref ou de mesme tele[2] assise, si ceo soit averré. Et ausi si le pleyntif se soit pleynt par bref pendaunt de autri seisine[3], ou[4] de plus haute nature, [5]pur le ordre de plee[5] nient gardé.

Brac. 188; Fle. 233 (§ 7). 5. Et ausi si le bref ne soit nient conceu solom le cas. Et ausi si le bref soit malement purchacé, cum si plusours pleintifs soint nomez en un bref, ou dussent estre deverses assises, ou la reverse. Et ausi en cas ou acun tenement est reconu a deus hommes a tener en commune, si le un soit en seisine, et puis soit engetté, s'il se pleyne [6]soul estre[6] engetté et disseisi del tut, si chet le bref, tut ne fust le autre parcener unques en seisine. Car la seisine ly[7] fust liveré ausi bien en noun de soen parcener cum [8]en soen noun demeyne[8]; et [123 *b.*] assetz est cil seisi en qi noun seisine est prise, s'il tienent estable ceo que en lour noun est fet.

Brac. 188, 188 *b*; Fle. 233, 234. 6. Le bref pora estre vicious en plusours maneres, cum si le bref soit purchacé sur celi qi est tenaunt en autri noun, sicum sur baillif ou fermer ou gardeyn ou chanoyne [9]ou

1—1. *so M.* mesme cele *L.* *sim. ACH.* sa demaunde par cel *ND.* 2. cele *L.* *sim. NACH.* tel *M.* 3. *so LSGM.* disseisine *ND.* 4. ou, *om. M.* e *NDSGA.* 5—5. *om. M.* 6—6. estre soul *M.* soulement estre *A,* 7. *so NM.* *sim. AH.* lour *L.* 8—8. *so N.* *sim. MACHS.* de soen demeyne *L.* 9—9. *om. M.*

has before withdrawn himself from a like writ, or a like assise, if this be verified. So likewise if the plaintiff has before made his plaint by a writ pending, founded upon the seisin of another, or by a writ of a higher nature, because the order of pleas has not been observed.

Misjoinder of plaintiffs. 5. The writ is also abatable if it is not well framed according to the case. So if the writ be badly purchased, as if several plaintiffs are named in a writ where there ought to be different Non-joinder. assises, or the reverse. So where any tenement is acknowledged to two men to hold jointly, if one has seisin thereof, and is afterwards ejected, and he brings plaint alone of being ejected and disseised of the whole, the writ fails, though the other parcener was never in seisin; for the seisin was delivered to him as well in the name of his parcener as in his own proper name; and he is sufficiently seised in whose name the seisin is taken, if he holds good what was done in his name.

Writ defective, if principal is not named. 6. The writ may be faulty in several ways, as if it is purchased against him who is tenant in the name of another, as against a bailiff, or farmer, or a guardian, or a canon, or a

serjaunt[9] sauntz nomer le principal en le bref. Et ausi par mesprisioun[1] de nouns nomables en bref, sicum Reynard[2] pur Reyner, Amice pur Avice; pur misprisioun de surnoun; et ausi pur omissioun de sillabes[1] ou des lettres des paroles ou de resouns; et ausi par defaute de surnoun de dignité, cum si Johan soit seculer homme et soit Mestre de Hospital, et se soit pleynt etres disseisi de acun fraunc tenement apendaunt a mesme cel hospital, et si n'est il mie nomé Mestre del Hospital. En mesme la manere [3]est de[3] persone de eglise, et touz prelatz et religious demaundauntz tenementz estre apurtenauntz a lour eglises ou a lour provendes, ou il ne se eyent fet nomer persone de tele Eglise, ou [4]arcevasqe ou evesqe ou chanoyn ou[4] prelat; ou si chanoyn seculer ad certeyne dignеté en[5] acune eglise dount il est chanoyn, a quele dignité il cleyme le tenement qe il demaund apendre, sicum [6]dené ou thresorie ou chaunterie[6], s'il ne soit nomé en le bref par mesme le surnoun de la dignеté ou del office, si est

Brac. 188 *b*; Fle. 234.

Brac. 189 (§ 6); Fle. 234 (§ 8).

1. *so L. sim SAR.* des surnouns auxi par omissioun des sillabes *ND.* de nouns nent nomablcs *M.* des nouns nomables *CH. sim. F.* 2. Richard *GAR.* 3—3. *so MCHF.* est *om. LA.* est de *om. N.* 4—4. Arceuasqe ou autre chanoun ou *L. sim. S.* Eueske ou autre chanoigne ou *N. sim. D.* Ercedeen ou autre chanoin ou *A.* Ercheuesqe ou Euesque ou chanoun ou *M.* Erceuesqe ou *C.* 5. *so NAMC.* ou *L.* a *H.* 6—6. done au thresorie ou chaunterie *L.* denrie tresorie ou chaunterie *N. sim. D.* dene ou tresorie ou chauncelerie *M.* denee ou tresorie ou chanterie *A. sim. GS.* al chauncellerie ou a la tresorie *C.* done a chauncelerie ou a tresorie *H.*

servant, without naming the principal in the writ. Also by mistake of Christian names in the writ, as Reynard for Reyner, Amice for Avice, or for mistake of surnames; likewise for omission of syllables or of letters in the words or sentences; likewise for want of a surname of dignity, as if John is a secular man, and Master of a Hospital, and complains that he is disseised of a frechold appendant to the same hospital, and is not named Master of the Hospital. The same rule holds in the case of a parson of a church, and all prelates and persons of religion, demanding tenements as appurtenant to their churches or prebends, where they have not named themselves parson of such a church, or archbishop or bishop or canon or prelate. So if a canon secular has a certain dignity in any church whereof he is a canon, to which dignity he claims the tenement in demand to be appendant, as to a deanery, treasury, or chantry, if he is not named in the writ by the same surname of dignity or office, the writ is abatable. So, in

Misnomer.

le bref abatable. Et en mesme la manere en dreit del tenaunt; [124.] si la dignité et le office ne soint especifiez, a quel il cleyme le tenement nomé en la pleinte annex.

Brac. 189 (§ 9), 211; Fle 234 (§ 12).

7. Et ausi par mesprisioun de vile, cum en cas ou hamelet est nomé la ou hom dust nomer la vile a quele le hamelet apent. Et de la difference qe est entre maners viles et hameletz serra dit en [1]la prise[1] de dreit. En mesme la manere [2]par defaute[2] de fere severauté en le bref de viles semblables as autres viles en mesme le counté; et ausi si le tenement[3] ne soit mie en la vile nomé en le bref.

Brac. 211 b; Fle. 242.

8. Et si de ceo soit debat entre les parties, de office soit enquise la verité, mes ne mie [4]en jeupartie de perdre ou[4] de gayner, tut le [5]voillent les parties[5]. Car excepcioun est mise avaunt pur le bref abatre, et nient encountre la assise. Et si les jurours dient qe le tenement ne est mie en la vile nomé en le bref, si chet le bref, et jalemeyns ne remeynt la assise et le tort determiné; et porra le pleyntif resorter a autre bref sem-

1—1. *so LGMH.* le chapitre *NA.* le prise *S.* 2—2. *so NAMCH. om. L.* 3. *so NAMCH.* tenaunt *L.* 4—4. de rien perdre a la partie ne *M.* en ren partie de perdre ou *H. sim. CF.* en partie de riens perdre ou *G.* 5—5. voleit la partie *M.*

case of the tenant, if the dignity and office to which he claims the tenement named in the plaint to be annexed are not specified.

Locality improperly stated.

7. The writ may also abate for mistake in the town, as if a hamlet is named where the town to which the hamlet belongs ought to have been named. The difference between manors, townships, and hamlets will be noticed in the chapter concerning Recovery of Right. So likewise for want of distinction in the writ between vills of a like name in the same county; as also if the tenement is not situate in the vill named in the writ.

Proceeding where situation is disputed. Writ, not action, prejudiced by this question.

8. If the situation be disputed between the parties, the truth shall be inquired by office, but not so that the gaining or losing of the action shall be at stake, though the parties be willing that it should be so. For the exception is put forward to abate the writ, and not against the assise. And if the jurors say that the tenement is not in the vill named in the writ, the writ abates, but the assise and the wrong nevertheless remain undetermined, and the plaintiff may resort to

blable, lequel il [1] se recrese [1] de soen bref par coungé ou sauntz coungé. Et s'il dient qe le tenement est en la vile nomee en le bref, adounc soit prise la assise. Et si les jurours ne sevent [2] en quele des deus viles le tenement soit, adounc soit demandé del pleyntif s'il cleyme rien de cel tenement en autre vile qe nomé ne est en le bref, et puis del tenaunt s'il cleyme rien en la vile nomé. Et si il dient [3] que noun, adounc soit comaundé as jurours del assise et as autres gentz del visnee qe renables devises et boundes soint mys par entre les deus viles. Et en mesme la manere soit fet de semblable distaunce ewe [4] entre [5] parties de par entre [5] deus maners ou deus countez, issi qe par puralez soit le plé et le contek detrié et terminé. Et si le pleyntif soit de eynz age, adounc soit le plee suspendu, et respité jekes a soen age. Car nul enfaunt de eynz age ne peut rien desclamer [6] en prejudice de ly, si il cleyme rien en tel counté ou noun, ou en tele vile, ou [7] en tel maner, pur [7] la puralé qe ensuit [8] qe detrie le dreit a [124 *b.*]

1—1. cesse *N.* se recesse *A.* se retret *MGC.* retreit *H.* 2. seuent certeinement *N.* *sim. AGHSM.* seuent mie certeinement *C.* 3. dit *MC.* die *NH.* 4. de ewe *LM.* eus *S.* ou *CH.* *om. NGA.* 5—5. parties par *N.* parties par entre *GA.* deus parties par entre *CH.* 6. so *NDGHC.* *sim. MF.* clamer *LS.* 7—7. *so verb. M.* *sim. AS.* en tele manere pur *L.* en tele manere purra *ND.* *sim. HF.* 8. *so G,* enfust *LMH.* *sim. CF.* en fuit *A.* rien ne fet for *N.*

another like writ, whether he withdrew himself from his writ with or without leave. And if they say that the tenement is in the vill named in the writ, then let the assise be taken. And if the jurors do not know for certain in which of the two vills the tenement lies, then let it be demanded of the plaintiff whether he claims anything of this tenement in any vill not named in the writ, and afterwards of the tenant, whether he claims anything in the vill named; and if they say no, then let the jurors of the assise and others of the neighbourhood be ordered to set up proper metes and bounds between the two vills. The like shall be done where a difference arises between parties concerning the boundaries of two manors or two counties, so that the plea and dispute shall be tried and determined by perambulation. And if the plaintiff is under age, the plea must be suspended and respited until he is of age; for no infant can answer to his own prejudice, whether he claims such a thing in such a county, or in such a vill or manor, or not, on account of the perambulation which follows, whereby

Boundaries of counties, vills, or manors settled by perambulation.

Infant cannot be party to such a settlement.

touz jours quant as devises; et issi remeyndra [1]le plee et la puralé[1] a fere deques al age [2]del pleyntif, qi avaunt soen age[2] ne porra point assenter en la puralé.

Brac. 211 *b*, 212; Fle. 242, 243.

9. Et si les jurours dient qe partie del tenement est en la une vile, ou en le un counté, et partie en l'autre, adounc soit prise l'assise pur cele partie del tenement qe est en la vile ou en le counté nomé en le bref, et nient del remenaunt. Et issi porrount par cas ambideus les parties remeyndre en nostre merci. Et en mesme la manere soit fete puralee pur contek des parties, ou destaunce est entre eux en queus feez ou queles baronies le tenement est, [3]cum le un dist[3] en un et le autre en un autre, et noméement si les jurours ne sevent mie la cer-
[125.] teyneté; sauve ceo qe en touz teus[4] cas soit demaundé des parties si ils cleyment rien ou noun cleyment, sicum avaunt est dit.

Brac. 207, 209.

10. Et ausi si hom demaunde tenement en soil privilegé, ou teus brefs ne courrount nent, sicum de nos aunciens demeynes, [5]ou nient ne court[5] for qe bref de dreit clos

1—1. *so verb. GM.* le plee et la parole *L.* *sim. NSCHF.* la parole *A.* 2—2. *om. MCH.* car ein *F.* 3—3. *so verb. NGSA.* cum le vn dust *L.* com bien dit *M.* com le dreit *CH.* 4. *so LS.* teus *om. NAGMCH.* 5—5. *so N.* cum nient ne curent *L.* ou nient ne oirent *A.* ou nent ni vnt *S.* ou riens ne vnt *G.* ou ne i courent *M.* *om. CH.*

the right as to the boundaries would be determined for ever. Therefore the plea and perambulation shall stand to be taken at the plaintiff's majority, for before that time he cannot give his assent to the perambulation.

Proceeding where part of the tenement is in the vill named.

9. If the jurors say, that part of the tenement is in one vill or one county and part in the other, then let the assise be taken for that part of the tenement which is in the vill or in the county named in the writ, and not for the rest. It may thus happen that both the parties remain in our mercy. In the same manner perambulation shall be made in case of a difference between the parties, where the contest is in what fees or in what baronies the tenement lies, where one says in one fee and the other in another, and in particular where the jurors are uncertain; saving that in all these cases it shall be demanded of the parties, as before mentioned, whether they claim anything or not.

Abatement by plea of ancient demesne.

10. The writ will also abate, if one demands a tenement in privileged soil, where such writs do not run, as in our ancient demesnes, where no writs run except a writ of right close

solom les usages des maners. A ceo [1]qe dist,[1] de soen fraunc tenement, porrount sourdre excepciouns: une pur ceo qe le fraunc tenement ne fust unques al pleyntif, mes a sa femme. Et si le baroun et sa femme seynt ambedeus pleyntifs, et il se soint pleyntz qe il sount disseisiz, par taunt supposent il qe il avoyent ambedeus fraunc tenement, et qe il tyndrent en commune; et de ceo sourd en cas excepcioun a[2] bref abatre. Et ausi par defaute de difference mettre entre le pere et le fiz en cas ou le fiz ad fet disseisine, et porte autel noun et autel surnoun cum soen pere. Et si acun eit deus surnouns, cel surnoun se tiegne dount il est plus conu. Plusours excepciouns sount a bref abatre, sicum dit serra entre les excepciouns del plee de dreit.

Ante, c. 17, s. 3, p. 315.
Brac. 202 *b*; Fle. 240; Ante, c. 13. s. 5. p. 297.
Brac. 188 *b*; Fle. 234.

12. Et si le bref soit perdu ou remué maliciousement [3]de filaz[3], adounc cesse le poer la Justice. Car sauntz garaunt de bref original de nostre Chauncelerie, ne ad Justice nul record. Mes si suspeccioun i courge de malice, tauntost soit enquis

Brac. 189 (§ 10); Fle. 234 (§ 14).

1—1. qe il dit *N.* qe dit *A.* qe dit est *M.* *sim. H.* 2. pur *N.* al *A.* pur le *MC.* de *H.* 3—3. des filles *N.* des filaz *SA.* des filez *M.* des files *C.* de Philatz *H.* *om. G.*

according to the custom of the manor. Exceptions may also be founded upon those words of the writ which say, 'of his freehold,' inasmuch, for example, as the freehold never was the plaintiff's, but his wife's; and if the husband and wife are both plaintiffs and complain that they are disseised, they thereby suppose that they both had a freehold, and that they held in common; and upon this an exception may chance to arise to abate the writ. So also, for not distinguishing between the father and the son, where the son has committed the disseisin and bears the same Christian name and surname as his father. And where any one has two surnames, that surname shall hold by which he is best known. There are several other exceptions to abate the writ which shall be noticed among exceptions in a plea of right.

Exception that freehold was not in plaintiff.
Disseisor not distinctly named.
Double surname.

12. If the writ be lost or maliciously taken off the files, then the authority of the Justice ceases; for without warrant by original writ out of our Chancery no Justice hath record. But if there be any suspicion of malice, let it be forthwith inquired by whose malice the writ was removed; and whosoever shall

If the writ be lost, the jurisdiction ceases.
Malicious abstraction of writ.

'par qi' malice la subtraccioun[2] avera este fete; et qi en ert atteynt soit pris et puniz par prisoen et gref rancoun.

[125 b.]

CHAPITRE XVIII. [XLIX.]

Des excepciouns a la persone le pleintif.

Brac. 190; Fle. 235.

1. Ratifié le bref, uncore se pora le tenaunt eyder par excepciouns encountre la persone le pleyntif, sicum par

Brac. 203; Fle. 235.

excepcioun de escumengé. [3]Car escumengé[3] est autaunt a dire cum [4]home qe est[4] hors de commune [5]pur lepre[5] del alme sicum meseyl [6]pur lepre[6] del cors. Et taunt[7] cum acun est escumengé, il ne deit communer ove nul homme, ne nul a[8] ly. Ne ceux ne sount en nul plee responables, sicum serra dit en plee de dreit.

Brac. 190; Fle. 235; Hengh. P. c. 8. p. 103.

2. Et ausi se porra le tenaunt eyder par excepcioun de villenage encountre le pleyntif en soen cas issi. Assise ne deit estre, car le pleyntif est moen vileyn. [9]Mes a ceo covent il[9]

1—1. *so verb. MCH.* par quele *LND.* *sim. SA.* de quele *G.* 2. substitution *S.* 3—3. *so verb. SGAC.* *om. L.* qe *ND.* car escomage *M.* 4—4. *so M.* home estre *LNA.* home *SG.* home est *CHF.* 5—5. pur le peril *M.* e lepre *C.* pur la pravite *A.* 6—6. pur la prauite *A.* lepre *C.* 7. tantost *M.* *sim. H.* 8. *so LSM.* oue *N.* home ouesques *G.* 9—9. Mes il couent *N.* Mes la couendra *M.* Mes couint *C.* *sim. H.*

be convicted thereof shall be taken and punished by imprisonment and heavy ransom.

CHAPTER XVIII.

Of exceptions to the person of the plaintiff.

Exception of excommunication.

1. The writ being established, the tenant may still aid himself by exceptions against the person of the plaintiff, as that he is excommunicated. For a person excommunicate is one that is out of communion on account of a leprosy of the soul, as a leper is for the disease of his body; and so long as a person is excommunicated, he ought not to commune with any one nor any one with him, neither is he entitled to be answered in any action, as shall be noticed in the plea of right.

Exception of villenage;

2. The tenant may also aid himself in a proper case by exception of villenage against the plaintiff in the following form: 'Assise ought not to lie, inasmuch as the plaintiff is my

qe il die qe il soit seysi de sa sute et de ses chateus ou qe il tient de ly en villenage, ne mie neqedent pur recoverer luy pur[1] soen vileyn, mes pur barrer la assise el accioun le pleyntif. Si le pleyntif neqedent par sa mise et par soen assent se seit mis en juré sur acune circumstaunce de soen estat, et s'il soit ausi cum atteynt pur le vileyn le tenaunt, bien list al tenaunt [2]de amener[2] et de encepper[3] et de chacer[4] cum fere deit soen vileyn; ne mie neqedent par jugement de nostre court sauntz autre bref, mes al peril qe apent. Car si il se peuse prover estre de fraunc estat sicum feffé a ly et a ses heirs par soen seignur, ou en autre manere, il avera accioun vers chescun qi tort ou grevaunce ly avera fet, par bref de trespas ou en autre manere.

Brac. 192 *b*, 193; Fle. 236 (§ 4). 237 (§ 11).

[126.]

3. Et en mesme la manere, si il peuse prover qe il eit demoré hors del fee [5]et hors de la seisine[5] le seignur, [6]par l'assise ou par le atteynte[6], par un an et un jour en cleymaunt fraunc estat sauntz cleym le seignur; si qe sauntz bref de

Glan. l. 5. c. 5; Brac. 190 *b*; Fle. 235 (§ 2).

1. cum *N.* sur. *M.* 2—2. *so LNM.* del amener *GS.* de mener *A.* dennoier *CH.* 3. *so LMA.* *sim SG.* encouper *NCH.* 4. *so L.* enchacer *NCH.* chastier *SGM.* 5—5. *om. CHF.* 6—6. *so LNSG.* par le assent de luy e par lauctorite *M.* *om. CH.* par la sise e par lautorite *F.*

villain.' But then he must also add, that he is seised of his suit and of his chattels, or that he holds of him in villenage;—not however for the purpose of recovering him for his villain, but to bar the assise in the plaintiff's action. But if the plaintiff has by his pleading or by consent put himself upon the jury concerning any circumstance of his estate, and he be thus as it were attainted for the villain of the tenant, the tenant may well take him away and put him in the stocks, or drive him off the land, as he should his villain, yet not so as to be justified by the judgment of our court without another writ, but at his own peril. For if the alleged villain can prove himself to be of free condition, as having been enfeoffed to himself and his heirs by his lord, or in any other manner, he shall have an action by writ of trespass or otherwise, against every one who has done him wrong or grievance.

holds only where the tenant can aver seisin of the villain.

The finding of the assise is not binding upon status;

and the lord acts on it at his peril.

3. So likewise the exception will fail if the plaintiff can prove by the assise or by attaint that he has lived out of the lord's fee and out of his seisin for a year and a day, claiming free estate, without claim by the lord; so that the lord cannot

The exception fails if the villain has been fugitif unclaimed for a year.

naifté ne le put il mie prendre ne recoverer[1] cum soen vileyn

Brac. 191; Fle. 236 (§ 8). [2]Car nuli ne pora clamer dreit en les apurtenances ne en les accessories qi nul dreit n'en ad en le princepal plé. Et pur ceo covendra en tiel cas qe le seignur demaunde primes le cors soen vileyn[2] par bref de naifté, et cum il avera le cors, si avera [3]les biens et la terre et[3] quant qe au cors apent. Et si le seignur toille rien a tiel futif sauntz jugement de nostre court, si fet encountre nostre pes. Et pur ceo voloms nous que teus futifs eynt accioun de recoverer de lour seignurs ceo qe lour seignurs averount tollet par force apres le an et le jour passé de lour feute[4], jekes autaunt qe le cors soit disreyné[5] pur lour[6] vileyn.

4. Et pur ceo fet[7] a examiner en ceste excepcioun, si les seignurs, qi mettent avaunt teles excepciouns, [8]soint en mesme le oure seisiz[8] de ceux qi il dient estre lour vileyns, et de lour seute et de lour chateus, ou qe il eynt esté lour [126 *b.*] vileyns et puis lour sount defuyz, et[9] adounc par cum bien de tens. Car si il eient esté [10]lour futifs[10] plus qe par un an, sicum

1. retener *M.* *sim. F.* 2—2. *omitted here, and added at the end of the section in ND.* 3—3. terre e *N.* terre e purchaz e *M.* *om. C.* 4. seute *L.* fute *ND.* sute *MF.* suite *AC.* 5. *so D.* *sim. NAM.* destreynt *L.* atteint *CH.* 6. *so N.* *sim. MCHF.* le *L.* sun *A.* 7. *so NAMCHF.* fet *om. L.* 8—8. seent eus mesmes en seisine *M.* suent eus mesmes leur seisine *C.* souent eus mesmes lour seiser *H.* 9. et *om. MCHF.* E si defuyz *G.* 10—10. lour fuiz *N.* sustret *C.* sustrez *H.*

And the lord must proceed by writ of naifty. take or recover him as his villain without a writ of naifty. For no one can claim any right to the appurtenances or accessories who has no right in the principal subject of action; and therefore the lord in such cases should first demand the body of his villain by writ of naifty; and after he has recovered the body, he shall have the goods and the land and all that belongs to the body. And if the lord take anything from such fugitive without judgment of our court, he acts against our peace. And therefore we will that such fugitives shall have their action to recover from their lords what their lords shall have taken from them by force after a year and a day from their flight, until the right in the bodies be proved.

Points to be examined in exception of villenage. 4. Therefore in this exception it is proper to examine whether the lords who put forward such exceptions are at that very time seised of those whom they allege to be their villains, and of their suit and chattels, or whether they were formerly their villains, and have since fled from them; and if so, how long since. For if they have been fugitives above a year,

dit est avaunt, la excepcioun ne tient mie leu; et si les seignurs pusent averrer lour seisine[1] de eynz le an et le jour, dounc sei teigne. Et en mesme la manere si il peuse averrer deligente seute de reclamer le et de purchacer cum soen futif et soen vileyn, tut ne eit il esté mie seisi de ly de eynz le an et le jour.

5. Et si le tenaunt die, que le pleyntif est autri vileyn, adounc covendra dire ovek, qe il ne tient mie les tenementz qe il demaund en soen noun demeyne mes en noun soen seignur, qi vileyn il est; en [2]quel cas l'assise[2] remeyndra, si[3] le pleyntif ne[4] puse moustrer par chartre de feffement, qe[5] il en fut feffé a luy et a ses heirs. Et [6]tut mette il[6] [7]a veer[7] tel purchaz, uncore ne vaudra nient tele proeve, s'il ne mette [8]a veer[8] oveke, [9]qe le seignur al vileyn ne[9] fust unques de ceo en seisine puis le purchaz le vileyn. Et si trové soit qe le seignur aveit seisi le tenement apres le purchaz fet par soen vileyn, tut le bailast il arere al vileyn a tener a sa volunté, en cel cas chet la assise, pur ceo qe le vileyn ne fu nent te-

Brac. 190, 190 *b*, 191 *b*, 193 *b*.

Brac. 192; Fle. 238 (§ 11).

1. *so NAM.* disseysine *LHF.* 2—2. *so N.* *sim. AMCHF.* quel assise *L.* 3. *so MCF.* et si *L.* *sim. NSGA.* 4. *so MG.* ne *om. LS.* 5. si *M.* 6—6. com il mette *M.* 7—7. auerreer *L.* a veir *DAR.* aueir *NGS.* *sim. MHF.* a voir *C.* 8—8. auerreer *L.* aueyr *N.* a veir *DARF.* a voir *M.* aueir *GH.* auoir cel proue *C.* 9—9. *so verb. ARMH.* le seignur al vileyn si il ne *L.* le seigneur al villein e qil ne *C.*

there is no room for the exception, as has been before said; but if the lords can aver their seisin within a year and day, then it holds good; and in like manner, if the lord can aver diligent suit to reclaim and recover him as his fugitive and villain, although he has not been seised of him within the year and day.

The lord must aver seisin within the year, or diligent suit.

5. If the tenant pleads that the plaintiff is the villain of another, he must further say, that he does not hold the tenements which he demands in his own name, but in the name of the lord whose villain he is; in which case the assise shall stand over, unless the plaintiff can show by charter of feoffment that he was enfeoffed to him and his heirs. And even if he proves such a purchase, this proof will not avail unless he further show that his lord was never seised thereof since his purchase; and if it be found that the lord seised the tenement after it had been purchased by his villain, although he afterwards delivered it back to the villain to hold at his will, the assise fails, because the villain was not tenant in his

Exception of villenage to another holds only when the villain held in his lord's name,

or at will.

naunt en soen noun demeyne, mes en noun de soen seignur. [127.] Et si le seignur n'en fust poynt seysi, adounc ne tiegne mie la excepcioun de villenage leu encountre nule estraunge persone.

Brac. 199; Fle. 237, 238.

6. Et si le pleyntif die en sa replicacioun encountre la excepcioun de villenage, qe il ne veut mie ne deit fere detrier soen estat, lequel il soit fraunc ou noun, par la assise, en tiel cas voloms nous qe l'assise soit prise par office del juge sur la disseisine, si le tenaunt ne voille weyver cele excepcioun, et solom le verdit se face jugement. Car nous voloms en favour de fraunchise, qe nul qi est en fraunc estat eit mester en tel cas de soi mettre en les jurours del assise pur fere detrier[1] soen estat, s'il ne voille; eynz est dreiture[2], qe la spoliacioun qe est foundé sur une simple possessioun soit primes detrié, et puis le dreit del estat qe est de plus haute nature.

7. Mes en brefs qe touchent la propreté et le dreit, [3]sicum en bref de dreit[3] [4]des custumes et des services, ou autres custumes ne autres[4] services ne soint demaundez qe de dreit ne

1. so *GASHF.* descrier *L.* trier *NDMC.* 2. dreit *NMC.* 3—3. so *LNDG.* om. *MCHF.* 4—4. et des custumes ne autres *L.* sim. *S.* e de coustumes qe autres custumes ne *ND.* de custumes ne autres *G.* e des customes e des seruices ou qe autres customes ne *M.* e les custumes e les seruices ouuesqe autres custumes e *C.* sim. *HF.*

own name, but in the name of his lord. And if the lord was never seised of the land, then the exception of villenage shall not hold against any stranger.

Replication objecting to the trial of status by assise.

6. If the plaintiff pleads in replication to the exception of villenage, that he will not nor ought to have his condition, whether he be free or not, tried by the assise, in such case the assise shall be taken upon the disseisin *ex officio judicis,* unless the tenant will waive the exception; and judgment shall be given according to the verdict; for we will that in favour of liberty no one of free estate be in such case obliged to put himself upon the jurors of the assise to determine his condition without his consent; but it is just that the spoliation, which is founded simply upon possession, be first tried, and afterwards the right concerning the condition, which is of a higher nature.

Assise taken upon the disseisin.

In proprietary actions, status may be incidentally determined.

7. But in writs which concern the property and the right, as in the writs of right of customs and services, where no other customs or services are demanded than those which are due

deyvent estre fetz, ou en autre brefs de dreit, tient ceste excepcioun si graunt force, qe si le vileyn, ou cil qi vileyn[1] est nomé, ne se voille de ceo mettre, qe par taunt serra jugement encountre ly. Et s'il se mette en la assise et la assise passe encountre le seignur, a touz jours mes iert le vileyn quites del cleym le seignur; et si encountre le vileyn, a touz jours mes remeyndra soen vileyn, ausi avaunt [2]cum s'il ly eust[2] [127 *b.*] recoveri par bref de naifté.

8. Mes en le bref de possessioun ne tient ele mie taunt de force; car[3] tut passe ele encountre soen estat, ja par taunt n'iert soen estat enpiré ne blemie taunt ne quant. Car excepcioun ne [4]seert fors a barrer[4] le pleyntif de sa demaunde, [5]et ne eschaunge[5] le estat en nul point, lequel qe la juree se face del pleyntif, ou de soen piere, lequel il morust vileyn ou cum fraunc, tut fust il vileyn; nent plus qe enqueste de bastardie. Car si ceste excepcioun cheet en enqueste, qe le piere ou autre auncestre le pleyntif morust bastard, tut soit [6]de ceo[6] par assent des parties [7]prise enqueste[7], qe

Brac. 194; Fle. 239 (§14).

1. *so NDSMA. sim. G.* il *add. L.* 2—2. *so verb. SAM. sim. GCH.* cum il eust *L.* cum il ly eust *ND.* 3. *so ND.* qe *LGSAH. om. M.* 4—4. seert fors abarrer *L.* sert fors qe a barrer *SA. sim. M.* fet fors qe abatre *C.* fet nent fors ke abarrer *H.* 5—5. e ne chaunge *NSGA.* ne chaunge *M.* ne chalenge *C.* ne en chalenge *H.* 6—6. *so M.* de *om. LASG.* de ceo *om. N.* ele *H.* 7—7. *so SAM.* prise en enqueste *LN.* qe lenquest seit prise *G.*

of right, and in other writs of right this exception is of so great force, that if the villain, or he who is alleged to be a villain, refuses to take issue upon it, judgment shall thereupon be given against him; and if the plaintiff puts himself upon the assise, and the assise passes against the lord, then the villain shall for ever after be quit from the claim of his lord; and if against the villain, he shall for ever after remain his villain as much as if he had recovered him by writ of naifty.

8. But in a possessory writ it has not so much force, for although it pass against his condition, it is not thereby impaired or prejudiced. For the exception serves only to bar the plaintiff of his demand, and does not alter the condition in any point, whether the inquiry of the jury be concerning the plaintiff or concerning his father, whether he died a villain, or in the condition of a freeman although he was a villain. An inquest upon bastardy is similar in its effect; for if an inquest be taken upon the exception that the father or other ancestor of the plaintiff died a bastard, although it be taken by consent

But in a possessory action status is not prejudiced by trial of the exception.

Exception of bastardy.

die qe il morust bastard, ja par taunt ne est nuli estat meu ne chaungé.

Brac. 202; Fle. 240.

Ante, c. 17. s. 3. p. 315.

9. Autres excepciouns sunt encountre la persone le pleyntif, cum si le bref soit purchacé en soen noun demeyne, en cas ou il se pleynt de tort fet a autre qe a ly, sicum est del baroun qi soul est nomé el bref ou le fraunc tenement est a la femme, forpris le cas de disseisine fete par la femme al baroun. Et si le bref soit purchacé en noun de baroun et de sa femme joyntement feffez[1] del fraunc tenement la femme, et le un de eus moerge pendaunt le bref, si est le bref par taunt abatable. Et en mesme la manere, si acune femme prenge baroun pendaunt soen bref [2]en le quel ele soule est nomé. Et ausi[2] sount acuns pleyntifs rebotables de lour pleyntes pur ceo qe [3]il ne ount nule severale accioun a demaunder rien en certeyne[3] severauté, sicum est des parceners et des autres qi tienent en

1. *so C. sim. NH.* feffe *LGM.* feffee *AS.* 2—2. *so L. sim. NSGA.* par taunt est il abatable. E en mesme la manere *M. sim. H.* 3—3. *so L. sim. SG.* certeyne *om. N.* i ne sieuent nule seuerale accioun demaunder en certeine *M.* qil ne seuent mie nul seueral accioun ne rens demaunder en *C. sim. H.*

of the parties, and the inquest find that he did die a bastard, yet the status of no person is thereby altered or changed.

Exception of non-joinder of co-plaintiff.

9. Other exceptions there are against the person of the plaintiff, as if the writ is purchased in his own name, where the complaint is of a wrong done to another as well as himself;

Husband and wife.

as where the husband alone is named in the writ, and the freehold is the wife's, except in the case of disseisin done by

Abatement by death or marriage, pending writ.

a wife to her husband. And if the writ be purchased in the name of the husband and his wife, jointly enfeoffed of the freehold of the wife, and one of them die pending the writ, the writ is thereby abatable. And the like, where any woman takes a husband pending her writ in which she alone is named[o].

Exception that plaintiff has no several action.

Some plaintiffs also may be debarred from their plaints, inasmuch as they have no several action to demand anything certain in severalty; as parceners and others holding in common, none of whom could ever tell where his own share

o '*Ex hoc nota,* that none can be party to the purchase, if he be not expressly named, as when the husband marries the disseisee after purchase of her writ. But it is not so of a *feme sole* disseiseress who takes husband after a writ purchased [against her]; because she may do it of malice [to defeat the action].' Note in MS. *N.*

commune, dount nul de eus savoit unques ou soen certeyn fu. [128.]
Mes s'il demaunde a tener en commune, soit oy.

10. Et acune foiz neest au tenaunt excepcioun de sa persone demeyne, sicum en cas ou il pora averrer par l'assise qe il ne est mie disseisour. Et ausi en cas ou le seignur del fee est pleyntif pur arrerage de sa rente, eynz ceo qe il eyt assayé a destreyndre soen fee, a la quele rente le tenement[1] est obligé dount la vewe est fete. Car si le tenaunt demaunde jugement si assise deyve passer eynz ceo qe le seignur eit assayé a destreyndre soen fee, ou eynz ceo qe il soit desavowé pur seignur, et le quel service il conust en tut ou en partie, en cel cas ne tient tele assise poynt de liu, mes destresce [2]sovent del service conustre[2]. Et si le seignur ne ad poer a destreyndre soen tenaunt pur poverté de ly mesmes, adounc soit comaundé al viscounte par precept des Justices qe il ly soit en eyde a destreyndre soen fee.

Brac. 203 b; Fle. 240.

Glan. li. 9. c. 8; Brac. 203; Fle. 240, 241.

1. so *NM.* tenaunt *LACH.* 2—2 so *LMH.* si noun del seruice cum en arrere *N.* *sim. D.* si noun del seruice com en otreit *G.* si noun del seruice com en octreie *A.* *sim. S.* si com del seruice conu e octreie *corr. R.* souient pur le service conustre *C.* couient del seruice conustre *F.* souent del seruice conystre *W.*

was. But if the plaintiff demands to hold in common, he shall be heard.

10. Sometimes an exception arises on behalf of the tenant, from his own person, as where he can prove by the assise that he is not disseisor. Also, where the lord of the fee is plaintiff for arrears of his rent, with which the tenement that has been viewed is charged, before he has tried to distrain his fee. For if the tenant demand judgment, whether the assise ought to pass, before the lord has essayed to distrain his fee, or is disavowed as lord, where the tenant acknowledges the services in whole or in part, in such case this assise does not lie, but distress from time to time for the service acknowledged[p]. And if the lord by reason of his poverty is not able to distrain his tenant, then let the sheriff be commanded by precept of the Justices that he aid the plaintiff in distraining his fee.

Exception to the person of the tenant; that he is the plaintiff's tenant, and might be distrained.

Sheriff commanded to aid distress.

[p] There appears to be some corruption in the text, which the MSS. do not enable us to set right. Possibly we ought to read, 'destresce soulement del service conu et otreié,' 'distress only for the service acknowledged and granted.'

CHAPITRE XIX. [L.]

De Excepcioun al Accioun.

Brac. 196, 205; Fle. 241.

[128 b.]

Fle 241 (§ 1), 243 (§ 3).

1. A ceo qe dit est el bref, a tort et sauntz jugement[1] pora le tenaunt dire qe par jugement. A ceo fet examiner lequel par jugement de nostre court, ou de autri court, [2]et lequel par noster bref ou sauntz noster bref[2]. Et si par jugement de nostre court ou de autri court sauntz noster bref, adounc vayle nient sa[3] excepcioun, eynz soit le fet cassé[4]. Car sauntz poer doné et limité par nous ne est nuly autri juge, nomément pur conustre [5]ou juger en[5] autri fraunc tenement. Et si le pleyntif graunte qe par bref original, mes a tort, en cel cas chete la assise, et soit dit qe il se purchace par bref de faus jugement. Mes ja pur nul[6] bref judicial issaunt de nuli original ne remeygne la assise.

1. so *NSGAMCH.* de nostre Court *add. L.* 2—2. sauntz noster bref *LND.* *sim. SG.* e le quel par bref ou saunz bref *MH.* *om. A.* 3. la *MH.* cele *C.* 4. cassable *MCH.* 5—5. en iugement de *M.* 6. nul *om. SGM.*

CHAPTER XIX.

Of Exceptions to the Action.

Exception of judgment.

1. To the words in the writ, 'unjustly and without judgment,' the tenant may plead that it was by judgment; and then it must be examined whether by judgment of our court or of that of another, and whether by our writ or without.

Judgment, without writ, void.

And if it was by judgment of our court or of another without our writ, then the exception shall not avail, but all that was done shall be annulled. For without an authority given and defined by us no one can be judge over another, especially to take cognizance of or determine concerning the freehold of another.

Judgment, if wrong, to be reversed by writ of false judgment.

If the plaintiff admits that the judgment was by original writ, but says that it was wrongful, the assise in such case shall fall, and he must be told to seek his remedy by writ of false judgment. But the assise shall not stand over for any judicial writ not issuing out of an original.

2. Et si acun mette en sa vewe tenement dedié par Evask ou autre chose qe ne deit estre en nuli biens, par taunt chet le accioun et l'assise, et le pleyntif remeyndra en la merci pur sa fause pleynte. Et pur ceo qe tiel tenement ne deit mie remeyndre al tenaunt, si soit enquis del tenement; et si trové soit qe le tenement ne deit remeyndre al tenaunt, si soit le tenaunt en la merci pur sa torcenouse occupacioun, et le tenement soit retourné en le estat qe il fust avaunt. Et en mesme la manere soit fet del tenement ocupé en severauté, qe deit estre comune a aucune universeté ou a autre communauté. Et de chemin real ou de autre [1]semblable chose chete[1] touz jours assise, et soit tourné en trespas, et soit enquis del trespas et del purpresture, et solom le verdit se face le jugement. Brac. 210 b; Fle. 241 (§ 2).

3. Et acune foiz cheet l'assise par noun certeynté, tut ne chete ele par taunt en juré ne en puralé, sicum avent par entre femme et le garraunt de sa dowarie avaunt le assignement fet a la femme de sa certeyne dowarrie; cum si ambideus soint [129.] Brac. 212 (§ 3); Fle. 243 (§ 4).

1—1. semblable chose *L.* semblable chose chite *M.* semblable chet *C.* tenement semblable chiete *NSG.* *sim. DAH.*

2. If any one puts in view a tenement consecrated by the bishop, or any other thing which ought not to be the property of any one, the action and assise thereby fall, and the plaintiff shall be in mercy for his false plaint. And as such tenement ought not to continue in the possession of the tenant, let inquiry be made concerning the tenement; and if it be found that the tenement ought not to remain with the tenant, let the tenant be in mercy for his tortious occupation, and the tenement be restored to its former state. Let like proceedings be taken with regard to a tenement occupied in severalty which ought to be common to any general body, or other community. With respect to the king's highway, or other like thing, an assise shall always fall and be turned into trespass; and inquiry shall be made of the trespass and purpresture, and judgment shall be given according to the verdict. If tenement is consecrated ground, the writ falls. Consecrated ground, how restored. Common soil. King's highway.

3. Sometimes the assise falls for uncertainty, although it is not on that account turned into a jury or perambulation[q]; as happens between a woman and the warrant of her dower before any assignment is made to her of her dower in certain, Uncertainty in subject-matter of assise. Dower not set out.

[q] See c. xvii. s. 8, p. 319. and c. xx. below.

engettez et la femme se pleynt soule, et met en sa vewe le tierz de tut le tenement sicum sa dowarrie, ele ne recovera poynt de tenement ne nule seisine par l'assise, pur ceo qe ele ne savoit unques sa certeine porcioun. Mes si generale seisine luy eit esté fete, adounc suffist a fere luy tele seysine cum ele eust avaunt. Et si especiale seysine luy soit fete, mes[1] ele [2]ne set ore a dire ou[2] en dreit, par ceo qe les[3] boundes par aventure sount ostez, ou par cas semblable, adounc luy soit assigné a la vaillaunce par ausmee[4] des jurours del assise, taunt cum il porrount ausmer[5] par entre eus qe le tenement amounta dount ele est disseisie.

Brac. 212 *b*; Fle. 243 (§ 5, 6, 7, 8).

4. Et ausi cheet assise par noun certeinté de la persone le pleintif, cum si les jurours ne ly conusent de rien; et ausi ou il ne sevent mie pur verité lequel il out la seisine en soen noun demeyne, ou en autri noun. Et ausi en cas ou les jurours ne sevent qi ad majour dreit le pleyntif ou le tenaunt, nent plus en la possessioun qe en la propreté. Et ausi en cas

1. la ou *A.* 2—2. ny fet ore a dire ou *L.* ni siet ore a dire ou *S.* ne siet ore *G.* ne siet dire ou *A.* ne siet ordiner ou *M.* ne fet mie ordeiner *C.* *sim. H.* 3. certeyns *add. N.* 4. aesme *N.* esme *M.* auisement *CH.* escient *A.* 5. aesmer *N.* esmer *AM.* auiser *CH.*

where if both are ejected, and the woman alone complains and puts in view the third of the whole tenement as her dower, yet she shall not recover any tenement or any seisin by the assise, inasmuch as her portion was never ascertained. But if general seisin has been made to her, then it is sufficient to put her in such seisin as she had before; and if special seisin was given her, but she cannot now tell in what place by reason of the boundaries being removed, or by a like accident, then let land of the like value be assigned to her by the estimation of the jurors of the assise, as much as they can estimate among themselves to have been the amount of the tenement whereof she was disseised.

General seisin of dower.

Identity lost.

Plaintiff unknown to jury.

4. The assise also falls for uncertainty in the person of the plaintiff, as if the jurors have no knowledge of him at all. So, where they do not know for certain whether he held the seisin in his own name or in the name of another. The assise also falls where the jurors do not know who has the better right, the plaintiff or the tenant, as well to the possession as to the property. Likewise, where the plaintiff claims by title of gift

Title, unknown.

Feoffee, not seised in life of feoffor.

ou le pleyntif cleyme par title de doun ou de feffement, s'il [129 *b*.] ne fust unques seisi en la vie le feffour. Et ausi chet assise en cas ou deus soers portent ceste assise, et se pleynent en commune ove lour barouns, ou le baroun de la une n'est nient nomé, lequel qe il soit feloun ou noun, mes qe il soit en vie. Et ausi si la vile principepale ne soit nomé. Car en une vile Brac. 211, 212; Fle. 242, 243 (§ 9). porrount estre plusours paroches, et en une paroche plusours maners, et hameletz plusours porrount apendre a un maner, sicum serra dit en le plee de dreit. Mes si la princepale vile ne soit nomé, l'assise remeyndra.

CHAPITRE XX. [LI.]

De Assises tournez en Jureez.

1. En plusours maneres sount assises targetz[1], et acunes Brac. 213, 215 *b*; Fle. 233, 244. jekes en tens, et acunes jekes a touz jours, [2]et acunes se chaungent[2] par assent des parties deques en jurez; et [3]cil qi

1. chargez *MC*. *sim*. *HF*. 2—2. *so verb*. *G*. et acuns se targent *L*. *sim*. *AS*. Acunes se chaungent *N*. e acuns tournent *M*. asqunes tournez *C*. *om*. *H*. 3—3. sil qi de ceo assentera *L*. cil qe de ceo se sentera grevee *ND*. sil qi desassentera *G*. si il de sa sentera *S*. si qe qi se assentira *M*. cil qe desassentera *H*.

or feoffment, if he was never seised in the lifetime of the feoffor. The assise also falls, when brought by two sisters, Non-joinder of co-plaintiff. who complain in common with their husbands, but the husband of one of them is not named, and this whether he be a felon or not, so long as he is living[r]. So if the principal town Town not named. is not named; for in one town there may be several parishes, and in one parish several manors, and several hamlets may Parish, manor, and hamlet. belong to one manor, as shall be mentioned in the plea of right; but if the principal town is not named, the assise shall stand over.

CHAPTER XX.

Of Assises turned into Juries.

1. Assises are put off several ways, some for a time, some Various modes of staying an assise. for ever; and some are turned into juries by assent of the

r 'A freeholder (un prudome) has four daughters, two of whom take husbands. The husband of one commits felony, for which he is outlawed, and abjures the realm. The father then dies. The inheritance is occupied by a stranger, and the four daughters are to purchase by the assise. *Qu*. Whether it is proper to name the felon, husband of one of the daughters, or not?' Note in MS. *N*.

desassentera[3] [1]cum il avera pledé[1] chete de sa pleynte, ou soit condempné a noun defendu; et acunes par office des Justices, sicum est en ceo cas, ou les parties descordent en quele vile ou en quel counté ou en quel maner ou en quel fee ou en quele baronie le tenement est. Jekes en tens, sicum par abatement des brefs, et par autres excepciouns dilatories; et a touz jours, par excepciouns paremptories.

[130.] Brac. 213; Fle. 244. 2. Et acunes se chaungent en jurez, sicum par excepciouns dedites, cum en ceo cas, si le pleyntif die qe il fust seisi par title de successioun apres le desces soen auncestre, qi de ceo morust seisi, et qi proscheyn heir il est, apres qi mort il entra freschement, et en seisine se tint jekes autaunt qe le disseisour a tort et saunz jugement l'engitta; si le tenaunt die encountre, qe le auncestre, dount il parout[2], n'en morut unques seisi en soen demeyne cum de fee, pur ceo qe il ne tint le tenement for qe a terme de vie, par quei qe par nuli title de successioun ne put il aver fraunc tenement; si le pleyntif die qe le auncestre morust seisi cum de fee, si chet l'assise et par assent des parties sount les jurours fetz cum juges arbitres;

1—1. *so verb. LNDSG.* de ceo qil avera comence deqes al plee *M.* 2. *so LMAC.* parle *NDG.* parolt *S.*

parties, where he who refuses his assent after he has pleaded shall be held to fail in his plaint, or be condemned as undefended; others *ex officio judicis*, as where the parties differ in what vill, county, manor, fee, or barony, the tenement is. Assises are put off for a time by pleas in abatement and dilatory exceptions. By peremptory exceptions they are barred for ever.

Assise turned into jury, where plea is traversed; as if plaintiff alleges title by descent, and defendant denies the ancestor's title.

2. Some are turned into juries by the exceptions being denied, as in this case, where the plaintiff says that he was seised by title of succession after the death of his ancestor, who died seised, and whose next heir he is, and after whose death he presently entered and kept himself in seisin until the disseisor wrongfully and without judgment ejected him,—if the tenant meets this by saying that the ancestor of whom he speaks never died seised in his demesne as of fee, inasmuch as he held only for term of life, and that therefore the plaintiff cannot have a freehold by any title of succession; and if the plaintiff replies that the ancestor died seised as of fee, then the assise shall drop, and by the assent of the parties the jurors

Jury by assent of parties.

et solom lour verdit passera jugement. Et sur teus verditz passez par communs assentz des parties ne ad jalemeyns leu atteynte.

3. Et ausi soit de debat eu[1] par entre les parties, lequel le auncestre tint le tenement en gage, ou autrement par condicioun, ou noun, et lequel satisfaccioun fust fete a la condicioun, ou noun. Et ausi en ceo cas, ou le puisnee frere ou bastard, ou autre, sount engittez par le verrei heir, si debat soit qi est eynznee ou legitime, de cel estrif serra enquise la verité par une juree par le assent des parties, ou en autres cas semblables, qe sount sauntz nounbre, [2]en queus[2] l'assise se tourne par excepciouns dilatories entre les parties en juree. [130 *b.*]

Brac. 213 *b.* (§ 4); Fle. 244 (§ 2, 6).

4. Et si le pleyntif die qe il fust seisi par title de doun jekes autaunt qe il fust a tort engetté, encountre ceo pora estre dit, qe cil de qi doun il cleyme title ne fust unques en seisine, par ount il ne pout[3] rien doner, ou si le donour fust de ceo en seisine, unqes de cele seisine ne se demist en sa vie,

Brac. 213 *b.* (§ 3); Fle. 244 (§ 5).

1. eu *om.* *NACH.* ou *M.* 2—2. einz ceo qe *M.* einz qe *C.* *sim.* *H.* 3. so *NSA.* pora *L.* *sim.* *CH.* puit *G.* poeit de ceo *M.*

become as it were arbitrators; and judgment shall pass according to their verdict[5]; nevertheless upon such verdicts, though passed by common assent of the parties, an attaint may lie.

Verdict of jury may be set aside by attaint.

3. So if it be disputed between the parties whether the ancestor held the tenement in gage or under any other condition or not, and whether the condition was satisfied or not. The like, where the younger brother, or bastard, or other, is ousted by the true heir, if the contest be which is eldest or legitimate, the truth of these questions shall be inquired by a jury by assent of the parties; and the like in other such cases which are numberless, in which the assise is turned into a jury by dilatory exceptions between the parties.

Other examples of disputed title.

4. If the plaintiff says that he was seised by title of gift, until he was wrongfully ejected, it may be said in answer, that he by whose gift he claims title was never in seisin, so as to enable him to make any gift; or if the donor was seised, he never divested himself of the seisin in his lifetime; nor was he

Jury to decide whether plaintiff claiming under gift was properly seised.

[5] 'These things are necessary to succession, true ancestor, true ownership in him, true succession, true heir, and true seisin; of which the four turn the assise, and the fifth makes the assise in its proper nature (en sa grasse nature).' Note in MS. *N.*

ne il qi est pleyntif unques en la vie le donour de ceo en seisine ne fust, mes apres la mort le donour se abaty en[1] cel tenement par sa propre force, hors de quel le tenaunt cum proscheyn heyr l'engetta [2]freschement, si ke ne out[2] for qe simple abatement. Et si les parties prient le averrement par commun assent, si cesse l'assise, et soit enquis par juree, lequel le pleintif fust seisi par socn propre abatement, ou par le bail ou la induccioun la seisine le donour en sa vie; et solom le verdit se face le jugement.

Brac. 213 *b*; Fle. 244 (§ 5).

5. Et si les jurours ne sevent riens, le pleyntif prenge rien par sa pleynte, eynz soit en la merci, pur ceo qe il ne ad mie prové sa intencioun. Et si les jurours soint [3]en un eoyr[3], si remeigne l'assise[4] et soit jugé encountre le pleyntif cum devaunt.

Brac. 213 (§ 4); Fle. 244 (§ 6).

6. Et si le pleintif prenge soen title de gage ou de purchaz condicionel, et la partie adverse[5] die, qe satisfaccioun soit[6] fete a la [7]condicioun, ou fust prest de aver esté fete, au jour[7]

1. *so NDGSAMCH.* en *om. L.* 2—2. franchement si ke ne out *L.* *sim. S.* freschement cum cely qe ne out *ND.* freschement si qil ne out *G.* *sim. A.* freschement e si ne out il *M.* *sim. CH.* 3—3. soint en awer *N.* *sim. DGM.* seient en ewer *A.* *sim. SF.* ne seient en Ewer *H.* 4. *so NDCH.* la seysine *LAF.* *sim. SGM.* 5. aduersarie *N.* diuerse *SG.* 6. ne soit poynt *N.* 7—7. *so LGSA.* condicion ou soit prest de auerrer qil fu fet al iour *M.* condicioun ou prest est dauerrer le fet al iour *C.* *sim. H.* partie condicionele e ceo soit prest de auerrer e estoit fete mencioun del an e del iour *N.*

who is plaintiff ever seised in the lifetime of the donor, but after the death of the donor he by his own force abated himself into the tenement, out of which the tenant as next heir presently ejected him, so that he was in only by mere abatement; and if the parties by common consent pray averment, the assise shall cease, and it shall be inquired by jury whether the plaintiff was seised by his own abatement or by the livery or induction of seisin by the donor in his lifetime; and judgment shall be given according to the verdict.

If jury is in doubt, plaintiff loses.

5. If the jurors know nothing of the facts, the plaintiff shall take nothing by his plaint, but be in mercy for not proving his contention. And if the jurors are in doubt, the assise shall be stayed, and it shall be adjudged, as before, against the plaintiff.

Fulfilment of condition, question for jury.

6. If the plaintiff derive his title under gage or conditional purchase, and the adverse party say that the condition was satisfied, or that satisfaction was ready to be made on the day

nomé el escrit, par desdire la partie cessera l'assise, et tournera en juree a enquere de la satisfaccioun, ou del offre, ou noun, si les parties voillent. Car[1] soit ore qe le pleyntif die qe il est disseisi de soen fraunc tenement, et prenge soen title de doun et de feffement, et die qe par le doun et le feffement le disseisour mesmes fust il de cel tenement seisi, et homage ly fist et esplez en prist et sa pesible seisine usa de la Pasche jekes a Nouel, qe celi feffour mesmes ly engetta a tort; si le tenaunt respoigne, bien porra graunter le doun et le feffement et la chartre et le homage, mes si il puse averrer touz ces fetz condicionels par escrit, sicum en ceste manere: jeo vous en feffai et en pris voster homage par tiele condicioun, qe si jeo puse enquere de eynz le an et le jour qe vous tenez acune part en chief du Roi, qe je me puse mettre en[2] seisine et vous engetter sauntz tort fere, si qe quant jeo [131.] Brac. 214: Fle. 245 (§ 6).

1. E *MCH.* 2. arere en *M.*

named in the deed, by denial of the party the assise shall cease, and shall be turned into a jury, if the parties consent, to inquire whether such satisfaction or tender was made or not. For suppose now that the plaintiff should say that he is disseised of his freehold, and should derive his title under a gift and feoffment, and say that by the gift and feoffment of the disseisor himself he was seised of this tenement, and did homage to him, and took the profits, and enjoyed his peaceable seisin from Easter until Christmas, when the feoffor himself wrongfully ejected him; if the tenant answer, he may well acknowledge the gift and the feoffment, and the charter and the homage, but if he can prove by writing that all these acts were conditional[t],—as thus, I enfeoffed you and took your homage upon this condition, that if I find within the year and day that you hold land anywhere of the king in chief, I may put myself in seisin and eject you without wrong, so that when I shall have found for certain that you hold elsewhere of Plea of condition.

t '*Nota, quod modernis diebus* no charter can be conditional on account of the statute *Quia emptores terrarum*. For the purchaser must hold either of his feoffor or of his chief; and of his feoffor only in fee tail. For when once the purchaser is in rightful seisin of the fee and freehold, he cannot be ousted except by his own consent; neither can the donor, who has once divested himself, have it again except by a new title. But as soon as he gives to hold of the chief lord, he divests himself entirely (se demet tot nettement). Wherefore the charter must be absolute (simple); and if there be any collateral deed of covenant, the donor cannot retake his seisin by his own force, but must use his writ of covenant.' (Note in MS. *N.*) See above, pp. 236, 238, and notes there.

averay enquis pur verité qe vous tenez aylours en chief del Roi, jeo vous engetteray a dreit, et par la condicioun a la quele vous assentetz[1]; si tieles condiciouns pusent estre moustrez par escrit de une part et de autre, adounc se passe le plee solom ceo qe les escritz serrount grauntez ou deditz.

[131 *b*.] Brac. 214, 214 *b*; Fle. 246.

7. Et s'il soint deditz fausement, tut soit cele fausine puis atteynte, uncore pora estre qe nule satisfaccioun ne est fete a la condicioun, par quei a force covendra de tele satisfaccioun enquere, et solom ceo [2]ayle le[2] jugement, sicum peert [3]en le chapitre de Dreit.[3] Car tut soit ele prové pur bone, uncore porra ele estre voide et de nule force pur soen faus testmoignage, qe dist, jeo ay doné, ou unques doun ne fust fet, coment qe il out acune purparlaunce de doun. Et de ceo est[4] qe ne suffist mie a soulement prover la chartre, si le doun ne est mie prové; car la chartre pora estre bone et verraye, et estre ceo [5]pora estre[5] qe le purchaceour ne purchacea mie le tenement par le doun cely qi fist la chartre, mes par soen propre abatement, ou par disseisine ou par[6] entrusioun. Et

1. assentistes *NGM*. assentates *C*. assentez *S*. 2—2. ayle al *L*. *sim*. *A*. aler a *NDCH*. aler al *S*. *sim*. *G*. aile le, *M*. 3—3. so *CH*. en chapitre de dreit *L*. en chartre desdite *S*. *sim*. *GA*. en la chartre de dyte *M*. de chartre dedite *N*. 4. so *NSGMCH* est *om*. *L*. 5—5. *om*. *NAM*. 6. sa *add*. *AM*. sa propre *add*. *CH*.

the king in chief, I shall lawfully eject you by virtue of that condition to which you assent,—if such conditions can be shown by writing on one side and on the other, then the plea shall proceed according as the writings are admitted or denied.

Conditional deed denied; question of fulfilment still material.

7. And if the conditional writings are falsely denied, although this falsity be afterwards proved, yet as it may happen that the condition has not been satisfied, an inquiry must of necessity be made concerning such satisfaction, and judgment shall go accordingly, as appears in the chapter concerning Right. For although the charter be proved good, yet it may be void and of no force by reason of its false testimony in saying, I have given, whereas no gift was ever made, although there was some proposal of a gift.

Both charter and gift to be proved.

Hence it is not sufficient to prove the charter alone, unless the gift is proved; for it may be that the charter is good and genuine, and yet the purchaser did not acquire the tenement by the gift of him who made the charter, but by his own abatement, or by disseisin or intrusion. So on the other hand, although

de autre part ausi, tut soit la chartre prové fause, uncore porra estre qe le doun fust bon et leal, par que i qe ambedeus covendra prover, le doun ausi bien cum la chartre.

8. Et si tieles condiciouns soint mises avaunt sauntz escritz, en tiel cas [1]se porrount[1] les parties adverses defendre par lour ley a lour xii. meyn, qe unques n'out tele condicioun. Et si la chartre soit de pur feffement sauntz condicioun, et le doun soit graunté ou[2] prové, adounc n'en est mester a crere nule vive[3] voiz a parler de condicioun pur la presumpcioun de la chartre qe ne testmoigne nule condicioun. Brac. 210 b; Fle. 247. [132.]

9. Et si le donour par acune condicioun contenu en le escrit par entre ly et le purchaceour ne se puise mettre en seisine et[4] engettre le purchaceour solom la condicioun, en cel cas ly covendra estre eydé par bref de covenaunt, qe serra pledé[5] par le graunt *Cape* et le petit, sicum[6] accioun reale. Brac. 214 b; Fle. 247.

10. Et sovent avent qe les pleyntifs sount destourbez qe il ne porrount nule seisine recoverer par lour pleyntes, sicum en Brac. 214 b (§ 5); Fle. 247.

1—1. *so verb. NM.* ne porrount mie *L.* purrount *ACH.* 2. *so NAC.* et *L.* e *M.* 3. vive *om. M.* 4. ne *NMCH.* 5. *so AMCH. sim. NSG.* emplede *L.* 6. solom *CH.*

the charter be proved to be false, yet it may be that the gift was good and lawful; wherefore both the gift and the charter must be proved.

8. If such conditions are set up without evidence of any writings, the adverse party may deny by their law, with eleven compurgators, that there ever was such a condition. And if the charter be one of simple feoffment without condition, and the gift be admitted or proved, then no credit need be given to an oral allegation of a condition on account of the presumption arising from the charter which does not mention any condition. Parole condition may be denied by *law.*

9. If the donor by virtue of any condition contained in the deed between him and the purchaser cannot put himself in seisin and eject the purchaser according to the condition, he must in that case be aided by writ of covenant, in which the process shall be by the great and little *Cape*, as is in a real action. Donor's remedy on breach of condition.

10. It often happens that the plaintiffs are prevented from recovering seisin by means of their plaints; as where the Various impediments to an assise.

cas ou les jurours del assise ne ount nule manere de conisaunce ne presumpcioun [1]des covenaunces[1] [2]en les persones des pleyntifs[2] ou[3] en la[4] chose dount la pleynte est fete. Et ausi lour propre volunté lour destourbe, sicum en cas de condiciouns; et ausi reles et quiteclemaunce; et ausi [5]accord, cum si ly engetté eit pris[5] par accord a la vaillaunce; et ausi chartre de confermement del engetté; et ausi consentement, cum si le disseisour doygne le tenement, a quel doun luy engetté fet chartre de confermement. Et ausi sunt il destourbez par lour propre force et usurpacioun, cum si il reprengent[6] par lour propre force ceo que il dussent[7] par jugement aver repurchacé. Et difficulté de jugement les desturbe ausi; et ausi dreit[8] jugement; et en [9]touz teus cas[9] par debat des parties cessera l'assise jekes en juré et en manere de juree serrount teus debatz terminez.

Brac. 216 (§ 4); Fle. 249 (§ 10). [132 *b*.] 11. Et si le pleyntif founde soen title par la ley de Engleterre, et le tenaunt die qe par cel title ne peut il aver fraunc

1—1. *so LND.* des Couenantz *G.* *sim. MW.* de couenantes *A.* des couenantes *S.* de couenaunt *C.* de Couenaunce *H.* 2—2. *so NDM.* les *om. LSW.* en la persone le pleintif *G.* entre eus les pleintifs *C.* entre les pleyntifs *H.* 3. ne *ND.* 4. *so NMCH.* la *om. L.* 5—5. *om. M.* 6. reprent *LNDSG.* repregnent *M.* preignent *CH.* reprene *A.* 7. dust *N.* 8. de dreit de *N.* 9—9. teuz cas *N.* touz ses cas *D.* teu cas *MCH.*

jurors of the assise have no kind of knowledge or presumption as to the agreements affecting the plaintiff[u], or concerning the thing whereof the plaint is made. They may also be impeded by their own will, as in case of conditions; also by release and quitclaim; and by accord, as where the person ejected has agreed to accept the value; also, by charter of confirmation from the person ejected; also by consent, as if the disseisor makes a gift of the tenement, and the person ejected executes a charter of confirmation. They may also be prevented from recovering by their own force and usurpation, as if they take back by their own force what they ought to have repurchased by judgment. Difficulty of judgment is another impediment. So also a legal judgment. And in all these cases upon a difference between the parties the assise shall be turned into a jury, and by way of jury such questions shall be determined.

Claim by courtesy of England, how met. 11. Where the plaintiff grounds his title on the 'law of England,' and the tenant pleads that he cannot have a free-

[u] The sense of the original is doubtful. There appears to be some corruption in the text, which I have found it impossible to remove.

tenement, par la resoun qe il unques ne out engendrure de tele femme, ou si poynt de enfaunt engendra, il fust mort nepurquaunt en la ventre sa mere, ou s'il fust nee en vie, si ne fust il mie enfaunt [1]einz moustre, ou tut fust il enfaunt[1], si ne fust il unques oy crier; et si le pleyntif die le contrarie, si cesse[2] l'assise et soit tourné en une juree. Et si les jurours dient qe il virent bien le pleyntif en pleyne seisine et de sa seisine estre engetté, mes qe il ne sevent nient de nuli enfaunt par la resoun qe la femme le pleyntif[3] morust de enfaunt en autre pays, adounc soit comaundé al viscounte del leu qe il prengne a ly le Corouner del pays, et en presence des parties, si il voillent estre, enquerge ou la femme tiel pleyntif morust et si ele morust de enfaunt ou noun, et si ele ne out unques enfaunt de tiel pleyntif puis ceo qe il la esposa qe fust oy crier ou noun, et solom ceo remaunde[4] a tel jour et a tiel leu ceo qe il trovera[5] par enqueste, et solom le maundement se[6] face le jugement.

12. Ou le tenaunt pora graunter qe la femme en qi persone Brac. 216 *b*; Fle. 249 (§ 11).

1—1. *so N.* *sim. MACH.* *om. L.* 2. *so LNA.* chiet *M.* chet *CH.* 3. *so NAMC.* ne *add. L.* 4. *so LMA.* soit remaundee *N.* seit maunde *CH.* 5. *so AM.* troua *L.* trouerent *CH.* 6. *so NAMCH.* se *om. L.*

hold by this title because he never had issue by such a wife, or if he ever begat a child the child died in the womb, or if born alive it was not a child but a monster, or supposing it to be a child it was never heard to cry; and if the plaintiff replies to the contrary, the assise shall cease and be turned into a jury. And if the jurors say that they saw the plaintiff in full seisin, and that he was ejected therefrom, but that they know nothing concerning any child by reason that the wife of the plaintiff died in childbed in another part of the country, then the sheriff of that place shall be commanded that he take with him the coroner of the country, and in the presence of the parties, if they choose to be there, inquire where the wife of the plaintiff died, and whether she died in childbed or not, and whether she ever had a child by this plaintiff after he espoused her, and whether it was heard to cry or not, and that he make his return, on such a day and at such a place, of that which he shall find by inquest; and judgment shall be given according to the return.

Inquiry concerning birth in another county.

12. Or the tenant may admit that the woman in whom the Marriage disputed.

reposa[1] le fee et le fraunc tenement out de luy enfauntz, mes ceo neqedent ne luy deit rien valer, car les enfauntz furent puis atteyntz bastardz. Et si le pleyntif ceo dedie[2], si cesse
[133.] l'assise et soit fete juré par commun assent des parties. Et si le pleyntif demaunde coment bastardz, et le tenaunt die pur ceo qe il furent neez avaunt ceo qe le pleyntif esposa lour mere, en tel cas [3]querra hom[3] la verité en manere de juree, et ne mie en fourme de assise. Et s'il die pur ceo qe le pleyntif ne esposa unques lour mere et le pleintif die le affirmative, adounc remeigne l'assise jekes autaunt qe [4]sceu soit de[4] Cristiene court, s'il la esposa unques ou noun. Et coment en tel cas fet a overer serra dit en les excepciouns en le Plee de Dreit.

Brac. 216 b; Fle. 249 (§12).

13. Et ausi tourne assise deques en juree acune foiz pur trespas; sicum en cas ou acun vodera user en[5] autri soil encountre le gré celi a qi le soil est; et si acun parcener ou autre vodera de commun fere several encountre la volunté des communers, ou si acun communer voille fere outrage et

1. *so LN.* repose *AMCH.* 2. *so NAMCH.* die *L.* 3—3. enquerra hom *N.* enquerra lem *M.* purra lem enquere *A.* 4—4. hom sache de *N.* deduit soit en *M.* deuorce seit en *CH.* 5. *so LNDGSAH.* en *om. M.*

fee and freehold were vested had children by the plaintiff, yet that the same ought not to avail him, inasmuch as those children were afterwards proved to be bastards; and if the plaintiff denies this, the assise shall cease and be made a jury by consent of the parties. And if the plaintiff demands how they were bastards, and the tenant answer, because they were born before the plaintiff married their mother, in such case the truth shall be inquired by means of a jury, and not in the form of an assise. And if he says, by reason that the plaintiff never married their mother, and the plaintiff alleges the affirmative, then the assise shall stand over until it be determined in court Christian whether he ever married her or not. The mode of proceeding in such cases shall be described in treating of exceptions in the Plea of Right.

Time of birth, question for jury.

Married or not, question for court Christian.

Assise turned to jury, where the act is only trespass.

13. Assises are sometimes also turned into juries on account of trespass, as where any one desires to use the soil of another against the consent of the owner. And if any parcener or other would make severance of what is common against the will of the commoners, or if any commoner commits excess by taking

prendre plus qe il ne devera, en tel cas est disseisine, et jalemeyns trespas, solom lour difference[1], cum s'il ne[2] cleyme nul fraunc tenement, adounc cesse l'assise et se tourne en un juree d'enquere del trespas et des damages. Mes pur ceo qe hom ne poet mie tauntost saver en[3] cas la volunté le trespassour, bien se purveit s'il se purchace par ceste assise. Mes si autre foiz le face, adounc se tiegne le assise, [4]si qe il purchace[4] sa pesible seisine par l'assise. Et si la tierce foiz le face, si chete en[5] la peyne de la reddiseisine. Et si le disseisor cleyme fraunc tenement, de ceo courge la assise; et si la assise die qe il ad fraunc tenement sicum communer et ne mie en severalté, si ly soit ajugé autele[6] seisine cum avaunt avoit; et pur le exces soit puniz cum disseisour. Brac. 216 b; Fle. 250. [133 b.]

14. Mes en communs tenementz de[7] teles covertes disseisines qe se comencent par poi et poi, si fet bien a prendre gages des trespassours et de enparker les bestes, si nul i face damage, [8]ou les[8] surcharge de aveers, issint qe par teles prises soint les trespas amendez par agard de veisins. Et si acun Brac. 216 b, 217; Fle. 250 (§ 12).

1. distaunce *M.* 2. so *NAMCH.* ne *om. L.* 3. teu *add. CH.* 4—4. e qil reporchace *M.* 5. en *om. MCH. interl. N.* 6. a tele *LC.* a[u]tiele *N.* au tele *M.* 7. en *M.* 8—8. en lour *N. sim. CH.* ou lour *A. sim. M.*

more than his due, the act amounts to a disseisin; and yet it may be a trespass according to the distinction, as where he does not claim any freehold; and then the assise shall cease and be turned into a jury to inquire of the trespass and damages. But because one cannot in such case immediately discover the intention of the trespasser, the plaintiff acts prudently if he proceeds by this assise. And if the act be done a second time, then the assise holds, so that the plaintiff may recover his peaceable seisin. If it be done a third time, the penalty of redisseisin shall be incurred. If the disseisor claims a freehold, upon this the assise shall take place; and if the assise say that he has a freehold as a commoner and not in severalty, let him be adjudged to have the same seisin as he had before, and be punished as a disseisor for the excess. Distinction between disseisin and trespass. Repeated trespass, treated as disseisin.

14. But in the case of common tenements where disseisins are made secretly and are begun by little and little, it is expedient to take pledges of the trespassers, and to impound the beasts, if any do damage in the commons or surcharge them with cattle, so that upon such seizures satisfaction may be made by Remedy for encroachments on common.

cleyme fraunc tenement, dounc a primes fra [1]qe sages[1] si ly detiegne[2] hors, issi qe il ne face nule disseisine et s'il ne puse estre destourbé, adounc tient leu ceste assise.

Brac. 216 *b*; Fle. 250 (§ 13). Brac. 217 (§ 6); Fle. 250 (§ 15); Ante, l. i. c. 22. s. 8, p. 89.

15. Et ausi pur trespas de guast et destruccioun, et ausi pur outrageouses destresces. Car [3]outrage en[3] destresce nurist acune foiz disseisine, et acune foiz trespas; disseisine, cum en cas ou acun distreint autre par quei gaynerie est destourbé quant nul enchesoun est a destreyndre; trespas[4] par la ou hom destreint [5]le tenaunt au tenaunt[5] pur le meen, ou le meen est assetz suffisaunt; et ausi ou les demeygnes[6] sount destreintz par la ou les villenages suffisent, ou par noun moebles ou il ad suffisaument a destreyndre par moebles, ou si [134.] de eynz mesoun ou asetz pora estre trové de hors, ou par les bestes de charues, ou autres udives[7] bestes sount asetz, ou par robe ou par mounture ou par vessel, ou hom pora destreyndre par autres chateus, ou si outrageouses destresces soint prises, cum xx. livres pur xx. south; ou si la destresce soit enchacé hors del counté ou hors del fee. Et solom ceo qe serra trové

1—1. so *LNDSM.* com sage *C.* qe sage *G.* 2. tiegne *NDM.* 3—3. so *LM.* outrageouse *N.* *sim.* *CH.* 4. si com *add. M.* 5—5. so *M.* le tenaunt *L.* le tenaunt del tenement *NDCH.* le tenant del tenant *GSF.* *sim.* *A.* 6. menes *MCH.* 7. odiefs *G.* eudiues *S.* odiues *AR.* vifs *CH.* viues *F.* *sim.* *W.*

the award of neighbours. And if any one claims a freehold, the owner will act wisely, in the first place, if he keeps him out, so that he may not do any disseisin; and if he cannot be prevented, then this assise takes place.

Excessive distress, when disseisin;

15. So likewise for trespass by waste and destruction, and also for excessive distress. For excess in distraining sometimes breeds disseisin, and sometimes trespass; disseisin, where any one distrains another, whereby husbandry is disturbed, whereas there is no occasion for the distress; trespass, where one distrains the tenant of the tenant instead of the mesne tenant, the mesne being of sufficient ability. So if the demesnes are distrained when the villenages are sufficient; or the distress is by immovables where there are movables enough to be distrained, or within the house when enough may be found out of doors, or by beasts of the plough where there are enough of other beasts of pleasure, or by apparel or riding-horse or vessel where the other chattels may be distrained, or if the distress taken be in excess, as twenty pounds for twenty shillings, or if the distress be driven out of the county or out of the fee. And according as it shall be found

when trespass.

disseisine ou trespas se tiegne l'assise cum assise ou se tourne en juré pur[1] enquere del trespas. Et plus i ad de excepciouns qe ne poent mie totes estre especefiez ici, dount partie tient leu en autres pletz, sicum aparra plus avaunt de[2] chalenges des jurours.

CHAPITRE XXI. [LII.]

De chalenge de Jurours.

1. Et cum les parties averount pledez deques a l'assise ou deqes a une simple juree sur acune excepcioun, en moutz de maneres porra la journee[3] estre delayé, sicum par defaute de jurours. Ou tut i eynt asetz des jurours, uncore porount acuns estre remuables par verreye chalenge des parties. Brac. 184 b, 185; Fle. 229.

2. Et ausi pur le tens en cas; car totes houres ne sount pas mures. Car en le Canoun est defendu par Sainte Eglise sur peyne de escumengement qe de la Septuagesme jekes as utaves de Pasche, ne del comencement del Advent jekes as utaves de Decret. Greg. l. ii. tit. 9. c. 5.

1. *so M.* del *L.* de *NACH.* lassise *N.* la Iuree *M.* *sim. CH.* 2. en les *M.* des *NA.* 3. *so LSGA.*

to be disseisin or trespass, the assise is held as an assise or is turned into a jury to inquire of the trespass. There are more exceptions that cannot all be particularly mentioned here, some of which hold in other pleas, as will further appear in treating of challenges of jurors.

CHAPTER XXI.

Of the challenge of jurors, and of the trial of the assise.

1. When the parties have pleaded to an assise or to a simple jury upon any exception, the day may be delayed many ways, as for default of jurors. Or if a sufficient number of jurors appear, yet some may be removable by the just challenge of the parties. Day delayed for default of jurors.

2. Sometimes the day is delayed on account of the season; for all seasons are not fit. For it is forbidden in the Canon by holy Church upon pain of excommunication, that from Septuagesima until the Octaves of Easter, and from the be- Prohibited days. Vacations.

[134 *b*.] la Tiphanie[1], ne en jours de [2]Quatuor Temple[2], ne en jours de majours letanies, ne en jours de Roveysouns[3], ne en la simeyne de la Pentechoste, ne en tens de syer blez et[4] de vendenges, qe durent de la Sainte Margarete jekes a la quinzeyne de Saint Michel, ne en solempnes jours festaus de Saintz nuli ne jurge sur les Saintz Evaungelies ne nul seculer plee [5]ne teigne ne somounse ne face en[5] tens avauntditz, issint qe tout cel tens soit doné a Deu préer et apeser contec et de acorder ceux qi serrount a descord, et pur coiller les biens de terre dount le poeple deit vivre. Les Evasques et les prelatz neqedent de Sainte Eglise fount acune foiz dispensaciouns qe assises et jurez sount prises de eynz cel tens par renables enchesouns.

Stat. West. 1 (3 Edw. I.) c. 51.

Brac. 185; Fle. 229.

3. Et cum la journé[6] ne pora estre delayé pur le tens descovenable, si porrount les jurours estre chalengez, qe il ne deyvent jurer ne estre en verdit encountre eus par suffisauntes et resounables excepciouns. Car autresi[7] sount eus rebotables[8] de serment fere cum sount testmoignes suspectz de test-

Glan. l. 2. c. 12.

1. Tiphayne *N*. Epiphanie *S*. Epyphanie *M*. epiphein *A*. 2—2. so *LGSCH*. iiij. tens *AM*. quatre temps *N*. *sim*. *D*. 3. oreysouns *CH*. 4. ne en temps *N*. *sim*. *D*. 5—5. ne seit tenuz ne somounce ne seit feit en lez *M*. 6. Iuree *NA*. *sim*. *CH*. 7. auxi *N*. ausi *AMCH*. 8. refusables *M*.

ginning of Advent until the Octaves of the Epiphany, and on Ember days, and on the days of the greater litanies, and on Rogation days, and in the week of Pentecost, and in the time of harvest or vintage, which last from St. Margaret's day until fifteen days after Michaelmas, and on solemn festivals of Saints, no one shall be sworn upon the holy Gospels, or hold any secular plea, or make any summons in the times aforesaid, so that all these seasons be set apart for prayer, and for appeasing of quarrels and reconciling those who are at variance, and for gathering the fruits of the earth which are to be the food of man. Nevertheless the bishops and prelates of holy Church do sometimes grant dispensations, that assises and juries be taken in such seasons for reasonable cause.

Prohibition dispensed.

Challenge of jurors.

3. When the day cannot be put off on account of the season being improper, the jurors may be challenged, and sufficient and reasonable exceptions alleged why they ought not to be sworn or be in verdict against the party. For the same objections lie against jurors taking the oath as against a sus-

Causes of exception.

monage porter[1], pur [2]ceo qe nul[2] ne deit jurer qi autre foiz eit esté atteynt de faus serment; car ceux sount forjugez de fraunche ley, issi qe mes ne soint cruz de nul serment qe il facent. Ne ceux ausi, qi ount suffert jugement [3]de vie et de[3] membre, ou juise de pillori ou de tumberel; ne ceux qe ne ount poynt de descrescioun; ne ceux qi sount escumengez; [135.] [4]ne meseeus degeez[4]; ne prestres ne clers de eynz saintz ordres; ne femmes; ne ceux qi sount demoraun'tz [5]hors del visnee[5]; ne ceux qi sount passez le age de lxx. aunz; ne charneus amis; ne ceux qi acun dreit porunt chalenger el tenement; ne vileyns; ne enditez ne appellez de felonie; ne [6]propres meynés[6] de acun des parties; ne ceux qi a acun des parties sount destreynables, ou seignurs, ou counseillers, ou countours.

4. Et cum les parties se serrount assentues [7]as jureez[7], adounc jurge le premer en ceste manere, paumez les saintz Evaungelies. Ceo oyez, vous Justices, qe jeo verité dirray de

Brac. 185; Fle. 230.

1. porter *om. MOH.* 2—2. *so NMC. sim. H.* ceo nuli *L.* ceo nul *A.* 3—3. de perdre vie e *N.* a perdre vie ou *AMC. sim. H.* 4—4. ne Meseels mys hors de commune des gentz *N.* ne mesels de comun de gentz ostez *C. sim. H.* 5—5. *so ND. sim. M.* den la vergee *L.* en hors de visne *C.* el visne *G. sim. A.* en veigne *H.* el vingnee *S.* 6—6. propre meysnee *N. sim. DG.* propre meigne *A. sim MS.* propres mahemes *C. sim. H.* 7—7. en Iureez *ND.* en iurours *M.* en iorre *CH.*

pected witness giving his testimony, inasmuch as no one who has been once convicted of perjury ought to be sworn, for such are held to have forfeited their free law, so as not to be credited upon any oath which they take. Nor ought those to be sworn who have suffered judgment of life and limb, or punishment of pillory or tumbrell; nor those who want discretion; nor excommunicated persons; nor lepers removed from society; nor priests or clerks within holy orders; nor women; nor such as dwell away from the neighbourhood; nor those who are above seventy years of age; nor allies in blood; nor such as can claim any right in the tenement; nor villains; nor persons indicted or appealed of felony; nor those of the household of any of the parties; nor those who are liable to be distrained by either of the parties; nor their lords, or counsellors, or accountants.

4. When the parties have agreed upon the jury, then let the first juror, touching the holy Gospels, swear after this manner. 'Hear this, ye Justices, that I will speak the truth

Form of juror's oath.

ceste assise, (si l'assise deyve estre prise en manere de assise et ne mie cum juree) del tenement dount jeo ay eu la vewe par le comandement le Roi; ou issi, del tenement [1]dount tele rente[1] est dite sourdre; ou issi, de la pasture et del tenement, ou de la comune, dount jeo ay eu la vewe. Et issi sount les motz del serment chaungeables[2] solom la manere del bref et de la moustraunce; et si la pleinte soit fete de [3]nusaunce, adounc soit dit issi: de la[3] nusaunce et del tenement a quel est dit qe la nusaunce est fete; ou issi, del mur, ou del estaung et del tenement, et ne mie dount jeo ay eu la vewe. Et adounc outre issi: et pur rien ne lerray qe verité ne diray, si Deu mei ayde et ses saintz. [4]Et puis jurgent les autres issi: autiel serment cum tel issi jura jeo tendray en dreit de moy, si Deu mei ayde et les saintz[4]. Et puis seint les Evaungelies beysez et en totes maneres honurez sicum
[135 *b*.] nostre fei et nostre sauvacioun. Et si plusours assises deyvent estre prises par un serment, adounc soit dit issi, des assises et des tenementz des queus jeo ay fet la vewe; ou issi, [5]de totes

1—1. *so M. sim. NA. om. L.* dount tel tenement *CH.* 2. *so N. sim. GM.* chalengables *LSACH.* 3—3. *so NM. sim. A. om. L.* 4—4. *so verb. MG. om. LNSACHF.* 5—5. *so verb. M. sim. H. om. LF.* de cestes assises e *A.* de ceste assise e de totes cestes assises *N.*

of this assise,' (if the assise is to be taken in manner of an assise and not as a jury,) 'of the tenement of which I have had the view by the king's precept;' or thus: 'of the tenement whereout such rent is said to arise;' or thus: 'of the pasture and of the tenement,' or 'of the common, whereof I have had the view.' Thus the words of the oath must be varied according to the form of the writ and declaration; and if the plaint be made of nusance, then it shall be said thus: 'of the nusance and of the tenement to which the nusance is said to have been committed;' or thus: 'of the wall, or pond, and of the tenement,' without adding 'whereof I have had the view.' Then it continues thus: 'and I will not fail for anything to speak the truth, so help me God and his Saints.' Then let the rest swear thus: 'The same oath which such a one hath thus sworn, I for my part will keep, so help me God and the Saints.' Then let the Gospels be kissed with all reverence as our faith and salvation. If several assises are to be taken under one oath, then it shall be said: 'of the assises and of the tenements whereof I have had the view;' or thus: 'of all

assises et[5] de ceux tenementz dount tele rente deit[1] sourdre; ou issi, de ces tenementz et de la commune de pasture, ou de turberie, ou de autre, et[2] des tenementz a queus dit est qe eles[3] deyvent appendre, dount jeo ay eu la vewe; ou issi, de ceste assise et del correy et del tenement, et issi des autres. Et en mesme la manere seynt sermentz fetz en les autres assises de mort de auncestre, et de dreyn present.

5. Et cum xii. averount juré et lour nouns serrount enbrevez, adounc lour seit le bref leu par le clerc prenotarie, qi dirra en ceste manere: vous dirrez par le serment qe vous avet fet, si tiel a tort et sauntz jugement eit disseisi le pleyntif de soen fraunc tenement en tele vile puis le terme ou noun. Et la Justice tauntost rehercera [4]mesme la force en ceste manere[4]: Johan qi ci est, se pleint de Pieres, qe il a tort et sauntz jugement ly ad disseisi de soen fraunc tenement en tele vile et dount il met en sa vewe x. acres de terre ove les apurtenaunces, ou plus ou meyns; et puis record le dit Brac. 185 b; Fle. 230 (§ 2).

1. est dit *M.* 2. ou *LSGAC.* e *M.* chose ou *N.* 3. so *NSMA.* eus *LC.* il G. 4—4. la fourme en ceste manere *M.* *om.* *CH.*

assises, and of those tenements whereout such rent is supposed to arise;' or thus: 'of those tenements, and of the common of pasture, or turbary, or other, and of the tenements to which it is said they ought to belong, whereof I have had the view;' or thus: 'of this assise, and of the corrody, and of the tenement,' and so of others. And in the other assises of mortdancester and darrein presentment the oath shall be taken in the same manner.

5. When twelve are sworn, and their names enrolled, then let the writ be read to them by the clerk prothonotary, who shall address them in this manner: 'You shall say by the oath you have taken whether such a one wrongfully and without judgment has disseised the plaintiff of his freehold in such a vill within the term, or not.' The Justice also shall straightway rehearse the substance of the plaint thus: 'John, who is present here, complains of Peter that he has wrongfully and without judgment disseised him of his freehold in such a vill, whereof he puts in his view ten acres of land (or more or less), with the appurtenances;' and then let him mention the

Writ stated by prothonotary.

Case explained by Judge.

le pleyntif, et les allegaunces[1] le defendaunt pur enfourmer[2] les jurours.

Brac. 185 *b*; Fle. 230 (§ 2). [136.]

6. Et tauntost voysent les jurours en une part par eus mesmes pur enparler. Et puis soint gardez, qe [3]nul de eus ne paroge as autres, ne autres ove eus fors entre les jurez mesmes[3]. Et si nul le face maliciousement, et soit de ceo atteynt, soit puni par prisoun et par fin, et les jurours soint amerciez, si il ne ly eyent encusé. Et estre ceo soint les jurours bien espiez, qe il ne garnisent nul [4]par encliner del oyl[4] ne par nul signe, encountre queles des parties il byent pronuncier lour verdit; et qi le face et de ceo soit atteynt soit amerciable ou autrement punisable solom le mal [5]qe en avent[5].

Glan. l. 2. c. 12; Brac. 185 *b*; Fle. 230 (§ 2).

7. Et si il ne se porrount accorder, soint autres mis [6]a la plus forte[6] partie des jurours, si[7] les parties le voillent, et si noun, soit jugé encountre ly qi ne le vodera; issi qe si le [8]pleyntif ne le[8] voille, adounc remeygne [9]la seysine sicum

1. allegaciouns *N.* *sim.* *SGMC.* 2. *so* *NACH.* *sim.* *M.* enfermer *L.* 3—3. nul ne parouge aueqes eus for soulement eus mesmes *M.* 4—4. *om.* *CH.* par colour del oyl *N.* 5—5. *so* *SG.* *sim.* *AF.* qe en auoynt *L.* qe en auendra *ND.* qe il en auoient fet. *M.* qen auoit *C.* 6—6. plus enforcer la *M.* 7. *so* *NDMCH.* et si *L.* e si *A.* 8—8. *so* *N.* *sim.* *GAMCH.* *om.* *L.* 9—9. *so verb.* *SAF.* lassise la seysine sicum auaunt *L.* lassise sicum auaunt *N.* *sim.* *MCH.* la seisine *G.*

declaration of the plaintiff and the allegations of the defendant for the information of the jurors.

The jurors retire.

6. The jurors shall immediately withdraw by themselves to confer together; and then let them be so kept, that none of them speak with any other person except the jurors, nor any other person with them. And if any do so maliciously, and be found guilty thereof, let him be punished by imprisonment and fine, and let the jurors be amerced, if they have not themselves accused him. Moreover let the jurors be watched, that they do not give warning to any one, by motion of the eye or by other sign, against which of the parties they intend to pronounce their verdict; and whosoever shall do so, and be found guilty thereof, shall be amerciable or otherwise punishable according to the mischief which may arise.

Jury not to give warning of their verdict.

Disagreement of jury. Additional jurors.

7. If the jurors cannot agree, let others be added to the majority of the jury, if the parties consent; and if not, let the judgment be against him who refuses to consent, so that if the plaintiff refuses, the seisin shall remain as before, and he be in

avaunt[9], et il en la merci, et si le disseisour[1] ne le voille, soit jugé cum noun defendu. Et si les jurours ne sevent pronuncier la verité ne rien del fet, si remaigne la seisine en le tenaunt, et le pleyntif en la merci, pur ceo qe il ne ad mie[2] prové sa entente en[3] sa pleynte. Et si il ne voillent le verdit pronuncier en ceo cas pur favour de une des parties ou par autre enchesoun, adounc soint enfermez sauntz manger et sauntz beyvere, si la qe il eynt lour verdit pronuncié. Fle. 230 (§ 2).

CHAPITRE XXII. [LIII.]

De Jugementz. [136 *b.*]

1. Et cum il serrount de un accord, tauntost voisent a la barre devaunt les Justices et dient lur verdit; et solom lour verdit soit jugement rendu pur une des parties, si nule doute i soit ne nule difficulté, pur quei mester soit de examiner le fet par les jurours ou par autres, ou de delayer le jugement jekes a un autre jour, issi qe en le meen temps en pusent les Justices estre avisez et counseillez quei en soit meuthz a fere. Brac. 185 *b*; Fle. 230, 231.

1. *so C. sim. M.* disseisi *L.* 2. *so NAMCH.* dounc *L.* 3. ne *NAHM.* e *GS.*

mercy; and if the disseisor refuses, he shall be adjudged as undefended. If the jurors cannot pronounce the truth, nor return any verdict as to the fact, let the seisin remain in the tenant, and let the plaintiff be in mercy for not having proved the case made by his plaint. If the jury refuse to pronounce any verdict in the matter through favour to either of the parties, or for any other reason, then let them be shut up without meat or drink until they have given their verdict.

If the jury are ignorant of the facts, plaintiff fails.

Jury, how compelled to give verdict.

CHAPTER XXII.

Of Judgments.

1. When the jurors are all agreed, let them immediately go to the bar before the Justices, and declare their verdict; and according to their verdict let judgment be given for one of the parties, unless any doubt or difficulty arise, which may make it necessary to examine the facts by the jurors or others, or to defer judgment until another day, so that the Justices may in the mean time be advised and consult what is best to do

Delivery of the verdict.

Si les Justices neqedent en[1] verditz [2]soint doutous[2], et les jurours ne soint mie asetz suffisauntment[3] examinez, et soint alez trop [4]avaunt al[4] jugement par la resoun de acun mot ou de acune resoun qe pout aver double entendement, en tiel cas tient leu certificatioun[5] par mesmes les Justices ou par autres. Mes plus beal et plus sayn est as Justices bien examiner les resouns des jurours, si qe il pusent [6]rendre bon jugement[6] et sayn, si qe nul errour ne soit trové en lour office ne en le proces.

Brac. 185 *b*; Fle. 230 (§ 3). 2. Et cum les jurours averount pronuncié le verdit sur le gros del assise, ou sour excepcioun, et le verdit se face encountre le pleintif, adounc soit agardé qe le tenaunt et les autres nomez en le bref voisent quite de cele assise sauntz jour, et le pleyntif ne prenge rien par soen bref, eynz soit en [137.] nostre merci pur la fause pleynte. Ses pleges de sure neqedent ne sount mie amerciables en tiel cas, quant le pleyntif ad suy jekes al fin.

1. entendent qe les *M.* 2—2. soint doutez *L.* se doutent *ND.* dotuz saient *S.* seent dotouz *M.* *sim.* *ACH.* de touz seient en awer *G.* 3. *so* *ND.* *sim.* *AMCH.* suffisauntz *L.* 4—4. folement auant en *M.* auaunt en *C.* 5. *so* *NGAM.* tiel certificacioun *L.* *sim.* *SCH.* 6—6. *so* *SGAMCH.* bien rendre les jugement *L.* rendre lour iugement bon *N.*

Doubtful verdict; proceeding by certification. therein. Where the Justices however are doubtful about the verdict, and the jurors have not been sufficiently examined, or have been too hasty in their judgment on account of some word or sentence which might have a double intendment, in such case a certification may be taken by the Examination of jurors by Judge. same or other Justices. But it is better and safer for the Justices thoroughly to examine the reasons of the jurors so that they may give a good and sound judgment, and that no error may be found either in their office or in the proceedings.

Judgment against plaintiff. 2. When the jurors have declared their verdict upon the substance of the assise, or upon any exception, and such verdict is given against the plaintiff, then let it be awarded that the tenant and the others named in the writ go quit of that assise without day, and that the plaintiff take nothing by his writ, but be in our mercy for his false plaint. Nevertheless his pledges to prosecute shall not in such case be amerciable, inasmuch as the plaintiff has prosecuted his suit to the end.

3. Et cum l'assise se[1] prent en manere de assise, adounc fet a prendre garde de la quantité et de la qualité de la pleinte, et cum bien le pleyntif eit mis en sa vewe et moustré en sa pleynte; car a ceo qe il ne avera mie mis en sa pleynte ne se estent mie le serment des jurours. Car si la Justice ly agarde plus qe le pleintif ne eit mis [2]en sa pleynte, et ausi si les jurours ly doignent la seisine de plus qe il avera mis[2] en sa vewe, [3]si fount il aperte disseisine al tenaunt[3], et le viscounte ausint, qi le comaundement de cel juge fornist; pur ceo qe en tiel cas, [4]ne en nul cas[4] ou soen poer ne se estent, ne ly deit nul bailiff obeier a forner les comaundementz; et celi ausi qi tele viciouse seisine receit. Et ausi en cas ou le pleintif purprent sur le disseisour plus qe dreit par colour de jugement. Et si le pleintif eit mis trop en sa vewe, en tel cas est il amerciable pur sa outrageouse demaunde. Fle. 251 (§ 19).

1. so *NAMCH.* se *om. L.* 2—2. *om. LNDSACHF.* en sa pleinte e ausi si les Iurours li doinent la seisine depuis qil auera mis. *M.* en sa pleinte si fount il aperte disseisine al tenant E ausi si le Iorours doignent la seisine pluis qil neit mis *G.* 3—3. *om. G.* 4—4. *om. M.* ne en nul autre cas *N.* ne en nul autre *A.*

The jurisdiction extends only to the land mentioned in the plaint and put in view.

3. When the assise is taken after the manner of an assise, regard must be had to the quantity and quality of the plaint, and how much the plaintiff has put in his view and set forth in his plaint; since the oath of the jurors does not extend to that which he has not put in his plaint. And if the Justice awards to the plaintiff more than he has put in his plaint, or if the jurors give him seisin of more than he has put in his view, they commit a manifest disseisin on the tenant[1]; as does the sheriff also, who puts in execution the command of the judge, because in such a case, or in any other where the Justice's jurisdiction does not extend, no bailiff ought to obey him in executing his commands. The plaintiff is in a like position who receives such defective seisin. So likewise where the plaintiff encroaches upon the disseisor more than right under colour of judgment. And if the plaintiff puts too much in his view, he is amerciable for his excessive demand.

[1] '*Ex hoc nota*, that the plaintiff's demand is the Justice's warrant, and the foundation of the judgment. Wherefore if the judgment is given upon a demand other than that which the plaintiff has truly made, whether more or less, the judgment is false.' Note in MS. *N.*

4. Et si le verdit soit pronuncié pur le pleyntif, tauntost soit enquis queus furent a la disseisine, et la manere del fet, si[1] la disseisine fust fete a banere desplaé, ou as chevaus covertz, ou par autre force des armes, et par quele force et queles

Brac. 162; Fle. 220, 221.

armes. Et dounc fet a saver, qe il i ad moutz des maneres des armes et sount moutz de maneres de force. Car nous dioums touz ces estre armez qi portent dount il porrount grevaunce fere a la gent, ou dount autres porrount poer aver, ausi bien arcs, et setes, et cotels, haches, et bastouns, cum haubercs, et launces, et espees. Et si est[2] force armé, et force

[137 *b.*] simple sauntz armes, sicum par multitude de gentz.

Brac. 186 *b*, 187; Fle. 222 (§ 6).

5. Et pur ceo qe meynt homme, qi nul dreit ad, purchace seisine par tele force, a la quele le tenaunt [3]qi dreit ad a retener ou a rester, en defut le tenement[3] pur [4]plus de[4] mal eschure, et les queles maneres de avenues[5] de seisine prendre est en partie encountre nostre pees, voloms qe les Justices enquergent queus vindrent en la force ovek le principal disseisour, si qe le disseisour et ceux de la force soint puniz par

1. E sĩ *NAM*. 2. ia *M.* ad *NAH.* 3—3. qe ad le dreit ne puit countre ester ne le tenement tener einz sen fuist *N.* 4—4. *om. N.* pour e pur plus de *M.* 5. venues *NA.*

Inquiry as to manner of disseisin and force used.

4. If the verdict be given for the plaintiff, it shall be forthwith inquired who were present at the disseisin, and the manner of the fact, whether the disseisin was committed with banner displayed, or horses harnessed, or by other force of

Force and arms.

arms, and by what force, and by what arms. And it should be understood that there are divers sorts of arms and divers kinds of force. For all those are said to be armed who carry anything wherewith they may do hurt to people or overpower others, as well bows, arrows, knives, hatchets, and staves, as hauberks, lances, and swords. So there is armed force, and simple force without arms, as by multitude of people.

Punishment of forceable disseisins.

5. And because many a man, having no right, gains seisin by such force, upon which the tenant who has a right to retain and abide in possession leaves the tenement to avoid further mischief, and forasmuch as such ways of obtaining seisin are in part against our peace, we will that the Justices inquire, who came in the force along with the principal disseisor, so that the disseisor and those of the force be punished by imprison-

la prisone et par fins, si[1] il soint [2]atteintz de disseisine fete a force, et si par armes, adounc soint reinz. Et si acuns soint[2] atteintz de disseisine fete par colour de dreit ovesque la pes, sicum par simple disseisine fete par jour et sauntz force et armes a[3] une blaunche verge en signe de pees, en tiel cas soint les disseisours amerciables par lour peers, et jalemeyns facent gré des damages al pleyntif. Et mesme la peyne dount Brac. 162 b; Fle. 221 (§ 5). dit est [4]a desus[4], qe fet a enjoyndre as disseisours qi engettent homme de fraunc tenement par force ou par armes, ou solom ceo qe fet a fere en manere de pees, soit enjoynt as disseisours qi a force ou par armes ou simplement [5]sauntz armes[5] detienent homme[6] de soen fraunc tenement, ou cum il quide leynz entrer pesiblement.

6. Acunes foiz avent en cestes assises, qe les disseisours se cuverent par nous, et dient qe il ne ount rien ne rien ne cleyment en le tenement, eynz ount fet en noster noun quant [138.] qe il ount fet, et sauntz nous ne poit la assise passer ne le fet estre mené en jugement sauntz prejudice [7]de nous[7]. En queus cas ne voloms ja qe par tele coverture remeigne la assise a

1. [E] si *N.* 2—2. so *verb. G.* *sim. M.* *om. LNASCH.* 3. oue *M.* ouuesqe *C.* ou *F.* 4—4. *so G.* *sim. NACF.* a dissuz *L.* de sus *H.* 5—5. *so N.* *sim. SAMCHF.* *om. L.* 6. hors *add. M.* 7—7. a nous fere *M.*

ment and fine if they are convicted of a disseisin effected by force, and if by arms, then ransomed. And if any be convicted of a disseisin done under colour of right, and without breach of the peace, as by a simple disseisin done in the daytime, without force and arms, with a white wand in sign of peace; in such case let the disseisor be amerciable by their peers, and also make satisfaction to the plaintiff in damages. The penalty above mentioned, which is to be imposed upon disseisors who eject people from their freehold, whether by force or arms, or, as it should be done, after a peaceable manner, shall also be imposed upon disseisors who with force or arms, or simply without arms, keep a man out of his freehold when he expects to enter peaceably therein.

Peaceable disseisin, with white wand.

Forceable detention, how punished.

6. Sometimes it happens in this assise that the disseisors shelter themselves by us, and say that they neither have or claim anything in the tenement, but whatsoever they did was done in our name, and that without us the assise cannot pass, nor the fact be brought in judgment without prejudice to us; in which cases we will not that under such pretext the assise

Defence, that the king is interested.

prendre; et si la disseisine soit clere et aperte, soit jugé pur le pleyntif, et soit commune ley encountre le tenaunt, sicum encountre autre del poeple; et si acune doute soit apercewe, soit le jugement respité deques a un autre jour, et en le meen tens soit le proces moustré a nous, si qe par conseil de nous soit ordeyné le jugement.

Brac. 186 (§ 4); Fle. 231 (§ 4).

7. Et pur ceo qe sovent avent qe le tenaunt ad fet nule disseisine ne nul tort, eynz ad purchacé le tenement par cas par feffement le disseisour, et en quel cas est bien resoun qe le tenaunt puse voucher le disseisour a garaunt, issint qe cil, qi nul tort ad fet, ne soit mie issi puniz del autri trespas, qe il ne recovere de soen feffour a la vaillaunce; et adounc soit tenu mesme le proces qe dit serra en garraunties de la assise de mort de auncestre. Et si[1] deus assises ou plusours soint aramez par diverses[2] persones vers un homme, la dreyne seisine soit primes a detrier, et issi arere meyn jekes a la premere disseisine.

Brac. 178 b; Fle. 219 (§ 22, 23).

Brac. 177; Fle. 219 (§ 23).

1. *so* NAMCH. si *om.* L. 2. plusurs e diuers *M.*

not to be regarded when the disseisin is manifest.

shall stand over; but if the disseisin be clear and manifest, let it be adjudged for the plaintiff, and let the common law take its course against the tenant as against any other person; and if any doubt be perceived, let judgment be respited to another day, and let the proceedings in the meantime be laid before us, so that judgment may be ordained by our advice.

Doubtful case to be referred to the king.

Vouching warrant.

7. And because it often happens that the tenant has not committed any disseisin or wrong, but has possibly purchased the tenement by feoffment of the disseisor; in such case it is reasonable that the tenant should be able to vouch to warranty the disseisor, so that he who has done no wrong may not be punished for the trespass of another, without recovering to the value from his feoffor; and then let the same proceeding be observed as shall be mentioned concerning warranties in the assise of Mortdancester. If two or more assises are prosecuted by several persons against one, the last seisin shall be first tried, and so backwards to the first disseisin[y].

Order of assises against one tenant.

[y] 'A is disseised by B. B continues seised, and is ejected by C. C is ousted by D, who enfeoffs E. A brings assise against B and E; B brings assise against C and E; C against D and E. *Quæstio*, whether E, tenant, ought to answer to all at the same time, or if not to all, to whom first? *Solutio:* The Justices *ex officio* ought to inquire of the last seisin

Brac. 187; Fle. 231 (§ 9).

8. Et puis soit enquis des jurours, queus damages les disseisours et les tenauntz eynt fetz en mesouns, en boys, en gardines et en garreynes, en vivers, en parcs, [1]en conigers[1] et aylours, et cum bien eit esté pris, ou pout aver esté pris par dreite gaynerie en le meen tens de totes maneres des issues del tenement, et quel profit et cum bien [2]vaillaunt pout le pleintif aver eu, si il[2] ne eust mie esté disseisi; et solom ceo soit agardé qe le pleyntif recovere pleynement ses damages. Et si les Justices veyent qe les jurours voillent allegger le disseisour par legers damages, par ceo qe il ly ount grevé de autre part [3]par la perte del tenement[3], adounc en presence des parties, si il voillent estre, par mesmes les jurours soint les terres estenduz a la verrey value, et solom la annuele value soint taxez les damages par les Justices, [4]sengles ou[4] [138 *b.*]

1—1. *om. ND.* 2—2. vaylent si le pleynteif *L.* qe le pleyntif eust eu si il *ND.* valent le pleintif eus en sil *S.* vailliaunt le pleintif eust ou sil *G.* valent e quel profit le pleintif eust eu sil *A.* vaillant poet le pleintif auer eu si i *M.* vaillent a eus le pleintif ou sil *C.* vaillent les espleez a eus ou si il *H.* il eussent auaille al plaintif si il *F.* 3—3. *so M.* *sim. NSGA.* par le par del tenement *L.* par le tenaunt *CH.* 4—4. *so NAMGCHF.* *om. L.*

Damages and mesne profits, how assessed.

8. Afterwards let it be inquired of the jurors what damages the disseisors and the tenants have committed in houses, woods, gardens, warrens, vivaries, parks, rabbit-warrens, and elsewhere; and how much has or might have been by good husbandry received in the meantime of all kinds of issues of the tenement, and what profit in value the plaintiff might have had if he had not been disseised; and it shall be awarded accordingly that the plaintiff recover his full damages. And if the Justices perceive that the jurors are disposed to relieve the disseisor by assessing light damages, because on the other hand they have made him suffer by the loss of the tenement, let the lands be extended by the same jurors at their true value in the presence of the parties, if they will be there; and according to the yearly value let the damages be taxed by the Justices, single or double, according to the ordinance of our statutes, and

in this manner: 'Good people of the assise, you shall tell us by your oaths which of these three, who bring assise of the same tenement against the same tenant E, was last seised, whether A or B or C.' And if they say C, and before him B, and before him A, then the judgment shall be thus: 'For as much as we find that B hath disseised A, and C hath disseised B, and D hath disseised C; therefore this Court doth award that B and C, being disseisors, do take nothing by their writs, but be amerced, and that A do recover his seisin against E by your views.'' (Note in MS. *N.*) Compare Bracton, 177, 178.

Stat. West. 1. (3 Ed. I.) c. 24; Stat. Glouc. (6 Ed. I.) c. 1; Stat. West. 2. (13 Ed. I.) c. 25, 26. Brac. 187; Fle. 231 (§ 9).

doubles, solom la ordinaunce de nos estatutz, et solom ceo qe l'assise avera esté fausement targé ou noun.

9. Et si les disseisours eint tollet ou detenu al pleintif vessel ou robes ou chatel[1], soit en eleccioun le pleyntif a sure ses chateus par apel de robberie, ou de trespas, ou a fere les taxer entre les autres damages. Et des bestes sauvages prises en parcs ou en chaces, ou des pessouns pris hors des vivers, soint les damages taxetz par les jurours. Car en tiel cas ne gist mie la peyne de la prisoun de iii. aunz, ne en nul
[139.] cas for qe ou felonie put estre jugé, si peril i gist de vie et de membre. Et si mesouns soint arses en le meen tens ou autre damage eit esté avenu, [2]tut eit il esté avenu[2] par despeiré[3] aventure sauntz malice de homme, ja par taunt ne ert le disseisour quite qe il ne rende les damages ausi bien [4]de ses chateus demeyne[4] cum de autri bien a tort detenu par le disseisour.

Brac. 187; Fle. 232.

1. vif chateal *G.* *sim. M.* 2—2. *so verb AM.* *sim. SGCH.* tut eit ceo estee *N.* *om. L.* 3. aspre *N.* 4—4. *so NMC.* *sim. SGA.* des chateus demeynes *L.*

according as the assise shall have been falsely defended or not.

Plaintiff may proceed by appeal for goods removed.

9. If the disseisors have taken away or detained from the plaintiff any vessel, robe, or chattel, it shall be in the election of the plaintiff either to sue for his chattels by appeal of robbery or trespass, or to have them taxed with the rest of his damages. The damages for wild animals taken in parks or chases, and for fish taken out of ponds, shall be assessed by the jurors; for in such cases the penalty of three years' imprisonment does not lie, nor in any case except where judgment of felony can be given, if the offender is in peril of life and limb. If houses have been burnt or other damage has happened in the meantime, although it was by an unforeseen accident, without any human malice, yet the disseisor is not thereby discharged from making satisfaction as well for the chattels of the disseisee as for the goods of others wrongfully detained by the disseisor.

Penalty of imprisonment.

Disseisor responsible for loss by fire or accident.

CHAPITRE XXIII. [LIV.]

De Apurtenaunces.

Brac. 220 *b*; Fle. 251.

1. Dit avoms de sus de disseisines des choses corporeles, ore fet a dire de disseisours de noun corporeles, sicum des aportenaunces. Car tut soit un tenement fraunc tenement solom la diffinicioun, quant a regard neqedent des services dount il est chargé [1]purra autre[1] tenement estre plus franc; et serrount jalemeyns ambedeus fraunes tenementz. Et dounc, si acun tenement soit chargé a acun service a autre tenement, cel service proprement est des apurtenaunces del autre tenement, a quel cel service est due. Des queles apurteinaunces nul ne deit disseiser autre; et si acun le face, ly disseisi porra estre eydé par ceste assise, ou par noster bref al viscounte sicum apres serra dit.

Brac. 220 *b*; Fle. 251.

2. Et fet a saver, qe acunes apurteynaunces sount fraunches, et [2]acunes enserveez. Fraunches[2], sicum [3]a regard[3] des persones et des tenementz as queus eles sount dues; enservez[4] [139 *b*.]

1—1. puit vn autre *N.* pur autri *MCH.* puit autre *A.* 2—2. *so N.* et acuns en seruices fraunes *L.* e ascuns en seruice fraunches *G.* e aucuns en seruices franches *S.* e acuns en seuerez fraunches *M.* e asquns fraunches *C.* *om. F.* 3—3. gardes *N.* 4. *so C.* en seruices *LGS.* enseuerez *M.*

CHAPTER XXIII.

Of Appurtenances.

Disseisin of incorporeal tenements.

1. Having spoken above of disseisins of things corporeal, we must now speak of disseisors of things incorporeal, as of appurtenances. For although a tenement be freehold according to the definition of it, yet in respect of the services wherewith it is charged another tenement may be more free; and yet both are free tenements. Wherefore if one tenement be charged with any service to another tenement, such service is properly an appurtenance to the tenement to which the service is due. Of which appurtenances no one ought to disseise another, and if any one does so, the disseisee may be aided by this assise, or by our writ to the sheriff, as shall be hereafter mentioned.

Nature of an appurtenance.

Remedy for disseisin of appurtenance.

Servitudes or easements.

2. It should be known that some appurtenances are free, others servile; free as in respect of the persons and tenements to which they are due, servile as regards the tenements

quant a regard des tenementz dount eles issent, et teus servages touz jours sount dues de autri tenement, et si ne put nul neqedent enserver nuly[1] soyl for qe le soen demeyne. Et issi sount[2] acuns tenementz plus fraunes qe autres. Car tiel soil est plus fraunc qe rien ne deit al[3] soil soen veysin, qe cely qe est obligé en servage.

Brac. 222; Fle. 254 (c. 18, § 3). 3. En plusours maneres porra homme enserver soen tenement, [4]sicum a graunter, qe[4] autre, qi rien ad, eit[5] leynz dreit [6]de pestre ou de syer ou[6] de pescher ou dreit[7] de chacer ou de aler ou de carier, [8]ou par autres servages[9] qe[8] porount estre sauntz fin et sauntz noumbre, solom ceo qe il sount simples ou [10]solom ceo qe il sount[10] compountz de autres apurtenaunces. Car il i ad apurteynaunce [11]et apurteinaunce de apurteinaunce. [12]Car a molin eweresce est le cours del ewe une des apurtenaunces[12] [13]et chemin une autre[13], a queles aportenent purgacioun et refeccioun[11], et si[14] sount apurtei-

Brac. 232; Fle. 267.

1. autri *M.* 2. so *NC.* sim. *M.* cum *L.* 3. so *NM.* a *L.* au *GSC.* 4—4. so *ND.* sim. *M.* sicum a garraunter qe *L.* sim. *GSF.* si asqun garaunt *C.* cum si asqun graunte a *B.* 5. qe il eyt *B.* 6—6. so *L.* sim. *GS.* om. *NDMCB.* 7. om. *NDM.* 8—8. for qe dreit de pestre ou de syer. E seruages *ND.* 9. so *MGCB.* services *L.* 10—10. om. *ND.* 11—11. om. *ND.* 12—12. so *M.* sim. *GW.* om. *LSARCFB.* 13—13. so *M.* sim. *GW.* ou chemin ou autre *L.* sim. *R.* en commun ou autres *CFB.* 14. ces *M.* seus *C.* ceus *B.* cel *F.*

from which they issue[z], and such servitudes are always due from the tenement of another; although no one can subject the soil of any one to servitude but his own. And in this way some tenements are more free than others; for that soil is more free which owes nothing to the soil of its neighbour, than that which is bound to a servitude.

Servitude, how created. 3. A person may subject his tenement to a servitude in several ways, as by granting that another, who has nothing therein, shall have a right of pasturing or mowing, or fishing, or of driving cattle, or of way, or of carrying therein, or by other servitudes which may be infinite and numberless, according as they are simple or compounded of other appurtenances. For there are appurtenances, and also appurtenances of appurtenances. For to a watermill, the course of water is one of the appurtenances, and way is another, to which cleansing and repairing are appurtenant, and are therefore

Appurtenances of appurtenances.

[z] Unless the text is corrupt, the above sentence appears to be a mistaken rendering of the parallel passage in Bracton or Fleta, when the sense is, that the same things which are rights or liberties (jura sive libertates) in relation to the dominant, are servitudes (servitutes) in relation to the servient tenement. This observation is found subsequently in Britton, *post*, s. 8, p. 367.

naunces as apurteinaunces; et dount remedie gist par ceste assise si nul en soit destourbé.

4. Et lequel qe cel servage soit due[1] de un soil a[2] autri soil ou a autri persone par la volunté des verrays seignurs pur certeyn service ou pur veisinage, pur ceo ne sount mie obligez soulement a autri [3]soil ne soulement a autri persone, einz sount obligez a autri[3] certeyn soil et al seignur del soil joyntment, qi qe unques en soit seignur. Et [4]de ceo ensuit[4], qi qe unqe purchace le soil, cil purchace les apurteynaunces [140.] dues a cel soil, si especiale forprise ne face destourbaunce; et dount acunes sount ordinez et establies par ceux qi poent le soil enserver, et acunes par loung usage des uns et par suffraunce et negligence des autres. Car presumpcioun oevere acune foiz en tel cas, qe suffraunce a escient par prescripcioun de tens suffit pur consente. Car tut ne soit acun tenement enservé a nule manere de servage a soen veisin par nule constitucioun ne par nul bon title du seignur del soil, si le veisin neqedent eit purpris[5] sour le soil soen veisin acun servage sicum de pestre la pasture del soil soen veisin et de

Brac. 221; Fle. 252.

1. *so GCFB. sim. SM.* due *om. LND.* 2. *so SGMCB.* ou de *L.* 3—3. *so G. om. LNDSMACB.* 4—4. de ensut *L.* de ceo ensiut *ND.* de ceo sut *S.* *sim. GM.* 5. forpris *MCF.*

appurtenances to appurtenances; and if any one be disturbed thereof, remedy may be had by this assise.

4. And whether the servitude be due from one soil to that of another or to the person of another by the consent of the true owners, for a certain service or by reason of vicinage, they are not bound to the soil only, or to the person only, but to the certain soil of another, and also to the owner of the soil, whosoever the owner may be. Hence it follows, that whosoever purchases the soil purchases the appurtenances due to the soil, unless hindered by special exception. Some of which servitudes are ordained and established by those who have power to charge the soil, and others by long usage on the one side, and by sufferance and negligence on the other. For in such a case it is presumed that sufferance with knowledge amounts by prescription of time to consent. For although a tenement be not burthened with any kind of servitude by appointment or other good title from the owner of the soil, yet if the neighbour has taken by encroachment upon the soil of his neighbour any servitude, as the depasturing

Servitudes run with the land.

Servitudes arising from usage and sufferance.

barrer le seignur del soil qe il ne puse pestre, et de ceo eit esté seisi en clamaunt fraunc tenement sauntz force et sauntz preere[1] fere al[2] seignur del soil, et continuelment et ne mie privément par mussesses[3] mes baudement et apertement, mes n'en pora estre engetté ne destourbé qe il ne soit disseisi. Et si cil a qi le tort est fet del[4] consentement disseisist tel purchaceour par force et ne mie par jugement, ja[5] ly ert tele presumpcioun si prejudiciele, qe, si ly engetté recovere sa seisine par jugement de nostre court, james ne le engettera for qe par plé el dreit par le bref de *Quo Jure.* Mes disseisine deprecative ou privé, sicum en la absence le seignur del soil,
[140 *b.*] tut se[6] soint les baillifs tel seignur [7]seyns ou[7] assentuz, ne accrest james fraunc tenement a ceux purchaceours.

Brac. 221; Fle. 252.

5. Et acune foiz est le soil enservé de dreit, tut ne soit il par constitucioun de homme ne par constitucioun de pesible seisine, sicum qe nul ne face en soen soil demeyne chose qe soit grevaunte ou nusaunte a soen veysin; et dount diverses nusaunces sount. Car acune nusaunce pora estre dreiturele,

1. priere *NM.* purpresture *CB.* 2. chief *add. MCB.* 3. muscestes *N.* muscettes *GSB.* musettes *M.* 4. de le *M.* e le *CFB.* 5. *so LNGS.* a *MCB.* 6. *so LSM. om. ND GRCFB.* 7—7. seins ou *ND.* feuz ou *M.* feinz ou *GSB. sim. W.* seinz ou *C.* leinz et *B.* seuz ou *F.*

of the herbage on his neighbour's soil, and the hindering of the owner from pasturing, and has been seised thereof, claiming freehold, without force and without asking leave of the owner of the soil, and this continually, and not privately by stealth, but boldly and openly, he can never be ejected or disturbed without being disseised. And if he to whom the wrong is done by his own consent, disseise such purchasor by force and not by judgment, that presumption shall be so far prejudicial to him, that if the ejected recover his seisin by judgment of our court, he shall not afterwards eject him but by plea in the right by writ of *Quo Jure.* But by a precarious or secret disseisin, as in the absence of the owner of the soil, although the bailiffs of such owner be present or consenting, a freehold never accrues to such purchasers.

Usage must be continued and open.

Writ of *Quo Jure.*

5. Sometimes the soil is subject to a servitude by law, although not by any man's appointment, or by the establishment of peaceable seisin, as, for example, to the obligation that no one shall do anything in his own soil that may be a grievance or annoyance to his neighbour; of which annoy-

Servitudes arising by law.

Sic utere tuo ut alienum non lædas.

et nomément cele qe nul veisin ne put defendre a autre de fere, sicum lever molyn en soen soil demeyne; et acune pora estre torcenouse, cum si acun face en soen soil demeyne chose grevaunte[1] a soen veisin qe par [2]dreit ly pora hom[2] defendre a fere; car dreit defend qe nuli ne leve ne enhauce soen estaung si haut par ount le tenement[3] soen veisin soit neyeez[4], ne qe il ne face fosse en soen soil propre par ount il tourne le ewe de soen veisin, ne par ount le ewe ne puse demorer en soen veuz[5] cours, ou qe nul ne face [6]en le soen[6] qe soen veisin [7]au meyns[7] ne puse user sa seisine del servage dount le soil ly est obligé et chargé, ou qe il ne puse user [8]sa pesible seisine[8] ou et quant il devera, en totes les maneres qe fere soleit et deveit, en noumbre et en gendre, qualité et quantité.

6. Car il i ad privé disseisine et aperte; pur[9] ceo qe [10]ausi bien cil est[10] disseisi qi ne est mie suffert de aver sa [11]chace entre[11] autri soil qe est enservé[12] a ceo, ou qe [13]il ne soeffre mie[13] Brac. 221 *b*; Fle. 252. [141.]

1. qe seit nusaunte *M.* nosaunte *C.* 2—2. dreite ley *ND.* ly *om. MCB.* 3. terre *M.* 4. meyns seurs *N.* neyez fors *M.* noee fors *C.* 5. auncien *M.* 6—6. ensi son soil *M.* 7—7. ialemeins *M.* 8—8. sa seisine pessiblement *N. sim. SGM.* 9. e pur *M.* 10—10. ausi bien si le *L.* ausi ben si ben li *S.* auxi bien est cyl *N.* cil est ausi bien *G.* ausi com il *M.* ausi qe le *C.* ausi si le *F.* 11—11. *so M.* chose outre *L.* chace outre *NSCB.* chace en *G.* 12. *so C.* en seuere *L.* enserui *N.* enceuere *S.* enseuere *G.* en seueraute *M.* 13—13. ne est mie soeffert *N.*

ances there are various sorts; for some annoyances may be lawful, and in particular such as no neighbour can forbid another to do, as to erect a mill on his own soil; and some Nusances. may be tortious, as if any one do in his own soil a thing which is a grievance to his neighbour, and which he by law may be prohibited from doing. For the law forbids any one to raise or heighten his pond so as to drown the tenement of his neighbour, or to make a ditch in his own soil whereby the water is diverted from his neighbour, or whereby it is hindered from remaining in its ancient course, or to do any act in his own soil whereby his neighbour may be less able to use his seisin of the servitude wherewith the soil is bound and charged to him, or to use his peaceable seisin where and when he ought, in all such ways as he was wont and ought to use it, in number, kind, quality, and quantity.

6. For there is secret as well as open disseisin; forasmuch as he is equally disseised who is not suffered to have his driftway over another's soil which is subject thereto, or is not permitted Disseisin may be by a partial disturbance.

de reperiler et redrescer le chemin, cum si tut[1] le chemin soit destrut, ou tut [2]le soil fet viver[2]; et cil[3] qi est distourbé de espurger le cours del ewe [4]a soen molyn ausi bien cum en cas ou tut le cours del ewe soit destourbé ou transtourné; car a cours de ewe apent purgacioun sicum redrescement a chemin. Et ausi fet cil disseisine qi en partie[4] destourbe autri[5] seisine, ausi bien cum si ly destourbat del tut. Et si acun eit commune en autri soil oveke fraunche entré et fraunche issue par certeyn leu, si le seignur del soil face destourbaunce par haye ou par mur ou par fosse par ount le entré et le issue est meyns oesé[6] ke devaunt, [7]cum il covendra chacer loinz entour la ou il soleit[7] chacer a dresces, en cel cas, et en cas semblables sount fetes disseisines, si par presentementz en[8] tourns de viscountes ou en vewe de frauncplege ne soint teles nusaunces redresceZ. Et ausi en ceo cas, cum si a acun soit graunté dreit de pestre a totes les foiz qe il vodera ovek ses avers, et s'il soit puis destourbez qe il ne les peuse pestre for

Ante, l. 1. c. 30. s. 8, p. 183.

1. so *NM.* *sim. SG.* toust *L.* *om. CB.* 2—2. le soil fet a viuer *D.* *sim. N.* le soil i fet viuers *M.* eit et fet viuer *C.* 3. si il *M.* 4—4. *om. CB.* 5. acuny *N.* 6. esce *N.* vsee *G.* eysez *M.* ese *C.* 7—7. cum il vodera *LNDS.* *sim. CB.* com il vodra chacer Com il couendra chacer loinz en tour la ou il soleit chacer *G.* com couendra chacer loinz entour la ou il se leyt *M.* 8. *so NMCB.* de en *L.*

to repair and put in order the way, as if the way was entirely destroyed, or the whole soil turned into a fishpond; and he who is hindered from cleaning out the watercourse of his mill is as much disseised as if the whole watercourse were disturbed or diverted; for to a right of watercourse the right of cleansing is appurtenant, as the right of repairing is appurtenant to a right of way. And he is as much guilty of disseisin who partly hinders another's seisin, as if he disturbed him of the whole. And if any one has common in another's soil with free ingress and egress by a certain place, if the owner of the soil commits disturbance by making a hedge, wall, or ditch, whereby the ingress and egress is less easy than before, inasmuch as he must drive his cattle a long way round where he could formerly drive them straight, these and like acts may be treated as disseisins, unless the nusances are redressed by presentment in the sheriff's tourn, or in view of frankpledge. So in this case,—where any one has a right of pasture granted to him for his cattle at whatsoever times he pleases, and he is afterwards disturbed so that he can put them

Way and water, rights appurtenant thereto.

Redress of nusance at sheriff's tourn.

qe a certein tens, ou cum [1]il les deit[1] pestre par tut, et s'il soit destourbé qe il ne les peuse pestre fors en certeyns leus; ou cum il deit aver pasture a totes maneres des avers, [2]et ne ly soit mie suffert for qe a une manere des avers[2], ou cum il deit aver a certeyn noumbre, et ne ly soit mie suffert for qe a meyndre noumbre; ou si graunté soit a acun homme qe il puse carier ewe de autri pusz a sa volunté, et soit destourbé sicum est dit de pasture; [3]et de tut autel[3] cas ad leu ceste assise, ausi bien cum si pleyne destourbaunce fust fete del tut. [141 *b.*]

7. Et en touz les cas ou ceste assise tient leu a cely a qi tele fraunchise est graunté, en mesmes les cas ausi tient leu ceste assise au seignur del soil, si celi a qi la fraunchise est graunté autrement use[4] sa seisine ou plus outrageousement qe fere ne deit. Bon est neqedent a destourber teus outrages en le comencement taunt cum hom put, si qe pesible seisine ne lour vaille pur title de fraunc tenement. Brac. 221 *b*; Fle. 253.

8. Les servages dount hom put soen soil enserver sount Brac. 221 *b*, 222; Fle. 253 (§ 2).

1—1. sil dust *M.* il deit *CB.* 2—2. so *L.* *sim. N.* *om. MCB.* 3—3. En touz autiels *N.* en tut teus *M.* en touz teus *CB.* 4. vodra user *M.*.

in only at a certain time, or when he has a right to pasture throughout the whole and he is hindered from having it except in certain places, or where he ought to have pasture for all manner of beasts and he is allowed to have it only for one kind of beasts, or where he ought to have pasture for a certain number and he is suffered to have it only for a less number; or if it is granted to any one that he may draw away water at his pleasure from another's well and he is disturbed as above mentioned concerning pasture,—in all these cases this assise is applicable, as much as if complete disturbance had been made of the whole.

Reciprocal remedy of owner of servient soil for excess.

7. In all cases where this assise lies for the grantee of such a franchise, it lies also for the owner of the soil if he to whom the franchise is granted uses his seisin in a different or more extensive manner than he ought. Nevertheless it is well to hinder such excesses, so far as possible, at the beginning, so that the disseisors may not avail themselves of peaceable seisin as title of freehold.

Purchase of servitude, complete without seisin.

8. The servitudes to which a man may subject his land are

sauntz noumbre; et tut en autele manere et par auteles enchesouns qe corporeles choses[1] sount purchacez, [2]sount teles dreitures ou franchises purchacez[2]. Mes a[3] teles fraunchises purchacer[4] ne covendra mie taunt de solempneté de seisines fere, cum covent [5]en le purchaz de chose corporele[5]. Car si les parties soint de une volunté, asetz suffist le bail des escritz ovek la vewe[6] des tenementz en presence des vesins, apres quel tens si le purchaceour soit destourbé a receyvere[7] la fraunchise qe graunté luy est, par cely qi graunter[8] le put, si serra il succurru par ceste assise, tut ne eyt[9] il pris nuls esplez. Cum si pasture soit graunté en autri soil en fee ou a terme
[142.] de vie, et les escritz soint liverez et le soil assigné par vewe de veisins, si[10] le purchaceour vodera lendemeyn ou loung tens apres pestre ses avers de la pasture de cel soil solom la manere de soen purchaz, et il en soit destourbé par le donour ou par autre, si serra il eydé par ceste assise, tut ne pust[11] il unques. Car teles fraunchises sount si simples qe eles ne soeffent point de bail de seisine cum fount choses grosses

1. *so NMCB.* choses *om. L.* 2—2. *om. CB.* 3. *so GSF.* a *om. L.* en *MC.* de *N.* 4. *so GS.* purchasez *LNMCB. sim. F.* 5—5. as choses corporeles *M.* 6. fere *add. NS. sim. G.* fete *add. M.* 7. *so L. sim. NSG.* retenir *M.* recouerir *C.* recouerer *B.* 8. *so NM.* garraunter *L. sim. CB.* 9. eynt *L.* eit *NB.* i eent *M.* 10. *so NSGMCB.* et *L.* 11. pessoit *M.*

innumerable; and such rights and franchises are purchased in the same manner and for the like causes as corporeal things. But for the purchase of these franchises the same formality of giving seisin is not requisite, as in purchases of corporeal things. For if the parties are agreed, the delivery of the deeds together with the view of the tenements in the presence of neighbours is sufficient; and if the purchaser be thereafter hindered from enjoying the franchise granted to him by one who had power to grant it, he shall be helped by this assise, although he has not taken any esplees. Thus, where pasture in another's soil is granted in fee or for term of life, and the writings are delivered, and the soil assigned by view of neighbours, if the purchaser, whether the next day or a long while after, has a mind to feed his cattle on the pasture of that soil according to the tenor of his purchase, and is hindered by the donor or another, he shall be aided by this assise, although he never enjoyed the pasture. For such franchises are so simple that they do not admit of delivery of seisin, as gross,

corsues et materieles. Et fet a entendre, qe quant al purchaceour sount teus purchaz fraunchises et dreitures, et ausi au tenement a quel sount assignez de appendre, et quant al seignur del soil[1] et au tenement a ceo obligé sount teus purchaz servages. Brac. 220 *b*; Fle. 251.

9. Mes tut soit le purchaceour issint en seisine, pur ceo [2]ne affie[2] mie qe cele seisine suffist pur touz jours. Car eynz ceo qe il eit pris autre seisine de la pasture, ne pora il mie cele pasture aliener, sicum est de avowesoun de eglise, qe ne put mie estre doné eynz ceo qe le donour eit esté seisi del avoweson par le presentement. Et ausi porra le purchaceour aver[3] barre pur sa seisine si le soil fust aliené a estraunge meyn eynz ceo qe autre seisine fust prise qe[4] soulement le bail de escritz. Et pur ceo fet bon[5] a mettre eynz les bestes tauntost. Car par le mettre de une beste suffit la seisine de totes les autres qe il porrount mettre, tut soit cele beste enpromté par le purchaceour de autre hom qe le donour, si en le doun ne[6] soit especialment forpris qe il ne fra pestre for qe Brac. 223, 223 *b*; Fle. 257. [142 *b*.]

1. chargee *add. M.* 2—2. ne sount [suyt *interl.*] il *N.* ne se afie il *M.* ne sue *GSC.* nen suyt *B.* 3. este *add. M.* 4. qe si *N.* mes qe *M.* 5. ben *M.* bien *CB.* 6. so *NMGCB.* *om. L.* ni *S.*

coarse, and material things do. It should be understood that such purchases, in relation to the purchaser and also to the tenement to which they are assigned to belong, are franchises and rights, and with regard to the owner of the soil which is charged, and to the tenement bound thereto, such purchases are servitudes. Franchises and servitudes.

9. But although the purchaser is thus in seisin, this does not prove that such seisin is sufficient for ever. For until he has taken other seisin of the pasture, he cannot alien the same; as in the like case of the advowson of a church, which cannot be granted before the donor has been seised of the advowson by presentation. The purchaser may also be barred of his seisin, if the soil be aliened to a stranger before any other seisin was taken thereof beyond the bare delivery of the writings. Therefore it is proper to put in the beasts forthwith. For the putting in of one beast is a sufficient seisin for all the rest which he might have put in, although the beast be borrowed by the purchaser of some other person, so it be not the donor, unless it be specially excepted in the gift that he Actual seisin must be had before alienation. Grant without seisin defeated by alienation of servient soil. Seisin of pasture, how acquired.

ses bestes demeyne, et ne mie [1]les autres[1]. Et s'il ne face, si porra il perdre soen purchaz par sa negligence pur la presumpcion qe est, qe il ne voleit nule seisine prendre.

Brac. 223 *b*; Fle. 257.

10. Et si il ne eit nule beste qe suue soit, ne autre a ceo pora enpromter, adounc suffit qe il destourbe celi [2]qi deit[2] le soil en quant qe il put, qe il ne le puse arrer et[3] semer. Et issi par tel contek retient il une manere de seisine, et issi porra mettre eynz ses bestes a quel houre qe il vodera veyer[4], tut soit la terre arree ou semé, ou tut soint les blez murs. [5]Mes si il[5] eit esté si negligent qe sauntz contek mettre eit suffert le seignur del soil arrer et semer, et en tens des blez a primes prenge la seisine par la pasture de ses bestes en les blez, en tel cas fet il disseisine al seignur del soil, et si le seignur recovere par ceste assise, le purchaceour ert barré [6]de la pasture[6] a remenaunt par sa negligence qe il demora trop de sa seisine prendre[7]. Mes ore poreit acun dire opposaunt[8] le contrarie, issi, qe si tu gaynes ma terre sauntz moen coungé et la semes, et jeo le suffre a escient, uncore ne mei

1—1. *so LN. sim. GS.* les bestes dautri *M.* les autris *C.* autris *B.* 2—2. *so LG.* qe deit *N. sim. DS.* qe deuoit *M.* qe doyue *B.* ke tient *F.* 3. ne *NGMCB.* ou *G.* 4. *so L. sim. SM.* venir voyre *D. om. G.* 5—5. *so NDS. sim. GMCB.* ou qe *L.* 6—6. del purchaz *MB.* del purchace *C.* 7. *so M.* prendre *om. LNSGCB.* 8. e posaunt *M.*

shall depasture his own beasts only, and not those of others; and if he omits doing this he may lose his purchase by his negligence, since it is presumed that he did not intend to take any seisin.

Quasi-seisin by hindering the tillage of the soil.

10. If the purchaser has neither beast of his own nor can borrow another for the purpose, then it is sufficient to hinder the owner of the soil as much as he can from ploughing and sowing, so that by such molestation he retains a kind of seisin, and may put in his beasts whensoever he chooses to send them, although the land be ploughed and sown, or although the corn be ripe. But if he has been so negligent as to suffer the owner of the soil to plough and sow without any dispute, and then takes seisin for the first time while the corn is growing by feeding his beasts in the corn, in such case he commits a disseisin against the owner of the soil; and if the owner recovers by this assise, the purchaser shall be barred of his pasture for ever after by his negligence in too long delaying the taking of seisin. But some one may say on the other hand thus, Although you till and sow my land without

est nul tort fet, jekes autaunt qe tu mei enportes la vesture; [1]coment est dounc ma negligence et[1] la soefferté[2] plus perilouse en le un cas qe en le autre? A ceo fet a entendre, qe [3]il ad negligente suffraunce[3] et suffrable cautele. Par suffraunce de arures se amendent les terres et par le semer ausi, et en [143.] tel cas est la suffraunce bone et[4] cautele a soeffrer qe home seme autri terre[5], ne nule disseisine est au seignur del soil, puis qe rien ne fust fet encountre soen gré. Mes par la ou nul profit [6]ne ly accrest par[6] la suffraunce mes damage, sicum est del premer cas, la est negligente suffraunce. Car en le un cas est la condicioun de celi, qi soeffre la arrure, amendé, et en le autre cas enpiré.

11. Acuns usent la seisine de commune en lour nouns demeynes et acuns en autri nouns. Et sicum gardein use seisine de commune en le noun del enfaunt de eynz age, qi gardeyn il est, ausi use persone de eglise en le noun de sa eglise. Car la eglise est touz jours supposé de estre en autel

Brac. 226 *b*; Fle. 258 (§ 9).

1—1. par ma negligence e est *M.* 2. *so LM.* soeffrance *N.* *sim. G.* suffert *S.* forfet *F.* 3—3. *so GS.* il ad negligence suffrante *LN.* lia suffraunce negligente *M.* 4. *so L.* e *MSG.* et *om. N.* 5. terre *om. M.* 6—6. *so verb. M.* ne accrest pur *L.* ne accrest al seignur *N.*

my leave and I knowingly suffer it, yet no wrong is done me until you carry the produce away; how then is my negligence and the sufferance more dangerous in the one case than in the other? In answer to this, it is to be observed that there is a negligent sufferance and a sufferable caution. For by suffering lands to be ploughed the lands are improved, and by sowing also; and in such case the sufferance is good and prudent to permit a man to sow another's land; and it is no disseisin to the owner of the soil, since nothing has been done against his consent: but where no profit accrues to him by the sufferance, but on the contrary loss, as in the case in question, then it is negligent sufferance; for in the one case the condition of him who permits the ploughing is made better, and in the other worse.

11. Some enjoy the seisin of common in their own right, and some in the right of others. And as a guardian enjoys the seisin of common in the name of the infant under age whose guardian he is, so likewise the parson of a church enjoys it in the name of his church. For a church is always supposed to be in the same state as an infant under age, by

Church seised of common by parson, as infant by guardian.

estat cum enfaunt de eynz age, par la resoun, qe ele est touz jours en la garde des persones, par les queus gardeyns eles poent purchacer et lour estat amender, sicum enfauntz par lour gardeyns; mes a lour damage ne poent il mie assenter. Par quei si acune eglise soit seisie de acune commune, tut moerge la persone, pur ceo ne perd mie la eglise sa seisine de sa commune, [1]ne nule[1] autre seisine, nient plus qe enfaunt de eynz age par le eschaunge de ses gardeyns, par quel eschaunge lour estat [2]ne empire ne eschaunge[2] en nul point. Et pur ceo put chescune persone user la seisine qe soen predecessour lassa a la eglise. Et si il en soit destourbé, si recovera par ceste assise. Mes si le predecessour eynz fust destourbé, ou si la eglise fu disseisie en tens de la vacacioun, adounc covendra autre remedie sicum par nos brefs de entré ou de *Quod permittat.*

Brac. 226 b, 227; Fle. 258 (§ 9, 10, 11).

[143 b.]

12. Et cum plusours servages sount, sicum avaunt est dit, et le plus renomé est dreit de pestre en autri soil, pur ceo fet primes a dire de commune de pasture.

Brac. 222; Fle. 254.

1—1. ne de nule *LNDGR.* ne de nul *S.* e de nule *M.* 2—2. ne puit estre enpiree ne chaungee *N.* ne empire ne enchange *S.* nest enpire ne amende ne en nule point chaunge *G.* ne enpire ne gaigne *O.*

reason of its always being under the guardianship of its parson, by which guardians churches may purchase and amend their estate, as infants may by their guardians; but they cannot assent to anything to their damage. Wherefore if any church is seised of a common, although the parson dies, yet the church does not in any manner lose its seisin of its common, or any other seisin, any more than an infant under age does by the change of his guardians, by which change his estate is not impaired or altered in any point. Therefore every parson may use that seisin which his predecessor left to the church; and if he be disturbed therein, he shall recover by this assise. But if the predecessor was before disturbed, or if the church was disseised in the time of its avoidance, then another remedy is required, as by our writs of entry, or of *Quod permittat.*

Infants and churches may amend, but not impair their estate.

Seisin of church not lost by change of parson.

For disseisin suffered by former parson, remedy is by writ of entry, or *quod permittat.*

12. Forasmuch as there are several kinds of servitudes, as we have before said, and the most important of these is the right of pasture in another's soil, we shall therefore first treat of common of pasture.

CHAPITRE XXIV. [LV.]

De Commune de Pasture.

1. Commune est un noun commun; et nule communauté ne put estre severale[1], qe au meyns ne soint [2]entenduz deus ou[2] plusours parceners, a queus ele deit estre commune. Et signifie proprement[3] qe acun deit communer ovekes[4] autre en autri soil. Et ausi est pasture un noun commun a herbage, et a glan, et a pesson, et as noiz, [5]et as foiles, et as flours[5], et a totes choses comprises de south[6] le noun de pesson.

Brac. 222; Fle. 254.

Brac. 222 *b*; Fle. 254 (§ 5).

2. Les purchaz de communes porrount estre larges ou estreites, sicum en touz tens, ou for qe en certeynes houres; et sicum par mi et par tut, ou for qe en certeyns leus; ou sicum a totes maneres des bestes ou for qe a certeyn. Renables defens sount neqedent forspris, et acune foiz espressement[7] et acune foiz covertement en teus purchaz. Car en [144.] tens de renable defens ne deit nul communer pur nul purchaz

Brac. 222 *b*; Fle. 255 (§ 7).

1. si seueraltee *ND*. 2—2. *so MS*. *sim*. *G*. attendauntz et entenduz de[us ou] *L*. entendu as deus ou *ND*. en deus ou en *C*. 3. *so ND*. priuement *LMCF*. *sim*. *GS*. primerement *R*. 4. *so N*. *sim*. *D*. a *LMCR*. 5—5. e a volites a az plusurs autres *M*. e a philbers *C*. 6. *so ND*. sus *L*. souz *M*. 7. apertement *M*.

CHAPTER XXIV.

Of Common of Pasture.

1. Common is a general name, and no community can be so restricted but that it be understood that there are at least two or more parceners to whom it is common. And it properly signifies that one person has a right to common with another in another's soil. Pasture likewise is a general name for herbage, acorns, mast, and nuts, and for leaves and flowers, and for all things comprised under the name of pannage.

Common defined.

Pasture, defined.

2. Purchases of common may be large or limited, as at all times, or only at certain hours; and as *per my et per tout*, or only in certain places; or as for all manner of beasts, or only for certain kinds. Reasonable prohibitions are nevertheless excepted in such purchases, sometimes expressly and sometimes tacitly; for none ought to common in respect of any purchase in seasons of reasonable prohibition, as in hay time

Various modes of granting common.

Limitation of right of common.

de commune; sicum en sesouns des prez et des blez; et sicum en[1] leus especiaument defenduz pur pasture aver as agneus et [2]as veals[2], et as boefs et as vaches, nient plus qe de eynz court ou de eynz gardins, ne en vergers[3] ne en parcs, ne en demeynes qe le seignur porra cortiner[4] ou enclore a sa volunté.

Brac. 222 b; Fle. 254.

3. [5]Commune est purchacé[5] en moutz de maneres; sicum par doun, cum si acun doigne acun soil ovek commune apurteynaunte; et par vente[6], cum si acun achate commune en autri soil, issi qe a touz jours mes soit apurteynaunte a soen soil, tut soint les deus soils de devers feez ou de deverses baronies ou de devers countez, mes qe il soint joynauntz; et ausi par veisinage, cum si veisin doigne commune a veisin et la reverse; ou par lounge soeffraunce sauntz autre title [7]al escient[7] et par la volunté des seignurs des soils. Car la volunté ne la suffraunce de lour baillifs[8] ne dounent[9] james title de fraunc tenement, ne nule propre usurpacioun, si cely, qi [10]issi se eit[10] purchacé, ne eit continué[11] et usé sa seisine al escient des seignurs; ne mie pur ceo, qe si acun, qi nul dreit

1. *so NMC.* en *om. L.* 2—2. *so G.* as veus *M.* a vaches *L.* *sim. SC.* 3. viuers *N.* vergeres *M.* 4. *so LG.* cotefier *N.* cotiner *S.* curtiner *M.* 5—5. *so MC.* *sim. N.* commun est purchaz *L.* 6. *so NM.* *sim. C.* vnite *L.* 7—7. et al escient *L.* a escient *NGSC.* a scient *M.* 8. *so NM.* baillies *LGSC.* 9. dorrount *N.* durreit *GS.* 10—10. *so NM.* se ci seit *L.* issi se seit *C.* 11. commune *N.* contenu *M.*

or harvest time; so in places particularly reserved for the pasture of lambs or calves, oxen or cows, no more than within the curtilage, or in gardens, orchards, or parks, or in demesnes, which the lord may fence in or enclose at his pleasure.

Purchase of common, by gift; by sale.

3. Common is acquired several ways; as by gift, where one gives to another any soil with common appurtenant; and by sale, as if one buy common in another's soil, so that for ever after it be appurtenant to his own soil, although the two soils be in different fees or different baronies or counties, so long as they are adjoining; by vicinage also, as if one neighbour gives common to another, and the reverse; or by long sufferance without other title, with the knowledge and consent of the owners of the soil; for neither the sufferance nor consent of their bailiffs will ever give title of freehold, nor will any arbitrary usurpation, if he who thus acquired it hath not continued and used his seisin with the knowledge of the owners; yet notwithstanding, if any one having no right but only recent seisin

Servient tenement may be in another lordship. Purchase by vicinage; by sufferance.

ad for qe tardive seisine de soen propre abatement, soit engetté par autre qi meyns de dreit eit, cil[1] qi engetté iert issi [144 b.]
de sa possessioun recovera soen estat, tel quel il out, par ceste assise. Car tut ne eust il dreit de estre issi en seisine, les disseisours nequedent ne ount nul dreit del engetter de sa seisine, tele quele. Mes si celi le engette, en qi persone la propreté repose, si toust cum il le savera, james ne recovera li engettez par ceste assise par title de pesible continuaunce de seysine.

4. Et si acun face purchaz de commune[2] pasture en autri soil, et ne eit nul tenement a qi cele commune porra apendre, tiel purchaz ne est mie proprement commune, eynz est louwage de pasture ou de herbage. Brac. 226 b; Fle. 255 (§ 9).

5. Et ausi cum ele est purchacé par volounté et par commun assent del donour et del purchaceour, en mesme la manere se estent ele et anientist par le commun desassent[3] des parties, issint qe le assent del un [4]soulement ne desassent del un[4] ne vaut nient a commune purchacer ou le purchaz weyver, si les assentz et desassentz ne se joynent par lour commune volunté. Et sicum ele est acune foiz purchacé par Brac. 222 b, 223, 227; Fle. 255.

1. *so M. sim. N.* si cil *LC.* 2. *so LM.* de *add. NGSC.* 3. dissent *N.* assent *G.* 4—4. *so M. om. LNSA.* soulement *G.*

by his own abatement be ejected by another who has less right, he who is thus ejected from his possession shall recover such estate as he had by this assise. For although he has no right to be thus in seisin, yet the disseisors have no right to eject him from his seisin, such as it is. But if he in whose person the property is vested ejects him as soon as he knows of the usurpation, the ejected shall never recover by this assise by title of peaceable continuance in seisin. Abator has assise against third party; not against true owner, if presently ejected.

4. If any one purchases common of pasture in another's soil, and has no tenement to which the common may belong, this is not properly a purchase of common, but a hiring of the pasture or herbage. Common must be appurtenant to a corporeal tenement.

5. As common is acquired by the will and mutual agreement of the donor and purchaser, so is it extinguished and destroyed by the mutual agreement of the parties to the contrary, so that the assent or disassent of one is of no avail either for purchasing common or for waiving the purchase, unless there be a union of assents or disassents by their common will. And as Waiver of common, by consent; by laches.

lounge suffraunce, ausi la perd hom par lounge negligence; mes ne mie si noun en cas ou la seisine ad esté apertement usé al escient des seignurs.

Brac. 227 (§ 14); Fle. 255 (§ 2).

6. Par commun assent ausi porra devener several ceo qe avaunt fust tenu[1] commun. Car ausi cum terre qe est commune entre parceners par divisioun put devener en severauté, en mesme la manere put acun tenement, dount la pasture est
[145.] commune, estre devisé entre les communers a tener en severauté. Mes a ceo covent le assent de trestouz les communers. Et cum il serrount [2]une foiz a ceo[2] assentuz, et les boundes fetes, et qe chescun sache soen several, mes ne vaudra nuli desassent.

Brac. 227 (§ 15); Fle. 255 (§ 3).

7. Et cum acun soil soit enservé, si porra cel servage estre amenusé et restreynt et eschaungé et estrescé, et en mesne la manere enlargiz et encruz, mes ne mie encountre les voluntez les donours et les purchaceours. Car si acun [3]le feist[3] encountre lour gré, si tendreit lu ceste assise en la persone celi qi soil hom vousist enserver plus qe [4]le dreit[4]; ou en cas a celi affert le remedie a qi le servage serreit due, si hom ly feist meyns qe le dreit.

1. so *LGRS.* tenu *om. NDMCF.* 2—2. venuz e *MC.* 3—3. le soit *M.* seit *C.* 4—4. dreit ne voleit *M.*

common is sometimes purchased by long sufferance, so it is lost by long negligence, but only in cases where seisin has been openly enjoyed with the knowledge of the owners.

Severance of common.

6. By mutual consent also that may become several which before was held in common. For as land which is common among parceners may by division become several, in the same way any tenement of which the pasture is common may be divided among the commoners, to be held in severalty. But for this the assent of all the commoners is necessary. And when they have once consented, and the boundaries are fixed, and every one knows his several, no dissent afterwards will avail.

Enlargement or restraint of easement.

7. Where any soil is charged with a servitude, the servitude may be lessened, restrained, altered, and limited, and in the same manner enlarged and increased, but not against the consent of the donors and purchasers. For if any one should do it against their consent, this assise would lie for him whose soil it was intended to burthen with more than was right; or, on the other hand, the remedy may belong to him to whom the servitude is due, where less is performed than is right.

8. Et cum acune commune deyve estre doné, si covendra translater de persone en autre, et de tenement a autre, et qe les persones et les tenementz soint especefiez de une part et de autre, ausi bien les persones des purchaceours et les tenementz a queus la commune est purchacé, cum les persones des donours et les tenementz qe serrount chargez a la commune. Car rule generale est qe commune ne porra point estre sauntz soil; ceo est a saver, sauntz soil a qi ele sert, ne sauntz soil chargé del service. Brac. 223; Fle. 255, 257.

CHAPITRE XXV. [LVI.]

De remedie de disseisine de commune.

[145 *b.*]

1. [1]A ceux[1] qi de commune sount engittez ou destourbez affert[2] remedie par nos brefs, puis qe eux ne porrount lour seisine retenir ne peisiblement joyer. De fourmes de remedies neqedent fet a destincter. Car solom les deversetez des cas covendra qe les brefs prengent variacioun. Car un soil porra estre chargé de plusours servages vers plusours soils, ausi bien Brac. 223 *b*, 224; Fle. 258 (§ 12, 13).

1—1. Acuns *N.* *sim. D.* Ceus *MC.* 2. a fere *MC.*

8. When a gift is to be made of a common, there must be a transfer of it from one person to another, and from one tenement to another, and the persons and tenements should be specified on both parts, as well the persons of the purchasers and the tenements for which the common is purchased, as the persons of the donors and the tenements which are to be charged with the common; for it is a general rule that there can be no common without soil, that is to say, without soil to which it is servient, nor without soil charged with the service. On a gift of common the persons and tenements should be specified.

CHAPTER XXV.

Of the Remedy for Disseisin of Common.

1. Those who are ejected or disturbed of their common may have remedy by our writs, when they shall be unable to retain or peaceably to enjoy their seisin. The forms of remedy however are to be distinguished. For according to the diversities of the cases the writs must be varied; for the same soil may be charged with several servitudes to several soils, as well in the whole as in part: and this may be true in Writ of assise of common.

par tut cum en partie; et ceo[1] porra aver diverses veies [2]de verité[2]; une par resoun de divers tenementz a queus les servages appendent, une autre par la resoun de diverses persones a queles il sount dues; et la terce est par la resoun de diverseté des persones et des tenementz. En la premere resoun suffist un bref pur la unité de la persone pleintive[3]. Mes en la secunde et en la terce sount divers dreitz, et de divers dreitz porrount estre diverses disseisines, et a diverses disseisines covendrount divers brefs.

Brac. 224; Fle. 258 (§ 13). 2. Mes si unité soit en le tenement a quel le servage est due, tut i eint diverses persones, ausi cum est de parceners qi tienent un tenement en commun, en tiel cas ne apent qe un bref, lequel[4] qe il eit un pleyntif ou plusours, et ceo[5] pur la unité de lour dreit, [6]tut soint il[6] deverses persones, et pur la unité del tenement qe est tenu en commun. Mes si le tenement soit departi entre les parceners, et puis soit acun dis- [146.] seisi de commune apurteynaunte a sa purpartie, en tiel cas gisent diverses pleyntes et divers brefs, issint qe chescun

1. *so NDMGC.* ceo *om. L.* 2—2. *so MSCF.* *sim. GND.* de verite *om. L.* 3. le pleyntif *N.* *sim. MC.* 4. *so NMC.* bref *add. L.* 5. *so MC.* ceo *om. L.* ceo est *N.* 6—6. tut i soint il *L.* tut eint il *N.* *sim. G.* tut i eyent il *S.* tut seent il *M.* tot seent *C.*

divers ways; one way, on account of the different tenements to which the servitudes belong; another way, by reason of the different persons to whom they are due; and the third way, by reason of a diversity both of the persons and of the tenements. In the first case one writ is sufficient, because of the unity of the person of the plaintiff; but in the second and third cases there are divers rights, and of divers rights there may be divers disseisins, and for divers disseisins there must be divers writs.

Single writ for common belonging to several tenements of one owner; *secus*, where several owners.

2. But if there be a unity in the tenement to which the servitude is due, although there are divers persons, as in case of parceners who hold a tenement in common, in such case, whether there be one plaintiff or more, there need be only one writ, and that by reason of the unity of their right, although they are divers persons, and on account of the unity of the tenement, which is held in common. But if the tenement be divided between the parceners, and any one of them be afterwards disseised of common belonging to his part, in such case separate plaints and separate writs lie, so that each parcener

Parceners sue by one writ; *secus*, after partition.

parcener portera severale assise. Et si un parcener soit disseisi de sa commune par soen autre parcener, adounc [1]ne covendra[1] nomer en le bref for qe le disseisour et [2]le disseisi[2], sauntz nomer autres parceners, lequel qe les parceners soint veisins ou cum un heir. [Brac. 224; Fle. 258 (§ 14).]

3. Et cum nous eoms grauntez issi nos brefs as pleyntifs, hastivement facent attacher [3]lour brefs[3] par pleges, et facent trier jurours, et veer le soil et le lu[4] de la commune et ausi le tenement a quel ele est due, issint qe les jurours soint certifiez de la graundour de la commune, et des boundes, et a quele manere des bestes, [5]et a cum bien, et de totes[5] les circumstaunces, dount il serrount chargez par nos Justices. [Brac. 179 (§ 3), 224 (§ 5); Fle. 259; Ante, c. 14, s. 3.]

4. Et cum les Justices vendrount en le counté, et la patente soit lue, tauntost soint les parties demaundez. Et si le pleyntif ne soit mie venu, [6]ne ne[6] soit essonié, lequel qe le disseisour i soit ou noun, en chescun plee soit jugé qe ly et ses pleges de [Brac. 224 b; Fle. 259.]

1—1. so *M.* ne *om. L.* ne couendra mie *ND.* 2—2. so *M.* *sim. N.* les disseisiz *L.* 3—3. so *LDC.* *sim. S.* lour brs *N.* lur br *G.* noz brefs *M.* les brefs *F.* 4. so *NDMC.* et le soil *add. L.* 5—5. so *verb. SG.* *sim. NDM.* et ausi bien do *L.* 6—6. so *N.* ne *MC.* ne ne *om. L.*

shall bring a separate assise. If a parcener is disseised of his common by one of his co-parceners, the disseisor and disseisee only are to be named in the writ, without naming the other parceners, whether the parceners be merely neighbours or entitled as one heir. [Assise between two parceners without the other parceners.]

3. When we have thus granted our writs to the plaintiffs, let them be forthwith attached by pledges[a]; and let jurors be chosen, and let the soil and place of the common be viewed, as well as the tenement to which it is due, so that the jury may be certified of the extent and boundaries of the common, and for what sort of cattle, and how many, and of all the circumstances as to which they will be charged by our Justices. [Proceedings in assise of common. View.]

4. When our Justices are come into the county, and the patent has been read, let the parties be immediately called; and if the plaintiff does not appear, or cause himself to be essoined, whether the disseisor be present or not, in every plea, it shall be adjudged that the plaintiff and his pledges [Proceedings in court. Non-appearance of plaintiff; writ abates.]

[a] The French text is somewhat obscure; but it is clear from the parallel place in Bracton that the pledges spoken of are pledges to prosecute. The expression *attachiato brevi* occurs in Fleta, 259.

sure soint en la merci; et par taunt est le bref abatu, ne james ne vaudra al pleyntif, eynz ly[1] covendra purchacer novel bref.
[146 *b*.] Et si le pleyntif i soit, lequel qe le disseisour i soit ou noun, soit lu le bref original.

Brac. 224 *b*; Fle. 259.

Ante, c. 15. s. 7, p. 309.

5. Et puis soit demaundé del pleyntif, de quele commune il se pleynt, et de cum bien, et a quel tenement il cleyme la commune appendre. Et puis die soen title, sicum de sus[2] est dit. Car si il ne eit point de fraunc tenement a quei la commune porra appendre, il cherra en sa pleinte sauntz autre reconisaunce de assise. Et dounc il porra dire, qe la commune est[3] apurteynaunte a soen fraunc tenement en tele vile, par la resoun qe il de tel tenement fust feffé, en quel tens icele commune fust apurtenaunte [4]a soen fraunc tenement[4], et par quel purchaz il en fust seisi, et sa seisine usa[5] pesiblement deques autaunt qe il fust engetté ou destourbé. Et si il die, qe il est disseisi de C. acres de commune, si pora cheier en sa pleynte, cum il deit dire qe il est disseisi de la pasture de C. acres de commune.

Brac. 224 (§5); Fle. 259 (c. 21, § 2).

1. ly *om. MC.* *om. NSGMCF.* 2. souz *M.* 3. porra apendre e est *M.* 4—4. *so L.* 5. pleinement e *add. M.*

to prosecute be in mercy; whereby the writ is abated, so as never after to be of service to the plaintiff, but he must purchase a new writ. If the plaintiff be in court, whether the disseisor be there or not, let the original writ be read.

Non-appearance of disseisor; assise proceeds.

Declaration of plaintiff.

5. Afterwards let the plaintiff be asked of what common he makes his plaint, and of how much, and to what tenement he claims the common to belong. And then let him declare his title, as above is said. For if he has no free tenement to which the common may belong, he shall fail in his plaint without any other recognisance of the assise. He may then say that the common is appurtenant to his free tenement in such a vill by reason that he was enfeoffed of such a tenement, at which time that common was appurtenant thereto, and by such purchase he was seised thereof, and his seisin peaceably enjoyed, until he was ejected or disturbed. If he says that he is disseised of one hundred acres of common, he may fail in his plaint, inasmuch as he ought to say that he is disseised of the pasture of one hundred acres of common.

Form of claiming common.

CHAPITRE XXVI. [LVII.]

De excepcioun de commune.

1. Moustré issi la entente al pleyntif, si le tenaunt n' i[1] soit ne soen bailliff, si courge la assise par sa defaute. Et [2]s' il i[2] soit, en primes se avise de sei ayder par excepciouns vers le juge, ou vers le pleyntif; vers qi il porra dire, qe la accioun ne la pleynte ne apent point a ly, pur ceo qe il ne est for qe fermer, ou bailliff, ou gardeyn; ou il porra dire qe il est soen vileyn. En cas neqedent ou le vileyn, dount le seignur ne est mie seisi, ad esposé fraunche femme, qe tient del heritage la femme le tenement a qel la commune est apurteynaunte, dount[3] le seignur al vileyn les ad disseisi, ja ne serra la assise targé par la excepcioun del villenage; et serra la commune ajoynte arere al fraunc tenement; et le seignur se purchace [4]a disreyner[4] le cors, si il quide bien fere.

Brac. 224 *b*; Fle. 259.

[147.]

Brac. 226 *b*, (§ 11); Fle. 261 (§ 10); Ante, c. 9. s. 12.

Brac. 224 *b*; Fle. 259; Ante, c. 11, s. 19.

1. ne *LMC.* ne i *N.* ni *S.* ny *G.* 2—2. so *G.* *sim.* *NS.* sil *LC.* si i *M.* 3. so *ND.* *sim.* *M.* adounc *L.* 4—4. so *ND.* a dreisner *L.* a dereiner *M.* adrescer *C.*

CHAPTER XXVI.

Of Exceptions to Common.

1. The plaintiff's contention being thus set forth, if the tenant or his bailiff does not appear, the assise shall proceed by his default; but if the tenant is in court, let him first consider how he may aid himself by exceptions against the judge, or against the plaintiff; against whom he may object, that the action and plaint do not belong to him, inasmuch as he is only a farmer, bailiff, or guardian; or he may say that he is his villain. Nevertheless, in cases where a villain of whom his lord is not seised has married a free woman, who holds of her own inheritance the tenement to which the common is appurtenant, and whereof the lord of the villain has disseised them, the assise shall not be barred by the exception of villenage, but the common shall be united again to the freehold; and the lord may take proceedings to prove his right to the person of the plaintiff if he thinks proper to do so[b].

Plea to the Judge; to the plaintiff.

Plea of villenage. Pasture belonging to freehold of wife of villain, recovered against lord.

[b] The above case is more fully explained in Bracton, where it appears that even though the villain was in the lord's seisin, yet the common might be recovered by the assise, as accessory to the wife's freehold. (Bracton, 224 *b*, s. 8.)

Brac. 225; Fle. 260 (§ 2). 2. Et autres plusours excepciouns,—a ceo qe dit est en le bref qe a tort ly ad disseisi, porra le tenaunt traverser, et dire, qe il ne fust unques seisi; et si il porra ceo averrer, si cheirra [1]la assise[1]. Mes eynz ceo qe hom courge a la assise, si fet a enquere del pleyntif, coment il fust seisi, et si il die par title de doun, adounc est la seisine plus tendre par la unité[2] des voluntez le donour et le purchaceour oveke la vewe et le assignement des tenementz en presence de veisins, qe par successioun. Car si en le cas de feffement soit le purchazour tauntost engetté apres le assignement le donour, tut ne eit le purchaceour mis ses bestes en la pasture, ja pur ceo ne remeyndra qe il ne recovera par ceste assise. Mes en cas de successioun est autrement. Car bien pora estre qe le predecessour eynz fust disseisi en sa vie; et ausi porra estre qe la seisine fut occupé par intrusioun le tenaunt en la vacacioun
[147 *b*.] de la seisine; en quel cas ne vaudra nient ceste assise al successour, sicum de sus est dit.

Ante, c. 23, s. 11, p. 370.

Brac. 225 *b*; Fle. 260 (§ 3, 4). 3. A ceo qe est contenu el bref, de sa commune de pasture apurteynaunte a soen fraunc tenement en tiele vile,—a ceo

1—1. le bref *M C*. 2. so *M S G C*. *sim*. *N*. amite *L*.

Plea, that plaintiff was never seised. 2. There are several other exceptions; thus, whereas writ says 'hath unjustly disseised him,' the tenant may traverse this statement, and say that he was never seised; and if he can verify this, the writ shall fail. But before proceeding to the assise, the plaintiff should be asked in what manner he was seised; and if he says by title of gift, then a slighter seisin is sufficient on account of the union of the wills of the donor and the purchaser, together with the view and assignment of the tenements in the presence of the neighbours, than where

Seisin, in case of gift; the title is by succession. For in case of a feoffment, if the purchaser be ejected immediately after the assignment of the donor, although such purchaser has not put his beasts in the pasture, yet it does not follow that he shall not recover by this

and of succession. assise. But in case of succession it is otherwise. For it may well be that the predecessor was disseised in his lifetime; or the seisin may have been usurped by intrusion of the tenant during the vacancy of seisin; in which case this assise will not avail the successor, as above is mentioned.

Plea, denying the right of common. 3. To that which is contained in the writ, 'of his common of pasture appurtenant to his freehold in such a vill,' it may

pora estre respoundu, qe le soil de la commune, et[1] le tenement a quel le pleyntif dit la commune apendre, sount de deverses baronies, ou de devers feez, et le fee en le quel la commune est demaundé est si fraunc, qe il ne est al autre fee de rien obligé [2]en servage[2], ne les pleyntif unques ne communa ne nul dreit out de communer ne par title ne par usage ne par veysinage, ne en[3] nule autre manere, et si unques neqedent il communa, ceo fust dounc a force, ou privément [4]par muscesses[4], ou par coungé, ou a volunté, et si autrement communa, [5]unques pesiblement ne communa[5], qe les bestes ne fusent enchacez ou enparkez, [6]et ly et ses gentz[6] desgagez[7]. A quei le pleyntif respoigne et die le contrarie, s'il quide bien fere.

4. Ou le tenaunt pora issi dire, qe le soil ou le pleyntif demaund commune est[8] soen several, qe il put arrer et semer et enclore a sa volunté et en touz tens [9]tener en closture[9]. Ou il pora dire, qe le pleyntif ne ad terre ne tenement a qi cele commune fust unques obligé ne apurteinaunte, ou s'il eit Brac. 225 *b*; Fle. 261 (§ 5, 6, 7).

1. en *LSGMC.* e *NF.* 2—2. *so M.* ne chaungie *L.* ne chargee *N.* *sim. G.* ne changee *S.* *om. C.* 3. *so SGM.* en *om. L.* par *N.* 4—4. par nutez *L.* par muscettes *NDS.* *sim. G.* ou par muscesces *M.* ou par mussettes *CF.* 5—5. *so verb. NSGMC.* *om. L.* 6—6. e ses gens *M.* 7. *so LG.* engettez *N.* des gages *M.* degagez *S.* 8. *so NG.* en *LSCF.* eit *M.* 9—9. tel tenement enclosa *M.*

be answered that the soil of the common, and the tenement to which the plaintiff alleges the common to belong, are of diverse baronies or diverse fees, and that the fee in which the common is demanded is so free that it is not charged with any sort of servitude to the other fee, and that the plaintiff never commoned or had any right of common either by title, usage, vicinage, or otherwise; and if, notwithstanding, he ever did common, it was by force, or secretly by stealth, or by leave, or at will; and if he otherwise commoned, he never did so peaceably, but his beasts were driven away or impounded, and he and his servants released upon security. To which the plaintiff may reply, and allege the contrary, if he thinks fit to do so.

4. Or the tenant may say, that the soil where the plaintiff demands common is his several, which he may plough, sow, and enclose at his pleasure, and at all times keep enclosed. Or he may say that the plaintiff hath no land or tenement to which that common was ever bound or appurtenant; or if he hath

Plea, claiming the soil as several.

Plea, that plaintiff has no land;

terre ou tenement, nule commune neqedent est apurteinaunte, car mesme cel tenement a quel il cleyme commune apendre soleit estre foreste, ou bruere, ou mareys, ou autre gastine, et
[148.] commun a touz ceux del visné, qe ore est assartié et arré, et
Post, c. 32, s. 10. nule commune put estre apurteinaunte a autre. Ou il pora dire qe le princepal disseisour nomé est mort. Ou il pora dire qe il recoveri[1] la commune par jugement de nostre court sicum apurteinaunte a tel tenement qe il recoveri[2].

Brac. 226; Fle. 261 (§ 9). 5. Ou il pora dire qe le pleyntif se pleint a tort; car tens[3] de la pleynte[4], et le jour de la date del bref, fust le pleyntif mesmes seisi, si qe cele pleynte ne put nuli fet detrier de plus tardif tens; et issi qe en le tens de la pleinte ne out il nul enchesoun de sei pleindre, par quei qe[5] la pleynte [6]ne fust[6] nule; ou s'il fust disseisi, quant il se pleint, uncore ne aveit il mie enchesoun de sei pleindre; car apres ceo qe il en fust disseisi, [7]si reprist sa[7] seisine sauntz jugement, par quei il est disseisour, et dounc[8] assise est de ceo arramé sur luy. Et

1. *so LN.* recouera *SGMC.* 2. *so LN.* recouera *SGMC.* 3. en temps *NG.* en tenz *S.* le iour *M.* 4. fete *add. M.* 5. *so LN.* qe *om. SGMC.* 6—6. nest *M.* 7—7. *so M.* *sim. G.* et si prist sa *L.* se prist il la *ND.* 8. dount *LNMG.* dont *S.* donk *C.*

or that his land was formerly common. land or tenement, yet no common is appurtenant thereto, for the same tenement to which he claims the common to belong used to be forest, or heath, or marsh, or other waste, and common to all those of the neighbourhood, though the same be now assarted and ploughed up, and that one common cannot
Plea, that principal disseisor is dead. be appurtenant to another. Or he may say that the principal disseisor named in the writ is dead. Or he may say that he
Plea of judgment. recovered the common by judgment of our court as appurtenant to such a tenement which he recovered.

Plea, that no cause of action existed at date of writ. 5. Or he may say that the plaintiff wrongfully complains, for that at the time of the plaint, and on the day of the date of the writ, the plaintiff himself was seised, and that the present plaint cannot try a fact of more recent time; and therefore at the time of the plaint he had no cause of action, and conse-
Plea, that plaintiff re-entered without judgment. quently the plaint is null; or that, if he was disseised at the time he complains, yet he had no cause of action, for that after he was disseised he took back his seisin without judgment, whereby he is become a disseisor, and that an assise is therefore commenced against him. And according as such excep-

solom le averrement des excepciouns se facent jugementz pur la une partie ou[1] pur la autre.

CHAPITRE XXVII. [LVIII.]

De Amesurement de Pasture.

1. Mes tut eit acun commune acune part, pur ceo ne deit il mie outrageus estre, de mettre plus de bestes, ne [2]a purprendre[2] plus de commune, qe ne apent a soen fraunc tenement ou qe il eit, mes soulement a celi a ki la commune est apurteynaunte. Car si[3] acun homme tient C. acres[4], et commune soit apurteinaunte a tote cele terre, et si il aliene cele terre et purchace autre a la quele la commune ne est mie apurteinaunte, en tiel cas ne porra il [5]rien retenir[5] de la commune, si noun par title de usage des avaunt le terme curraunt en assise de mort de auncestre. Et si il eit retenu une acre a la quele la commune est apurteinaunte, ja pur ceo ne deit il aver commune for qe solom la quantité qe il avera retenu. Brac. 229; Fle. 262. [148 *b.*]

1. *so NGSM.* et *L.* 2—2. *so GM.* pur prendre *LNCS.* 3. *so NMF.* sicum *L.* 4. de terre *add. NMCF.* 5—5. *so M. sim. C.* mie rien tenir *L.* mie retenir *N.*

tions shall be made good, judgment shall be given for one party or the other.

CHAPTER XXVII.

Of Admeasurement of Pasture.

1. Although a person has some right of common, yet he ought not to exceed by putting in more cattle or usurping more common than he is entitled to, or than belongs to his freehold, but only to that to which the common is appurtenant. For if any person holds an hundred acres of land and common be appurtenant to all the land, and if he aliens this land and purchases other to which common is not appurtenant, in such case he cannot retain any part of the common, except by title of usage beyond the term of limitation running in an assise of Mortdancester. And although he has reserved one acre to which common is appurtenant, yet he ought to have common only in proportion to the quantity of land so reserved. Surcharge of common. Common in proportion to tenement.

Brac. 229; Fle. 262 (§ 1). 2. Et si plus voille aver a force, adounc i deit le seignur del soil mettre remedie par enparkement del[1] surcharge ou[2] [3]del utrage des bestes[3]. [4]Et si fere ne le peuse par ly, adounc ly vaudra remedie par ceste assise pur la partie del utrage[4] des bestes[5], autresi cum ceste assise tendreit leu entre le seignur del soil et acun qi vousist communer maugré le seignur, ou nule manere de dreit ne de title ne avereit de clamer commune.

Brac. 229; Fle. 262 (§ 2). 3. Et si le seignur ne se vodera entremettre, adounc apent remedie a la pleinte de acun des communers par noster bref al viscounte du pays de chescun utrage ouster et de chescun exces remener[6] en certein, par le quel bref nous maunderoms issi. Pleynt est a nous Johan qe Pieres a tort ad surchargé sa commune de pasture de N., issi qe il ad plus de bestes mis qe a li apent de mettre; et pur ceo tei comaundoms[7] qe sauntz delay facetz cele commune amesurer, issint qe celi [149.] Pieres ne eit plus des bestes qe a ly apent aver, solom le

Brac. 229; Reg. Brev. Orig. 156 *b*.

1. *so MW.* de *LNDSG.* 2. *so SM.* et *L.* e *NDGW.* 3—3. del utrage *L.* *sim. W.* de outrage *NS.* par enparkement des bestes *G.* 4—4. *so verb. MGW.* *om. LNDRSCF.* 5. prises *G.* 6. *so GMS.* remouer *L.* remuer *NDCF.* 7. maundoms *NM.* *sim. CF.*

Lord's remedy for surcharge, by impounding beasts, 2. If he will perforce have more, the lord or owner of the soil should apply a remedy by impounding the surcharge or excess of his cattle. And if he cannot do it by himself, he may avail himself of the remedy by this assise for the excess of the cattle, in like manner as this assise would also lie between the owner of the soil and any one who in spite of the owner insisted upon commoning where he had no manner of right or title to claim common.

or by assise.

Commoner's remedy, by writ of admeasurement. 3. If the lord will not interpose, a remedy is afforded at the plaint of the commoners by our writ to the sheriff of the county, to remove every outrage, and bring every excess to a certain limit; in which writ our command runs thus:

Form of writ. 'John has complained to us that Peter has unjustly surcharged his common of pasture in N., and has put in more beasts than belongs to him to put; therefore we command thee, that without delay thou cause the aforesaid common to be admeasured, so that the same Peter shall not have more beasts than to him belongs to have according to the free tenement which he holds in the same vill; and that the aforesaid

fraunc tenement qe il tient en mesme la vile, et qe le avaunt dit Johan eit autaunt de commune cum a ly apent, et qe mes ne oyoms pleynte.

4. En quel cas le viscounte deit reteinere pleges de sure, et puis deit fere somoundre le seignur del soil et trestouz les communers et autres veisins, et celi de qi la pleinte est fete, qe il soint sour la commune mesmes a certeyn jour de fere mesurer cele commune solom noster comaundement; et qe les parties soint dounc instructes, le un a moustrer ses grevaunces[1] et le autre a moustrer soen dreit, si il voille estre. A quel jour si le pleyntif ne viegne, si remeigne en la merci le viscounte, et les pleges ausi, et nient plus soit fet [2]par ceo[2] bref. Et si le pleyntif viegne al jour, tut ne viegne mie soen adversarie, pur ceo ne remeigne mie le amesurement a fere. Brac. 229; Fle. 262 (§ 4).

5. Et si le defendaunt veigne et moustre ses munimentz et ses resouns, adounc face le viscounte trier xii. prodeshommes, qi voisent jurer de leaument fere ceo qe le viscounte les

1. seruages *C.* 2—2. a tel *M.* a cel *C.*

John have as much common as belongs to him, and that we hear no further complaint.'

4. In such case it is the sheriff's duty to take pledges to prosecute, and afterwards to cause the lord of the soil and all the commoners and other neighbours, as well as the person against whom the plaint is brought, to be summoned, to be upon the same common at a certain day, to cause the common to be measured according to our command; and that the parties be then prepared, the one to show his grievances, and the other his right, if he chooses to appear. At the day named, if the plaintiff does not come, he and his pledges shall remain in mercy of the sheriff, and nothing more shall be done upon that writ. If the plaintiff appears at the day, although his adversary does not appear, yet the admeasurement is not to be put off. Pledges to prosecute. Summons of parties. Non-appearance of plaintiff. Amercement to sheriff.

5. If the defendant comes and produces his muniments and explains his title, then let the sheriff cause twelve good men[c] to be chosen, who are to swear that they will lawfully do what the sheriff shall charge them on our behalf. Then let them Jury sworn. Charge of jury.

c The word *prodehomme*, as well as the similar expression *good and lawful man*, implied the possession of a freehold. Compare the note in p. 333.

Brac. 229, 229 b; Fle. 262 (§ 4). chargera de par nous. Puis lour soit chargé a dire si celi de qi la pleinte est fete eit point de fraunc tenement a quel cele commune est apurteinaunte, et cum bien des bestes il porrount communer par resoun de chescune acre, et quele manere des bestes[1], et si totes houres par mi le an, ou for qe en certeines houres, et si totes maneres des bestes, [2]ou a[2] certein noumbre, et si par mi et par tut, ou for qe en certeins lus.

6. Et si le defendaunt cleyme commune par title de doun, adounc soit enquis, lequel il fust de ceo seisi eynz ceo qe le [149 *b*.] soil fust graunté de estre commune as autres communers, ou noun. Et si devaunt, si remeigne en sa seisine; et si apres, adounc fet a demaunder, si il usa sa seisine par cel doun, ou noun, et si le donour fust mesmes seisi de la chose qe il dust aver doné. Et solom ceo se face jugement. Et si le doun soit prejudiciel as communers, si ne vaudra le doun, for qe solom la quantité qe le donour peut doner sauntz nuli prejudice.

7. Et si il cleyme sa seisine et soen title par usage et en mesme la manere qe les autres communers, et cel title

1. *so NDMW.* il porrount communer par resoun *add. L.* 2—2. *so DGSW.* ou au *L.* ou for qe a *M.* ou [a *interl.*] *N.*

be charged to declare whether he against whom the plaint is brought has any freehold to which the common is appurtenant, and how many beasts the commoners may common there in respect of every acre, and what sort of beasts; and whether at all times in the year, or only at certain times; and whether all kinds of beasts, or only a certain number; and whether in each part and all parts, or only in a certain part.

Special inquiries where common is claimed by gift. 6. If the defendant claims common by title of gift, then it shall further be inquired whether he was seised thereof before the soil was given to become common to the other commoners, or not. And if before, let him remain in his seisin; and if after, then it must be asked whether he enjoyed his seisin under that gift or not, and whether the donor was himself seised of the thing which he is supposed to have given; and judgment shall be given accordingly. And if the gift be prejudicial to the commoners, the gift shall be good only to the extent to which the donor might give without prejudice to any.

Title by usage established. 7. If he claims his seisin and title by usage in the same manner as the other commoners, and can verify this title, then

puse averrer, adounc chete la pasture en hochepot entre les communers solom chescun fraunc tenement a quel la commune est apurteinaunte, issint qe chescune acre i seit fete autri soer.

8. Et cum les jurours averount presenté lour verdit, tauntost soit lour verdit mis en scrit[1], et enselé de south les seals les jurours, et jalemeyns enroulé, issi qe si le defendaunt voille mes surcharger la[2] pasture [3]qe le pleintif eit remedie par la peine purvewe en nos estatuz de la secunde surcharge de pasture[3].

Fle. 263 (§ 5, 6).

Stat. West. 2. (13 Ed. I.) c. 8.

9. Et de tenement tenu en commun entre parceners, fet[4] commun par lour commun assent, si[5] le un des parceners voille surcharger cele commune de plus des bestes qe il ne deit, ou en autre manere qe solom la constitucioun del premer assent, si gist remedie par noster bref de amesurement, et ausi par ceste assise, si les autres parceners le voillent, solom la resoun qe [6]dite est de sus[6] del [7]seignur del soil[7]. [150.]

Brac. 229 *b*; Fle. 262 (§ 2), 263 (§ 4).

Ante, s. 2.

1. escrit *NGSAMC.* 2. commune de *add. N.* 3—3. *so GMW. om. LNDSARCHF.* 4. forfet *M.* fetz en *G.* fors *H.* 5. E si *MCH.* Si *N.* 6—6. *so G. sim. SACHF.* dist de sus *L.* de sus *om. N.* dit est de souz *M.* 7—7. soil le seignur *GM. sim. SCHF.*

let the pasture fall into hotchpot among the commoners according to every freehold to which the common is appurtenant, so that every acre be put on equal terms with the others.

8. When the jurors have brought in their verdict, let it be immediately put in writing, and sealed under the seals of the jurors, and also entered on the roll, so that if the defendant would again surcharge the pasture, the plaintiff may have his remedy by the penalty provided in our statutes for a second surcharge of pasture.

Verdict to be sealed and enrolled.

Remedy for repeated surcharge.

9. With regard to a tenement held jointly among parceners, and turned into common by their mutual consent, if one of the parceners will surcharge this common with more cattle than he ought, or in any other manner than according to the purport of the first agreement, a remedy lies for the other parceners by our writ of admeasurement, and also by the assise if they please[d], as is above explained concerning the owner of the land.

Joint tenement turned into common by parceners; Remedy for surcharge.

[d] That is, if they decide upon treating the wrong as a disseisin of their freehold, and not merely as a surcharge of common. See Brac. 229 *b*; Fle. 263 (§ 4).

CHAPITRE XXVIII. [LIX.]

De Quo jure.

Brac. 229 b; Fle. 263.

1. Tut soit qe acunes gentz purchacent communes par negligence des seignurs de soils par lounge usage, et par peisible seysine et par fole soeffraunce des seignurs a escient, et dount[1] si acun qi[2] eit issi usé sa seisine, soit engetté ou destourbé, si recovera sa seisine par ceste assise, mes, pur ceo qe graunt defaute de ley serreit, si commune issi purchacé demorast en tele manere oveke tiel purchaceour; de sicum cel title prent plus nesaunce del tens[3] qe del dreit, et dreit ne soeffre mie, qe les seignurs n'eyent remedie en le dreit de la proprete, fust purveu un bref sur le dreit qe est appelé, *Quo jure*; par le quel le seignur [4]recovera el dreit[4] de la propreté ceo qe il avera perdu el dreit de la possessioun.

Brac. 229 b, 230; Fle. 263.

2. Chescun neqedent ne ad mie accioun par cest bref. Car a nul ne apent accioun par ceo bref si noun a chef seignur del

1. *so L.* des quels *N.* donqe. *G.* *sim. SMAC.* 2. *so GAC.* *sim. interl. N.* qi *om. LSM.* 3. tort *CH.* 4—4. *so G.* *sim. W.* el dreit *S.* eit dreit *L.* [recouera *in*] el dreit *A.* recouera le dreit *M.* eit le dreit *CH.*

CHAPTER XXVIII.

Of Quo jure.

Seisin recovered by assise may be lost by *Quo jure.*

1. Although some acquire common through negligence of the owners of the soil by long usage and peaceable seisin, and by the folly and sufferance of the owners with knowledge of the fact, and although, if any one who has thus enjoyed his seisin be ejected or disturbed, he may recover his seisin by this assise, yet because there would be a great defect in the law if the common thus purchased should remain in that manner with the purchaser, such title arising rather by time than by right, and because the law will not deprive the owners of their remedy in the right of property, therefore a writ upon the right called *Quo jure* has been provided, by which the owner shall recover in the right of property that which he has lost in the right of possession.

Writ of *Quo jure* lies between lords of diverse fees.

2. Not every one however can proceed by this writ. For no one is allowed to have his action by this writ except the

maner ou de la vile, [1]en la quele la commune[1] est, ou sovereyne partie de la vile. Estre ceo covent a ceo qe ceo bref teigne leu, qe le tenement a quei le pleyntif dit la commune appendre et le soil de la commune soit de devers feez ou de deverses baronies ou de devers feffementz, issi qe le pleyntif [150 *b.*] et cil de qi il se pleint ne tiegnent mie lour tenementz et lour pastures en commun, mes en severalté. Car en cas ou (Brac. 230; Fle. 264 (§ 2).) plusours sount feffez de un seignur en un maner ou en une vile, ne tient mie leu cest bref par entre veysins, pur ceo qe entre veysins reseauntz en un fee plus proprement est cele commune appellé veysinage qe commune, ausi cum est en cas ou veisin[2] soeffre [3]nul autre[3] communer oveke ly[4], ou[5] si il ne ly soeffre, la reverse. Cum acun seignur dounc eit perdu par jugement el[6] dreit possessorie, et autre eit gayné par assise de novele disseisine pur soen usage et sa seisine, uncore porra perdre par ceo bref, si il ne peuse moustrer autre title, si il ne eit usé sa seisine des avaunt le terme especefié el bref de

1—1. *so NAMCH.* ou la quele commune *L.* 2. *conj.* ne. *add. LNDMGAHF.* ni *S.* 3—3. *so MCHF.* mie le autre *L.* mie autre a *ND.* mie lautre *S.* *sim. GARW.* 4. eus *S.* eaus *G.* 5. *so L.* e *NDGSAF.* *om. HW.* *eras R.* 6. *so MF.* et le *L.* e le *ND.* en le *ABHW.*

chief lord of the manor or vill in which the common lies, or of the principal part thereof. It is moreover necessary, in order that this writ may lie, that the tenement to which the plaintiff alleges the common to belong, and the soil of the common be of different fees or of different baronies or of different feoffments, so that the plaintiff and the person of whom he complains do not hold their tenements and their pastures in common but in severalty. For in cases where there are several feoffees of one lord in the same manor or vill, this writ does not take place between the neighbours, because between neighbours resident in one fee such common is more properly called vicinage than common; as where one neighbour allows another to common with him, provided the other allows the same, but not otherwise. When therefore any lord has lost by judgment in the possessory right, and another has gained by assise of Novel Disseisin by reason of his usage and seisin, yet the latter may lose by this writ if he can show no other title, unless he has enjoyed his seisin before the time limited in a writ of right.

dreit. Et pora un chef seignur, ou plusours, enpleder un chef seignur ou plusours ausi bien cum un[1] seignur un[2] autre, lequel qe il ount lour tenementz en une vile ou en deverses, sauve qe lour tenementz soint en devers feez.

Brac. 230 (§ 2); Fle. 264 (§ 3). 3. Et cum ceo soit venu al plee, si porra ly empledez estre essoniez le premer jour ausi bien cum le pleyntif, et avera autre jour par soen essoniour. A quel jour si il face defaute, si serra agardé le attachement sicum en personels pletz, pur ceo qe nule pasture ne est issi demaundé, sicum par bref de dreit est acune foiz demaundé. Mes cum ly enpledez vendra en court, et il est[3] especifié en nostre court, quele commune
[151.] il cleyme, adounc a primes se tiegne le proces, sicum en le bref de dreit. Et si li enpledez dounc face defaute, si soit la pasture prise en nostre meyn par le petit *Cape.*

4. Al jour del plee, presentes les parties, die le pleyntif sa demoustraunce en ceste manere[4]. Ceo vous moustre Johan, qe ci est, qe Piers, et les autres nomez en le bref, qi illokes sount (si plus i ad [5]qe sount[5] enpledez) a tort demaundent commune en ses terres en N. qe aver ne deyvent:—et

1. soen *ND.* sun *A.* 2. ou *NAM.* 3. eit *NM.* *om. W.* 4. fourme *AMCH.* 5—5. qe vn *M.*

And one chief lord or more may implead one chief lord or more, as well as one lord another, whether their tenements lie in one or several vills, so long as they are of diverse fees.

Appearance; essoins. 3. When this plea comes into court, the person impleaded may be essoined on the first day as well as the plaintiff, and shall by his essoiner have another day; at which day if he

Process by attachment, for default of appearance. makes default an attachment shall be awarded against him, as in personal pleas, because no pasture is here demanded, as is sometimes demanded in a writ of right. But when the person impleaded has appeared in court, and it is specified in our court what common he claims, then from this point the same

Subsequent process as in writ of right. process lies as in a writ of right; and therefore if the party impleaded afterwards makes default, the pasture shall be taken into our hand by the little *Cape*.

Form of plaintiff's declaration. 4. At the day of plea, the parties being present, the plaintiff shall state his declaration in this form: 'This showeth to you John, who is here, that Peter and the others named in the writ, who are there, (if there are more than one impleaded,) wrongfully demand common in his lands in N., which they

covendra especefier [1]en quant[1] des acres, et [2]as quantz[2] des bestes, et en [3]queles sesouns[3], solom ceo qe ly enpledez clama especefiaunt en nostre court:—et pur ceo a tort qe mesme celi Piers ne les autres nule rente ne ly rendent ne service ne ly fount, ne il ovekes eux ne commune aylours, par quei qe[4] en ses terres deyvent communer; et si il ceo vodrount dedire, [5]il le tent de[5] averrer par seute [6]et dreyne[6].

5. Et dounc soit demaundé par la Justice, quele commune il cleyment, et cum bien; et lour respounse soit enroulé. Et puis soit enquis de eus, quel service il fount pur la commune aver; ou, s'il furent de acun tenement feffez, a quel la commune est appendaunte [7]et adounc fust, adounc seit especifié[7] quel service [8]et quel[8] tenement et la quantité et qi en sount tenauntz; et ausi en cas ou il allegent pesible seisine pur title. Brac. 230; Fle. 264 (§ 4, 5).

6. Adounc respoignent [9]les defendauntz et se defendent[9] par motz defensables en ceste manere. Piers (et les autres [151 *b.*]

1—1. quantz *N.* qant *S.* kaunz cenz *M.* 2—2. en quant *L.* cum bien *N.* as quantz *G.* quantes *A.* kotes *H.* 3—3. *so M.* *sim. GA.* queles seisines *LS.* quele seisine *N.* ki seisine *H.* 4. il *M.* 5—5. il tende ceo de *M.* il le tend *C.* 6—6. *so LND.* e derreine *G.* *sim. SMH.* dereinee *A.* de drein *C.* 7—7. *so verb. SMACHW.* et dounc fu adounc fust especifie *L.* e dount fu: E adounc soit especifiee *N.* *sim. D.* e adonques fu. e adonqes seit especifie *G.* 8—8. est due a cel *L.* ouesques le *G.* *sim. S.* e quel *M.* ou quel *NAC.* ou ki le *H.* 9—9. les defendauntz *om. LNDGSARW.* et se defendent *om. M.*

ought not to have:' he should also specify the quantity of acres and number of cattle, and in what seasons, according as the person impleaded specifically claimed in our Court:—'and herein wrongfully, in that the same Peter or the others do not pay him any rent, or perform to him any service, nor does he elsewhere common with them, whereby they ought to common in his lands; and if they deny it, then he tenders averment by suit and proof.'

5. Then let it be asked by the Justice what common they claim, and how much, and let their answer be enrolled. And then let it be inquired of them what services they perform for having such common; or, if they were enfeoffed of any tenement to which this common is and then was appurtenant, let it be specified what service and what tenement, and the quantity, and who are tenants thereof. So likewise, where they set up peaceable seisin as a title. Inquiry by Justice as to defendant's title.

6. Then let the defendants answer and defend themselves by proper words of defence in this manner: 'Peter (and the Form of defendant's answer.

nomez en le bref) defendent tort et force, et bien vous moustrent qe a dreit demaundent a communer en la terre mesme celi Johan en N., et par la resoun qe eus et lour auncestres et lour tenauntz de N. i ount communé par continuaunce de pesible seisine devaunt [1]le terme[1] especifié en le bref de dreit, fesaunt a Johan tiel service qe chescun homme astrier de mesme la vile soleit doner a mesme celi Johan et a ses auncestres, une geline par an a Nouwel, dount il se mettent bien en Deu et en la graunt assise, lequel eux et lour gentz de N. eint meillour[2] dreit de communer en la terre le avauntdit Johan en N. par tiel service qe chescun communer [3]qi ad astre[3] en mesme la vile de N. deyve doner al avauntdit Johan une geline par an a Nouwel, sicum dit est avaunt, ou mesme celi Johan de tener sa terre en N. sicum soen several sauntz ceo qe le avauntdit Piers et les autres i deyvent communer.

Brac. 230; Fle. 264 (§ 6).

7. Moutz des maneres des services i sount, qe gentz fount [4]al seignur[4] del fee pur commun aver en soen fee, sicum en deners, en syer par jours en Aust, ou par un jour, et ausi par

1—1. so *NAGMH.* le terme *om. L.* 2. so *ACH.* mie lour *L.* meur *N.* maiour *MG.* *sim. S.* 3—3. so *G.* qe a astre *L.* qe ad astre *SMH.* *sim. C.* que ad estee *N.* *sim. A.* 4—4. so *AM.* *sim. SGH.* as seignurs *LN.*

others named in the writ) defend the wrong and force, and well show unto you that they rightfully demand to common in the land of the same John in N. by reason that they and their ancestors and their tenants of N. have commoned there by continuance of peaceable seisin before the term limited in the writ of right, performing to John the following service, to wit, that every astrier in the same vill was used to give to the same John and his ancestors a hen yearly at Christmas, whereof they put themselves on God and the great assise, whether they and their people of N. have better right to common in the lands of the aforesaid John in N. by such service that every commoner who has his hearth in the same vill of N. ought to give to the aforesaid John one hen by the year at Christmas, as is aforesaid, or the same John to hold his land in N. as his several, without the aforesaid Peter and the others having any right to common there.'

Services by which common may be held.

7. There are several sorts of services which are performed to the owner of a fee for having common in his fee, as service in money, or by reaping at harvest time so many days or one

faucher[1] ou arrer par un jour ou par plusours, ou par acun autre regard [2]de annuele courteisie, mise[2] en certeyn [3]et par certeyn[3] pris, issi qe cele rente chete en le estente del maner. [152.]

8. Ou issi: et bien vous dient, qe il demaundent commune en dreit par la resoun qe mesme celi Johan ad communé par totes les terres mesme cesti Piers et les autres deques ore a treys aunz, qe il de soen gree maliciousement s'en ad sustret, par quei il put issi forclore cesti Piers et les autres de communer en ses terres. Et si ceo soit averré par juree, ou ambideux se assentent, si retenderount Piers et les autres, et Johan remeyndra en la merci; mes il porra neqedent communer en lour terres sicum il soleit, et s'il en soit destourbé, il recovera par assise de novele disseisine, [4]si il par[4] sa folie [5]ne eit reconu en nostre court[5] qe il ne cleyme nule commune.

9. Et si les enpledez ne pusent assigner service ne encheson de vesinage, adounc covent qe il moustrent autre title[6], Brac. 230; Fle. 264 (§ 6).

1. scrcler *MH.* sarcler *C.* 2—2. de annuel seruice mis *N.* de generale curtoisie mise *S.* general de annuele corteisie ou mise *M.* 3—3. *om. N.* 4—4. *so NGAMCH.* si il pora par *L.* 5—5. *so N.* *sim. SAMCH.* en nostre Court ne ęit reconu *L.* ne *om. G.* 6. *so NACH.* article *LM.*

day; so likewise by digging or ploughing one day or more, or by some other recompense of annual courtesy reduced to certainty and of a certain value, so that such rent may be comprised in the extent of the manor. The service should be certain.

8. Or the defence may run thus: 'well and truly say that they lawfully demand common by reason that the same John hath commoned throughout all the lands of the same Peter (and the others) until within three years last past, when he of his own accord maliciously withdrew himself therefrom, with the intent thereby to exclude the same Peter (and the others) from commoning in his lands.' And if this be verified by a jury, or acknowledged by both parties, Peter and the others shall retain their common, and John shall remain in mercy; but he may nevertheless common in their lands as he used to do; and if he be disturbed thereof, he shall recover by assise of novel disseisin, unless he has by his own folly acknowledged in our court that he does not claim any common. Form of defence when mutual common is alleged.

9. If the persons impleaded can neither assign any service or consideration of vicinage, then they must show some other Other titles.

sicum title de purchaz, ou lounge seisine par prescripcioun[1] de tens. Ou il porrount dire, qe, si Johan ne commune mie ore ovekes eux, ceo porra il retter a sa negligence [2]ou a la negligence[2] de ses auncestres, car il soleynt communer en lour terres en N. pour cele commune aver qe ore est en debat,
[152 b.] mes les auncestres Johan furent engettez, et suffrirent, qe le soil fust arré ou edefié, la quele commune il porroit[3] uncore purchacer, si il [4]ne se fust[4] mesmes forclos de accioun par noun clamer. Et si les parties descendent de ceo en juré, soit de ceo enquise la verité par cestes paroles: si Johan et ses hommes de tele vile, et Pieres et les autres et lour hommes del autre vile soleint unques communer ensemble en tel leu ou en tel ou noun; et solom le verdit, se face le jugement. Autres excepciouns i pount tener leu, dount partie sount dites avaunt et partie serrount apres.

Brac. 230 b; Fle. 265 (§ 7).

10. Et si les tenementz soint de un fee, adounc ne pora nul veisin autre defendre a communer renablement pur le veisinage, si noun par acune especiale forprise, qe ly destourbé ne recovere sa seisine par ceste assise.

1. so *NAMH.* presumpcioun *LC.* 2—2. so *NAMCH.* om. *L.* 3. so *M.* sim. *NACH.* porrount *L.* 4—4. se fust *L.* ne se fut *S.* ne se suit *AG.* ne seut *M.* ne fust *NCH.*

Mutual common lost by negligence of plaintiff.

title, as title of purchase or long seisin by prescription of time. Or they may say, that if John does not now common with them, he may impute it to his own negligence, or to the negligence of his ancestors, inasmuch as they used to common in their lands in N. in return for having this common now in dispute; but that the ancestors of John were ejected, and suffered the soil to be ploughed or built upon, the which common he might still obtain if he had not excluded himself from his action by non-claim. If the parties go to a jury upon this point, the truth thereof shall be inquired by these words, whether John and his men of such a vill, and Peter and the others and their men of the other vill, were ever used to common together in such a place or not; and according to the verdict judgment shall be given. Other exceptions may be used, some of which have been before, and others shall be hereafter mentioned.

Common within a lordship by vicinage.

10. If the tenements are of one fee, then one neighbour cannot hinder another from reasonable common in respect of vicinage, unless by virtue of some special saving, but that the person disturbed shall recover his seisin by the assise.

11. [1]En dreit de seisine de commune de pasture repurchacé par ceste assise[1], et puis perdue[2] par le *Quo jure*, sicum dit est en cest chapitre, voloms qe ausi soit entendu, qe ausi put[3] la seisine estre recoveré et puis autre foiz reconquise par celi qi meillour dreit avera par la vertue del *Quo jure*, de totes autres communes, sicum de foyer[4], pescher, enbeverer, chacer, et autres qe sount sauntz noumbre, oveke lour apurteynaunces, qe sount fraunche entré et fraunche issue. Brac. 230 *b*; Fle. 265 (§15).

CHAPITRE XXIX. [LX.]

De renables Estovers. [153.]

1. Une autre manere de commune est sicum de faucher ou [5]de syer ou de foyer[5] ou de couper en autri boys ou en foreste ou quarrere ou mareys ou bruere ou gastine a renables estovers, qe covent pur arder edefier ou enclore, et a teles autres necessaries fere, solom ceo qe acun tenement serra Brac. 231; Fle. 265, 266.

1—1. *so verb. NDGSMA. om. and add. in marg. L.* 2. *conj.* lo ad perdue *L.* lad perdu *GSARM.* la perdu *W.* lad perdue *C.* le ad perdu *NDH.* lad perdue *F.* 3. *so NSMW. sim. G.* par *add. L.* 4. fower *N.* fuyr *G.* fuier *S.* syer *M. sim. CH.* 5—5. de syer *NH. sim. G.* de shier ou de foer *M.* de foier *A.*

11. With regard to seisin of common of pasture recovered by the assise, and afterwards lost by a *Quo jure* in the manner pointed out in this chapter, we will have it understood that seisin may also be recovered, and then got back again by him who has the better right by means of a *Quo jure* in the case of all other commons, such as common rights of mowing, of fishing, of watering cattle, or of chase, and others which are innumerable, with their appurtenances, which are free ingress and egress. Proceeding by *Quo jure* applies to all common rights.

CHAPTER XXIX.

Of reasonable Estovers.

1. There is another sort of common, as of mowing, lopping, digging, or cutting in another's wood, or in a forest or quarry, marsh, heath, or waste, to the extent of such reasonable estovers as are required for burning, building, or fencing, and doing such other necessary things according as one tenement Estovers.

enservé et chargé a fere a[1] autre, au meyns a terme de vie receivere; et dount[2] si acun seit engetté de sa seisine ou destourbé, si avera remedie par ceste assise, mes qe il puse averrer certein soil estre obligé ou assigné, ou il dust ses estovers receiver, ou il pora fere la vewe as jurours de la assise. Et dount[3] a plusours maneres purra il estre destourbé; cum si le seignur del boys face couper tut le boys nettement, [4]si qe rien[4] ne remeygne, ou au meyns qe taunt cum covent a communer ne soit remis[5], ou si hom ne li soeffre de rien prendre, ou ne mie suffisaument, ou nient for qe par liveré, ou nient for qe a [6]certeyns tens[6].

Stat. West. 2. (13 Ed. I.) c. 25.

2. Et pur ceo qe graunt debat porra estre apesé par bon especefier en les escritz del [7]contract premer[7], bon est qe apertement soint touz[8] estovers notez[9] [10]en escriptz[10], si par mi et par tut, ou si en certeyn lieu, ou si en totes houres, ou for qe en certeynes, et de queus boys, et des queus places, et entre queus boundes, et as queus tenementz, et si qe totes

Brac. 231; Fle. 266.

1. e *MCH*. 2. dounc *L*. adounc [t *corr.*] *N*. donqz *G*. donc *S*. dunk *H*. *sim. A*. dont *M*. 3. dounc *LN*. donqes *MG*. doncqz *S*. dont *AH*. 4—4. *so NGA*. si rien *LS*. qe rien *M*. 5. *so M*. *sim. N*. riens *LC*. leinz *A*. 6—6. certeines houres *MC*. *sim. NSGAH*. 7—7. premer contract *N*. *sim. SGMC*. 8. tiels *N*. teus *M*. 9. moustrez *H*. 10—10. *om. A*. e estrices *M*. e escritz *G*.

shall be subject and charged to another, to be enjoyed at least for term of life; and if any one be ejected or disturbed in his seisin thereof, he shall have remedy by this assise, provided that he can aver certain soil to be charged or appointed where he is to receive his estovers, and which he can cause to be viewed by the jurors of the assise. He may be disturbed thereof many ways, as if the owner of the wood cause the whole of the wood to be cut down to the ground, so that none remains, or at least if as much as is required for common is not planted again; or if he is not permitted to take any, or not sufficient, or only by delivery, or only at certain times.

Remedy for disturbance of estovers, by assise.

Disturbance of estovers, what.

2. And because great dispute may be set at rest by proper specification in the writings upon the first contract, it is well that all estovers should be plainly expressed in writings, whether they are to be taken in every part, or whether in a certain place, and whether at all times or only at certain times, and of what woods, and in what places, and within what boundaries, and for what tenements; so that all things be reduced to a

Specification of estovers in charters.

choses [i] soint mises en certeyn[2] et [en dreite mesure, issi qe le un ne puse fere wast, ne le autre defendre mesurer. [153 *b.*]

3. Mes si turberie, ou bruere, ou herbage, ou pesson, ou boys, ou gastine, ou autre [1]oure nomé[1] soit tenu[2] en commun[3] par entre [4]parceners ou[4] veisins, et acun face exces, ou gast, ou destruccioun, adounc [5]soit le remedie[5] [6]solom ceo qe ordiné est[6] en nos estatutz.

Stat. West. 2. (13 Ed. I.) c. 22, 25; cf. Brac. 231; Fle. 266.

CHAPITRE XXX. [LXI.]

De Nusaunces.

1. Uncore sount autres maneres de disseisines qe sount a redrescer par ceste assise, et qe sount fetes par torcenouses nusaunces [7]de veisin au veisin[7]; sicum est de cours de ewe a tort trestourné ou estopé a nusaunce de fraunc tenement de acun veisin. [8]Car a[8] acun tenement apent[9], qe il puse mener ewe hors de autri soil, et par mi autri soil jekes en le soen a

Brac. 231 *b*; Fle. 266.

1—1. our nome *L.* ouere nomee *N.* oeuere nomee *D.* oure nome *G.* houre nomee *S.* chose qe *AR.* commune *MW.* ore nome *CH.* 2. en certein *add. MC.* en certein ou *H.* 3. *so GC.* commune *LSM.* 4—4. *om. CH.* 5—5. seit fet remedie *G.* seit remedie fet *M.* 6—6. sicum est contenuz *M.* sicum est *C.* 7—7. de veisins *M.* de veisin *CH.* 8—8. qe [come a *interl.*] *N.* qe a *M.* pur *H.* 9. apurtient *N.* apurtenaunt *H.*

certainty and to just measure, and that the one party may not commit waste, nor the other hinder a measurement.

3. But if turbary, heath, herbage, mast, wood, waste, or other thing just above named, be held in common between parceners or neighbours, and any one of them commit excess, waste, or destruction, then let such remedy be applied as is ordained in our statutes.

Remedy of parceners by Stat. West. 2. c. 22.

CHAPTER XXX.

Of Nusances.

1. There still remain other kinds of disseisins, which are to be remedied by this assise, and which arise from tortious nusances done by one neighbour to another; as when a water-course is wrongfully diverted or stopped, to the annoyance of the neighbour's freehold. For it is a right which may belong to any tenement that the tenant may convey water out of another's soil and through another's soil to his own, at all

Nusances may be remedied by assise.

totes hures, ou en certeynes, et a quele quantité qe il vodera, ou for qe a certeyne quantité; et si[1] de ceo soit destourbé a tort en tut ou en partie, adounc apent remedie par ceste assise. Et ausi en cas ou acun fet en soen soil chose qe greve au fraunc tenement soen veisin, cum si acun enhauce soen estaunc taunt qe il [2]ennuye le fraunc[2] tenement soen veisin.

Brac. 231 *b*; Fle. 266 (§ 2).

[154.]

2. [3]Des nusaunces[3] sount neqedent acunes torcenouses et damageouses, [4]et acunes damageouses[4] et nient torcenouses. Et pur ceo covent a chescun pleyntif en ceo cas moustrer a quel damage [5]de ly[5] la nusaunce est fete. Et si la nusaunce soit trové torcenouse et damageouse, dounc [6]ceo est a tut[6] remettre en le estat qe estre soleit. Et si nient torcenouse, uncore fet a suffrir, tut soit ele damageouse. Car a communer en autri soil apent [7]chace et[7] fraunche entré et fraunche issue, tut soit [8]la chace[8] damageouse. Et si [9]cil a qi le soil est[9] deface le entré et estope par mur ou par haye ou par fossé, issi qe il face aperte nusaunce al communer, [10]cele nusaunce est torce-

1. *so W.* si *om. LNDGSAMCHF.* 2—2. ennuye fraunc *L.* ennoye al fraunc *N.* anuie le franc *A.* enneye le fraunc *G.* empire le fraunc *M.* 3—3. *so ND.* *sim. GFW.* des acuns *L.* des quels *A.* 4—4. *so verb. NAMH.* *om. LC.* 5—5. *om. M.* de qi *CH.* 6—6. soit a tut *N.* fait tuit *G.* fet tout a *M.* ceo a tut *A.* 7—7. cas et *LS.* *sim. HF.* *om. ND.* chace e *GMW.* en cas ou *C.* en cas e *A.* 8—8. *so GW.* le cas *LSA.* ele *NDMCHF.* 9—9. *so verb. GM.* si soit qe le soil de ceo *L.* *sim. SCH.* si issi soit qe le seignur del soil *N.* *sim. D.* si seit qe le seignour del soil de ceo *A.* *sim. F.* 10. *conj.* et *add. L.* e *add. NDGSMAWCH.*

times or at certain times, and in what quantity he pleases, or only to a certain quantity; and if he is wrongfully disturbed thereof in the whole or in part, then the remedy by this assise is applicable. So in case any one does in his own soil something injurious to the free tenement of his neighbour; as if one raise his pond so high as to damage his neighbour's freehold.

Some nusances are *damna absque injuria.*

2. Of nusances, however, some are both tortious and hurtful, others hurtful yet not tortious; therefore it behoves every plaintiff in this case to show what damage is occasioned to him by the nusance. And if the nusance be found to be both hurtful and tortious, then matters are to be entirely restored to their former condition. If not tortious, it must be tolerated, however hurtful it may be.

Disturbance of access to common.

For unto common in another's soil always belong a drove-way and free ingress and egress, although the drove-way may be hurtful; and if the owner of the soil destroys the ingress, and stops it by a wall, hedge, or ditch, so as to commit an evident nusance to the commoner, nouse et damageouse; et pur ceo fet tut a oster et a remettre en le premer estat par ceste assise, ou tut sauntz bref par quei qe home le face freschement sour le fet.

3. En[1] mesme la manere est a fere en cas ou hom ad dreit de aler par mi autri soil, et qe le[2] chemin soit estopé ou estrescé, si qe homme ne puse mie aler, [3]ou nient[3] ausi esement cum homme soleit. Et ausi, en cas ou cours de ewe est du[4] de auncien usage ou autrement graunté par mi autri soil, si le cours soit estopé ou trestourné en partie ou en tut. Et ausi de estaunck fet de novel ou enhaucé ou abatu, par quei le autre tenement joynaunt [5]en est neyé ou grevé[5], en tiel cas est la nusaunce torcenouse et damageouse, tut veigne tel servage plus de dreit qe de establisement de homme; et pur ceo fet tut a redrescer par ceste assise en le estat qe estre soleit as custages le fesour. Et ausi si celi a qi le servage de fraunche chace aver par mi autri soil apent soit destourbe en tut ou en partie qe il ne puse aver sa chace, solom ceo qe aver dust et soleit.

Brac. 231 *b*; Fle. 266 (§ 2).

Brac. 232; Fle. 267.

[154 *b*.]

1. so *NAMCH.* Et *L.* 2. so *MCH.* le *om. LNA.* 3—3. ne venir *M.* *sim. CH.* 4. donee ou *N.* su *M.* deuenue *C.* *sim. H.* 5—5. en est anoye ou greuee *N.* est greuez *M.* ne est mie greue *C.* nest pas greue *H.*

this nusance is both tortious and hurtful; and therefore the whole is to be removed and restored to its former condition by this assise, or even without writ, so as it be done immediately upon the fact.

Remedy by assise; remedy by immediate removal of obstruction.

3. The like proceedings must be taken where one has a right to go through another's soil, and the way is stopped or straitened in such a manner that he cannot go, or not so conveniently as he used. The like where the free course of water through another's soil is due by ancient usage or grant, if such course be stopped or diverted in part or entirely. So if a pond be newly made, or heightened, or lowered, whereby the adjoining tenement is drowned or injured; in such case the nusance is both tortious and hurtful, although this servitude be rather created by law than established by man; and therefore all is to be restored by this assise to the condition it used to be in, at the cost of the offenders. So if he to whom belongs the servitude of having a free chase in another's soil be disturbed entirely or in part, so that he cannot enjoy his chase according as he ought and used to have it.

Disturbance of way.

Disturbance of water-course.

Nusance heightening pond.

Disturbance of free chase.

Brac. 232, 232 *b*; Fle. 267 (c. 27. § 2).

4. Et tele nusaunce pora estre assigné par[1] une voie devaunt Justices en plusours maneres, cum si [2]un homme soit[2] del tut deveié[3] ou destourbé en acune manere, ou si chemin soit tourné a la nusaunce del communer, issi qe ly covendra aler loyntz en tour, ou il soleit aler et chacer adresces[4], ou si le chemin soit estrescé issi qe il ne puse mes carier de charre ne de charette sicum il dust et soleit, tut [5]lesse il[5] chemin as chivaus et as bestes. Et ausi en cas ou acun eit fet [6]taunt qe soen veisin, qi[6] deit communer oveke ly par enbeverer a soen beverour[7] ou par ewe trere de soen puis ou autrement communer, [8]ne puisse communer[8] sicum il dust, par destourbaunce del chemin alaunt et retournaunt al ewe, ou par destourbaunce del ewe mesmes. Car ausi aperte disseisine fet celi, qi ne [9]ad suffert[9] redrescer le cours del ewe [10]en quei[10] est estoupé, par ount le molyn moist[11], cum cil qi ne soeffre mie moudre.

1. en *M.* 2—2. un homme soit *L.* le chemyn ly soit *N.* *sim.* *DMWRCHF.* 3. viee *N.* devee *MCH.* 4. adrescez *M.* adrescer *AC.* 5—5. eit il lessee *N.* *sim.* *AMCHF.* 6—6. taunt cum soen veisin qi *L.* *sim.* *A.* taunt cum soen veisin qe *N.* taunt qe sun veisin qe *M.* *sim.* *GW.* taunt qil *C.* *sim.* *H.* taunt com bon veisin qe *S.* 7. *so* *N.* beuerer *L.* enbeuerer *S.* ewe *G.* estang e en son beuerer *M.* 8—8. *om.* *LNDMGSCHFW.* e il ne puisse *AR.* 9—9. soeffre *NSGAMCH.* 10—10. encreu la quel *M.* en qi *C.* 11. muet *ND.* moelt *SG.* most *A.* meust *M.* moet *CH.* mot *F.* mout *corr.* *R.*

Assignment of disturbance of way.

4. And such nusance may be assigned before the Justices in various manners; as if a man be entirely turned out of his way or disturbed in any manner; or if a way be diverted to the nusance of the commoner, so that he is obliged to go far round, whereas he used to go and drive straight; or if the way be narrowed, so that he cannot drive a wagon or cart therein as he ought and used to do, although room enough may be left for horses and beasts. So where any

Common watering-place.

one has done an act whereby his neighbour, who has a right to common with him either by watering his cattle at his watering-place, or by drawing water from his well, or otherwise, is hindered from commoning as he ought, either by disturbance of the way leading to or from the water, or by

Mill-race.

disturbance of the water itself. For as manifest a disseisin is committed by him who does not suffer a watercourse which should move a mill to be repaired where it is stopped, as by him who does not allow the mill to be used.

5. Acune foiz neqedent est cours graunté a acune persone et acune foiz a autri tenement. Mes le graunt fet as persones se esteint mortes les persones. Mes ceo [1]qe est a moen soil purchacé[1] remeynt perpetuel; et solom le purchaz et le usage et la seisine covendra repurchacer, si homme en soit disseisi; en quel cas et en cas semblables gist[2] remedie de cele nusaunce redrescer par ceste assise as custages des disseisours.

Brac. 233; Fle. 269 (§ 13).

[155.]

6. Et quant al servage, qe est, qe il ne list point a nul veisin de fere en soen soil molyn, [3]ou gors[3], ou escluse, ou autre chose semblable, a la nusaunce del fraunc tenement soen veisin, gist ausi remedie par ceste assise de tut abatre, si nule nosaunce soit fete hors de soen dever. Et ausi de nusaunce fet par[4] abatre [5]ou a countrefere[5] ceo qe a dreit fut primes levé, sicum de mur abatu, ou fosse paremplé, ou pescherie destrute, ou [6]estaung ou pount ou escluses[6] ou auteles autres choses, par ceste assise serrount teles choses redrescez

Brac. 232 *b*; Fle. 268 (§ 4, 5).

1—1. *so verb. M.* qe a moi soul pur purchaz *LS.* qe est a moen soyl pur purchaz *ND.* qest al soil purchaz *AR.* qest annex al soil par purchaz *G W.* qest a moi soil pur purchace *C.* *sim F.* 2. eit *M C H.* 3—3. *so G.* *sim. M.* *om. L N S A C H.* 4. *so G M.* pur *L.* 5—5. e par ouster *M.* *sim. G.* 6—6. estaung ou puiz ou pount ou escluse *N.* estang ouste ou escluses *M.* puitz enclose *H.* *sim. F.*

5. A watercourse is sometimes granted to a person, and sometimes to the tenement of another. A grant made to a person becomes extinct upon the death of the person. But that which is purchased to my soil remains perpetual; and according to the purchase, and usage, and seisin, the right is to be recovered, if the owner is disseised of it; and in this and the like cases there lies a remedy by this assise, for redressing the nusance at the cost of the disseisors.

Grant of easement to a person, ceases on death. Grant to a tenement is perpetual.

6. With regard to the servitude which consists in this, that it is not lawful for any neighbour to erect in his own soil a mill, or weir, or sluice, or other like thing, to the damage of the free tenement of his neighbour, a remedy also lies by this assise to abate the whole, if any nusance be done contrary to this obligation. So likewise, where a nusance is committed by pulling down or destroying that which at first was lawfully raised, as by pulling down a wall, filling up a ditch, destroying a fishery, pond, bridge, or sluice, or other such thing, the thing shall be restored by this assise to its former condition

Right to hinder erection of mill, &c. Remedy by assise to abate nusance. Remedy to restore lawful erections.

en lour premer estat as custages les fesours, et issi serrount les nusaunces oustez.

Brac. 232 b; Fle. 268 (§ 6).

7. Et sicum hom porra fere tort et disseisine par overe [1] a fere [2]ou a defere[2], ausi put hom fere disseisine par negligence sauntz rien fere, sicum en cas ou acun est tenu de clore, ou [3], de fere repariler, [4]et de purger[4], et teles autres choses semblables, et il ceo soeffre sauntz rien fere, la quele soeffraunce est prejudiciele al fraunc tenement soen veisin, et la quele negligence est punisable par ceste assise. Et [5]sicum acun [155 *b*.] poet[5] fere torcenouse nusaunce par rien fere, ausi la pora il fere par sa nounsuffraunce, cum cil qi ne soeffe mie celi de clore ou de seyer[6], qi fere le deit al esement de soen fraunc tenement; et ausi porra cel tort par ceste assise estre amendé.

Brac. 233, 233 b; Fle. 269 (§ 16).

8. Acunes nusaunces neqedent sount qe sount grauntez as viscountes [7]a redrescer[7], et a nos hundreders et a plusours autres fraunes hommes, qi ount la vewe de fraunc plege pur

1. *so SHW.* *sim. GMA.* ouerer *LND.* 2—2. vn e defere vn autre *NDA.* vn a defere *S.* vn e a defaere *G.* vne chose e defere *M.* 3. *so NDM.* ou *om. LSGA.* 4—4. despurger *L.* de purger *SGA.* 5—5. *so verb. NW.* *sim. MCH.* si acun puse *L.* *sim. SGA.* 6. scier *N.* foier *SA.* foyr *G.* foer *MH.* fere *C.* 7—7. *so NMW.* a drescer *LS.* a [re]drescer *N.* a deescer *A.* redrescer *G.* de redrescer *CH.*

at the cost of the offenders, and thus the nusance shall be removed.

Disseisin by omission.

7. As one may do a wrong and a disseisin by an act, in doing or undoing, so a person may commit a disseisin by negligence without doing anything; as where one is bound to fence or repair or cleanse or the like, and lets the matter be without doing anything, which omission is prejudicial to the free tenement of his neighbour; and this neglect is punishable by the assise. And as one may commit a tortious nusance by not doing something, so the like may be done by not permitting something; as where a person will not suffer him to fence or to reap who is bound to do so in easement of the complainant's freehold; and this wrong may also be remedied by the assise.

Disseisin by not permitting a lawful service.

Remedy of nusance in sheriff's tourn, hundred-court, and view of frankpledge.

8. There are however some nusances which sheriffs are authorised to redress, as are also our hundreders, and many other freemen, who have view of francpledge for the com-

commun profit, sicum de chemin estopé, qe les trespassauntz[1] ne soint mie trop destourbez de lour chemin, et sicum de autres plusours nusaunces. A nul nequedent ne list de teus tortz[2] redrescer sauntz noster bref for qe tortz fetz puis la dreyne vewe, [3]et puis le dreyn tourn de viscounte[3]. Et tut soit qe teles nusaunces porrount estre redrescez par ceste assise, pur ceo ne remeynt mie qe eles ne porrount estre amendez par autre remedie, sicum par oster les nusaunces freschement sur le fet, si hom put; ou si noun, [4]par bref de *Justicies*[4] au viscounte, par le quel bref le viscounte ad poer de cel tort [5]redrescer, et est fet nostre Justice[5] de fere amender le tort, et en chose [6]qe touche[6] le bref qe[7] porte record. Brac. 233 *b*; Fle. 269 (§ 16). Ante, l. I. c. I. s. 7; c. 28. s. I.

1. so *NDG*. *sim*. *SACHW*. trespassours *L*. 2. so *NG*. *sim*. *MASHFM*. cours *L*. 3—3. so *NMCH*. *sim*. *A*. *om*. *L*. 4—4. so *G*. par bref des Iustic' *LND*. par les Iustices *MCHFW*. par bref les Justic' *A*. 5—5. redrescer fet et nostre Iustice *L*. redrescer qe est fet nostre Iustice *N*. redrescer qe est fet e nostre Iustice *D*. fet redrescere nostre Iustic' *AR*. redrescer [*a vacant line*] fet nostre Iustic' *M*. redrescer fet nostre Iustice *CW*. *sim*. *F*. fet redrescer nostre Iustice *H*. 6—6. touche *ACH*. toche en *M*. 7. qe de ceo *ND*. qi *A*. i *M*.

mon benefit[e]; as in the case of a way being stopped, in order that passengers may not be too long deprived of their way, and in the case of several other nusances. But it is not lawful for any one to redress such wrongs without our writ, except those which have been done since the last view, or since the last sheriff's tourn. And although nusances may be redressed by the assise, yet it does not follow that they may not be set right by another remedy, as by removing the nusance immediately upon the fact, or if this be not done, by writ of *Justicies* to the sheriff, whereby he has authority to redress the wrong, being made our Justice to cause the wrong to be remedied; and of matters which concern the writ he is to bear record. Remedy by immediate removal; Remedy by *Justicies*.

[e] 'It should be known that the sheriff ought not to redress any nusance presented at his tourn, if it be not wrongful and injurious to the community (a commune des gentz). For nusance done to a single person shall be redressed by a single suit and not otherwise.' Note in MS. *N*.

CHAPITRE XXXI. [LXII.]

[156.]

De remedie de nusaunces.

Brac. 233; Fle. 269 (§ 16).

1. Si [1] le *Justicies*, ou le[1] bref de novele disseisine, deyve estre purchacé de chose fete en un counté, qe soit nusaunce a tenement [2]gisaunt en[2] autre counté, tutz jours soit le purchaz fet au viscounte en qi baillie la nusaunce avera esté fete.

Brac. 234 b; Fle. 271 (§ 8, 9).

2. Et de estaungs et des gors levez ou haucez ou abatuz a torcenouse nusaunce, fet a prendre garde lequel il soint levez en le tenement le pleyntif, issi qe le soil soit soen de une part et de autre, sicum en acun rivere; et en cel cas tient leu assise de Novele Disseisine del fraunc tenement le pleyntif. Et si en le tenement celi de qi la pleynte est fete, adounc tient ceste assise de nusaunce. Et si partie en le un soil, et partie en le autre, cum avent acune foiz en rivers, [3]ou les soils[3] de une part et de autre sount a diverses gentz, adounc[4] quant a proprement parler tient lu ceste assise de fraunc

1—1. so *S.* les Iustices ou le *LAW.* les Iustices ou les *ND.* le iusticies en *G.* le Iustic' ou *M.* *om.* *HF.* 2—2. so *M.* *sim.* *GARW.* corsaunt en *L.* tochaunt *NDS.* 3—3. ou en soils *LM.* ou en les soyls *N.* *sim.* *SGACH.* 4. so *G.* et adounc *L.* *sim.* *NSAMCH.*

CHAPTER XXXI.

Of remedy of nusances.

Writ to sheriff in whose bailiwick nusance is committed.

1. If a *Justicies*, or a Writ of Novel Disseisin is to be obtained for a thing done in one county to the annoyance of a tenement lying in another county, the writ is always to be directed to that sheriff in whose bailiwick the nusance has been committed.

Distinction where act is done in plaintiff's tenement; or in defendant's;

2. Of ponds or of weirs raised, heightened, or demolished, amounting to a tortious nusance, it must be seen whether they are raised in the tenement of the plaintiff where the soil is his own on both sides, as in a river;—for in such case an assise of Novel Disseisin of the freehold of the plaintiff will lie. But if it be in the tenement of him of whom the plaint is made, this assise of nusance is applicable.

or in both.

And if part is in the one soil and part in the other, as it sometimes happens in rivers where the lands on either side belong to different persons, then properly an assise of freehold lies for the act

tenement a regard del meynovere fet en le soil le pleyntif, et del remenaunt [1]de la nusaunce meynoveré[1] en le autre soil tient lu ceste assise pur la nusaunce oster, et si tendrount lu deus assises de un [2]soul fet[2]; mes [3]pur eschure la charge de deus assises sure[3] assetz suffit la assise de nusaunce [4]pur tut le tort redrescer[4].

3. Et de autre part de un fet porrount estre plusours disseisines de fraunc tenement, et jalemeyns[5] de plusours nusaunces torcenouses, ausi cum en cas ou aucun [6]leve ou face[6] fossé en autri soil maugré le seignur del soil, par taunt fet il a ly disseisine de soen fraunc tenement, pur ceo qe il meynovere soen soil maugré soen, et par cas est le fossé fet en tiel lu, qe le seignur del lu est destourbé de chacer, par quei acun chemin est estopé, ou acune ewe trestourné hors de soen dreit cours ou en partie destourbé de coure. Et en [7]ceo cas et en cas[7] semblables gist remedie par ceste assise del fraunc tenement le pleintif; et par ceste assise serra tut determiné,

Brac. 235; Fle. 271 (§ 10).

[156 *b.*]

1—1. del nusaunt meyn ouere *L.* de la nusaunce meyn ouere *NS.* *sim. AMCH.* de la nusaunce meynoure *G.* 2—2. *so SAC.* soil fetz *L.* soyl fet *N.* *sim. GMH.* 3—3. pur plus de peril eschure *M.* pur eschure *CH.* 4—4. parount le tort purra estre redresce *M.* purrount le tort redrescer *H.* 5. *so G.* de *add. LSMA.* 6—6. *so NDGSAR.* leue ou ou *L.* homme fet *M.* homme face *CH.* 7—7. *so MCH.* *sim. A.* ces cas *L.* tiels cas [e en cas] *N.*

done in the soil of the plaintiff, and an assise of nusance for the rest of the nusance committed in the other's soil, to remove the nusance; and thus two assises would take place upon a single fact. But to avoid the charge of bringing two assises, the assise of nusance is sufficient to redress the whole wrong.

One remedy for disseisin and nusance.

3. Again, for a single act there may arise several disseisins of freehold, as well as several tortious nusances; as where a person makes a ditch in another's soil against the consent of the owner of the soil, he thereby disseises him of his freehold, inasmuch as he works his soil against his consent, and the ditch perhaps is made in such a place that the owner is either disturbed of his right of driving cattle, because some way is stopped, or some water is diverted from its right course, or partly hindered from running. And in this and the like cases a remedy lies by this assise of the freehold of the plaintiff, and by this assise the whole matter shall be termi-

Several disseisins and nusances by one act, remedied by one assise.

ausi bien del fraunc tenement recoverer, cum [1]de les[1] nusaunces oster et redrescer. Et pur ceo qe touz les tortz nescent[2] de un soul fet, par un soul jugement porrount estre redrescez.

Brac. 235; Fle. 272 (§ 10).

4. Et acun porra tele chose fere en soen soil de un fet qe porra grever a soen veisin en diverses maneres, cum s'il estoupe acun chemin, tut soit le chemin soen soil demeyne, par ount soen veisin ne pora aver fraunche chace et entré et issue pur pestre ses avers, sicum il soleit, en ceo cas ly tout[3] il sa commune, et par taunt ly fet il disseisine de sa commune, et estre ceo disseisine de soen chemin estopé; et tut neqedent porra estre redrescé par une assise, sicum par assise de chemin estopé.

Brac. 235; Fle. 272 (§ 11).

5. Estre ceo sount acuns cas, ou [4]acun de un[4] soul fet [5]porra fere[5] plusours disseisines[6] et a plusours gentz, cum si acun fet clore acune commune, ou tenement, en le quel un homme ad fraunc tenement, et un autre ou plusours commune de pasture, et le tierz dreit de [7]foyer ou[7] de couper, et le

1—1. *so N.* de ces *L.* des *M.* de ses *GCH.* *sim. S.* 2. ne soint *L.* nessent *N.* ne esteient *M.* ne seient *GSA.* 3. *so G.* tient *L.* detient *NAM.* touit *S.* 4—4. de alcun *N.* 5—5. *so verb. GARM.* porrount estre *L.* *sim. N.* purra estre *SHW.* *sim. F.* 6. disseisiz *N.* 7—7. sier ou *S.* sier foyr e *G.*

nated, as well for the recovery of the freehold as for the removal and redress of the nusances; and since all the torts arise from a single act, they may be remedied by a single judgment.

Several disseisins by act *in proprio solo.*

4. A person may likewise do such an act on his own soil as may injure his neighbour in several ways; as if he stops a way, although the way be his own soil, whereby his neighbour cannot freely drive his cattle and have free ingress and egress for his pasture as he used; in this case he deprives him of his common, and consequently disseises him of that, and also disseises him of his way by obstructing it; and yet the whole may be redressed by one assise, as by assise of way stopped.

Disseisin of several by single act.

5. There are moreover some cases where a person may by a single act commit several disseisins, and to several people; as if any one cause a common to be enclosed, or a tenement in which one man has a freehold, another (or several others) common of pasture, a third the right of digging or of cutting,

quart dreit de embeverer, et le quint chemin de[1] chace, et issi des autres servages qe sount sauntz noumbre, en teus cas [157.] serrount fetes plusours disseisines, qe totes poent estre remenez en lour dreit estat par ceste assise del fraunc tenement, si celi qi deit le soil, se pleyne; et si il ne fet, adounc covent qe chescun se pleyne [2]qi estat vodera aver et recoverer[2], et qe chescun soit[3] pur sei.

6. Et cum le viscounte avera resceu noster bref [4]de *Justicies*[4] de commune de pasture, ou de renables estovers, ou de commune de pescherie, ou de mareys, ou de autre, et eit trové au viscounte pleges de sure, al viscounte apent tauntost de[5] somoundre la partie de qi la pleynte est fete, et les veisins del hundred, qe il soint al[6] proscheyn Counté, ou al lu ou la nusaunce ou la disseisine est fete, et qe les veisins en le meen tens voisent et veent la nusaunce, et la pasture, et le tenement en le quel la nusaunce est fete, et le tenement le pleyntif, a quel ele dust estre fete.

Brac. 233 *b*; Fle. 269 (§ 18).

7. Au quel jour nul essoine soit allowé al defendaunt, nient

1. e *S.* a *G.* 2—2. qe voudra estat recouerer *M.* *sim.* *SA.* qi vodra soen estat recouerir *G.* 3. ensiwe *N.* 4—4. *so* *GSC.* des Iustices *LA.* *sim.* *MR.* de Iustic' *NH.* 5. fere *add.* *M.* *sim.* *G.* 6. *so* *NSAMH.* a *L.*

a fourth the right of watering his cattle, a fifth a drove-way, and thus of numberless other services, in such case several disseisins are committed, which may be all restored to their right condition by this assise of freehold, if the owner of the soil will be plaintiff; but if he will not, then every one who would have and recover his estate must bring his plaint, each for himself.

Remedy by one assise, if owner of soil be plaintiff; if not, by several assises.

6. When the sheriff has received our writ of *Justicies* of Common of pasture, reasonable estovers, common of fishery, marsh, or the like, and the plaintiff has found pledges of suit to the sheriff, it is the sheriff's duty immediately to summon the party against whom the plaint is made, and the neighbours of the hundred, to be at the next county court, or at the place where the nusance or the disseisin is committed, and that the neighbours in the meantime go and view the nusance, and the pasture, and the tenement in which the nusance is done, and the tenement of the plaintiff to which it is supposed to be done.

Proceeding by *Justicies*; Summons; View.

7. At the day named no essoin shall be allowed to the

No essoin allowed to defendant.

plus qe al disseisour, eynz soit prise la[1] enqueste, lequel qe le defendaunt viegne ou noun. Et solom le verdit soit par la vewe des jurours redrescé en soen dreit estat, sicum estre soleit as custages le fesour[2], et amende[3] al pleyntif ses damages, et remeigne en nostre merci.

CHAPITRE XXXII. [LXIII.]

De Excepcioūns des Nusaunces.

[157 *b*.] Brac. 234; Fle. 270.

1. Cum ceste assise soit arramé sur acune nusaunce, par plusours excepciouns se pora celi eyder de qi la pleynte est fete. En une manere, pora il dire, qe il ne fit poynt de nusaunce, ou ne leva point de mur, ou point ne haucea estaung, ou point ne abati le fossé, eynz fit autre nent nomé en le bref; et si ceo soit averré ou nient dedit, si chet le bref. Ou il porra dire qe le pleyntif ne aveit mie le tenement, a quel la nusaunce fut fete, quant la nusaunce fust primes fete, eynz le tint[4] dounc un autre, et nul ne se deit pleyndre de tort fet a autre qe a ly.

1. bone *NM*. bon *CH*. 2. *so NGMA*. disseisour *L*. 3. *so G*. demaund *LCH*. *sim*. *S*. doigne *N*. damand *A*. rende *M*. 4. *so SAM*. tient *LNG*. aueyt *H*.

Inquest. defendant, any more than to a disseisor, but the inquest shall be taken, whether the defendant come or not; and according Judgment. to the verdict by view of the jurors the right condition of things shall be restored as it used to be, at the cost of the offender, who shall also repay to the plaintiff his damages, and remain in our mercy.

CHAPTER XXXII.

Of Exceptions in the Assise of Nusance.

Exceptions of defendant; 1. When this assise is brought for any nusance, he against whom the plaint is made may aid himself by several excep- denying the act to be his; tions. Thus, he may say that he did not commit any nusance, or raise a wall, or heighten a pond, or throw down the ditch, but that another person not named in the writ did it; and denying the plaintiff's possession of the tenement. if this is verified or not denied, the writ falls. Or he may say that the plaintiff had not the tenement to which the nusance was done, at the time when it was first done, but another then held it, and none ought to complain of a wrong done to any except himself.

2. Ou il pora dire qe il ne ad point de nusaunce, ou tut i eit il nusaunce, pur ceo ne deit mie la assise passer; car la nusaunce ne est mie torcenouse, pur ceo qe le pleyntif [1]ne le put mie[1] defendre par nul dreit; sicum est de molyn qe veisin porra lever en soen soil sauntz tort fere a soen veisin, tut chete cel molyn a la nusaunce le veisin; et sicum est de autres nusaunces qe ne sount mie torcenouses, et les queles si acun[2] abate ou ouste a force, il fet apert trespas encountre nostre pes. Brac. 234; Fle. 270 (§ 3).

3. Et cum les parties eint pledez [3]a la assise, soit l'assise[3] prise, et si ele passe pur le pleintif, adounc soit comaundé al viscounte, qe la nusaunc soit osté et remené[4] en le estat qe estre soleit as custages le trespassour, lequel qe ewe deyve estre remené en soen auncien cours, ou qe le cours deyve estre reparilé [5]et vertie[5], ou overte, ou fossé paremplie ou abatu, ou estaung avalé, ou mur ou haye refete[6], ou chemin enlargi, ou tele autre nusaunce amendé solom soen auncien estat. Et totes cestes nusaunces soint remendez[7] en le auncien Brac. 234, 234 b; Fle. 270 (§ 4). [158.]

1—1. *so verb. NM.* ne put nient *L.* ne puit il mie *G.* no puit mie *A.* *sim. SCHW.* 2. veisin les *add. NM.* *sim. ACH.* 3—3. *so verb. NMHF.* *sim. A.* et la assise soit *L.* 4. remeigne *M.* 5—5. *om. A.* ou reuerti *N.* ou nette *M.* 6. *so ARMCHF.* refeti *LS.* refetee *ND.* refet *G.* refaytee *W.* 7. amendeez *N.* reamendez *GM.* *sim. SAB.* remaundez *W.*

2. Or he may say that there is no nusance, or if there be any, yet the assise ought not to pass, inasmuch as the nusance is not tortious, because the plaintiff has no right to forbid it; as in the instance of a mill, which one neighbour may erect in his own soil without committing a tort to another neighbour, although the mill may happen to be an annoyance to that neighbour; and the like of other nusances which are not tortious, and which if any abate or remove by force, he is guilty of a manifest offence against our peace. Exception, justifying the act. *Damnum absque injuria.*

3. The parties having pleaded to the assise, let the assise be taken, and if it pass for the plaintiff, then let the sheriff be commanded to cause the nusance to be removed, and the place restored to the condition in which it used to be, at the cost of the trespassor, whether water is to be brought back into its ancient course, or the course cleansed and turned, or opened, or a ditch filled up or abated, or a pond lowered, or a wall or hedge repaired, or way enlarged, or any other such nusance set right according to its former condition. And in all these Assise taken; Judgment for plaintiff. Former condition to be restored.

estat solom [1]la leure et la loungure[1] et la haucesce et la parfondesce; et qe le cours del ewe nient plus soit fet curraunt ne meyns curraunt, ne plus bas ne plus haut, ne en nule manere chaungé, si noun [2]en meuz[2], qe estre soleit.

Brac. 234 *b*, (§ 9); Fle. 271 (§ 5, 6). 4. Et touz jours [3]garde sey chescun[3] qe nul ne prenge par sa force ceo qe il dust [4]recoverer par jugement. Car qi le fet et le autre puse[4] recoverer par jugement, a peyne recovera james le verray seignur de joyndre la seisine par jugement a la propreté.

Brac. 234 (§ 7); Fle. 271 (§ 6, 7). 5. Et a ceo qe dit est en le bref, a tort, fet a prendre garde si la nusaunce soit torcenouse, ou noun. Car si ele ne soit mie torcenouse, par taunt acrest excepcioun al responaunt. Mes si ele soit torcenouse et damageouse, adounc fet ouster et redrescer. Si ele soit damageouse, adounc fet a destincter. Brac. 232 *b*; Fle. 268 (§ 7). Car si ele soit damageouse a plusours autres, tut ne soit damageouse al pleyntif, uncore fet a ouster par office des Justices. Car touz jours voloms qe commun profit soit gardé et fet avaunt le profit de privé persone. Et si ele ne est mie torce-

1—1. le laour e la lungure e le leour *M.* 2—2. en le estat *M.* 3—3. *so G.* garde sa enchesun *L.* soi garde chescun *N.* se garde chescun *N.* *sim. AR.* garde chescun *W.* garde son cheson *SC.* garde sen chesoun *F.* *om. H.* 4—4. *so G.* recouerer par iugement *LSCHF.* recouerir par iugement [quar si il face *interl.*] *N.* recouerir par Iugement e si ceo face *A.* recouerere recunquere, qar ki le fet e lautre le puisse recouerer par iugement *M.*

cases the thing is to be restored to its ancient condition, in breadth, length, height, and depth; and the watercourse is not to be made more or less running, or lower or higher, or in any manner altered, unless for the better, from what it used to be.

Danger of righting oneself without judgment.

4. Every one should always beware of taking by his own force what he ought to recover by judgment; for if he does so, and the other party recover by judgment, the true owner shall hardly after succeed in uniting by judgment the seisin with the property.

Exception that the nusance is not tortious.

5. With regard to the word 'wrongfully' contained in the writ, care must be taken to see whether the nusance be wrongful or not; for if it be not wrongful, an exception thereby accrues to the respondent. But if it be both tortious and hurtful, then it is to be removed and redressed. If it be hurtful, a distinction is to be made. For if it be hurtful to many others, although it be not hurtful to the plaintiff, yet it ought to be removed by the Justices *ex officio*. For we will always, that the general advantage be regarded and promoted before the advantage of a private person. And if it be not

Common nusance to be abated *ex officio*, although the plaintiff be not damnified.

nouse, tut soit ele damageouse, si cheet la accioun al pleyntif quant devers ly mesmes, tut ne chete ele mie quant devers autres.

6. Ou il porra dire qe en acun tens fust torcenouse al pleyntif, et[1] il ad neqedent perdu sa accioun, pur ceo qe il, de sa propre auctorité et sauntz jugement, bien un an ou plus puis qe ele fust fete, la abati, et overa par sa force ou il dust aver overé par jugement, tut le put il bien aver fet freschement sur le fet, ou au meyns tauntost cum il le savoit; et ceste excepcioun averré ou nient dedite, voloms qe soit alouwable. [158 *b.*] Brac. 233. 233 *b*; Fle. 269 (§15, 16).

7. Et a ceo qe dit est el[2] bref, de nusaunce fete en ewe, fet a prendre garde en quel counté, ou[3] en quele vile, ou en quel lu le tort est fet, ausi cum de estaung, des gorz, et des autres nusaunces, et lequel[4] le ewe en la quele nusaunce est fete en[5] tut ou en partie est[6] commune, [7]et lequel[7] le pleyntif ou le autre eint[8] la pescherie ou solement dreit de pescher. Et Brac. 235; Fle. 272 (§12, 13).

1. et *om. SGM.* 2. *so AM.* al *L.* en le *NCH.* 3. e *AM.* 4. *so M.* qe *LA.* quel *N.* 5. ou en *ND.* 6. *so ND.* en *LARM.* ou *G.* ou en *CHW.* 7—7. *so verb. G.* en la quele *LNAM.* 8. ieint *L.* auoynt *N.* eent *M.* *sim. AH.*

tortious, although it be hurtful, the plaintiff's action ceases so far as respects himself, although it may not as it regards others.

6. Or he may say, that although at one time it was tortious to the plaintiff, yet he has now lost his action; for he of his own authority and without judgment, a year or more after the nusance was done, abated it, and proceeded by his own force, whereas he ought to have proceeded by judgment,—although he might have so abated it immediately after the fact, or at least as soon as he knew of it. And this exception, if verified or not denied, shall be allowed. Exception that plaintiff has abated the nusance by force.

7. And whereas the words in the writ are, 'of nusance done in the water, &c.' regard must be had in what county, in what vill, or in what place, the wrong is done; and the like of a pond, weir, or other nusance; and whether the water in which the nusance is done be in all or in part common[f]; and whether the plaintiff, or the other, has the fishery, or only a right of Exceptions founded upon the locality of plaintiff's tenement; and nature of plaintiff's estate.

[f] The text is probably corrupt. The sense, following Bracton, would be: whether the water is *appropriated* in the whole or in part, *or* is common.

[1]par teus avisementz[1] porrount estre allouwables excepciouns. Car si le ewe soit tut a celi de qi la pleinte est fete, et en la vile nomé en le bref, [2]et le tenement soit ausi en mesme la vile ou en mesme le counté, al quel la nusaunce est fete, adounc est le bref[2] bon et bien purchacé; et si noun, par taunt est le bref abatable, par ceste parole, a la nusaunce de soen fraunc tenement en mesme la vile. Et si le pleyntif ne ad rien en le ewe [3]si commune de pescherie noun[3], et eit levé gorz en mesme le ewe, et [4]le seignur[4] del ewe eit graunté a acun autre[5] dreit de pescher en mesme le ewe, si le dreyn purchaceour leve gorz a la nusaunce [6]del autre[6] gorz, soit la nusaunce
[159.] ousté par ceste assise, cum en cas de marché, ou de autre fraunchise, graunté, issi qe ne soit nusaunt a autre[7] marché joynaunt.

1—1. par teus anusaunces *L.* pur tieles nusaunces *N.* par teles auisementz *G.* par teles anosances *AR.* par teus anosaunz *C.* *sim. H.* par teles nusaunces *M.* *sim. W.* 2—2. *so verb. G.* *sim. MW.* *om. LNDARCHF.* 3—3. si qe commune de pescherie noun *L.* for qe commune de pescherie *N.* fors qe commune de pescher *GAM.* *sim. SRCW.* 4—4. *so G.* les issues *LNDSAR.* le fiers *M.* ly syres *W.* de issue *C.* del issue *H.* le issue *F.* 5. *so ACH.* autri *LNSGM.* 6—6. de autri *SG.* del autri *M.* 7. *so SMH.* *so corr. on eras. N.* countre *LC.* nule *G.* contre *A.*

fishing. And with reference to such considerations, exceptions may be allowable. For if the water belongs entirely to him against whom the plaint is made, and is in the vill named in the writ, and the tenement to which the nusance is done is in the same vill, or in the same county, the writ is good and well purchased; but if not, the writ is abatable by reason of these words, 'to the nusance of his freehold in the same vill.' And if the plaintiff has nothing in the water but a common of fishery, and has erected a weir in the same water, and the owner of the water has granted to another a right of fishing in the same water, if the last purchaser erect a weir to the damage of the other weir, the nusance shall be removed by this assise; as where a market or other franchise is granted, so that it be not a nusance to another adjoining market[g].

Grantee of a common of fishery may bring assise against subsequent grantee.

So grantee of market.

[g] 'A fair is a market of all manner of victual, and of all manner of other things, as of horses and other beasts, and birds, and also of *aveer de poyz*, as spiceries and other such things; also of gold, silver, tin, and other metals, of precious stones, linen, cloth, furs, arms, and all kinds of merchandise; and this once a year. But markets in country towns may be one day in the week; in boroughs, two days; in cities, three. But in London and in a town having the same liberties as London, (enfranchie come en Londres) every day of the week, save Sunday.' Note in MS. *N.*

8. Et dounc fet a destincter de veisinage[1] de marché, quel deit estre joynaunt et quel noun, et de eynz cum bien [2]de chemin[2] hom se put pleyndre de nusáunce, qe un marché soit nusaunt a un autre. A ceo qe marché deit estre ousté par ceste assise cum nusaunce a autri marché joynaunt, covendra qe le pleintif assigne la nusaunce issi, qe par la ou il ad soen marché par acun jour de la symeine en tele vile, la ad celi, de qi la pleinte est fete, fet[3] crier et lever marché par mesme le jour en mesme la vile, ou en autre vile en[4] meyns de[5] vi. lues[6] et demi et la terce partie de une lue de soen marché. Car si le pleintif die, qe il ad levé marché par un autre jour ou s'il die, qe les marchéz ne se joynent mie par vii. lues, si ne prendra il rien par sa pleynte. Car commune journé est au meyns de xx. lues; soit dounc la journé departie en iii. parties, issi qe la une partie soit assigné a ceux qi vount [7]vers le

Brac. 235, 235 *b*; Fle. 272 (§ 13).

1. so *G.* *sim. M.* homage *LSACH.* 2. so *MCH.* *sim. NG.* chescun *LA.* de chescun *S.* 3. so *SAM.* fere *LNCH.* *om. G.* 4. ou *LMSC.* *om. A.* ou en *NDF.* al *GW.* au *H.* 5. de *om. G.* 6. de voie *add. N.* 7—7. marchaunder *H.* vers marchaunder *W.*

8. In the case last mentioned, a distinction must be made as to the proximity of a market, what may be called adjoining and what not, and within what distance by road a man may complain of a nusance done by one market to another. In order to justify the removal of a market by this assise as a nusance to another adjoining market, the plaintiff must assign the nusance thus: that whereas he hath his market on a certain day of the week in such a town, he against whom the plaint is made has caused another market to be proclaimed and set up on the same day in the same town, or in another town within six miles and a half and the third part of a mile[h] from his market. For if the plaintiff say that he has set up a market on another day, or if he say that the markets do not adjoin by seven miles, he shall take nothing by his plaint. For a common day's journey is at least twenty miles; let therefore the day be divided into three parts, and one part be

Disturbance of ancient market by new.

New market, within 6⅔ miles from the old, and on the same day.

[h] It should be by the calculation six miles and a half and the third of a half mile, and is so in the parallel passages of Bracton and Fleta. The following clause is in the Charter of Edward III. to the city of London: 'Item, Quod nullum mercatum de cætero teneatur infra septem leucas in circuitu civitatis prædictæ.' (Liber Albus. 147.) The Latin word *leuca*, French *lue*, appears to have been used in England for the English mile. (See Spelman, Gloss. s. v. *leuca*.)

marché[7], l'autre partie [1]soit assigné a marchaunder, et la terce partie est[1] [2]de retourner del[2] marché[3], par si qe gentz puessent tut fere de jour, issint qe ne covendra point as gentz
[159 *b*.] aler ne retourner de[4] nutauntre[5] pur peril de maufesours. Si acun marché dounc soit levé joynaunt a autre de eynz la terce partie de xx lues, et mesme le jour qe l'autre marché est, ceo est aperte nusaunce. Et tele nusaunce put estre redrescé ou ousté par ceste assise, pur ceo qe ele est damageouse et torcenouse.

9. Et si acun se sent grevé par acune fraunchise graunté par nous par acune nusaunce [6]a acune sue[6] fraunchise, et overe par force a destourber cele fraunchise ou de tut anienter noster fet, en taunt semble qe il despise la ley[7], par ount il est grefment amerciable; et en despit de sa force retendra l'autre sa fraunchise, lequel qe ele ly soit prejudiciele ou noun. Car nul ne deit entrepreter nos douns ne nos voluntetz, sauve[8] nous. Et pur ceo voloms nous en touz cas qe teus qi se

1—1. *conj. om. LNDARGSF.* soit assigne a ceus qe vount marchaunder e lautre partie est *M.* est *H.* seyt assigne a ceux qe sount marchaunz *W.* 2—2. a demorir enle *G.* 3. e la terce partie pur marchandeer [*interl. N.*] 4. par *M.* *om. G.* 5. nuit *A.* 6—6. *so verb. GAM.* a suue *L.* e asqun sue *C.* *sim. HF.* 7. *so LNSACHF.* e de receyuere dreit par iugement de nostre Court *add. M.* *sim. G.* 8. sauntz *N.* *sim. GSMCH.*

allowed for going to market, another for marketing, and the third for returning home; so that people may do all in the day, and not be obliged to go or return in the night for fear of evil doers. If therefore any market be set up adjoining to another market within the third part of twenty miles, and on the same day as the other market, it is a manifest nusance; and such nusance may be redressed or removed by this assise, because it is both hurtful and tortious.

Person aggrieved by royal grant, not to right himself by force.

9. If any person feels himself aggrieved by any franchise granted by us on account of a nusance accruing to a franchise belonging to him, and sets himself by force to disturb this franchise, or entirely to defeat our act, he thereby appears to despise the law, and is therefore liable to be heavily amerced. And, by way of punishment for his force, the other shall retain his franchise, whether it be prejudicial to him or not. For none ought to interpret our grants or our will except ourselves. Therefore we will that in all cases those who think

sentent grevez par nos douns ou autrement, [1]par nos ordinaunces covenable eynt[1] remedie.

10. Et voloms [2]qe sceu soit qe en les[2] cas de disseisines, ou nul disseisour ne soit en vie [3]en le tens[3] qe la assise deyve estre prise de fraunc tenement ou de commune ou de renables estovers ou de nusaunce, qe la assise chete, et qe le pleintif ne prenge rien par soen bref ne par sa pleinte, eynz soit en nostre merci, et le tenaunt se voise quite sauntz jour; et qe remedie soit doné al pleintif par bref de entré foundu sur disseisine, par le quel le tenaunt ert tenu a la restitucioun, tut ne soit il punisable [4]pur le premer tort[4], et ou la vewe serra fete en touz pointz ausi cum en la disseisine. Brac. 235 *b*; Fle. 273 (§16). Brac. 172, 234; Fle. 270 (§1).

11. De reddisseisines suffit ceo qe dit est en nos estatuz. Prov. Mert. (20 Hen. III.) c. 3; Stat. Marl. (52 Hen. III.) c. 8; Stat. West. 2. (13 Ed. I.) c. 26.

1—1. *so N.* *sim. CH.* par ordinaunces couenable eynt *L.* par ordenance couenable eent de ceo *M.* 2—2. *so verb. MSCH.* qe sune soit qe en les *L.* qe sauuez soint qe en le *N.* *sim. D.* qi issint seit qe en touz les *G.* qe en le *AR.* qe seuwe chose seyt qe en touz les *W.* 3—3. *so A.* *sim. N.* en le tenement *L.* en tens *MCH.* 4—4. *so NM.* par la premere Court *LA.* par le premer tort *D.* *sim. HF.*

themselves injured by our grants, or otherwise, have a suitable remedy by our orders.

10. It should be known that in all cases of disseisin, where no disseisor is alive at the time when the assise of a freehold, or of a common, or of reasonable estovers, or of a nusance, ought to be taken, the assise shall abate, and the plaintiff shall take nothing by his writ or by his plaint, but be in our mercy, and the tenant go quit without day; and remedy be given to the plaintiff by writ of entry founded upon disseisin, whereby the tenant will be bound to restitution, although he is not punishable for the first tort, and in which the view shall be made in all points as in the assise of disseisin. When the disseisor is dead, plaintiff must proceed by writ of entry.

11. Concerning redisseisin, enough is said in our Statutes. Redisseisin.

CHAPITRE XXXIII. [LXIV.]

[160.]

Des Fermes.

Brac. 220; Fle. 275, 276.

1. Une manere de accioun ad en partie semblable a disseisine, sicum destourbaunce ou spoliacioun de terme. Car ausi graunt dreit ad le fermer a recoverer soen terme, et soen chatel, cum le fraunc tenaunt soen fraunc tenement. Par ceste assise neqedent ne ad il nul recoverer, pur ceo qe ele ne tient james leu en certeyn terme, si[1] ne soit agardé al termer par jugement de nostre court pur dette ou pur autre chose, et[2] en teus termes tient bien leu ceste assise, et la peyne de la reddisseisine ausi pur mester.

Stat. Mercat. (13 Ed. I.)

Brac. 220, 220 b; Fle. 275, 276; Reg. Brev. Orig. 227 b.

2. Mes quant au premer cas, ou le fermer ne ad rien del fraunc tenement, s'il soit engetté, dounc fet a prendre garde [3]de soen terme, si en soen lessour[3] remeint le fraunc tenement

1. *so AB.* si *om. LDGSMCHFW.* si il *interl. N.* 2. ou *L.* *om. N.* e *SGAMCH.* 3—3. *so LNDSGAMR.* quant al remedye qil couyent qe ly engettee de soen terme lequel le leessour en qi persone *W.*

CHAPTER XXXIII.

Of Farms.

Term of years not recovered by assise;

1. There is a kind of action somewhat resembling that of disseisin, for the disturbance or spoliation of a term. For the farmer has as much right to recover his term and his chattel as the freeholder his freehold. Yet he hath not any recovery by this assise, because it never lies for a certain term except where it is awarded to the termor by judgment of our court for a debt or for other cause; for in the case of such terms this assise doth well lie, and the penalty of redisseisin if necessary.

except in case of judgment creditor.

Remedy of farmer against lessor.

2. But with regard to the first case, where the farmer has nothing of freehold, if he be ejected, the nature of his term is to be regarded, whether the freehold remains in his

ou en autre, [1]et si en le[1] lessour, adounc appent remedie par tel bref. Comaundez a Piers qe il rende a Johan taunt de terre ove les apurteinaunces en tele vile, la quele mesme celi Piers ly lessa a terme qe ne est mie uncore passé.

3. [2]Et si[2] le lessour doune le fee et le fraunc tenement, ou le fraunc tenement soulement, a estraunge persone, et de ceo [3]il met[3] en seisine autre, et en ouste le fermer, issi qe nul gré ne ly est fet de soen terme, et si al lessour par cas ne soit demoré par quei il porra estre attaché a fere ly tener covenaunt al termer, ou de autrement fere soen gree de ses damages, en tel cas [4]ne ad[4] uncore ordeyné nul certeyn remedie vers le lessour; et [5]pur ceo le[5] meillour counseil en tel cas est, qe les fermers se tienent en seisine taunt cum il porrount; et si il soint engettez, jalemeyns ne mettent peyne de user lour seisine et destourber le [6]purchaceour de user[6] taunt cum il purrount, si la qe lour gré soit fet [7]en acune manere. [160 *b.*]

1—1. *conj.* issi a le *L.* issi qe a *N.* issi qe al *DSAR.* issi qe le *G.* issi qe a ki [*a blank space*] al *M.* 2—2. issi qe *LNDSAM.* *sim.* *GCF.* issint ke si *H.* E si *W.* 3—3. qe il met *L.* *sim.* *G.* mette *ND.* qe i mette *M.* qil mette *SC.* *sim.* *AH.* 4—4. ni ad *SA.* ny est *G.* nest *MCH.* 5—5. *so* *NSGACHW.* pur le *L.* pur ceo qe *M.* 6—6. purchaceour *N.* disseisour *M.* disseisour de vser *CH.* purchaceour deuers lour seisine *A.* 7—7. *conj.* en acune manere en cas. Sount *L.* en acune manere *om.* *NMGCH.* en asquns cas sount *A.* *sim.* *S.*

lessor or in a stranger; for if in the lessor, he may have his remedy by the following writ: 'Command Peter that he render to John so much land with the appurtenances in such a vill, which the same Peter leased to him for a term which is not yet expired.'

3. But if the lessor gives away the fee and the freehold, or the freehold alone, to a stranger, and he puts another person in seisin and ousts the farmer without making him any satisfaction for his term, and if it happen that the lessor retains nothing by which he can be attached to make him keep his covenant with the termor, or otherwise satisfy him for his damages; in such case there is not yet any certain remedy provided against the lessors; and therefore the best advice in such a case is, that the termors should keep themselves in seisin as much as they can; and if they are ejected, should nevertheless do their utmost to use their seisin, and hinder the purchaser from using it as much as they can, until satisfaction be in some way made to them.

Farmer has no remedy against stranger, donee of the reversion.

Brac. 220 *b*; Fle. 276 (§ 9); Ante, c. 5, s. 13; Post, l. iii. c. 2. s. 4.

4. Et acuns cas sount[7] neqedent ou hom ne deit pas encountre ester de estre engetté, sicum en cas ou le chief seignur engette termers pur la garde des terres de acun enfaunt qi cheet en sa garde. Et ceo[1] deivent les fermers suffrer, pur ceo qe averount recoverer[2] del remenaunt de lour terme, quant teus gardes[3] averount atteynt lour plener age[4].

5. Et sount acuns cas ou les fermers sount engettez sauntz ceo qe les seignurs des tenementz se soint assentuz[5]; et en tel cas gist recoverer par assise de novele disseisine a la pleinte le seignur del soil, et les damages neqedent deyvent de office des Justices estre deliverez al termer. Et si le seignur, quant il avera issi repurchacé soen tenement, ne voille rebaillier[6] al termer, par bref de covenaunt si se covendra purchacer; le quel bref serra pledé par somouns et par attachement[7]. [8]Et quaunt[8] il i ad plusours, dount les accions sount acune foiz affermez a eus et a lour heirs, acune foiz a lour assignez, acune foiz a lour executours, et acune

1. *so MW.* si *LNDGSACHF.* 2. *so M.* *sim. W.* retourn *LNA.* *sim. S.* recovery retourne *G.* returner *F.* 3. heirs G. 4. *so LNDSAR.* Car tut delaient gardes fermes pur ceo ne les tollent mye *add. G.* *sim. M.* 5. qe sunt engettez *add. M.* 6. relesser *M.* relaxer *F.* 7. sicome persónel plee *add. G.* *sim. W.* 8—8. *so L.* *sim. NDARSCHF.* autres personels torz i ad *G.* *sim. MW.*

Guardian may oust the farmers of his ward.

4. There are however some cases in which a person has no right to oppose his being ejected, as where the chief lord ejects the termors on account of the wardship of the lands of an infant who falls in his ward. And this the farmers ought to permit, because they shall have their recovery of the remainder of their term when such wards had attained their full age.

Recovery against stranger at suit of freeholder for benefit of termor.

5. There are some cases where the farmers are ejected without the consent of the owners of the tenements, and in such cases a recovery lies by assise of novel disseisin at the suit of the owner of the soil, where the damages however ought to be delivered by the Justices *ex officio* to the termor. And if the owner of the soil when he has thus recovered his tenement will not deliver it again to his termor, he must recover it by writ of covenant; in which writ the process is by summons and attachment. And whereas there are several whose actions are sometimes limited to them and their heirs, sometimes to their assigns, sometimes to their executors, and

Process in writ of covenant.

Personal actions.

foiz vers executours et vers autres, dounc remedies gisent par nos brefs fourmez solom chescun cas.

[1]*Ci finist le livere de disseisines*[1]: [2]*et comence le livere de Mort de Auncestre*[2].

1—1. Explicit liber secundus de disseisinis *ND*. *om*. *S*. 2—2. Incipit liber tertius de Morte Antecessoris *ND*. e comenco le liure de dreit de possession *AR*. Ci comence le ters lyure de intrusion. *M*. e comence le tierce liure dentrusion. *C*. *sim*. *H*.

sometimes against executors and others; therefore remedies lie by our writs formed according to the particular case[1].

Here ends the Book of Disseisin; and begins the Book of Mortdancester.

[1] This passage is somewhat obscure, and it will be seen that in some valuable manuscripts a reading is found which gives a totally different aspect to the whole sentence. The following note, from the margin of MS. *N*, appears to explain the expression, 'dount les accioun sount affermez,' as referring to what in our modern terminology are called the limitations introduced into the lease.

'In this part a recovery is given against the lessor where he is not guilty of the ejectment; with an example of a demise in large terms (ovesques une touche de ferme lessee largement). Wherefore when the deed of lease makes mention thus: habendum et tenendum prædictis B. et C. et eorum hæredibus et assignatis sive legatariis: if one of the termors keep out the other, or if the executors keep out the heirs, or the heirs the executors; or if one die within the term, and his heirs or executors be kept out by the other joint farmer, the recovery appears in the writing which commences thus: 'Every possession' (en la escrowette qe comence issi. Chescune p'on, etc.).' Note in MS. *N*. I am unable to explain to what treatise or other writing the last words refer. The same contraction is used for *possession* elsewhere in the same handwriting. See li. iii. c. 15. s. 2, note.

END OF VOL. I.